Meaning Matter Memory

Selections from the Studio Museum in Harlem Collection

MEANING
MATTER
MEMORY

Selections from the Studio Museum in Harlem Collection

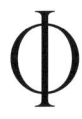

Director's Foreword

Thelma Golden, Ford Foundation Director and Chief Curator

The Studio Museum in Harlem has always offered a corrective to the omissions of the art world. We were founded at a time when the near exclusion of artists of African descent across galleries and museums nationally was commonplace. Our founders identified this absence and responded by instituting our beloved Museum in a second-floor loft on Fifth Avenue, just down the road from our magnificent new home. This was both an urgent need and a brave act of advocacy, central to which was a clear sense of the people we served: Black artists, our vibrant Harlem community, and the Black community.

Though we started as a noncollecting museum, the outstanding directors within our institutional lineage identified the need to steward a collection and uplift the incredible creative work being made by artists of African descent. We received our first work in 1970, and in 1977, under the leadership of Dr. Mary Schmidt Campbell, we officially implemented a collecting policy. Our aim was simple: the preservation, presentation, and interpretation of work by these very same artists. No other museum had taken on this critical duty. And I use the word "duty" in its full definition as a moral obligation and responsibility, because that is how our directors approached the acquisition of works into our collection during a pivotal moment of vastly reimagining the global art historical canon. This was especially important as artists of African descent—nationally and abroad—pursued practices that defied and exceeded narrow art historical categories that constricted the many ways Black art manifests. Soon enough, the artists on the peripheries of art history's rigid center found themselves justly at the core of a cultural shift that reimagined the canon itself.

Our permanent collection has allowed us to plant seeds for the future of Black culture, a future where our material achievements are properly preserved, writers are able to produce rigorous scholarly articles and publications out of which new art histories will surface, emerging artists can be inspired by a wealth of objects and ideas created by other artists of African descent, and where our communities can access a rich artistic heritage that illuminates our past and defines so much of our present.

Just as our permanent collection testifies to the innovation and diversity of artists of African descent and their varied practices, so too does this collection catalogue. This necessary sequel to our 2010 catalogue *Re:Collection* celebrates the tremendous growth of our permanent collection, and, by extension, our storied institution. Animating the works in this volume are over one hundred talented scholars, museum professionals, poets, and artists, whose vocations have at times intimately entwined with the Museum's evolving ecosystem of voices. The texts take on a range of writing styles, including poetry, lyrical reflections, traditional didactics, and a script. Many of the artists highlighted in this book are now well known, and there are those whose legacy is only now being brought to light. Writing these histories is a momentous privilege. Read together, the book presents breadth, depth, and specificity, providing a truly special opportunity to facilitate further discussion around this affecting selection of works.

Thank you to all Studio Museum staff, past and present, for their part in producing these pages. In particular, I would

ike to thank the Curatorial Department—specifically
Connie Choi, Curator, who shepherded this book to publication with a deft eye and exacting knowledge—and Adria
Gunter, Habiba Hopson, Yelena Keller, Jayson Overby, and
Kiki Teshome for their critical support in all aspects of this
publication; and a special thanks to Henry Luce Foundation
Publications Fellow June Kitahara for her indispensable
organizational work, and Meg Whiteford for her editorial
dexterity and attentive care throughout this monumental
process. This book was supported by Abigail Gordon, Studio
Museum and MoMA Curatorial Fellow, and the Collection
and Exhibitions Management team, who coordinated the
documentation of works in our permanent collection:
Maya Herdigein, Divine Jones, and Emily Nazarian, and former colleagues Sydney Briggs and Rachel Hansen. We are
forever grateful to former directors Dr. Mary Schmidt
Campbell, Kinshasha Holman Conwill, and Dr. Lowery Stokes
Sims for their leadership, guidance, words, and wisdom.

Thank you to WeShouldDoItAll for their thoughtful design,
which represents so astutely this manifold, complex
selection of works; John Berens for photographing the
objects in our collection with care; the galleries, museums,
and individuals who provided us with images to reproduce
here; our copyeditor, Jedd Hakimi at Point Line Projects,
and to Maki Nakada for her kanji translation of "love."

What appears here is just a glimpse of our collection. Yet
each work carries with it a unique understanding of life
in its many forms, and serves as an appropriate expression of our entire collection, which altogether weaves
a glorious tapestry of diverse artists of African descent.
It is with great hope that readers will come see these
spectacular works in person, especially as new works are

added to our collection and new stories demand telling—for our permanent collection is not just a repository of objects, but a crucial site of Black cultural formation.

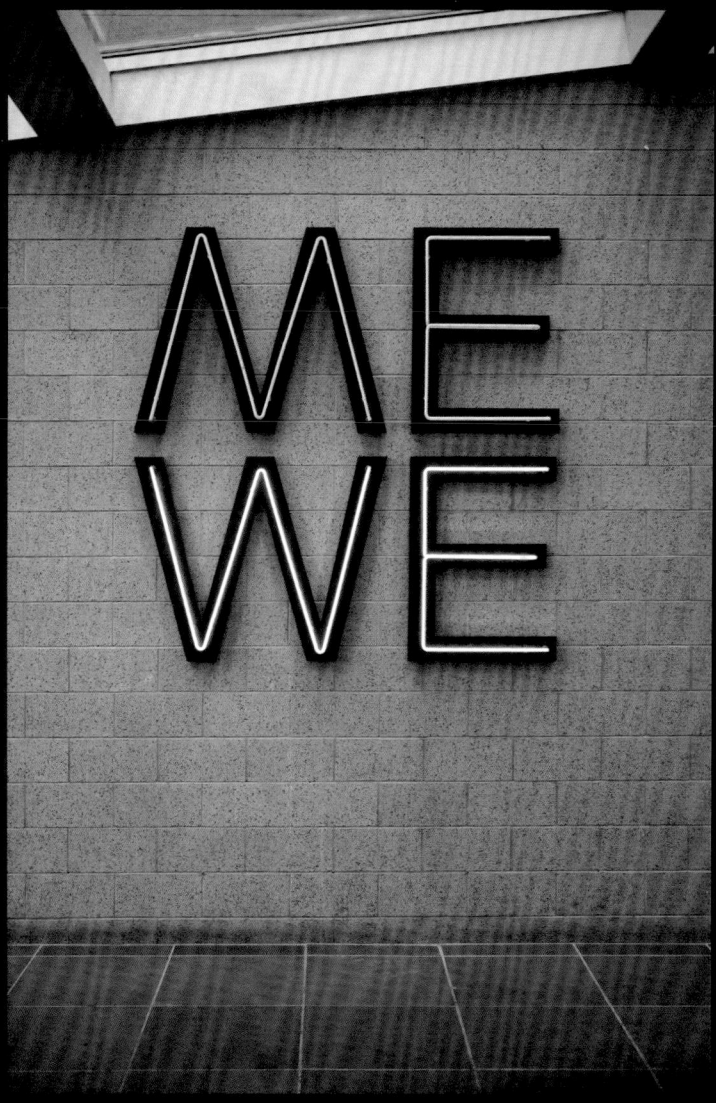

Glenn Ligon, *Give Us a Poem*, 2007.
Neon and Sintra PVC, 75 ⅝ × 74 ¼ in.
Gift of Glenn Ligon 2007.32

Introduction
Connie H. Choi

When the Studio Museum in Harlem opened in 1968, its founders—a diverse group of activists, artists, community members, and philanthropists—clearly stated a commitment to both living artists and the general public by foregrounding contemporary art and arts education. The Museum thus began as a noncollecting institution, announcing that it had "forsworn a permanent collection, a traditional feature of art museums" since "meeting new needs requires a free-wheeling approach, which could, in its view, be impeded by a vested interest in any artist or art style."[1] For the first few years, the Museum resisted collecting in order to focus its efforts on exhibitions and initiatives for living artists, including the signature *Artist-in-Residence* program. However, works began to be gifted to the Museum within two years of its opening, demonstrating that others— primarily artists, who were the first donors—understood the importance of an art collection for the Museum, for Harlem, and for the artists themselves.

While the founding idea of a radical, experimental space established the Museum's artist-driven mission, which it continues to center as the core of its work, the institution quickly realized that the needs of its community of artists and Harlem residents necessitated a shift toward becoming a fine arts museum.[2] In 1976, the Museum, under the leadership of Courtney Callender, formed a Curatorial Council—an advisory committee of artists, educators, and scholars, including Benny Andrews, Elizabeth Catlett, David Driskell, Jacob Lawrence, Norman Lewis, and Hale Woodruff—who identified as a priority the building of a collection.[3] The following year and nearly a decade after its founding, the Museum, with Dr. Mary Schmidt Campbell at the helm, officially changed its collecting policy, thus formally establishing the institution's permanent collection.

During Campbell's tenure as Director, the Museum's collection more than tripled in size, buoyed by a series of collection exhibitions starting in 1980, the excitement around the institution's move to its first permanent home on West 125th Street in 1982, and the first purchases of artwork in the mid-1980s. In 1985, just eight years after formally instituting a collection policy, the Museum received the Award of Merit from the Municipal Art Society of New York City for "establishing the premier collection of Black art in the country."[4] The Museum continued to build its collection, even calling the 1990s "The Decade of Collecting" in its 1991—92 annual report. That decade, with Kinshasha Holman Conwill as Director, saw the addition of works by many artists not previously represented in the collection, as well as a substantial increase in art from the Caribbean.[5] In 1993, in celebration of its twenty-fifth anniversary, the Museum organized *The Studio Museum in Harlem: Twenty-Five Years of African-American Art*, the first traveling exhibition of works from the collection. The exhibition went to twelve venues across the United States over a three-year period, introducing audiences around the country to the Museum's holdings.

In 2001, under the direction of Lowery Stokes Sims, the Museum established the Acquisition Committee, which meets three times a year to bolster the growth of the collection. With the committee's support, the Museum has since been able to add to the collection well over three hundred works, with many purchased directly from exhibitions organized by the Museum. Individual members have also funded the acquisition of additional works, extending their generosity to the Museum and its collection. The contributions of the committee have strengthened the important connection between the collection and the Museum's exhibition and institutional history, including its *Artist-in-Residence* program, which provides studio space and institutional support to emerging artists of African and Afro-Latin American descent.

Prior to the formation of the Acquisition Committee, works by artists in residence only entered the collection if they were gifted by the artists themselves or individual collectors. In committing to acquiring works from artists in residence whenever possible, the Museum and the committee have ensured that over eighty percent of alumni are represented in the collection. Many artists during their residency have been impacted and inspired by their time in Harlem, creating works that express their connection to the neighborhood. The Museum's collection thereby uniquely reflects the history of its location, demonstrating the institution's commitment to the communities that surround it.

Since the 1970s, the Museum has acquired many works that reference Harlem and the ways the neighborhood has inspired artists for generations. In 2021, the Studio Museum and the Metropolitan Museum of Art jointly announced the establishment of the James Van Der Zee Archive, a partnership between the institutions that comprises, in part, a shared collection of about six thousand works made by the famed photographer. These photographs serve as an incredible visual resource, allowing the Museum to richly represent the Harlem of the first half of the twentieth century alone and in dialogue with the many portrayals of the neigh-borhood that have followed in the decades since.

The Museum's permanent collection has experienced tre-mendous growth under Thelma Golden's leadership, and specifically in the years leading up to its new building, in large part due to major bequests by two trailblazing women: Peggy Cooper Cafritz (1947—2018) and Nancy L. Lane (1933—2022). Cafritz, a DC-based activist, collector, and educator committed to supporting the work of emerging artists of African descent, gifted more than four hundred works to the Museum, which introduced over one hundred new artists—including many from outside the United States—to the collection. Lane, a corporate executive and the Museum's longest-serving Trustee (1973—2022) and Founding Chair of the Acquisition Committee (2001—22), championed the work of Black artists with a specific focus on photography. In particular, her gift deepened the Museum's holdings of works by its artists in residence.

For a museum that began as a noncollecting institution, the Studio Museum has firmly established itself as hold-ing the leading collection of works by artists of African descent. This volume celebrates the incredible strength and depth of the collection and is a testament to all of the artists, individuals, and Museum staff who have contrib-uted to the growth and care of this unparalleled collection.

Interviews with Former Directors Mary Schmidt Campbell, Kinshasha Holman Conwill, and Lowery Stokes Sims

From its opening in 1968 to the time of this publication, the Studio Museum in Harlem has been led by seven inimitable directors: Charles E. Inniss (1968—69), Edward Spriggs (1969—75), Courtney Callender (1975—77), Mary Schmidt Campbell (1977—87), Kinshasha Holman Conwill (1988—99), Lowery Stokes Sims (2000—05), and Thelma Golden (2005—). In 2023, the Museum interviewed Mary Schmidt Campbell, Kinshasha Holman Conwill, and Lowery Stokes Sims about its permanent collection.

Interview with Mary Schmidt Campbell

What does it mean for the Studio Museum to have a permanent collection?

When the Studio Museum in Harlem opened in 1968, the founders avoided amassing artifacts. It was a museum for working artists. Hence, the name— Studio Museum. William T. Williams, one of our brilliant abstract painters, suggested that an artist-in-residence program, along with exhibitions and accompanying publications, was a bold way for the Studio Museum to realize its ambition of being a "living museum" for working artists. There were some in the art world who believed collecting was passé, a relic, an old way of thinking about the rationale for a museum.

As bold an idea as it was to establish a living museum, the original mission neglected to take into account a glaring reality: few institutions were collecting the work of Black artists. Without the capacity to preserve the material culture of its artists, how does a culture come to know and understand its heritage— the full meaning of its past? Despite the original mission, artists who exhibited at the Museum often expressed the desire to have some representative piece of their work preserved. Many would gift a work of art as an expression of gratitude, either after a residency or an exhibition. So, in fact, the museum was engaged in de facto collecting, even before it formally became a collecting institution. Moreover, by the time I arrived at the Studio Museum, the Board had determined that the Museum needed to be a fully accredited fine arts museum. Accreditation without a permanent collection did not seem feasible.

As I look back on our decision to establish a permanent collection—along with the need, therefore, for a permanent facility and professional staff—I believe the Studio Museum, even as it maintained a robust exhibition and publishing efforts, may not have fully realized how radical and

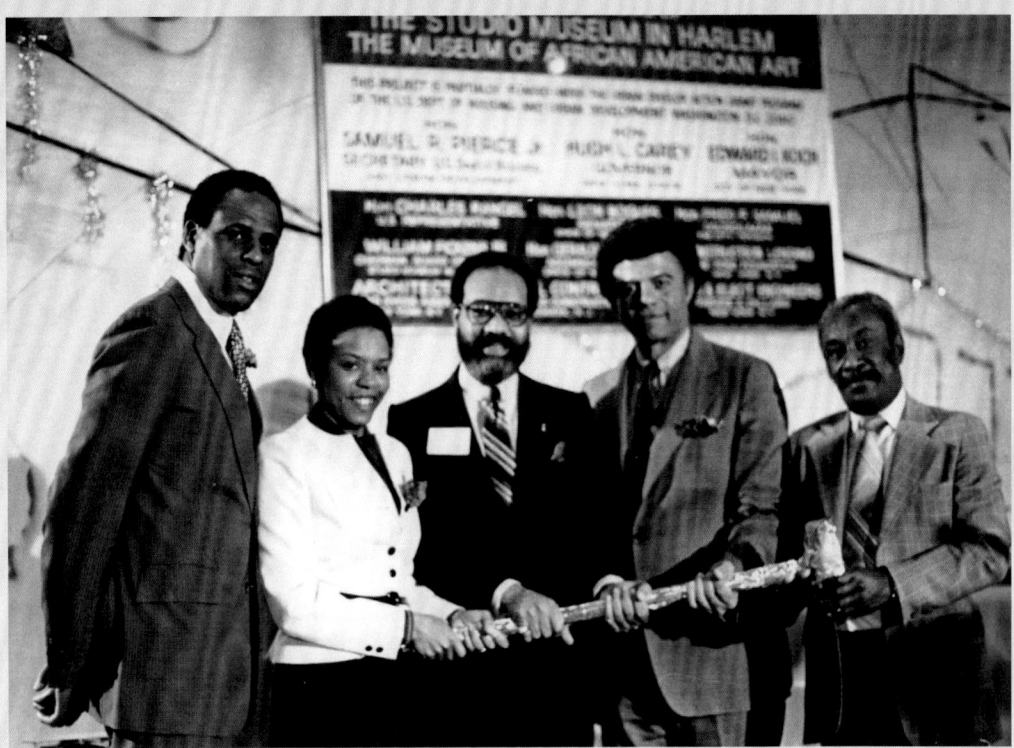

(L to R) Carl McCall, Mary Schmidt Campbell, Arthur Barnes, Robert Carroll, and Fred Samuel at the groundbreaking for the Studio Museum in Harlem at 144 West 125th Street, 1981

pioneering a decision it was both to institutionalize the *Artist-in-Residence* program and to launch the permanent collection. To this day, there are few (if any) other museums that support working artists by offering studio space and an exhibition combined with ongoing exhibition, publication, collecting, and educational programming. That this set of activities has been sustained for over fifty-five years testifies to the idea's durability and the determination of the Museum's leadership. The result has been generative. The Studio Museum is fueled by the energy of working artists, an energy that is a magnet for other artists, even as it preserves history and heritage, in part by serving as the principal producer of museum professionals of color and as a major source of scholarship and research on art of the African diaspora.

What work in the collection is significant to you, and why?

Romare Bearden was the subject of my dissertation and, later, a biography I authored—*American Odyssey: The Life and Work of Romare Bearden* (Oxford, 2018). Bearden had gifted his 1964 black-and-white photo projection *Conjur Woman*, a masterpiece, before my arrival. When we moved from the loft on Fifth Avenue to 144 West 125th Street, into what was then the Museum's own building, I hung *Conjur Woman* in my office. She felt like an old friend who kept me company every day. When I walked down 125th Street across from the Museum, I would look up and see *Conjur Woman* seeming to project from the lit office, as if she were a guardian keeping watch over the street below. Her unconventional majesty reminded me of the potency of image-making.

What collection-related advancement are you most proud to have

accomplished during your
time at the Museum?

In 1977, when I arrived at the Studio Museum in Harlem, you could count the number of Black curators on one hand. If the Museum were to build a permanent collection, we would need to develop a professional staff. I remember vividly when Terrie Rouse walked into the Museum clutching her resume looking for a job. Though she had not been an art history major, she had studied African American history and culture at Cornell. In her interview, it was clear she was whip-smart, energetic, and curious. I said to her, "If you are willing to learn to become a curator, your capstone project will be the organization of the permanent collection of the [then] Adam Clayton Powell State Office Building." The state of New York had assembled an outstanding collection of over one hundred pieces by major artists; but without curatorial attention, the collection was in a state of disarray in a basement storage room.

The Museum managed to obtain a state grant to organize, catalogue, and assist in obtaining or building proper storage. I made the project Terrie's fieldwork after she had studied at the Smithsonian's seminars on curatorship and visited a number of New York museums as part of her on-the-job training. Other Studio Museum staff learned on the job or trained through CETA, the labor department's Comprehensive Employment Training Act. (Some clever person at the Department of Cultural Affairs appropriated a federal program designed to train manufacturing workers and applied it to areas of expertise at cultural institutions, museums included.) We also engaged the Metropolitan Museum of Art to assist with training a registrar and offering a seminar on their photography collection.

Additionally, every now and then, someone who had training or experience or the right educational background would walk through the door—such as Grace Stanislaus, who had studied art history at Columbia University, or Kellie Jones, who came to the Studio Museum from Amherst bursting with knowledge about individual artists, starting out researching and writing brilliant chronologies that accompanied the catalogues. Or Sharon Patton, who entered the Studio Museum as Chief Curator. The Museum was a magnet for curatorial talent, even as it attracted aspiring museum professionals, whom the Museum willingly trained and apprenticed. But my key advancement was setting the tone for the Studio Museum in Harlem to become a laboratory within which curatorial talent and museum professionals could be cultivated.

What is a challenge
that arises with being
a collecting institution?

Collections grow. Space will always be a problem. Every museum has to have a thoughtful deaccessioning policy and clear guidelines for the acquisition of work. Resources are a challenge because of rising space costs. Maintaining proper conditions is an especially acute challenge given the variety of materials and media used by contemporary artists as well as the ongoing wear and tear of more traditional materials. Conservation is particularly expensive, and maintaining the means to periodically assess the condition of works and to remedy those in need of maintenance and repair requires active caretaking and vigilance. Expertise in managing these requirements is not plentiful, and the Studio Museum's tradition of training and developing expertise on-site will continue to be a strength.

What is your hope for the
future of the Museum?

Watching the directors who came after me, I have been impressed by the Board's ability to choose the right director for the right time. For over forty years, the Studio

Museum has enjoyed an unbroken lineage of directors, each of whom advanced the Museum in one way or another. I hope that—given the splendid and longstanding tenure of Thelma Golden, who stewards the Museum with a combination of grace, deep understanding of art and artists, deft managerial expertise, and clear-thinking business sensibility—the Museum will be able to continue a legacy of outstanding cultural leadership far into the future.

How did your experience
at the Museum
shape your work?

The Studio Museum was my incubator. As a scholar, I was given the opportunity to organize one solo exhibition after another and write catalogue essays on a number of artists who went on to become masters of art. Getting to know them and their work has been a highlight of my career. Though I resisted it at first, I became intensely entrepreneurial in order to establish business models that would allow the Museum to thrive as it sought to perform professionally at the highest level. That business acuity has followed me in every job. Fundraising— presenting a narrative in which others can believe and see themselves—was a skill finely honed at the Studio Museum. Like the best nonprofits in this country, the Studio Museum has understood that development is about developing relationships among a community of believers.

Working with a sense of community is another aspect of the Museum that has stuck with me. The Studio Museum made it absolutely clear that institutions have a responsibility not only to their core stakeholders but also to the community in which they operate. Once, I was walking down 125th Street during the renovation of the building at 144 West 125th, when someone tapped me on the shoulder. He asked if I was the director. "Yes," I replied. "Are y'all renovating that building and turning it into a museum?" he continued. "Yes," I replied

proudly. "Well," he advised, "you better get it right; because if you don't, we comin' after you with the hook." The Studio Museum had to perform well, like Ella Fitzgerald and James Brown did at the Apollo, to avoid the community coming after us with the hook! I loved that we meant that much.

A question that needs posing but is rarely asked is: "Why was the Studio Museum— an organization of modest resources, located in what was then one of the most resource-depleted neighborhoods in the city—not only able to survive but thrive and move so rapidly and emphatically to occupy the core of the city and global cultural community?"

Would you answer?

At the outset, our Board was one of modest resources. Despite the fact that we did not have access in the early days to resources, we did have an unshakable sense of shared purpose. That purpose is shared among working artists, scholars and historians, the community, and the Museum's leadership. Critical too has been an unsentimental clarity about the need for sound fiscal and governance practices, as well as an unerring sense of excellence— avoiding the hook. The new building is the latest and most visible example of that.

Describe the Studio
Museum in one word.

Miraculous.

Interview with Kinshasha Holman Conwill

There is a river whose streams make glad the kingdom of God. In *There Is a River* (1981), the African American historian Vincent Harding explicates the text of the history of Black people in the United States, linking it to the flow of a mighty river with major tributaries that contribute to its power and richness. In the United States, the Mississippi River, the country's second longest, stretching from the height of Lake Itasca in Minnesota to the Gulf of Mexico, flows like Harding's poetic river. The Mississippi's tributaries include other major rivers, such as the Missouri—the country's longest river—Ohio, Arkansas, Illinois, and Red rivers. The Mississippi also indirectly connects to other significant US rivers, including the Allegheny, Tennessee, and Wabash. Many of these storied rivers resonate with the history of African Americans, and hence with the Studio Museum in Harlem, a major tributary of that history.

Like the Mississippi River, the Studio Museum has many tributaries. They comprise the artists, the collections, the exhibitions, the publications, the programs, the collectors, the donors, and the communities that contribute to this major museum's flow through the history of the United States and the world.

The interconnected nature of the Mississippi is akin to that of the Studio Museum. It feeds and is fed by waters from Canada, Mexico, Africa, the Caribbean, all of the many states of the United States, and more. The profound role that the Museum plays in the cultural streams of the United States, the world, and the African diaspora through the art it collects is as fluid and powerful as that storied river.

What does it mean for the Studio Museum to have a permanent collection?

It ensures that the art of the African diaspora will have an evergreen place

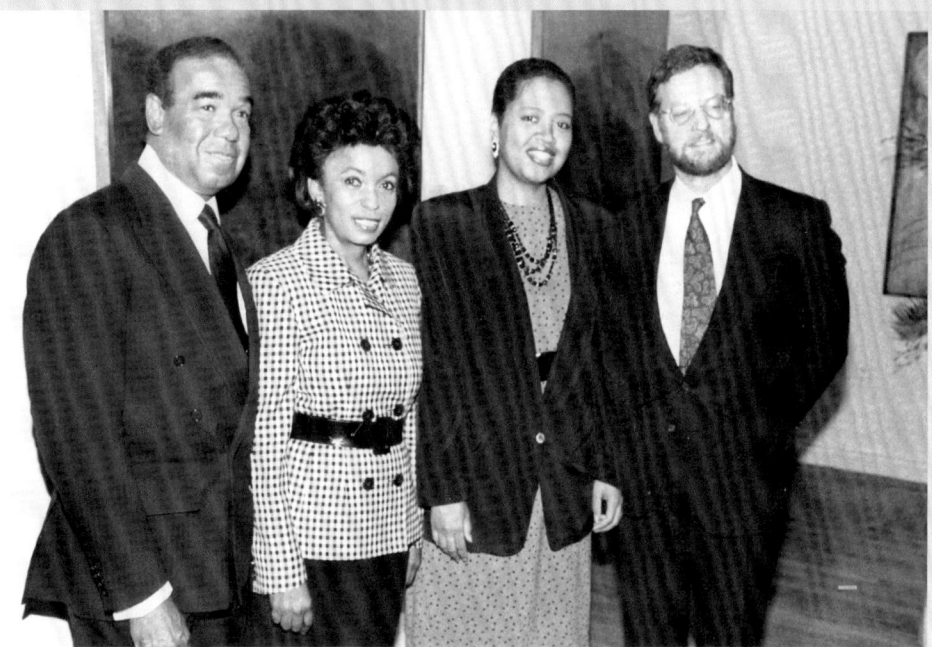

(L to R) Bobby Short, Nancy L. Lane, Kinshasha Holman Conwill, and David Rockefeller Jr.

in the history of art and that the represented artists will be safeguarded through their artworks' care and preservation, interpretation, and documentation. Given the years of erasure and neglect of Black artists by the larger art world, the Studio Museum's singular attention to acquiring an unparalleled collection secures this legacy for posterity.

What work in the collection is significant to you, and why?

Betye Saar's mixed-media assemblage *Indigo Mercy* (1975) is a work of audacious beauty. It stands on its own as an object of lyrical vision and has become a decades-long touchstone for audiences. In its references to the spiritual practices of diverse cultures, it is both powerful in its presence and empowering to its viewers. Saar's ability to activate a sense of mystery both ancient and timeless has attracted visitors, who, without instruction, left written messages, coins, photographs, and flowers as offerings when the work was exhibited.

The potency of the work derives in great part from how it stands as an invitation to enter the artist's world. Its physical composition, including an open palm—a symbol of welcome and protection in various cultures—votive candles, beads, and other emblems collected from the artist's prodigious haunting of flea markets (among other rich sources of her unique bricolage), makes it a vessel of individual and community secrets and narratives. With nods to everything from the works of Joseph Cornell, fellow Los Angeles artists John Outterbridge and Noah Purifoy, Kongo nkisi, and personal histories of the vanity table as an object of Black women's agency, Saar forges a potent and unforgettable work of art. That the work was the donation of the Nzhinga Society, an African American women's organization, makes it even more meaningful and resonant, amplifying its importance.

What collection-related advancement are you proud

to have accomplished during your time at the Museum?

The organizing and travel of the Museum's *25 Years of African American Art* exhibition (1994—97). Working with curator Valerie Mercer, the exhibitions and collections staff of the Museum, and the Studio Museum's traveling partner, the Gallery Association of New York State (GANYS), we were able to share our diverse collection with an amazing array of a dozen national museums of all sizes, in venues in every major region of the country, including the RISD Museum, the Modern Art Museum of Fort Worth, the National Museum of Mexican Art (known then as the Mexican Museum), and the Lowe Art Museum at the University of Miami. While other important exhibitions of art by Black Americans had traveled nationally, most notably the exhibitions organized by pioneering artist and curator David Driskell (including *Two Hundred Years of African American Art* and *Hidden Heritage*), they were usually large—and important—historical surveys. In many cases, the *25 Years* exhibition provided the first opportunity for audiences in some communities to view a range of significant contemporary art by African Americans, including Romare Bearden, Fred Brown, Nanette Carter, Colin Chase, Ed Clark, John Dowell, Melvin Edwards, Sam Gilliam, Barkley Hendricks, Richard Hunt, Kerry James Marshall, Norman Lewis, Howardena Pindell, Betye Saar, Jack Whitten, and William T. Williams.

Writing in the exhibition catalogue, then curator of collections Valerie Mercer spoke of African American artists over-turning formalist conventions, and subverting tenets of "fleeting stylistic trends," while making evident that these artists were well aware of the larger art world and forging their own paths.

What is a challenge that arises with being a collecting institution?

Collecting in real time is about knowing—in the institutional bones—both what matters now and what will resonate over time. It is not about being trendy or crowd-pleasing, but rather about trusting the art and artists that will help define meaning-making in a way that stands the test of time. It is about being courageous and risk-taking and following the mission-driven heart of the organization. Those qualities become more critical when the art is of the African diaspora, given the ebb and flow of interest in and understanding of that vast and deep corpus of creativity, which has been crucial to defining US and world art. It is a major responsibility.

What is your hope for the future of the Museum?

That it continues to be at the center of shaping the discourse around the art of Black America and the African diaspora—defining ideas, lifting up artists, and preserving a culture that is essential to understanding how art and ideas shape all of our lives.

How did your experience at the Museum shape your work?

It became the marker for all my future work, in and outside of the museum field. The rigor, the expansive thinking, the sense of possibility, the belief in the power of art and community—in all senses of the word "community"—were forged there.

Describe the Studio Museum in one word.

Extraordinary.

Interview with Lowery Stokes Sims

What does it mean for the Studio Museum to have a permanent collection?

This issue was intensely debated in 2004 among the Board when I was Director of the Studio Museum. It was a moment when we were beginning to realize the budgetary commitment that would be required to acquire, store, and care for art objects. At the same time, under the visionary leadership of longtime board member Nancy L. Lane and Thelma Golden, then Deputy Director for Exhibitions and Programs, an engaged and supportive Acquisition Committee formed, which significantly impacted the nature of what was then described as the Studio Museum's "collection of gaps."

The argument was made at the Board level that the Museum should affirm this institutional role and continue to collect— and accept that the collection would have the same lively, idiosyncratic character as its acquisitions and donations.

For me, this decision was in line with the argument made by the esteemed artist, curator, and educator David Driskell in a conversation I had with him at the Hatch-Billops Collection in 1998. Professor Driskell was unequivocal in his conviction that Black institutions must collect the work of Black artists as a commitment to the greater Black community. He saw a time when white institutions would finally catch on to the importance and value of Black art, and he didn't want Black institutions to then be priced out of the market. I was particularly inspired by his observations that our institutions see themselves as the keepers of our culture and that they work to create their own legacies.

What work in the collection is significant to you, and why?

Heirlooms & Accessories (2002) by Kerry James Marshall is very significant for me. It came to the Museum through the generosity of an anonymous donor, who was a close associate of mine. The donor came to the opening of the 2004—05 exhibition of Kerry's work that we hosted at the Museum, which had been organized by the Museum of Contemporary Art in Chicago. I was instantly drawn to this work. And who wouldn't be? Kerry pointedly turned the voyeurism of the perpetrators of a lynching back on themselves, singling out the women who look out at us, making them into locket mementos— something the lynchers would do with their victims. It is a fierce indictment.

What collection-related advancement are you proud to have accomplished during your time at the Museum?

Certainly the donations of the Acquisition Committee helped the Museum survey contemporary and occasionally historical art by Black global creators, setting the existing collection on a new trajectory.

What is a challenge that arises with being a collecting institution?

Principally money and space. But also identifying key works that represent a time, era, or epoch.

What is your hope for the future of the Museum?

It's being fulfilled through the new building.

How did your experience at the Museum shape your work?

It gave me experiences, skills, and perspectives that have served me well in my life ever since.

Describe the Studio Museum in one word.

Catalytic.

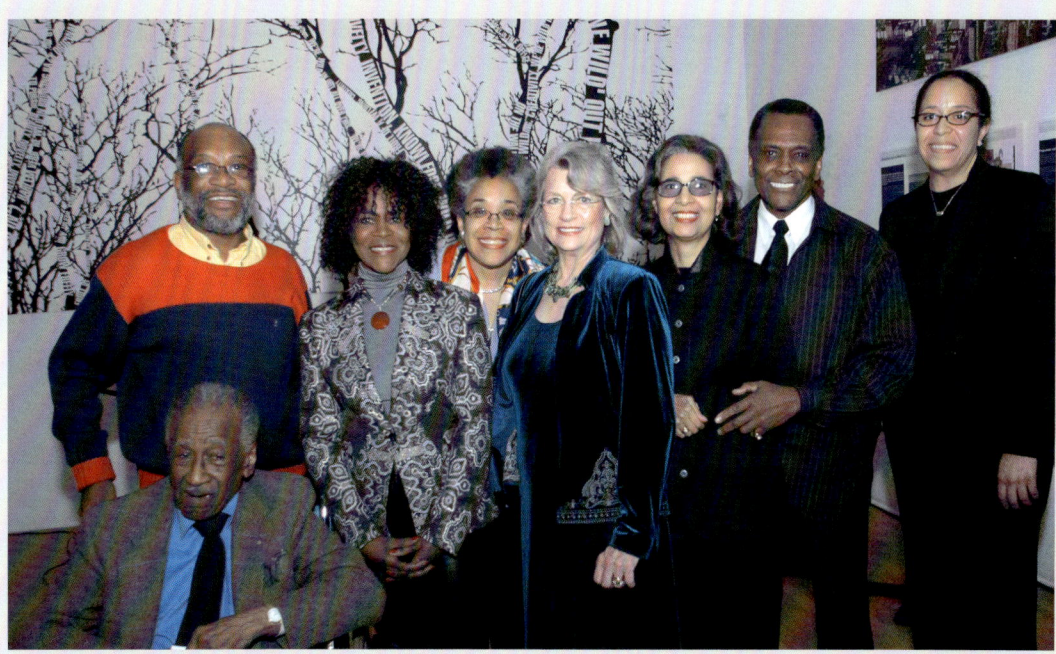

(L to R) Albert Murray, Chester Higgins Jr., Cicely Tyson, Lowery Stokes Sims, Louise Kerz, Gail Lumet Buckley, Arthur Mitchell, and Sandra Jackson Dumont at the book launch of *Hirschfeld's Harlem: Manhattan's Legendary Artist Illustrates This Legendary City Within a City*, 2004

Joshua Johnson

c. 1763—1826

In this tender Federal-era portrait, Sarah Maria Coward is two or three years old. The artist, Joshua Johnson, demonstrates the toddler's growing independence by depicting her stepping on to a garden path. Dressed in a white muslin frock, a sheer overlay, and red slippers, Coward holds a rose in her right hand and gestures slightly behind with her left, toward a butterfly or moth. In the background, a lush highland rises. Berries, flowers, and butterflies operate as symbols of curiosity, good humor, maturation, and fleeting youthful wonderment in Johnson's representations of children.

Johnson was one of the most important portraitists working in the Federal and proto-Romantic eras in the United States. His preference for strong, direct passages of contrasting color, geometric shapes, and crisp, graphic use of line and mass made him a sought-after composer of like-nesses. Born to an Anglo-colonial father and an enslaved mother, Johnson apprenticed with a Baltimore blacksmith, completing his work there at age nineteen. Shortly thereafter, in December 1798, Johnson placed the first of two advertisements for his skills in the *Baltimore Intelligencer*, proclaiming himself "a Portrait Painter" and a "self-taught Genius."[6]

Across Johnson's nearly four decades of portrait painting, the artist painted over a hundred members of Baltimore and northern Virginian society of all ages, including Black subjects—free and enslaved— as well as Catholic, Jewish, Quaker, and Protestant people, and abolitionists and slaveholders. His art is proof of a Black entrepreneur who navigated adroitly across the social boundaries of race, class, and religion in the first decades of the United States.

—Horace D. Ballard

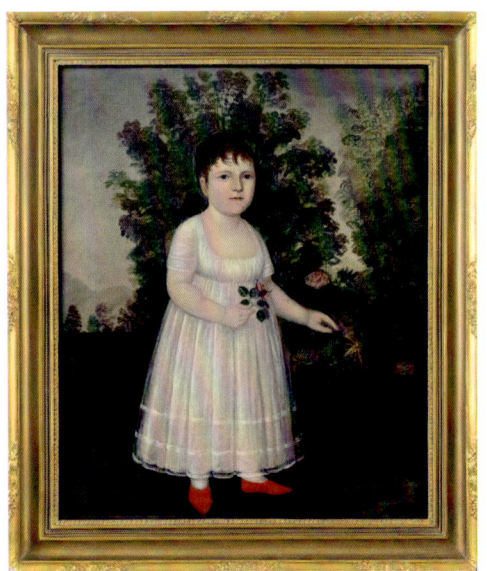

Portrait of Sarah Maria Coward, c. 1804. Oil on canvas, 36 × 30 in. Museum purchase and a gift from E. Thomas Williams and Auldlyn Higgins Williams, New York 1997.9.16

Edward Mitchell Bannister

1828—1901

Untitled, c. 1878. Oil on canvas,
19 ½ × 27 ½ in. Museum purchase and
a gift from E. Thomas Williams and
Auldlyn Higgins Williams 1997.9.3

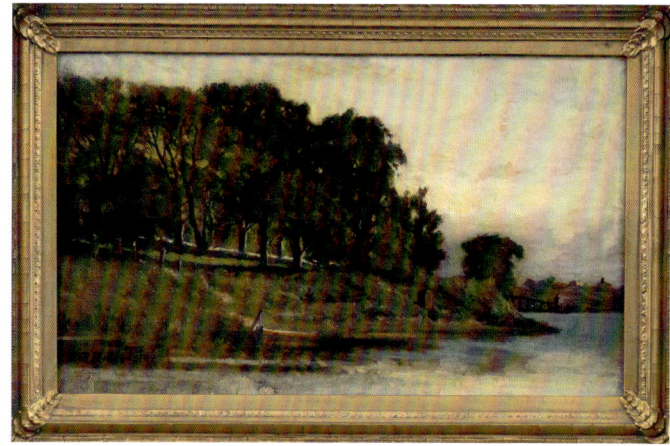

Edward Mitchell Bannister was one of the few African American painters
to gain widespread attention in the nineteenth century. Known for his
picturesque New England landscapes, such as this painting, Bannister
captured the serenity of nature through impasto techniques and muted
tones. This is a study of trees, water, and sky after an early frost. The trees
at center, portrayed with browning leaves, are covered with a thin layer
of snow. While the snow is painted delicately, Bannister applies heavy
brushwork to the leaves, the patches of grass, and the water, where he
has built up paint to portray the reflection of heavy clouds. With only
a moored boat and backgrounded houses, lack of human activity amplifies the quietness of the scene. Bannister's paintings never dealt with
race. When they did include figures, they were usually white. Bannister's
commitment to nineteenth-century North American and French landscape traditions meant that his works dealt with nature above all and
largely eschewed details, human or otherwise, that might distract from it.

Born in Canada to a father from Barbados and a mother whose background is unknown, Bannister moved to Boston at the age of twenty,
where he worked as a barber and took art classes at night with noted
sculptor-anatomist Dr. William Rimmer. While in Boston, Bannister was
exposed to the work of William Morris Hunt, a painter from Vermont who
was inspired by the French Barbizon paintings of Jean-Baptiste-Camille
Corot and Charles-François Daubigny, and who was known for rustic landscapes. After moving to Providence in 1870, Bannister became a painter
full-time and won a bronze medal for a Hunt-style work, *Under the Oaks*,
at the Philadelphia Centennial Exposition of 1876. Though the committee
initially rescinded the award upon learning Bannister was Black, he ultimately received the prize, and commissions, including this work, followed.
By the end of his life, Bannister had become one of Providence's most
prominent painters.

— Eliza Butler

Charles Ethan Porter

1847—1923

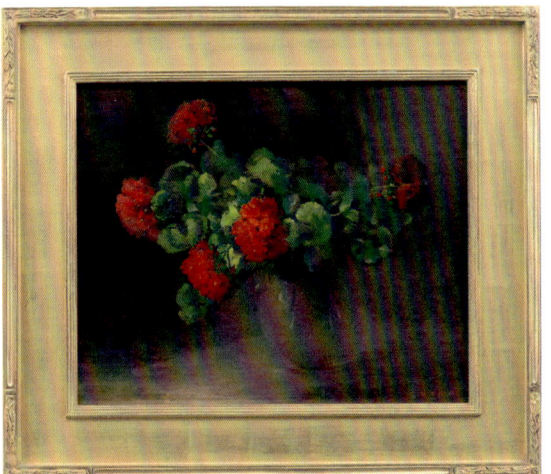

Charles Ethan Porter was born into a free African American family in Rockville, Connecticut, in 1847. His mother's garden and the fields, marshes, and woodlands of his home state compelled his lifelong fascination with cultivated species and the natural world, as well as with drawing and painting from life. In 1869 Porter became the first Black artist to attend classes at the National Academy of Design. By 1878 Porter had set up a commercial studio in Hartford, Connecticut, and he quickly amassed a following among notable artists and celebrities, such as Frederic Edwin Church and Mark Twain. After two years in Paris taking classes at the École des Arts Décoratifs and the Académie Julian (1881—83), Porter returned to Hartford and there composed virtuosic compositions in the style of Henri Fantin-Latour: sumptuous still lifes and landscapes built from compressed gestures, translucent glazes of contrasting color, and layers of fresh paint laid on to a previous, still-wet layer. He revisited the theme of geraniums in bouquet, bowl, and demijohn vessels multiple times during the 1880s.

The species of geranium depicted in Porter's painting originated in South Africa. In the seventeenth century, the plant and its seeds were brought to the Netherlands from the peninsula of the Cape of Good Hope, shipped to the Leiden Botanic Garden by Paul Hermann, a medical officer with the Dutch East India Company. They then entered the North American colonies of Britain and France in the early eighteenth century as a perennial. The flower immediately became a favorite of visual artists, most notably among the Peale family of Philadelphia, and later, Henri Matisse. As such, geraniums have come to symbolize artistic achievement and innovation, distanced friendship, good health, well wishes, and, sometimes, folly. These transatlantic histories and affective realities seem apropos when viewing a still life of geraniums rendered in the luminous precision of Porter's brushstrokes.

—Horace D. Ballard

Henry Ossawa Tanner
1859—1937

The son of an African Methodist Episcopal (AME) Church bishop, Henry Ossawa Tanner became one of the first internationally renowned African American artists. Tanner received formal training at Pennsylvania Academy of Fine Arts under the mentorship of realist painter Thomas Eakins. Disturbed by racial tensions and systemic oppression, in 1891 Tanner departed for Paris, where he lived for the remainder of his life. Tanner first painted genre images with African American figures and later shifted to biblical themes. A devout Christian and religious practitioner, Tanner made works post-1900 that evidence motifs of meditation, spiritual inspiration, and the witness experience.

Tanner's undated *The Three Marys* portrays the biblical tale of the "myrrhbearers," the women who discovered Christ's empty tomb following his crucifixion. The story narrates three women, whose identifications differ depending on religious denomination, arriving to anoint Christ's body with incense and spices, only to discover his vanished body. In Tanner's rendition of this metamorphic event (sketched and painted on numerous occasions), the women showcase an immediate emotive response to Christ's resurrection. Mary Magdalene, leading the group, lifts her right arm, and Mary and Salome follow behind, appearing surprised, frightened, or perhaps concerned. Typical of Tanner's religious depictions, the event surrounding *The Three Marys* is kept out of sight. Instead, the viewer must consider the emotional residue of what has just occurred. Through this technique of "watching others watch," the artist invites the viewer to reflect on miraculous observations of the unseen, for almost all can relate to the sentiment of wonder after witnessing that which cannot be explained.[7]

—Habiba Hopson

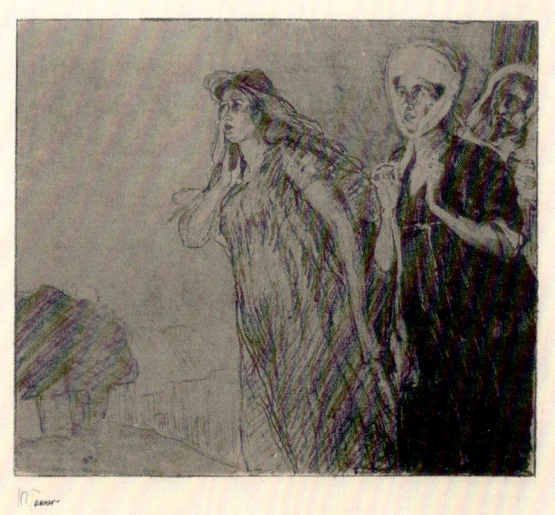

The Three Marys, n.d. Lithograph, image: 13 ¾ × 17 ⅜ in. Gift of Onyx Gallery 1984.7

Martha Jane Pettway

1898—2003

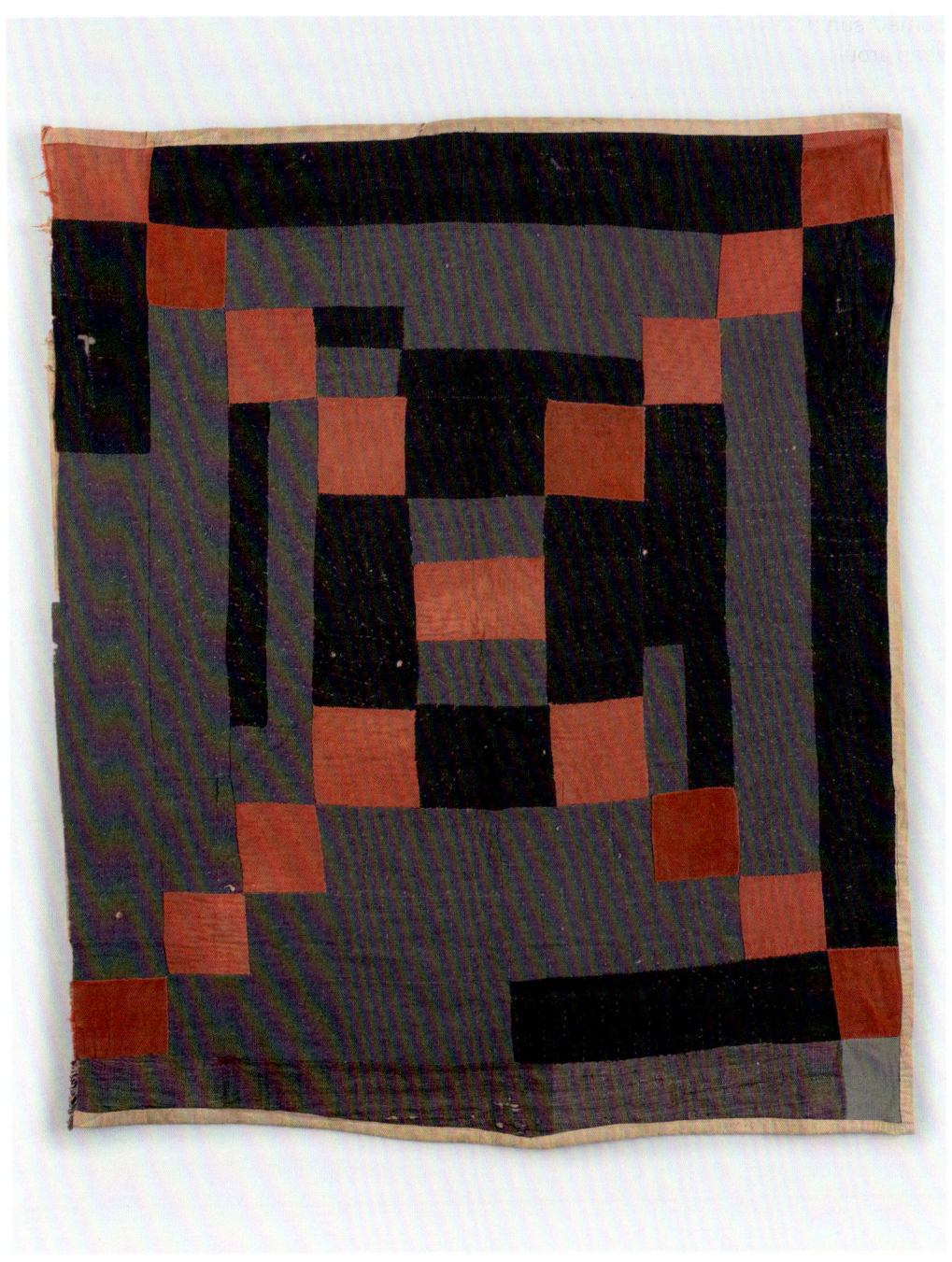

*Center medallion strips with multiple borders
and cornerstones*, c. 1920. Wool, corduroy,
and cotton, 76 × 66 in. Gift of The Souls
Grown Deep Foundation, 2020 2020.12.14

Hmm-mmh   In Gees Bend / in Boykin / in Bama
                                          hands stretch / toward / wide swatches of
hands dig deep / into /
soil / sea / sky
come / sun up / sun down / rays /
wrap around
                                                                    let me
                                          reach / till / plant / thread / rows
                    in stitches / tiny / stitches / with these / with my / Black / hands
                                          warm you up / in / a familial embrace
                    of / mama / sister / daughter / auntie / play cousin / grandma's
                                                                    hands
                                          quilting / circles / squares / inlets / outlets
                    blurring / lines / foreground / background / fade in / out / lost

                                          this **X**

          rising up / target / compass / align / constellations / sightings / pathways /
          merge / intersect / three - sided border / follow me follow me / find the gate / we're all /
          in / seal the edges / look to the / Queen / check / as she / mate / places this /
          inter / cross / sectional cover of / love / all the / ways / in all / the ways / over / you

                                          marks / home

found / where we / mended / repaired / passed them / on / to the next / and the next /
bowed down / kneeled down / laid down / (a)cross channels / ripples / foundations /
enmeshed with / red dirt / bloodied threads / workmen's / secondhand / denims / and /
sweat stained / gray twills / worn in / that / weathered / through / storms / seasons / and /
Sonny's Blues

          my prayers / my tears / my dreams / are woven / in / this shield / every patch /
          each square / for / one child / plus one / for me / and one / for Little

          my soul / grows / deep in / the knowing / this patchwork / tree / preserves / our
                    memories / our histories / abstracted / coded / only / to those / who
                                                          shouldn't be / knowing
from margins /   to center /
                                                          we made / our name /
as   / the Pettway /   People.
Hmm-mmh   hmm-mmH

—Daonne Huff

Aaron Douglas

1899—1979

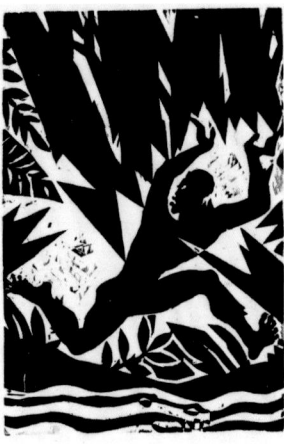

Flight, 1926. Woodcut, 8 × 5 ½ in.
Promised gift of Crystal McCrary and
Raymond J. McGuire to the Studio
Museum in Harlem and the Whitney
Museum of American Art, New York
PG.2022.4.2

COLLECTION

Aaron Douglas arrived in Harlem in 1925. As an art student in Nebraska
and an art teacher in Missouri, Douglas had read of Harlem's burgeoning cultural scene in *The Crisis*, the monthly magazine of the NAACP,
and *Opportunity*, the journal of the National Urban League. Before the
year was out, Douglas began contributing to these publications. With
the encouragement of artists and writers active in the New Negro
Movement—including Alain Locke, W. E. B. Du Bois, and Winold Reiss—he
developed a signature visual language informed by both African art and
European modernism. He quickly established a career as an illustrator,
not only for *The Crisis* and *Opportunity*, but also for other magazines,
for Locke's criticism, and for Langston Hughes's poetry. In 1926, when
Theatre Arts Monthly published Locke's article "The Negro and the
American Stage," Douglas contributed two black-and-white illustrations inspired by Eugene O'Neill's play *Emperor Jones*. In *Flight*, the
titular Jones—a former Pullman porter turned disgraced Caribbean
emperor—flees from his rebelling subjects through a jungle. Carving
negative space into a wooden block, Douglas crafted angular, exaggerated foliage that seems to threaten, even pierce, the similarly exaggerated form of the antihero. The original caption lauded the image's
"sharply defined sense of dramatic design—of drama in design."[8]

As Douglas gained prominence and expanded his artistic practice over the
course of the 1930s, he continued to use figures in profile, limited color
palettes, and overlapping flat forms to cultivate a sense of drama. He produced numerous illustrations, paintings, and murals—including the *Aspects
of Negro Life* mural cycle at Harlem's Schomburg Center for Research
in Black Culture, completed in 1934. From the pages of influential magazines to the walls of cultural institutions, Douglas established not only
a unique personal style but a defining aesthetic of the Harlem Renaissance.

— Katherine Fein

Malvin Gray Johnson

1896—1934

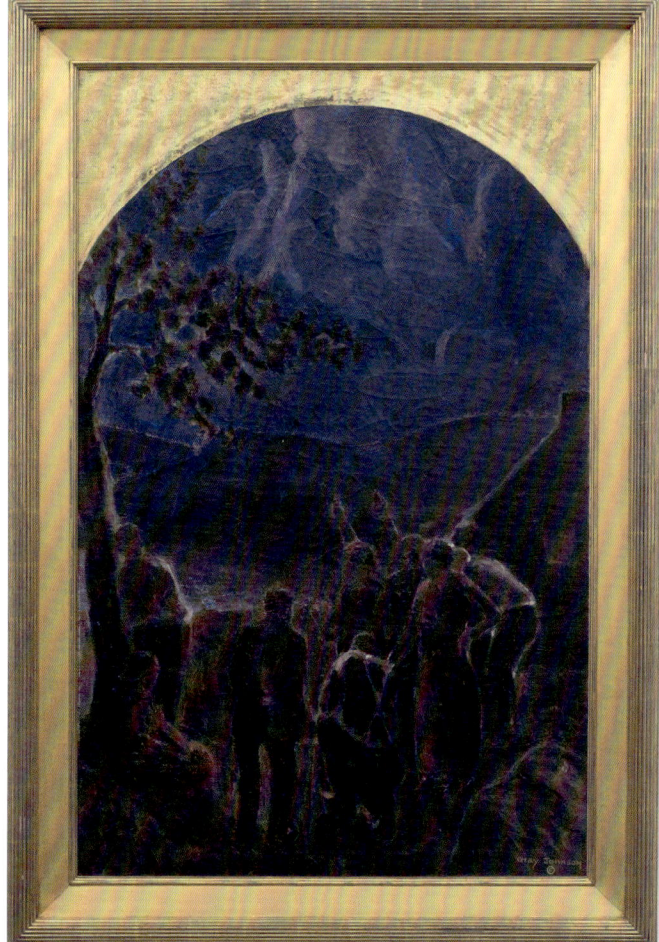

Malvin Gray Johnson's *Swing Low, Sweet Chariot*, a visual imagining
of the Black spiritual of the same name, emphasizes African American
vernacular traditions within a modern painting style. Framed by a gilded
arc, black- and burgundy-tinted figures huddle together near a tree.
They direct their attention to the dark blue sky, where a chariot pulled
by three horses appears out of the clouds. According to Johnson, the
figures represent enslaved African Americans, who, after a grueling day
of work, call up to God to ask for freedom. The chariot, driven by angels,
symbolizes God's attempt to rescue the slaves, referring to the lines
in the second verse: "I looked over Jordan and what did I see / Coming
for to carry me home / A band of angels coming after me / Coming
for to carry me home." Johnson depicts this scene through techniques
inspired by the French Post-Impressionist painter Paul Cézanne, such
as the use of flattened space and the inclusion of blocky forms with
little volume or detail; the intensely dark palette derives from the work
of Symbolist painter Albert Pinkham Ryder. While Johnson was never

especially religious, he saw in the spirituals an opportunity for experi-mentation, a chance to combine a Black idiom with modernist practices.

Swing Low, Sweet Chariot was the first major painting of Johnson's career, and in 1929, it earned him a top prize at the Harmon Foundation's annual exhi-bition. Born in Greensboro, North Carolina, the artist studied at the National Academy of Design and spent most of his adult life living in New York, until his sudden death in 1934. As an active member of the Harlem Renaissance, Johnson was influenced by Alain Locke, who called on Black artists to look to African American subject matter for inspiration. In painting scenes from spirituals, such as *Swing Low, Sweet Chariot,* Johnson offered images of Black resistance and perseverance in the face of hardship—a picture of hope for Black Americans dealing with racism and inequality in the 1920s.

— Eliza Butler

Doris Ulmann

1882—1934

Traveling along the coastal region of the Southern United States, photographer Doris Ulmann made a lasting impact with her momentous photo series, which captured the rural lives of the Gullah Geechee people, formerly enslaved people and their descendants living on a plantation in the 1930s. To accompany the publication *Roll, Jordan, Roll* by Julia Peterkin, Ulmann photographed the group and their long-standing folk traditions. Through her meticulous approach and unique perspective, Ulmann created a compelling body of work that both documented a specific time and place and celebrated the resilience and dignity of this community.

Ulmann took a deeply personal approach to her photographic process. Rather than merely observing, she immersed herself in the Gullah community. In *The Choir*, Ulmann fully embraced the pictorialist approach. She employed a soft-focus technique and carefully composed her subjects, lending the photograph a mysterious, dreamlike quality. Though their full-bodied figures are made visible, each face is unrecognizable. Upon close inspection, the photograph reads like a charcoal drawing with characteristics of an Impressionist painting: airy lighting effects, an unprocessed look or lack of definition, and practically fleeting. Ulmann elevates her subjects beyond documentation, creating a deeply empathetic portrait that was not often seen in documentary photography of Black people in the United States at the time.

When Peterkin's *Roll, Jordan, Roll* was published, the images were reproduced as ninety lavish hand-pulled photogravures. The high-quality production and attention to detail in the printing further emphasized the artistry and significance of Ulmann's work. The photogravures allowed the subtleties of light and shade, as well as the intricate textures, to be faithfully represented, enhancing the emotional impact and immersing the viewer in the world of Ulmann's subjects.

— Jayson Overby Jr.

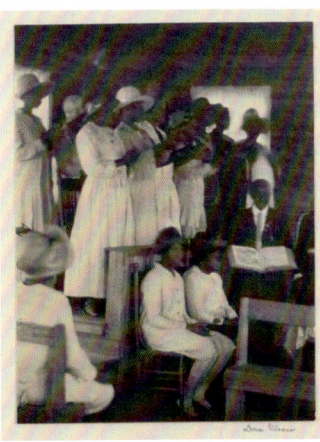

The Choir, c. 1928—30. Platinum print, 7 ⅞ × 6 ⅛ in. Gift of Joy of Giving Something Inc. 2018.47.43

Augusta Savage

1892—1962

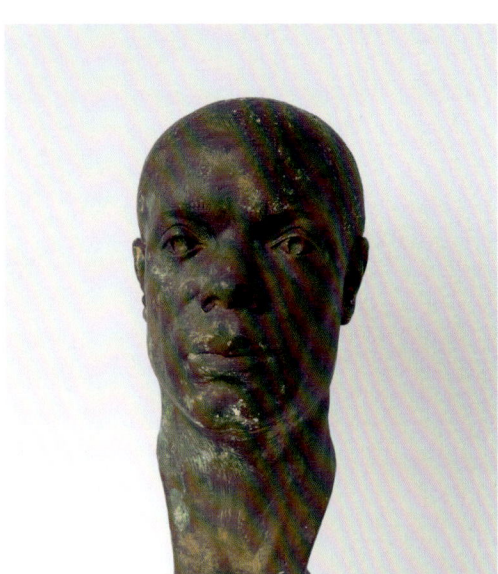

Bust of Dr. William Pickens, Sr.,
1932—33. Plaster, 16 ½ × 7 × 9 in.
Gift of Mr. William Pickens III, New
York 2002.28

William Pickens (1881—1954) was an author, educator, and prominent leader of the civil rights organizations the National Association for the Advancement of Colored People (NAACP) and the Niagara Movement. Born in South Carolina and raised in Arkansas, Pickens studied at numerous institutions— Talladega College, Yale University, Fisk University, and Selma University—and authored several books, including an autobiography, *Bursting Bonds* (1923). In sculptor Augusta Savage's plaster bust, Pickens appears calm and resolute. The work's surface is painted to approximate the metallic and weathered patina of a bronze sculpture, further enhancing a sense of monumentality.

A resident of Harlem since 1921, Savage completed this bust of Pickens shortly after her return to New York after three years of study in Paris under the auspices of the Julius Rosenwald Fund, which gave hundreds of grants to African American artists during the 1930s and 1940s. Savage was by this point well known for her astutely modeled portraits, earning acclaim in previous years for sculpting the likenesses of Black luminaries such as W. E. B. Du Bois and Marcus Garvey. Savage's portrait busts were but one part of her broader practice as both an artist and activist. In the same years she sculpted this bust of Pickens, for instance, she established the Harlem Community Art Center (then the Savage Studio of Arts and Crafts) and worked as an influential teacher and mentor to a new generation of African American artists in New York and beyond.

—Caitlin Meehye Beach

James Van Der Zee
1886—1983

James Van Der Zee is renowned for his compelling narrative studio portraiture. Born in a racially segregated United States, Van Der Zee chose to portray his subjects in a dignified manner, irrespective of white society's views. In doing so, he not only humanized African American narratives of his time but also spun a poignant cultural tapestry of Harlem, all through the lenses of art and empathy. Indeed, amid the collective strides of the Harlem Renaissance, Van Der Zee was a beacon of representation and innovative creativity.

Through his deliberate choices in lighting, composition, and subject matter, Van Der Zee transformed ordinary scenes into astonishing works of art. Van Der Zee was recognized for his meticulous attention to detail and his ability to capture the spirit of his subjects. In *Christmas Morning*, a family of five stands in front of an ornately decorated Christmas tree. Caught in a moment of laughter and glee, the father beams at his son, who stares into the camera, same as his mom and two siblings. Van Der Zee was known for using props and costumes to create elaborate and visually striking backgrounds. He also retouched his images to alter the appearances of his photographed sitters; this technique also included applying color to heighten and add detail to the stylized photographs. Here, all of the hand-painted ornaments and other decorations gleam brightly across the otherwise black-and-white image. Van Der Zee's surrealistic approach to portraiture, and also his process, set him apart from other photographers; across his photographs, at times viewers may not be able to distinguish reality from fantasy.

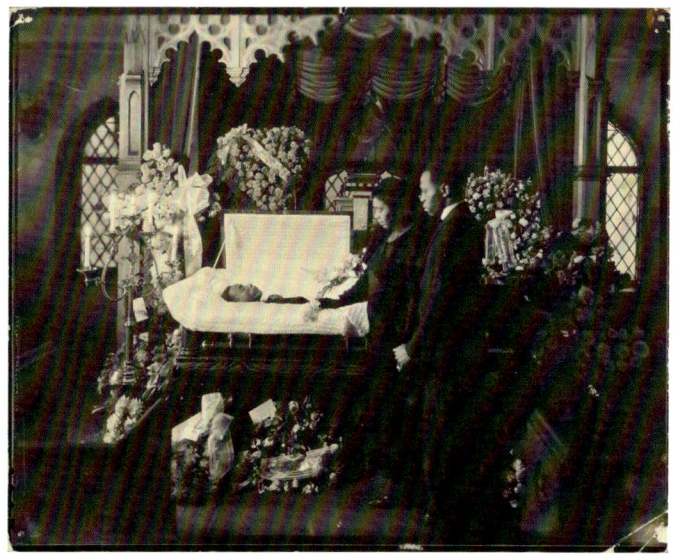

Funeral Portrait: Man in Casket, with Mourners, 1920s—30s. Gelatin silver print, image: 7 ⅝ × 9 ⅝ in.; sheet: 8 × 10 in. James Van Der Zee Archive, The Metropolitan Museum of Art; print from the shared collection of the Studio Museum in Harlem (2021.30.28) and The Metropolitan Museum of Art (2021.444.28)

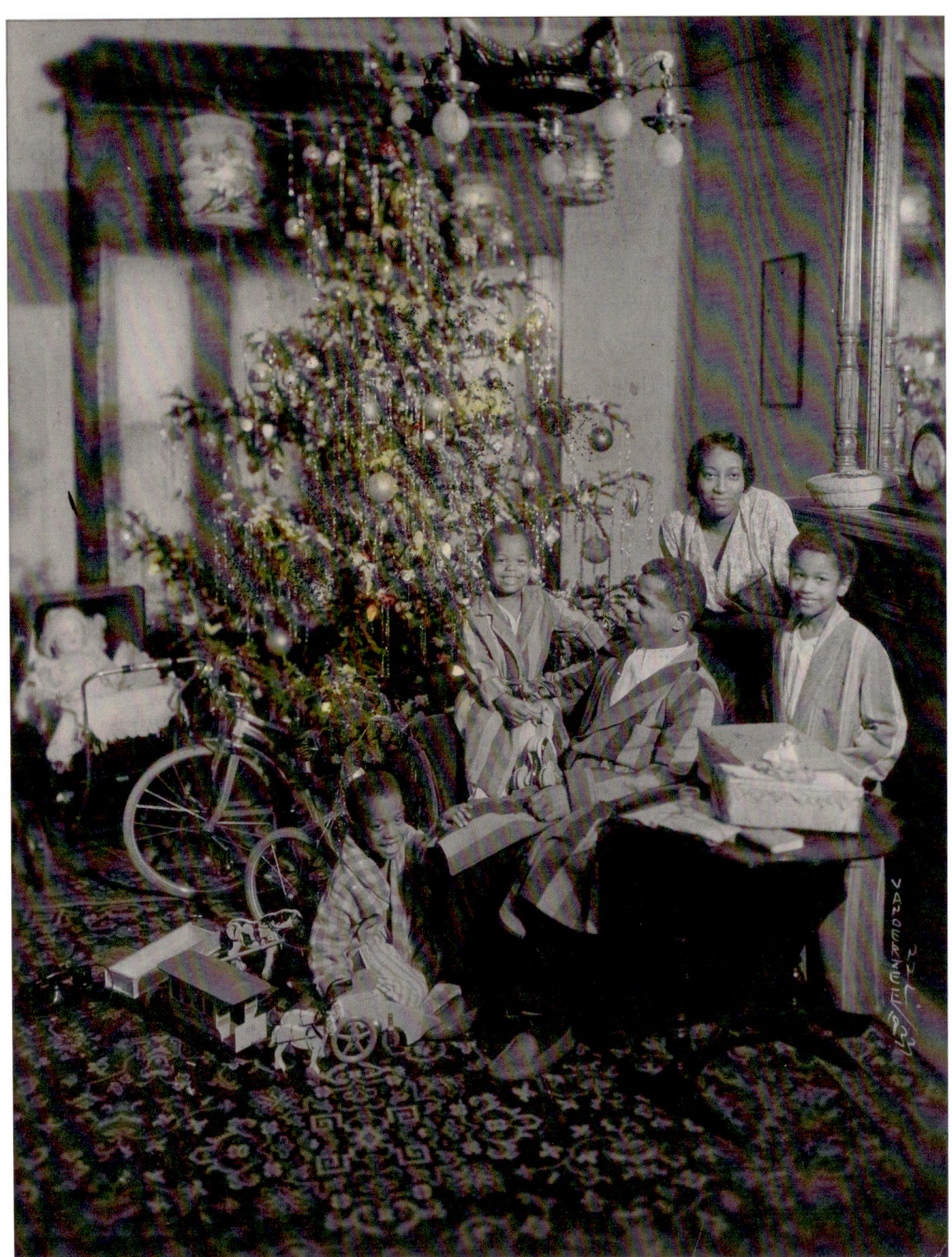

Christmas Morning, 1933. Hand-painted
gelatin silver print, 9 ½ × 7 ⅜ in. Gift of
the Sandor Family Collection, Chicago
2000.11.10

In *Choir Boy*, a young man sings as he gazes upward. He is ethereal, nestled between an assortment of flowers and plants. In the right corner, Van Der Zee manipulated the image to integrate a group of putti using the photo-montage technique known as "combination printing" to layer the images. He used this photographic technique often, mainly in his mortuary portraits.[9]

In *Funerary Portrait*, a deceased man lies in his casket surrounded by bouquets of flowers. On top of the picture, Van Der Zee overlaid the church hymn "Goin' Home," a widely popular funeral song. The line "I'll be going home" is front and center. It is repeated, attesting that God's disciples are eager and ready to join ancestors and return to a place of home, heaven. Photography historian Deborah Willis says, "We know of no one else who photographed the rites of the dead so imaginatively, although postmortem photography has been widely practiced throughout American history. Such photographs must have had a special resonance in a Harlem where Victorian spiritual sentiment still found many eager adherents."[10]

Throughout his career, Van Der Zee dexterously blended his cutting-edge techniques with much sincerity. His dedication to each of his subjects—the famous and the everyday people—and determination to document their lives traced a legacy of Black excellence. The hand-coloring, the meticulous manipulation, and the bold exploration of themes—from prosperity to mortality—affirm Van Der Zee's impact and his contribution to the canon of photography and Black portraiture.

—Jayson Overby Jr.

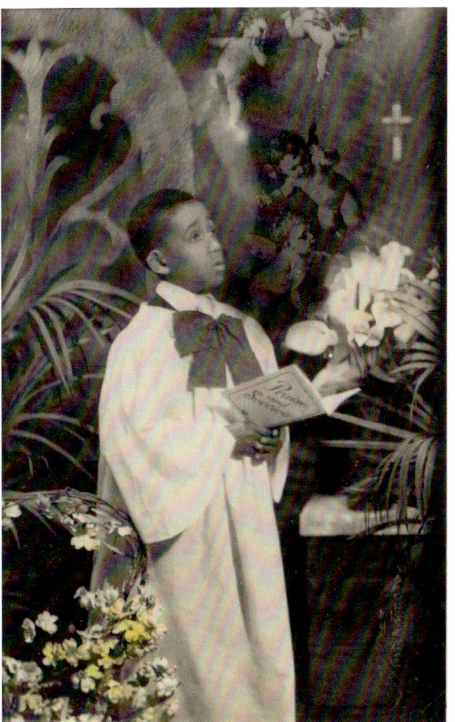

Choir Boy, 1937. Gelatin silver print, 8 × 5 in.
Gift of the Sandor Family Collection,
Chicago 2000.11.13

Meta Vaux Warrick Fuller

1877—1968

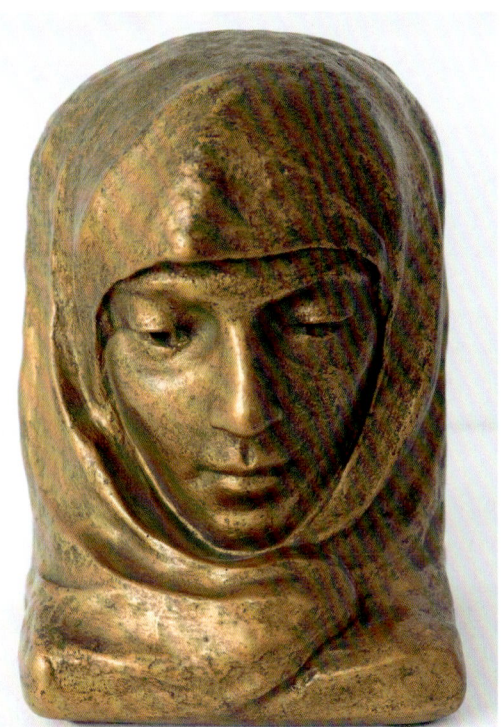

Silence, 1934. Painted plaster, 7 × 4 ½ × 5 in.
Gift of Buel A. Staggers, MD 1991.2

By the time she modeled the bust of *Silence* in 1934, Meta Vaux Warrick Fuller was well known as a sculptor committed to exploring human expression and emotion. From the beginning of her career, at the turn of the twentieth century, Fuller honed her skills in figurative sculpture through studies at art academies in Philadelphia and Paris and garnered international acclaim for works that expressed, in the words of one contemporary, "horror, pain, and sorrow."[11] *Silence* depicts a shrouded figure who lowers her eyes in contemplation. The artist conceived this work as one of a pair, with the pendant *Repose* (1934), a bust with its head tilting back in respite, complementing the downward gaze of *Silence*.

Fuller addressed the theme of silence before, most notably in her statuette *Mary Turner: A Silent Protest Against Mob Violence* (1919), which paid tribute to Mary Turner, a Black woman who was lynched by a mob of white men in Georgia in 1918. *Silence*, by contrast, is more enigmatic. It does not seem to refer to any one individual or event, and along with *Repose*, could be read simply as a study of emotion. Yet in the broader context of Fuller's oeuvre, with works often depicting resilience in African American history, the sculpture perhaps bespeaks what the Black feminist scholar Patricia Hill Collins has described of silence as something that is borne not of passivity but a knowingly strategic and opaque form of resistance.[12]

—Caitlin Meehye Beach

Carl Van Vechten

1880—1964

Photographer, arts patron, and writer Carl Van Vechten peered into the world that unfolded during the Harlem Renaissance. Along with his curiosity, he took with him a camera. He was an amateur to the medium but nonetheless was ushered into the close circles of the Black artists, musicians, philosophers, and writers who called Harlem their home. Though he photographed social gatherings, he found success building a portfolio of portraits of influential people of the twentieth century who were central to the Harlem Renaissance.

In 1983 the Eakins Press, in collaboration with master printers Richard Benson and Thomas Palmer, produced a portfolio of fifty selected portraits in an editioned series of one hundred.[13] The images were reproduced using a "customized hand-pulled gravure process," a technique that includes ink printing from copper plates made from negatives.[14] Among Van Vechten's famous portraits from this portfolio is one of the sociologist W. E. B. Du Bois. When photographing Du Bois, Van Vechten

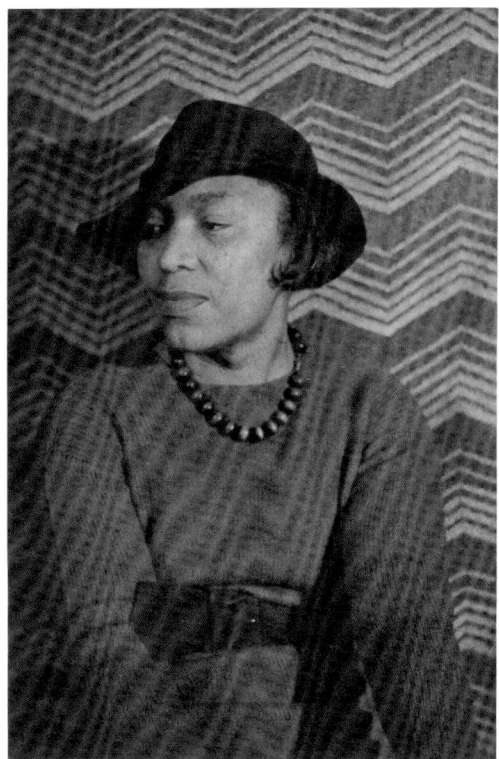

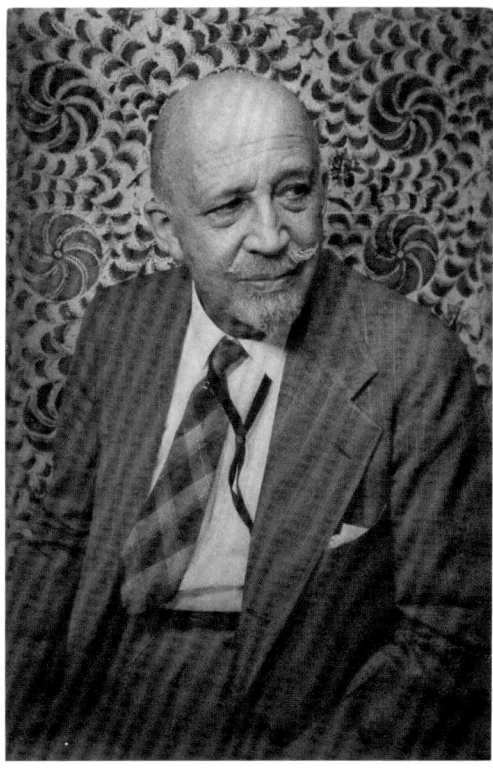

Zora Neale Hurston (from the portfolio "'O, Write My Name': American Portraits, Harlem Heroes"), 1935, printed 1983. Printed by Richard Benson (1943—2017) and Thomas Palmer (b. 1957), Published by Eakins Press Foundation, New York. Photogravure, sheet: 22 × 14 in. Museum purchase 1985.2.1

W. E. B. Du Bois (from the portfolio "'O, Write My Name': American Portraits, Harlem Heroes"), 1936, printed 1983. Printed by Richard Benson (1943—2017) and Thomas Palmer (b. 1957), Published by Eakins Press Foundation, New York. Photogravure, sheet: 22 × 14 in. Museum purchase 1985.2.7

sought to convey his intellectual and authoritative presence.[15] He captures Du Bois with an imposing pose and averted gaze; the strong lighting and sharp focus accentuate Du Bois's features, showcasing his intensity. This photograph of Du Bois is one of many that was captured; in one of the others he offers Van Vechten a slight smile.

In another photograph from the portfolio, a forty-four-year-old Zora Neale Hurston sits against a zigzag background. Unlike Du Bois's look, her slight smirk feels like an invitation, very hopeful. Hurston, an anthropologist and writer, formed a long-lasting friendship with Van Vechten, and sat for the photographer often. In a 1934 letter to the photographer, she wrote, "I love myself when I am laughing. And then again when I am looking mean and impressive."[16] Van Vechten's photograph of Hurston would become one of the most circulated images of the writer.

—Jayson Overby Jr.

Aaron Siskind

1903—1991

The entrance of the stately building has been boarded up. Ornate moldings, testaments to better days, no longer frame the front door but the words "danger, keep out." Ignoring this warning, four children gain access through the ground-floor window. Two boys perch on the ledge, peering into the dark interior, and a third has climbed to the second floor, looking down at his companions below. The fourth child stands just inside the lower window, entirely obscured except for their hand. Illuminated by the bright sun, this hand offers assistance to the two boys on the ledge in a gesture that suggests both caution and camaraderie.

Aaron Siskind produced this photograph as part of the "Harlem Document" series. In the midst of the Great Depression, he collaborated with other photographers and writers to establish the Feature Group, a suborganization within New York's Photo League dedicated to advocating for social change through documentary photographic essays. "Harlem Document" became their most visible project, with selections published in *Fortune* and *Look* magazines and exhibited in Harlem and elsewhere in New York City. Although World War II interfered with further publication plans, Siskind returned to this project decades later, producing a photo book of the same name in 1981. Together, the photographs of "Harlem Document" paint an unsparing yet often joyful portrait of Depression-era Harlem. With signature attention to texture and composition, Siskind captured scenes of domesticity, street life, architectural facades, nightclubs, and more. Like *Boys in Empty Tenement*, many "Harlem Document" photographs feature children. Through their eyes, viewers witness dereliction, hardship, and struggle, but also playfulness and resiliency. Come with us, that outstretched hand seems to say, and we will explore together.

—Katherine Fein

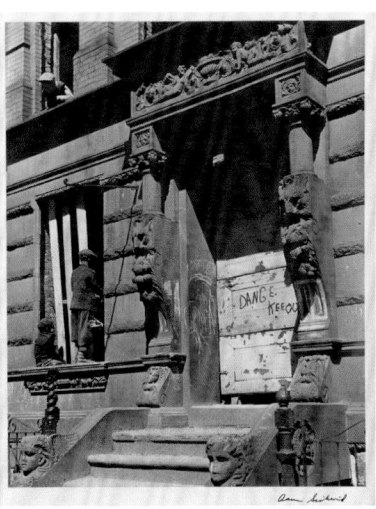

Boys in Empty Tenement (from the series "Harlem Document"), 1935. Vintage gelatin silver print, 14 × 11 in. Gift of Barbara Doty, Iowa City, IA, in partnership with Robert Mann Gallery, New York 2002.12.3

Clementine Hunter

1886/7—1988

Untitled (Man Dying) is a poignant depiction of the liminal moment between life and death. Its formal qualities epitomize Clementine Hunter's large oeuvre. A prolific, self-taught "memory painter," Hunter illustrated the landscape of the Louisiana plantation life that occupied her daily life. Producing between five and ten thousand works, she rendered colorful, abstract scenes of fieldwork, baptisms, and weddings on an array of materials, such as discarded items, bottles, canvases, and quilts.

This intimate and dreamlike oil painting shows a dark-skinned figure on their deathbed accompanied by a loved one. She paints both figures in flat profile—a standard of figuration in Hunter's practice. Their hands and bodies connect at the midpoint of the composition, rendering their bodies indistinguishable from one another. In a surrealist turn, the figures lay somewhere on the threshold between outside and inside, life and death, sheltered by a colorfully painted tree in full bloom and a facade-less house. The near-black roots of the tree and foundation of the house interlock, similar to the figures' hands, in a gesture of support and comfort. A solitary chair at the bottom of the painting hovers in space, expressing—with the dark blueish hues throughout—the scene's solemnity. The active brushstrokes that make up the natural elements, details, and figures of the painting pop against an otherwise untouched paper background.

Although she received little formal schooling, it is clear from her work that Hunter studied in the storied Cane River region of Louisiana. Her unparalleled level of detail and intuition allowed her to establish an artistic career on her own terms. Her dedication to creatively commemorating Southern Black life garnered her great acclaim within her lifetime despite starting her career as a painter in her late fifties. Like the backward C and H with which she signed each of her works, Hunter left an indelible mark on US art history.

—Rachell Morillo

Untitled (Man Dying), c. 1940—45. Oil on paper, 13 ¾ × 12 ¼ in. Gift of Maurice C. and Patricia L. Thompson Jr., CT 1995.4.2

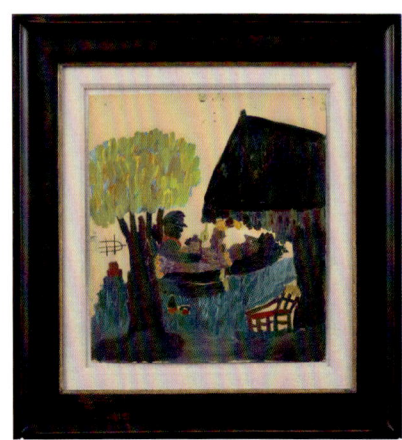

Loïs Mailou Jones

1905—1998

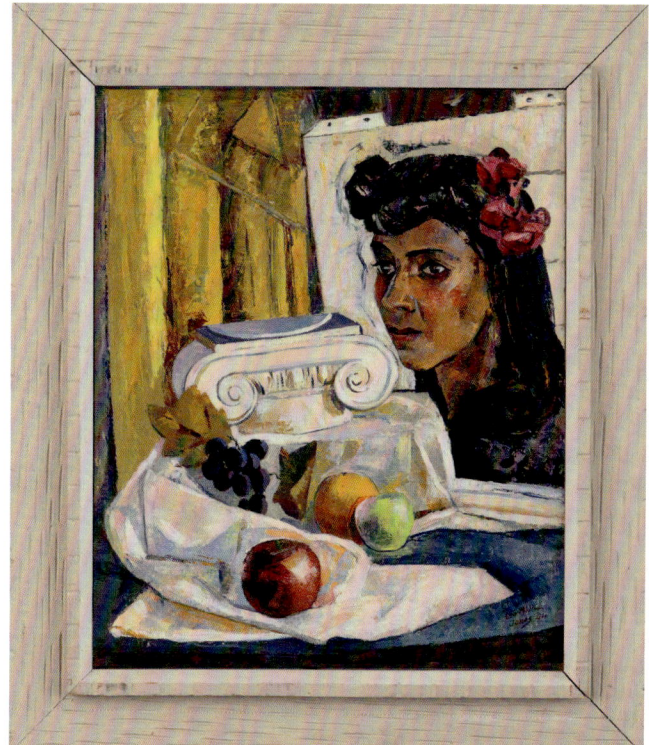

Still Life with Portrait, 1944. Oil on canvas, 25 ½ × 21 ½ × 1 in. Gift of Loïs Mailou Jones Pierre-Noel Trust 2014.1.2

In 1996, the Studio Museum in Harlem named Loïs Mailou Jones "Artist of the Year." At ninety years old, Jones used the occasion to reflect on her long career: "My friend Dorothy West tells people she's the last surviving writer from the Harlem Renaissance. Well, I'm the last artist."[17] Indeed, Jones came of age at the height of the Harlem Renaissance, and one of her earliest accomplishments was designing the cover for the August 1928 issue of *Opportunity*, a leading journal of Black culture. By the time she accepted the Studio Museum award seventy years later, she had made a profound mark as an artist and teacher.

Born and raised in Boston, Jones studied at the School of the Museum of Fine Arts, becoming its first Black graduate in 1927. She worked briefly as a textile designer before pursuing teaching, and in 1930 she became the first woman to serve as a faculty member of the art department at Howard University. Jones taught at Howard for almost fifty years, impacting generations of students, several of whom went on to become prominent artists themselves. As she taught, she remained committed to her artistic practice, taking inspiration from her travels across the country and around the world. During the 1930s, she spent summers in New York, where she mingled with the leading figures of the New Negro Movement, including her Howard colleague Alain Locke and artist Aaron Douglas. From 1937 to 1938, a sabbatical in France immersed Jones in the vibrant

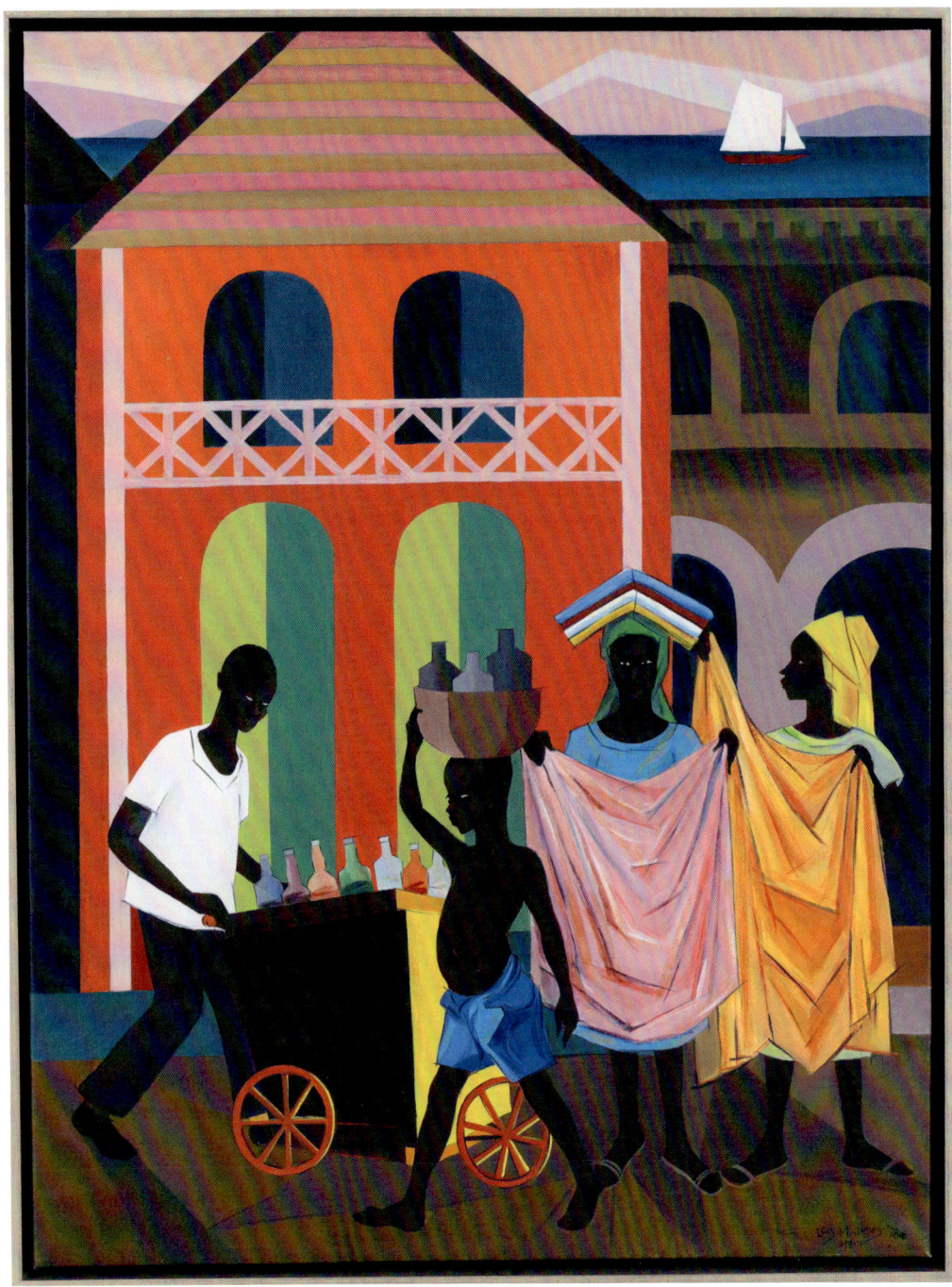

Street Vendors, Haiti 1978, 1978. Acrylic
on canvas, 53 × 40 ¼ in. Gift of
Loïs Mailou Jones Pierre-Noel Trust
2014.1.5

Afrodiasporic community in Paris and afforded her firsthand access to African and European art in French museums. She would return often over the following years, and this community and these art traditions had a lasting influence on her work.

In *Still Life with Portrait*, for example, Jones riffs on the European still-life genre, wielding the bold brushwork of Post-Impressionism to represent four pieces of fruit and an Ionic capital arranged on a white sheet. Behind these posed elements, a portrait of a young Black woman rests on an easel. Rendered just as vividly as the objects on the table, the woman seems present with them, rather than confined to the painting within the painting. Yet this portrait is not complete—bare canvas surrounds her face, unfinished and unframed. Here, Jones simultaneously lays bare the artifice of painting and asserts her proficiency in multiple genres. She reflects on the role of Black women in art as both subjects and artists, claiming a place for herself in art history.

In the 1950s, Jones began traveling regularly to Haiti, and in 1970, she made her first of several trips to West Africa. The people, landscapes, art, and spiritual practices of these places took center stage in many paintings during the second half of her career, including *Street Vendors, Haiti 1978* and *Les Jumeaux Du Longo*, both in the Studio Museum's permanent collection. In the 1970s, Jones received overdue recognition on a national level, including a retrospective at the Museum of Fine Arts, Boston—the first solo show dedicated to a Black woman artist at that museum. She left behind an oeuvre that spans the twentieth century, transcends genres and geographies, and honors the richness and complexity of Black life.

—Katherine Fein

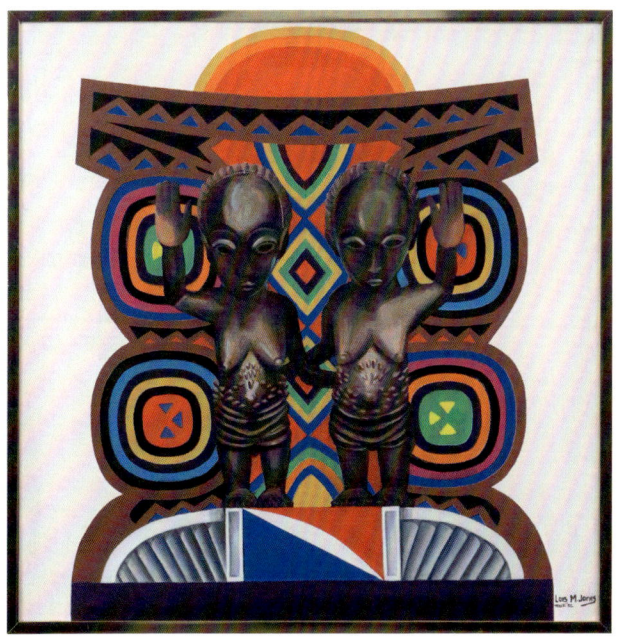

Les Jumeaux Du Longo, 1982. Acrylic on canvas, 36 × 36 in. Gift of Loïs Mailou Jones Pierre-Noel Trust 2014.1.1

Hayward Oubre

1916—2006

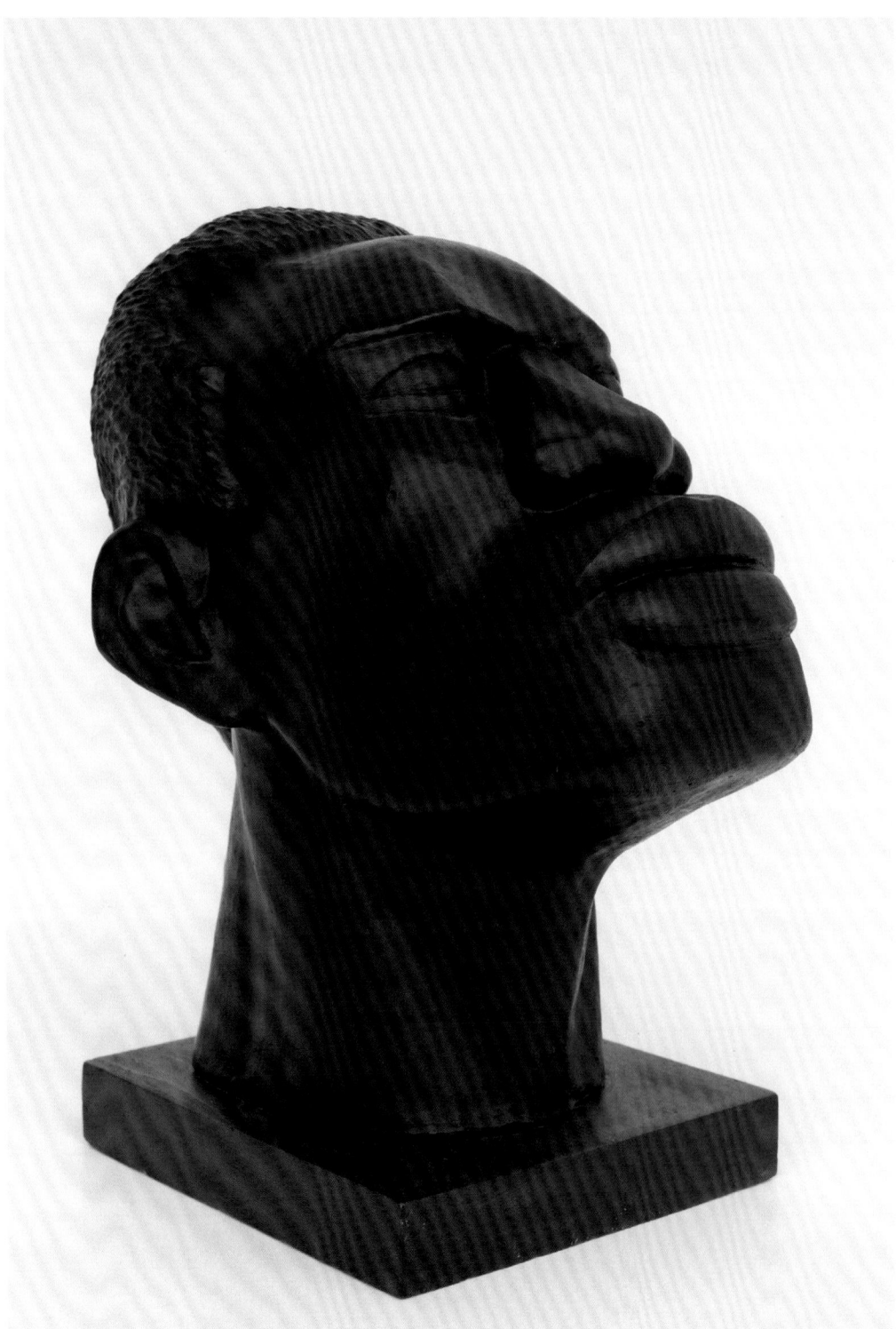

Following his undergraduate degree in art from Dillard University and his continued study as a special student at Atlanta University with Hale Woodruff, Hayward Oubre joined the United States Army in 1941. He served in the 97th Regiment until 1944, and alongside 3,700 other Black soldiers and engineers, he constructed the Alaska-Canadian Highway. As a military engineer, Oubre and many Black soldiers performed specialized work during World War II, even as the press largely represented Black soldiers as only serving as unskilled laborers, including stevedores.[18]

Oubre sculpted *Stevedore* in 1945, shortly after he was honorably discharged from the army. For artists in the United States at the time, stevedores represented the hardworking people who grounded industry in the country. Instead of focusing on broad shoulders and a defined body—as Richmond Barthé did in his sculpture of the same name, created in 1937—Oubre represents only the upturned face and powerful jaw of his figure. He avoids the overt indications of labor that Barthé built into his sculpture, including the rope and navy cap held by the figure, instead emphasizing this man's strength of character.[19] Born in New Orleans, Oubre would have seen the stevedores who labored at the city's ports. With Oubre's familiarity with both civilian and military dockworkers, his sculpture presents an idealized, heroic symbol of the dignity of the Black worker.

This Social Realism, as well as the sculpture's grounding in Renaissance portraiture, emerged from Oubre's study with Woodruff at Atlanta University. After sculpting *Stevedore*, Oubre pursued a master of fine arts degree at the University of Iowa before returning to the South to teach, ultimately chairing the art departments at both Alabama State University and Winston-Salem State University. His early plaster sculptures, like *Stevedore*, later inspired his best-known body of work, his wire sculptures.[20] Revealing a version of the armature of such plaster works, these dynamic linear sculptures were created with coat hanger wire.

—Katelyn D. Crawford

Stevedore, 1945. Black painted plaster with wood base, 15 × 9 × 12 ½ in. Gift of Michael Rosenfeld and halley k. harrisburg 2003.2.6

Eldzier Cortor

1916—2015

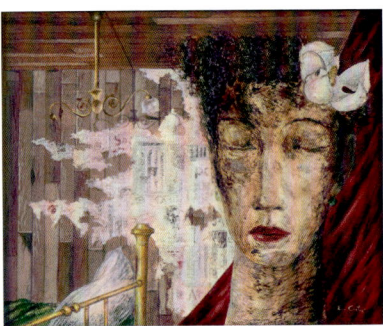

The Room, 1949. Oil on Masonite,
7 ⅞ × 9 ⅞ in. Gift of Katrina McCormick
Barnes 1971.1

Eldzier Cortor was a master of tensions, cultivating with brush and pigment complex microcosms of Black life. Trained at the Art Institute of Chicago and later under László Moholy-Nagy at Chicago's Institute of Design, Cortor synthesized his academic and modernist training to produce ethereal imagery of Black people, particularly women; his elongated forms were dually inspired by the African sculptures he studied at Chicago's Field Museum.

The Room exemplifies Cortor's distinctive style par excellence. In 1971 the painting was the very first the Studio Museum in Harlem accepted, leading up to the formation of its official collection in 1977. Strong lines cut across the intimately scaled composition, framing a poised Black woman in a moment of serenity and quietude. Part of a series of urban interior scenes, similar features appear across each of the paintings—otherworldly Black figures in states of rest or meditation, their limbs graceful and strong, their skin radiant. A crimson cloth complements a green bedcover, both of which are echoed in the figure's lips and earring. The red lipstick and jade jewelry can be excavated for their period significance: the first an indicator of feminine beauty during and following World War II, and the latter a powerful symbol of serenity. A white magnolia flower nestles into the figure's lush curls at her temple, possibly symbolizing the Southern origins of the woman herself and the durability of the magnolia tree; its shapely blooms also suggest stability and resilience.

An expert mark-maker, Cortor builds further depth and richness by exploiting the pull between delicate hatching and thick impasto, as seen in the figure's tightly coiled hair. Often described as surreal, Cortor's work regularly presents the affecting luminescence of Black interiority. Despite the disarray of poverty, as evidenced by the papered walls and broken light fixture, Cortor's figures are dignified, self-assured, and caught in states of tranquility, a masterclass in narrative tension. Against the harrowing backdrop of US racial inequality, Cortor's work manifests Black peace as beauty and resistance.

—Stephanie Sparling Williams, with research assistance from Grace Billingslea

Robert Blackburn
1920—2003

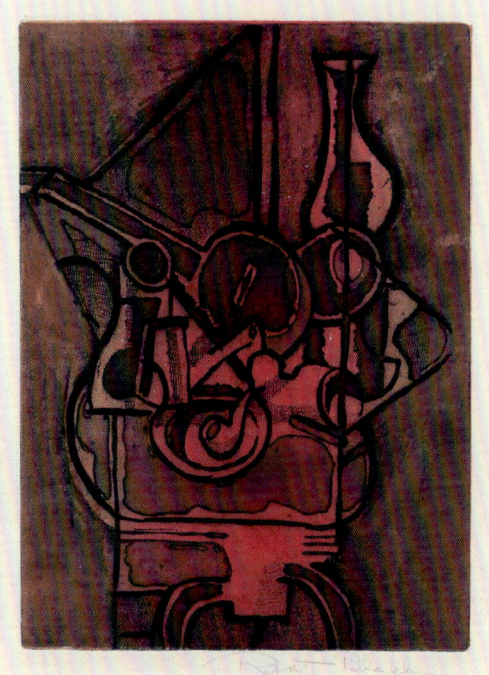

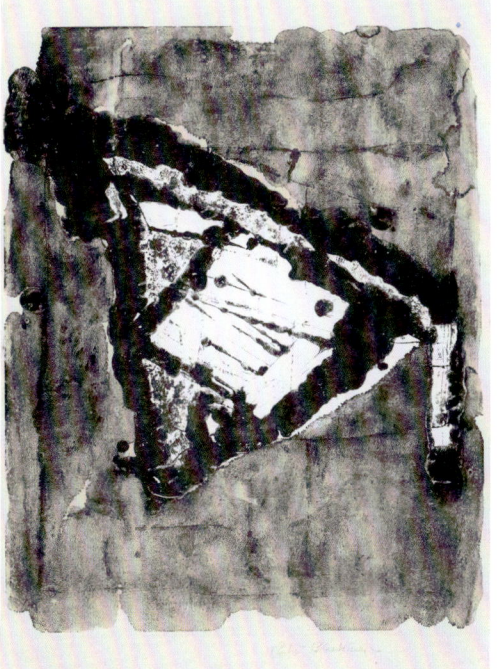

Artist's Table, 1957. Intaglio with color
additions, 9 ¾ × 7 ¾ in. Gift of anonymous
donor 2014.14.2

Ominous Shape (aka Ominous Black),
1970s. Lithograph on paper, 23 ½ × 19 in.
sheet: 28 × 20 in. Gift of the Estate of
Robert Blackburn 2016.1.10

Community-based and artist-run initiatives launched the career of Harlem
native Robert Blackburn. As a youth, he attended classes at the Harlem
Community Arts Center, the Harlem Art Workshop, and the Uptown Art
Laboratory. Through these programs, he befriended and learned from some
of the century's leading Black visual artists. His teachers included Selma
Burke, Sargent Johnson, Norman Lewis, and Augusta Savage. Blackburn also
studied alongside the artists Ernest Crichlow, Roy DeCarava, and Jacob
Lawrence. Printmaking, lithography in particular, was fundamental to these
community arts projects and, as a result, Blackburn's introduction to the
artistic profession. He embraced the medium of printmaking at a time when
his teachers and peers steered toward the more popularized art forms
of painting and photography.

As his career unfolded, two dimensions of printmaking animated his
practice: first, the relationship between the artist and printer; second,
how the painterly process translated to printmaking. In the end, his
visual language shifted from Social Realism to abstraction. The Mexican
muralist movement initially inspired him to depict the life conditions
of workers. In 1941 he enrolled at the Art Students League, where he met
the painter and printmaker William Barnett and received an introduction

to Euro-American art movements such as Cubism. In this period, he also developed an interest in the intaglio printing promoted by Stanley William Hayter and his workshop Atelier 17. In 1947, with Barnett's help, Blackburn opened his own studio, which transformed into a printmaking workshop. Together with Barnett, he adopted techniques unfamiliar to printers in the United States. For example, he used multiple stones in one print to create still-life works. When black-and-white was the norm in lithography printing, he incorporated color to allow for diverse compositional forms. Works like *Untitled (boats)*, *Artist's Table*, and *Red Wine Glass* reflect these interests. While operating his studio, Blackburn served from 1957 to 1963 as the master printer at the United Limited Artist Editions. There he pulled the first prints made by the highly celebrated artists Jasper Johns, Robert Motherwell, and Robert Rauschenberg.

Blackburn understood from personal experience that printmaking tapped into the most powerful aspect of the visual arts: community building. In 1971 he incorporated his commercial studio into the nonprofit organization named "Printmaking Workshop." For the next four decades, he operated one of the few Black artist-run spaces in New York City. Many of the artists included in the Studio Museum's permanent collection—Emma Amos, Romare Bearden, Betty Blayton, and Mavis Pusey,

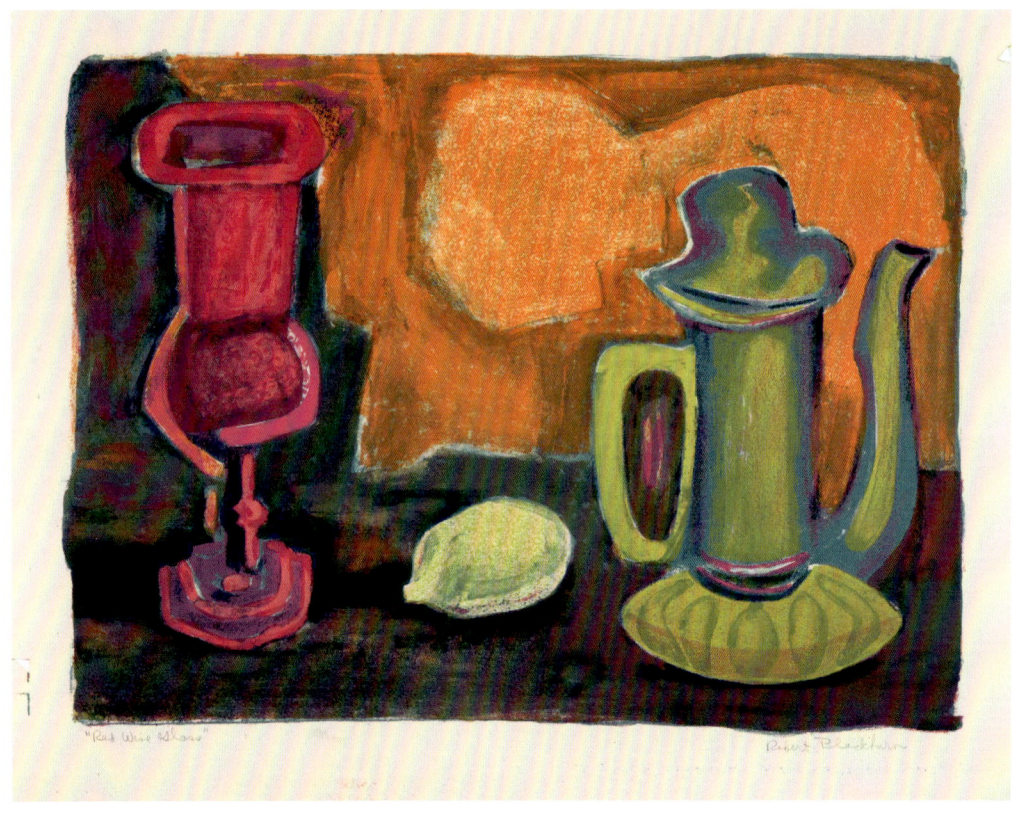

Red Wine Glass, c. 1950. Lithograph on paper, sheet: 15 × 20 ½ in. Gift of the Estate of Robert Blackburn 2016.1.5

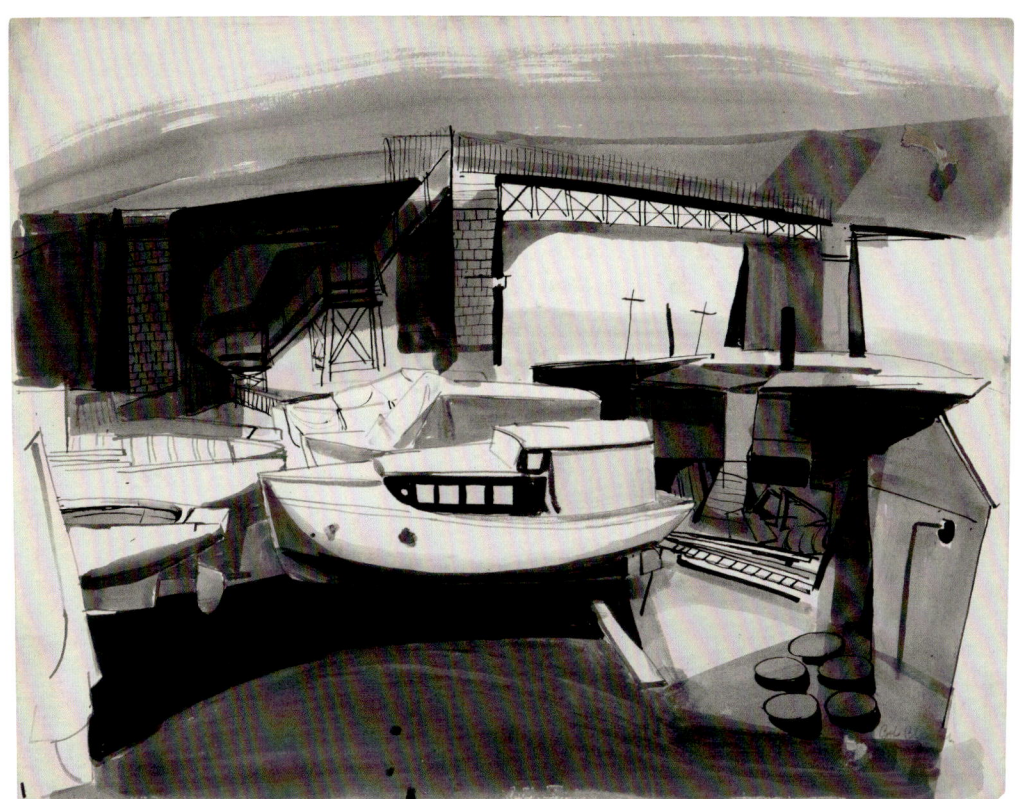

Untitled (boats), 1950—52. Ink and pencil on
paper, sheet: 17 × 22 in. Gift of the Estate of
Robert Blackburn 2016.1.2

to name a few—made prints at the Printmaking Workshop, often for
the first time and assisted by aspiring artists who served as the printers.
At Blackburn's encouragement, Bearden incorporated photo etching
and monoprint into the making of his signature collages. A work by Amos
appears on the verso of Blackburn's print *Ominous Shape (aka Ominous
Black)*, which signaled Blackburn's return to black-and-white lithography.
In addition to encouraging his peers' experimentations with printmaking,
he recycled blocks and stencils from past prints and explored methods
in etching and woodcuts. The artistry of Blackburn ultimately elevated
the standing of printmaking within the art canon, and it provided a lasting model for artists to craft a socially engaged practice.

— Drew Thompson

Roy DeCarava
1919—2009

Roy DeCarava deeply understood the world around him—and his photographs are a testimony to that. Known for his ability to capture the glory of Black life in subtle tones of gray, DeCarava left an indelible mark on the canon of American art from the mid-twentieth century on. His style can be characterized as intimate, introspective, and humanistic. His silver gelatin black-and-white images have an ageless quality about them; they transcend the confines of time and place and capture the essence of his subjects with immense compassion and sensitivity. Throughout his practice, DeCarava skillfully photographed emotions and narratives within his frame, often exposing everyday scenes and private moments that might otherwise have gone unnoticed.

In *Couple Dancing*, DeCarava photographed the closeness of a couple in a low-light environment, with each figure's face obscured. The man gently grasps the middle of the woman's back; she holds his and both move away from the light—as if their dancing is taking them away from the image itself. The interplay between light and darkness adds texture and brings the subjects closer to the forefront. Yet DeCarava maintains their privacy by creating just enough distance between the subject and viewer. There is a sense of rhythm and movement, almost as if music can be heard in the photograph. Here he photographed subtleties of human expression and interaction. The painting technique chiaroscuro, or the integration of dark and light, lent DeCarava the inspiration to produce enigmatic photographs such as *Couple Dancing*. Making use of the technique, DeCarava explores shadows and highlights, building a unique and distinctive visual language.

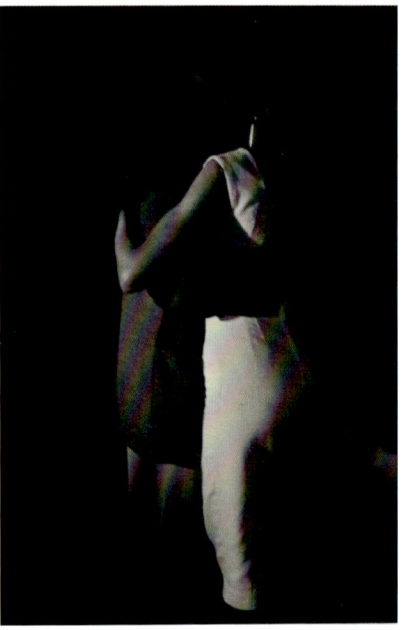

Left: *Couple Dancing*, 1956. Gelatin silver print, 14 × 11 in. Museum purchase with funds provided by the Acquisition Committee 2006.10

Right: *Lingerie*, 1950. Gelatin silver print, image: 8 ¾ × 12 ¾ in., sheet: 11 × 14 in. Gift of Wendy DeCarava and Laura DeCarava, New York 2006.12.2

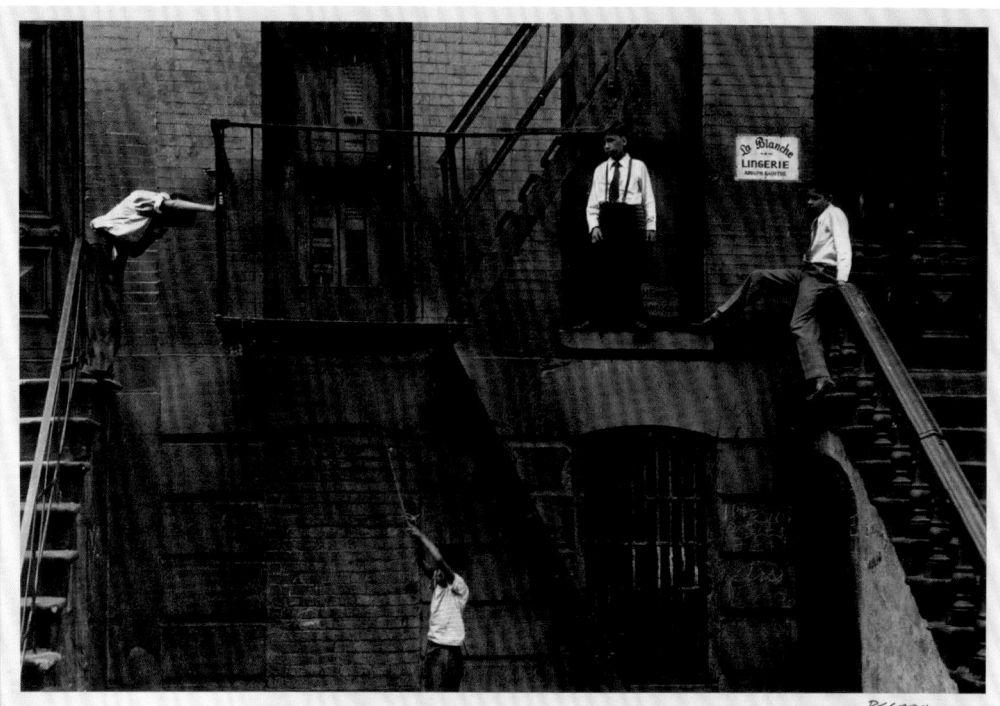

Across his practice, DeCarava consistently surveyed themes of identity, race, and social inequality. He was able to depict both the grittiness and vibrance of life, which resonated with his viewers. In *Lingerie*, titled after the La Blanche lingerie shop outside of which four young boys are pictured hanging out, the boys dawdle near the emergency fire escape, stand in the window, and sit on the stoop banister. Against the static backdrop of the worn-down building—almost like that of a photo studio—each of the boys is carefully composed; they're nearly positioned like a clock, mimicking "the rhythm of an hour, a day, a world."[21] In the darkroom, DeCarava worked routinely to improve and perfect his printing techniques. He taught himself how to make the images softer by printing in deep tones, which produced his distinctive photographs.

DeCarava developed a unique language that set him apart from his contemporaries. His compositions are meticulous, with a keen eye for framing and arrangement. As part of an early working philosophy, DeCarava wanted to provide a counternarrative to the biased representations of Black people. His deliberate focus on Black people invited folks to engage not only with the subjects' emotions, but more importantly their stories—capturing their humanity and resilience.

—Jayson Overby Jr.

Seydou Keïta

1921—2001

Seydou Keïta creatively captured the ambitions, self-projections, and tastes of thousands of people in Bamako, Mali. For the most part, his clients were part of a burgeoning middle class, resultant of a growing post—World War II economy and the loosening grip of French imperialism.[22] At the peak of his practice, between 1948 and 1962, queues of waiting clients, both the local populace and foreign visitors from neighboring countries, would form around his studio.[23] During this period he produced tens of thousands of images.[24]

Keïta's studio, built on inherited land near a prison, was centrally located. Though ease of access increased the demand for his work, his devotion to detail was the reason for his popularity. Keïta focused on highlighting the contrast between adorned, textured fabric and dark skin, which in turn was often accentuated by natural light, such as in *Untitled, #59*.[25] He explored symmetry as he negotiated whether his subjects should sit, stand, or lie down. Patrons appreciated the extent to which he directed their suits, boubou, zerebou, or other flowing garments folded or spread out against patterned backdrops—as showcased in the regal pair posing against a swirling floral motif in *Untitled, #290*. He often choreographed the gestures made by bangled wrists, the degrees to which proudly adorned necks turned, the crossing or raising of a knee, as well as the boldness of the gaze.

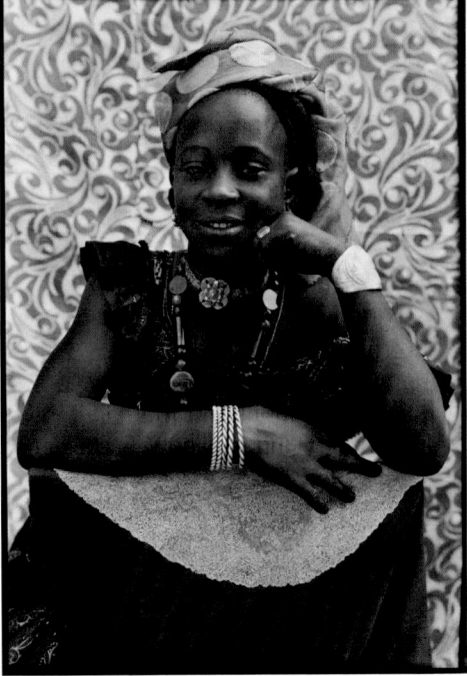

Untitled, #59, 1956—57. Gelatin silver print, image: 22 × 15 ½ in. Edition 3 of 10. Gift of Anne Ehrenkranz 2008.2

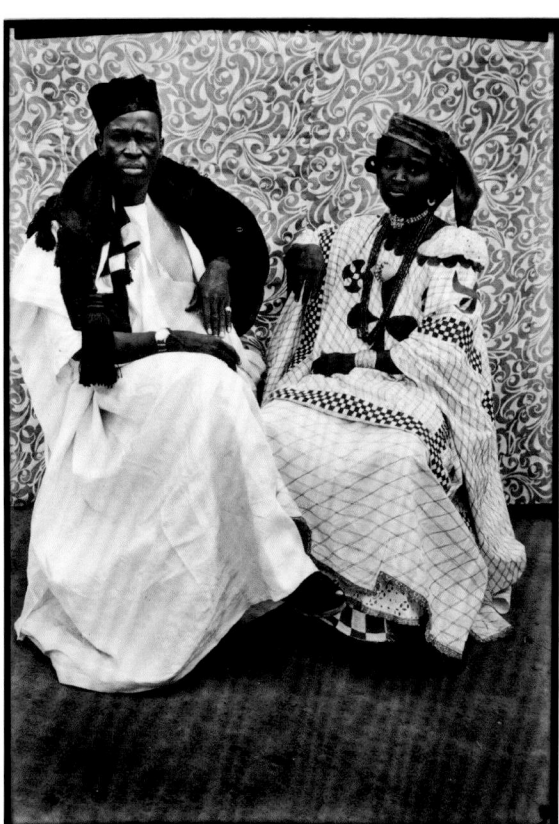

Untitled, #290, 1956—57. Gelatin silver print, image: 21 ¾ × 15 ½ in. Edition 3 of 10. Museum purchase made possible by a gift from Anne Ehrenkranz 2008.6

In his studio, the ordinary person was posed reverentially, thus appearing graceful and refined. This was often aided by the assortment of desirable props they could use, which included motorbikes, artificial flora, a radio, a television, or pens, among others. From myriad images emerge faces carrying an array of sentiments—from tempered to smiling whimsy. Over decades, Keïta captured the confidence and camaraderie of families, the tenderness of spouses leaning ever so slightly toward each other, solemn heads of home surrounded by their households, as well as wide-eyed children dressed as impeccably as adults.

In 1935 Keïta's uncle Tiemoko Keïta gave him his first camera after a visit to Senegal.[26] If gifting the fourteen-year-old with a 6 × 9 Kodak Brownie implanted in him the idea of becoming a photographer, then it was Pierre Garnier and Mountaga Kouyate who nurtured that intent. Both men equipped Keïta with the technical skills and confidence to shoot and develop his work.[27] After Mali gained independence in 1960, he spent less time in his studio, becoming more preoccupied with documenting the young country's transition to democracy and becoming an official state photographer.[28] By 1977, he had closed his studio; however, over a decade later, he was pulled out of retirement, as his meticulously archived life's work began to gain international acclaim with ever-increasing demands for exhibitions, from Paris to New York and beyond.

—Tandazani Dhlakama

Hale Woodruff

1900—1980

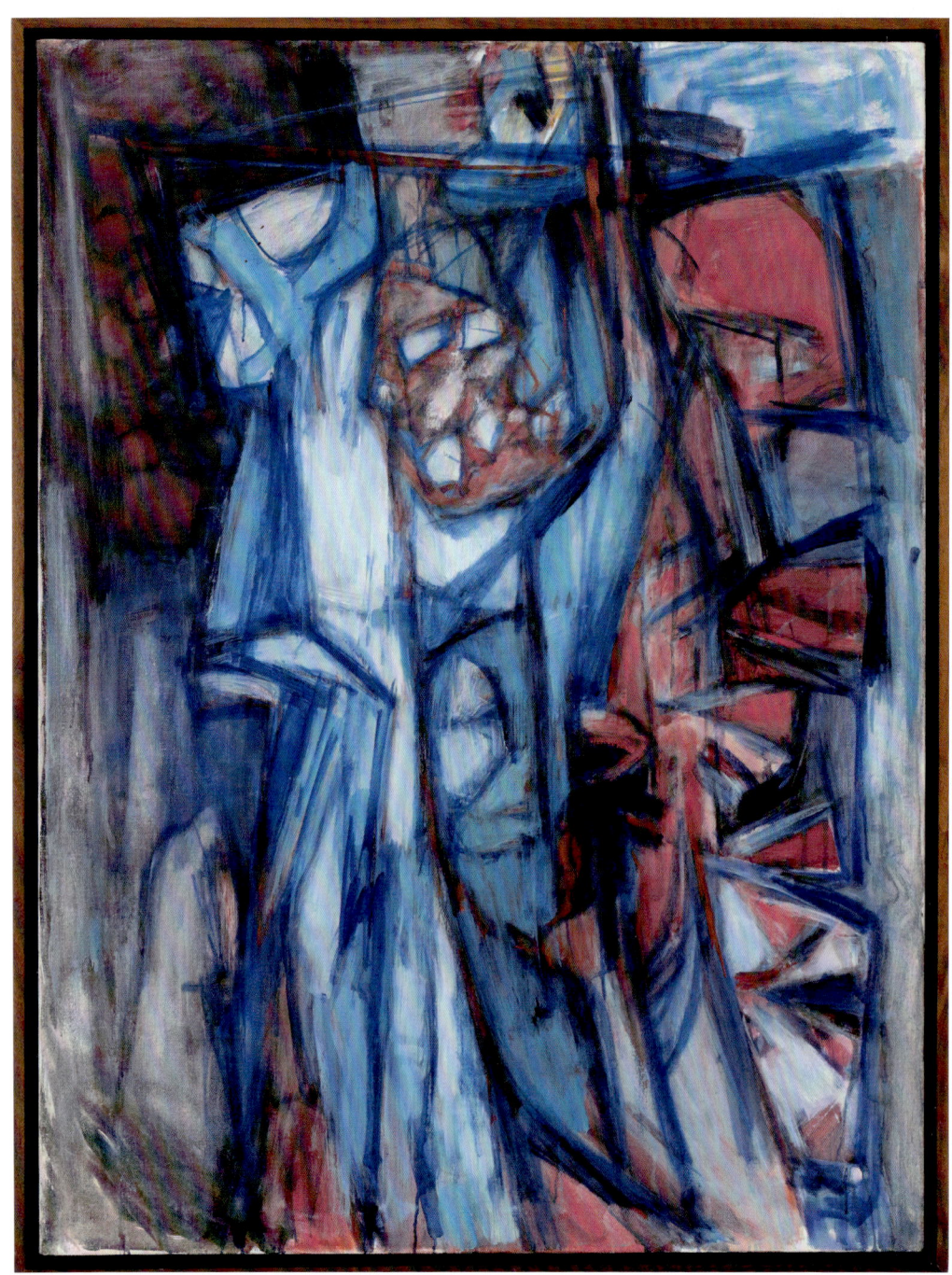

Portal, n.d. Oil on canvas, 42 ⅜ × 32 in.
Gift of E. Thomas Williams and
Auldlyn Higgins Williams, New York
1987.5.1

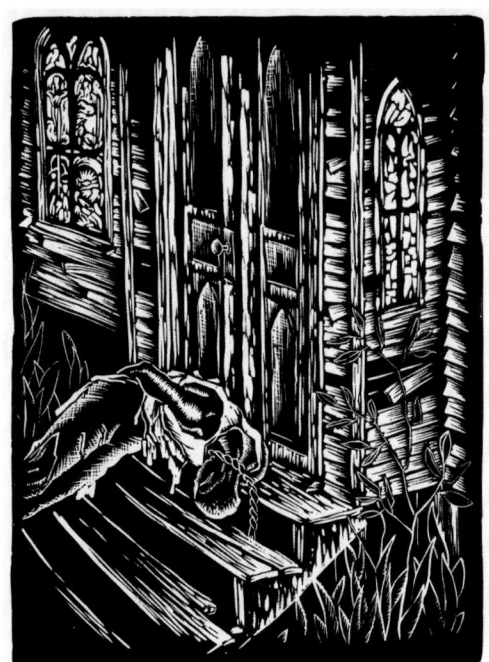

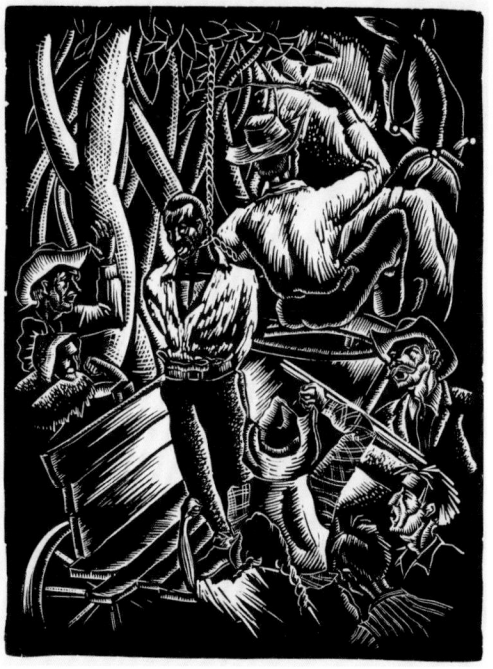

By Parties Unknown (from the portfolio "Hale Woodruff: Selections from the Atlanta Period 1931—1946"), 1931—46; printed 1996. Linoleum cut with chine-collé, image: 11 ¹⁵⁄₁₆ × 8 ⅞ in., sheet: 19 × 14 ¹⁵⁄₁₆ in. From an edition of 75. Gift of Auldlyn Higgins Williams and E.T. Williams, Jr. 2020.23.2

Giddap (from the portfolio "Hale Woodruff: Selections from the Atlanta Period 1931—1946"), 1931—46; printed 1996. Linoleum cut with chine-collé, image: 12 × 8 ¹⁵⁄₁₆ in. sheet: 19 ⅛ × 15 in. From an edition of 75. Gift of Auldlyn Higgins Williams and E.T. Williams, Jr. 2020.23.4

Hale Woodruff's *Africa and the Bull* reconfigures the myth of the abduction of Europa by Zeus (in the guise of a bull) by way of Titian's *The Rape of Europa* (1560—62). In addition to replacing Europa with a personification of Africa, Woodruff deviates from Titian's work by cropping the composition tightly around Africa and the bull. The bull, rendered in multiple shades of white with black outlines for his trunk and muscles, takes up most of the composition. In this way, Woodruff's painting expands the myth toward the transatlantic slave trade and its aftermath. (The title, one notices, is less specific about the crime between Africa and the bull.) The softest, roundest forms (like cotton balls) in the painting, white like the bull itself, surround Africa. She lies stiff and angular on the bull's back like a Senufo sculpture; or like one of Picasso's African-influenced figures, a reminder that the colonial powers for generations stole not only millions of people from the African continent but also cultural objects and influence—with European artists looking to Africa much like Woodruff's bull looks at the continent's personification. As Woodruff wrote to a student in 1955: "These cubists were struck by the bold yet controlled form of African sculpture. Picasso's 'Demoiselles d'Avignon' is definitely influenced by the African mask . . . . However, the modern artist rarely delved into the cultures of these peoples."[29]

Woodruff, for his part, made learning, preserving, and teaching the culture of Black people his vocation. He studied in various places in the United States, Paris, and Mexico from the late 1920s to the mid-1930s, developing relationships with Palmer Hayden, Alain Locke, Diego Rivera, and Augusta Savage, among others.[30] Part of his project of representing Black American life included a series of linocuts produced between 1931 and 1946 that showed events, both awful and joyous, from the South. *Giddap* captures a lynching in progress, with a rowdy white crowd of men and women surrounding a Black man wearing a noose on the back of a horse-drawn wagon—one that is just about to drive away. *By Parties Unknown* shows a prostrate body, also wearing a noose, on the steps of a wooden shack with unusually ornate windows. The central figure in *Trusty on a Mule* is, one would guess, lucky to be alive; he wears striped prison gear, bandanas, and a hat, with no shirt. The mule lopes forward and Trusty looks over his shoulder, sitting sidesaddle, perhaps ready to run.

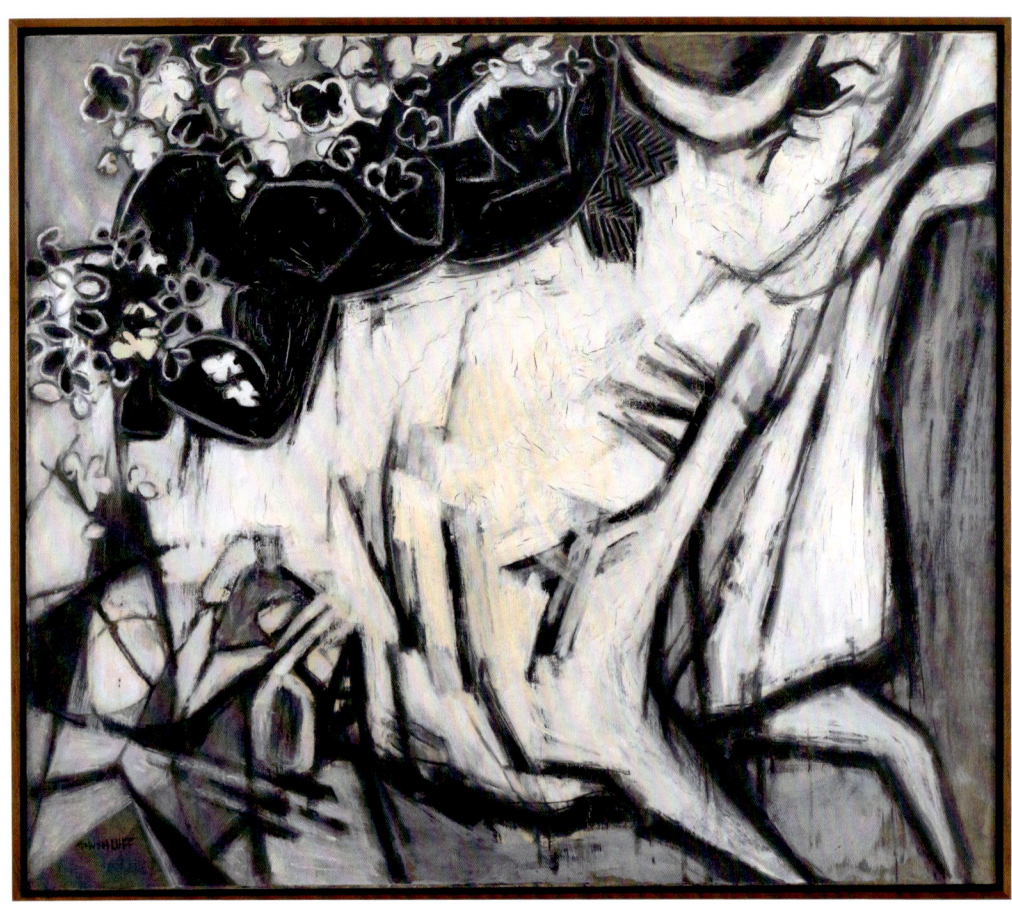

Africa and the Bull, c. 1958. Oil on canvas, 44 ¼ × 52 ¾ in. Gift of E. Thomas Williams and Auldlyn Higgins Williams, New York 1987.5.3

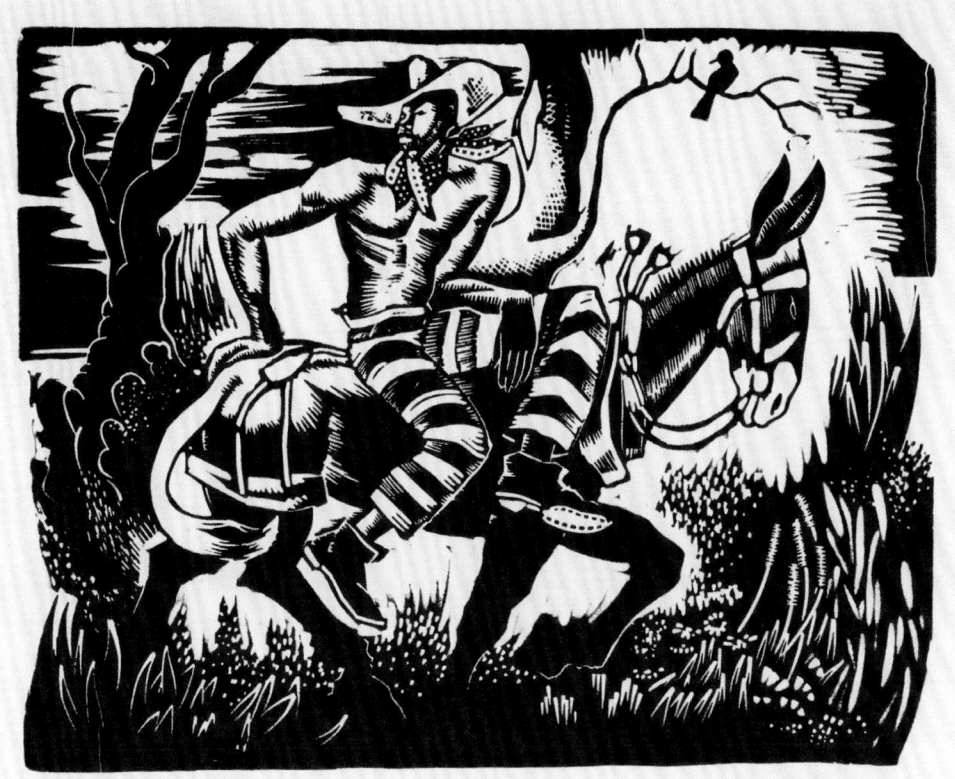

Trusty on a Mule (from the portfolio
"Hale Woodruff: Selections from
the Atlanta Period 1931—1946"),
1931—46; printed 1996. Linoleum cut
with chine-collé, image: 8 ³⁄₁₆ × 10 ³⁄₈ in.,
sheet: 19 × 15 in. From an edition of 75.
Gift of Auldlyn Higgins Williams and
E. T. Williams Jr. 2020.23.8

Woodruff was deeply invested in both the past and future of Black
artistic practices. In 1950, he focused on the past, completing "The Art
of the Negro" mural series at Atlanta University; these murals depict
his interpretation of African art's history and future, rendering historical
events, conversations among artists from different time periods, and
forms of art from all over the world—and all of this, importantly, in the
art school he had established in 1931. Woodruff's own practice shifted
in the 1960s, when he likely painted *Portal*; his confident lines and
drips of paint crisscross in dynamic, abstracted space that still some-
how looks like African masks. It appears to have been painted quickly,
as if the painting were itself a portal about to flicker shut.

— Terence Washington

Jacob Lawrence
1917—2000

Born in New Jersey to parents from Virginia and South Carolina, Jacob Lawrence came to Harlem in the early 1930s. It was in Depression-era Harlem that Lawrence developed as a young artist situated within a dynamic cultural community. During this time, Lawrence frequented Augusta Savage's art studio, the Savage Studio of Arts and Crafts; took classes with Charles Alston at Utopia Children's House; attended Harlem Art Workshop courses at the Schomburg Center for Research in Black Culture (then the 135th Street New York Public Library branch); and spent time with the collaborative 306 group.[31] He was also part of the Harlem Artists Guild, which lobbied the Works Progress Administration to support Black art spaces and public art commissions, and whose organizing created the Harlem Community Art Center.[32] These spaces activated interdisciplinary conversations and nurtured Lawrence. In these settings, his historical education and political development took shape alongside his artistic practice.

His first solo show, in 1938 at the Harlem YMCA, focused on street scenes of Harlem. That same year he was also constructing a series highlighting the life of abolitionist Frederick Douglass and conducting research for a series on Haitian revolutionary Toussaint L'Ouverture and another on abolitionist Harriet Tubman.[33] Artworks that focus on Black history, the role of historical research, and the central importance of the library as a space of knowledge and creativity recur throughout Lawrence's practice. In *The Schomburg Library*, figures explore a maze of bookshelves, fill their arms with books, get lost in their research, and huddle closely to read together. This artwork references Lawrence's formative experiences in Harlem libraries and also speaks specifically to the legacy of Arturo Alfonso Schomburg,

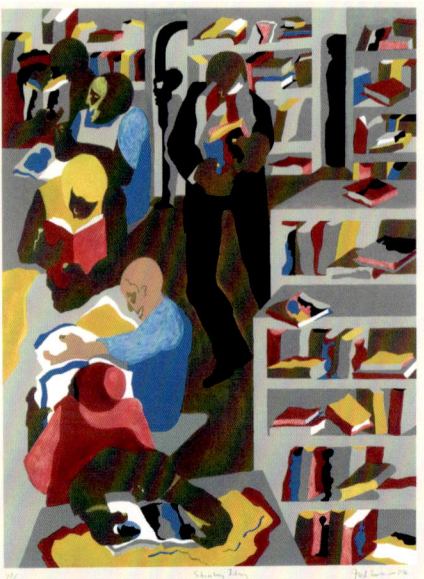

The Schomburg Library, 1986—87. Serigraph, 27 ¾ × 21 ½ in. Gift of Altria Group, Inc. 2008.13.4

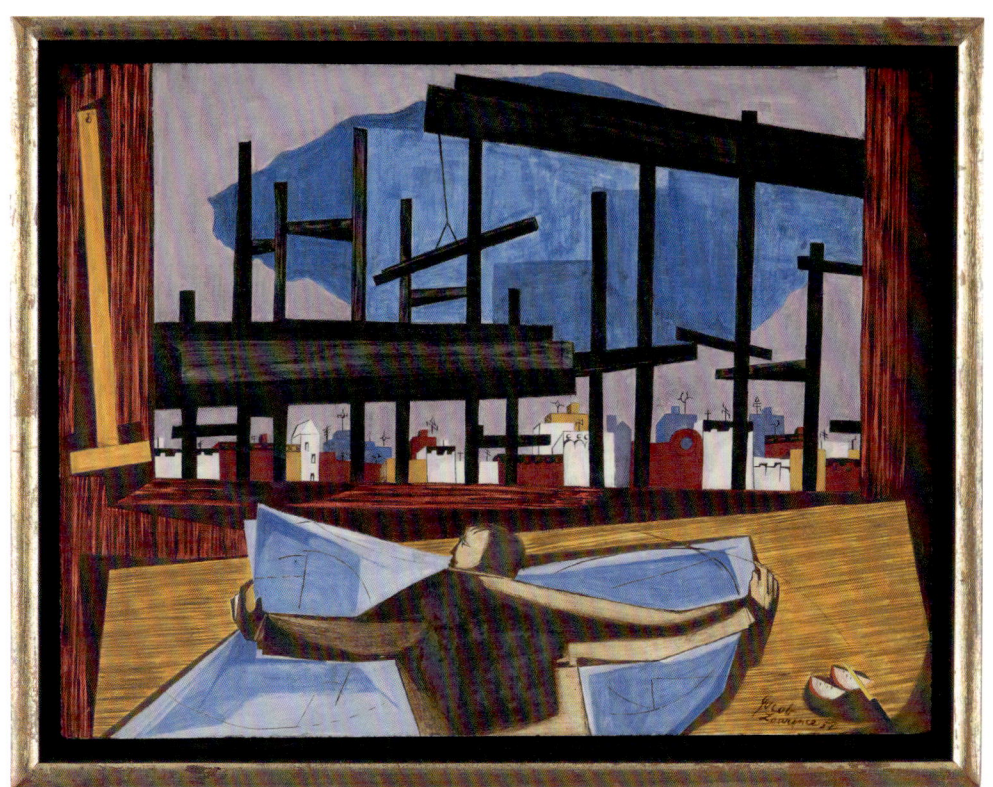

The Architect, 1959. Egg tempera on
Masonite, 13 ⅝ × 17 ½ in. Gift of Mr. and
Mrs. James Harithas 1982.1

whose collection formed the core of the Schomburg Center. Historical
and oral history research was also central to Lawrence's best-known series,
"The Migration Series" (1940—41), which details—in sixty paintings—the
narratives of Black people's migrations out of the South and the complex
experiences they encountered in their new homes.

Throughout his long career, Lawrence focused on political subjects in addition to quotidian Black life—depicting work and leisure experienced in the
street, on the stoop, around the home, and in the community. He returned
to the subject of the builder often. In *The Architect*, a person looks out over
an active construction site, consulting plans for a building that, even in its
beamed form, is strikingly different from the city rendered in the background. This artwork can be understood as connected both to the long
history of Black carpenters and construction workers whose labor built the
United States and to the building of creative and intellectual Black spaces
and institutions.[34] Lawrence's graphic use of color, flattened spaces, and
abstracted forms masterfully creates whole worlds layered with social and
political complexity. With his keen understanding of space, rhythm, and
composition, combined with his interest in history and sharp attention
to the contemporary moment, Lawrence produced hundreds of artworks
that narrate the Black experience in Harlem and beyond.

—Jennifer M. Harley

Bob Thompson

1937—1966

Bob Thompson's colorful, figurative paintings reveal his engagement with the Western art historical tradition through vibrant silhouettes of people, animals, trees, and monsters. With expressionist style, Thompson paid homage to the old masters' paintings and prints, such as those from Fra Angelico or Francisco de Goya. He also drew inspiration from modern European paintings by Pablo Picasso and Paul Gauguin and found that scenes from Greek mythology and biblical narratives resonated with the bohemianism and social turmoil of the 1960s. He states, "When in 1962 I went to Europe, the museums were driving me crazy. I was seeing so much art. And then I thought that, well, I had better go back into this . . . I look at Poussin and he's got it all there. Why are all of these people running around trying to be original when they should just go ahead and be themselves and that's the originality of it all, just being yourself . . . I work with these things that are already there . . . because that is what I respond to most of all."[35]

On the right side of *Painting (Four Figures)*, Thompson depicts a gathering of women in shades of pink, brown, green, and purple. They engage in conversation, perhaps about what the pink figure points toward on the left side of the painting. In that direction grows a leafy green tree near the base of a yellow and red hill. Dark vertical lines indicate other trees, but one doubles as the silhouette of a man wearing a wide-brimmed hat.

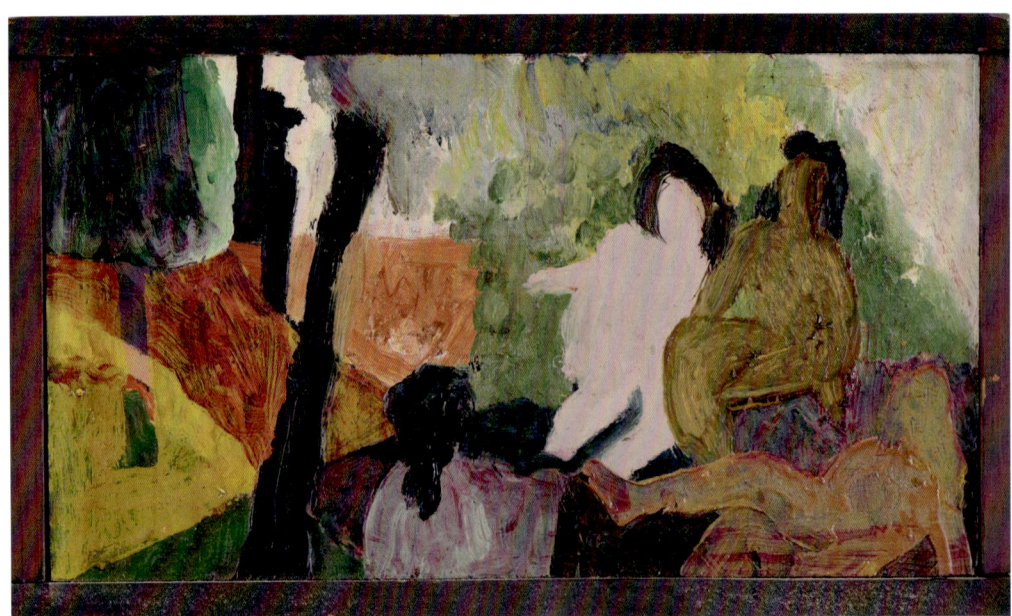

Painting (Four Figures), 1960. Oil on board, frame: 7 ¼ × 12 ½ × 2 in. Gift of Lillian and Abraham Feinberg 2017.35

He could be easily missed among the other shapes in the forest. The painting thus suggests a tense moment when the women discover that they are being surveilled.

Two silhouetted men wearing hats appear with a horse in *Untitled*. They stand in a wooded clearing staring at a purple figure just ahead, who may be approaching the group or walking away. The reason for their meeting is as mysterious as their appearance. Uninterested in providing visual details, Thompson uses minimal brushstrokes to gesture toward ambiguous activity. However, his anthropomorphic treatment of animals and trees accompanying the figures often gives clues about the tone of the subject matter. In this work, the trees gather together like the men. Their trunks lean toward each other from opposite sides, and two touch limbs as if readying for an embrace—or fight.

Thompson's forest scenes are also places for erotic play. In *The Gambol*—which recalls Gauguin's 1897 painting *Where Do We Come From? What Are We? Where Are We Going?*—a nude woman at center reaches one arm up into the branches of a tree. She is flanked on the left by a couple entwined on horseback and nude horseback riders on the right. The narrative of this group scene emblematizes Thompson's often enigmatic work. His eccentric technique and visual idiom leave viewers to speculate about the meaning of uncertain situations.

—Bridget R. Cooks

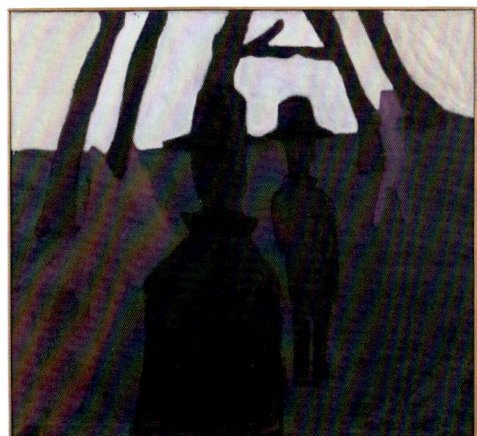 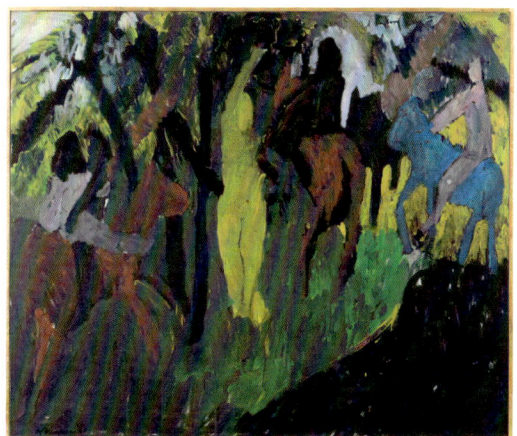

Untitled, 1959. Oil on canvas, 50 × 56 in. Gift of Nancy Ellison Rollnick, New York 2002.2

The Gambol, 1961. Oil on canvas, frame: 49 ¾ × 60 in. Gift of the Feinberg Family 2016.31

Charles Alston

1907—1977

In the mid-1950s, artist and educator Charles Alston began creating works in a black-and-white palette. As part of this series, he painted *Black and White II*, a vertical composition grounded by intersecting blocks of black and gray that gradually transition into less defined light gray and white forms near the top of the canvas. The works in this series underscore Alston's belief that artists could shift freely between abstraction and figuration, and between media, working however best suited their subject.[36] Even as he painted *Black and White II*, Alston described himself as primarily a figure painter, invested in people and how art represented the Black community.

Alston was a founding member of the artist collective Spiral, established in 1963, alongside Romare Bearden, Norman Lewis, and Hale Woodruff. In search of "mutuality of direction," the Spiral group adopted Alston's limited range of tones in anticipation of their first exhibition: "We had people who painted hard-edge abstractions, sort of romantic landscapes and figures. All kinds of people were in it. We just felt that we needed to get together and discover whether we had things in common, and, if possible, work out some kind of general broad philosophy."[37] Members of the group took up Alston's preoccupation with black-and-white, exploring the political and formal resonances of the dichotomous colors to consider the role of art in the civil rights movement. In 1965, Spiral staged their only exhibition, *First Group Showing: Works in Black and White*.

—Katelyn D. Crawford

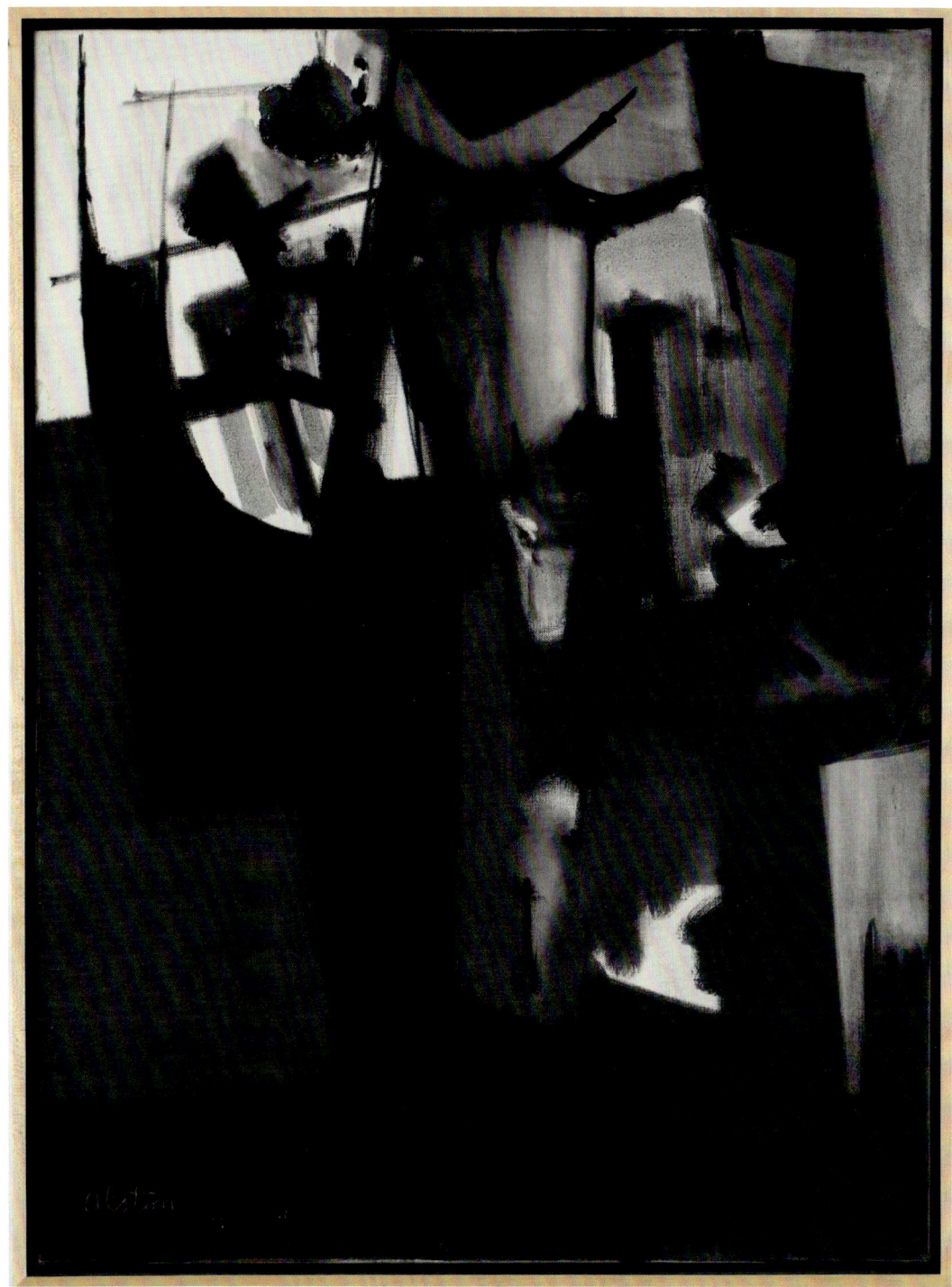

Black and White II, c. 1960. Oil on canvas,
48 × 36 in. Gift of Aida Winters, New York
2000.8.1

Malick Sidibé
1935/6—2016

Photographer Malick Sidibé captured the energy and excitement of Bamako youth at the cusp of Mali's independence.[38] As their new state attempted to shake off the stubborn residue of French colonialism, young men and women sought their autonomy and found solace in popular culture. They danced to the music of Aretha Franklin, James Brown, Jimi Hendrix, the Jacksons, Bob Dylan, and Led Zeppelin, to name a few.[39] They emulated Black power leaders in the United States, proudly donning Afros and bell-bottoms. This is evidenced in photographs such as *Le faux musicien derriére sa voiture*, in which a man beside a car, likely a Renault 8, ecstatically strums a guitar like his funk heroes. The young people discreetly socialized late at night, way beyond state-imposed curfews, as observed in the animated dancing in *Regardez Moi!* and *Danser* le TWIST *[Dance the TWIST]*. They formed competitive cliques with names like "the Soul Brothers."[40] On Sundays, they spent time relaxing and listening to battery-powered record players on the banks of the Niger River, as pictured in *Pique-Nique a la chaussée*. Sidibé's flash memorialized them, and they could identify themselves among hundreds of images in his studio days after their photo was taken.

Sidibé feverishly documented this revelry, which meant attending as many as four parties before daylight.[41] Though he had a studio practice, and was commissioned to photograph special occasions, his ability to move around with his camera made him highly sought after. This urban lifestyle vastly

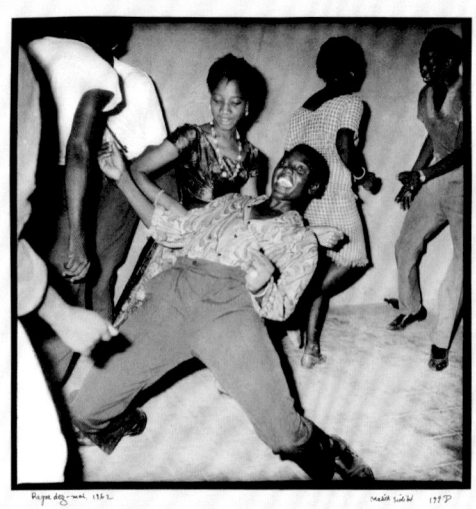
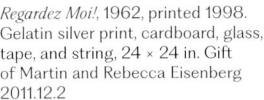

Regardez Moi!, 1962, printed 1998. Gelatin silver print, cardboard, glass, tape, and string, 24 × 24 in. Gift of Martin and Rebecca Eisenberg 2011.12.2

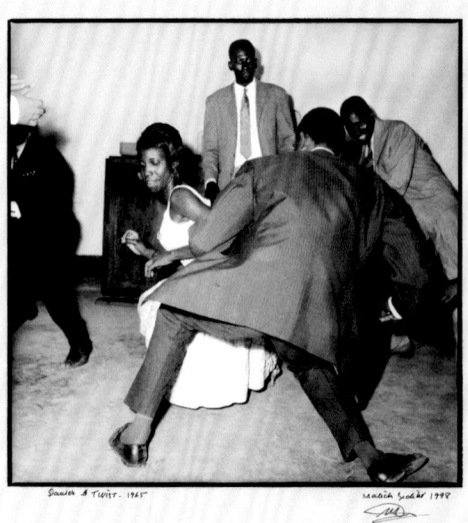

Danser le TWIST [Dance the TWIST], 1965, printed 1998. Gelatin silver print, 13 ⅜ × 13 ¼ in. Gift of Joy of Giving Something, Inc. 2018.47.24

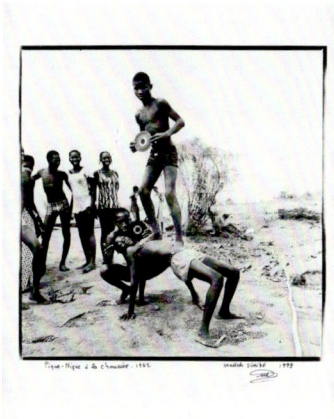

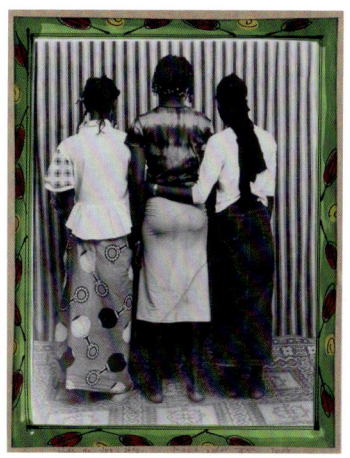

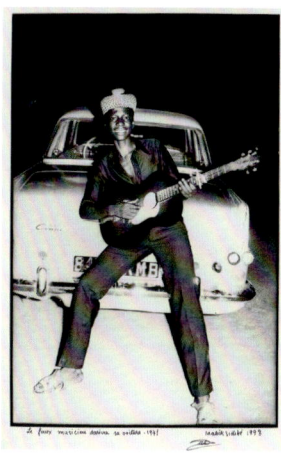

Pique-Nique a la chaussée / Picnic at Chaussee, 1972, printed 1999. Gelatin silver print, 16 × 12 in. Gift of Jean Pigozzi, Geneva, Switzerland 2002.1.3

Vue de Dos, 2002, printed 2004. Gelatin silver print, painted glass, cardboard, tape, and string, 17 × 13 in. Gift of Martin and Rebecca Eisenberg 2011.12.3

Le faux musicien derrière sa voiture / The Wannabe Musician Behind His Car, 1971, printed 1998. Gelatin silver print, image: 16 × 12 in. Gift of Jean Pigozzi, Geneva, Switzerland 2002.1.4

differed from his rural farming upbringing in Soloba, Mali, where Sidibé was one of the first in his family to obtain a formal education.

His creativity was evident in his student drawings, eventually earning him a position at the Institut National des Arts de Bamako (then the École des Artisans Soudanais) in 1952. There, Sidibé enjoyed the medium of painting; however, he later preferred the immediacy of photography. In 1955, he was invited to decorate the photography studio of Gérard Guillat, where he later apprenticed.[42] In the studio, Sidibé attended to African clients, while Guillat gave attention to European customers. In 1957, as Guillat's studio closed, Sidibé acquired his first camera, a Brownie Flash he used to photograph social events.

By 1963, Sidibé opened his own studio in Bagadadji, Bamako, and by the 1970s was capturing fewer parties and more portraits. Unlike his documentary work, his studio photography was more choreographed. Using electrical lighting, he helped his clients feel at ease by allowing them to pose with their own beloved objects or various aspirational studio props, including hats, ties, and even motorcycles. The early 2000s saw Sidibé critiquing photographic portraiture through series such as "Vue de Dos." In these works, heads turn away from the camera, proving that it takes more than a face to create a telling portrait.

—Tandazani Dhlakama

Norman Lewis

1909—1979

Throughout his career, Norman Lewis remained skeptical about the power of art to effect change. He sought to separate his aesthetic endeavors from his activist ones and left behind early-career explorations of Social Realism for abstraction. Yet Lewis's form of Abstract Expressionism still centers his activist concerns: his practice derives from the emotions he felt—fear, sorrow, anger, frustration, grief—about the state of the world and the place of Black people within it.

At the center of Lewis's *Bonfire* burns a bright orange flame. With a blue center, the fire glows vividly, with splashes of pink, green, yellow, and red throughout. Atop a haze of dark blue, abstracted figures curve, bend, and stretch around the edge of the blaze. A sky-blue cloud floats toward the edges of the canvas. Taking into consideration Lewis's approach, one might be drawn to the work's sinister undertones, such as the dangers that the fire itself—and the suggested human bodies around it—can inflict. The dashes of white among the figures call to mind Ku Klux Klan gatherings and echo contemporary events such as the Unite the Right white supremacist rally in Charlottesville, Virginia, after in 2017.

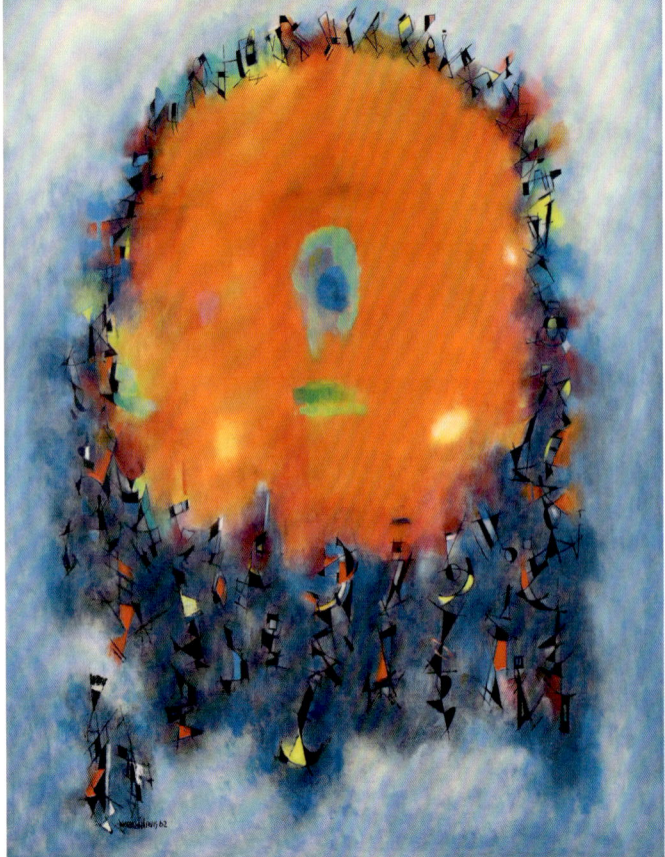

Bonfire, 1962. Oil on canvas, 64 × 49 ⅞ in.
Gift of the Estate of Norman Lewis
1981.1.2

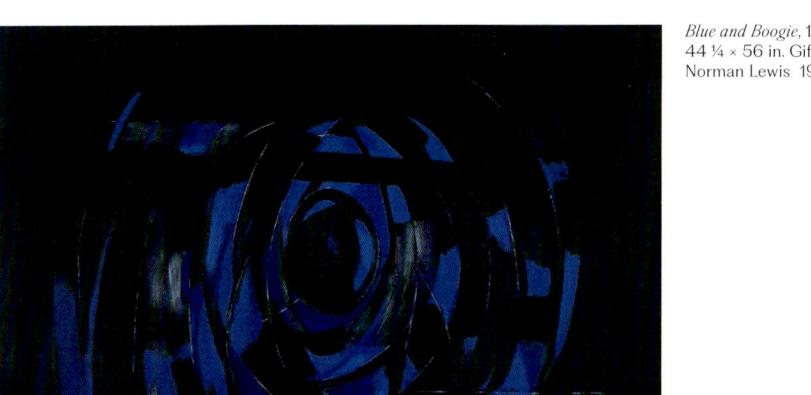

Blue and Boogie, 1974. Oil on canvas, 44 ¼ × 56 in. Gift of the Estate of Norman Lewis 1981.1.1

An altogether different interpretation can be found by giving added weight to the impact of Lewis's collaborative experiences. Lewis participated in and led groups of artists and activists throughout his lifetime, which animated and advanced his work. He was a regular attendee at 306, the shared studio of Charles Alston and Henry Bannarn, where discussions of Black history and art exhibitions drew in the likes of Ralph Ellison and Augusta Savage. He described these sessions as fostering a "feeling of belonging without ostracism."[43] He also cofounded Spiral, a collective of African American artists whose work wrestled with questions regarding the responsibility of the artist in social justice movements, and Cinque Gallery, a space dedicated to showcasing and supporting the work of artists of color.

The effects of these community-driven experiences undergird *Blue and Boogie*, Lewis's nod to Harlem's nightlife culture. The circular, kinetic movement of blue suggests a repetition and return—perhaps to the refrain of a song, a venue, or a connection found through music. During the Harlem Renaissance, clubs such as the Savoy Ballroom and Smalls Paradise offered evenings of lively jazz music and attracted writers, entertainers, athletes, and artists like Lewis. The music and dancing within these spaces echoed these performances through Harlem's streets, fostering a sense of community, kinship, and belonging.

Lewis's career was deeply informed and inspired by practices of collaboration, discourse, and connection across Harlem and New York City. While *Bonfire* could be a cautionary tale about an event ripe with potential for violence, it also offers an ode to the power and promise of these collective experiences. In foregrounding the spirit exemplified in *Blue and Boogie*, *Bonfire* reads as a portrait of a gathering brimming with energy and vitality, a group working together to nurture an artistic spark.

—Kate Claman

Romare Bearden

1911—1988

Romare Bearden has had a profound impact on my artistic journey and approach to creating art. His innovative use of collage in *The Farmer, Jazz II, Two Women,* and *Conjur Woman* shows an ability to convey narrative through work that resonates with many artists and art lovers. His work inspired me to break free from strict formalities and to embrace a more multiplicitous and unconventional style.

Bearden's approach to composition, particularly his willingness to leave elements unfinished or extend them beyond the paper/canvas, has influenced my artistic choices. His collages allow the viewer's imagination to complete the narrative, a technique he used so effectively. People sometimes think collage is easy. They don't truly understand the work involved in creating these images. I love the simplicity of the figure in *The Farmer*, as I have a lot of works featuring girls with their hands on their hips. Bearden played with scale; he played with abstraction and figuration; and he played with color here. He put orange straight down the middle, which draws the viewer's eye all the way into this work.

I use a lot of bright colors to explore movement in my work, and I see the same in Bearden's practice. In *Jazz II*, the brightness of the colors creates a beautiful sense of movement. You can almost hear the music coming from the work, which also seems to radiate the heat of the performance, of the cluster of so many bodies packed together. However, Bearden and I differ in that he often used color throughout his compositions and white only sparingly, as in *Two Women*, while I don't use any color in the background. Although we both are telling stories, albeit in different time periods, my work suggests that we don't need to be centered around whiteness and that whiteness is all around us, while his work barely uses white because the story is more important.

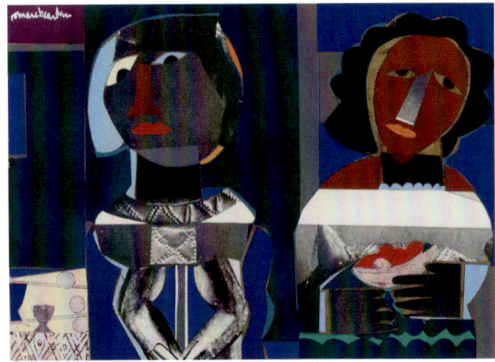

Two Women, 1969. Collage on paper, image: 17 ¼ × 23 ¾ in. Gift of the Ralph and Fanny Ellison Charitable Trust 2011.9

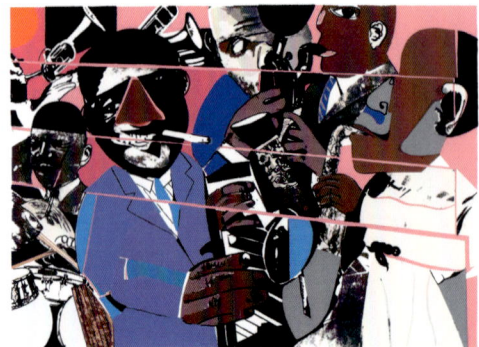

Jazz II, 1980. Serigraph on paper, 31 × 41 ½ in. Gift of ACA Galleries, New York 2002.4

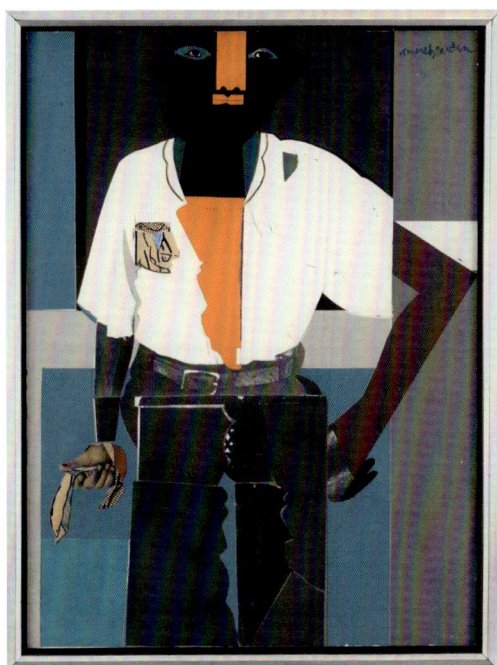

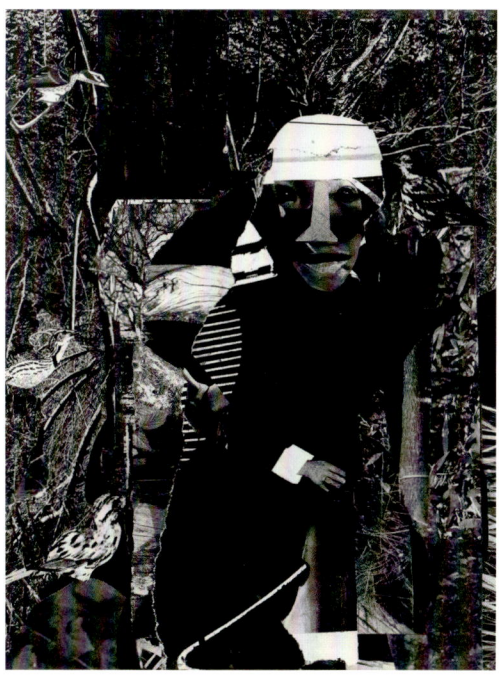

The Farmer, 1968. Mixed-media collage on
Masonite, 39 ½ × 29 ¾ in. Museum purchase
and a gift from E. Thomas Williams and
Auldlyn Higgins Williams 1997.9.12

Conjur Woman, 1964. Photo projection on
paper, 64 × 50 in. Gift of the artist 1972.5

Even in works that are mainly black-and-white, Bearden's application
of moments of white makes a profound impact. In *Conjur Woman*, the
striped arm of the figure and the small section of wider stripes over her
shoulder suggest prison uniforms. This strategic use of black-and-white
stripes influenced my work, as they appear within my collages as a way
to discuss mass incarceration in the United States.

Bearden's artistic influence is both a conscious and subconscious process;
artists working in collage today are indeed shaped by the work they encounter, even when they may not be fully aware of it. This process of assimilation
and reinterpretation showcases how art is a continuum, building upon the
legacy of those who came before while introducing personal interpretations
and innovations. It's clear that Romare Bearden's legacy continues to reverberate through many living artists working today, enriching them with layers
of inspiration, innovation, and a fresh perspective on artistic expression.

—Deborah Roberts

Kwame Brathwaite

1938—2023

Untitled (Garvey Day, Deedee in Car),
c. 1965, printed 2018. Archival pigment
print, 40 × 60 in. Museum purchase
with funds provided by the Acquisition
Committee, Ruthard C. Murphy II in
memory of Anderson dos Santos Gama,
and Anonymous 2019.10

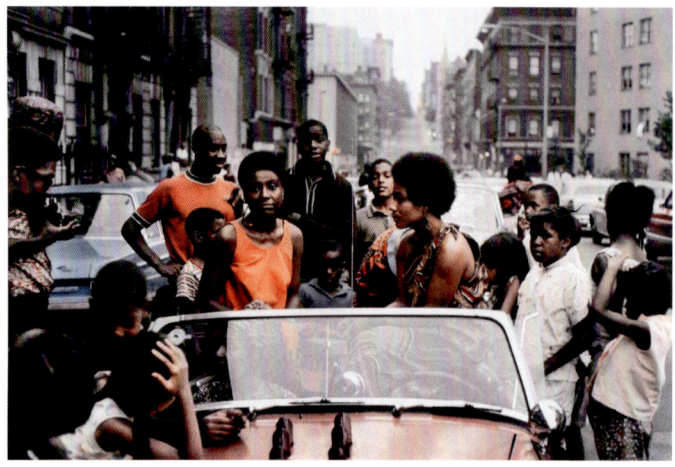

Kwame Brathwaite documented the beauty of everyday cultural life. He produced some of the most compelling and striking images of Black women, jazz musicians, and the Black freedom movements of the mid-1950s, 1960s, and 1970s. With "Black is beautiful" as his mantra, a phrase originally coined by Marcus Garvey and the Universal Negro Improvement Association, Brathwaite's photographs reframe the notion of blackness by highlighting its power, potential, and beauty—naturally.

Untitled (Garvey Day, Deedee in Car) embodies the spirit of the "unofficial photographer of New York's annual Marcus Garvey Day celebration."[44] This color photograph deliberately shows off the splendor of hundreds of people gathering on the streets of Harlem to witness a parade full of regalia, pomp, African dancing, and the Miss Natural Standard of Beauty pageant. Children of all ages and complexions surround a convertible with a trio of Black women sitting inside. One of the women in the car meets the camera's gaze; she wears an orange dress, appearing like a rose that grew through concrete. Her brown, almond-shaped eyes; dark, glowing skin; and full lips are further accentuated by a neatly cropped Afro and long, beaded earrings. The honey-brown-skin-toned woman next to her has a striking profile; she wears a large, beautifully coifed Afro and an earth-toned, off-the-shoulder West African print dress. The third woman, sitting below in the foreground, dons an animal-print head wrap and matching top. Brathwaite, with the expertise and savoir faire of an artistic director, coupled with the patience and fearlessness of a master photographer, beautifully represents the array and vibrancy of Pan-Africanism that lined the streets of Lenox Avenue, Adam Clayton Powell Jr. Boulevard, and 125th Street—not only during this annual celebration but throughout this monumental era.

—Rhea Combs

Richard Mayhew

1924—2024

Gorge, 1966. Oil on canvas, 60 × 50 in.
Gift of David L. Schneider, PhD 1986.11.1

Richard Mayhew's distinctive fiery vistas and cool misty fields have kept him at the forefront of landscape painting for the past seventy years. Inspired by the Hudson River School painters who worked in the nineteenth century just northwest of his childhood home in Amityville, New York, his oeuvre features a strategic combination of saturated colors and welcoming views that express his unique interpretation of the land. He did not work from life. Instead, he created imagined landscapes that drew on his memories and expressed his creative consciousness. Simultaneously representational and abstract, Mayhew's luminous compositions, and captivating color and light, visually transport viewers to another place.

Mayhew created compelling visions of spatial freedom during the civil rights movement in the United States and envisioned *Gorge* as a place of peace in the face of tumultuous social and cultural transformation. In the foreground, he presents blended clusters of cobalt, navy, and Prussian blue. What could be Impressionist flowers are scattered on an ocher-colored field and lead viewers further into the picture plane. In the background, a lush green pathway winds along the crest of a hill, receding into an atmospheric haze. The peach above the horizon suggests the dawn of a new day.

The journey in a Mayhew painting is more than a representation of the natural environment. He generated these painted places in a seemingly insatiable quest to share with viewers the beauty of what he saw, dreamed, and felt, so that they can feel it too.

—Bridget R. Cooks

Melvin Edwards

b. 1937

In Melvin Edwards's *Cotton Hangup*, a cluster of welded metal objects is encased in a rebar frame. Three chains tether the cluster in place as it hangs from the ceiling and walls, such that it splays across the corner of a room. It can also be exhibited dangling from a single hook against a wall. In either scenario, the gravitational pull of its weighty materials compels the viewer toward *Cotton Hangup.* The work is composed of what Edwards describes as "familiar form objects," commonplace scrap metals—in this case, steel joinery and mechanical casings—that have been fused together into a singular construction.[45]

Edwards is perhaps best known for his series "The Lynch Fragments" (begun in 1963), which condenses blades, chains, machinery, and other discarded metal objects into dense nuclei of forms. While Edwards's approach is formally abstract, his use of recognizable objects—tools and utensils—alongside poignantly political titles resists easy categorization or resolution. *Cotton Hangup* is emblematic of this practice. The work's title evokes the cotton gin, which, together with its suspended compositional form, triangulates the industrialized cotton trade and the racialized violence of lynching.

Edwards studied painting before taking up welding in 1960. The shift from two to three dimensions opened up all sorts of spatial possibilities for the artist, who was interested in breaking free from the containment of the picture frame. And as he moved away from painting, the pictorial field became increasingly elastic in his work. Whereas in work such as *Chaino* (1964) the rectilinear frame operates as a totalizing force, in *Cotton Hangup*, produced only two years later, it is completely upended. Sculpture allowed Edwards to work environmentally, to consider the floor, walls, and ceilings in equal measure.[46] It also allowed him to work relationally, as in *Cotton Hangup*, implicating the viewer in acts of spectatorship by interrupting and disturbing architectures.

—Alexis Lowry

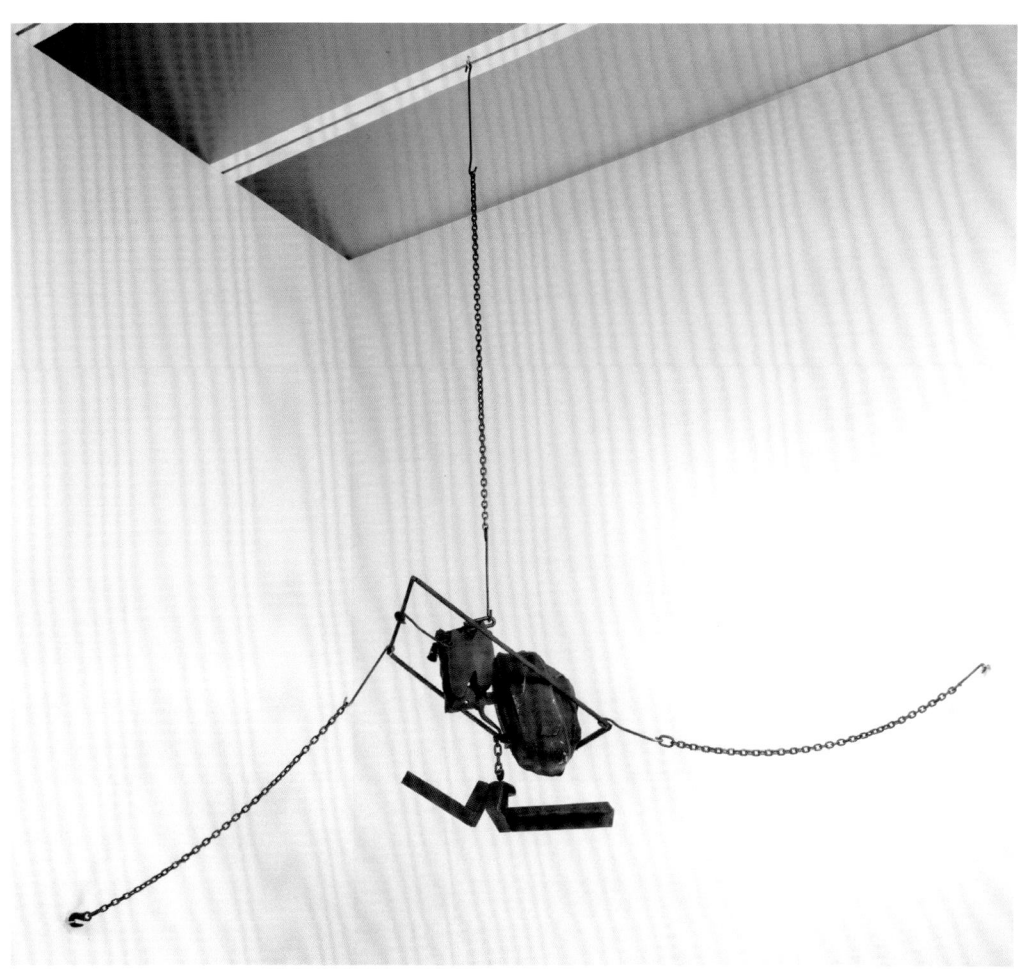

Cotton Hangup, 1966. Welded steel,
32 × 30 × 30 in. Gift of Mr. and Mrs.
Hans Burkhardt 1991.21

Emma Amos

1937—2020

While studying abroad in London, Emma Amos wholeheartedly embraced abstract motifs and themes that transcended specific narratives and identity politics. While there, Amos experienced a sense of liberation and discovered an artistic community not solely organized around her racial identity. Notably her encounter with exhibitions such as the Tate Gallery's 1959 *The New American Painting*, which highlighted Abstract Expressionists from the United States, further shaped her artistic trajectory.

Amos's identification with Abstract Expressionism placed her within a discourse dominated by white men. But she developed her own distinctive language of abstraction. Although printmaking was her primary focus, she ventured into painting, infusing her compositions with spontaneity and improvisation. *Untitled (Tan Abstraction)* is among the works produced during her time in London. Amos's composition contains several box-shaped brushstrokes of blended yellowish-brown earth tones. These blocky brushstrokes overlap with intermittent hints of red or grayish-black shapes underneath.

In the 1960s, Amos's artistic direction shifted toward figuration, particularly after joining the Spiral collective. Unlike her older Black peers in the collective, who initially pursued Social Realism before abstraction, Amos had begun her artistic career with abstraction. However, Amos's time with Spiral provided fertile ground for her artistic experimentation. Inspired by her surroundings in New York City and nature, she began to incorporate more variations in color and form into her work. Her use of color exploded, and her figures became more varied and spatially dynamic. *Baby*, a notable painting from this period, reflects her experiences and inspirations from spending time at the beach and, as the title suggests, her first pregnancy. This artwork is characterized by a composition featuring circular shapes

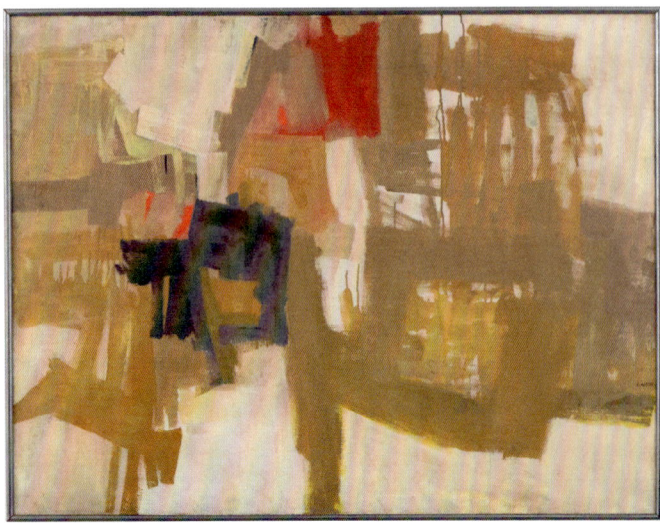

Untitled (Tan Abstraction), 1958. Oil on canvas, 36 ¾ × 49 in. Gift of Sandy and Bill Michael in honor of their friendship with Emma Amos 2019.28

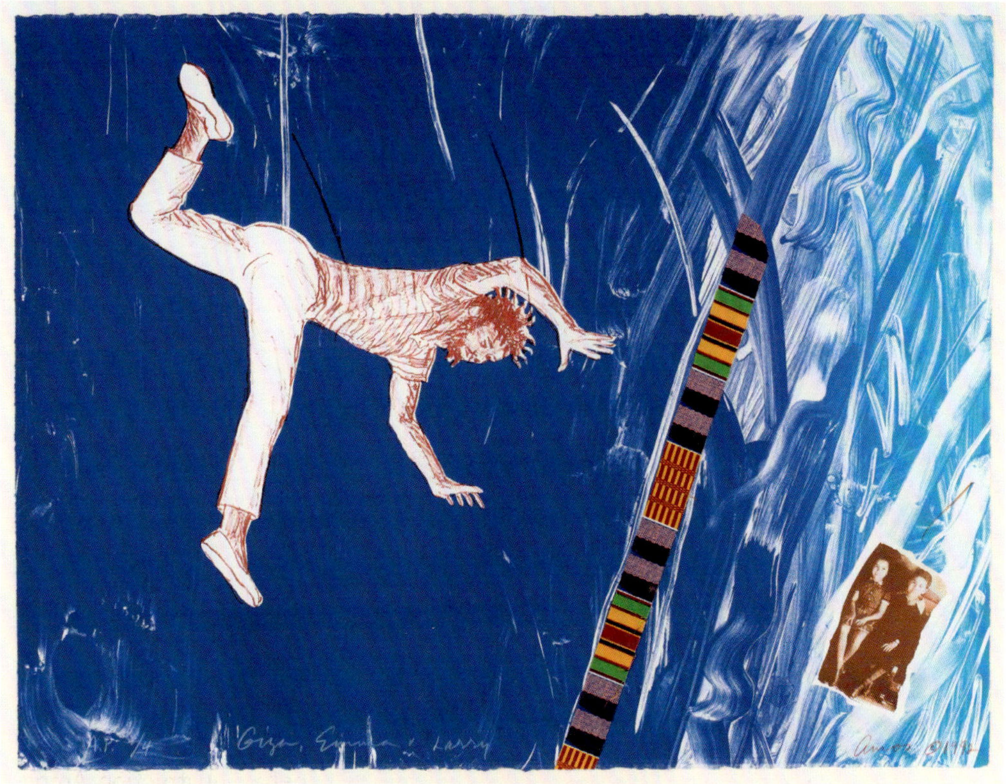

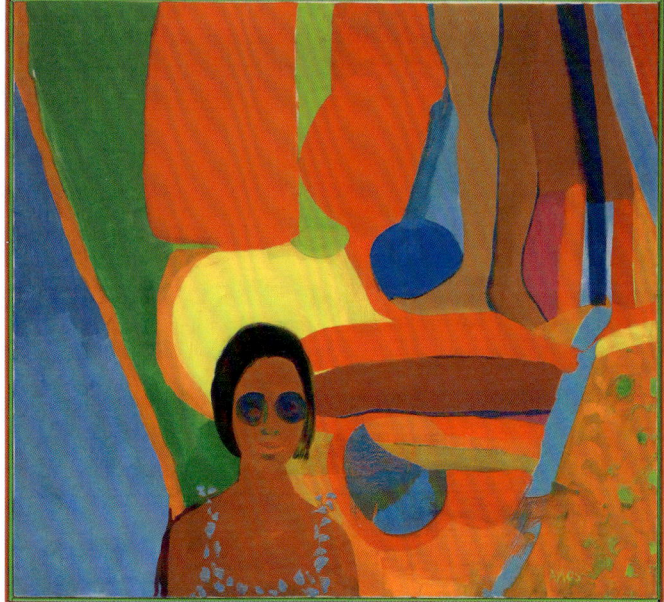

Above: *Giza, Emma and Larry*, 1992.
Lithograph with photo transfer
and African fabric collage, image:
22 ½ × 30 in. AP 2/4. Gift of
Sylvan Cole Jr., New York 1993.7

Left: *Baby*, 1966. Oil on canvas, 45 × 50 ⅓ in.
Purchased jointly by the Studio Museum
in Harlem, Museum purchase with
funds provided by Ann Tenenbaum and
Thomas H. Lee; and the Whitney Museum
of American Art, with funds from the
Painting and Sculpture Committee
2018.32

in bold red, blue, and green hues. The circular forms in the painting—like beach balls, the sun, or sunglass shades—suggest the energy and playfulness associated with beach activities and Amos's emerging life as a mother.

Amos first started printing at Robert Blackburn's cooperative workshop in the mid-1960s, and it quickly became a vital space for her artistic development. As a Black woman artist navigating an art world governed by white men, Amos found herself in a multiply marginalized position. However, at Blackburn's workshop, she discovered a lively community of printmakers and printers with whom she could collaborate. For Amos, working with skilled printmakers such as Blackburn and, more frequently, Kathy Caraccio, allowed her to explore the complexities of various printmaking methods and themes of both fragmentation and possibility, as she probed the complexities of race and gender.

As Amos's work matured, she combined various media and techniques. She depicted moving figures—often diving, running, dancing, or falling—that came alive against vibrant, colorful backgrounds. She sometimes used fabric to complicate her surfaces, redirect the viewer's eye, and inject more color. *Giza, Emma and Larry* commemorates the life of one of Amos's former students, Giza Daniels-Endesha. The artist shows her subject falling through the air, separated by a strip of kente fabric from a phototransfer image of Amos and her brother, Larry, as children. This artwork encapsulates Amos's ability to infuse her pieces with emotional resonance and layered narratives, weaving together personal, historical, and cultural elements into a rich tapestry of expression.

—Shawnya Harris

Alma Thomas

1891—1978

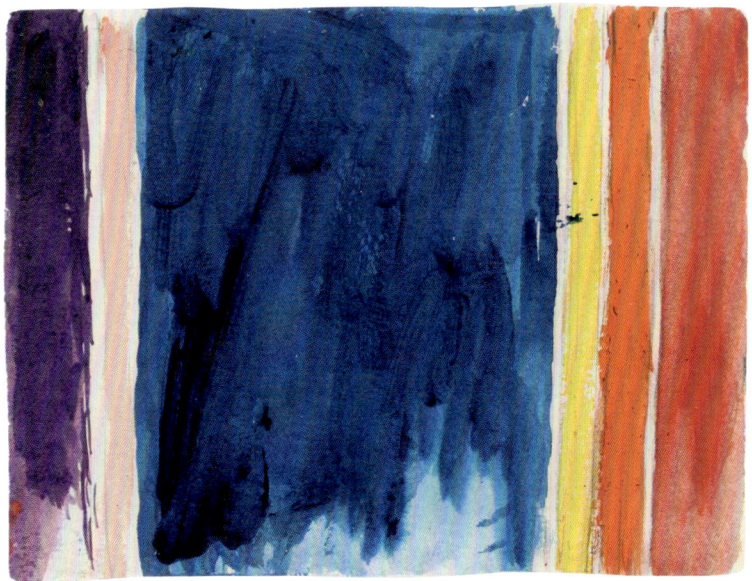

Space, 1966. Acrylic on paper, image:
6 × 7 in. Museum purchase and
a gift from E. Thomas Williams and
Auldlyn Higgins Williams 1997.9.19

Alma Thomas's abstract works are widely celebrated for their vibrant colors and diverse subject matter, which includes flowers, music, and outer space. Thomas made many artworks inspired by the wonder of space travel and images she saw on television broadcasts of NASA's Apollo shuttle launches in the 1960s. The title of *Space* likely refers, then, to the celestial space that so fascinated the artist. Formally, too, Thomas explored space in her work, asking—through paint—how different colors jostle for position in the visual field. *Space*, like many other works Thomas painted, features stripes outlined in sketchy pencil lines with colors painted on top in acrylic, indicating that the artist planned the composition before coloring it. She then laid on stripes of violet, peach, deep blue, lemon, orange, and brick red, with thin strips of the white paper left untouched in between these colors. Looking at this work, one might ask: In what order did Thomas paint these stripes? Which colors look like they are in the foreground or background? What makes the colors seem to move? The bright streaks to the left and right of the composition frame the multi-hued, active blue field as if viewers can travel into it. Elsewhere evidence of motion can be seen in the marks Thomas made; visible brush-strokes animate the blue field, and a small splash punches into the yellow stripe. The pencil lines set walls that the stripes breach—rules the colors cannot help but break in all their vigor.

—Terence Washington

Al Loving

1935—2005

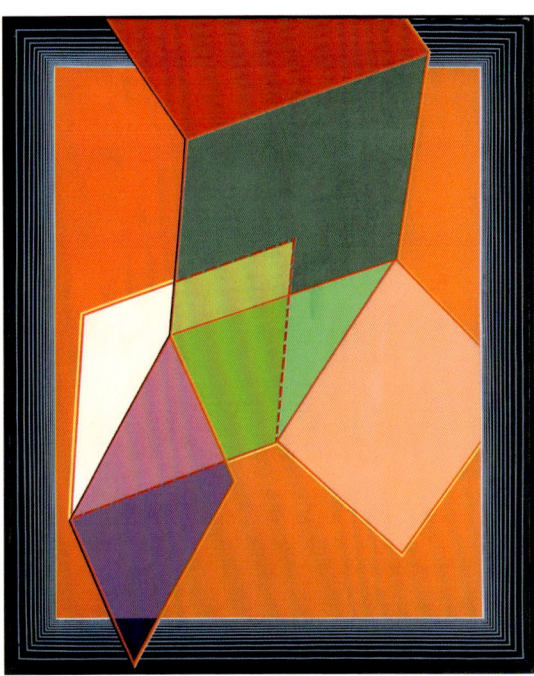

Variations on a Six Sided Object, 1967.
Acrylic on canvas, 72 ¾ × 61 in. Gift of
Ruth Weisberg and Kelyn Roberts 1983.20

Al Loving is celebrated for his meticulously structured paintings and
collages that explore the indeterminacy of space as a way to question
perceptions and experiences of the painted canvas. During the height of his
artistic production, in the 1970s and 1980s, Loving was part of a cadre
of African American abstract painters—including Howardena Pindell, Jack
Whitten, and William T. Williams—who probed the relationships between
painting, space, and illusion, and who took a profound interest in pushing
the boundaries of geometry and form. Loving's tireless investigations
of color theory, abstract composition, and the materiality of painting made
him a pioneering figure in the history of late twentieth-century abstraction.

Loving's works in the collection of the Studio Museum present a holistic
view of his stylistic and thematic trajectory. *Hex 4* emblematizes Loving's
minimalist, hard-edged abstractions, from which he first rose to prominence
in the late 1960s. These early works take the cube as a basic modular unit
for deconstructing the pictorial plane and for imagining painting beyond the
flat surface. Deeply inspired by the oeuvre of artist Josef Albers, this phase
of Loving's career was characterized by a rigorous engagement with color
theory and serial repetition of form.

Painted on a hexagonal canvas, the appropriately titled *Hex 4* is structured
with carefully delineated bands of thick, bold color rhythmically layered
to form an illusion of a three-dimensional cube that betrays the supposed
flatness of painting. This painting and other works, like *Variations on a Six*

Sided Object, are rendered with an almost confrontational chromatic intensity that heightens their illusory effect: colors are schematized such that they variously pulse from or recede into space, revealing Loving's remarkable understanding of the unity between color and depth.

In the early 1970s, Loving departed from the linear precision of his geometric canvases to embrace an approach freed from the cohesive, stretched canvas. Instead of working with a brush, Loving cut canvas or cardboard into strips that he subsequently dyed. Works like *Roger*—an ambiguously shaped agglomeration of corrugated cardboard—convey the radical change that Loving's style underwent during this decade.

Evoking an archipelago with its clustered, independent forms, *Roger* is void of the formulaic architecture of Loving's previous works. On the one hand, this work along with others of the 1970s and 1980s demonstrate that his thinking remained guided by geometry's complexity. In fact, the effect of these colorful ribbons of canvas recalls the rectangular swathes and blocks of color undergirding his hard-edged paintings. On the other hand, working with loose pieces of canvas allowed the artist more freedom to experiment with varied, less fixed forms, resulting in new spatial con-figurations and an emphasis on the physical process of arriving at a work via cutting, dyeing, configuring, and reconfiguring. Ultimately, Loving's adventures with space, color, and form—as witnessed both in his geomet-ric paintings and his unclassifiable collages—opened up a new language of abstraction, and new ways of understanding the genre's foundations.

—Zoë Hopkins

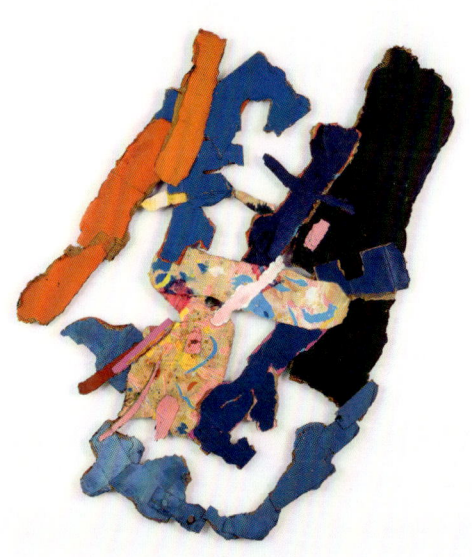

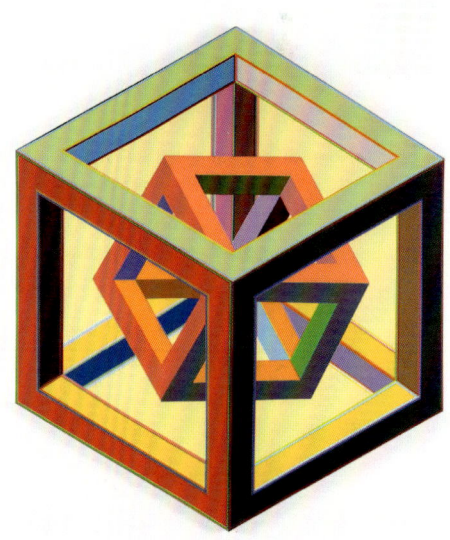

Roger, c. 1975. Corrugated cardboard collage, 91 × 83 ¼ × 2 in. Gift of the artist 1977.6.1

Hex 4, 1968. Acrylic on canvas, 70 ½ × 82 ½ in. Gift of Eileen C. and Major E. Thomas 1991.19.1

Gordon Parks

1912—2006

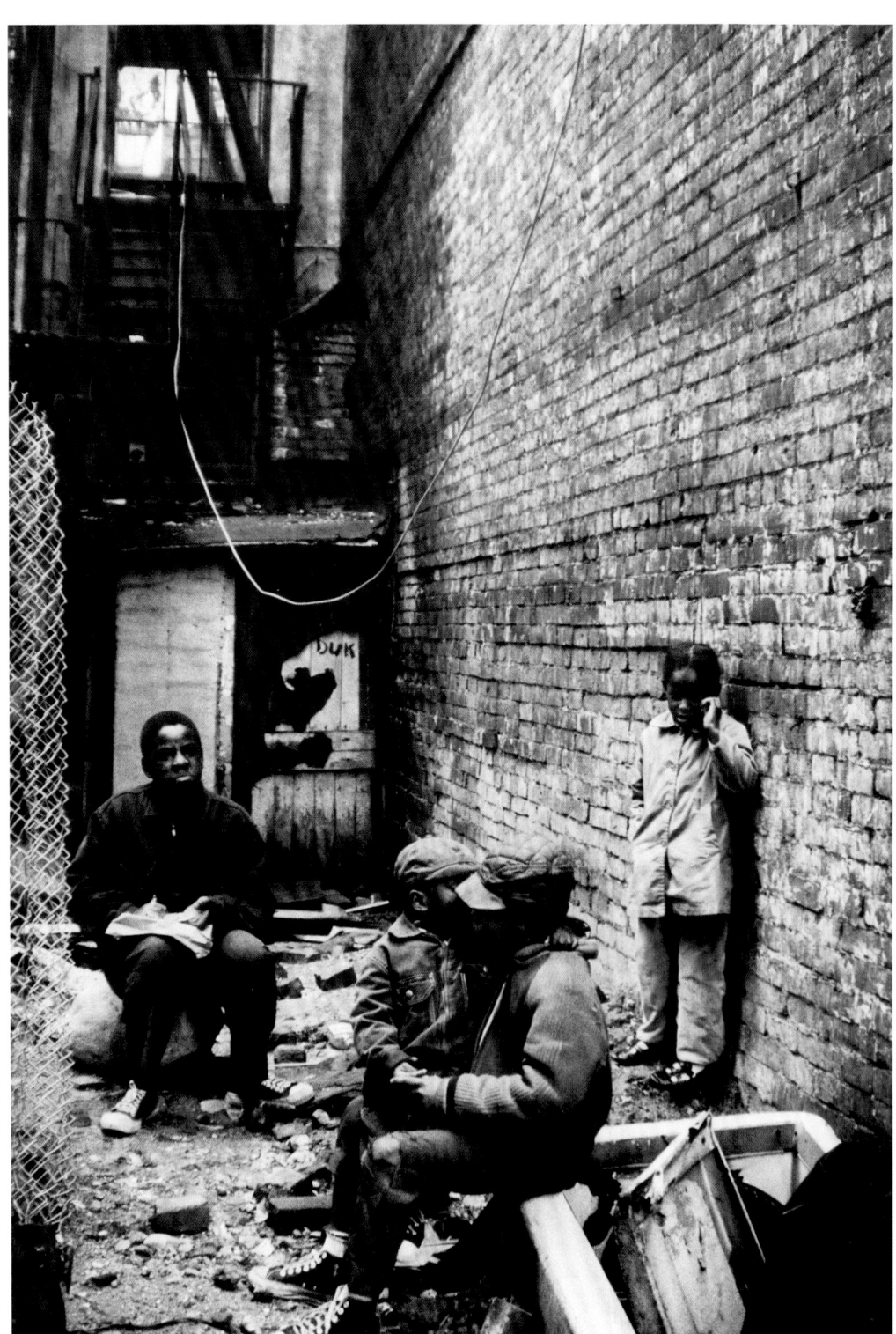

In the winter of 1967, *Life* magazine assigned Gordon Parks, the first and only Black photographer on staff at the time, to document the painful realities of poverty in Harlem. Over the course of a month, Parks captured the lives of Norman Fontenelle Sr., his wife, Bessie, and their eight children. After bonding with the family and earning their trust, Parks took hundreds of images of their daily lives and published a photo essay titled "A Harlem Family" in *Life* the following March. Parks was acutely aware of his position as an outsider and observer, and approached this assignment with immense care and empathy—his resulting photographs, such as this closely cropped image of four of the Fontenelle children in a desolate outdoor area, are humanizing and intimate. Parks's candid scene of the four children is a poetic balance of light, shadow, and texture. While the details of individual faces are obscured in shadow, their personalities shine through—an older brother protectively sits with his siblings, a curious child returns the camera's gaze, and the two other siblings whisper to one another. The childhood innocence dramatically juxtaposes the roughness and grit surrounding them, inspiring empathy in the viewer.

A self-taught photographer, Parks began his career with the Farm Security Administration in the 1940s, during which time he developed his signature style—honest depictions of how people lived. Parks would remain at *Life* for two decades, and he produced memorable photographs of US culture as well as the nation's turbulent histories, with a focus on civil rights, systemic racism and poverty, and urban life. Throughout his nearly sixty-year career as a photographer, filmmaker, and composer, Parks remained committed to social justice and activism, using his skills to advocate against oppression and violence against Black people across the United States.

—Doris Zhao

Fontenelle Children Outside Their Harlem Tenement, 1967. Gelatin silver print, 24 × 20 in. Museum purchase with funds provided by the Acquisition Committee 2001.25

Betty Blayton

1937—2016

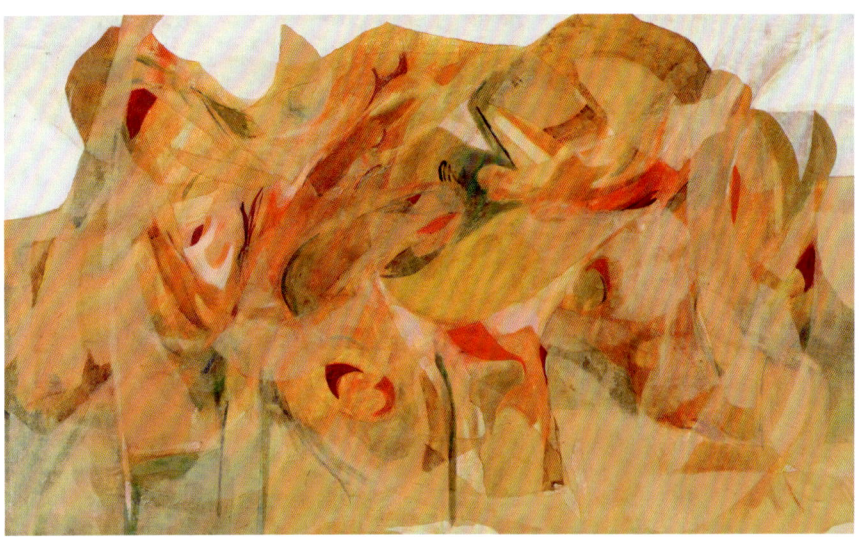

Untitled, 1968. Oil and collage on canvas,
35 ¾ × 60 ⅛ in. Gift of anonymous donor
1975.3

Betty Blayton describes her paintings as "the working out of an inner symbolic language of sensory impressions and intuition . . . an effort to get closer to my own being and by so doing hopefully opening up for those who view them as a sensory language (through the use of color, line, and form) which we all share."[47] Her work thus argues that viewers innately have access to an understanding of abstraction, that it only needs to be opened up.

For Blayton, the process of making art is meditative and self-reflective, and this space for contemplation is also something she hopes viewers might be able to find while looking at her work.[18] Though the sensory impressions she seeks to document are intangible, Blayton called her work "Spiritual Realism." She explains: "The more you look at it the more it is real, not necessarily as abstract as initially perceived. I am very aware that color has sound, and lines have rhythm and motion."[49] Spending time with *Untitled*, the painting does shift into motion; the curved shapes and pieces of paper swoop around pockets nestled into a larger form. She builds up the composition with layers of translucent, organic shapes in earthy tones cut through with moments of pink and burgundy. "I think when I say 'spirit,' it has to do with the energy that motivates me," Blayton says. "I think that everybody has a spirit . . . . So when I say 'spirit,' I am talking about that energy that manifests us into motion, whether it is something concrete, or an idea or a thought or a feeling."[50] Behind her abstractions, such as *Untitled*, is a motivation of spirit that can be found either by making art or spending time with it.

— Jordan Jones

Tom Lloyd

1929—1996

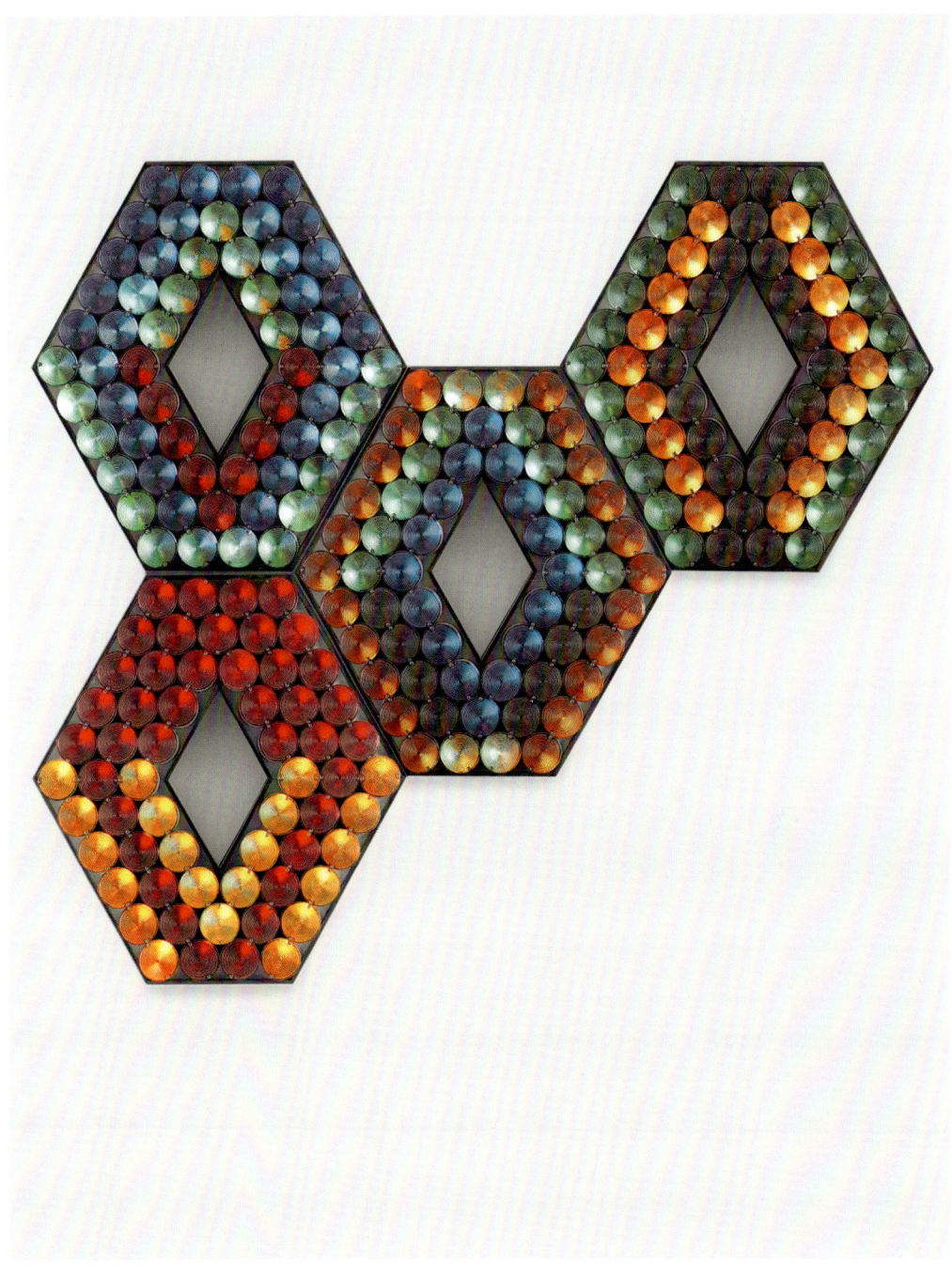

Moussakoo, c. 1968. Light bulbs, plastic
lenses, aluminum, laminated plywood, each
approximately 35 × 33 × 15 in. with overall
dimensions variable. Gift of the Lloyd
Family and Jamilah Wilson 1996.11

Baby, you alright?

I got to feeling like a machine,

that's no way

to feel . . . [51]

mechanized motorized

numbed   plain

out of light.

So let's take a beat

oscillate til

we syncopate

re-configurate to

re-imaginate

resisting the static noise

the same ol' same ol' SAME

OL'

THING

in favor of   a jump   A LEAP

into

primary and secondary HUES

bending & REFRACTING

follow the

WARNING WARNING

red LIGHTS

blue LIGHTS

SLOW   it   dooooown!

lights OFF lights OUT

this ain't no kids game

STOP

unplug reset

in 1968

unplug reset

in 1992 in 2008 in 2020 in in in

cause THE TIME is

done come

again AND

again

they said

DIM DOWN now son

Dim down now son

STAY

IN

YOUR

PLACE!

no no I

WON'T!

Say it loud
SAY IT LOUD say it CLEAR for the folks

in the back!

NO, NO! I said

a switch

[Power flipped]   Lights UP
                           Lights ON

Are YOU ready?

SPEED IT UP

flashing yellow READYREADY

green LIGHTS

GO

cause THESE lights MY lights
gonna SHINE
make 'em STAND DOWN concede SO BRIGHT gonna light a NEW way
make 'em put on their SHADES

it's a new DAY

BEHOLD!

Those marquee SIGNS blink BLINKING you

PULLING you
CALLING you

in
along Broadway
across 125th Street
at 2033 5th Avenue
like a moth to a like a beacon of

singing shouting declaring:

MY Black is

We're ALIVE!

my Black IS

We're ELECTRIC!

my Black is my Black is My   Black   IS   **BLACK !**

Baby, we gon' be alright[52]

——Daonne Huff

Diane Arbus

1923—1971

The year 1968 was full of tragedy with the back-to-back assassinations in April and June of civil rights leader Martin Luther King Jr. and Senator Robert F. Kennedy. These brutal killings led to widespread rioting, national disillusionment, and sociopolitical upheaval.[53] The landmark Fair Housing Act was perhaps the only positive outcome of the horrific year. This legislation, which prohibits discrimination concerning the sale, rental, and financing of housing based on race, religion, or national origin, was dear to King, who had for years helped organize nonviolent marches for fair housing for African American communities.[54] On April 11, 1968, just one week after King's assassination, and during the ensuing Holy Week Uprising protests that engulfed more than one hundred cities from coast to coast, President Lyndon Johnson signed the Fair Housing Act into law. This is the necessary backdrop for any consideration of Diane Arbus's portrait of King's widow, Coretta Scott King, posing on the front lawn of their family home in Atlanta.

Arbus emerged in the early 1960s as one of the most distinctive and influential photographers in the United States. Alongside Lee Friedlander and Garry Winogrand, her work was featured at the Museum of Modern Art in *New Documents*, the watershed 1967 exhibition that soon changed the course of photography in the United States. As the museum curator John Szarkowski wrote, the artists had "directed the documentary approach toward more personal ends. Their aim has been not to reform life, but to know it. Their work betrays a sympathy—almost an affection—for the imperfections and the frailties of society."[55]

In October 1968, six months after King's death, Arbus flew to Atlanta to make a portrait of Coretta Scott King for *Harper's Bazaar*.[56] She worked extensively inside the Kings' home, which was filled with the leader's honorary awards and memorial tributes, but preferred using the symbolic form of the house's exterior for the portrait's stage. Subject and photographer are at arm's distance, and the camera's lens does not record King's feet—she is heaven- not earth-bound, and clasps her hands peacefully, looking skyward. For her part, although unseen, Arbus holds her 2 ¼-inch Rolleiflex and looks down into its ground glass, where King appears as a latent image. The malevolence of the world is, for a moment, far, far away.

—Jeff L. Rosenheim

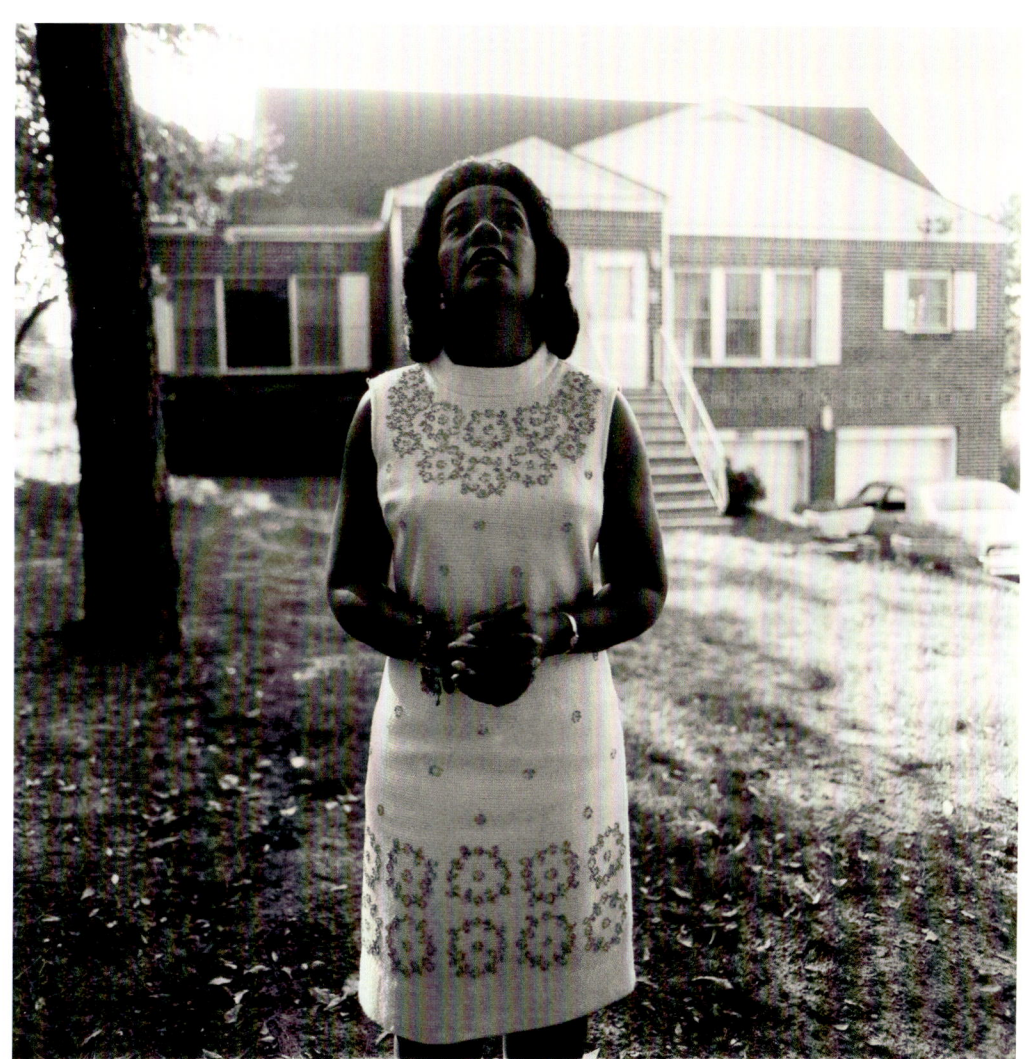

*Mrs. Martin Luther King, Jr. on her front
lawn, Atlanta, GA, 1968*, 1968. Gelatin
silver print, 14 ½ × 14 ½ in. Gift of
Jeffrey Fraenkel and Frish Brandt 2018.2.1

Mavis Pusey
1928—2019

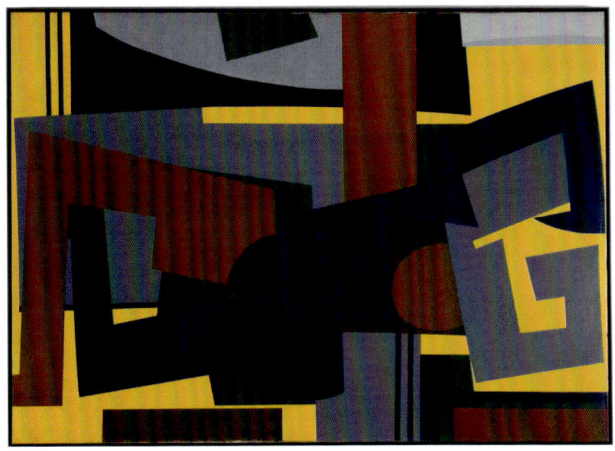

Purir, 1968. Oil on canvas, 40 × 56 ½ in.
Museum purchase with funds provided by
the Acquisition Committee 2018.4

Mavis Pusey was a prolific printmaker and painter whose work reflected the dynamism of the world around her. The painting *Puriv* epitomizes her distinctive style. Anchored by a mustard yellow along with brown, gray, blue, and green geometric forms that collide, overlap, and entangle on the canvas, *Puriv* synthesizes color and form. Its elongated, intertwined forms are hybrids—melding hardline, abstract shapes with organic, circular shapes—evoking contours of clothing pattern pieces. Much of Pusey's work from this period seems tied to the fashion industry, which she navigated as a student and professional. Pusey moved from Retreat, Jamaica, in 1959 to study at the Traphagen School of Fashion in New York City. By 1961 Pusey was working part-time at a bridal gown boutique while enrolled at the Art Students League.[57]

The year 1968, when Pusey painted *Puriv*, proved to be a watershed year for the artist. She had moved to London the year before to work with printmaker Birgit Skiöld, and also found employment as a patternmaker and clothes designer.[58] During these years, a robust, graphic style emerged from Pusey's work; the artist was inspired by her new surroundings in England, jazz music, as well as fashion and its interactions with the human figure. Her work as a clothing designer took her to Paris, where she witnessed the student and worker uprisings of 1968. This turbulent time, and the years leading up to it, inspired prints such as *Paris, Mai-Jun* (c. 1968) and *Eric* (n.d.); both pieces have strong, parallel black lines—evocative of musical staves—that encapsulate the chaos of the city. Pusey carries over these powerful lines to *Puriv*, in both the upper left and lower segments. Though she would later return to New York to print at Robert Blackburn Printmaking Workshop before settling in Orange, Virginia, it is evident from her subsequent works that the period surrounding the creation of *Puriv* and her time in the fashion industry were crucial to her artistic development.

— Hallie Ringle

David Driskell

1931—2020

The year 1968 is regarded as one of the most tumultuous years in modern US history. The activist and spiritual leader Martin Luther King Jr. was assassinated in Memphis, the Vietnam War had reached its thirteenth year, and—given the white supremacist terror in the United States—Black Nationalist groups began to gain steam, rejecting nonviolent philosophies touted by their predecessors.

Driskell created *Woods at Skowhegan* in this tense environment. Here he depicts expressive, relaxed strokes of earth tones, likely made from watercolor, that render a dense forest of tall trees. In 1961 Driskell and his wife purchased a home in Falmouth, Maine, where they would visit each summer. He has said of these summers, "On going to Maine, and being reinvigorated by nature, I became very much taken with the countryside and with the landscape. I then moved my art through phases of looking at nature."[59] Natural and spiritual elements had long been an inspiration for Driskell's abstract and figurative work. He used trees as conceptual devices to remark about spirit and revered trees as material that could be turned into lumber for shelter.

At Catholic University, he wrote his master's thesis on the evergreen tree as a symbol of eternity. Driskell shared: "I was searching for other ways of connecting the pine tree to another dimension in life . . . I did not always see it as landscape. But I saw it as part and parcel of something larger."[60] Against the backdrop of 1968, Driskell's art practice could not exist outside the influence of the aforementioned realities. Nonetheless, his view and admiration of nature offer a wider aperture on Black leisure that celebrates engagements with fauna and flora—and perhaps, a covert response to the intensities of sociopolitical unrest in 1968.

—Taylor Renee Aldridge

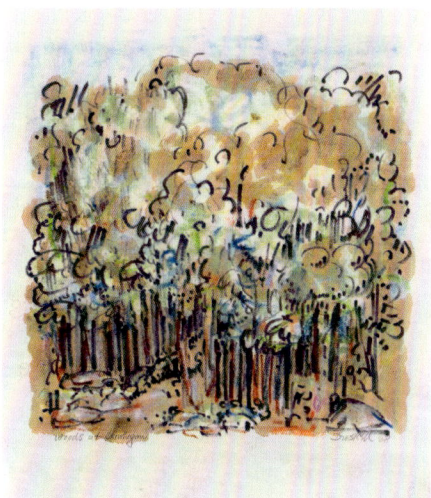

Woods at Skowhegan, 1968. Work on paper, image: 8 ½ × 8 ½ in., sheet: 10 ⅞ × 9 ½ in. Bequest of Peggy Cooper Cafritz (1947—2018), Washington, DC, collector, educator, and activist 2018.40.72

Barkley L. Hendricks

1945—2017

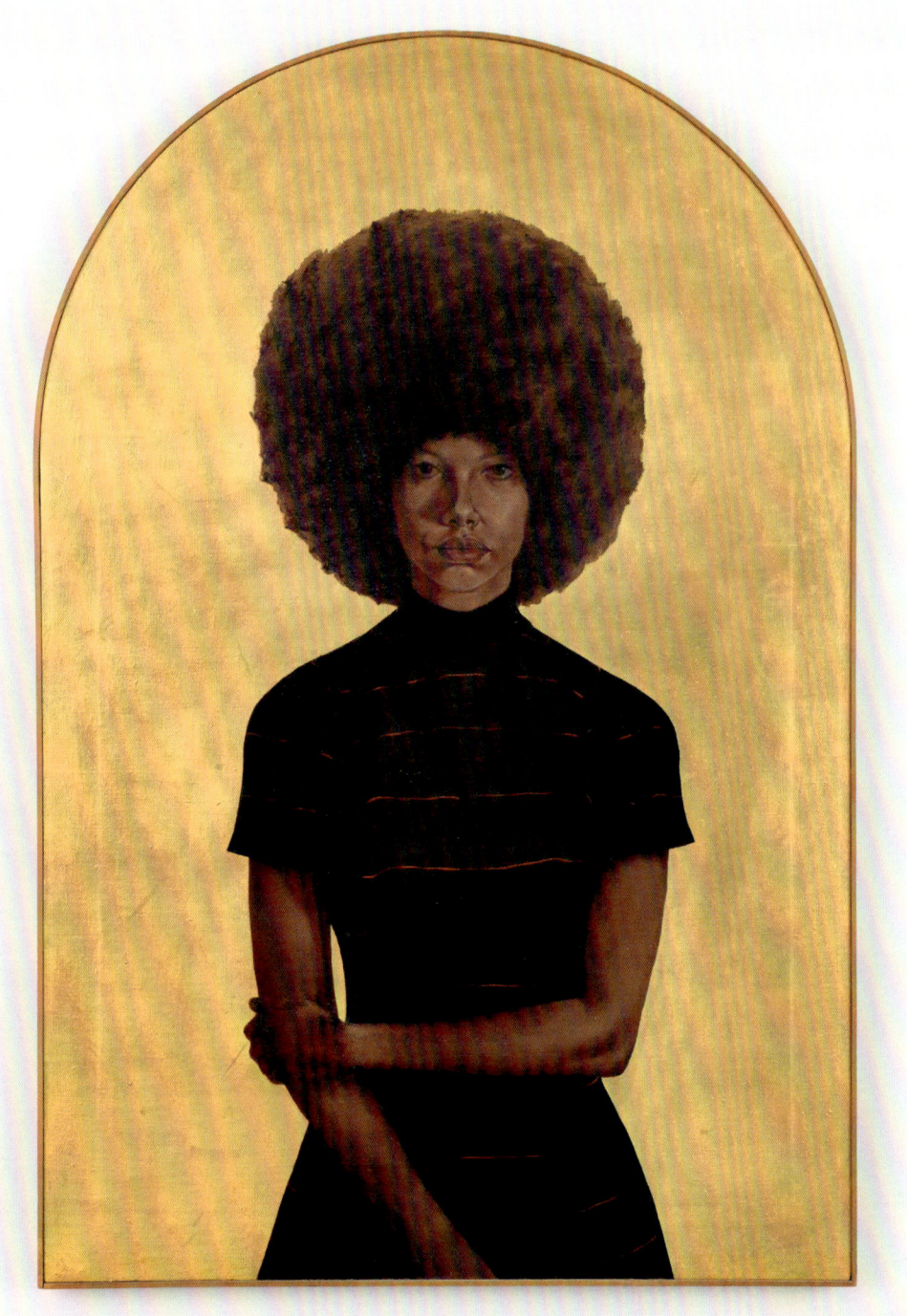

Lawdy Mama, 1969. Oil and gold leaf on
canvas, 53 ¾ × 36 ¼ in. Gift of Stuart
Liebman, in memory of Joseph B. Liebman
1983.25

Lawdy Mama is one of Barkley L. Hendricks's earliest portraits, painted between his academic training at the Pennsylvania Academy of the Fine Arts (PAFA) (1963—67) and Yale University (1970—72). At PAFA he was the first Black student to be awarded two consecutive travel scholarships, which brought him to Europe in 1966 and North Africa in 1968. There he encountered works by the old masters of European painting. Hendricks derived inspiration from the technical virtuosity of the old masters, but his subjects boldly challenged the status quo of both art history and contemporary society through representations of his reality as a Black person in the United States. While his portraits reflect the Black Power ideology, style, and popular culture of the era, he eschewed conventional impressions of recognizable figures in favor of honest portrayals of everyday people.

Lawdy Mama is a portrait of his cousin Kathy Williams, though it visually recalls Black Power activist and Black Panther Kathleen Cleaver. The subject's spherical hairstyle is reinforced by the curved lunette frame, common to European religious paintings that Hendricks saw in his travels. Hendricks explored the reflective potential of gold leafing, a feature historically reserved for religious icons as in the gold-ground paintings of Italo-Byzantine and early Renaissance art. However, his subject is not the Madonna nor any other saint, but a family member depicted with a natural Afro in place of a halo. Transcendental light radiates behind her, warmly emanating the notion "Black Is Beautiful." Through these stylistic and technical devices, Hendricks elevates a Black woman to iconic status.

The painting also shows the artist's early exploration of his "limited palette" concept, a signature style in which he painted the clothes of his subject on top of a solid, flat background within the same color field. While Hendricks had not yet fully committed to a gold-on-gold approach here, a golden hue permeates everything, from the highlights on Williams's hair to her bronze skin and the orange stripes on her dress. The artist seamlessly tied the work together through a thread of golden light.

The title of the painting nods to Hendricks's deep love of music, particularly jazz, as he sometimes quoted songs, albums, or lyrics in the naming of his works. "Hey Lawdy Mama" (or "Oh Lordy Mama") is a Piedmont blues song first recorded by Buddy Moss in 1934 and further popularized by Louis Armstrong in 1941. In 1967, not long before Hendricks created this painting, Nina Simone released her song "Blues for Mama," which began with the lyrics "Hey, Lordy Mama." Whatever the primary inspiration for his title might be, Hendricks was well-versed in the music of both Armstrong and Simone, and he often borrowed from vernacular language and popular culture for his titles.

Lawdy Mama is a pivotal early portrait by Hendricks, significant in the development of his painting style, as well as in his use of handcrafted frames and gold-leafing, which he continued throughout his career. His artistic vision stands out as unique among his contemporaries, and his work has profoundly impacted a younger generation of artists.

—Trevor Schoonmaker

William T. Williams

b. 1942

Inspired by growing up in North Carolina and New York, as well as contemporaneous social and cultural affairs, the art of William T. Williams opens modernist modes of abstraction to subjects beyond the canvas.

In the early 1960s, Williams abandoned figuration to explore his fascination with paint, color, and mark-making. Among competing perspectives on art and art history as a graduate student at Yale, he knew he had to sharpen his views and create his own path. Williams absorbed the principles of modernist aesthetics, retaining only those he found useful, and by 1968, he developed a rigorous geometric style infused with a bold, expressionistic quality.

In his first series, "Diamond in a Box," Williams centered multicolored diamond forms that repeat and radiate into the depths of the picture planes, as arcs, bands, and rectangles intersect the central shapes. The untitled screenprints (all 1969) in the Studio Museum's collection evince how Williams explored numerous arrangements, perspectives, and color combinations with this format. Paintings in the series are imbued with dynamic tension, as seen in *Trane*, and thus are indicative of the political context of the late 1960s. At the same time, *Trane*'s discordant forms and colors also evoke its namesake's turn to avant-garde jazz—the multiphonics of John Coltrane's late music—demonstrating Williams's facility for merging cultural references with abstraction.

Williams's practice has bridged divides between artists, museums, and their surrounding communities. In 1968 he developed the *Artist-in-Residence* program at the Studio Museum and formed Smokehouse Associates with artists Melvin Edwards, Guy Ciarcia, and Billy Rose. The latter group consulted with local organizations and residents to paint vibrant abstract designs on Harlem buildings, aspiring to improve the aesthetics of the environment and lives within.

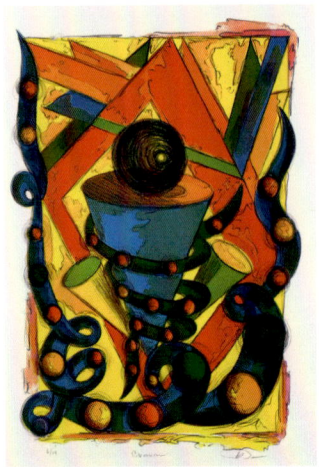 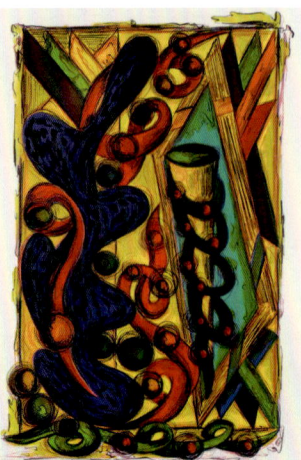

Left: *Caravan*, 1991. Lithograph with linoleum cut, image: 41 × 29 ½ in. Edition 6 of 27. Gift of William T. Williams and Oberon Press Inc. 1993.12.3

Right: *Perdido*, 1991. Lithograph with linoleum cut, image: 39 ¾ × 26 ¼ in. Edition 6 of 27. Gift of William T. Williams and Oberon Press Inc. 1993.12.4

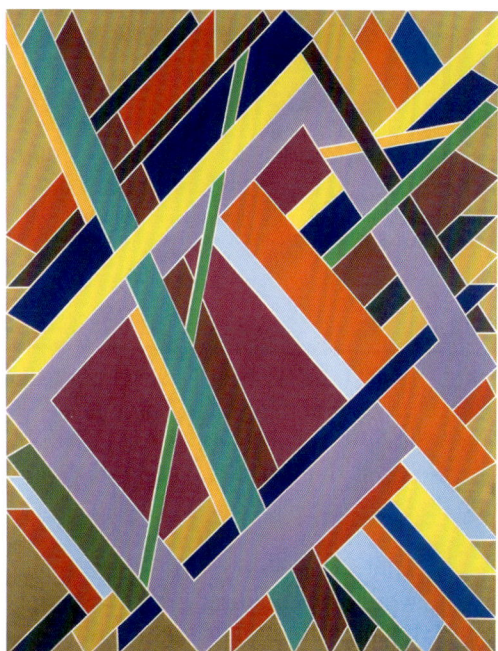

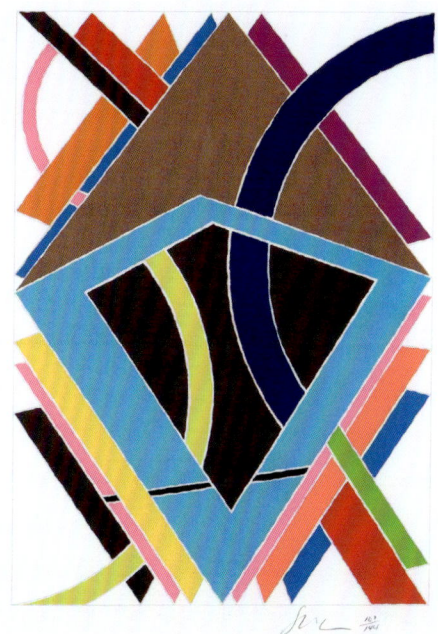

Trane, 1969. Acrylic on canvas,
109 ½ × 85 ½ × 2 in. Gift of
Charles Cowles, New York 1981.2.2

Untitled, 1969. Screenprint on paper, sheet:
23 ⅜ × 17 ½ in. Edition 107 of 144. Gift of
Charles Cowles, New York 1981.2.4

For his 1970s "Shimmer" series, he subdued his palette and modified his paint application. Williams added pearlescent bases to his pigments and painted with rhythmic brushstrokes covering the entire canvas. In the 1980s Williams worked with similar tones, as his mark-making became more gestural and his surfaces more textured. By the early 1990s, a fuller range of colors returned. Works such as *Caravan* and *Perdido* exemplify the vibrancy of Williams's palette and interest in revisiting earlier motifs. Both lithographs feature conical, spherical, and serpentine forms interplaying with the diamonds from his first series, creating new, dynamic formal relations.

The colorful grid compositions of Williams's "465" series refer to his home address. They exemplify how he has experimented with color and paint application, and expanded on earlier formats and techniques throughout the 2000s.[61] While Williams has noted that later works are records of "place as a specific type of poetry," the expression of specificity within the abstract has been one of the hallmarks of Williams's entire career and will remain a long-lasting contribution to the language of modernism.[62]

——Kanitra Fletcher

Barbara Jones-Hogu

1938—2017

Vibrant colors, rhythmic compositions, bold lettering, and subjects inspired by people of African descent—these are the key elements of Barbara Jones-Hogu's prints. A lifelong resident of Chicago, Jones-Hogu was a founder of the African Commune of Bad Relevant Artists (AfriCOBRA), a collective of Black artists formed in 1968 during the civil rights and Black Power movements. She and other founders had been associated with the earlier Organization of Black American Culture (OBAC), best known for the 1967 Wall of Respect mural in the Bronzeville neighborhood of Chicago. At a time when Black artists were coming together in solidarity, AfriCOBRA created a visual language and philosophy that defined a Black aesthetic, one that emphasized self-determination and empowerment of people across the African diaspora.

Jones-Hogu studied various forms of printmaking—etching, lithography, screen printing, wood engraving, and woodblock printing—at the School of the Art Institute of Chicago and the Institute of Design at Illinois Institute of Technology. The artists in AfriCOBRA chose printmaking as their medium of choice for its democratic possibilities: works could be made at low cost and in multiples, allowing the works, and their political and inspiring messages, to be seen by many and acquired for display in Black homes. Jones-Hogu also embraced printmaking as a means to create works with positive images that fostered confidence and uplifted Black communities. Her training as a printmaker helped establish the AfriCOBRA aesthetic, with works such as *One People Unite* and *Unite* becoming emblematic of the group's oeuvre.

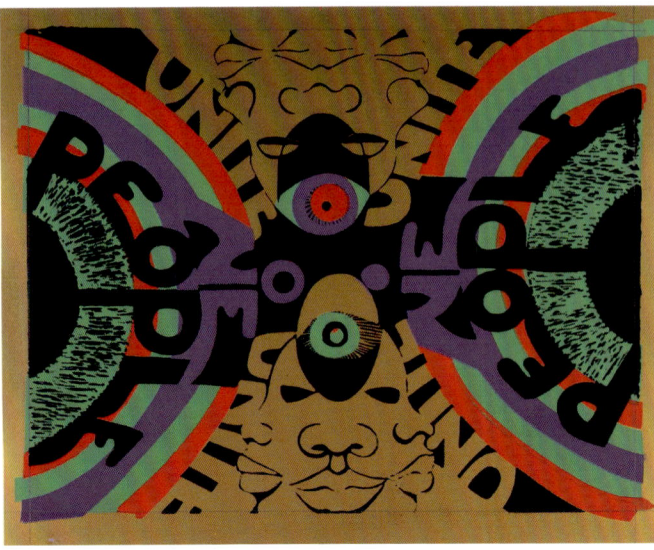

One People Unite, 1969. Screenprint on gold paperboard, image: 19 ¾ × 25 ¾ in., sheet: 22 ½ × 28 in. From the edition of fewer than 10 impressions printed by the artist. Museum purchase with funds provided by the Acquisition Committee 2018.17

AfriCOBRA's mission to create works that educate to encourage change is evident in *One People Unite*. Jones-Hogu advocated for the use of text in AfriCOBRA works. Clear messaging of uniting as one people was used as a rallying directive. The near symmetry of the work was also understood to be accessible and based on what artists in the group saw as the syncopated rhythms of African movement and music. Jones-Hogu often experimented with papers and printing across various impressions of the same work. Here, she left the gold paperboard bare, allowing the lustrous color to act as the base for the heads and multiples of "UNITE" in the vertical center. In other impressions of *One People Unite*, the artist applied brown ink over this section, giving the work a more somber tone overall.

The message of solidarity can also be found in *Unite*, Jones-Hogu's best-known work. The repeating and overlapping triangles of the word "UNITE" appear as shouts increasing in intensity by the Afroed crowd with fists raised in the Black Power salute. Rhythm is incorporated in the sharp diagonals of text that contrast with the rounded fists and heads, suggesting the energy and possibilities of a unified front. Throughout these works, Jones-Hogu visually expressed Black pride and unity, ideas central to both her practice and the Black Power movement.

—Connie H. Choi

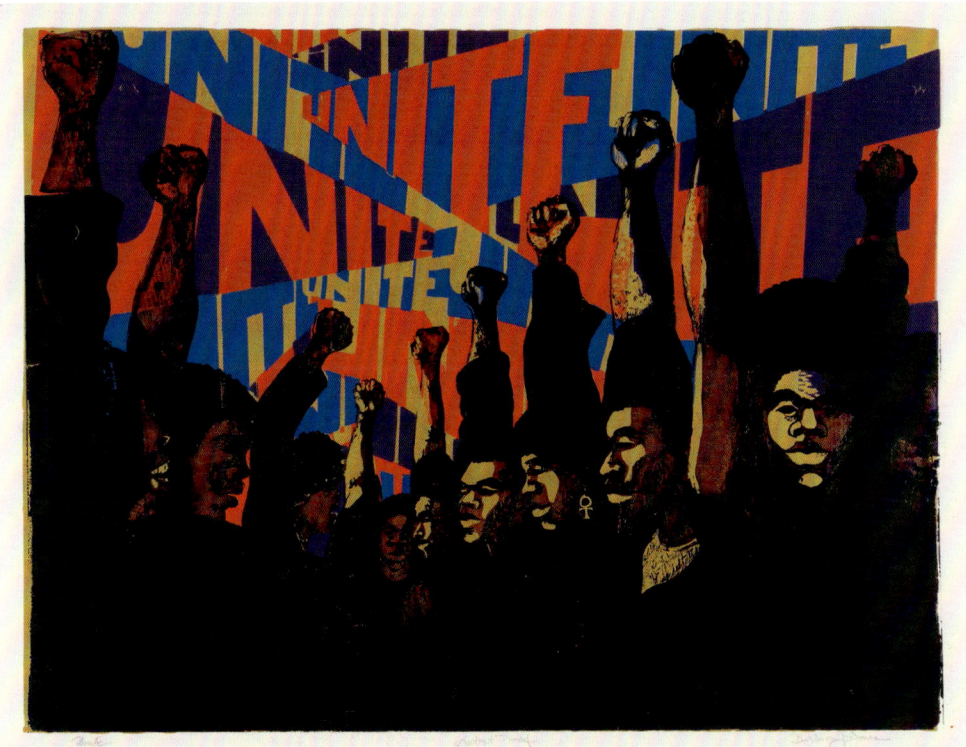

Unite, 1969. Screenprint on cream wove paper, image: 22 ½ × 30 ¼ in., sheet: 26 ¼ × 35 in. Museum purchase with funds provided by the Acquisition Committee 2018.18

Ademola Olugebefola

b. 1941

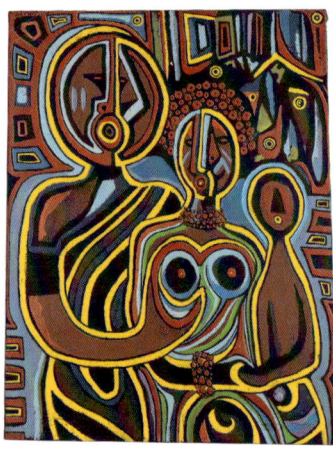

The Family, 1969. Acrylic on canvas, 36 × 28 in.
Gift of the artist 1981.7

In *The Family*, Ademola Olugebefola uplifts the traditional nuclear family to the status of ancient African royalty. A father wraps his arm around a mother's shoulder, his hand intimately cupping her breast; a child to her left holds her hand. He renders the triad in rich and thick red, yellow, blue, and brown lines—the effect encases the man, woman, and child as if in a halo, only unlike the pieta, this is the complete unit. Everyone in this family is holy.

Born in St. Thomas, Virgin Islands, Olugebefola (then Bedwick L. Thomas) moved to the United States at age five, and to Harlem in 1963—a fraught year considering the Birmingham bombings, March on Washington for Jobs and Freedom, murder of Medgar Evers, and countless civil rights demonstrations. Just two years later, he cofounded the Harlem-based WEUSI Artist Collective, spinning off the Twentieth Century Creators to form an offshoot collective more focused on art that directly cited African symbolism and cosmologies. As a member of the Black Arts Movement, Olugebefola made it his mission to "create an art that was independent of European aesthetics, one that exemplified excellence and portrayed much of our positive, constructive history and contributions to the world."[63]

The Family indicates Olugebefola's activist background and training in graphic design, woodcuts, illustration, and theater. Expressing his belief that African peoples originated in the heavens, the artist venerates a domestic subject (a family) into the realm of gods. He works in a signature blend of plane and color. He frames the regal trio with a concentric square pattern, symbolic of structure and order, and reminiscent of geometric motifs of textiles like bògòlanfini, the Malian mud cloth, or kente, the cloth of Akan royalty. The parental figures' faces split in half, like a Janus, or more aptly, a tribal mask—Olugebefola defiantly rending back the Cubist interest in the cultural material of the African continent to face this appropriation eye to eye.

—Meg Whiteford

David Hammons
b. 1943

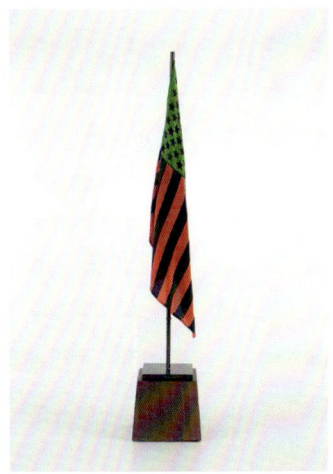

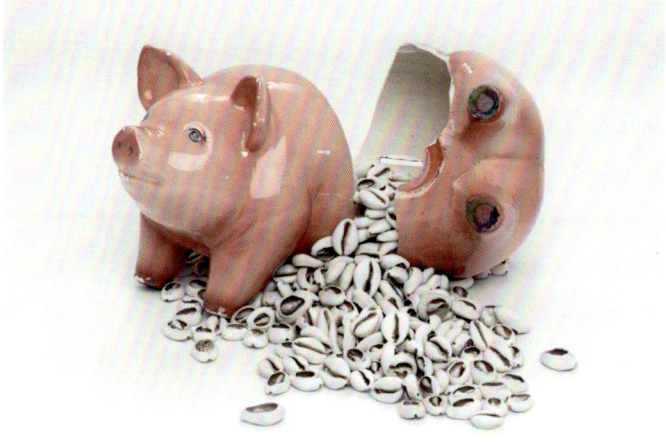

African-American Flag, 1997. Printed fabric stapled on a painted wooden pole, flag: 8 × 11 in., pole and base: 22 in. Bequest of Peggy Cooper Cafritz (1947—2018), Washington, DC, collector, educator, and activist 2018.40.109

Too Obvious, 1996. Cowrie shells and porcelain, 7 × 12 × 14 in. Gift of Edward Clark, New York 2002.7

On United States Flag Etiquette:
In elementary school, I was on safety patrol. During the morning drop-offs, we kids would greet arrivals and open car doors. We were also tasked with raising the flag. A slow and mindful unraveling of the perfectly folded triangle, never should it touch the ground. One morning, a dilemma. A car approached as we began the unwind. Serve the people or the flag? I let the flag touch the ground and was reprimanded.

On Black Flag Etiquette:
As I move from a side street to an avenue, I hear it before I see it. A few more steps and I'm swept into the current of a weeknight parade. Pan-African flags of small scale and large scale are waved vertically, right side, flipside, marched horizontally held tautly from each corner, drop a penny and it might bounce, worn as capes and togas, plastered on T-shirts and totes. If not in flag the marchers remained on brand in head-to-toe red, black, and green; even the trees were wrapped all in. A Marcus Garvey impersonator helmed the lead, complete with plumed fore-and-aft cap.

Decades earlier
You saw those abstract Italian bars
and felt compelled to remix them into
the US stripes and stars
We already knew[64]

A limited edition turned mass-produced commodity
trickle down trickle down down now
how many knockoffs are on full display

and I hear of no lawyers' cease and desisting along 125th
so we all getting paid today

Because we deserved one too

The design is yours and the production is theirs but the profit is ours
You do it for the ~~money~~ culture

Because we deserved one too

'Cause we can't take it with us, right?
Money's like snowballs it's here it fades it melts away until another snowy
or rainy day when we break the piggie and make it rain in cowrie shells and
ancestral prayers

Get your money, Black man! Get your money! [65]

Dear Brother David,

As a child in church, we learned that a proper prayer was done through
ACTS. [66]
I observed you. Eyes closed. Jaw relaxed. Swaddled in a cameo cocoon.
Oh prophet, oh seer, oh justice! Is it as shield as camo as comfort?
Not in a state of helplessness or ambivalence but
a liminal wait for it holding the pause the beat
with silent lips. Give me your tired, your poor,
your huddled masses yearning to breathe free. [67]
Before we act move decide what's next because
there is always a next.

Can You Dig It?
                              Lead on
Lead on

Oh! *Oh!* Say. Say, can *you*? Say can you, say can you, *see? Can you see* can
you cc sea see? Yes, I can. It was a time where we said Black Lives Matter,
every day. When so proudly we waved down and up the rich green avenues
with broad red hearts and brave Black bodies all these bright BLACK stars
shining through the seemingly always ongoing perilous fight. Lifting every
voice to sing in to ring in harmonies of Black Power of Black Pride of Black
    Beauty of the regular Black folks who always tell it, see it like it is. [68]
    Third eye unblocked locked in pressed down made it holding steady
                              steady.
Ready to receive making my way through this ornate coalmine of my mind
                              to find
                          the shape of
                  wonderment and possibility still
                              to
                          come.

—Daonne Huff

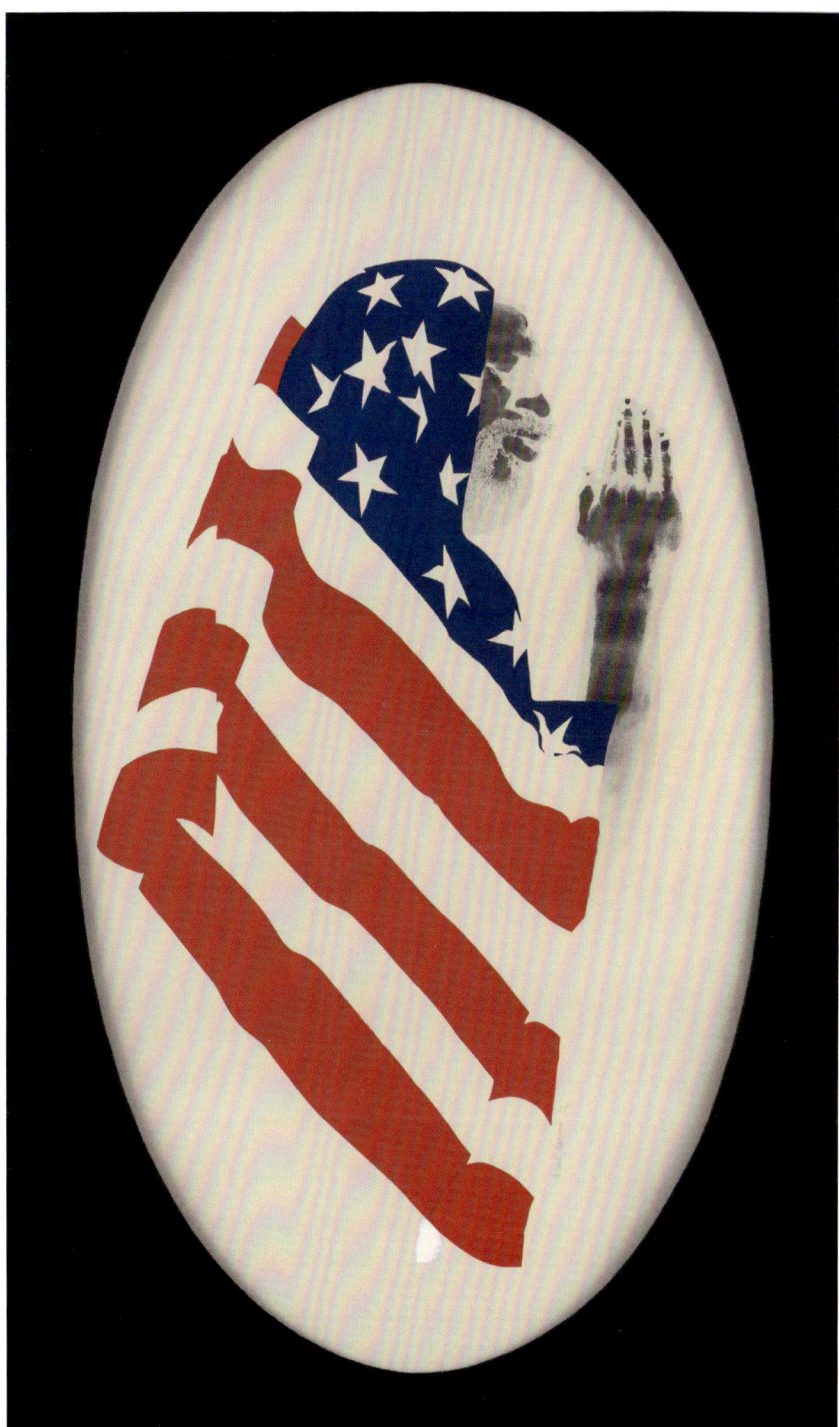

Pray for America, 1969. Screenprint and
pigment on paper, 60 ½ × 30 in. Studio
Museum in Harlem and the Museum of
Modern Art; gift to the Studio Museum in
Harlem and the Museum of Modern Art
by the Hudgins Family in honor of David
Rockefeller on his 100th birthday 2018.38

Margaret Taylor-Burroughs

1915—2010

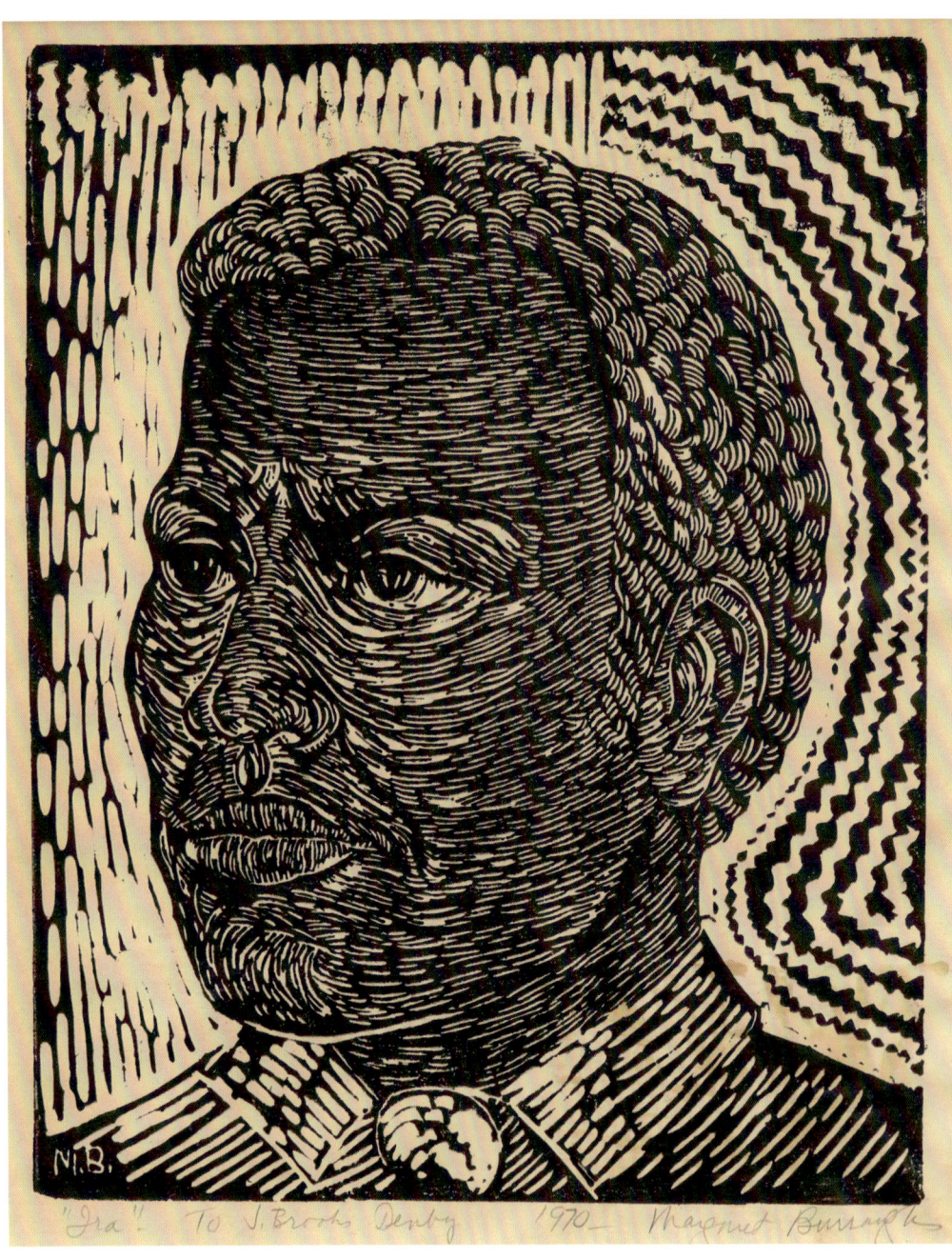

Ira, 1970. Woodblock on paper, image:
11 × 9 in. Gift of Vivian D. Hewitt 2012.31.3

While best known as a community organizer, educator, and museum founder and director, Margaret Taylor-Burroughs was also an accomplished artist. Receiving her master's degree from the School of the Art Institute of Chicago, Taylor-Burroughs went on to teach art at DuSable High School for twenty-seven years, where she was committed to exposing Chicago public school students to art and Black history.

Ira exemplifies Taylor-Burroughs's interest in historically significant Black figures and her dedication to imagery that promotes social uplift. Likely a portrait of either pioneering Black British American actor Ira Aldridge or a young Lieutenant Ira L. Cooper, a famous Black detective in St. Louis known for fighting crime and solving high-profile cases, the print was produced the year after the artist's retirement from public-school teaching and at the start of a decade-long tenure at Kennedy-King College. Bearing greater resemblance to Cooper, the work is one of dozens of extant portraits Taylor-Burroughs created of notable figures such as W. E. B. Du Bois, Mahalia Jackson, and Jean Baptiste Point du Sable, among many others. Her graphic style reflects her studies in 1952 at Mexico City's Taller de Gráfica Popular, a workshop where fellow Black American artist Elizabeth Catlett was also working and teaching at the time. Equally significant was Taylor-Burroughs's work as a National Endowment for the Humanities fellowship at Chicago's Field Museum of Natural History in 1968, which led to travels in Ghana the same year. From process to form, these contexts exposed Taylor-Burroughs to site-specific cultural inspirations and fresh visual dialects, observed in the reinvigorated sculpting of her figures, particularly through stylized lines and patterning.

In *Ira*, the artist carved energetic lines into wood, carrying ink across a classical composition—upright figure, formally dressed, evocative gaze—that connotes dignity and self-determination. Taylor-Burroughs's mission to share Black history, inspire racial pride through art, and promote mutuality left an indelible mark on the history of art and on the cultural landscape of the Chicago communities the artist dedicated her life to serving.

—Stephanie Sparling Williams, with research assistance from Grace Billingslea

Beauford Delaney

1901—1979

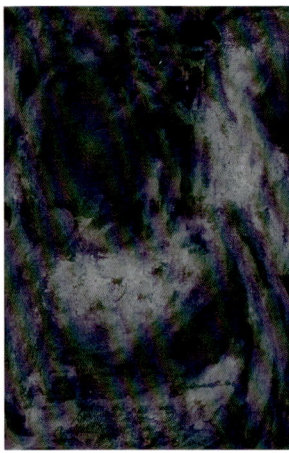

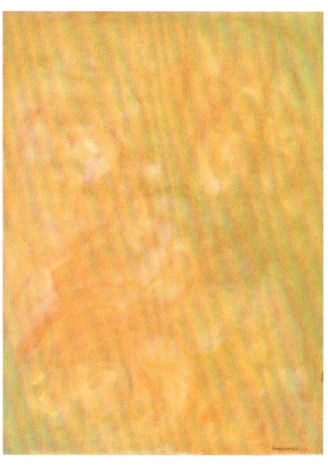

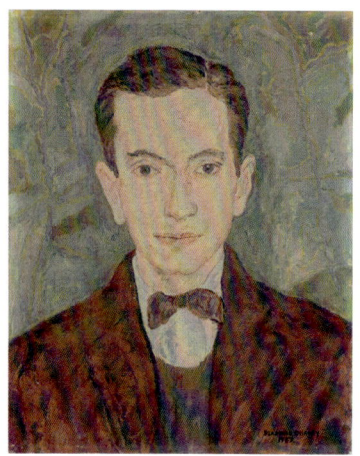

Something to Remember Me, 1960.
Gouache on paper, image: 8 × 5 ⅜ in.
Gift of Babette New 1986.17

Untitled, 1963. Gouche on paper,
30 × 22 ½ in. Gift of Mr. and Mrs.
David K. Anderson 1984.5.2

Untitled (Portrait of Ted Wilentz), 1952. Oil on
canvas board, 20 × 15 ¾ in. Gift of Ted and
Joan Wilentz 2012.29.1

Something to Remember Me announces itself in a whisper of thin black gouache. It is a small, mysterious painting—a shadow taking shape at the edge of a void. The painting is unusual for Beauford Delaney, an artist known for his exuberant, near-impressionistic abstract paintings and portraits rendered in thick strokes of saturated color, especially shades of luminous yellow. Much of the story of Delaney, who expatriated to Paris in 1953 in search of something else, centers his struggles with mental health, his queer identity, his blackness back at home. Yet this somber, intro-spective painting and its title's proposition posit another direction—looking instead to what he leaves behind: the legacy of his variable, dynamic body of work.

In 2013, I organized the exhibition *Brothers and Sisters* for the Studio Museum, which hosted Delaney's retrospective in 1978, a year before his death. Brothers and Sisters focused on a selection of Delaney's paintings in the Museum's collection, positioning them as anchors of post-painterly abstraction with creative genealogies across generations of Black artists. Delaney's intimate gouaches and oils produced between 1958 and 1969, among them *Untitled* and *Untitled Abstraction*, present two different tendencies: atmospheric, diluted hazes of color, and surfaces densely stippled with beads and streaks of oil paint. The viewer either gets pulled into their depths or ensnared in the thickened draw of their surfaces. This tension is part of the pleasure.

Yellow is the heart of many of Delaney's paintings, from creamy pastel to mustard to surprisingly acidic. The last is most often seen humming in the background of his portraits, as in the assertive backdrop behind the relaxed sitter of *Portrait of a Young Musician*. Delaney's mastery of the color has yet to be surpassed. His expressionistic portraits, often painted from memory, are exuberant even as the sitters have a stern look, evidenced in his early portrait of Ted Wilentz, owner of Eighth Street Bookshop in Greenwich Village, a haunt for the New York literati near Delaney's home at 181 Greene Street. The brushwork animates and enlivens the subject, imparting warmth and a sense of Delaney's care for and appreciation of his sitter. Other portraits memorialize the kinships he fostered throughout his life, notably his friendships with Marian Anderson, James Baldwin, and Jean Genet. These works are predictive of a later generation of portraitists, such as Jordan Casteel, Jennifer Packer, Andy Robert, Henry Taylor, and Lynette Yiadom-Boakye, who likewise use portraiture to document times and places, people, and moments—some things to remember.

Delaney's paintings are enigmatic yet open. They provide solace, and they located a community of artists and thinkers who felt they had no place and who, like Delaney, sought something more somewhere else. He navigated both abstraction and portraiture, each carrying a different social charge for Black and queer artists then and now. His quietly audacious experiments in color and light "breath[ed] slowly, evenly, gently, deliberately."[69] They live because he lived, and we could never forget.

— Jamillah James

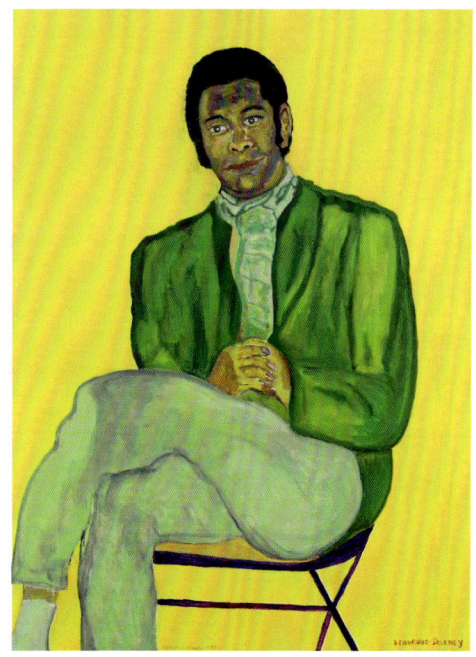

Portrait of a Young Musician, 1970. Oil on canvas, 51 × 38 in. Gift of the Estate of Beauford Delaney 2004.2.27

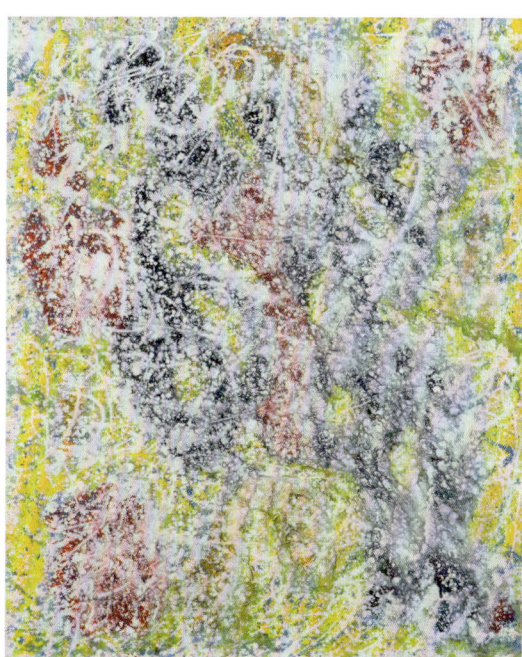

Untitled Abstraction, 1969. Oil on canvas, 25 × 21 in. Gift of Addie Herder, Philadelphia 2001.2.2

Dana C. Chandler Jr.

b. 1941

With its large star, stripes, and deeply lined face of its central figure, Dana C. Chandler Jr.'s *What Amerika Means to the Black Man circa 1775—1970* recalls another work about nationhood and profound waiting: Charles White's lithograph of a mother of a US soldier, *Mother (Awaiting His Return)* (1945). Whereas White's work dramatizes the perhaps futile wait for a soldier's return home after World War II, Chandler's print depicts a Black man in a prison cell embedded in a version of the US flag. To compound the feeling of confinement, Chandler flattens the cell, trapping the man between the picture plane and the room's opposite corner, visible just over his shoulder. In the top right of the cell, a barred window opens to an inky blackness that matches the man's Afro. Chandler's one-starred flag forms the prison wall closest to the viewer. Making the flag part of the very structure of the prison argues, along with the work's title, that the United States is to Black people here a prison, and that they have been waiting for liberation since the country's establishment.

In bold, capitalized text, *What Amerika Means* demands all political prisoners be freed "TODAY." The figure in the image, with his round Afro and the slight cleft in his chin, resembles the mugshot of George Jackson, a prominent revolutionary imprisoned in California's San Quentin and Soledad State prisons in the late 1960s. With this possible reference to Jackson, who argued for the use of guerilla warfare against police and the military, Chandler's exhortation to "FREE ALL POLITICAL PRISONERS" might well be as much a directive for revolutionaries as it is a demand made of the state.

—Terence Washington

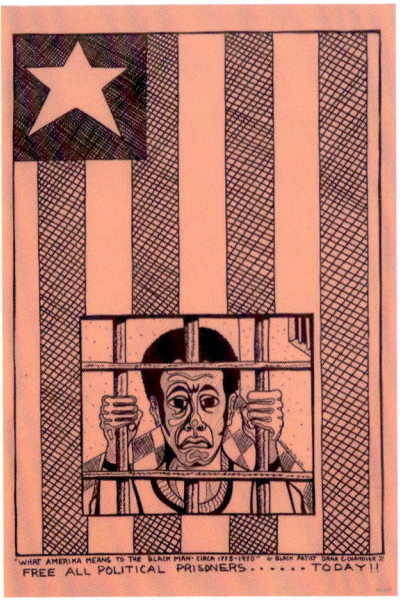

What Amerika Means to the Black Man circa 1775—1970, 1970. Offset print, 20 × 14 in. Gift of the artist 1970.1.4

Elizabeth Catlett

1915—2012

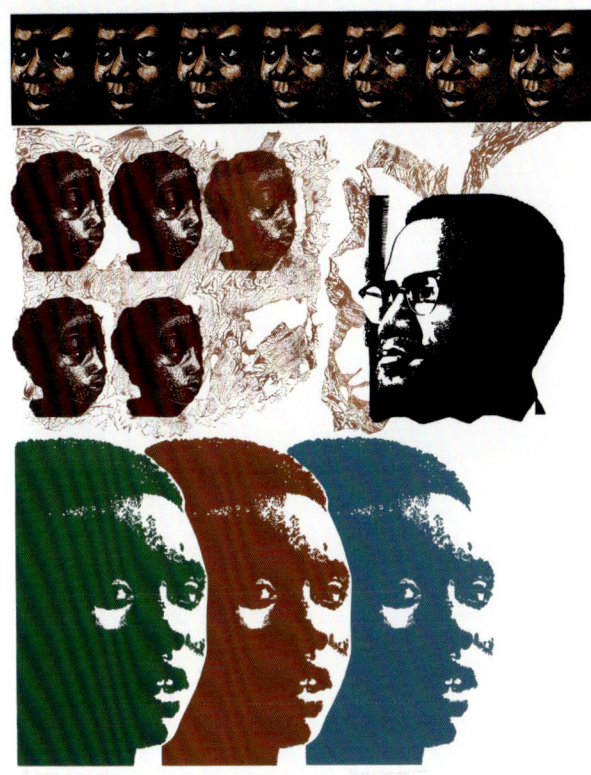

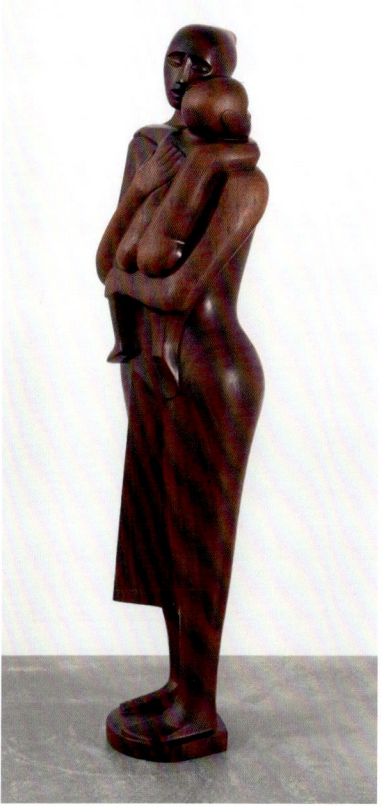

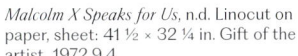

Malcolm X Speaks for Us, n.d. Linocut on paper, sheet: 41 ½ × 32 ¼ in. Gift of the artist 1972.9.4

Mother and Child, 1993. Mahogany, 67 ½ × 16 ½ × 8 ¾ in. Museum purchase 1996.13

Elizabeth Catlett's practice comes out of both solitary and solidarity work. Catlett describes this: "We work alone but we also work with and for others, and it is expressed by two words: one is 'solitary,' in which we create out of what is in us, from our innermost feelings, ideas, emotions, knowledge . . . we also create from 'solidarity,' which is what we have in our innermost selves that comes from what we have gotten from our solidarity with other people."[70]

The "I," the solitary and singular nature of Catlett's work, comes from a practice shaped by all her nested identities: she is a Black woman, a sculptor, a printmaker, a wife, a mother, a grandmother; she was born in the United States, and she later became a citizen of Mexico. She shares, saying, "I believe that all of these states of being have influenced my work and made it what you see today."[71] These states are the innermost spaces she pulls from across her prints and sculptures.

The "I" behind her work is critical. The majority of Catlett's subjects are Black women. This is exemplified by her early series "The Black Woman," in which Catlett depicts the full breadth of Black women's experiences—their labor, art, excellence, struggle, grief, and survival.[72] Similarly, images of mothers and children, such as the mahogany sculpture *Mother and Child* and the lithograph *Danys Y Liethis*, are spread throughout Catlett's practice. In these works, Black mothers hold their children close. These are awesome figures rendered in bold, caring, curving shapes, as Catlett reflects on the complexities of motherhood.

Catlett's work also engages a broader "we," and her sense of solidarity lies with the work of collective liberation. She finds that "art is important only to the extent that it helps in the liberation of our people . . . . Art for me now must develop from a necessity within my people. It must answer a question, or wake somebody up, or give a shove in the right direction—our liberation."[73] Her practice is in service to a "we" looking to get free. Linocut prints like *Homage to the Panthers* and *Malcolm X Speaks for Us* align themselves with the Black liberation work of the Black Power movement. She approaches this work with certainty: "There is no question as to who we are and where we are going—black people are on our way to liberation."[74] This "we" grows to encompass the people of Mexico and Latin America

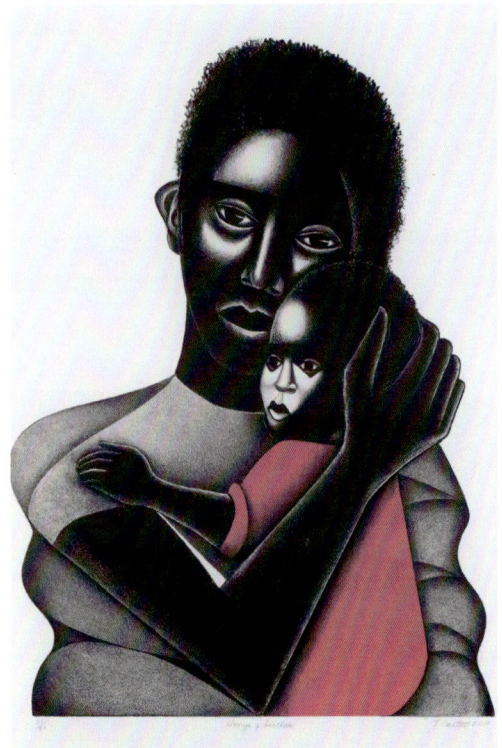

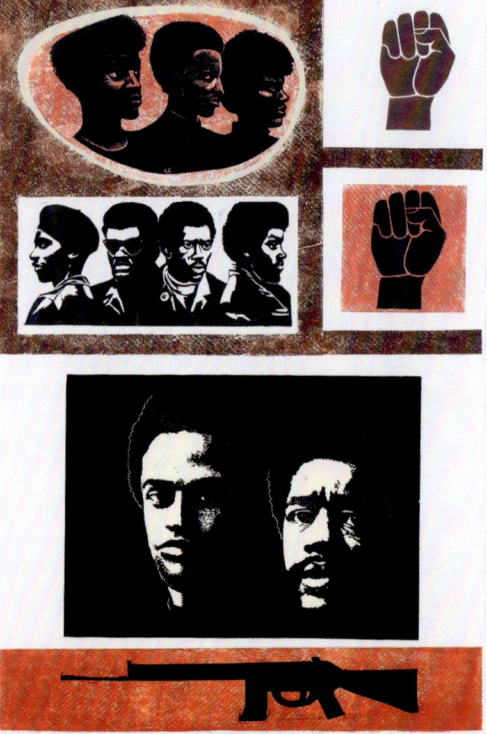

Danys Y Liethis (Mother and Child), 2005. Three color offset lithograph on Somerset Velvet Paper, sheet: 28 × 20 in. Promised gift of Nancy L. Lane PG.2023.010.6

Homage to the Panthers, 1970. Linocut on paper, sheet: 37 ¼ × 27 ½ in. Gift of the artist 1972.9.3

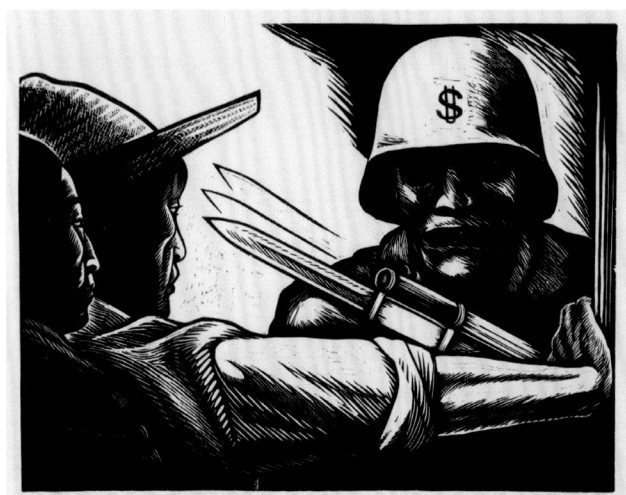

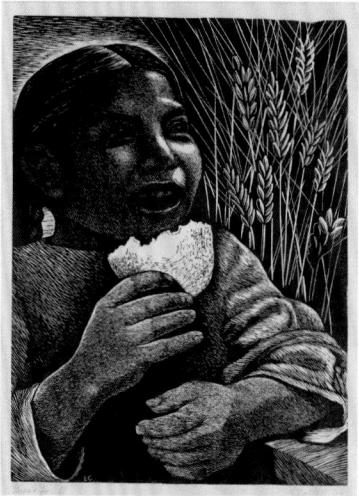

Latina America Dice "No!", 1963. Linocut on paper, 16 × 20 in. Gift of the artist 1976.42

Bread for All, 1954. Linocut on paper, image: 17 × 12 ¾ in. Gift of the artist 1972.9.8

more broadly, as seen in the linocuts *Latina America Dice "No!"* and *Bread for All*. In the former, a couple defiantly blocks entry to an armed US soldier, a symbol of US imperialism; the latter celebrates the agricultural reforms of the Mexican Revolution, depicted via a young girl holding a loaf of bread against a backdrop of wheat stalks.[75] This "we" grows further—her works serve an ever greater and ever-growing group of people aligned in similar struggles.[76] With urgency and conviction, with care and an unwavering eye toward liberation, Elizabeth Catlett created art reflective of herself as well as her people—a clear, singular "I" and an open, expansive "we."

— Jordan Jones

Richard Hunt

1935—2023

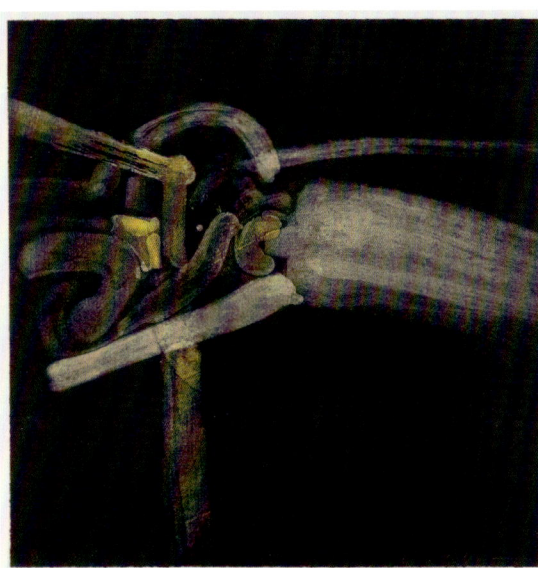

Untitled, 1965. Lithograph, 15 × 15 in.
Gift of Dr. Leon Banks 2004.1.1

In 1953 Richard Hunt visited *Sculpture of the Twentieth Century* at the Art Institute of Chicago, an experience that profoundly impacted the young artist's work. The exhibition's artists, including Julio González, Pablo Picasso, and David Smith, inspired Hunt to manipulate form through the use of direct metal and fabrication techniques. The artist purchased a soldering iron, set up a studio in his parents' basement, and began to make sculptures out of discarded metal, a cheap and accessible material. He discovered that welding allowed for an intuitive means of making, a process that would unleash the expressive potential of his industrial material.

Hunt quickly earned recognition for his linear abstract compositions through a series of exhibitions throughout the mid-1950s and early 1960s.[77] While traveling in Europe on a fellowship, he learned bronze casting in Florence and saw the work of Constantin Brancusi and Auguste Rodin along with the *Winged Victory of Samothrace* in Paris. Such experiences allowed Hunt to metabolize the sculptural history of line, volume, and space, leading him to fuse heterogeneous elements together to create hyphenated forms.

By the mid-1960s, Hunt began to create more volumetric sculptures. While at the University of Chicago zoological laboratory, the artist acquired a visual vocabulary inspired by plants, animals, and forces of nature. His "Hybrid" series—biomorphic sculptures cast in bronze, aluminum, welded chrome, and Cor-ten steel—graft human and nonhuman forms into industrial constructions. *Hybrid Form #3*, realized a year before Hunt became the first Black sculptor to receive a major solo exhibition at MoMA, demonstrates his mastery as well as his singularity. A thick, four-sided column tapers as it rises from the floor, transfiguring midway into two gnarled limbs. Winglike appendages sprout from one, while a bulbous claw extends from the other. Solid yet fluid, semi-figural yet abstract, *Hybrid Form #3* borrows elements from classical sculpture, Surrealism, and Abstract Expressionism while remaining entirely distinct. The same might be said for Hunt himself. The artist developed his expansive abstract language amid the height of the Black Power movement, a period in which political and aesthetic demands were placed on Black artists to create overtly figurative messages of Black empowerment.

Throughout his career, Hunt explored the possibilities of space in a variety of forms. In the late 1960s, the artist began to push his practice into the public environment, embracing industrial-scale fabrication to realize monumental outdoor commissions. Hunt's printmaking practice demonstrates the artist's engagement with sculpture as a "three-dimensional corollary of drawing."[78] A fellowship at the Tamarind Lithography Workshop in 1965 enabled Hunt to experiment with various techniques, exploring spatial complexity in a different form. *Untitled*, a color lithograph from this time, insinuates a three-dimensional construction within two-dimensional space. Gestural yellow forms project off black paper, incorporating negative space and extending beyond the frame. An untitled lithograph from 1980 features lightning bolt-like forms that cascade across the paper. Rendered in positive and negative shapes with alternating colors, the editioned work demonstrates the artist's continual reinvention of form. As Hunt wrote in an artist statement from 1967, "One hopes to see from what has been done, what can be done."[79]

— Eric Booker

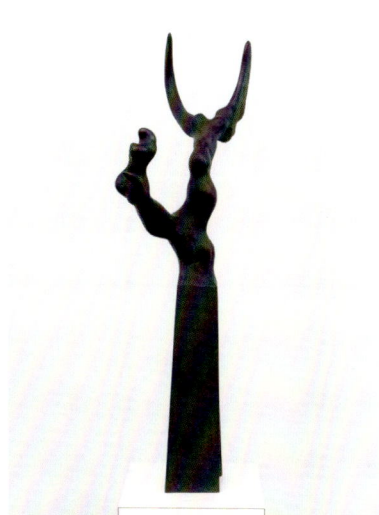

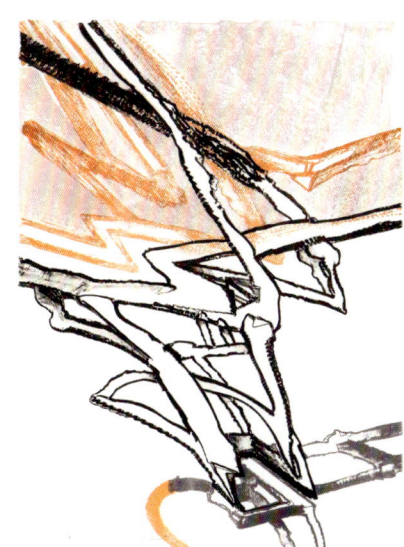

Hybrid Form #3, 1970. Cast bronze, 55 ½ × 23 × 16 ½ in. Gift of Mr. and Mrs. Samuel Shore 1983.11

Untitled, 1980. Lithograph, 30 × 22 ⅜ in. Edition 8 of 50 + 6 APs. Gift of Dr. Leon Banks 2004.1.2

Robert Rauschenberg

1925—2008

Robert Rauschenberg's *Signs* is a frenetic tableau of trauma and tragedy evoking the cataclysmic panic of the late 1960s. When commissioned by *Newsweek* magazine to design a cover heralding the arrival of the 1970s, Rauschenberg produced a photomontage "to remind us of the love, terror, violence of the last ten years."[80] Echoing the collective anxieties engendered by the Vietnam War, heightened racial tensions, and the death of cultural luminaries—such as President John F. Kennedy, Robert F. Kennedy, and Martin Luther King Jr.—Rauschenberg's juxtaposition of printed news materials underscores the omnipotence of mass media over the public imagination.

Eschewing compositional hierarchy, *Signs* reflects the visual excess of the postmodern age with images competing against one another in a futile game for attention. Its pasted fragments refuse representational overde-termination, becoming not so much a mirror of society but a lens on its operations. The work's conceit reveals itself at the visual ruptures between its constituent images. At these junctures—where Janis Joplin sings to the drum of mechanized infantry and the wonder of space exploration meets the specter of death—a stark dissonance renders a traditional icono-graphic reading ineffectual.

Signs highlights the heavily mediated construction and memorialization of collective histories. While void of any implied political statement, such a work may have read as too damning for an outlet such as *Newsweek*, who eventually rejected the image for publication. Rauschenberg's long-time gallerist, Leo Castelli, wanted to see the work live on and issued an editioned set of screenprints. Their subsequent circulation across art institutions and private collections further complicates the dialectical relationship between mass media and art.

—Sheldon Gooch

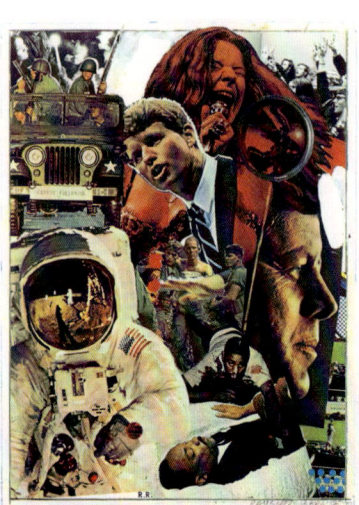

Signs, 1970. Silkscreen,
43 × 34 in. Edition 144 of 250.
Gift of Jean-Christophe Castelli
2003.29.6

Jeff Donaldson

1932—2004

Victory in the Valley of Eshu, 1971. Screenprint, 35 ¾ × 26 ¾ in. Edition 146 of 280. Gift of the artist 1976.53

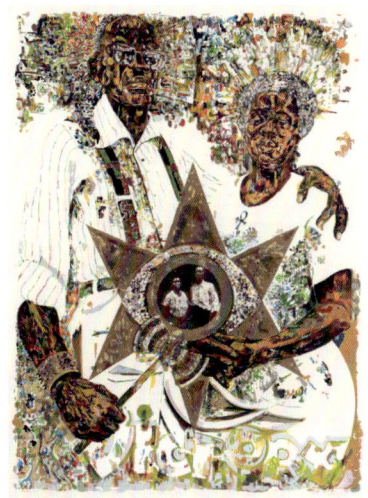

In the manifesto for the African Commune of Bad Relevant Artists (AfriCOBRA), Jeff Donaldson wrote, "It's NATION TIME and we are searching."[81] Cofounded by Donaldson alongside Wadsworth Jarrell, Jae Jarrell, Barbara Jones-Hogu, and Gerald Williams in 1968, the AfriCOBRA collective sought to propose a transnational Black aesthetic in service of Black people. The "NATION" for which Donaldson called was one of community and empowerment, deeply informed by history.

In *Victory in the Valley of Eshu*, a couple stands together, arms around each other, with the word "victory" printed at the bottom of the work. The woman holds a six-pointed star with an eye at its center. In its pupil is a black-and-white photograph of the couple in their youth. Their portrait references Afrocentric imagery and history, including an ankh, the ancient Egyptian symbol of life; a double axe used in Yoruba ceremonials; the red, black, and green of the Pan-African flag; and the star, a symbol of Eshu, the Yoruba deity of fate. The couple's victory—an example to be emulated—is the presence, affirmation, and representation of their ancestry in their daily lives.

With the addition of colorful halos, Donaldson elevates Black people to the level of gods. His work underscores the second syllable of AfriCOBRA's name, read phonetically as "FREE," a recognition of complex connotations of freedom across Black history and the creation of a Pan-African visual aesthetic that refuses and subverts the expectations and limitations imposed by the mainstream art world.

—Kate Claman

Dindga McCannon

b. 1947

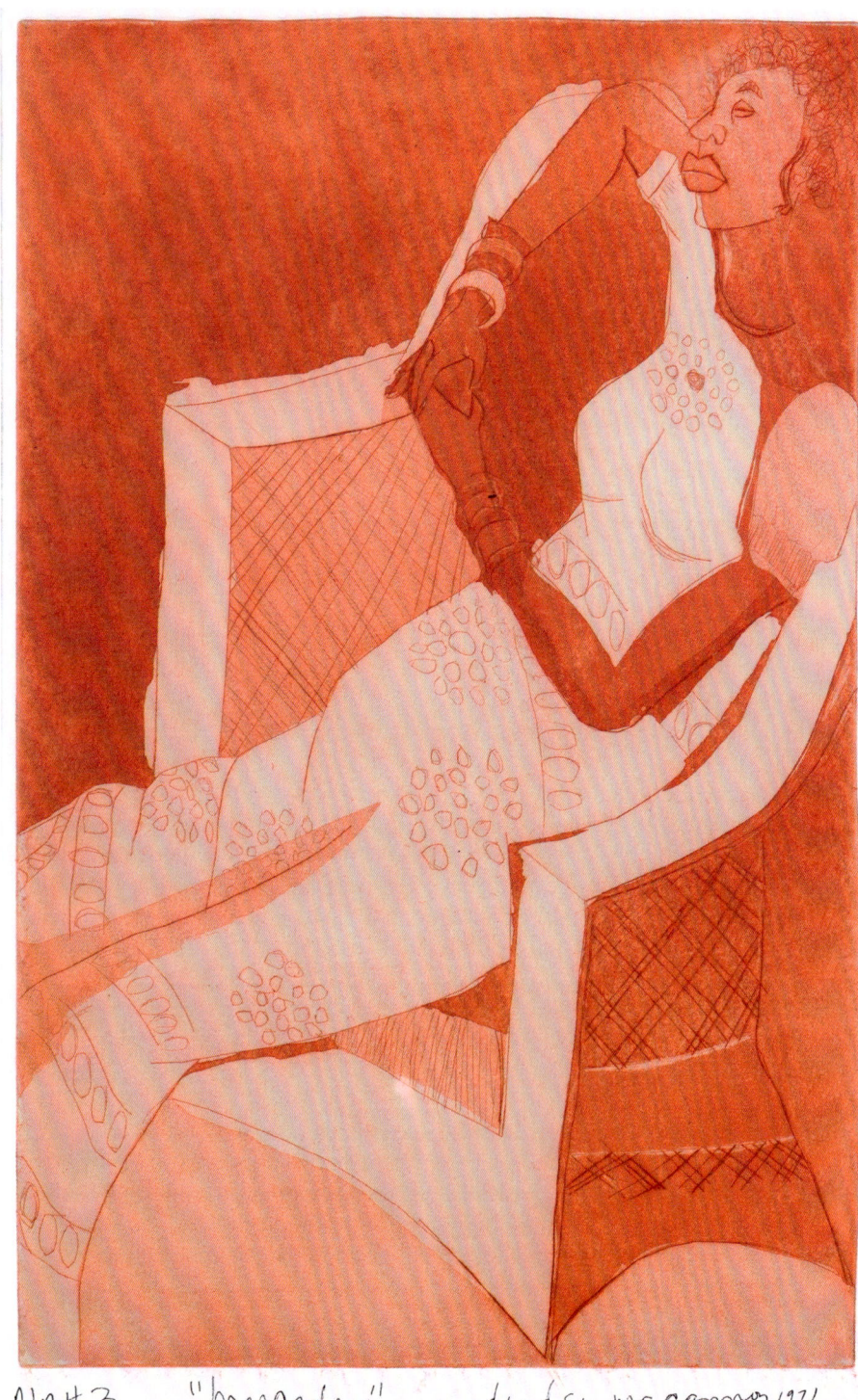

A/P #3　　"mercedes"　　dindga mccannon 1971

In Dindga McCannon's monochromatic print *Mercedes*, a woman is enveloped in a wash of red ink as she reclines on a rattan chair. She sits with her arms propped and fingers gently intertwined; the details of her resting profile, bangles, and the circular patterns of her dress are exposed on the white paper. Named after her friend and fellow Harlemite Mercedes, this etching was one of several proofs McCannon created while she worked at the Robert Blackburn Printmaking Workshop. This space offered collaborative and accessible training for local artists, enabling McCannon to experiment early in her multimedia practice. Yet at age twenty, as one of two women in the Weusi Artist Collective and a new mother, the opportunity to show her work in galleries alongside her male peers were few and far between.[82]

Early works, such as *Mercedes*, serve as a reminder of a deserved rest amid the multiple roles Black and women-identifying bodies command in the domestic and public spheres. Created during a period in which the artist observed the disconnect between the Black Arts and feminist movements, she incorporated her lived experience and her admiration of the Black women in her community into both her work as an artist and as an activist. Utilizing the skills she acquired in the workshop, McCannon prioritized experimentation and opted to forgo editions within the multiple prints she created. Instead, through numbering and alternating colors of ink, she indicated distinct differences between each proof. This not only allowed her to exercise spontaneity within the printmaking process, but further enabled McCannon to breathe new life into each version of the work. *Mercedes* emits a timeless regality, as the varying saturation of red ink adds texture and depth to the composition. Contrasting with the negative space of the white paper and the lighter tones of the foreground, the chair's frame further emphasizes and cradles the sitter. The position of the subject and application of a single hue work together to create a scene of softness and warmth. Whether it is one of contemplation or daydream, McCannon captures a moment in which the everyday woman is elevated and immortalized.

—Starasea Camara

Mercedes, 1971. Etching, image: 12 × 8 ¾ in.
AP 3. Gift of anonymous donor 1976.51

Benny Andrews

1930—2006

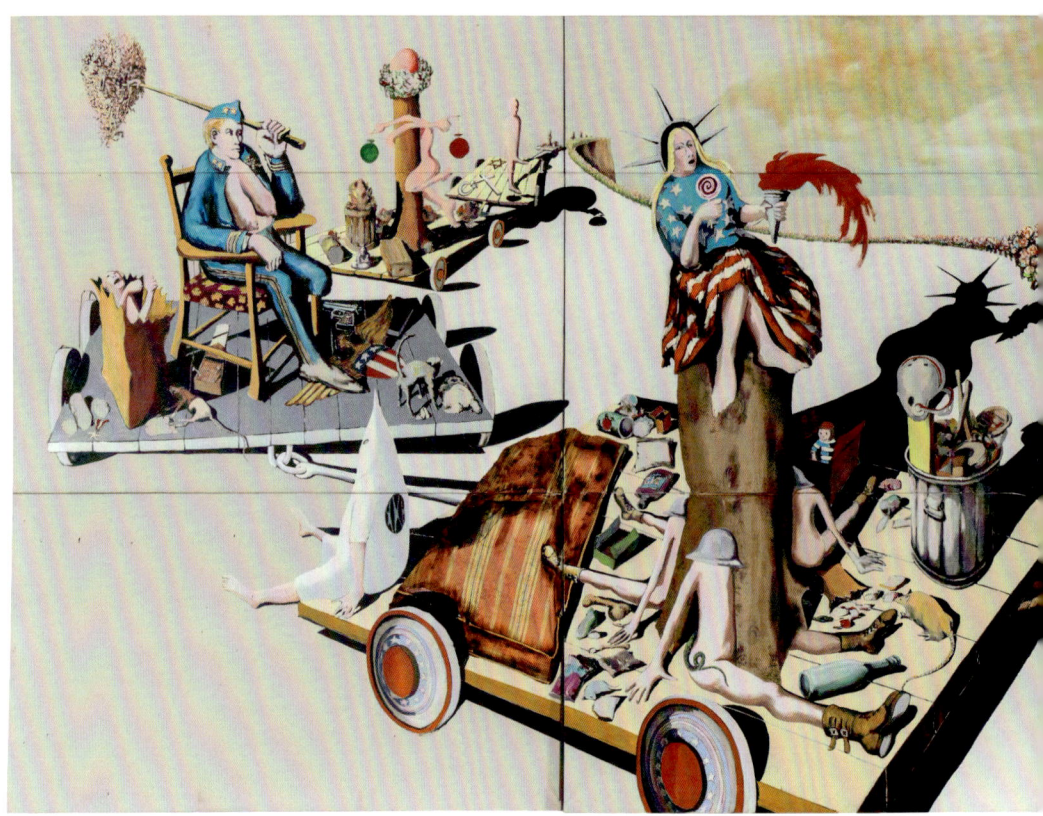

Trash, 1971. Oil and mixed-media collage on linen, overall: 120 × 336 in. Gift of Mr. and Mrs. Stanley Katz, New York 1981.14.1a–l

Trash does not depict any normal garbage pickup day. Like many of Benny Andrews's works, this twelve-panel, collaged painting tells an allegory of the contested lands that make up the United States of America. Working primarily in oil and mixed media, Andrews made stylistic figurative works that include the application of fabric and other materials. His investment in collage is a key element of his practice, providing depth and dimension to the formal quality of his work, as well as an emotional component through the dressing and enlivening of his subjects. In *Trash*, the nation's detritus, placed on wheeled wooden platforms, overspills with symbolism—Lady Liberty, football helmets, Klan hoods, large rodents, and glass bottles. No story of the United States, however, would be complete without the labor of Black people, and here Black figures strenuously drag the trash by rope and chain to a larger pile. For Andrews, the work of cleaning up the land was not just an extended metaphor but a lifelong practice.

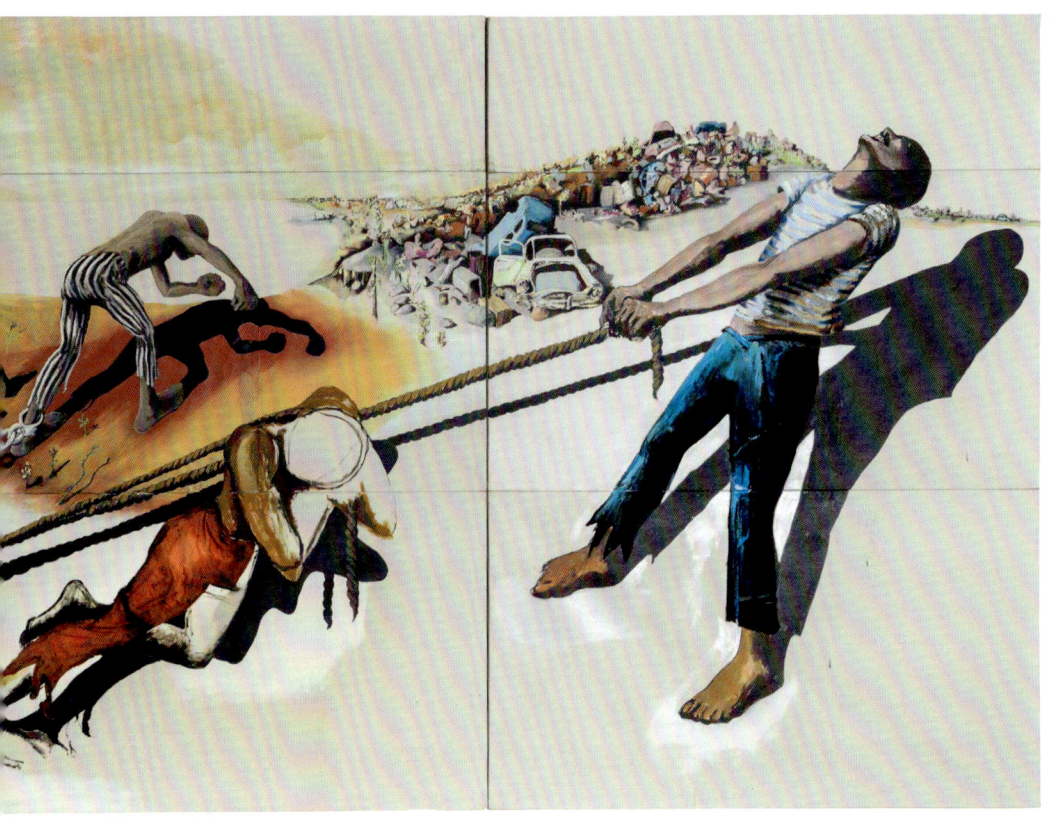

He created several series of works that captured a particular personal or political theme. From 1970 to 1975, the artist was at work on his "Bicentennial Series," which resulted in five monumental-sized works and hundreds of preparatory drawings and paintings. By rendering the injustices of race, gender, labor, and war through surreal compositions, such as in *Trash*, the series visually combats the revisionist histories Andrews expected would proliferate during the celebration of the country's two hundredth anniversary. In the sketch *Liberty on Top of the World # 2 (Study for Trash)*, the artist drew an early version of the statue that appears in the finished painting, presented here on top of a globe meant to represent the worldwide reach of the country's impact. Andrews drew extensively to capture his thoughts and numerous iterations of an idea before they took their final form, even creating a preparatory painting for *Trash* through *Composition (Study for Trash)*. Together, these drawings and paintings display the intentionality and striving present in Andrews's practice and life.

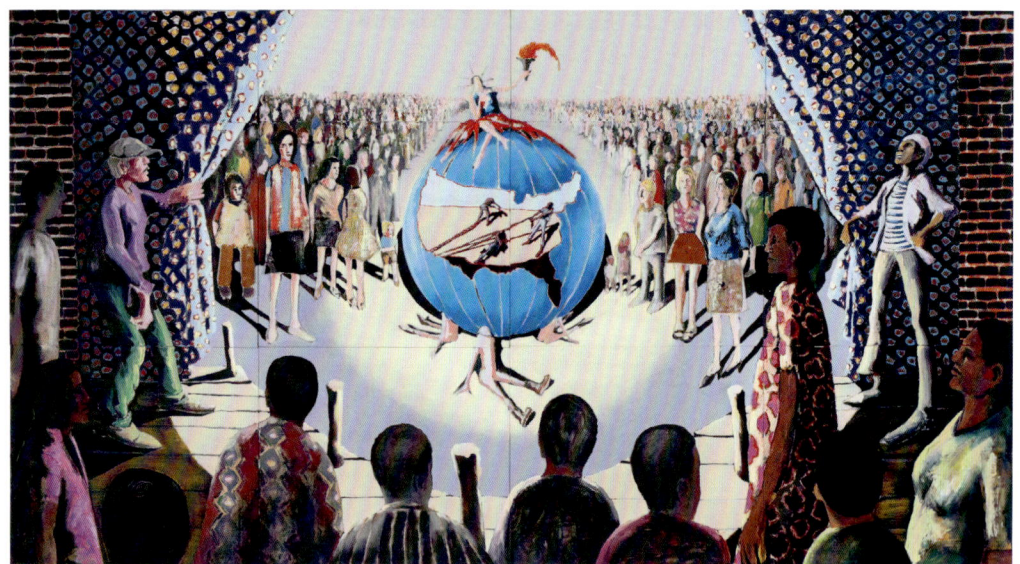

Composition (Study for Trash), 1971.
Oil and collage on twelve joined
canvases, 50 × 92 in. Gift of Mr. and Mrs.
Stanley Katz, New York 1981.14.2

The commitment to highlight the grievances of Black people in the United
States and uphold the legacy of their contributions to the country also
appeared through Andrews's advocacy. Andrews was a founder of the
Black Emergency Cultural Coalition (BECC). The BECC was created
by a group of artists in 1969 to protest the controversial *Harlem on My
Mind: Cultural Capital of Black America, 1900—1968* exhibition at the
Metropolitan Museum of Art, which was staged without including the
curatorial and artistic involvement of African Americans. The BECC
organized protests, published newsletters, and conducted programs
to advocate for greater representation and employment opportunities
from major arts institutions in New York City. Through the BECC, Andrews
led art education programs in prisons and detention centers. In 1976,
he organized an exhibition of artwork by incarcerated and formerly
incarcerated artists at the Studio Museum, providing institutional legit-
imacy to incarcerated artists decades before it became a field-wide
issue. The artist's work as an organizer and arts advocate supported
the efforts of institutions like the Studio Museum and the continued
preservation and study of Black cultural production.

—Kiki Teshome

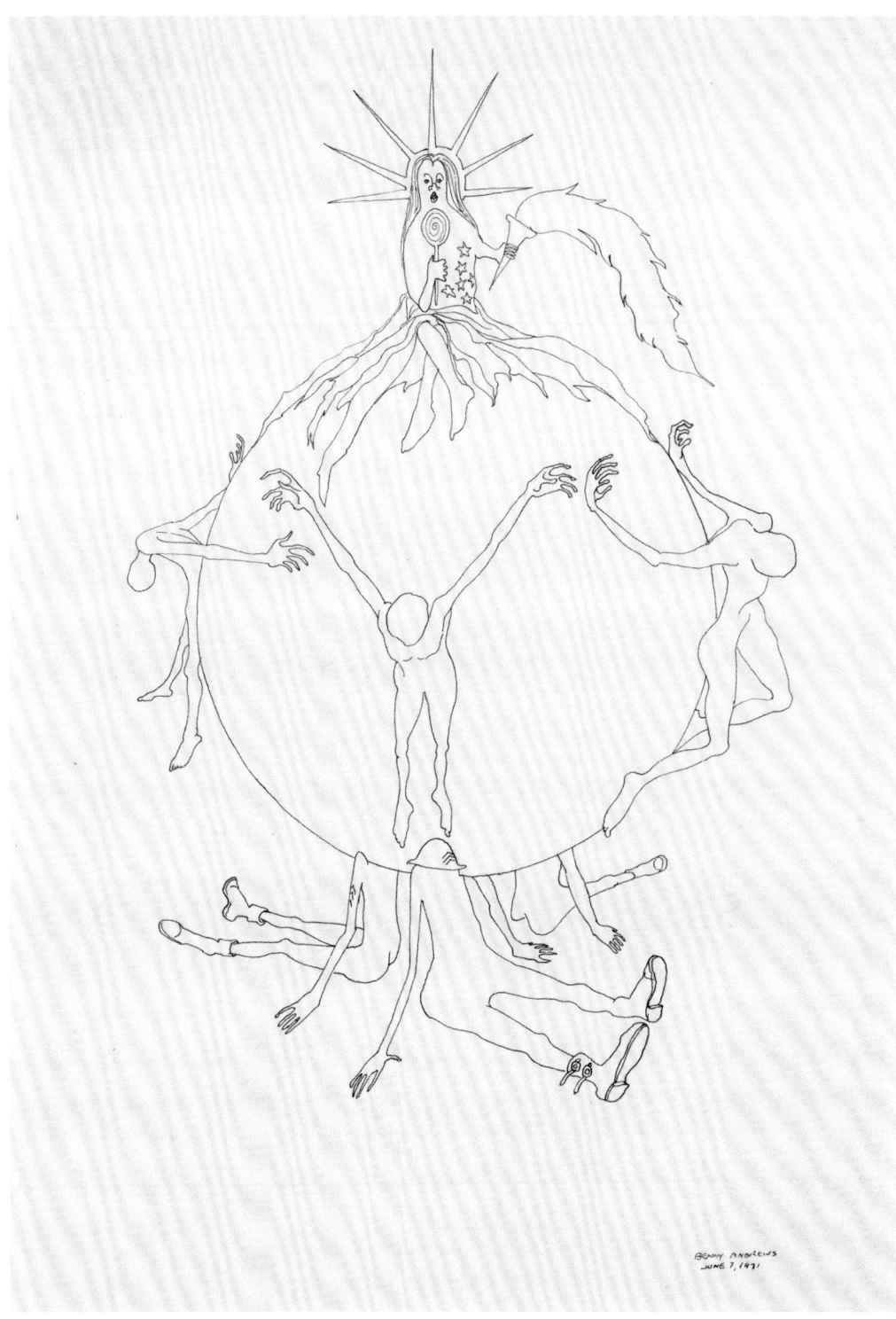

Liberty on Top of the World # 2 (Study for
Trash), 1971. Pen and ink on paper,
image: 16 ½ × 10 ¾ in. Gift of Mr. and Mrs.
Stanley Katz, New York 1981.14.5

Stephanie Weaver

b. 1946   Artist in Residence 1971—72

In the early 1970s, Stephanie Weaver depicted scenes from Black life from memory and her surroundings in Harlem, where she was an artist in residence at the Studio Museum from 1971 to 1972. Weaver painted on board that she then varnished or left exposed to achieve different skin tones for her subjects. *Hallelujah* depicts Black people at church amid all that comes with it: the colorful patterns, the hats, the movement of the crowd against itself, the Os of mouths (and a tambourine!) in mid-song. Weaver painted all the way to the edge of the board as if the congregation might process out of the spare wooden frame into the room around it. In addition to modeling the colors of skin tones, the grain of the wood in *Hallelujah* sometimes looks like a pattern on clothing such as in the red-and-green choir robes interspersed throughout or the pink dress in the top left. The wood unifies the congregation: even with the diversity of dress, complexions, and facial expressions among the church members, the exposed grain of the wood throughout belies the individuality of the congregants by revealing them to be fundamentally one body. In this way, even down to its materials *Hallelujah* provides an image of fellowship both Christian and Black. Weaver conveyed this idea with *Hallelujah*'s composition—she connects the subjects' bodies like a single sheet—in the bottom quarter of the painting, around a chair where a gray-haired church elder leans for support. There, Weaver signed her name: "Stephanie."

—Terence Washington

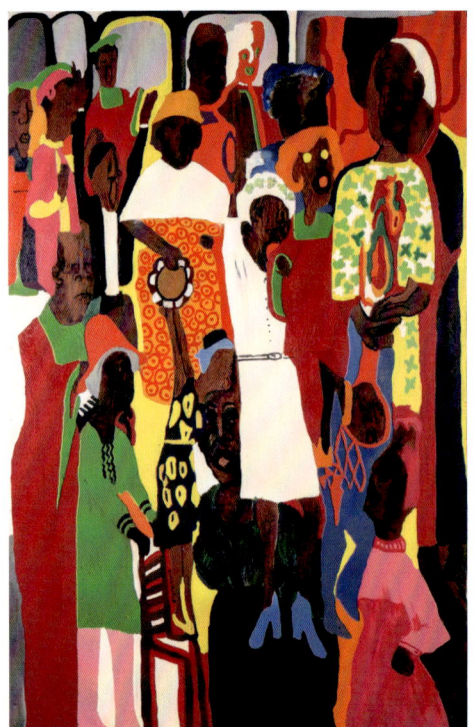

Hallelujah, 1971. Oil on board, 72 ¾ × 48 in.
Gift of the artist 1972.7

Alexander "Skunder" Boghossian

1937—2003

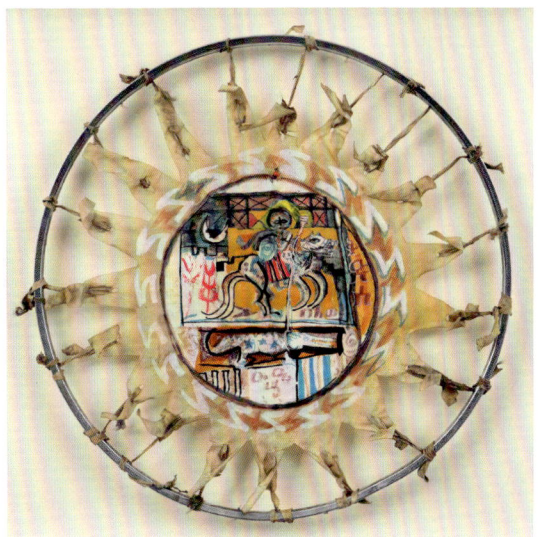

Alexander "Skunder" Boghossian was a giant of African and African diaspora art. Over the course of his nearly fifty-year career, Boghossian lived in London, Paris, Addis Ababa, Atlanta, and Washington, DC, where he circulated among some of the most influential thinkers, artists, and musicians associated with Negritude, Pan-Africanism, Surrealism, and various Black artistic movements in the United States. From 1966 to 1969, Boghossian spent time in Ethiopia, where he taught at the Fine Arts School in Addis Ababa. In this period, he began to incorporate direct references to the illuminated manuscripts and icons of the Ethiopian Orthodox Church and to the archaeological and religious sites that he visited during extensive travels around the country. Boghossian developed a singular artistic language that combines elements of Ethiopia's rich traditions and religious art with Western art, West African traditional art forms, and magical realism of mid-century African literature.

Cowboy U.S.A. is an oil and tempera on animal skin work that demonstrates the blending of Ethiopian and American contexts, two worlds that Boghossian straddled beginning from the 1970s until his death in 2003. The lone figure on horseback, sparse landscape, and architectural outline with stained glass windows in the background draw from the Coptic convention of flat icons and square formatting. The crocodile on a leash in the foreground is a metaphor for the uncanny or malevolence in the Ethiopian animist tradition. Using a satirical title, Boghossian repurposes the visual imagery of his Ethiopian heritage to portray his perception of the US military adventurism in Vietnam. "I see myself as a 'witnesser' of my kind," the artist explained. "I am conscious of the happenings at all times, and this inevitably appears in my work, via my dreams, or my experiences."[83]

—Smooth Nzewi

Antony Charles Robert Armstrong-Jones

1930—2017

Taken by renowned British photographer and royal Antony Charles Robert Armstrong-Jones, also known as Lord Snowdon, these nine black-and-white bromide prints feature the 1972 company of a young Dance Theatre of Harlem (DTH). Created in the wake of Martin Luther King Jr.'s assassination in 1968, the company was founded in 1969 by Arthur Mitchell, who was the first Black principal dancer at the New York City Ballet, and Karl Shook, virtuosic dancer, choreographer, and writer. Snowdon befriended Mitchell in the 1960s and was commissioned to photograph rehearsals and performances as early as 1971. Interested in highlighting people and places considered marginal and deeply invested in perfecting the pose, the photographer was particularly enamored with capturing dancers and performers. Snowdon began taking pictures in his youth at Eton College and began his professional career in the society pages of some of Britain's well-known tabloids, such as *Tatler*, *Picture Post*, and *The Sketch*. By twenty-eight, he had been working for *Vogue* for two years and became known for his documentary-style images of high society.

Several of the photographs in the portfolio feature the theater's principal dancers, including a portrait of Lydia Abarca and Walter Raines, cast as the leads in Ruth Page's imagining of *Carmen*, entitled *Carmen and José*, which a contemporary review called "a ratatouille of spicy ideas."[84] In it, the duo gazes at each other as Raines, on bended knee, supports Abarca's graceful perch, with her outstretched back leg asserting her power and grace. Other dancers featured include Paul Russell and Gayle McKinney.

Mitchell is prominently featured in two of the photographs. In one, his arms encircle Abarca and his hands cradle her illuminated face in a rehearsal for some future performance. In the other, a youthful Mitchell reposes alone on the studio floor—eyes closed, lying on his stomach with arms crossed and his head resting on his hands with a smile dancing at the corners of his mouth. Taken together, the portfolio of images richly captures classes, rehearsals, performances, and promotions, and describes a burgeoning moment in the theater's history.

—Key Jo Lee

Untitled (from the portfolio "Dance Theater of Harlem"), 1972. Black and white bromide prints, each: 12 × 16 in. Photograph by Snowdon, copyright Armstrong-Jones, gifted by Snowdon to the Studio Museum in Harlem 2016.3.3, 2016.3.6

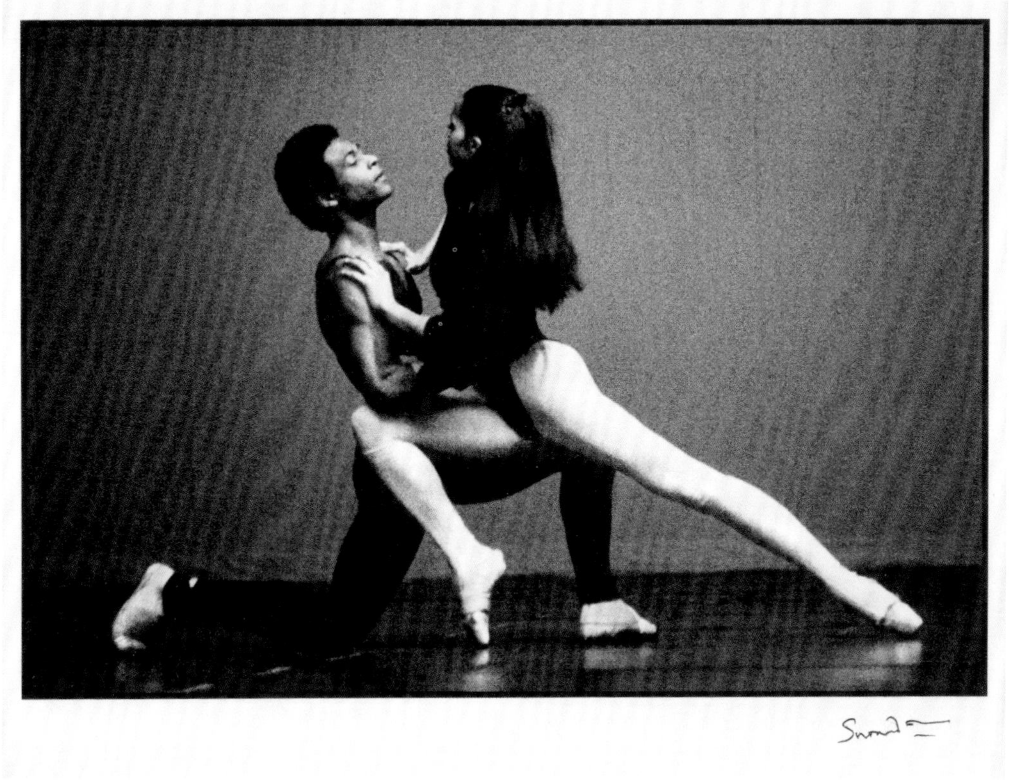

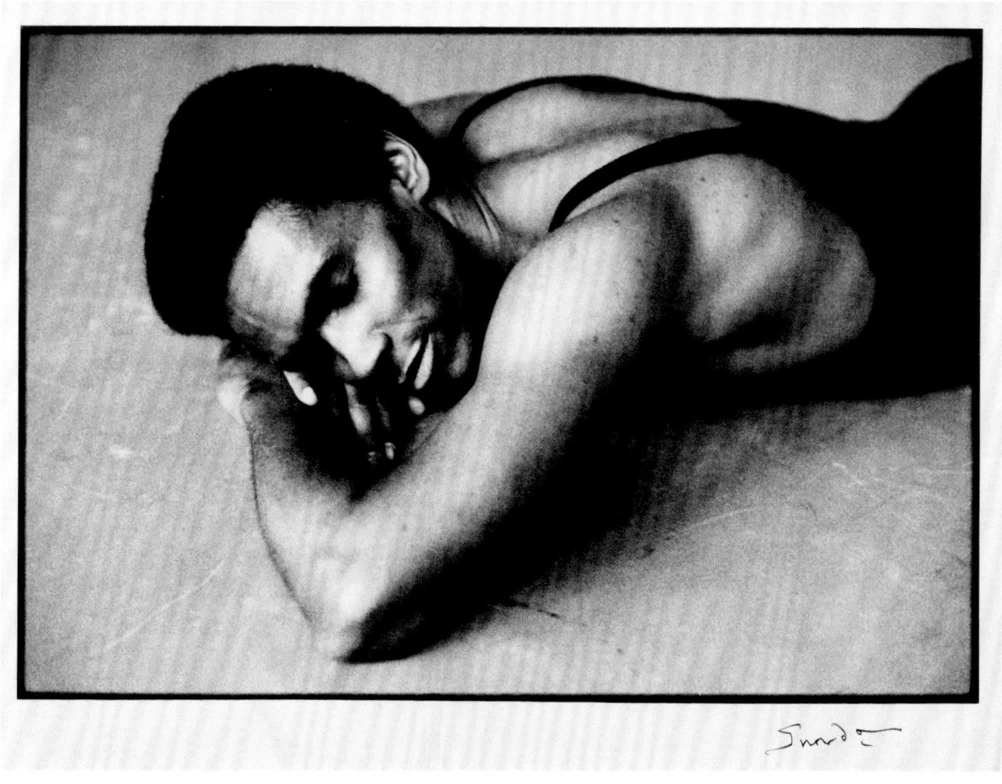

Maren Hassinger

b. 1947   Artist in Residence 1984—85

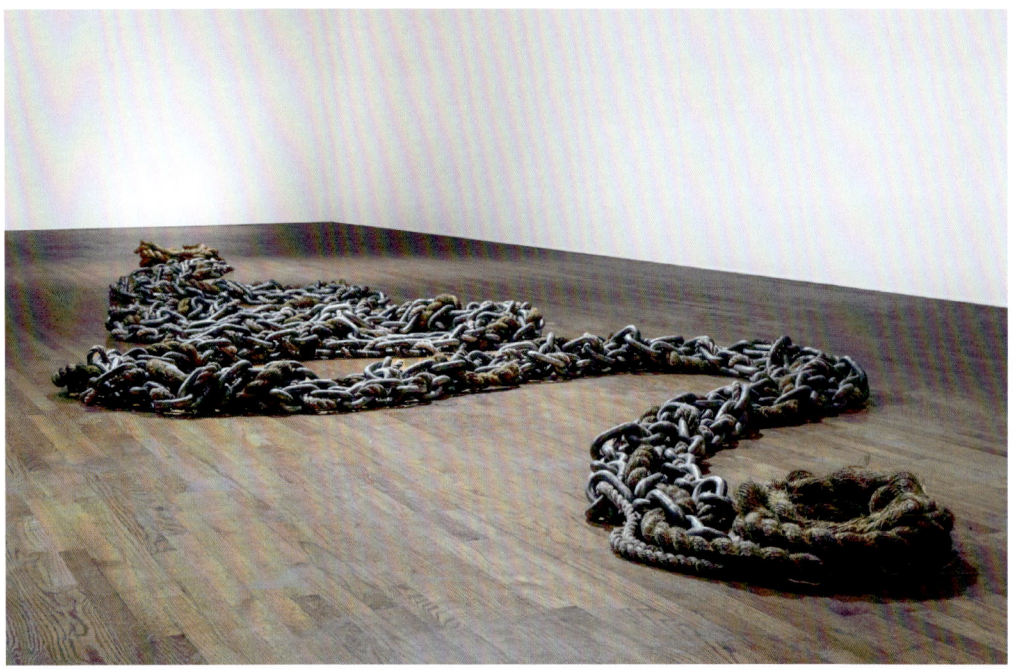

River, 1972/2011. Mixed-media installation with steel chains and rope, dimensions variable. Gift of the artist 2012.34

Maren Hassinger is known for a practice that brings together industrial materials, movement, and the natural environment. While pursuing her MFA at the University of California, Los Angeles, in the fiber arts program in sculpture, she was part of the interdisciplinary art scene alongside artists such as Houston Conwill, David Hammons, Ulysses Jenkins, Senga Nengudi, and Frank Parker. Each artist explored the newfound capacities of performance and sculpture in a loose collective called Studio Z, a community of Black artists now recognized as being at the vanguard of conceptual practices that emerged in the 1970s.[85] Hassinger developed her work in sculpture and performance as she began to experiment with metal and galvanized rope to convey natural elements such as wind, trees, or rivers.

River, one of her earliest works, includes tightly tangled steel chain-links and rope wound together to create a single line. The materials, traditionally used as hauling lines on maritime ships made for "tremendous physical expenditure of energy to make this kind of work," suggest the way movement is enmeshed into Hassinger's process and the intensive labor required by Hassinger's practice.[86] The title and materials point to the natural world as an inspiration for how people relate to one another, and how history is entangled with an individual's experiences. The alluded-to river can be interpreted as the Middle Passage—the route across the Atlantic Ocean to the Americas as part of the horrific journey of enslavement for Black people. It can be the infrastructure and interpersonal lines that cross and carve the place the work was made—including the Los Angeles River, a natural waterway that was channeled and federally controlled by 1960—or the connections between Hassinger and the Studio Z artists. Their relationships meandered from the 1970s onward throughout the course of each artist's career. *River* can be such connections that weather the course of life, as durable as the concrete of the engineered waterway or the chain-links that Hassinger uses to bind the work.

—Lilia Rocio Taboada

Wadsworth Jarrell

b. 1929

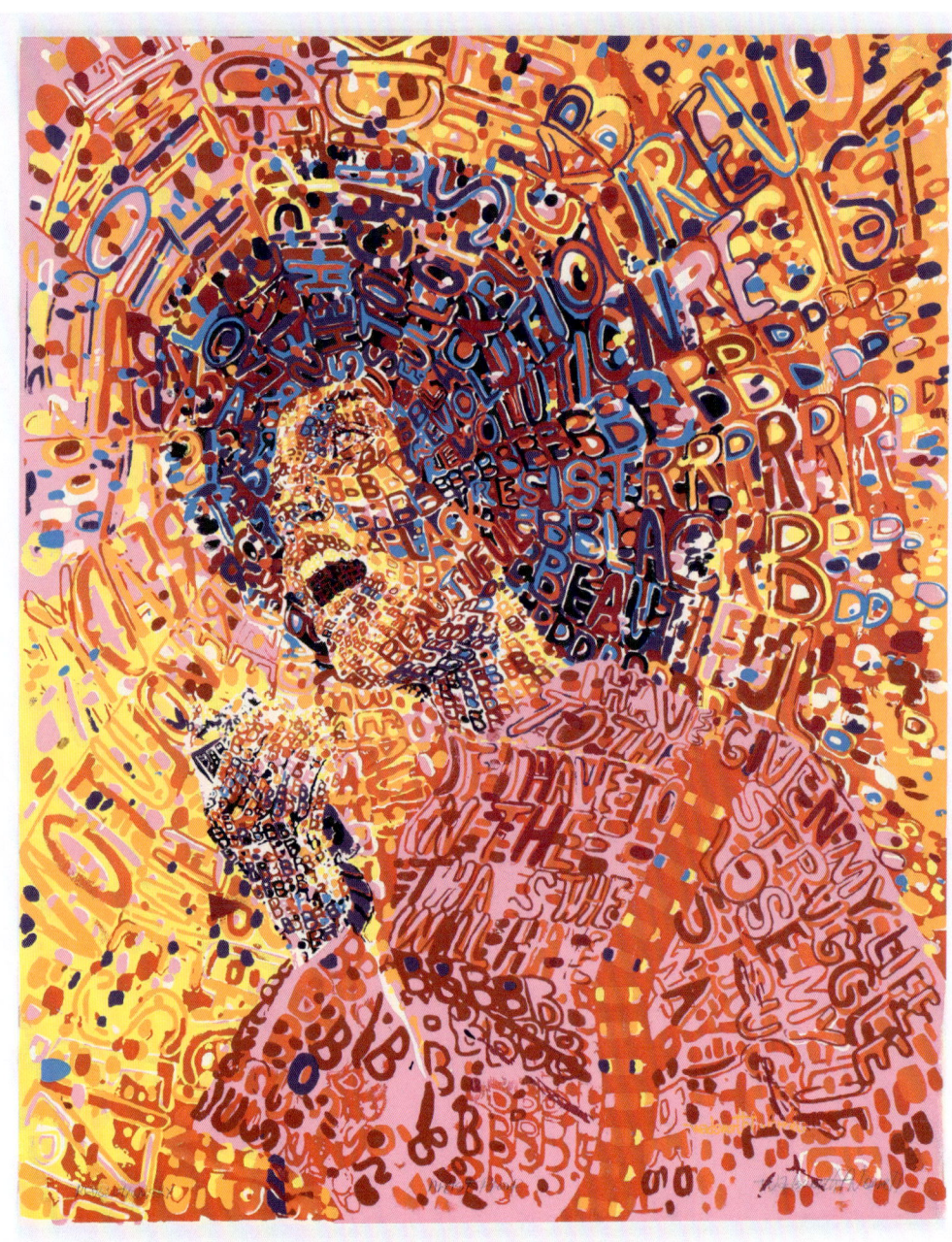

Revolutionary, 1972. Screenprint on off-white
heavy wove paper, 32 ¾ × 26 ½ in. AP.
Museum purchase with funds provided by
the Acquisition Committee 2018.16

Wadsworth Jarrell is a founding member of the Chicago-based group AfriCOBRA (African Commune of Bad Relevant Artists), which included Jeff Donaldson, Jae Jarrell, Barbara Jones-Hogu, and Gerald Williams. Wadsworth Jarrell's print *Revolutionary* exemplifies the highly chromatic and boldly graphic style for which the collective is known. *Revolutionary* replicates a portrait of activist and author Angela Davis that Jarrell painted the year before. While painting is a significant part of Jarrell's practice, AfriCOBRA collectively pursued printmaking as a democratizing medium, as the relatively low cost of production and dissemination increased access and affordability.

With vigor and energy that rivaled the action painters of the era, but without the desire to eliminate figural or political content, AfriCOBRA sought to create a collective aesthetic, or visual language, to describe—and celebrate—the revolutionary ideas and figures connected with the Black Arts Movement. Consider the outward arc of letters and words that create *Revolutionary*. The text emanates from every cell of the work, combines with the figure's surroundings, and returns in a perpetual and reciprocal exchange. Even the interior of Davis's mouth, which might otherwise appear dark and empty, shows itself as a space of creation. Upon close inspection, we see that Jarrell has inscribed that space too with individual letters that build and blend on their way to the implied masses.

Davis's clothing and adornment also conspire to heighten the potency of the message. Her jacket is a direct reference to Jae Jarrell's *Revolutionary Suit* (1970), including the elegantly draped ammunition belt holding brightly colored bullets. Jarrell has said that the suit is "strickly [sic] for Black people in the present revolution, with a show of force for liberation."[87] When the clothing melds with her posture—eyes and body leaning forward delivering open-mouthed, microphone-amplified proclamations—we receive a call toward a more radical future.

—Key Jo Lee

Barbara Chase-Riboud

b. 1939

Le Manteau (The Cape) or Cleopatra's Cape is the earliest sculpture in Barbara Chase-Riboud's multimedia series devoted to Cleopatra VII of Egypt.[88] The monumental work comprises 3,500 multicolored bronze and copper patinated squares woven together with wire and draped over a steel armature frame. Long strands of twisted hemp rope cascade down the cape's aperture. The sculpture appears to rest softly on the ground, evocative of the divine-like description of the Egyptian queen, whose reputation precedes her as a powerful, authoritative, intelligent, and strikingly beautiful ruler. Chase-Riboud explains: "The genesis of my interest in Cleopatra is based on my fascination with power as wielded by women throughout the ages … she is an icon for modern women."[89]

In 1968 upon receiving Marc Riboud's letter describing the excavated Han dynasty tombs of Liu Sheng and his wife Dou Wan, Chase-Riboud began reimagining the details of ancient Chinese funerary objects. Complete with square-patterned jade plaques bound with gold wire, the burial suits armed the monarchs' physical bodies and spirits, so as to carefully transport them to the afterlife. Chase-Riboud's adaptation, by way of a bronze cape, reimagines Cleopatra's immortality. To achieve the cape's glistening appearance, Chase-Riboud embraced an alchemical process in the foundry that produced unpredictable color changes in the bronze.

An artist, bestselling novelist, and award-winning poet, Chase-Riboud is renowned for a multimedia practice that engages memory and history across different cultures and epochs. After graduating from the Tyler School of Art at Temple University, Chase-Riboud embarked on international travel through Europe and Egypt, where she discovered ancient bronze casting techniques and a wealth of creative inspirations. *Le Manteau (The Cape) or Cleopatra's Cape* evidences the artist's steadfast inquiry into historical remembrance, impressive facility of the bronze medium, and fusion of visual cultures.

—Habiba Hopson

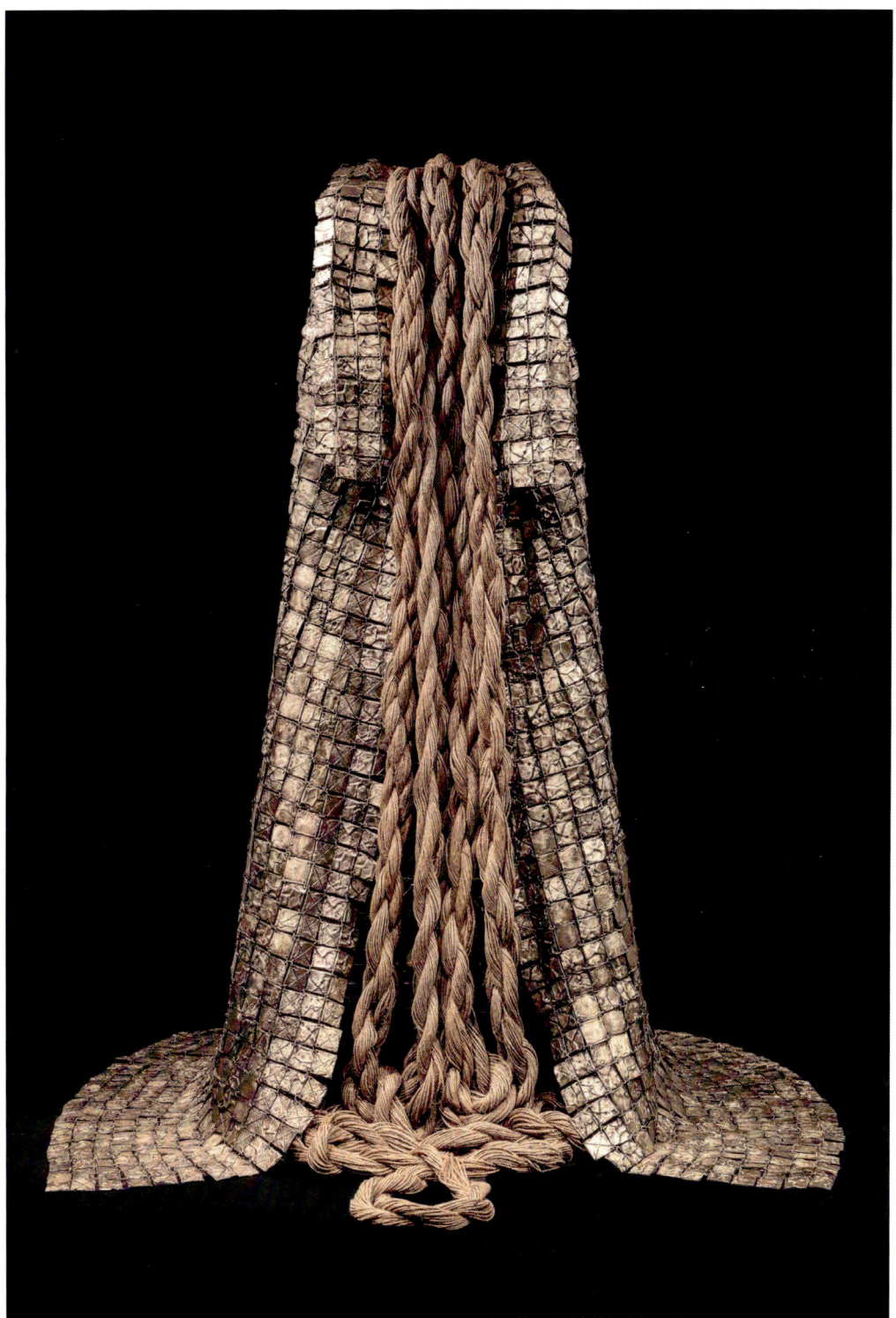

Le Manteau (The Cape) or Cleopatra's Cape,
1973. Bronze, hemp rope, and copper,
99 ½ × 84 × 72 in. AP. Gift of the Lannan
Foundation 1998.7.4

Sam Gilliam

1933—2022

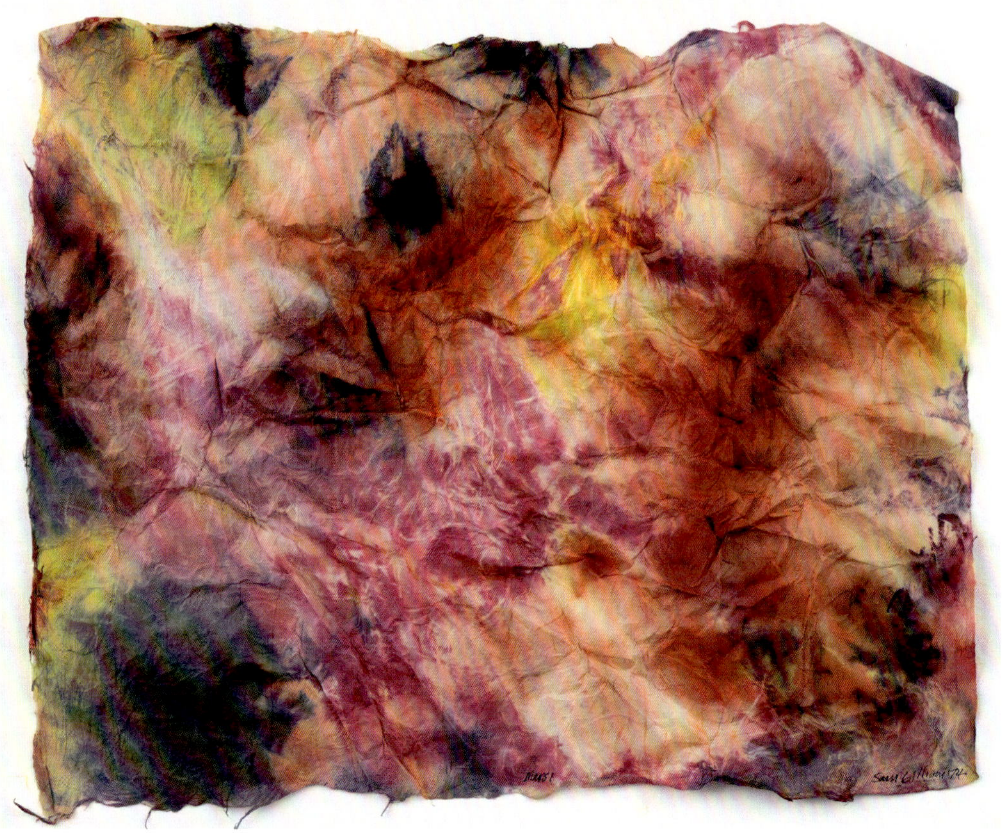

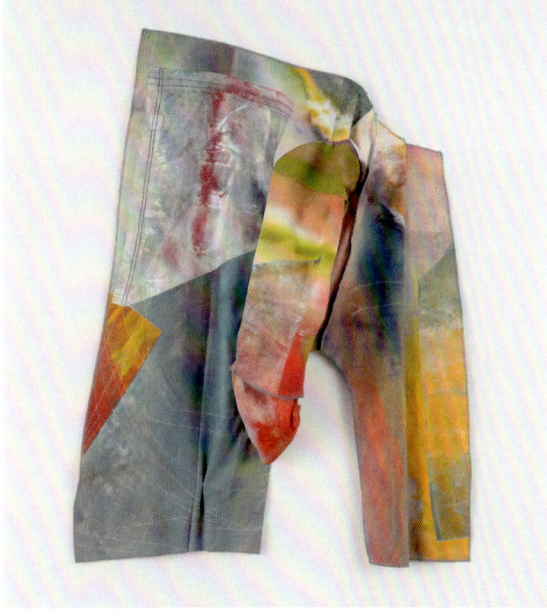

Above: *Mars I*, 1974. Acrylic on rice paper, 21 × 25 ½ × ⅝ in. Gift of Charles Cowles, New York 1981.2.1

Left: *D'Artagnan (Musketeer Series)*, 1997. Acrylic on constructed stretched cotton canvas, 56 ½ × 44 × 7 in. Promised gift of Nancy L. Lane PG.2023.010.13

First there is the color—letting it blur and blend and become shades that are also works of art. Then there is the daring use of the canvas—letting it slip and sway from convention—now it hangs, drapes, and suspends, and it often implicates movement and complicates the viewer's sense of space. The work of Sam Gilliam is most often noted and recognized for these interventions in the field of abstract color field painting.

Notably, Gilliam's work situates several methodologies, such as experimentation and improvisation, that align with African American experience and idiom (jazz, for instance). Yet the work also offers some crucial wiggle room—around, out of, and sometimes back into the centrality of Black experience. The sense of motion and other digressions away from traditional abstract painting in Gilliam's work might portend other, more imaginary detours that, however momentary, offer ways into other registers of experience beyond the overpowering predominance of racial consciousness. Or stated differently, Gilliam's work locates race by rousing its dislocation. Instead, Gilliam's work excites explorations of how race, while significant, fails to subsume all aspects of our complex humanity, encouraging a multifarious, knotty set of additional interests and commitments.

Gilliam, who stated in a 2018 interview that "my work is as political as it is formal," makes work that stages both of these as correlated projects.[90] For an artist such as Gilliam, who worked from the 1960s until his death in 2022, social distresses in the United States from the past fifty years could be interpreted as the soft targets of his constant formal resistance to a straightforward painting practice or style. Gilliam perhaps instigates an oppositional stance toward the painting form, but the social and political significance of his refusal reverberates well beyond the specificity of form. This refusal implicates a wide range of social norms, procedures, and expectations, all in need of adjustments and formal experimentation.

Works from Gilliam's early career, such as *Mars 1*, as well as those from the 1990s, such as *D'Artagnan*, equally expose his divested interest in explicitly political or representational art making. It is true that Gilliam's works do not often depict or narrate freedom or liberation from racism. They do not spell out hope in the face of the "race problem." Rather, the work as a whole incites a liberatory experience—it spurs the viewer into an encounter full of interpretive options and choices, which include those related to the social, political, and racial, as well as those related to other varied subjects and themes. Gilliam's paintings formally unfix and recalibrate the hold of race. This is itself an experiment as poignant as his experiments that free the canvas and make colors careen and sway together.

—Romi Crawford

Louise Nevelson
1899—1988

A six-and-a-half-foot black box, an eight-and-a-half-foot-tall maze, a one-foot-deep labyrinth.

I have a dream that one day every valley shall be exalted,

Eight small black wood boxes, surrounded by eight larger ones, sit on a base created by four vertical boxes of equal size. The small ones are open, holding space for smaller, open, cubic shapes containing black forms. The abstracted still-life arrangements of uneven geometric shapes attract the gaze, competing only with the horizontal- and diagonal-striped molding Louise Nevelson inserted in several larger shapes.

every hill and mountain shall be made low,

The twelve surrounding boxes provide peep spaces, containing and protecting their interior space. An arc on the left, placed vertically, is balanced by three long rectangles, superimposed like a low relief above the boxes, further shielding these internal spaces from the viewer's gaze.

the rough places will be made plain,

The sturdy, seemingly simple construction and the hermeticism of *Homage To Martin Luther King, Jr.*, are characteristic of Nevelson's assemblages and the formidable strength of the piece. More than formal compositions, Nevelson's works attempt to tame and organize an interior space. What keeps viewers coming back to the work is the tease—the implied, silent promise that they will be allowed in that inner world, in the artist's interiority.

and the crooked places will be made straight . . .[91]

The total balance of Louise Nevelson's construction, impenetrable yet seductive and harmonious, may have been a mirror of the fourth dimension, a concept influential to many artists of the twentieth century. The artist's goal may have been "to awaken in the authority of instinct . . . and consciousness of soul, brain, and body in a coordinated whole," that is, the dance of creation itself.[92] Shall we dance, Martin?

—Vladimir Cybil Charlier

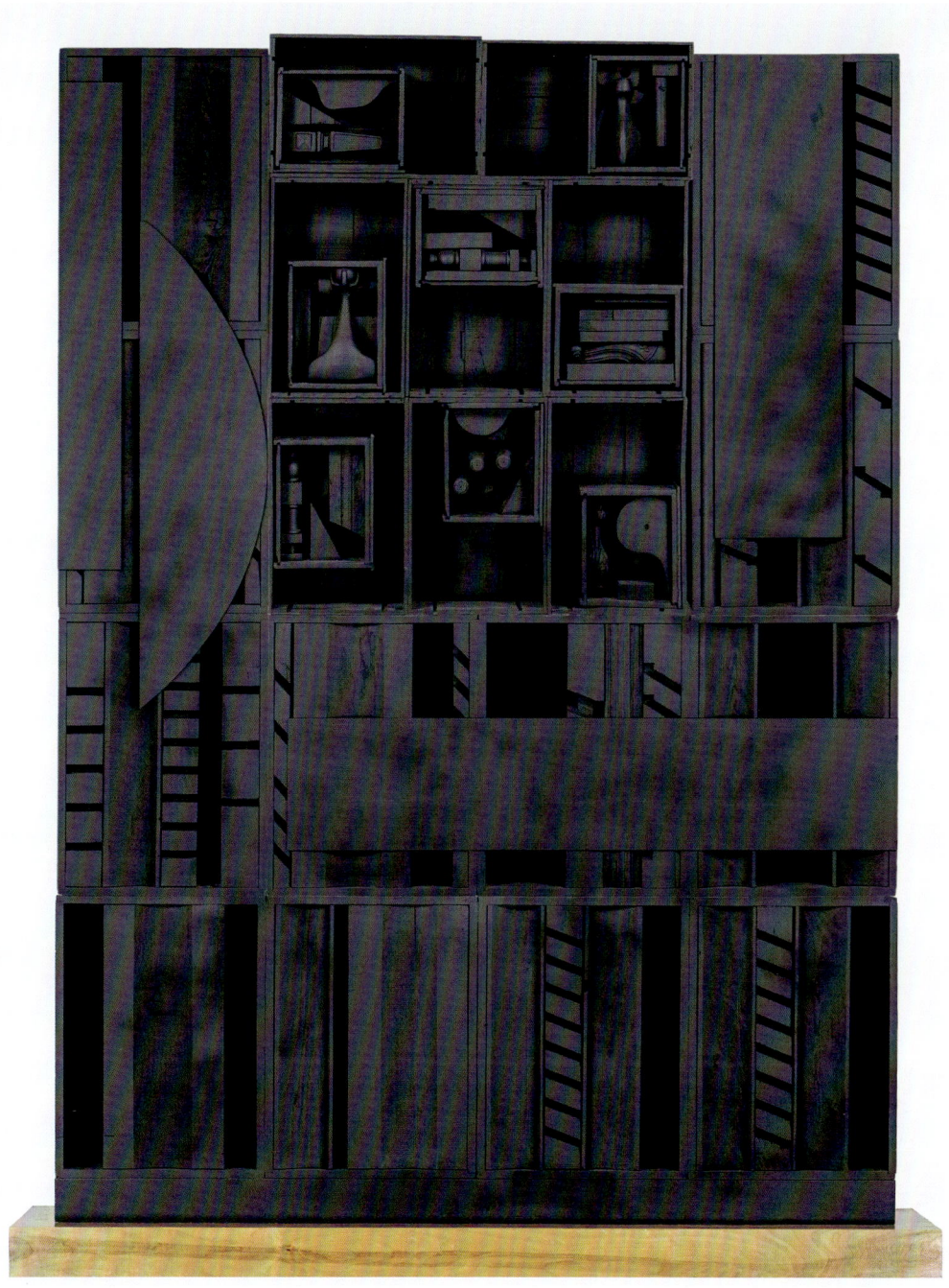

Homage To Martin Luther King, Jr., 1974—85.
Painted wood, 104 × 78 ½ × 12 in. Gift of the
artist 1985.6a-e

Peter Bradley

b. 1940

Peter Bradley invites spontaneity, chance, and movement into his paintings through a variety of methods of application to explore the material possibilities of color and texture. The artist explains that through art making he "can almost dance with color."[93]

Bradley aims to eliminate predictability in the painting process by using techniques that allow for improvisation. In the 1960s, he ceased using paintbrushes, instead opting to toss, drip, and spray acrylic gel paint on to his canvases. The artist plays with proximity and force to yield a variety of marks—from heavy splatters thrown from a distance to clouds of finely misted paint. His ever-changing methods allow for textural variation and buildable surfaces, giving each canvas a unique topography and a sense of tactility. The resulting color-dappled paintings retain the gestures of his application and expand the possibilities of his palette. The layered artworks resist a single focal point and morph with changing light and perspectives.

In *Chinese Snowball II*, Bradley closes the distance between himself and the canvas; in addition to interacting from afar, he wipes a white layer of paint directly on to the surface. The markings dominate the composition, mapping the slippery impact of his wide, sweeping gestures. The effect is a flurry of activity and motion. Beneath the stormy white strokes are his signature layered clouds and webs of color, including muted mauves and stark mustards. On the bottom-left of the canvas, sharp linear splatters of white climb outward to the edge of the canvas, showing the traces of forceful impact. The combined gestural markings bloom from the center point toward the outer edges, alluding to the titular bulbous flowers and evoking the dynamism that was crucial to the painting's creation.

—Mia Matthias

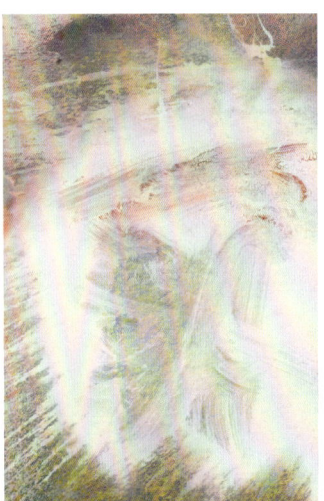

Chinese Snowball II, 1974. Oil on canvas, 76 × 51 in. Gift of Andre Emmerich 2001.17

Houston Conwill
1947—2016

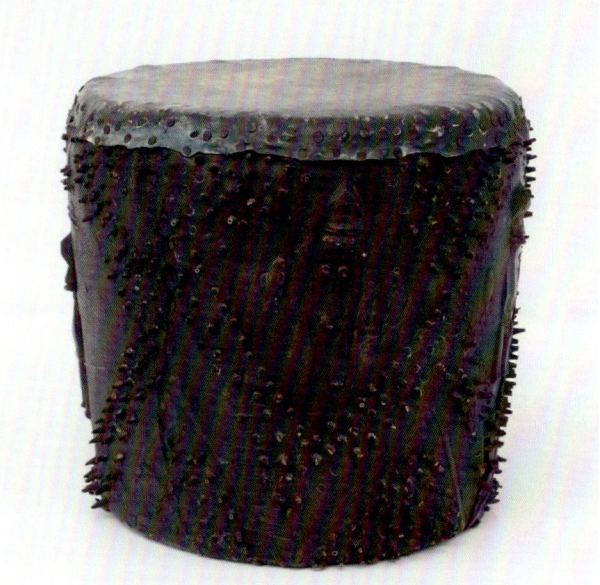

Sculptor, performer, and installation artist Houston Conwill merged personal mythology, African spiritualities, and African American folklore and rituals to explore African diasporic practices. Conwill, raised Catholic, spent time in a Benedictine monastery prior to formally studying art at Howard University and then the University of Southern California. He extended his interest in religion and ritual into his practice. Conwill referenced art found throughout the continent of Africa, such as rock carvings and paintings in Tassili n'Ajjer in Algeria, in his "petrigraphs"—the artist's wall sculptures made of sheets of latex embossed with charged symbols such as bones, crucifixes, and animals. With time, Conwill began to wrap these petrigraphs around cylinders, resulting in objects situated in the same visual landscape as *Drum*.[94]

Circling the surface of *Drum* are symbols seen often in Conwill's work—diamonds of spiky protrusions, abstracted human figures, fish, and a crocodile. *Drum* may have emerged from work Conwill did with artist Senga Nengudi for their 1980 performance *Getup*.[95] Conwill used his sculptures in performances and installations, further engaging with the diasporic traditions on which he called—as some African objects hold functions, ritual or otherwise, outside of aesthetic pleasure. How might one's experience of *Drum* change if seen alongside performers, if heard alongside singing or chanting? With no written word in prehistoric cultures to explain work such as the Tassili n'Ajjer rock art, Conwill connected past to present visually, staging ritualistic performances with potent sculptures rooted in a "history of a people embedded, recorded, and suspended."[96]

—Amber Edmond

Betye Saar

b. 1926

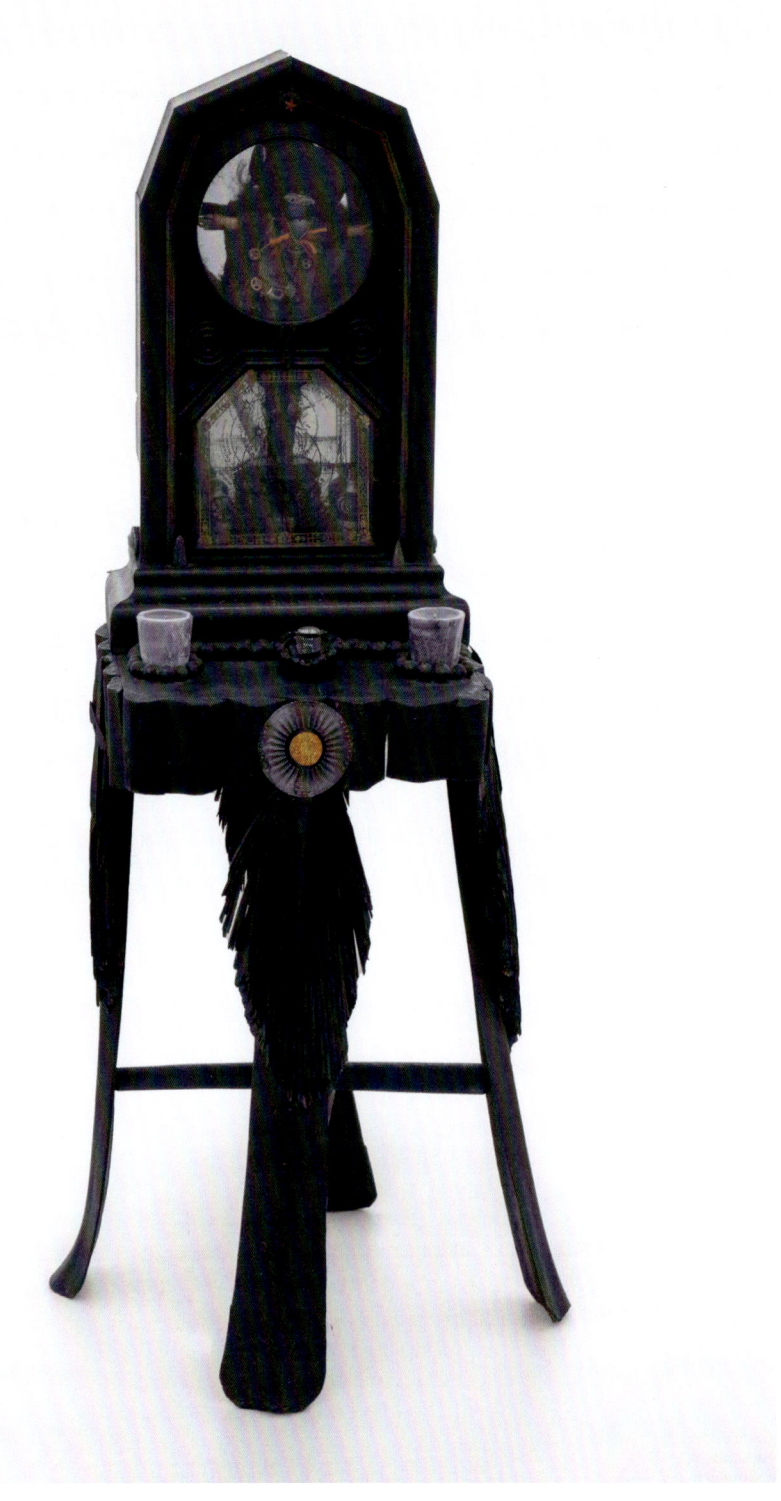

Although short in stature, standing at less than forty-two inches high, Betye Saar's *Indigo Mercy* commands any space it inhabits. Like much of her work, this is an assemblage of everyday objects whose complex composition is shrouded in mystery and invites inquiry and careful consideration. Visually sobering, the piece resembles an altar—a place of divination, a space for prayer—and thus offers a moment for worship.

In her approach to the act of making, and through materiality and form, Saar contends not only with notions of race, politics, and gender, but also religion, spirituality, and mysticism. The indigo table sits on four legs adorned with palm leaves. Candles, perhaps placed as offerings, are affixed to the tabletop in front of what was once a wooden clock. The clock, with its internal mechanisms removed, is filled with symbols and imagery, while a central figure—draped in cloth and jewelry—stands with outstretched arms gazing at the viewer. By incorporating photographs, vintage toys, cultural artifacts, and Black memorabilia in her work, Saar challenges the stereotypes of African Americans as fabricated by white America. The repurposing of objects of subjugation used to reinforce abhorrent views of Black Americans is overturned, upended, and reimagined in Saar's rich assemblages of found objects and often-discarded items. While Saar's work is critical to the Black Arts Movement, it was the Watts Riots of 1965 and assassination of Martin Luther King Jr. in 1968 that deeply informed and impacted her art practice over the next several years. Over her nearly sixty-year career, Saar left indelible marks on contemporary art, addressing some of the most pressing social and political issues of our time through material and form.

—Folasade Ologundudu

Indigo Mercy, 1975. Mixed-media
assemblage, 41 ½ × 13 × 13 in. Gift of the
Nzingha Society, Inc. 1979.9

Senga Nengudi

b. 1943

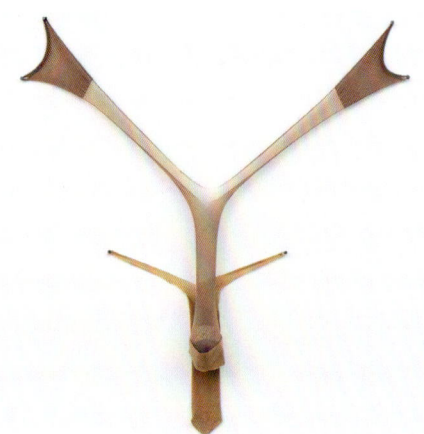

R.S.V.P. V, 1976. Nylon, mesh, and sand,
48 × 36 × 2 in. Museum purchase
with funds provided by the Acquisition
Committee 2003.10.22

Senga Nengudi's artistic practice emerges from the intersection of multiple disciplinary traditions. In her "R.S.V.P." series, sculpture, installation, and dance are the most prominent forms, and the primary materials of nylon pantyhose and sand reference the mutable architecture of the human body. Pantyhose are nailed to walls and crisscross as if tangled arms and legs seeking space. Sand weights these nylon limbs by collecting at the bottom of the pantyhose to form dense hanging balls. Dancers activate the "R.S.V.P." installations—they explore the possibilities for physical movement, entanglements, and somatic pathways beyond the elasticity of the pantyhose. In *R.S.V.P. V*, nylon hose extend into elongated wishbone shapes affixed to the wall by the legs, the necks stretched downward by sand and knotted at the hanging base. The larger of the two shapes hangs in front of the smaller one, which is about half its size.

After Nengudi went through childbirth, pantyhose became the material through which she explored her curiosity around the nature of changing bodies. The stretched nylon signifies the resiliency, defined by the tension between strength and fragility of both the body and the spirit. Through illness, aging, intentional reshaping, and death, humans transform and ultimately disintegrate into new material.

R.S.V.P. V is a request to respond to an invitation, to explore how identity is understood through the body—in mobility and constraint—even as identity exceeds and is betrayed by the ever-evolving body. Pantyhose evoke social norms of feminine respectability and decorum, and Nengudi's pantyhose appear in shades of brown. The dark-hued nylon, along with the weight of the sand inside the fabric, compel considerations of the burden carried by Black women, who are always seen as outside of or transgressing notions of femininity, even as they stretch the boundaries of what can be contained within the categories: woman, Black, body, and human.

—Aimee Meredith Cox

Frank Bowling
b. 1934

Within Frank Bowling's *Blond Betsey*, dynamism, momentum, and space resound throughout and showcase the energetic charge characteristic of many of his works. Bowling extends the language of artistic production through his handling of color and form. The effect is a piece laden with visual tension. Bowling infuses this work with a multidimensionality that speaks to his complex engagement with his chosen medium, and his creative methods draw upon his engagement with narratives of modernism.

Named after former *Art in America* editor Elizabeth Baker, *Blond Betsey* follows the trend of many of Bowling's works produced in the 1970s—poured paintings that reflect his noted experimentation with abstract formalism, process, and material. The strong vertical lines of the bright yellow and blue result in a pillar-like form, commanding in shape and compelling in hue. As the paint extends horizontally down the length of the canvas, the thin, solid stripe of blue blends into the yellow, creating a chartreuse hue seen at the base. Similar strips of peach, salmon, and citrine are also present, adding further spatial and visual dimension to the piece.

On full display is Bowling's desire to, as he describes, "invent ways of using the traditional ways of applying paint."[97] An inherent resonance in *Blond Betsey* comes through via his intentional manipulation of paint and exploration of its effects. The piece challenges understandings of modernism that laud orthodox methodologies at the expense of innovative modes of production. The affective draw of the work lies in the innumerable possibilities presented through medium and technique.

—Arese Uwuoruya

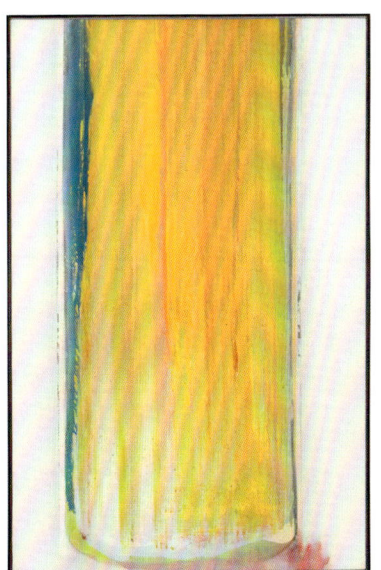

Blond Betsey, 1976. Acrylic on canvas, 70 ¼ × 46 ½ in. Gift of Ninah & Michael Lynne 2015.22

Dawoud Bey

b. 1953

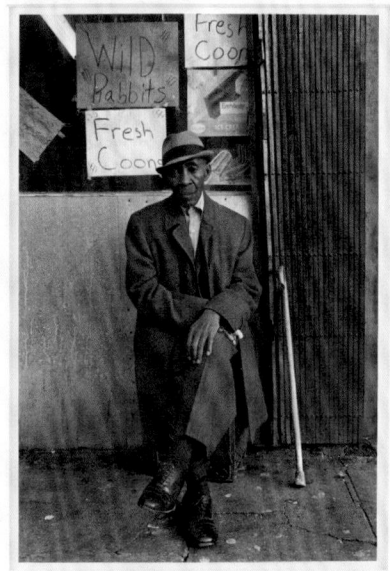

Fresh Coons and Wild Rabbits (from the series "Harlem U.S.A."), 1976. Silver print, 8 ⅜ × 6 in. Gift of the artist 1979.1.17

Artist Dawoud Bey makes photographs that portrait-ize his subjects, whether it is his images of street scenes and sites in Harlem, such as *Fresh Coons and Wild Rabbits* from the "Harlem U.S.A." series, or his more historically inflected work, such as "The Birmingham Project" series. Even his images of sites along the Underground Railroad, in the "Night Coming Tenderly, Black" series, are portraits of hallowed locations. In effect, Bey has been actively reconceptualizing portrait photography since the mid-1970s, demanding more of the genre—whether it is forcing a more accountable rapport between the subject and the photographer or portrait-izing the landscape.

Bey's book *Street Portraits* (2021) most decisively demonstrates his affinity for classical street portraiture and photography, which I describe as an established and notable category, especially among Black photo makers from the 1960s and 1970s. These photographers were often making a concerted effort to transgress the "Sunday best" representations indicative of studio-based portraiture from the 1920s to 1950s, such as that of noted Harlem photographer James Van Der Zee.[98] In effect, Bey's work negotiates the potential of both Black street photography, which often fails to register an adamant Black gaze, and Black studio portraiture, which, with its pronouncement of composure, often curtailed the beauty that follows from Black everydayness.

Bey's "Street Portraits" text also fastens a close formal connection to noted photography books that explore this form, including *The Sweet Flypaper of Life* (1955) with photographs by Roy DeCarava and text by poet Langston Hughes, and *In Our Terribleness (Some Elements and Meaning in Black Style)* (1970), a collaboration between photographer Fundi (then Billy Abernathy) and poet Amiri Baraka (then LeRoi Jones). True, Bey's "Street Portraits" aligns with, and forms a genealogy with, these previous book projects; yet his practice, in a wider sense, regularly reveals shrewd and careful alterations and updates to the portrait form and category.

An example is Bey's "The Birmingham Project." Made in memory of the 1963 murder of four young girls in the bombing of the Sixteenth Street Baptist Church in Birmingham, Alabama, as well as the two young boys who died in the ensuing racial violence, the series reveals Bey's innovative and conceptually insightful take on portraiture. Pairing portraits of ado-lescents who are the ages of the victims alongside portraits of adults who are the age of the victims had they survived, Bey couches an inciting, pivotal historical event within the context of the present and within the photographic portrait form. The diptych *Imani Richardson and Carolyn Mickel*, part of "The Birmingham Project," is poignant as a marker and reminder of US civil rights history. It also points to the history of Black por-trait photography, a genre that Bey conceptually advances and challenges, renews and fine-tunes with each new project.

— Romi Crawford

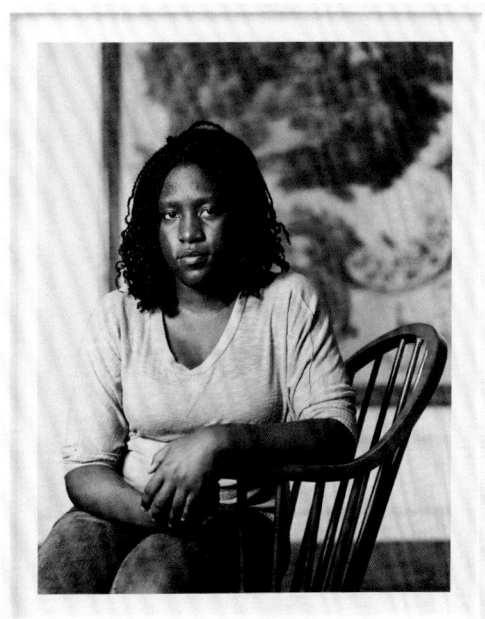 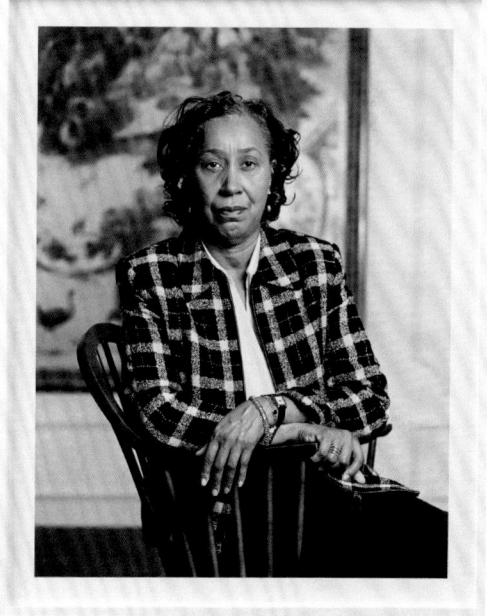

Imani Richardson and Carolyn Mickel (from the series "The Birmingham Project"), 2012. Archival pigment print mounted on Dibond, each: 43 × 33 × 2 in. Gift of Agnes Gund 2014.11a-b

Samuel Fosso

b. 1962

Photographer Samuel Fosso has garnered international recognition for the fashioning of his own self-image. Employing self-portraiture and performance, Fosso uses photography to explore social histories, personal and shared memories, and experiences of the human condition. Fosso was born in Cameroon to Nigerian parents, raised in Nigeria until the Nigerian-Biafran War (1967–70), and, as a result of the war, moved as a refugee to Bangui, Central African Republic (CAR). He began his photographic career through curiosity and spontaneity—at just thirteen, Fosso established a commercial portrait studio, where he gained clientele from his professional reputation for quick service. To finish unused rolls of film, Fosso would take self-portraits as promotional material for his studio business, or to send back to his adored grandmother in Nigeria. His images catapulted into the art world when, in 1994, his self-portraits earned an award at the inaugural photography biennial Rencontres Africaines de la Photographie in Bamako, Mali.

Inspired by images of African Americans in magazines (brought by US Peace Corps volunteers to the CAR) and Cameroonian-Nigerian high-life musicians such as Prince Nico Mbarga, Fosso would adorn himself in Western clothing (such as bell-bottoms and platform boots) to embody these Black personalities. *Self Portrait* showcases a teenage Fosso dressed in a long-sleeved shirt tucked into high-waisted black flare pants. His long and slender physique is accessorized with a loose watch, necklace, bulbous metallic-framed sunglasses, and a Kodak cap. The adolescent Fosso reads as undeniably confident, nonchalant, and well beyond his years. To stage images, Fosso adorned custom-made outfits from the merchant tailor and, in so doing, transformed his personhood to match his subject of inspiration. As a result, self-portraiture became a conduit for self-affirmation, a theatrical act, and an expression of universal archetypes.

—Habiba Hopson

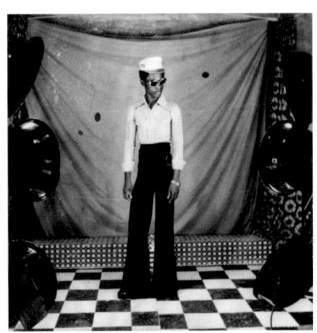

Self Portrait, 1976. Gelatin silver print, 40 × 40 in. Museum purchase with funds provided by the Acquisition Committee 2003.10.23

Daniel LaRue Johnson

1938—2017

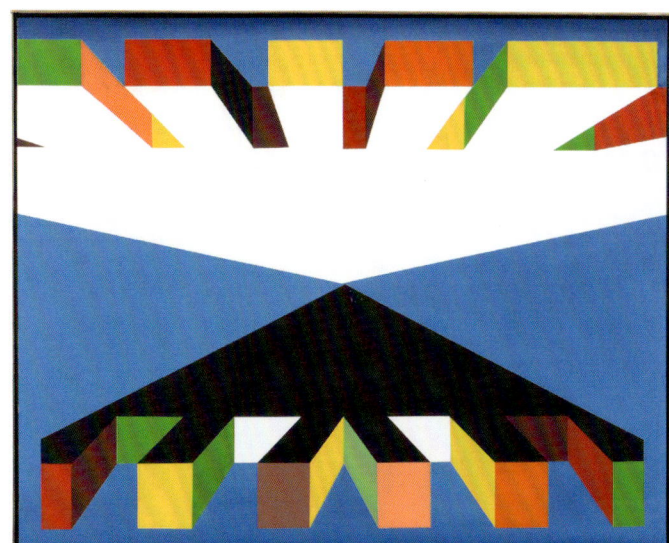

Nations, 1976. Acrylic on canvas,
48 × 60 ⅛ in. Gift of Shirley Williams
1993.18.1

For much of his career, Daniel LaRue Johnson aligned with the sentiments of the civil rights movement, as he constructed artwork of various media to capture the rapidly changing social climate of the United States in the twentieth century. Spanning five feet in width, Johnson's painting *Nations* reflects his tendency toward large-scale abstract works later in his career. The title of the work offers a clue into Johnson's abstraction, which harkens to key tenets of nations—patriotism, symbolism, unity—as a commentary on the fraught state of US politics.

Johnson created *Nations* during a time when the United States was still reeling from the scandal of President Nixon's resignation—the only US president to resign his seat—and just a year after the end of the controversial Vietnam War. The arrangement of colors and forms on the canvas resembles a country's flag, arguably a nation's most important unifying symbol. Two triangles, one black, one white, hover at the center of the composition like a crest or emblem. Although the shapes reflect one another, the points of each triangle do not touch as the viewer might initially suspect, signaling further disconnect. Given Johnson's political affiliations, this could be a reference to race relations in the United States. But one can also make the connection to political rhetoric that plays on extremes, leaving little room for nuance and forcing sides on complex national issues. The sliver of space between the two points highlights the often-irreparable divide between both sides, no matter how small the difference. *Nations* identifies anxieties about rebuilding a national identity in the face of conflict and diverse experiences, which are pervasive discussion points in any political landscape.

—Elana Bridges

Valerie Maynard

1937—2022   Artist in Residence 1969—74

The prints of Valerie Maynard, pioneer of the Black Arts Movement and the Studio Museum in Harlem's first artist in residence (1969—74), celebrate Black pride and resilience. Among the works that joined the institution's permanent collection in its first decade, *Dope Cry* is a rare etching, printed in brown ink and signed with a stylized monogram at bottom right. Multiple figures overlap within the composition, anchored by an exaggerated profile and neck wearing a large collar. While iron collars were common torture devices in the plantation South, the design can alternatively be interpreted as a reference to the ornamental neck-piece of the Benin ivory featured on the catalogue for the Second World Black and Africa Festival of Arts and Culture (FESTAC) in Lagos, Nigeria, where Maynard exhibited in 1977. Another impression of the print in the artist's archives is inscribed with a different title, *125 Street & Lexington Ave*, suggesting that Maynard found inspiration in Harlem residents for her figures, including the headscarf-wearing elderly woman clutching her purse who is depicted twice: once in the center of the image and again at the right margin. Maynard layers tone by varying the depth of her etched lines, leaving residual ink on the copper etching plate and pulling ink from within the recessed lines up and on to the surface of the plate in a technique known as "retroussage." These interlocked gradations create what she later referred to as "depth of feel," a play on the term "depth of field"—a conventional measurement of visual focus—to emphasize the emotional impact and connective appeal of her work.[99] They also allow Maynard to represent historical and contemporary temporal registers as multiple facets of the same image.

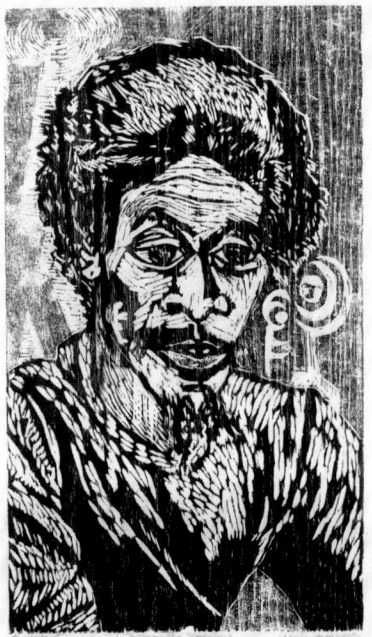

Tyrone the Sculptor, 1973. Woodcut, image: 19 × 11 ¼ in. AP. Gift of the artist 1981.12.1

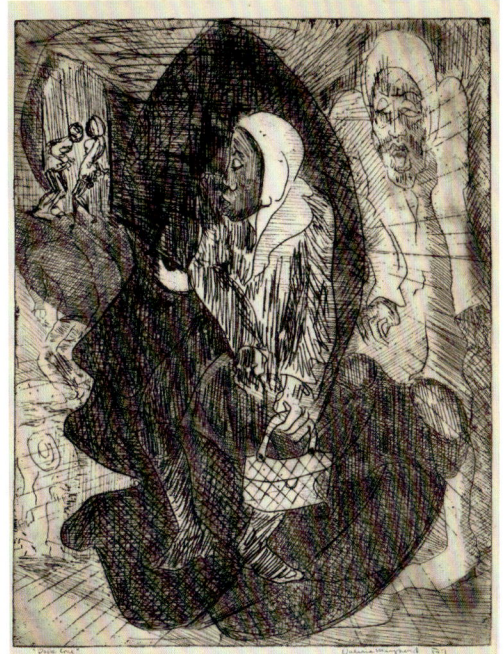

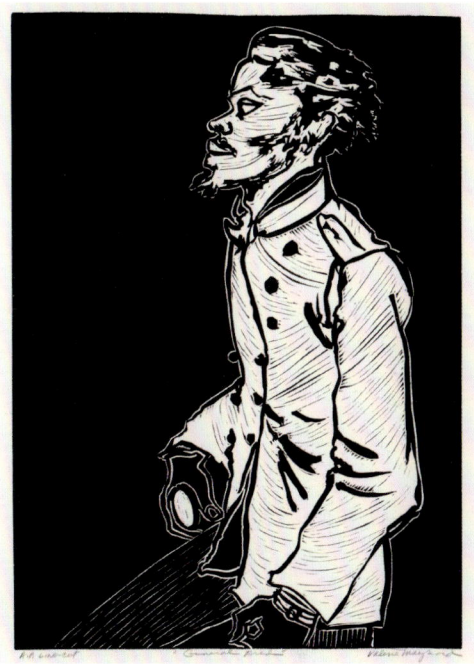

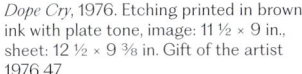

Dope Cry, 1976. Etching printed in brown
ink with plate tone, image: 11 ½ × 9 in.,
sheet: 12 ½ × 9 ⅜ in. Gift of the artist
1976.47

General Fred, 1973. Linocut, image:
17 ⅞ × 13 in. AP. Gift of the artist 1981.12.2

Additional prints in the Studio Museum's collection demonstrate the formative relationship between artist and institution. Maynard established the Museum's community-centered print studio in the early 1970s, which welcomed children and adult visitors interested in seeing and learning printmaking into a working studio. Visitors to that space served as impromptu models for her linocuts, Maynard's preferred media for executing rapid portraits. Such is the case with *General Fred*, an occasional visitor whose Civil War—esque sack coat inspired the work's title. A prolific sculptor, Maynard remembers sharing salvaged trees with Tyrone Mitchell, who was later an artist in residence at the Studio Museum between 1981 and 1982 and who was the subject for *Tyrone the Sculptor*, one of the few woodcuts Maynard created.[100] Here, Maynard deftly manipulates the grain of the wood to create diverse patterns and textures. Mitchell is surrounded by signifiers of their shared métier, with carefully stippled logs above his right shoulder and an abstract sculpture above his left. Maynard's deft transformation of a slab of wood into three things at once—the likeness of a sculptor, sawed logs, and a finished three-dimensional work—reflects the centrality of community, self-reliance, and aesthetic economy within her practice both as an artist and as a teacher, and to the foundations of the Studio Museum itself.[101]

—Leslie Cozzi

McArthur Binion

b. 1946

McArthur Binion's abstractions merge the structural logic and analytical geometries of Minimalism with expressive mark-making and autobiographical narrative. In works such as *History of Application: Talking to You,* Binion begins with meticulously hand-drawn grids, then builds up an abstract field of monochromatic variations, typically deploying two or three colors in a restrained palette. For Binion, the grid is a platform for improvisation, more akin to a musical score than a restrictive device. Riffing within this systematic framework, his compositions operate at the intersection of order and indeterminacy, seriality and sentiment.

Binion developed a singular style of applying oil stick and industrial wax crayon on aluminum sheets. The blob-like accumulations of discrete, contrasting colors of wax in *History of Application: Talking to You* exemplify this method, which effects a three-dimensional quality and registers the pressure of the artist's hands. His methods and unconventional materials garnered the attention of Minimalist sculptors Dan Flavin and Ronald Bladen—the latter invited Binion to participate in the second exhibition organized at New York's Artists Space in 1973, cocurated by Carl Andre, Bladen, and Sol LeWitt. While aspects of Binion's formal methodologies are rooted in Minimalist tenets, his commitment to interlocking his identity within the grid complicates Minimalism's objective and cerebral underpinnings, infusing the work with emotion and Black subjectivity.

His work indexes his intensive and process-driven labor—charged by his biographical connections to rural Mississippi cotton fields and Detroit assembly lines. Chromatically split down the center, the double image of diagonally oriented rectangles in *History of Application: Talking to You* contributes to a dynamic optical effect that accentuates left and right. Binion learned to paint with both hands due to his arduous process, and the visual bifurcation of this piece reflects his ambidextrousness and exceptional bodily choreography. The painting's embodiment of aspects of the artist's lived experience presaged later works such as his "DNA" series, which integrates address book reproductions and personal ephemera into his abstract matrix.

—Jordan Carter

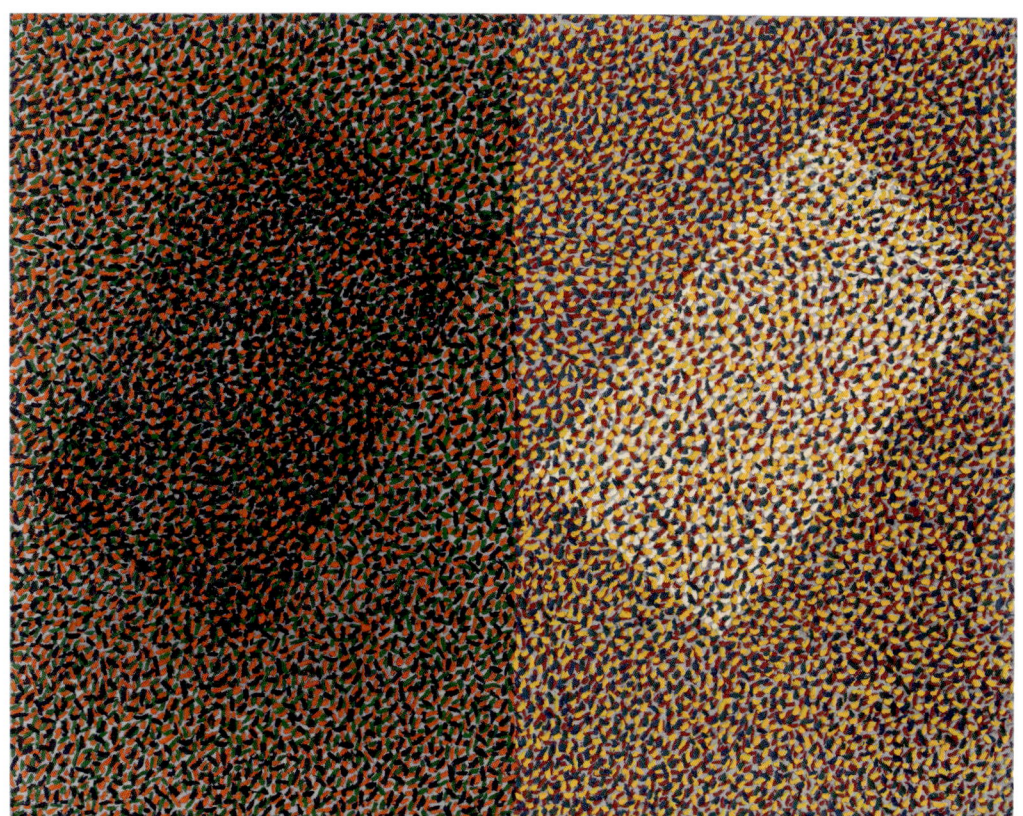

History of Application: Talking to You, 1977.
Dixon wax crayon on aluminum, 46 × 59 in.
Museum purchase with funds provided by
Barbara Bluhm-Kaul and Don Kaul, Chicago,
and a gift of the artist and Kavi Gupta
Gallery, Chicago 2016.20

Ming Smith

b. 1947

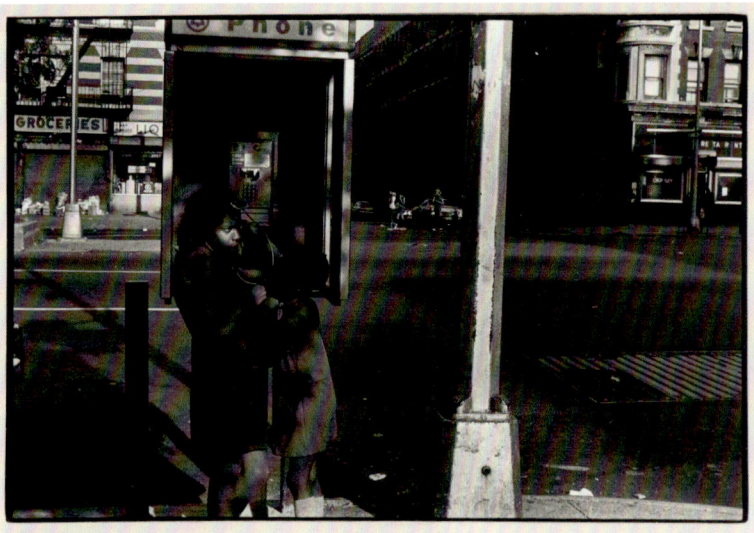

Mother and Child, 1977. Vintage gelatin
silver print, 11 × 14 in. Museum purchase
with funds provided by Betsy Witten
2018.31

A woman with a roller in her hair leans against a pay phone, her expression intense as she listens to the person on the other end of the line. A young girl waits patiently, staring up at the woman. One of her earliest photographs of Harlem, photographer Ming Smith's *Mother and Child* reveals the artist's deep empathy for the neighborhood and those who inhabit it. The work exemplifies the artist's ability to capture moments in time, often mundane and quiet, that celebrate the complexities of blackness and a commitment to the play of light and shadow. There is a tenderness between the two subjects, with the girl nearly mirroring her mother's stance. While largely in shadow, the woman's face is partially bathed in light, emphasizing the heated look in her eyes and stirring the viewer to wonder about the source of her agitation.

Five years prior to taking this image, Smith was invited to join the Kamoinge Workshop, a collective of Black photographers formed in New York City in 1963. The group met weekly to discuss and critique each other's work and share professional and technical advice. There, Smith honed her photographic eye and conceptual focus. Her intuitive and thoughtful approach to photography is clear, with cropping and an embrace of darkness poetically used to focus attention within the scene. The stillness of her images—with the figures in *Mother and Child* standing on an eerily empty city street—contrasts with the emotion emanating from her subjects. Smith's photographs vibrate with energy and tension, offering multitudes in understanding Black life.

—Connie H. Choi

Nanette Carter

b. 1954

The concept of the "scape" is a rich field of study in Nanette Carter's practice; she is a "scapeologist." For Carter, the scape refers to "underwater, sea, land, sky, and outer space. All of the natural scapes the universe has offered." Though considering the environment, Carter's work is not filled with realistic scenes of nature. Instead, she makes use of abstraction. She explains: "Metaphorically, scapes have allowed me to weave various political themes and concepts into my work. I have subscribed to calling my work conceptual abstractions . . . . My topics are universal—like denouncing wars, which are usually based around land, or if I am celebrating nature, I am most comfortable using scapes to deliver my themes."[102] Thus Carter's scapes tap into the full breadth of the word "landscape": the natural and the political (while understanding that both are connected).

An early work, *Syncopated Scape 1*, employs some core visual strategies of Carter's practice. Printmaking is foundational for Carter—she made linocuts as early as the first grade.[103] Woodcuts eventually captured her attention in college because the medium allowed her to explore texture.[104] In *Syncopated Scape 1*, subtle striations cause the forms to buzz with energy. The collage-like composition draws on her childhood experience of watching her mother sew dance costumes, cutting patterns and combining tulle, taffeta, and sequins—discrete parts brought together to make a whole.[105] Red space is cut through by a wave of white lines; curling teal forms seem to ride this wave. A confetti of colorful rectangles and white dots descends from above. Meanwhile, a sharp blue front rises from below. With the title's first word, "Syncopated," the work also pulls from the language of jazz. Dots, bars, and lines score a melody. Describing her process like that of a musician, Carter shares, "I improvise off of scapes, thus creating new worlds."[106]

—Jordan Jones

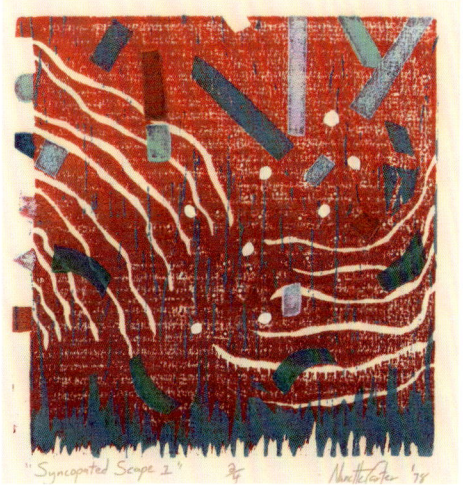

Syncopated Scape 1, 1978. Woodcut, 13 ¼ × 13 ¼ in. Edition 2 of 4. Gift of Mr. and Mrs. Matthew G. Carter 1980.1.1

Jack Whitten

1939—2018

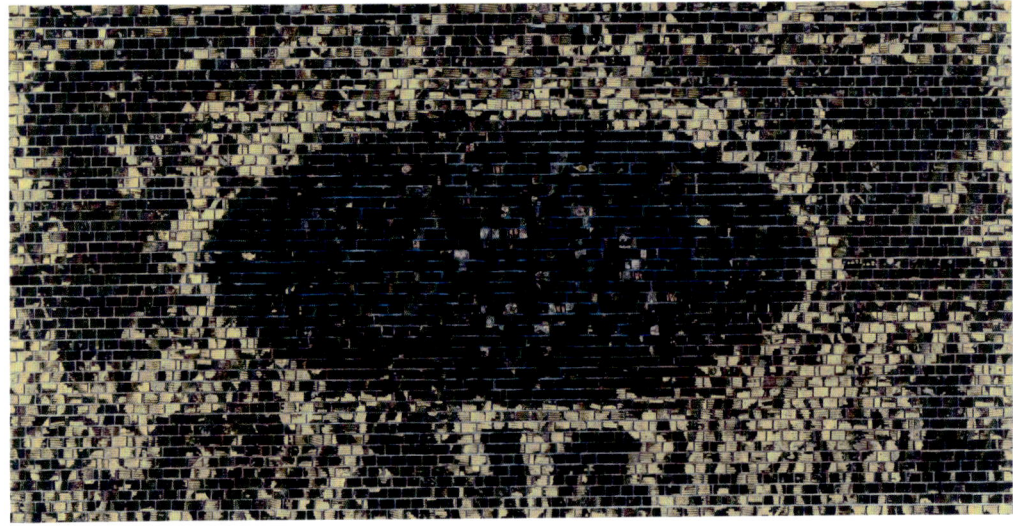

Quantum Wall, V (Inside The Soul Of Time),
2017. Acrylic on canvas, 48 × 96 × 3 in.
Promised gift of Mr. and Mrs. Lee Broughton
PG.2019.2

Jack Whitten was always searching for and testing new methods of art making. He characterized his early works as "abstract figurative expressionist."[107] Influenced by artists such as Arshile Gorky and Willem de Kooning, Whitten composed brightly hued, surrealist mixes of figures and landscapes. The 1970s would be a career turning point. In an intense period of experimentation, Whitten switched from oil to acrylic paint and abandoned symbolic and narrative elements such as color, figures, and gesture. His palette became predominantly black-and-white and his compositions purely abstract, as seen in *Khee I.*

Khee I dispenses with illustration and points to Whitten's investigation into processes with acrylic paint, development of new tools, and incorporation of found objects. Whitten placed objects, such as stones and wire, underneath his canvas and spread layers of acrylic paint on top, creating surprising textures across the surface. He then raked the canvas with his "developer," a serrated metal blade attached to a twelve-foot-long apparatus.

The resulting striations revealed the layers of paint beneath the surface and allowed light to interact with the added dimensions, creating an opticality Whitten termed "vibration."[108]

The 1980s saw Whitten create a series of paintings that suggest the significance of place in informing one's identity and aesthetics. From references to navigational charts and cosmological maps in works such as *Dead Reckoning I*, to his "Site" paintings, constructed from acrylic casts of objects found in New York City, Whitten eventually determined that a sense of place was a mental site rather than a physical location. As a Black abstract artist at that time, Whitten found that much of his career was overlooked by both Black and mainstream art communities. Feeling he was "politically . . . caught between a rock and a hard place," Whitten developed his own agenda and an intentionality about who he was and what he was doing.[109]

A major creative breakthrough in the form of a singular style of working came in the 1990s. Using small pieces of paint cut from dried slabs of acrylic, he assembled these tesserae on the canvas, building mosaic-like, multitextured works. Depending on how Whitten positioned the chips, he was able to direct the light and "build anything [he wanted] to build," including *Quantum Wall, V (Inside The Soul Of Time)*, and the majority of his acclaimed "Black Monoliths" series (1988—2017) dedicated to distinguished Black cultural figures.[110]

Up until his passing in 2018, a relentless curiosity and fearless drive guided Whitten throughout his career, resulting in a body of work that reflects his stated ambition "to change the course of painting through innovation."[111]

— Kanitra Fletcher

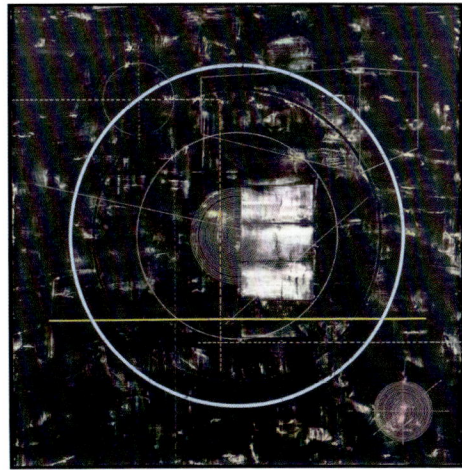

Dead Reckoning I, 1980. Acrylic on canvas, 73 × 73 ¼ in. Gift of Bill Whitten 1984.16

Khee I, 1978. Acrylic on canvas, 72 × 84 in. Gift of Lawrence Levine, New York 1981.9

Louis Delsarte

1944—2020   Artist in Residence 1979—80

In Louis Delsarte's drawing *Ship Going Northward Despite the Frozen Wind*, a ship and its cargo lurch in a windstorm. The ship bows upward to vertically fill the composition. Thick, smoky clouds coat the sky. Wind moves the crew across the deck—a figure at portside and another, rendered as a blink-and-you'll-miss-it sketch, hiding by the rigging. Delsarte depicts the focal figure's head whipping side to side in short marks reminiscent of comic book action, turning this static drawing into a time-based depiction of a possibly capsizing ship. Another figure, who wears a patterned mask, grips the mast. Behind him, a woman, naked save for underwear, reels against the sails. Keeping in mind the artist's long admiration for and study of music, this drawing showcases Delsarte's unique ability to render shifting tones and rhythms in a two-dimensional medium. Amid the tempest, Delsarte's presto sensibility breaks through.

The cargo is pomegranates and three leopards shown in the act of escaping the cage. The wooden rails of a crate shatter as one cat shoves its powerful neck out, furthering the intensity and potential for mutiny. The title indicates the direction of the ship: northward. The animal freight suggests the vessel's origins: Africa. Thus, it can be deduced that this trade-north journey is perilous in many ways, despite the storm. *Ship Going Northward Despite the Frozen Wind* alludes to relentless change—with no potential for calm given what awaits at the destination.

—Meg Whiteford

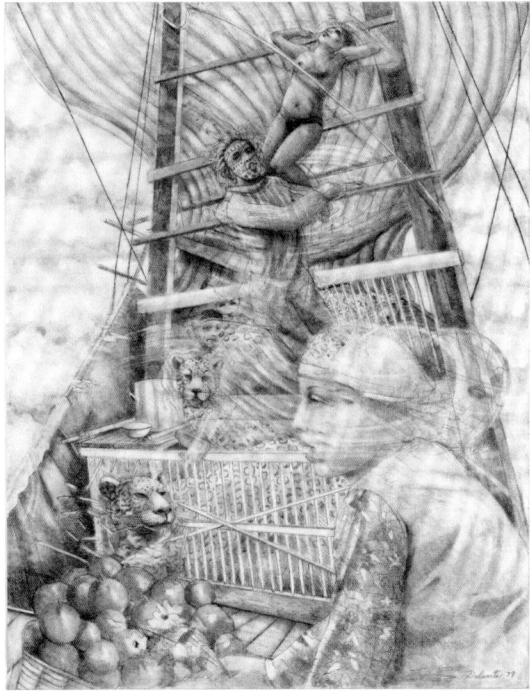

Ship Going Northward Despite the Frozen Wind, 1979. Graphite on paper, 25 ½ × 20 × 1 in. Gift of David Mann 1997.5

Candace Hill-Montgomery

b. 1945   Artist in Residence 1979—80

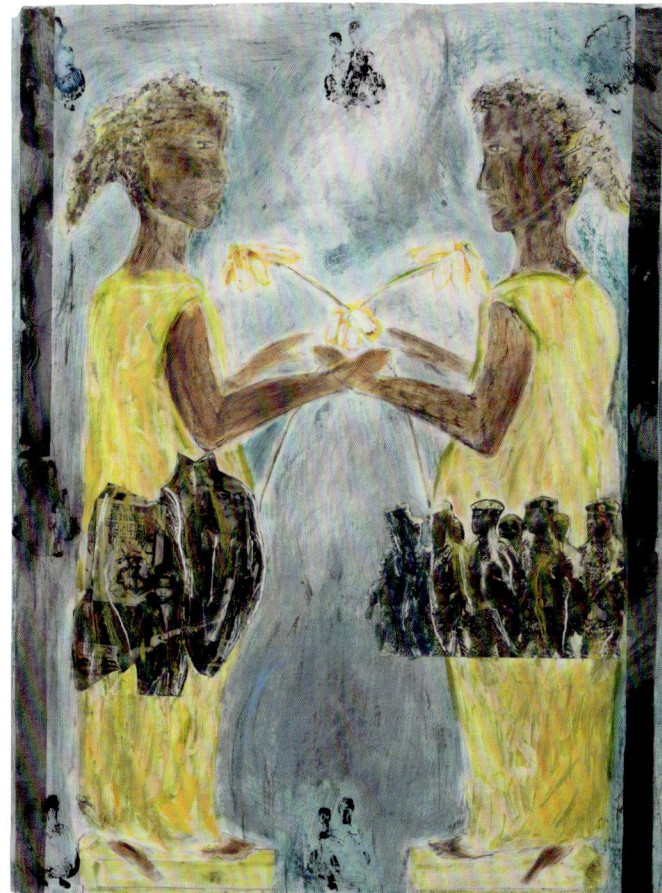

Birth of a Nation II, 1979. Mixed media and photo collage, 72 × 52 in. Gift of the artist 1980.17

Two figures in yellow draped dresses, reminiscent of Classical and Neoclassical statuary, stand on pedestals against a turquoise background. From their bodies, yellow flowers sprout. Photographs from the Black Panther Party archive lay on top of them, referencing global Black freedom struggles.[112] Bordering the composition is the stamped image of a parent and child, alluding to the "birth" of its title.

The words "birth of a nation" may first bring to mind the 1915 D. W. Griffith film of the same name, a foundational work in the history of film that also centered anti-Black tropes and invigorated support of the Ku Klux Klan. *Birth of a Nation II* is part of Candace Hill-Montgomery's series "Historic Extinctions," which was created as a response to the film and other manifestations of anti-Black racism in contemporary culture. Making this work while in the Studio Museum's *Artist-in-Residence* program, Hill-Montgomery expertly visualizes multiple meanings of "birth" and "nation" to explore Black radical traditions in the United States and around the world.

"Birth," in the Classical tradition, anthropomorphizes concepts such as liberty and justice via stoic women like the Statue of Liberty or Lady Justice. Hill-Montgomery depicts similar figures in color. In the face of oppression, when liberty and justice are not extended to all, the desire to live under these ideals drives people to birth new states. Additionally, the parent-child relationship—biological or familial—points to the inherited, long history of anti-blackness and to its resistance. "Nation" recalls movements in the United States such as Black Nationalism or the Black Panther Party and the decolonization of Africa as people fought for and built independent states starting in the mid-twentieth century. These contexts, alongside Hill-Montgomery's collaged imagery, allude to a Pan-African urge to free all colonized Black peoples and honor histories of resistance against white supremacy across the world.

—Amber Edmond

Gerald Jackson

b. 1936

Part of the larger "Divine Providence" series, this collage by multidisciplinary artist Gerald Jackson assembles his ruminations on love, hope, and spirituality. Mixing paintings, found images, and original writing, the materiality of this work also sheds light on the material conditions of his everyday life.

Central to the collage is a Black figure, Jackson's version of "Black Marilyn," wearing a fringed leotard and with flowing hair; her wide-legged stance suggests a moment of transcendence and recalls the stage presence of actors such as Marilyn Monroe. This embodiment of both strength and grace echoes in the silhouette of a rose, thorns, and buds to the left. To the right are a line drawing of an ankh amulet with "Isis" written below it and a photograph of a statue of Selket—references to the Egyptian goddesses of healing, magic, and death. Together they evoke divine feminine energy as found in the ancient cultures and contemporary music that Jackson voraciously consumes. The maneki-neko "beckoning cat" and calligraphy, including the Japanese kanji for "love," are emblems often encountered on the Bowery, an artist enclave in New York City where Jackson lived from the 1970s to the mid-2000s before relocating to New Jersey. They too charge the artwork with good fortune and welcome.

Raised in Chicago and spending a formative part of his career in New York City, Jackson melds formal artistic references and the grittiness of the cities in which he lived. Packed with metaphysical meaning, he encodes his work to evoke rather than directly communicate a spiritual message.

—Rachell Morillo

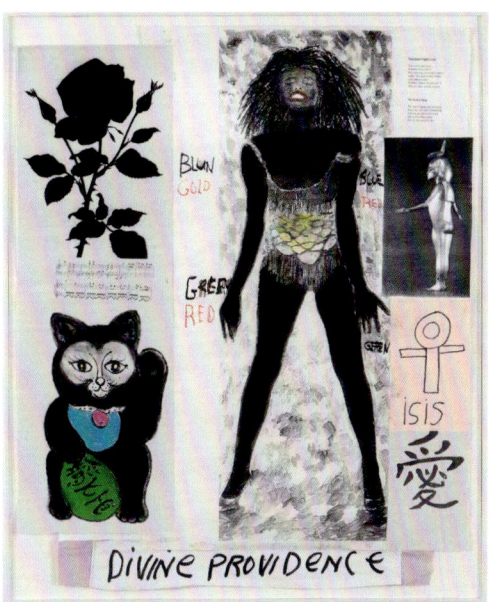

Untitled, n.d. Mixed-media collage on paper, 38 × 32 in. Museum purchase with funds provided by Martin and Rebecca Eisenberg 2021.20

Faith Ringgold

1930—2024

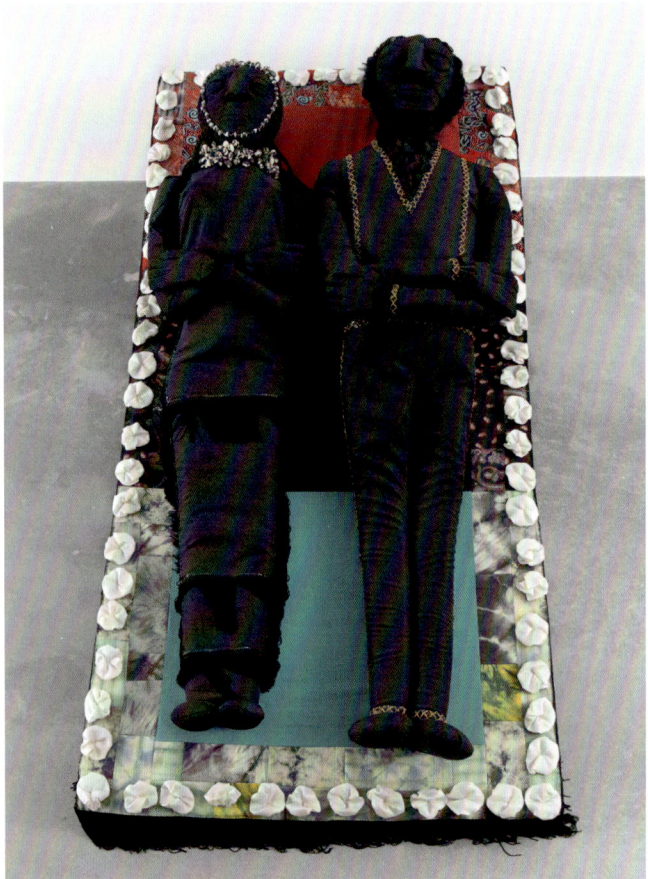

Buba and Bena #2 (from "The Wake and Resurrection of the Bicentennial Negro"), 1987. Foam, mixed media, wood, fabric, and fringe, 74 × 40 × 12 ½ in. Gift of an anonymous donor 1987.15

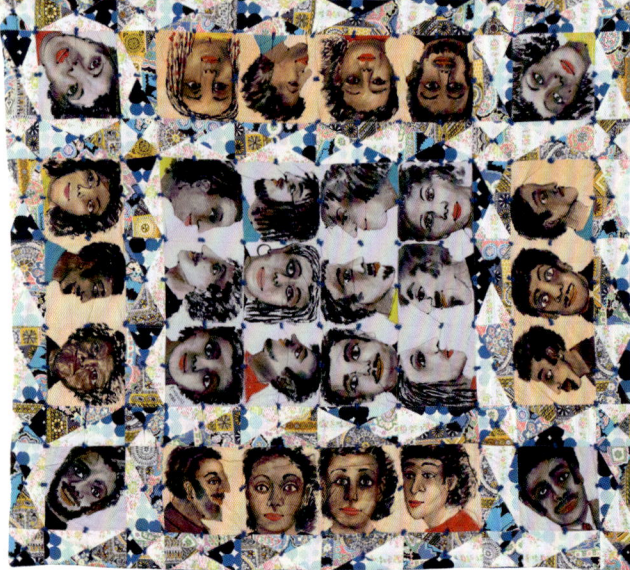

Echoes of Harlem, 1980. Hand-painted cotton, 80 ½ × 89 ½ in. Gift of Altria Group, Inc. 2008.13.10

Throughout her long and storied career, Faith Ringgold created prescient bodies of work that celebrate Black lives and engage in institutional critique. The artist came of age just after the Harlem Renaissance and started her career as an elementary school educator. Her work has captured the attention of children, the Black community, and the art world alike. Alongside her career as an artist, Ringgold is equally lauded for her activism. In the late 1960s and 1970s, she was active in the civil rights, Black Power, and women's rights movements. The artist also protested against the egregious absences and exclusion of Black artists, and Black women particularly, in mainstream art museums.

Ringgold provides social commentary on race relations in the United States with the installation *The Wake and Resurrection of the Bicentennial Negro*, which includes the discrete sculpture *Buba and Bena #2*. Buba and Bena are the two decedents and the focus of the composition. Buba has died from a drug overdose, a social ill that has plagued urban communities, and Bena, overcome by grief, has also died. Buba and Bena lie on a Pan-African flag draped on a cooling board (an older Southern term for the table cooled by ice on which a body was lain for viewing at a wake). The mise-en-scène also includes two other figures, the elegantly dressed mourners Moma and Nana amid a backdrop of stained glass, soft sculpture, windows, and flowers. The work is activated by recordings of Martin Luther King Jr.'s "I Have a Dream" speech, hymns such as "Amazing Grace" and "He Arose," and an improvisational dance by students the artist hired when it was displayed at colleges. This swell of energies contributed to the resurrection of Buba and Bena. *The Wake and Resurrection of the Bicentennial Negro* is an exemplar of the Bible verse from Psalms 30:5, "weeping may endure for the night, but joy comes from the morning."

Echoes of Harlem is Ringgold's first "story quilt" and the last work she created with her mother, Willi Posey Jones, before her mother's death in 1981. The quilt celebrates the multiplicity of voices in the artist's tight-knit Harlem community. Inspired by the African American quilting tradition, the quilt is a symphony of painted portraits of the people Ringgold knew in her Harlem neighborhood framed by scraps of fabric fashioned by the artist's mother. *Echoes of Harlem* was created for the 1980 exhibition *The Artist and the Quilt*. The exhibition featured women artists such as Alice Neel, Charlotte Robinson, Betye Saar, and others who were charged to create works in collaboration with a "traditional" quiltmaker.

Faith Ringgold was a womanist artist. She exemplified that women's work is indeed making art. She affirmed: "I don't feel restricted by being female, any more than I feel restricted by being Black or being American— these are the facts of my life. It is powerful to know who you are."[113] Over a consummate and prolific career, her works stand the test of time. Faith Ringgold has crafted and said what she pleases.

—Anne Collins Smith

Hughie Lee-Smith

1915—1999

The paintings of Hughie Lee-Smith are like tableaux vivants or theater sets where a cast awaits their cue. In the absence of trees and shrubbery, Lee-Smith fills his surreal landscapes with figures who wander, play, and seek respite. In some cases, he interchanged these figures with a variety of symbols and objects as he worked to develop his visual language.

In *Festive Vista*, gray skies color an urban landscape. Atop a building, three ribbons anchored by three poles flow with the wind. A shadow is cast on to the conjoining buildings. There in the shadows, Lee-Smith paints two question marks, a pointing finger, and a target. Certainly, he is contemplating the deep questions that those who live within the margins of society wrestle with.

For the artist, the target—along with balloons and ribbons—was a motif that represented his fondness for the circus. His maternal grandmother, who took care of the young Lee-Smith, restricted him from attending such "low-class" activities as the circus. Reflecting on those days, he said it "must have sunk into my unconscious and manifested itself years later in my paintings: the balloons, ribbons, pennants."[114] After relocating to Cleveland, Lee-Smith found solace from this exclusion in drawing, painting, and eventually theater. As an adult, he taught at the Karamu House, the nation's first and oldest Black theater company. This would heavily influence the works made later in his career.

Often depicted as decrepit, near destruction, or completely destroyed, the buildings in Lee-Smith's artwork typically add anxiety and uncertainty to his compositions. However, the buildings in *Festive Vista* are well-kept. Though his paintings overlapped on themes of solitude, alienation, exclusion, and existentialism, he also created work emblematic of the experiences and emotions of so many Black people in the United States. He invited viewers to reflect on social inequities but to also hope for resilience.

—Jayson Overby Jr.

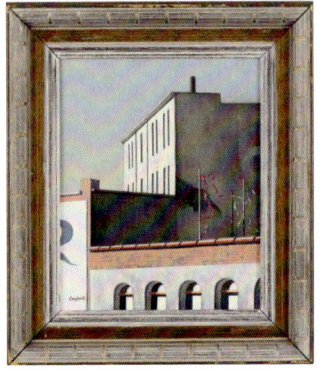

Festive Vista, 1980. Oil on canvas, 15 × 13 in. Museum purchase and a gift from E. Thomas Williams and Auldlyn Higgins Williams 1997.9.17

Nellie Mae Rowe

1900—1982

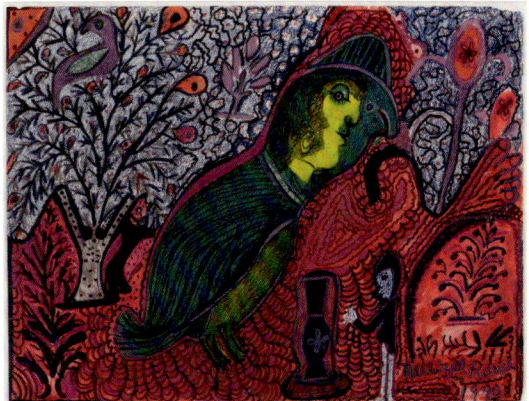

Though Nellie Mae Rowe received acclaim as an artist late in life, the origins of her craft can be traced back to the formative years she spent on her family's farm in Vinings, Georgia. In between the laborious tasks she was assigned by her parents, Rowe spent her time on creative pursuits. In these moments of retreat, the young artist fashioned dolls out of clothing and scrap materials, took to the woods surrounding her home to construct playhouses with her siblings, and put graphite to paper to create drawings inspired by life and the vast imaginative world in her head. Rowe's childhood exuberance for art making carried into her adult life—her residence, which she aptly nicknamed her "playhouse," functioned as both dwelling and studio. From the late 1960s until her death in 1982, Rowe's home facilitated a return to the drawing, doll making, and "yard art" of her youth.

Across her drawings, Rowe often turned to motifs found in Christian scripture; she commonly repeated birds, fish, trees, and cattle as imagery. The artist combined her knowledge of the Bible and reverence for religious teachings with her personal mythologies. Evidence of her deep spiritual conviction and expansive imagination came together in works of art that privilege both religious doctrine and fantasy.

Green Parrot is one of the numerous fantastical scenes Rowe created following her recognition as an artist. The titular figure stands at the center of the image against a bold red background and is surrounded by sky, trees, animals, a bird, a human figure, and a sea of amorphous and botanical patterns. The various elements of Rowe's composition cohere in an avantgarde style—her otherworldly figures and environment resist spatiotemporal placement and discernible classification. Though the exact inspiration for this work is not known, Rowe often turned to Black American folkloric and oral traditions when conceiving her drawings. Perhaps nestled amid this tangle of imagery are stories passed on by friends and family or remnants of the biblical messages she held dear.

—Alexandra E. Adams

Howardena Pindell

b. 1943

Feast Day of Iemanja II, December 31, 1980. Acrylic, dye, paper, powder, thread, glitter, and sequins on canvas, 86 × 103 in. Gift of Diane and Steven Jacobson, New York 1986.2

Known for her monumentally scaled paintings, Howardena Pindell plays with and breaks "the grid" that was largely a preoccupation of many of her peers working in abstraction. She layers her large-scale paintings with glitter and sequins that act as beacons for the eye. Created in a highly methodical process, these works act as a meditation for the artist. Carefully punched out paper circles are affixed to a canvas that is cut and reworked, stitched together, and remade into a new form. In this way, the artist injects what has traditionally been aligned with craft into the visual language of fine art painting—a subversive reaction to an art canon and medium largely dominated by white men.

Much of Pindell's work from this time period, the late 1970s to the mid-1980s, was influenced by her travels for research related to both her art practice and curatorial work. *Feast Day of Iemanja II, December 31* pays homage to the orisha Lemanjá, a deity with origins in West Africa that evolved through time to Brazilian candomblé as the goddess of the sea. Intrinsically linked to the divine feminine, Pindell represents the goddess as blue or white, which makes up the palette of this work. During her feast day, practitioners release offerings to the goddess into the water in the hope that she accepts and then provides them a blessing. The rippling glitter of the surface of this painting recalls the reflection and shimmer of the sea and cresting waves. It also nods to those who traversed the ocean during the transatlantic slave trade. Thus, Pindell deftly illustrates her ability to tackle complex and harrowing themes and reconfigure them into beautiful objects that speak to the resilience of the diaspora.

—Adeze Wilford

Marilyn Nance

b. 1953 Artist in Residence 1993—94

Two inhales, two exhales, at the same time. A whisper, a glance, a smile.
Two breaths at a time. Warmth, joy. Two breaths at a time. Gratitude,
excitement. Two breaths at a time. Wonder, hope. Two breaths at a time.
Pride, comfort. Two breaths at a time. Worry. Can this moment last forever? Captured by the camera, it instantly becomes archival.

In the photograph *Al and Ali* by Marilyn Nance, we see a Black man—
the artist's husband, Al Santana—in a homey setting amid the bliss
of early fatherhood. A few-weeks-old baby sleeps on his chest. It is Ali,
Al and Marilyn's firstborn child.

Nance shares this intimate moment with the world in a small but generous gesture. The work gives private insight into the lives of a Black
family in the United States in the 1980s. It is a powerful visual statement
against a persistently present stereotype of "the absent Black father."
Here is not the space to dispute this idea and to unpack its complexities;
Nance's work is powerful enough to speak on its own terms.

Nance possesses the great ability to interweave big as well as small
moments of life by creating narratives encompassing the Black human
condition. Over the past five decades, her black-and-white photographs
have become reflections of the life, the bodies, the histories, as well
as the economies of African American and further African diasporic existence. Nance holds a deep sensitivity for the intricacies of these narratives,
which she translates into a mosaic of relations: private and public; past
and present. Underneath: a constant awareness of how race and class
determine every aspect of these moments.

—Yvette Mutumba

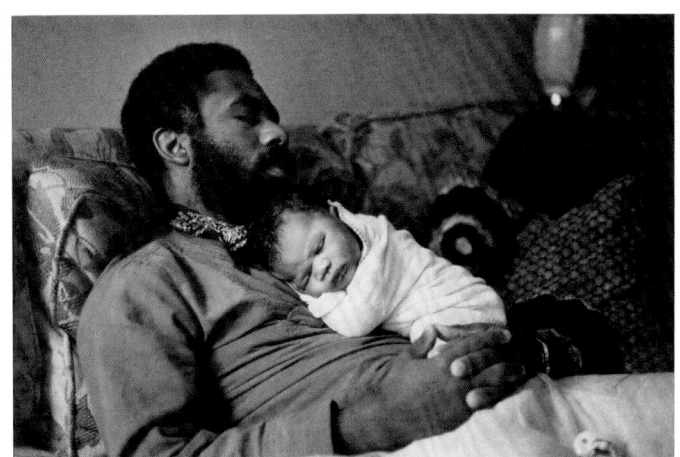

Al and Ali, 1981. Gelatin silver print,
14 ½ × 21 ¾ in. Gift of the artist 1994.6

Ed Clark
1926—2019

Ed Clark's *Untitled (Paris Series)* exemplifies the artist's lifelong experimentation with abstract visual language, the materiality of pigment, and luminous color. The interplay of curvilinear and straight strokes, rendered here in lush pastel hues, characterizes the works in this series. Clark achieved the broad, bold strokes of this painting with aid of a push broom, an implement he adopted into his process in the 1950s when he was unable to find a brush wide enough to achieve his desired effects. The breadth of the push broom allowed him to "sweep through the paint," thus quickly manipulating the pigment he applied to canvases on his studio floor.[115] The luscious, tactile surfaces of the resulting works embody and preserve the energetic movements and gestures that went into their making. The critic John Yau aptly notes the ways Clark's technique transformed a janitorial activity into high-minded lyricism.[116]

Clark's painting pays tribute to Paris, a city that played an enormous role in shaping his artistic vision. He arrived there in 1952, and with financial support provided by the GI Bill, he enrolled at Académie de la Grande Chaumière to continue a course of study he had started a few years earlier at the Art Institute of Chicago. Clark embraced the rich cultural life of Paris, becoming part of a multiracial, intellectual, and artistic community of US expatriates. He immersed himself in French modernist painting, including that of Pablo Picasso and Henri Matisse, who were still alive and making their artistic presence felt. Contemporary French painting also appealed to him. In particular, he responded strongly to a painting by Nicolas de Staël, noting the power of the surface and paint as material fact.[117] The painting fed into Clark's interest in highlighting the brush-

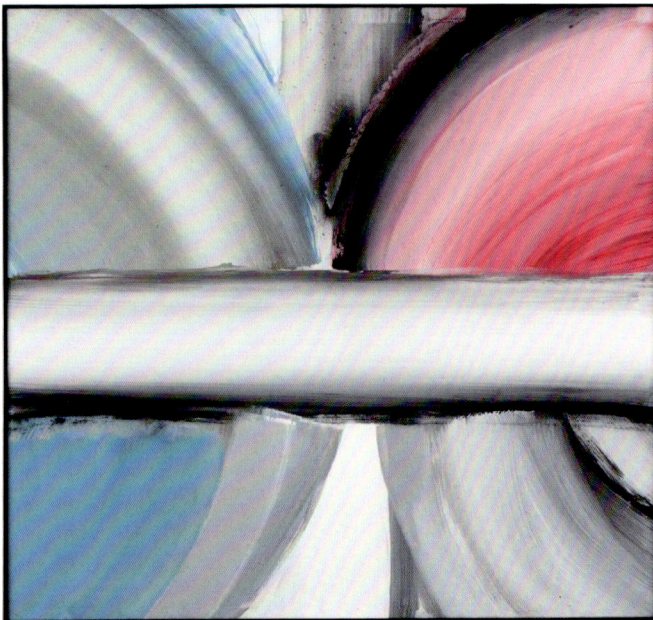

Untitled (Paris Series), 1987. Acrylic on canvas, 74 × 81 ½ in. Gift of Schaina and Josephina Lurie Memorial Foundation 1987.17

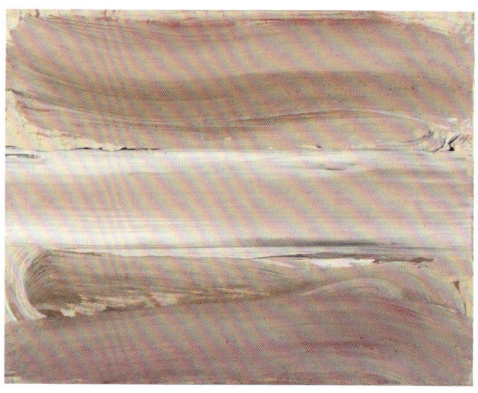

Untitled, 1974. Color etching on paper,
22 × 30 in. Gift of Lowery Stokes Sims
2000.3.3

Taos Series, 1982. Acrylic on canvas,
61 × 76 in. Gift of David Hammons
2002.11.1

stroke as subject and led to his eventual adoption of the push broom.
Clark's second visit to Paris, in the 1960s, led to another artistic innovation: the oval canvas. He considered this shape, which resembles a human
eye, a more accurate reflection of a human's field of vision. In the 1970s,
he superimposed the elliptical shape on to rectangular canvases, creating
subtle figure-ground relationships that provide a backdrop for the oval.
He explored this new compositional format in smaller works on paper
as well, including the etching *Untitled*, with its soft curves visible on the
upper and lower edges of the sheet of paper.

Although Clark returned to New York City, and it became his home base,
he continued to visit Paris throughout his life. He also traveled widely,
including to Taos, New Mexico. The earthen tones of the uneven bands
composing *Taos Series* suggest the distinctive desert landscape of the
southwestern United States. The darker palette he used to brush the
horizontal bands provides a striking contrast to *Untitled (Paris Series)*,
painted five years later. The colors and light that appear in his paintings
are unconscious responses to the places in which they were made.

Inspired by his years in Paris, Clark reconsidered the potential of the formal
elements of painting: brushstroke, surface, color, and light. He reinvigorated
these elements, seeing how they could be marshaled to create works
of art that embody the dynamism, vitality, and beauty of modern life.

— Eugenie Tsai

Randy Williams

b. 1947

Over a fifty-plus-year career as an artist, Randy Williams has offered a prolific understanding of the power of assemblage—the material practice of grouping together unrelated objects. Williams's practice was profoundly influenced by decades of teaching with the Metropolitan Museum of Art's collection and his work amid downtown Manhattan in the 1970s and 1980s. His mixed-media works form a visual encyclopedia through the combination of art historical references, objects found traversing the city, and text. Williams's work often includes backdrops made of found wood as a material ode to the artist's father's work as a carpenter, and *Tic Tac Doe* features wood partitions that create small vignettes. Assemblages by Williams are mini-lessons composed of materials symbolic of his experiences while also remaining open to interpretation, analogous to the close-looking Williams championed through his work in nonprofit institutions.

Tic Tac Doe bridges these two aspects of the artist's life's work with a title featuring a pun on the game tic-tac-toe and "DOE," the acronym for the phrase "depends on experience" often listed on job applications. Aptly, the work includes a blue book by Robert N. Anthony and Regina Herzlinger, *Management Control in Nonprofit Organizations* (1975). The lottery ticket embedded into the book is "symbolic of the altruistic probability of good fortune."[118] The ticket is also a vernacular symbol of chance—a component of Dada, the early twentieth-century art movement responding to the atrocities of World War I in which artists embraced chance and absurdism, and an art historical reference that Williams readily looks toward. The ticket sits above twine sprayed with gold and wrapped around a tree branch, alluding to the fabled idea of spinning straw into gold by making do. These elements suggest the good fortune that Williams found through arts institutions and his road into nonprofits with his version of "depends on experience," which was informed as much by carpentry and the streets of New York as his training and education.

—Lilia Rocio Taboada

Tic Tac Doe, 1983. Mixed media on wood, 42 × 55 × 6 in. Gift of the artist 1989.7

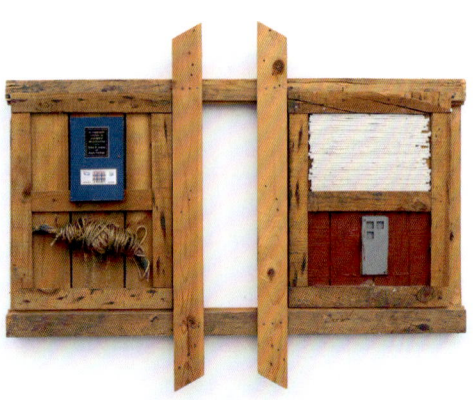

Sana Musasama

b. 1957   Artist in Residence 1983—84

Orange Interior, 1983. Painted ceramic, 44 × 12 × 14 ½ in. Gift of Alison Saar 1987.4

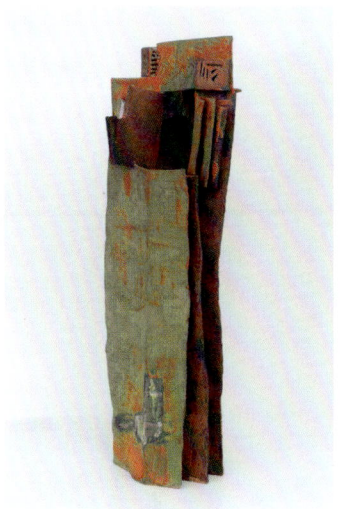

"Clay is everywhere," says ceramicist Sana Musasama, "and it is this ubiquity that makes it such a powerful communicator of cultural values."[119] For about fifty years, Musasama has centered clay as her sculptural medium, establishing a body of work that reflects a belief in clay's ability to encapsulate personal and social narratives. Upon graduating from City College of New York in 1974, the artist spent the following years honing her skills and artistic vision by traveling and participating in residencies, studying Mende pottery in Sierra Leone, and participating in a residency at the Archie Bray Foundation in Montana. Musasama spends years working through concepts, and in the 1980s, her oeuvre focused on home, architecture, and archeology—ideas that come together in *Orange Interior*.[120]

This work was created during Musasama's residency at the Studio Museum in Harlem from 1983 to 1984. A slab-built, faceted ceramic column, *Orange Interior* is painted mostly with green, charcoal gray, and orange, the paint appearing weathered and revealing the structure's foundation. The paint even appears "chalky," as curator Deirdre L. Bibby describes the artist's work of this period from another series, "Echoes & Excavations."[121] *Orange Interior* is a slightly bent and torqued tower with a folded element on one of its sides and a small perforated decorative structure capping off the object. During this period, the artist's involvement with a public arts organization and participation in an architectural ceramics seminar led to her desire to focus on the environment and find a universal symbol that was "communicative, cross-cultural, and panoramic."[122] Referring to these works as her "House" series, Musasama drew inspiration from the dwellings she lived in while in West Africa, Asia, and the Western United States. Here, she amalgamates many references into a single artwork yet centers the cross-cultural symbol of home.

—Zuna Maza

Lorraine O'Grady

1934–2024

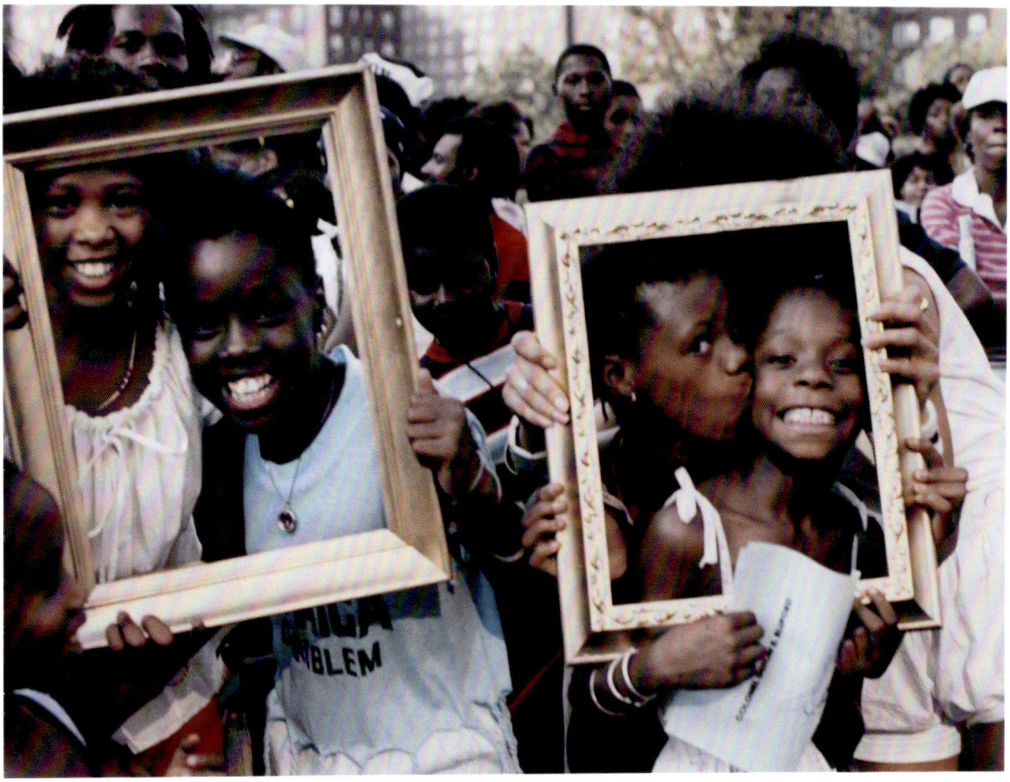

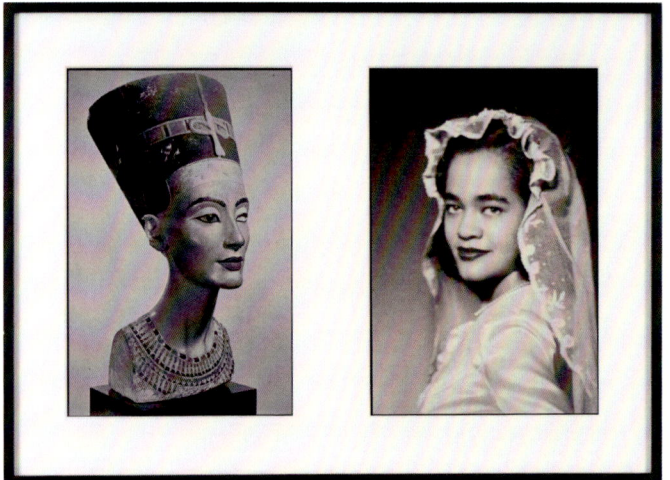

Above: *Art Is. . .(Girlfriends Times Two)*, 1983/2009. Chromogenic digital print, image: 16 × 20 in. Edition 4 of 8 + 1 AP. Bequest of Peggy Cooper Cafritz (1947–2018), Washington, DC, collector, educator, and activist 2018.40.240

Left: *Miscegenated Family Album (Sisters I), L: Nefernefruaten Nefertiti, R: Devonia Evangeline*, 1980/1988. Silver dye bleach photograph (Cibachrome), image (each): 20 × 16 in. Gift of Peg Alston 2010.19.1

Lorraine O'Grady called her practice a "writing in space," an apt entry point to understanding the artist's oeuvre as a manifestation of choreography, a word etymologically arcing from the Latinized Greek khoreia, "to dance," and graphia, "writing."[123] Her career, across a rich intersection of creative disciplines, kept the written word—and the scores that follow—as central protagonists that she spurred into action as collaborators, avatars, and coconspirators. O'Grady's foundational performance project *Art Is. . .*, which took place at Harlem's African American Day Parade in September 1983, applies this methodology directly. When an acquaintance declared that "avant-garde art doesn't have anything to do with black people," O'Grady took up the task to illustrate otherwise, with the streets of New York City as her inspiration.[124]

Amid the throngs of people celebrating their blackness at the parade, O'Grady traveled with fifteen actors and dancers all wearing white who held gold picture frames as they posed for pictures with Harlem pass- ersby. The group was also accompanied by a nine-by-fifteen-foot gilded antique-style frame mounted atop a gold-skirted float. In traveling along Adam Clayton Powell Jr. Boulevard, this float framed onlookers, connecting the proposition of "art is . . ." with "Harlem" definitively, with all its creative vibrance and rich history. In reflecting on the work, the artist recalls the people in the parade shouting, "We're the art!"[125] In the resulting photo- graph *Art Is. . .(Girlfriends Times Two)*, O'Grady challenges the frameworks of both who belongs within art historical traditions of representation and what shape a creative institution can take. By using gold frames typifying a canonized idea of museums as institutional settings and bringing Black people "into view" via the lines of the frame's visual edit, the artist makes plain the stark contrast between who is seen and who is rendered invisible within the vast arc of visual culture.

In the series "Miscegenated Family Album" the artist again reclaims the frame, this time deploying the diptych as a visual strategy and technique. This format exemplifies O'Grady's emblematic "both/and" approach used to push back at the binary of "either/or" and instead suggest an endless interconnectivity. The installation consists of sixteen diptychs selected from sixty-five image pairs that first appeared in her 1980 performance *Nefertiti/Devonia Evangeline*. The originating piece combined a projection of slides depicting the artist's late sister Devonia Evangeline with the unceasingly mythologized Egyptian royal Queen Nefertiti and both their families; O'Grady performed live in front of the images as they rotated in different combinations. O'Grady writes, "The female body in the West is not a unitary sign. Rather, like a coin, it has an obverse and a reverse: on the one side, it is white; on the other, non-white or, prototypically, black."[126] Through these bodies of work, the artist instructs the viewer to extend beyond a Western and Eurocentric readership of the Black form, complicating assumptions surrounding Black heritage and identity and the porous boundaries these histories traverse.

—Legacy Russell

Alison Saar

b. 1956   Artist in Residence 1983—84

Alison Saar grew up in a family of artists, each of whom made a profound impact on her art. Her mother, Betye, and older sister, Lezley, are celebrated artists whose work is also represented in the Studio Museum's collection; her father, Richard, was a ceramist and art conservator, and her younger sister, Tracye, is a writer. Saar is known for sculpture, installation, and prints that center the human figure, often women, often carved from wood—"figured but not figurative" as Thelma Golden wrote in 1992—and that are voracious in their art historical, literary, cultural, spiritual, and material references.[127]

Saar's turn to the figure happened at the end of her MFA at Otis Art Institute in Los Angeles. As she has narrated it, she completed her thesis work months early and so decided to make a work just for herself. Art historian Judith Wilson describes the resulting sculpture, entitled *Si j'étais blanc* (1981), as an "eloquent conflation of things African with things American."[128] Pleased with the result, Saar made all new work for her thesis and had her solo debut in June 1982 at Jan Baum Gallery in Los Angeles.

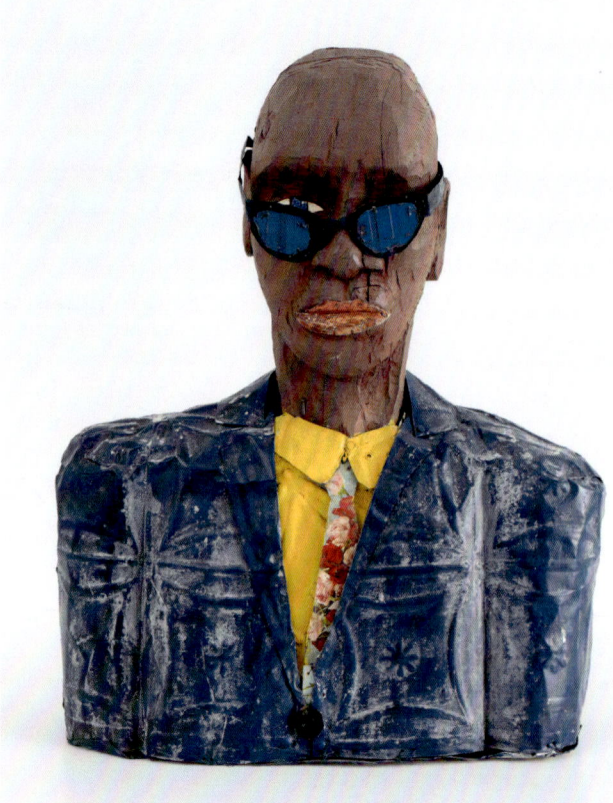

Bullit Head, 1984. Mixed media; metal, wood, tin, nails, 24 × 18 ¾ × 6 ½ in. Gift of Sana Musasama 1987.9

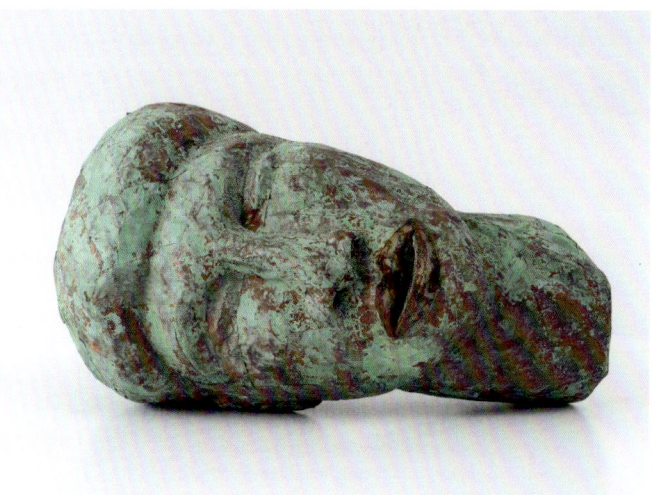

Soon after completing her MFA, Saar moved to New York. In 1982, Robert Blackburn invited her to work in his printmaking studio, and from 1983 to 1984 she was an artist in residence at the Studio Museum.[129] This time in New York was essential for Saar's creative development.[130] It was then that Saar began layering tin over her carved sculptures. Although she first used tin to make monotypes in a printmaking course as an undergraduate at Scripps College, in New York she incorporated stamped tin that had previously lined ceilings in townhouses around Harlem.[131] As she explained to curator Mary Nooter Roberts, she saw wisdom in this material that had witnessed so much of twentieth-century life in Harlem. Wrapping it around carved wooden pieces felt to her like creating a skin for the figures, with the patterned texture creating tactility and evoking scarification.[132]

Two works in the Studio Museum's collection, made a decade apart, evidence different ways Saar has employed this technique in her sculptures: *Bullit Head* and *Caldonia*. In the former, the marks from Saar's carving of the wood remain visible on the figure's head, neck, and opaque sunglasses, while she uses painted tin to create the figure's textured suit, shirt, and floral tie. With *Caldonia*, the entire sculpture is covered with tin, which has acquired a rich green and caramel patina. Consisting of a human head and neck lying on its right ear, *Caldonia* aligns with a number of works that Saar created in the mid to late 1990s in which she rotates the head ninety degrees to evoke a state between worlds. She later described it: "I always see [the turned head] as being either in reverie or in limbo, trancelike between two worlds, and I think that dream state is also between two worlds, that you're not here but haven't trespassed into the other thing."[133] Together, these sculptures speak to the material and conceptual reach of Saar's practice: artworks made from the stuff—even detritus—of this world that evoke the in-between worlds that her figures inhabit but, with their closed or covered eyes, do not necessarily welcome viewers to join.

—Emma Chubb

Jean-Michel Basquiat

1960—1988

Jean-Michel Basquiat's *Bayou* is one of many paintings inspired by the history of the Black Atlantic and Southern United States diasporas. The title points toward the artist's deep exploration of the Mississippi River as a charged site for the African diaspora in the United States. A metaphorical spine of the country, the Mississippi flows southward from Minnesota through New Orleans and into the Gulf of Mexico—what is known as the Mississippi River Delta—creating numerous bayous. Basquiat spent some time in New Orleans and considered it a central node in his construction of global blackness in the "New World."

This painting, like several by the artist, is still to be explored in deeper scholarly fashion. It may have been shown in January 1985 at Bruno Bischofberger Gallery in Zurich in a show of eleven works. The following year, *Bayou* was presented in Hanover, Germany, in one of Basquiat's early museum exhibitions. The show was subtitled "To Repel Ghosts," a phrase that appears frequently in the painting and is the title of at least two other works. "To Repel Ghosts" refers to the artist's belief in the spiritual nature of his work and in art as an incantatory device, something that can be used for protection in a cold, crude, and often cruel world. In this painting, that phrase emerges written and painted over in white, but remains legible, in the lower right corner.

"South" is also written and crossed out on both the left and right sides of the painting, emphasizing the locale's importance in the painting and the story the word tells of US history. The skinny green branches at top left and center right, by virtue of the painting's clues noted above, may conjure a "pastoral scene of the gallant South," as Billie Holiday sang in "Strange Fruit," the haunting song about lynching. Holiday's singing, her art, made beautiful creations out of evil histories, not unlike Basquiat's paintings.

—Franklin Sirmans

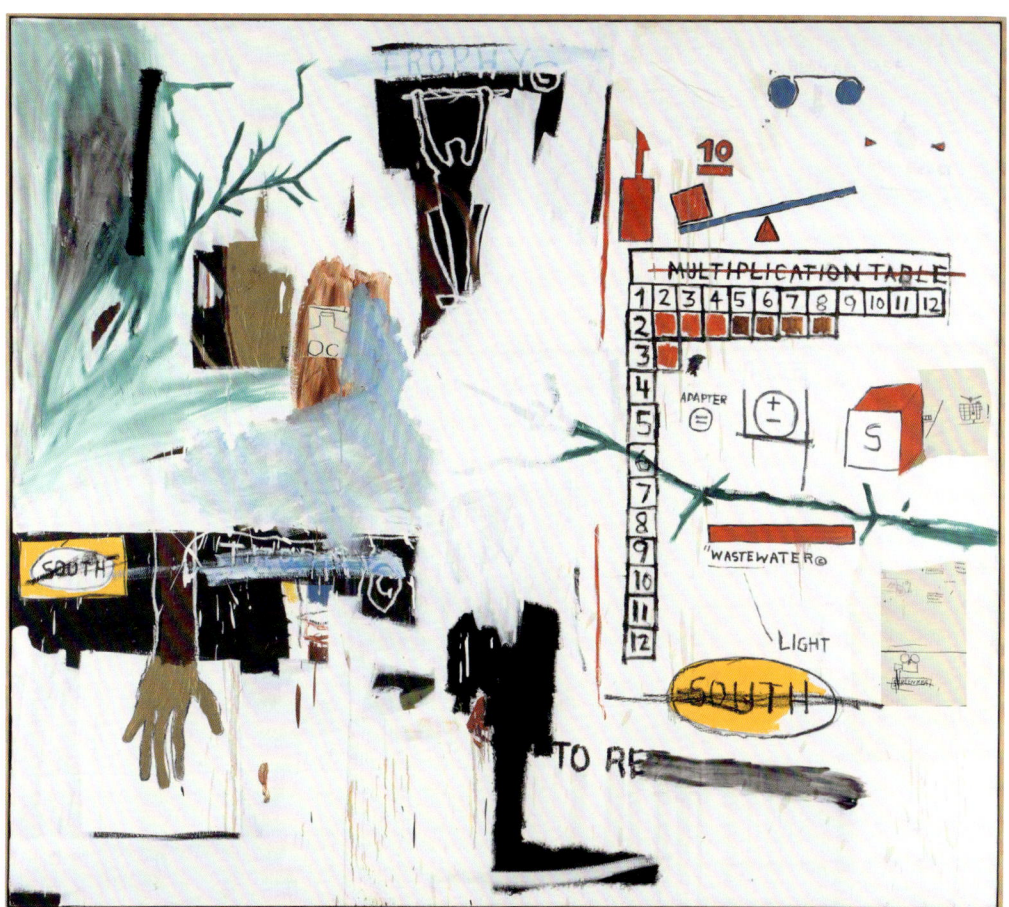

Bayou, 1984. Oil, acrylic, collage, and wax on canvas, 85 ¾ × 98 in. Gift of Joseph and Amy Perella 2023.23.1

Candida Alvarez

b. 1955   Artist in Residence 1984—85

COLLECTION

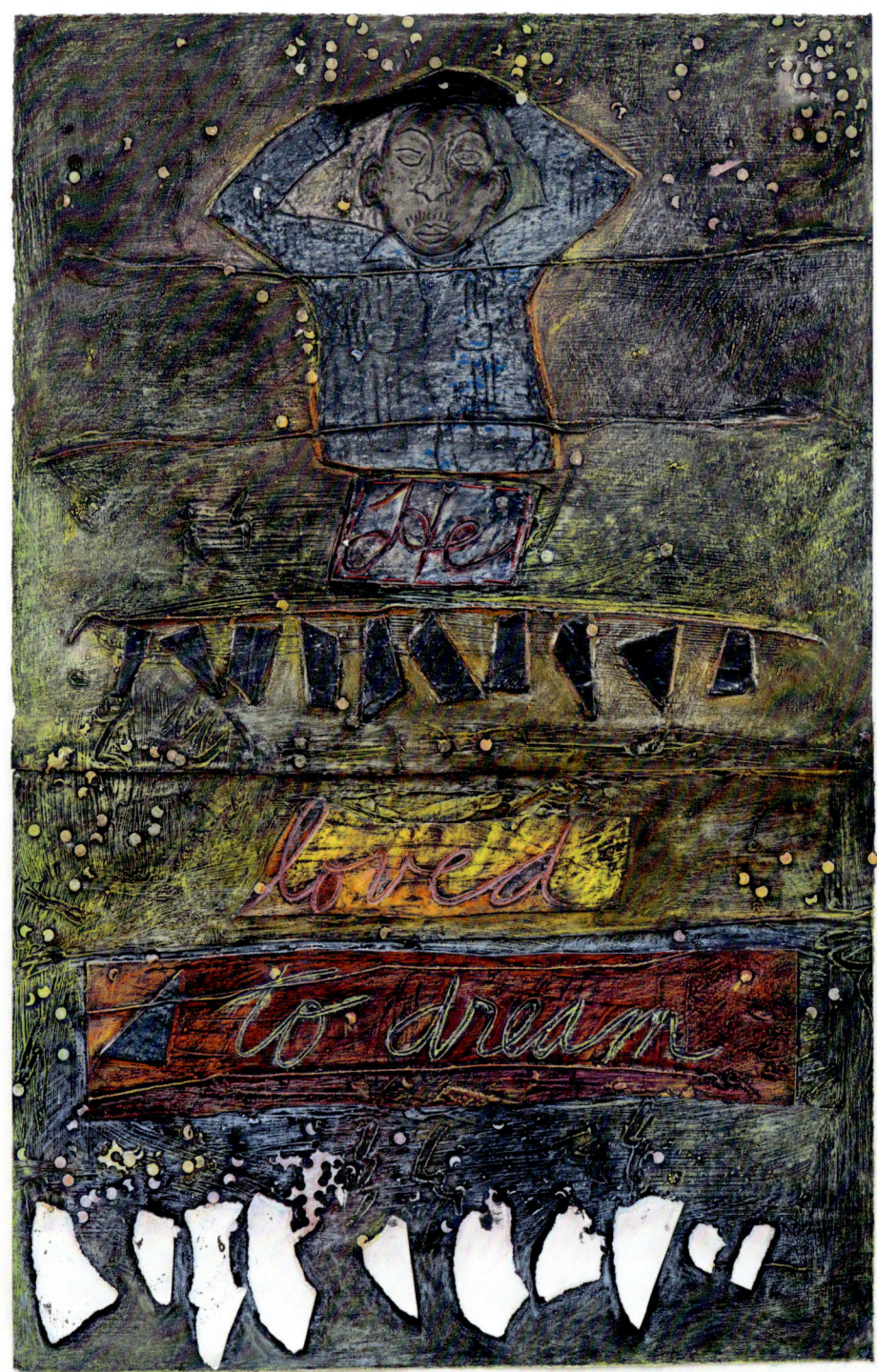

Created during Candida Alvarez's participation in the Studio Museum's *Artist-in-Residence* program, *He Loved to Dream* depicts the artist's late father, Maximino, enveloped in reverie. Through texture and a deep green and blue color palette, the artist renders a recurring childhood memory wherein her father would release his weight and, along with it, the residue of the day on to his favorite armchair. Alvarez recalls that he would place his hands at the nape of his neck and tenderly cradle his head, such that his arms took on a form that reminded her of wings.

She came to believe that this bodily arrangement allowed her sleeping father to take flight into his unbridled subconsciousness. Such a proposition led her to wonder where exactly he went when he closed his eyes—a question that informed her decision not to figure his likeness from an external point of view (as she did in another work by the same title) but to render him as if she were inside the dream with him. Long interested in exalting the magic entombed in seemingly ordinary acts and experiences, Alvarez positions sleeping as both a respite for the body and a technology of imagination that harnesses the existential mysteries lurking below the realm of that which is sayable, doable, and thinkable amid our waking hours.

He Loved to Dream also memorializes the intimacy between Alvarez and Maximino. A testament to the boundless subconsciousness she inherited from witnessing her father rest, this composition suggests the value of dreaming in the name of expanding one's self-perception and, by extension, the realm of possibilities one deems achievable.

—Camille Bacon

He Loved to Dream, 1985. Mixed media on paper, 29 × 19 in. Gift of the artist 1986.5

Kerry James Marshall

b. 1955   Artist in Residence 1985—86

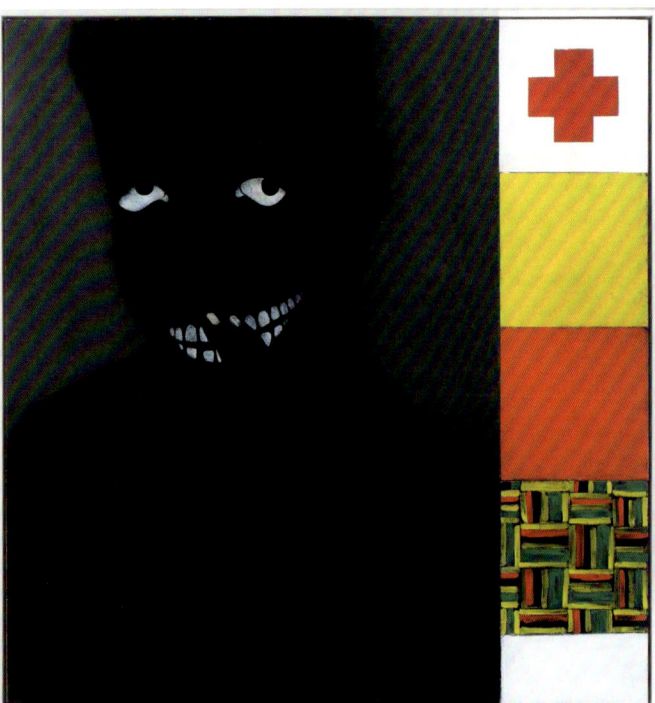

Silence is Golden, 1986. Acrylic on panel, 49 × 48 × 2 in. Gift of the artist 1987.8

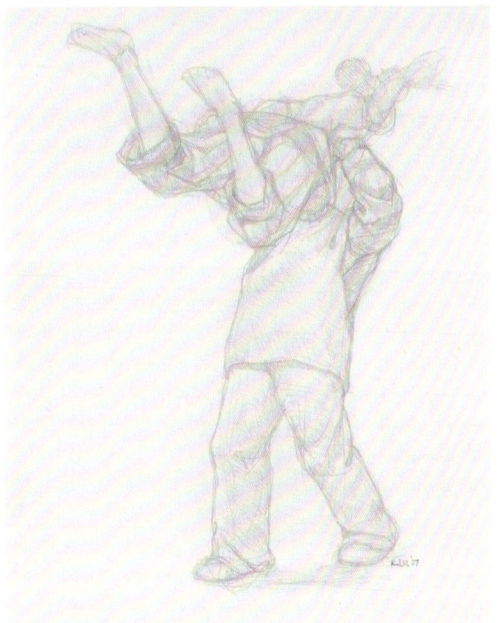

Untitled, 2007. Graphite on paper, image: 11 × 8 ½ in. Gift of anonymous 2014.14.6

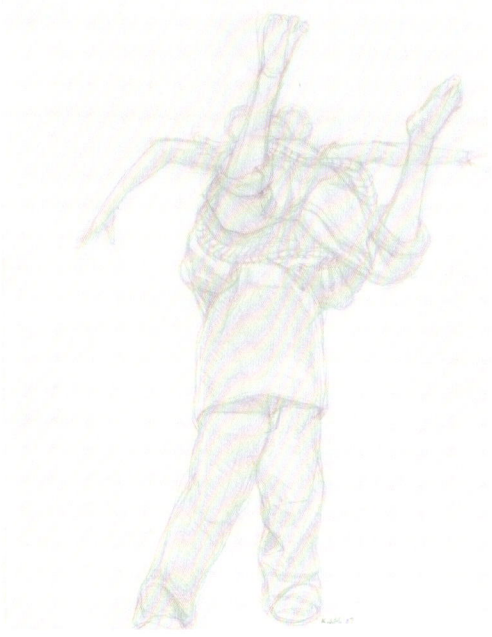

Untitled, 2007. Graphite on paper, image: 11 × 8 ½ in. Gift of anonymous 2014.14.7

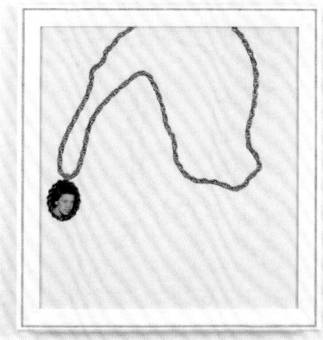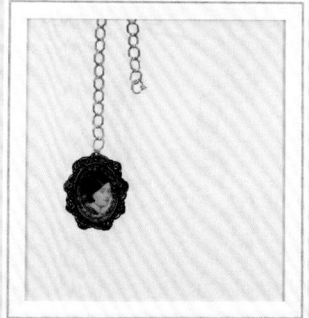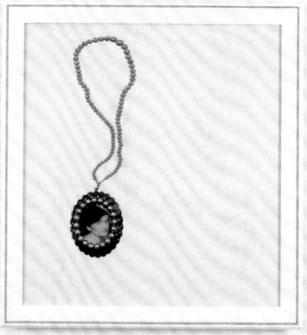

Heirlooms & Accessories (triptych), 2002.
Inkjet prints on paper with rhinestones
in wooden artist's frames, image (each):
51 × 46 in., frame (each): 57 × 54 × 2 in.
Museum purchase made possible by a gift
from an anonymous donor 2005.7a–c

Kerry James Marshall, who works in painting, sculpture, printmaking, and photography, intervenes in art history by replacing its focus on white Europeans with positive scenes of Black people who are variously and vibrantly alive. Marshall explicitly rejects depicting trauma in his work; in the inkjet prints *Heirlooms & Accessories (triptych)*, for example, he leaches out the image of lynching victims Thomas Shipp and Abram Smith from Lawrence Beitler's 1930 photograph. Instead, Marshall places in lockets the heads of three white women who were in the crowd. These lockets extend to hang, noose-like, from the lynching tree. Marshall's study of the Western art canon (along with reading Ralph Ellison's *Invisible Man* in 1980) taught him that what Western culture values is both visible and pointedly invisible. *Heirlooms & Accessories (triptych)* reverses the custom of depicting Black people's traumatic experiences, as well as hiding the complicity of white people, especially white women, in that trauma. Marshall's reframing points to the women as accessories to the lynching and to the inheritance of that collusion. A thin line of rhinestones frames each photograph, winking at the connection between visibility and value. With the rhinestones also emphasizing the surfaces, Marshall depicts value systems both in content and form.

The artist's works instruct viewers how to look. A pair of untitled drawings from 2007 modestly rejects the viewer's gaze. Each graphite drawing— from Marshall's "Vignette" series—depicts a different viewing angle of the same scene. A man swings a woman high in the air, her feet kicking above both their heads in a pose that reworks Jean-Honoré Fragonard's *The Swing* (c. 1767—68). Marshall places plainly dressed Black subjects where Fragonard painted white aristocrats in fineries. Fragonard's painting has the man brazenly looking up his beloved's dress mid-swing. One of Marshall's drawings situates its viewer in the lover's position—with the woman's open legs swinging toward the picture plane—except she is wearing pants. There is nothing salacious to see; here the potential violence in the Western gaze is both revealed and thwarted.

Marshall's practice can be read as a continuous proof: if Western art has taught his viewers how to look, then he can leverage the canon's methods to redirect the focus. After reading *Invisible Man*, he gave up making abstractions and collages and began painting Black figures as impossibly, richly black. One of the works he created during that period was *Silence is Golden*. While the particulars of the figure disappear into Marshall's flat, coal-black rendering of the torso, its facial features are almost brash and self-consciously minstrel-like. A careful viewer might see the thin curves of the figure's knuckles just under the arresting, contrasting center of the subject's face. Two white fingernails *shush* against a Cheshire cat smile, while the face is punctuated by eyes alternately laughing and coy. Silence is golden where invisibility has worth. The figure and the viewer share a joke, a secret: "If you can see me, don't tell." Somewhere between being rendered invisible and claiming invisibility lies personhood, Marshall seems to say. If it is there, he would be the artist to find it.

—Terence Washington

Lyle Ashton Harris

b. 1965

Situated within Lyle Ashton Harris's *Americas* triptych and his larger "Americas" series, *Miss America* features an unnamed Black woman with her face painted matte white. The textured black of brows, lashes, and darkly tinted, tightly pursed lips peek and punch through the paint as her face turns in a blur of clench-jawed motion. A slice of light bifurcates her body, which is nude save for a US flag hung across her collarbone and shoulders. In step with other works in the series and with Harris's broader preoccupations, the image's invocation of national personifications like the titular pageant queen or the Columbia figure—a virginal, feminized embodiment of the United States, draped in stars and stripes—invites a critical consciousness of how race and gender configurations are built into the history and very notion of nationhood. Moreover, it points to how such configurations lead to severe and multivalent consequences in the face of perceived deviance, failure, or illegibility. Complementing the critiques in *Miss America*, then, might be the figure of *Miss Girl*, another photograph in the triptych, depicting Harris dressed not only in whiteface but in the drag of a blond blunt-cut wig and color-saturated lips.

Harris worked on his "Americas" series at Wesleyan while studying with Hazel Carby. Beyond challenges to flat readings of figures such as the tragic mulatta, Carby and other Black feminist scholars write extensively on oppressively distorted views of Black women's sexual and subjective characters—as well as their access to a category of womanhood itself. This points viewers to the curiously strategic imprecision of *Miss America*'s whiteface. Where the white pigment dusts the subject's hair and draws the application and contrasting color into sharp relief, Harris perhaps nods wryly to the Black feminist practice of unmaking these distortions by pronouncing whiteness as a furtively silent and overdetermined qualifier of womanhood, beauty, sexual agency, and gendered citizenship.[134]

—Jakeya Caruthers

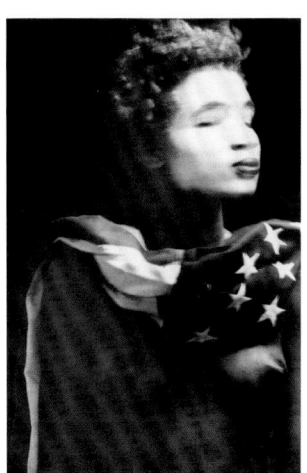

Miss America, 1987—88. Gelatin silver print, 30 × 22 in. Anonymous gift 2003.6.1

Nadine DeLawrence-Maine

1953—1992   Artist in Residence 1985—86

Nadine DeLawrence-Maine began experimenting with sheets of metal in 1986 while in the *Artist-in-Residence* program at the Studio Museum in Harlem. The artist wanted a method that translated her canvas works on to material that could easily take sculptural form.[135] In *Chamma*, she interlaces variously shaped aluminum panels into an abstract configuration covered in layers of paint. DeLawrence-Maine vacillates between broad swathes of color, thinly applied wisps of white and blue, and coarse textural swirls, revealing her formal training as a painter and a fondness for the exploratory and playful.

DeLawrence-Maine drew much of her inspiration from the craft and religious traditions of West and Southern Africa during a time when Black artists routinely looked beyond the United States for inspiration. Travel to Mali in 1979, and later to Botswana in 1990, further cultivated a burgeoning investment in looking to these regions for aesthetic guidance.[136] In *Chamma*, the artist's use of curvature and her calculated placement evoke a likeness to tribal masks and shields.

The word "chamma" (alternately spelled "shamma") refers to the toga-like garb long worn by populations in Ethiopia. It is also a colloquial term for the distance between the back of the heel and the tip of the big toe.[137] In the brochure for *From the Studio: Artists-in-Residence, 1985—1986*, DeLawrence-Maine describes her works of art—with their overlapping forms, techniques, traditions, and vocabularies—as "an exploration in to the multiplicity of dimensions of self."[138] Just as the artwork represents hybridity, coexistence, and discovery, the artist's chosen title may too speak to amalgamation. Rather than pointing to any one concept, "chamma" could very well be an invented word, further exemplifying DeLawrence-Maine's prowess with experimentation and the lexical.

—Alexandra E. Adams

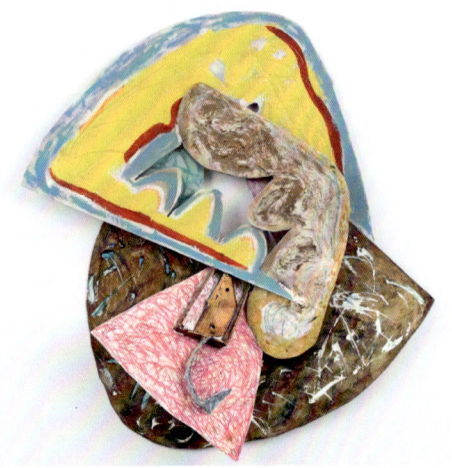

Chamma, 1987—88. Polychromed painted aluminum, 56 × 40 × 4 in. Gift of Mrs. Ruth DeLawrence 1995.7

Terry Adkins

1953—2014   Artist in Residence 1982—83

An artist and musician, Terry Adkins took an interdisciplinary approach
to his practice, often melding music, spoken-word performance, sculpture,
and video to create works that exist outside of the traditional bounds
of any one genre. In these works, Adkins used his deep knowledge of both
US history and a wide range of art and music traditions to forge new ways
of understanding and honoring the legacies of culturally significant, but
largely unheralded or underknown individuals. These individuals included
John Brown, the nineteenth-century abolitionist, and Matthew Henson, the
Black explorer of the Arctic in the late nineteenth and early twentieth centuries. In his early sculpture *Magus and Adnachiel*, the artist demonstrates
his extensive interest in mysticism and spirituality by referencing obscure
figures from ancient and astrological texts.

"Magus" is a word with several meanings, including in its plural form the
biblical wise men; but for this work, it more likely refers to a magician
or sorcerer of the dark arts. Adkins represents this figure in a dark wood
with black pigment covering the convex proper front. Adnachiel, the
guardian angel of independence and the zodiac sign of Sagittarius, is rendered in a blond wood with yellow pigment on the concave proper front.
While not directly related to music, the two forms evoke certain musical
instruments; they project a sense of movement and vibration even in their
stillness. Dark and light; outward and inward; danger and protection;
silence and sound—the sculpture embodies contradiction even as its
two components complement each other in shape and structure. The
side-by-side placement of these oblong forms suggests the expansive
and generative nature of Adkins's practice or, perhaps, the duality inherent
in all individuals.

—Connie H. Choi

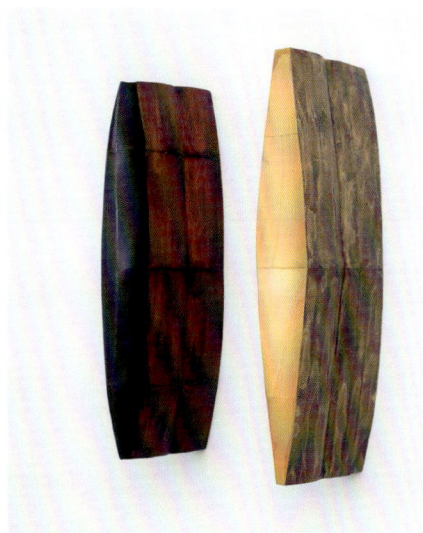

Magus and Adnachiel, 1988. Wood and
pigment, in two parts, left: 40 × 7 × 15 ¾ in.
and right: 38 ¾ × 7 × 11 in. Gift of Nina and
Frank Moore 2002.3

Cynthia Hawkins

b. 1950   Artist in Residence 1987—88

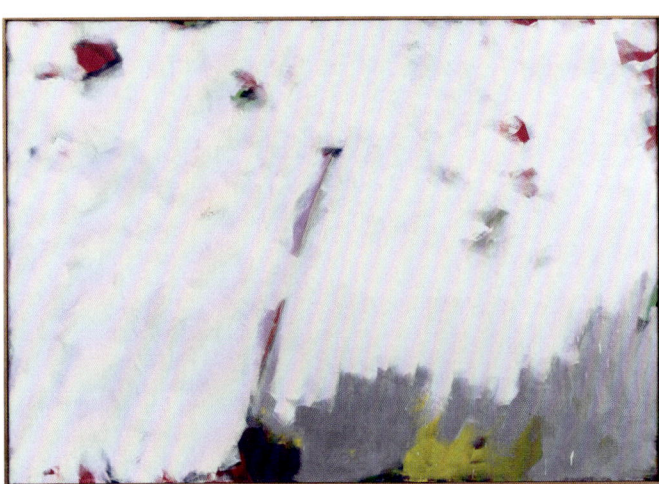

The Well, 1988. Oil on canvas, 66 × 96 in.
Gift of the artist 1989.3

Cynthia Hawkins's approach to abstraction is characterized by a distinct artistic language of motifs, colors, and forms. Hawkins's enduring interests in the environment, luminosity, and the cosmos guides the artist's intuitive approach to light, form, and color, as evidenced in a work such as *The Well*.

As an undergraduate student at Queens College and into her first years as an artist, Hawkins would take the train from her studio on Eighty-Third Street to visit the galleries on Fifty-Seventh Street and in SoHo, where she frequented the Black-owned galleries of the 1970s and 1980s. Despite the art world's barriers to artists of color and women, Hawkins actively visited and exhibited her work in galleries such as Just Above Midtown (JAM), Clocktower, Artists Space, Cinque Gallery, and Kenkeleba House. It was during her participation in the *Artist-in-Residence* program at the Studio Museum in Harlem, from 1987 to 1988, that *The Well* came into being.

In *The Well*, Hawkins employs swaths of white paint intersected by strokes of lavender, gray, lime, and lemon hues, revealing pentimenti. Denying translucency in her white paint, Hawkins affirms the potential of light in creating density instead of negative space. This painting reflects Hawkins's interest in the relationship between art and physics, as she experiments with paint's capacity to either respond to or resist the pull of gravity. The physical resistance and longevity of oil paint reveal Hawkins's experimental approach to abstraction that incorporates the environment as a material in its own right.

— June Kitahara

Lorna Simpson

b. 1960

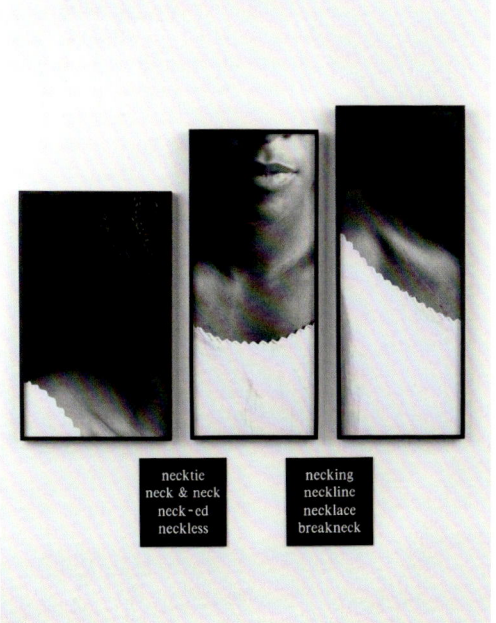

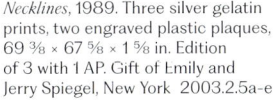

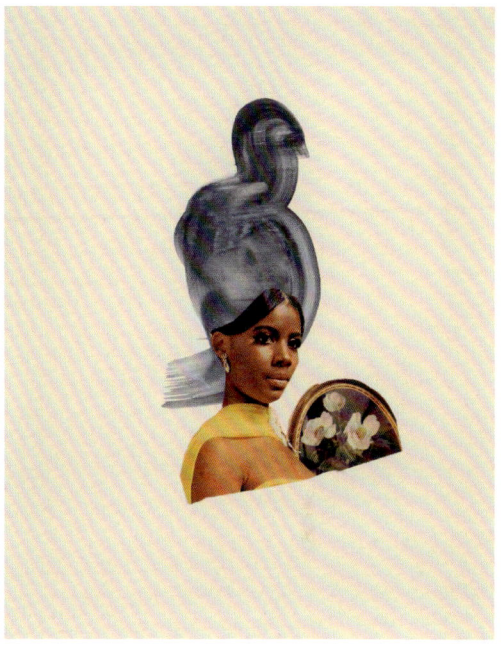

Necklines, 1989. Three silver gelatin prints, two engraved plastic plaques, 69 ⅜ × 67 ⅝ × 1 ⅝ in. Edition of 3 with 1 AP. Gift of Emily and Jerry Spiegel, New York 2003.2.5a–e

White Roses, 2011. Ink drawing and collage on paper, 11 × 8 ½ in. Gift of the artist on the occasion of the Romare Bearden (1911–1988) Centennial and *The Bearden Project* 2012.13.3

Lorna Simpson's artistic practice explores the complex interplay between power and visuality. Across her early photography, conceptual phototexts, and recent paintings and collages, Simpson challenges ideologies that posit the Black body as the visual index of racial difference.

Necklines illuminates the dynamics of race and gender that shape experiences of seeing and being seen, by inhibiting the viewer's access to the Black female body. Simpson makes portraits of part of a shoulder, the top half of the sternum, and the right collarbone. Challenging the myth of the passive observer, Simpson's withholding undermines the viewer's voyeuristic desires, which ascribe significations of race and gender on to the body. Below the images, Simpson affixes two panels that feature lists of words where all but one begins with the word "neck." Here, the signifying powers usually reserved for captions are displaced by the unruly web of associations between image and text. Whereas captions act as narrative frames, the texts in *Necklines* are more akin to poetry. Words like "Necktie," "Necking," and "Necklace" float, and at the end of the list, Simpson incorporates "neckless" and "breakneck," which conjure lynching and the gruesome display of broken Black bodies that served to maintain the racial order.

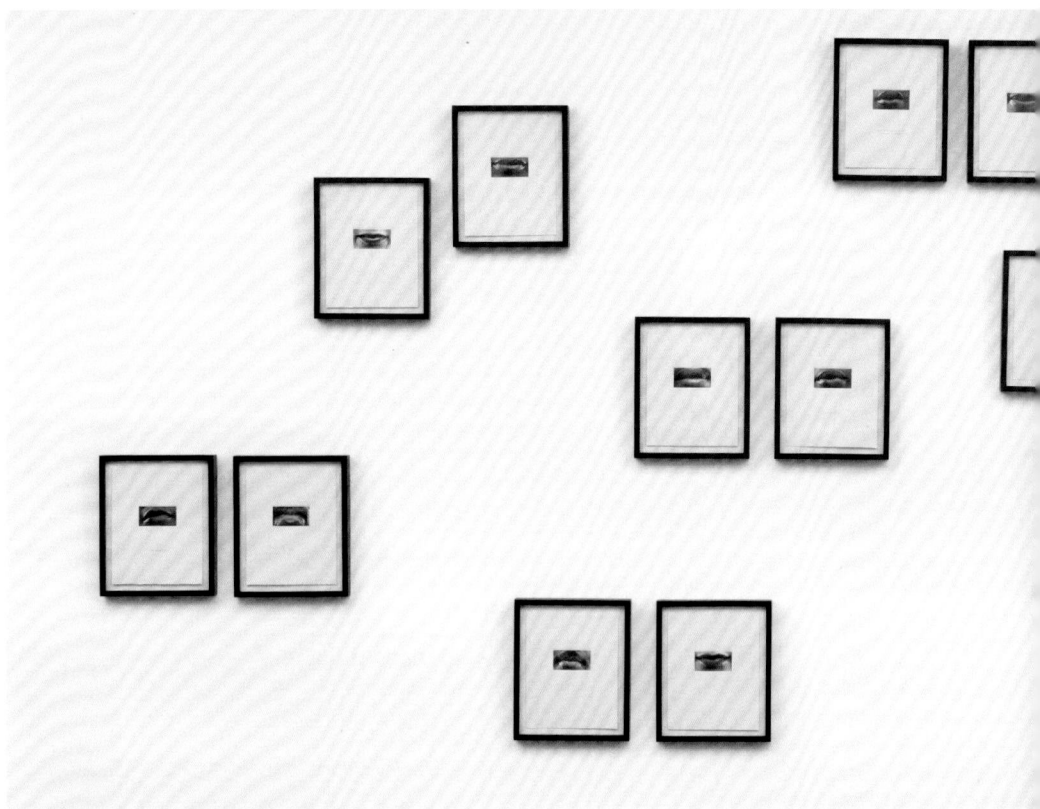

15 Mouths, 2002. Fifteen Iris prints on velour paper mounted on Hahnemuhle copperplate paper with letterpress text on each page (individually framed), image (each): 10 × 8 in. Edition 38 of 40 with 10 APs. Museum purchase with funds provided by the Acquisition Committee 2002.10.9a—o

Simpson also plays with the relation of image and text in *15 Mouths*. Her anti-captions resemble the labels used in science and medicine to evaluate and classify body parts. Yet when she pairs the images of lips with texts of ambiguous phrases, she frustrates science's perverse fascinations with the Black body—a commentary on techniques of observation and strategies of power that reduce Black people to objects of knowledge to be studied, prodded, and mutilated.

While departures from her earlier conceptual art, works such as *White Roses* and *Appeared* illustrate Simpson's continued concern with the ways power structures visual experience. In both artworks, Simpson uses images sourced from *Ebony* and *Jet* advertisements from the 1930s to the 1970s. She traces her interest in these images to her grandmother's collection of these Black publications, which, as she explains, not only "hearken back to my childhood, but are also a lens through which to see the past fifty years in American history."[139] In *White Roses*, Simpson crowns the head of a Black model with a shadowy purple ink wash that flares out behind her neck. The artist's mark-making amplifies subtle aspects of the found image—in this instance, the subtle depth established in the

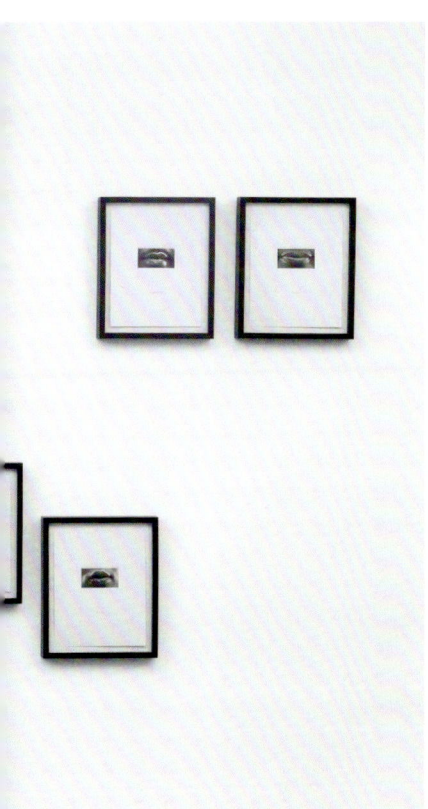

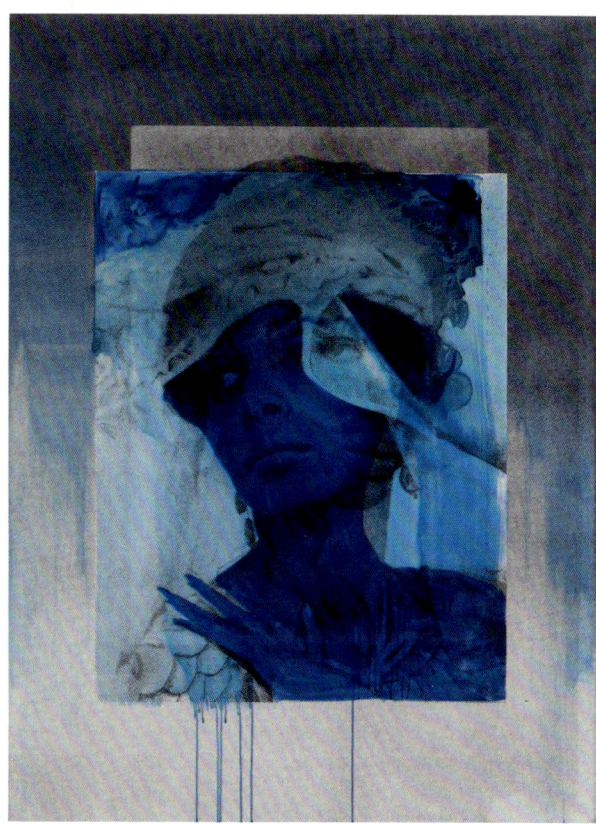

Appeared, 2019. Ink and screenprint on gessoed fiberglass, 67 × 50 × 1 ⅜ in. Museum purchase with funds provided by Rodney Miller 2020.15

two-dimensional image by the picture of white roses in the background. As with her allusion to this spatial dimension, Simpson is drawn to show how context is encoded in the found images. For example, consider the positioning of the face and model's expressions in *White Roses*. Whether joyful, aloof, or, as in this instance, reserved, Simpson treats the model's look as a window into the past. "I found [the images] really satisfying to look at," she explains, "because they're so contextual—from a particular time and for a particular audience."[140] Whether through the unique glimpse into past worlds, as she offers in *White Roses*, or through the "surreal portraits" like *Appeared*, in which faces blur into a spectral plane, Simpson's experiments with found images cultivate novel ways of looking at history.[141]

—Nijah Cunningham

Beverly Buchanan

1940—2015

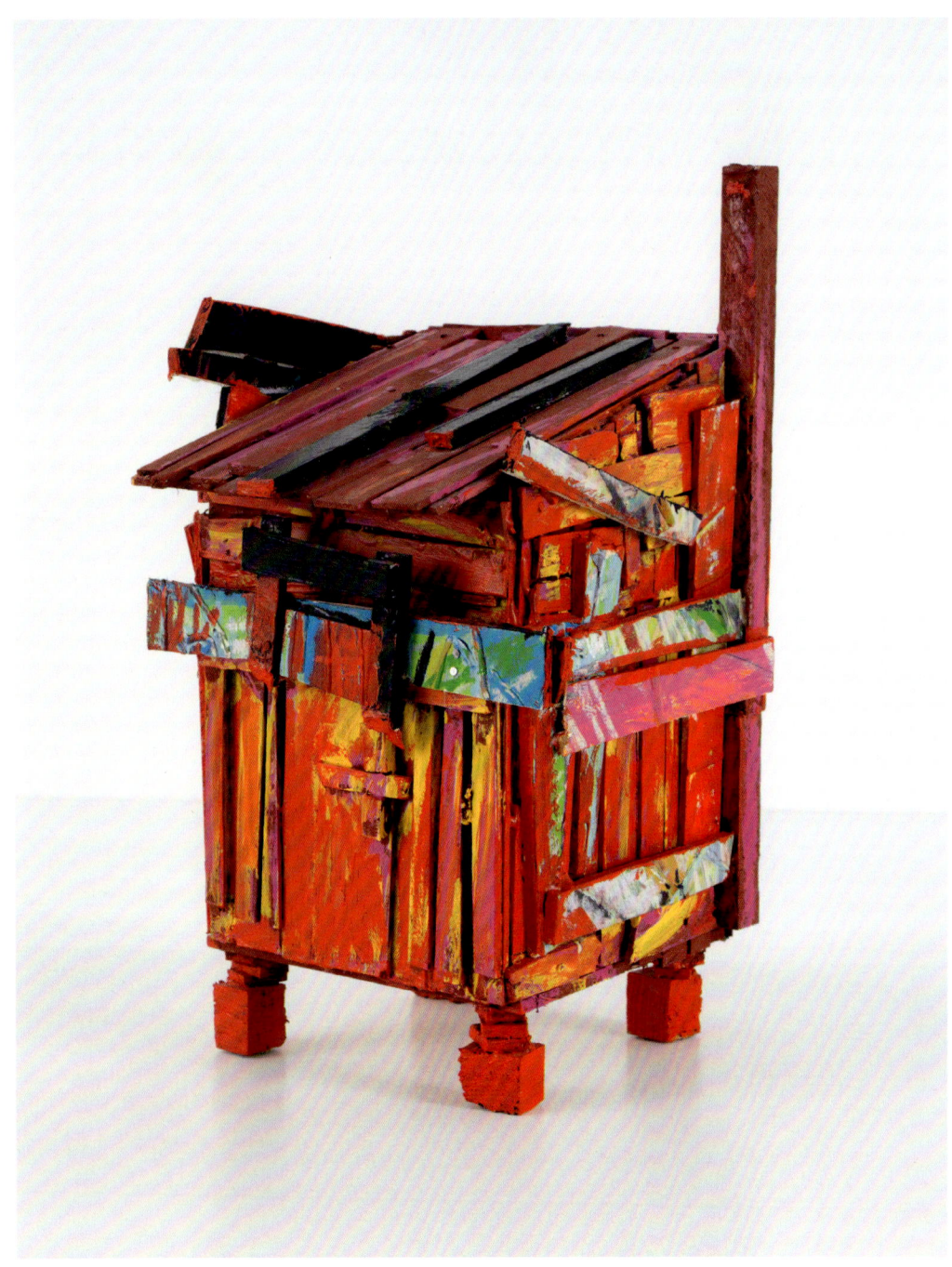

Sassy Shack, 1989. Painted wood
construction plus foam core,
14 ¼ × 8 × 7 ⅜ in. Gift of Lowery
Stokes Sims 2000.3.1

Sassy Shack stands nimble on four hoof-like stilts. The dwelling comprises wooden slats placed in ad-hoc uniformity and is painted with scribbles and blocks of color in rhythmic precision. *Sassy Shack* sways as if lifted by a strong wind; it is dancing. It is a disco shack of all colors.

Buchanan tenderly documented the houses, via memory and notes, that she passed while roaming her home state of Georgia in her pickup truck. This resulted in a series of works that spanned from 1985 to her passing in 2015. Through photographs and writing, she narrates the lives of the inhabitants with an unclear line between fact and fiction—the truth held in suspension. Buchanan's documents are now held in the Smithsonian's archive; they are a gift of insight into her methodical practice. The shacks are not so much a carbon copy of what she has seen, but through color and gesture, they amalgamate all that was sensed, known, observed, and recorded—a personal and collective archive. The shacks betray inherited vernaculars of unwieldy architectures vital to slave-descended communities across the Americas and the Caribbean, where iterations continue to stand as homes to this day.

Buchanan noticed the often disregarded, as Alice Walker shared in her poem dedicated to Buchanan:

To see the shacks,
You rescued from our shame,
And transformed with your wit,
Small nails, old boards,
And paint.[142]

Buchanan describes the earthly compounds that make up our common habitats. They conjure my childhood Victorian brick home in London, England, with its outdoor toilet-turned bathroom accessed by a corrugated-plastic roofed alleyway made by my Jamaican dad. He cut holes all over the house to let the light shine in, a metaphor for resistance. It was not until I reached Jamaica in my late twenties that I understood the root of these memories. How are the stories of flesh and psyche told through architecture?

—Phoebe Collings-James

Inge Hardison

1914—2016

The Making of a Legacy: Albert A. Diop,
Tribute to 20 Years of Service, 1970—1990,
1990. Bronze, 19 × 11 × 11 in. Gift
of Geri Ruth-Diop from the estate
of Albert A. Diop 2018.39

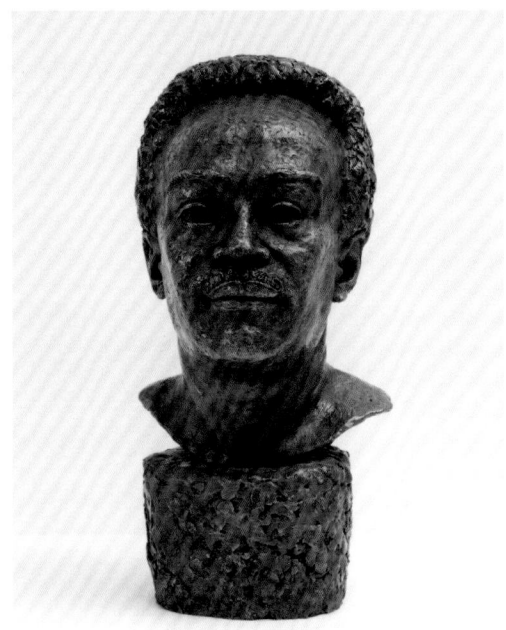

Sculptor Inge Hardison celebrated Black achievements through portraiture made with clay, wax, or plaster molds, which were then cast in stone or bronze. Born in Virginia but spending most of her life in New York, Hardison began her career as a Broadway actress. She later turned to sculpture, studying at the Art Students League under modernist painter and sculptor William Zorach. In 1963, she received critical acclaim for her sculpture series "Negro Giants in History," which included likenesses of W. E. B. Du Bois, Frederick Douglass, and Harriet Tubman. She made other notable series throughout her long career, such as "Ingenious Americans," which featured portraits of Black inventors, and "Our Folks," a collection of sculptures of everyday people.

The Women's Committee of Local 1549 commissioned *The Making of a Legacy: Albert A. Diop, Tribute to 20 Years of Service, 1970—1990* to honor Albert Diop, a then powerful member of New York City's influential District Council 37 union. The sculpture is typical of Hardison's oeuvre: highly naturalistic with careful attention paid to every detail of Diop's visage, including his deep inset eyes, receding hairline, and broad forehead. Diop's expression is one of quiet calm as his face is frozen just as he starts to smile. The bronze bust is roughly textured, like most of her sculptures, calling attention to the medium and adding a sense of tactility to the work. Like Hardison's other work, *The Making of a Legacy* is rendered in an exacting likeness.

—Eliza Butler

Willie Cole

b. 1955   Artist in Residence 1988—89

Willie Cole's *Domestic ID II* features scorches of twelve steam irons on paper affixed to two window frames. Arranged in a three-by-four grid, the scorches in this work share a common, recognizable form, yet also contain differences that grant each an individuality; some bear extensive markings and patterns, some are darker around the edges, and some are plain, save for a few small unburnt circles. The almond-shaped outlines resemble faces, thus prompting the viewer to discover other forms within the composition—circles become open mouths, and lines become scars or adornments.

The form of the iron is suffused with layered meaning when repurposed in this piece. Cole, who began using irons in his work in 1988—the same year that his residency at the Studio Museum in Harlem began—employs the motif for its visual similarity to Dan masks from the Ivory Coast and Liberia, and for the thematic connections to his family's history of domestic labor, as suggested by the work's title. In searing the paper with the iron's heat, Cole imprints the surface of *Domestic ID II* with converging legacies that simultaneously look inward, toward past familial generations, and outward, toward the arts and culture from the wellspring of the Black diaspora. By placing these legacies behind a window frame, Cole opens a portal—we look through, perhaps seeing other faces, or perhaps seeing ourselves reflected.

—Simon Ghebreyesus

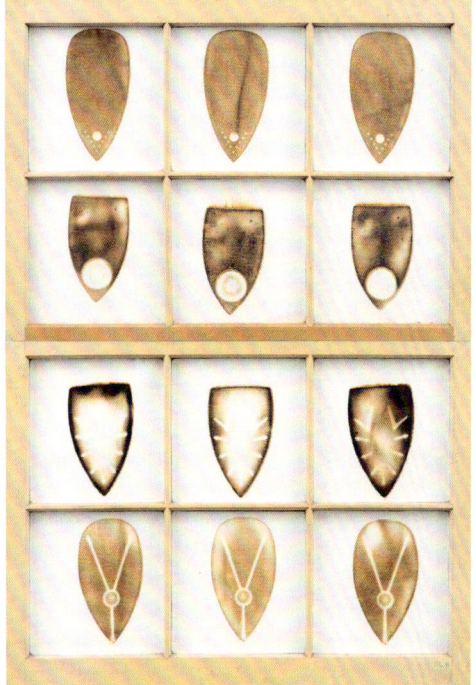

Domestic ID II, 1991. Iron scorches on paper in two double-panel window frames, 52 × 35 ¾ × 2 in. Gift of Martin and Rebecca Eisenberg 2012.27a-b

Thornton Dial

1928—2016

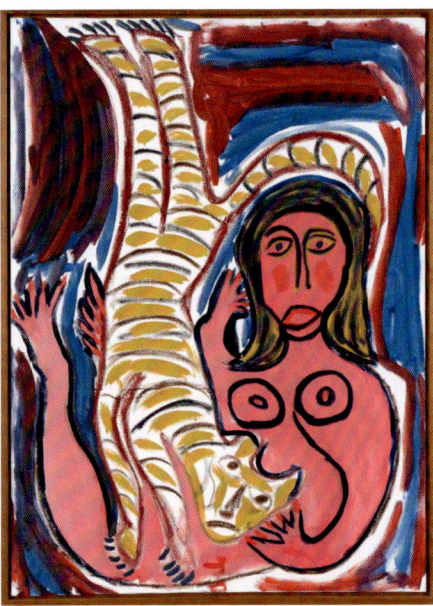

Lady Holds Her Tiger, 1991. Acrylic on canvas, 48 × 36 in. Gift of Ron Shelp, New York 1992.10.1

In *Lady Holds Her Tiger*, a nude woman rendered almost entirely in red acrylic engages in a full-frontal encounter with her viewer. An outstretched tiger, with the same simplicity of line and color as its human companion, falls into the woman's lap. The cat's body covers portions of the woman's as if a shield, and the animal also meets the spectator's gaze.

Thornton Dial repeatedly included wildlife in his artwork, typically depicting a central woman figure surrounded by cascades of bright color. His roosters, birds, fish, and tigers often functioned as proxies for Dial as he explored the complexities of identity, especially as it concerned his experiences as a Black man living in the rural South.[143] In interviews, Dial noted the influence of his upbringing on his work. His paintings reflect a childhood surrounded by farm animals, demonstrate a deep reverence for the women who raised him, and examine his relationship to manhood and masculinity by way of whimsical visual scapes.[144]

Lady Holds Her Tiger displays the figurative expressionism for which Dial was known. While Dial did not receive formal artistic training, one can see through his uses of color and his exaggerated, affective style the artist's penchant for gestural techniques and his dedication to physicality as a compelling compositional method.[145] As is common in the artist's work, the relationship between the figures is not entirely clear—is the tiger meant to be a protector, a figment of the woman's imagination, or does their relative positioning suggest Dial's commentary on eroticism and dynamics of power?

—Alexandra E. Adams

Frank Stewart

b. 1949   Artist in Residence 1975—76

Whether they are practically gazing into the lens or averting the moment of being photographed, the subjects in Frank Stewart's photographs play a lead role in the artist's image-making process. Subjects, composition, and framing are the unifying elements and mainstays of an image made by Stewart. His careful intentions are displayed in what he sees and then decides to capture.

Across his practice, dating back to his first images from the March on Washington for Jobs and Freedom in 1963, he sensed the importance of framing—knowing the moment to insert and then withdraw. Over the years, Stewart learned from other authorities in photography to hone his skills, including folks such as Roy DeCarava, Joel Meyerowitz, and Garry Winogrand. Particularly, DeCarava's landmark work *The Sweet Flypaper of Life* (1955), a collaboration with writer Langston Hughes, encouraged Stewart to seek DeCarava for mentorship. Stewart's interest in people, and more importantly Black life, led him to align himself with organizations such as the Kamoinge Workshop, a New York—based collective of Black photographers. The group established a set of "aesthetic goals based on shooting, timing, framing, and darkroom techniques," rules that Stewart took up, especially those concerning frame and focus.[146]

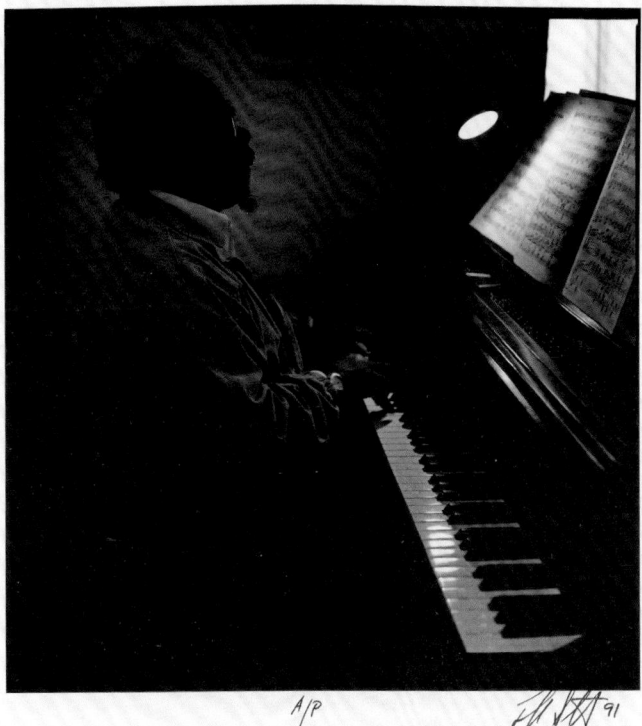

Untitled, 1991. Gelatin silver print, sheet: 14 × 11 in. AP. Gift of Joy of Giving Something, Inc. 2018.47.26

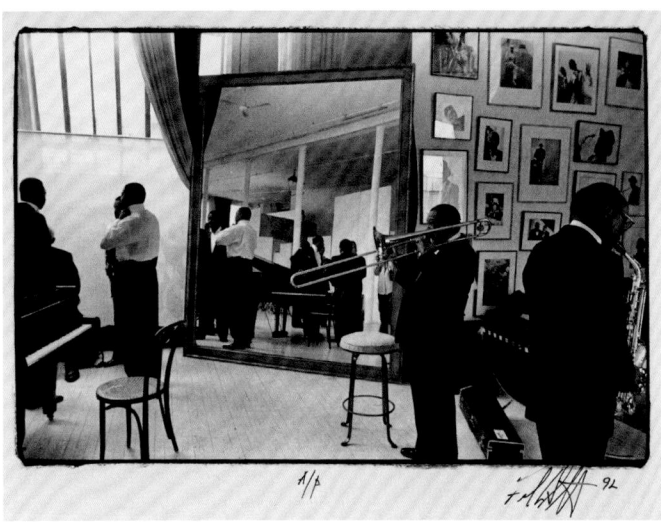

Untitled, 1992. Gelatin silver print, sheet: 11 × 14 in. AP. Gift of Joy of Giving Something, Inc. 2018.47.29

Many of those signature elements, aesthetics, and focuses began to show up in the work Stewart created during the three decades he spent as the senior staff photographer at Jazz at Lincoln Center (JALC). In *Untitled* (1992)*,* Stewart photographs a group of jazz musicians, surviving members of Duke Ellington's orchestra and Wynton Marsalis's septet. Careful to frame each subject, he positions everyone in the photograph in a way that guides the viewer's eyes across the image plane. To the immediate left, three men stand and another sits in conversation. Stewart himself is captured briefly in the large mirror that splits the image into thirds. Then, the slide of the trombone shifts the viewer's focus to the foreground. With his back turned, the figure on the right playing the saxophone denotes that this might be where the image abruptly ends. But, moving to the various photos along the wall, one could also argue this is where the image begins. The inclusion of the framed photos is intentional; there is a push between both background and foreground, past and present. The mirror and photos pull us into a refracted reality.

In contrast, works such as *Untitled* (1991) explicitly highlight Stewart's admiration for the chiaroscuro technique of depicting the extreme differences between light and darkness. He captures a strip of light from the lamp as it falls on to the piano, only illuminating music sheets and keys. The seated man playing the piano seems to float into, or out of, the darkness.

Former Studio Museum in Harlem director Mary Schmidt Campbell says, "Stewart's photographs are never evidence; rather they are invitations to remember time, places, and people—whether those are circumstances in which people are trapped or alone. In extending the invitation, he is inviting us to know these people, places, and situations."[147]

—Jayson Overby Jr.

Selma Burke

1900—1995

Primarily known as a sculptor, Selma Hortense Burke was famously commissioned to create the bas-relief portrait of Franklin Delano Roosevelt that became the inspiration for the president's likeness on the dime. Born in North Carolina in 1900, Burke saw her career span sixty years, from 1935 during the Harlem Renaissance until 1995, when she passed away. She focused on arts education all her life, and opened the Selma Burke School of Sculpture in 1940, and the Selma Burke Art Center in Pittsburgh, which operated from 1968 to 1981. There, she taught scores of children the skills and relevance of art making, as well as good citizenship and self-determination. Her final sculpture, a nine-foot bronze memorial statue of Martin Luther King Jr., was completed in 1980.

Made only two years before her death, *Butterfly* marks a departure in Burke's oeuvre. In this print, a butterfly hovers amid dense morning glory vines, which get their name from their response to the morning sun. Burke's butterfly's bright red, orange, and green wings draw the eye to the center of the composition. She flattens the picture plane such that the flora and fauna are pushed up—rather than back—toward a hidden horizon. Though rendered in two dimensions, this print bears many similarities to Burke's sculptures. The closely packed and overlapping curves of the leaves, through which the flowers push their throats forward toward the light, recall the sinuous curves of the feminine form that Burke repeatedly etched into stone.

—Key Jo Lee

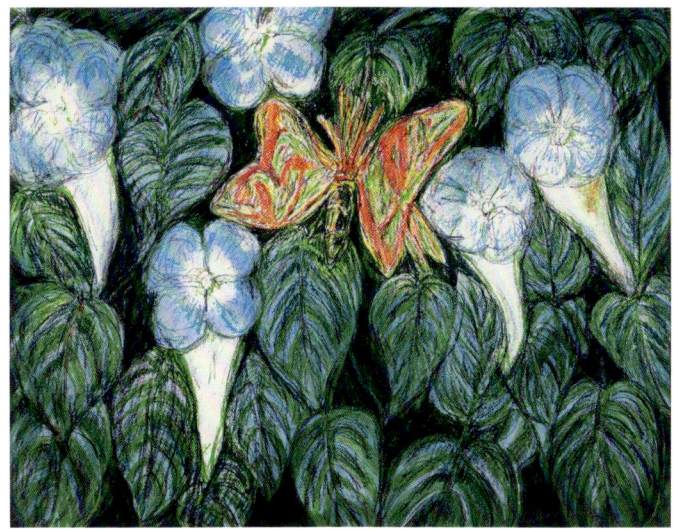

Butterfly, 1993. Silkscreen on paper, 19 ½ × 35 ½ in. Edition 100 of 150. Gift of Vivian D. Hewitt 2012.31.2

Gary Simmons

b. 1964

Gary Simmons's conceptual practice sits at the intersections of visual culture and collective memory, uncovering forgotten or willfully ignored social histories. Well-versed in pop culture, Simmons critically redeploys appropriated images to reveal the traces of racism and classism that remain hidden in plain sight within United States material culture.

In the early 1990s, Simmons honed his signature erasure technique in a series of works executed in white chalk on slate boards. Pairing icons from children's entertainment with the pedagogical connotations of the chalkboard, Simmons reveals how the educational system shapes our entrance into the world of racial ideas. His earliest chalkboards confront the racist stereotypes embedded in cartoons from the 1930s to 1950s, which were often based on the caricatures developed in minstrel shows. *Green Chalkboard (Toothy Grin)* features a haloed figure with a bone threaded through a wisp of hair. Bearing a stupefied grin punctuated by a prominent bucktooth, the character evokes the passive and foolish Sambo stereotype. After completing each chalk drawing, as with *Green Chalkboard (Toothy Grin)*, Simmons effaces the image by dragging his hands across the chalkboard surface in a pointed act of rupture that undermines the potency of such stereotypes.

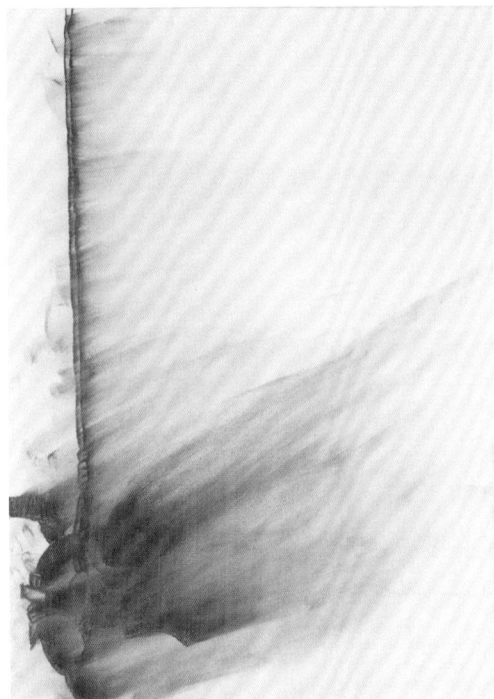

Study for Swingin', 1993. Charcoal and gesso on paper, image: 28 × 20 ¼ in. Gift of Martin and Rebecca Eisenberg 2011.11.11

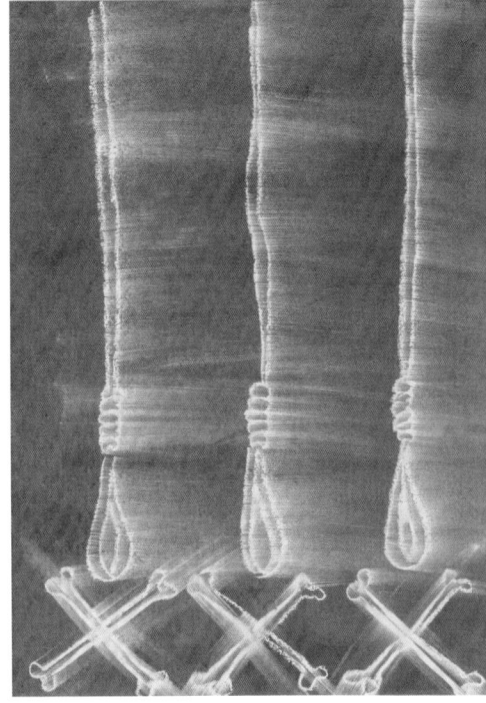

Untitled, 1997. Gouache and chalk on paper, 28 × 20 ⅛ in. Bequest of Peggy Cooper Cafritz (1947—2018), Washington, DC, collector, educator, and activist 2018.40.304

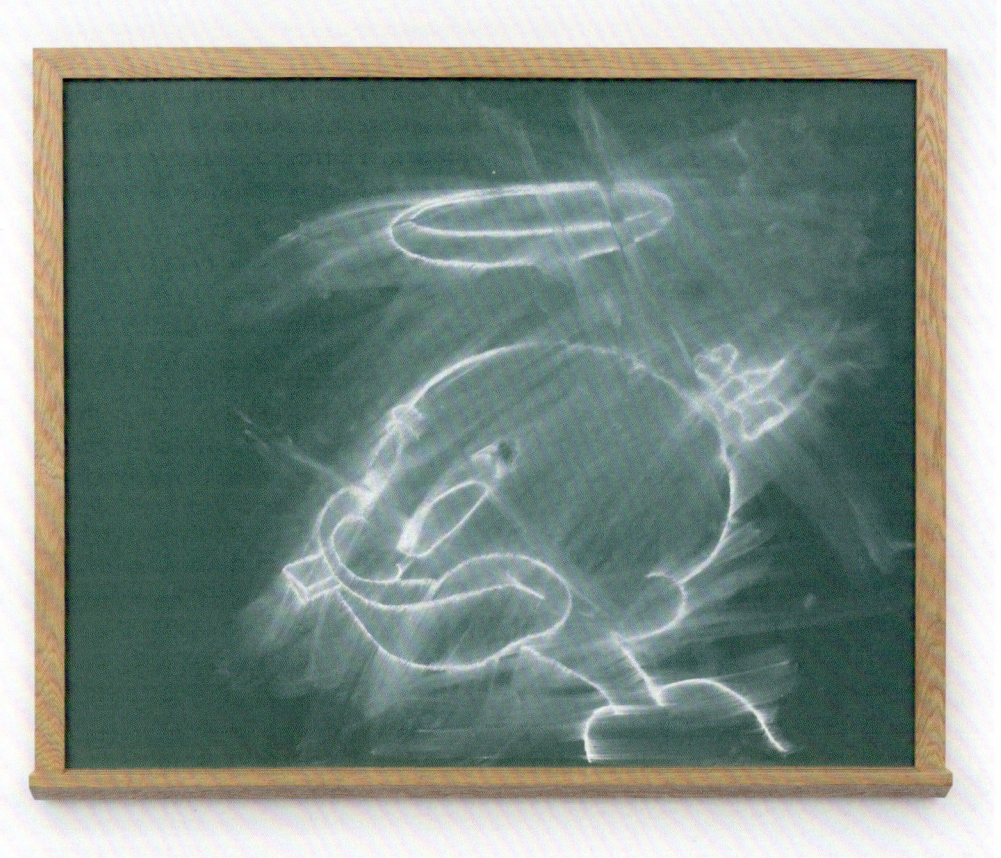

Green Chalkboard (Toothy Grin), 1993.
Chalk, fixative, chalkboard paint,
fiberboard, and wood, 48 × 60 × 3 ¼ in.
Gift of Zoë and Joel Dictrow, New York
2005.16

In subsequent works, Simmons executed drawings on the wall, engaging in a direct dialogue with the architecture of the institution. Underlining the concept of erasure, these ephemeral works exist only for the duration of an exhibition and are eventually painted over. *Study for Swingin'* is a preparatory sketch for a wall drawing. The work relates to the *Little Ol' Bosko* MGM cartoon series featuring Bosko, a little Black boy with exaggerated features who must deliver a bag of cookies to his grandmother. On his wild adventures, he always encounters a sinister band of frogs who attempt to steal his cookies. Depicting a frog hanging from a swinging rope, *Study for Swingin'* references a scene in which a jazzy frog is hanged from the ship's bow in "Little Ol' Bosko and the Pirates." The charged symbol of the noose appears in several of Simmons's works, including *Untitled*, wherein three isolated ropes appear above three crossbones. In both pieces, Simmons points to the racial violence often embedded in cartoons.

In the early 2000s, Simmons's visual repertoire expanded beyond cartoons; works such as *Lean/To* delve into the iconography of the rural South. This pastel drawing depicts a simple log cabin leaning at a strong angle. Horizontal smears evoke motion to conjure a structure fighting against gale-force winds in a futile attempt to remain standing. Simmons returns to the cabin as a motif often in a further investigation into potent oppositions—urban versus rural, North versus South, for example—that undergird cultural constructions of otherness.[148]

In 2020, after a nearly thirty-year hiatus, Simmons returned to the cartoon imagery of his early career. *More to the Point* revisits the character Bosko with heightened urgency. Set against a white ground, the painted figure yells and points to something outside of the canvas frame, as if demanding a call-to-action. Simmons's revisitation of his earlier references underscores the weathered truth that while so much has changed, so much remains the same. In this way, the artist's work insists that memories that seem too contested or too traumatic to ever truly be settled are the very ones we must resolve to stare down.

—Jadine Collingwood

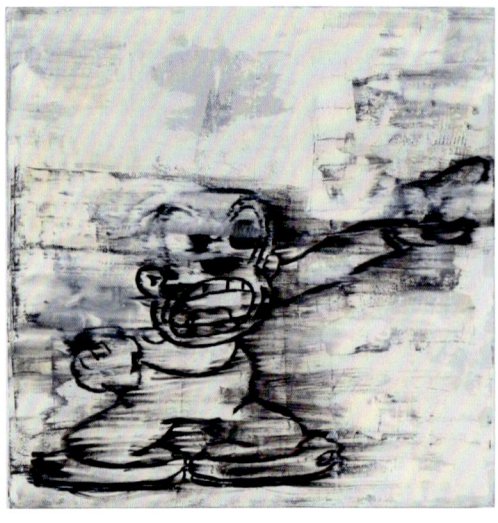

Lean/To, 2000. Pastel on vellum, 51 ¼ × 51 ½ in. Museum purchase with funds provided by the Acquisition Committee 2002.23.18

More to the Point, 2020. Oil and cold wax on canvas, 60 ¼ × 60 ⅜ in. Museum purchase with funds provided by Neda Young 2020.14

Fred Wilson

b. 1954

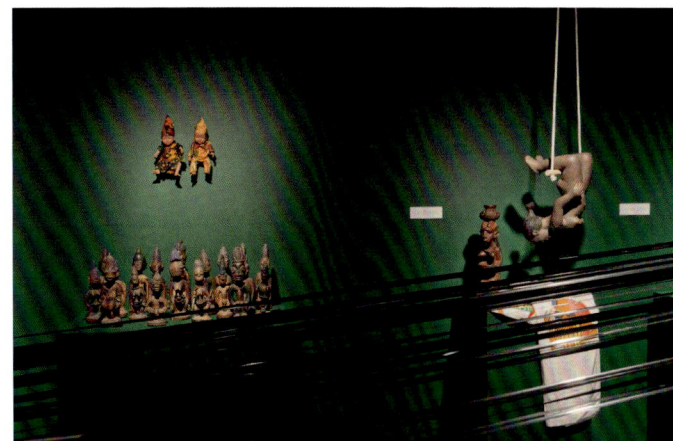

Local Color (installation view), 1993. Twenty-four African and Caribbean objects from the Studio Museum in Harlem collection, two plastic dolls, carved wooden standing figure, brass mask, wood mask, folding table, T-shirt, video cassette, video monitor, VCR, unreeled videotape, and thirty-two empty video tape boxes, dimensions variable. Gift of Fred Wilson 2009.12

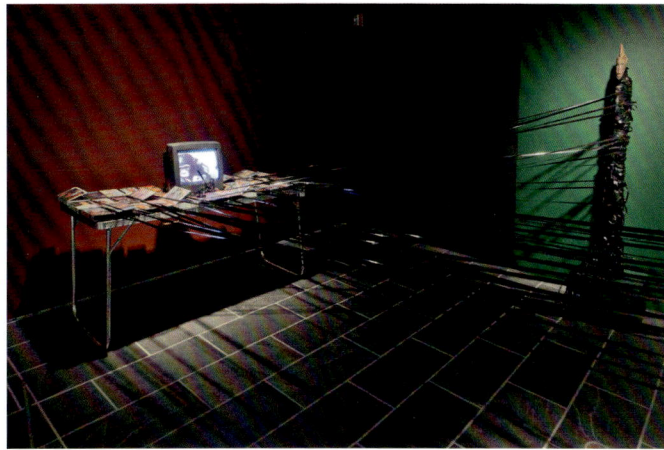

From local color to lack of color, Fred Wilson's work defies expectations, provokes inquiry, and enriches aesthetic experience. In 1993, Bronx-born conceptual artist Wilson created *Local Color*, an installation at the Studio Museum in Harlem that underscored the institution's role as a culturally specific space sited within a rich, diverse, and historically Black community, even as the installation upended museological conventions. *Local Color* called into question institutional collecting criteria and, by extension, societal value systems, and blurred the distinction between objects deemed worthy of exhibition and those kept outside of institutional visibility. For the work, Wilson assembled traditional African and Caribbean artifacts from the Studio Museum's permanent collection and a variety of items purchased from vendors on Harlem's 125th Street, thus affirming the pervasive presence and connective commonalities of the African diaspora. Furthering this stance, Wilson tinted the walls of the installation with the Marcus Garvey tricolor of red, black, and green. This politicized disruption of the white cube, soothing to select sensibilities, exemplifies Wilson's use of color to create "an emotional field."[149]

Wilson also plays with the political significance and emotional impact of color with *Untitled (African Union)*—in this case, withholding it. Part of a series of paintings inspired by the designs of flags of Africa and the African diaspora, *Untitled (African Union)* recasts the graphic elements of the flag of the continent's fifty-five-state body as an abstract geometric composition devoid of its characteristic colors. Painted in black outlines on unprimed canvas—an allusion to permanent potential—the flag's familiar symbols open a multitude of meanings. With *Local Color*, Wilson brought the street into the realm of the art museum; *Untitled (African Union)* transforms a symbol of a geographic location into an art object—down to the characteristically contemporary art (un)titling device.

Flags can elicit feelings of pride and belonging; they also thereby distinguish members of a group from others. In heraldry, color is a vehicle of values. Thus, Wilson's defamiliarized emblem raises a host of questions: Can the aspirations ascribed to a flag withstand the evacuation of color? Without its green, can the African Union flag inspire hope? Without its gold, can it convey Africa's prosperity? Without its white, Africa's purity? Without the red, is there no solidarity or remembrance of bloodshed? Whereas the works in Wilson's untitled flags series are typically displayed in grids—the aggregation symbolic of pan-African unity—in representing multiple countries, *Untitled (African Union)* serves as a concentrated metaphor. Moreover, as it documents a design that would be retired in 2010, the work commemorates a particular bygone vision of continental cooperation.

—Akili Tommasino

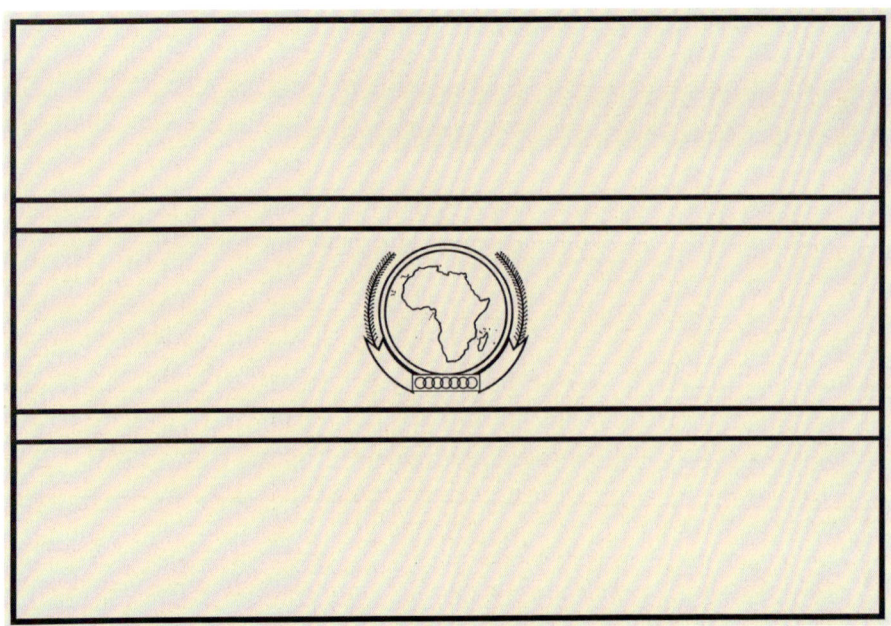

Untitled (African Union),
2009. Acrylic on canvas,
27 × 40 in. Gift of the artist
2013.2

Chris Ofili
b. 1968

Chris Ofili constructs intricate and meticulously labored-over paintings and works on paper; his compositions merge abstraction and figuration to explore established narratives from religion, folklore, myth, and popular culture. Ofili's practice embraces juxtapositions. His subject matter includes the sacred and profane, and the prized and discarded. Casting a wide net of aesthetic and cultural inspirations across space and time, Ofili manifests his own worlds, where "beauty is a simple exploration of line, form, and shape."[150]

His works made mid-graduate school evidence an elaborate layering of materials including paint, resin, glitter (which came slightly later), and most notably—elephant dung. A trip to Zimbabwe in his early twenties left an indelible mark on the artist, catalyzing his use of elephant feces (considered medicinal in African contexts). In *Elephantastic*, uniform and curved lines of red acrylic paint adorn the surface in a manner similar to the cohesive and repetitive designs of Zimbabwean cave paintings. The resulting abstract pattern forms the backdrop for three piles of elephant dung arranged in the lower half of the composition. This target of curiosity for the artist—of dung elevated to art—caused an uproar in the art world in the late 1990s.

Bridging abstract language with figurative elements, Ofili's creations in the mid-1990s display an exuberant and energetic visual expression, inspired by a range of references, from the Bible to Black culture. The artist's series of 181 watercolors titled "Afro Muses" (which debuted at the Studio Museum in Harlem in 2005) showcases imagined Black men and women in an Afrocentric world, where ornate appearances reign.

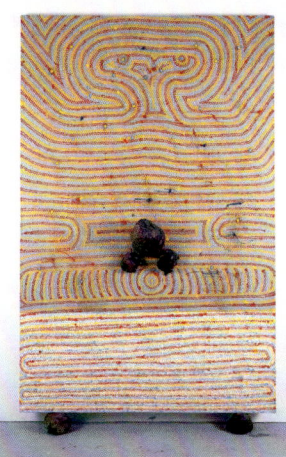
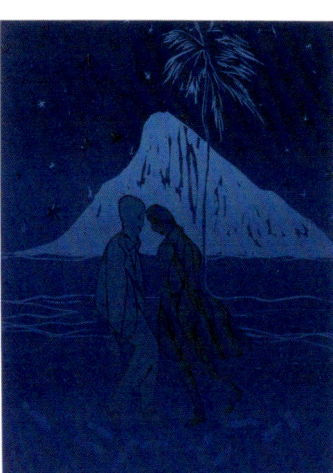

Left: *Elephantastic*, 1994. Acrylic, oil, polyester resin and elephant dung on linen, 72 × 48 in. Gift of Ninah and Michael Lynne 2018.44.14

Right: *After the Dance* (from "The Rivington Place" portfolio), 2006. Silkscreen on Somerset Velvet, image: 16 × 12 in., sheet: 30 × 20 in. Edition 1 of 50. Museum purchase with funds provided by the Acquisition Committee 2008.10.6

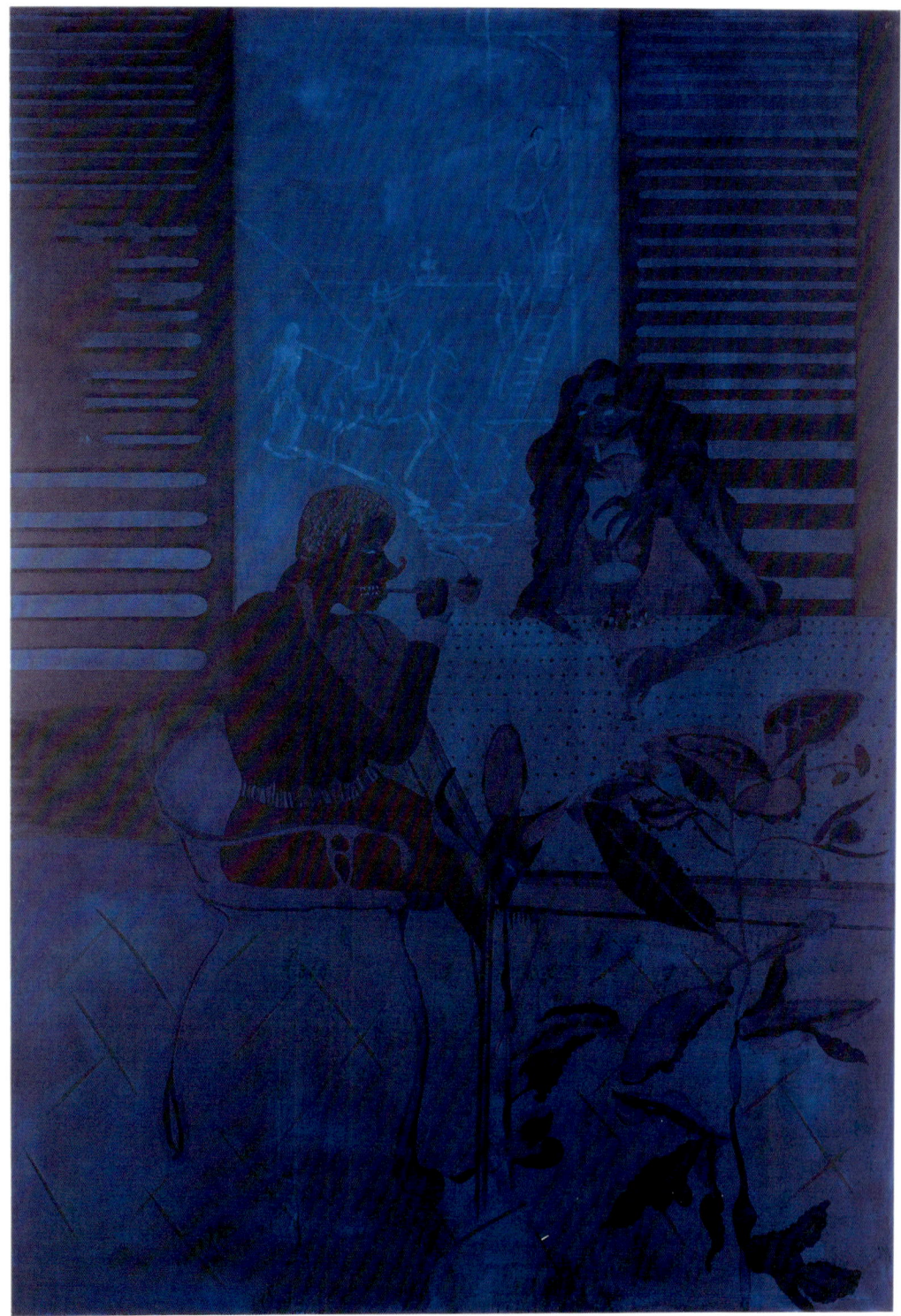

Blue Smoke (Pipe Dreams), 2011. Oil on
linen, 110 ¼ × 77 ¼ in × 1 ⅝ in. Gift of
anonymous donor 2019.20

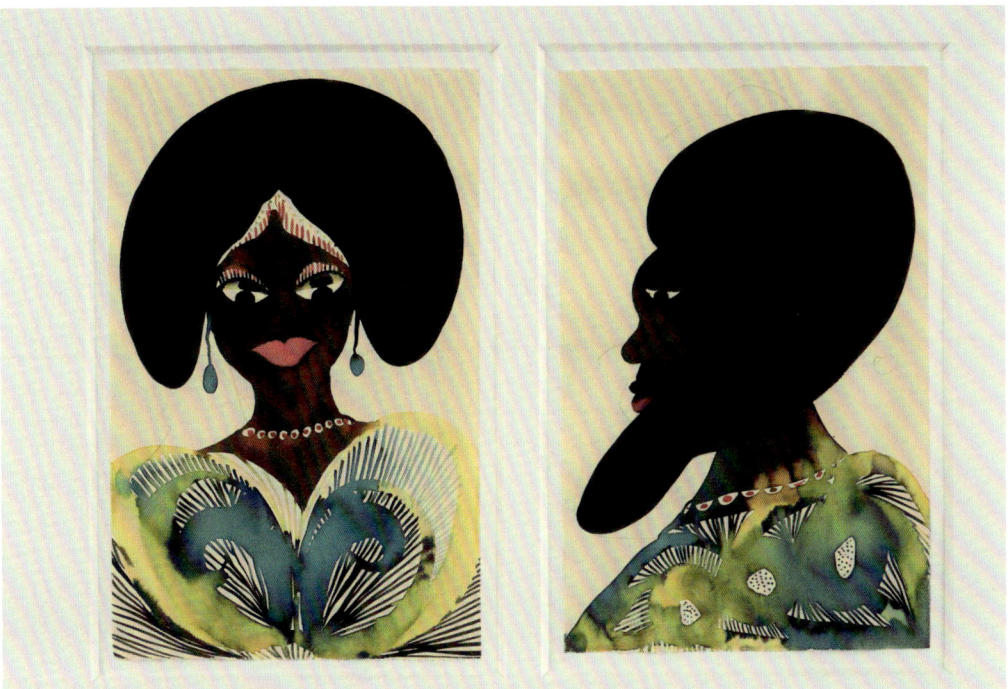

Untitled (diptych from the "Afro Muses"
series), 1995—2005. Watercolor and
graphite on paper, each: 9 ½ × 6 in. Gift of
Anne Ehrenkranz in honor of Nancy L. Lane
2006.22

In 2005, Ofili's paintings experienced another metamorphosis after the
artist relocated from London to Trinidad. Impacted by the island's vibrant
colors and lush landscape, Ofili's works from this period echo his new
home's magical terrain, as well as the slow transition from daytime
to evening when shapes remain visible yet details obscure. Employing
blue—near black—as his primary painting ingredient, Ofili began to,
as artist Glenn Ligon elucidates, "use blue as a kind of dark matter, a force
not easily quantified but which holds the universe he creates on canvas
together."[151] *Blue Smoke (Pipe Dreams)*, among a series of blue canvases
produced after the artist's move to Trinidad, portrays a bearded man
smoking a pipe and a woman holding glassware seated together at a table.
Taking on a similar palette, *After the Dance*, from "The Rivington Place
Portfolio," presents a dancing couple in a sensual paradise drawn directly
from the iconic photograph *Christmas Eve* by the late Malian photographer Malick Sidibé. Within these dark compositions, Ofili has developed
"another way of representing light," encouraging the viewer's consideration
of an "appreciation of the darkness and darkness being associated with
quiet and introspection."[152]

—Habiba Hopson

Nari Ward

b. 1963   Artist in Residence 1992—93

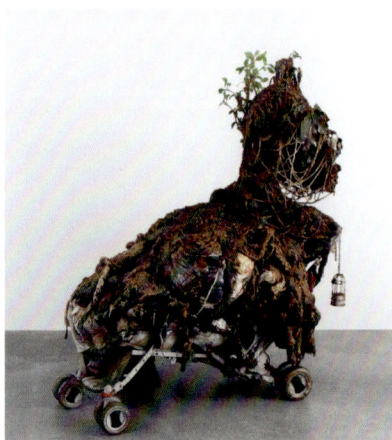

Trophy, 1993. Baby stroller, Tropical Fantasy soda with sugar, and mixed media, 71 × 31 × 48 in. Gift of Nicole Klagsbrun 2023.33.1

Produced during his 1992—93 residency at the Studio Museum in Harlem, Nari Ward's *Trophy* started—as many of his early-career projects did—with the artist traversing his Harlem neighborhood in search of ordinary, abandoned materials to turn into art. A cast-off baby stroller forms the sculpture's base, its wheels marked by many journeys—first holding infants as their caretakers navigated city streets and later being pushed by community members who transported other precious cargo: discarded bottles and cans to recycle for money. Ward considers the relative value of materials, asking what distinguishes trash from trophy; being cared for from being marginalized.

The dense accumulation of objects that Ward stacks atop the stroller includes personal items, such as crumpled clothing, soiled blankets, and threadlike strands resembling hair, that allude to the lives and struggles of Harlem's residents in the 1990s amid the ongoing HIV/AIDS crisis, drug epidemic, and housing insecurities. Ward binds these items with an old firehose, further fusing them with a caramel glaze derived from boiled sugar and Tropical Fantasy soda.[153] By introducing the sugary coating, Ward traces transhistorical paths between "the sugars of the plantation, the sugar of the slave trade," and present-day overabundance and consumption. "There's a historical dialogue but also a corner store dialogue," he adds, highlighting the ongoing brutality of racialized capitalism in the United States.[154]

Ward invites a grappling with these heavy and entangled histories through the sculpture's massive and decaying bulk. His construction of the top portion, however, lightens the conversation. He loosely arranges tendril-like ropes, from which green leaves and branches emerge. Crowning the work's hulking body, the plant rises up, suggesting triumph, dignity, and renewal hinted at by Ward's title.

—Tamara H. Schenkenberg

Chakaia Booker

b. 1953   Artist in Residence 1995—96

Repugnant Rapunzel (Let Down Your Hair) presents a sculptural retelling of the classic fairy tale from which the piece borrows its title. Through contorted, tangled pieces of car tire, Chakaia Booker takes the story, most famously recorded by the Brothers Grimm, and emphasizes the grotesque, mysterious, and dark tone of the original narrative.

Booker began making her tire assemblages in the 1980s after years spent observing the material accumulation of Manhattan's East Village and her native Newark, New Jersey. Booker's sculptures are reminiscent of the "junk art" that was a recognized staple of the Los Angeles art scene of the 1960s and 1970s, where artists routinely looked to the discarded, the everyday, and the utilitarian as material teeming with aesthetic and communicative potential. In Booker's care, repurposed rubber, which she collected from city streets and landfills when first adopting the material into her practice, becomes both a visual symbol and an ode to sustainable praxis.

In *Repugnant Rapunzel,* typically unyielding rubber is made supple and is woven to resemble thickly braided locks of hair. Booker's technique positions a style often associated with Black hair care traditions as a stand-in for the golden tresses at the center of the original fable. In addition to the artist's allegorical investment, the work speaks to an array of visual and cultural topics including histories of craft. Booker's process, for example, calls to attention the histories of weaving and basketry found within the African diaspora. Her work also displays an awareness of the exploitation of labor in developing raw goods and the effects of rampant consumerism on the environment. Her use of automotive rubber is a penetrating gesture toward the material and human investment in commerce and the maintenance of industrialization.

—Alexandra E. Adams

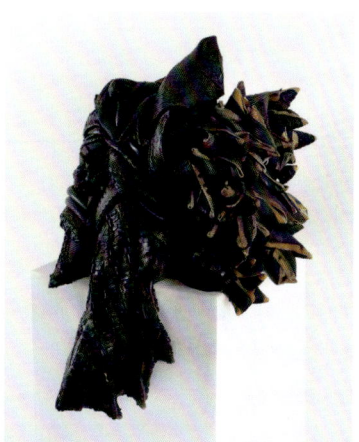

Repugnant Rapunzel (Let Down Your Hair), 1995. Rubber tires and metal, 59 × 24 × 24 in. Gift of Friends and Family of Chakaia Booker 1996.7

Adrian Piper

b. 1948

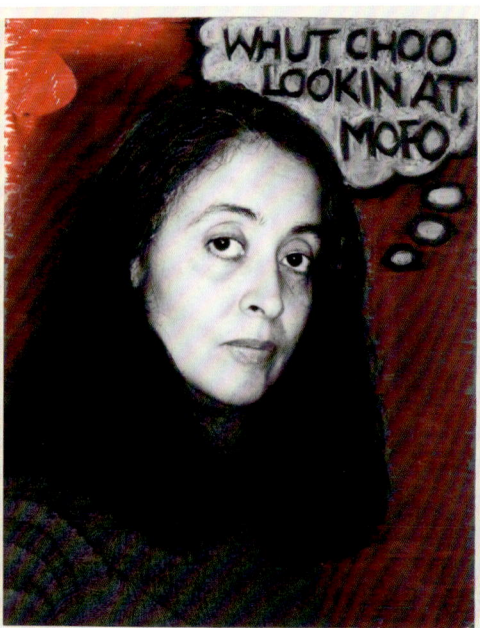

Self-Portrait as a Nice White Lady,
1995. Black-and-white autophoto with
oil-crayon drawing, 18 ¼ × 14 ¼ in.
Museum purchase made possible by a gift
from Barbara Karp Shuster, New York
2004.2.5

In this work, conceptual artist and philosopher Adrian Piper presents a self-portrait that emphasizes the often-jarring contradictions created by human classification. She was born and raised as a Black woman, despite presenting as white to the wider world. The color of her skin, the texture of her hair, and her middle-class upbringing often led to misidentification and general mistrust of Piper's identity, from both Black and white peers. This greatly influenced her artistic practice. The fallacies of phenotypical classification allow Piper to act as a trickster figure who, through performance and visual art, pushes the boundaries of race, gender, and class. Piper's conceptual explorations reveal the humor, violence, and power experienced by those who fall between and beyond Black and white.

Piper's practice relies on existential explorations of the "self" to hold a mirror to society. *Self-Portrait as a Nice White Lady* plays with the existential in content and form, which undermines its ability to be taken at face value. The black-and-white "autophoto" is framed by playful, imperfect strokes of red oil crayon compromising the integrity of the machine-made image. The title alerts the viewer to Piper's performance of whiteness, of gender, and of social acceptability. "Nice," which is typically interpreted as "good," but is not intrinsically so, leaves room for much deception. The jive talk found in the speech bubble humorously contradicts her role as the "nice white lady" while offering a clue to her true Black identity at the time. The ultimate result is an image that borders on the absurd, a figure actively working against the racial classifications deemed most appropriate by society.

—TK Smith

Renee Cox

b. 1960

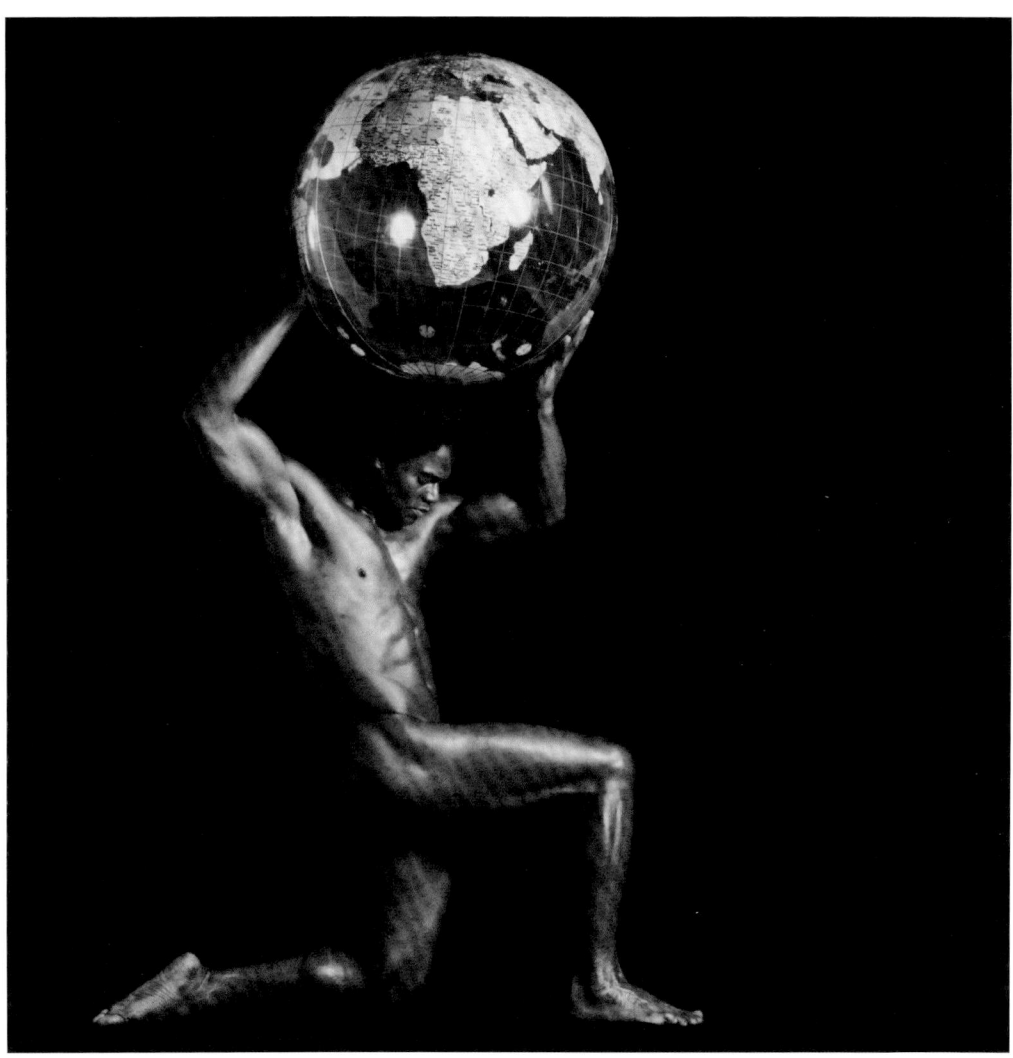

Atlas, 1995. Gelatin silver print,
10 ½ × 10 ½ in. Gift of Joy of Giving
Something, Inc. 2018.47.7

Renee Cox often works in photographic series to explore and challenge preconceived notions about race and gender across history, popular culture, and religion. *Atlas* is from the early series "Flipping the Script" (1994—97), which controversially reinterpreted a number of iconic images and religious masterpieces by placing a Black figure at center. Here a kneeling, nude Black man holds the globe aloft, his muscles seeming to flex and strain. While keeping the world up is clearly taxing, the man does so with grace and beauty. Cox utilizes chiaroscuro, a technique of contrasting between light and shadow, to highlight the figure's strong form, which she heightens even more with the photograph's stark black background.

Cox references the story of Atlas, a Titan from Greek mythology. After the Titans, an older generation of gods, were defeated in battle by the Olympians, the younger generation led by Zeus, Atlas was sentenced to hold up the heavens for eternity. This mythic figure is commonly represented in imagery as a white man carrying the world on his shoulders. By casting a Black man in the role of Atlas, Cox calls attention to the transatlantic slave trade and the history of Black labor, whereby Black people profoundly contribute to, but do not benefit from, the development of industries and economies in the United States and Europe—literally bearing the weight of the world's responsibilities. Cox emphasizes this further by showing Africa as the center of the world, a view that repositions global centers of power and influence. In photographs such as *Atlas*, Cox problematizes the removal of the Black figure from representations and histories, flipping the script to deconstruct long-standing narratives and to empower Black people.

—Connie H. Choi

Michael Richards

1963—2001   Artist in Residence 1995—96

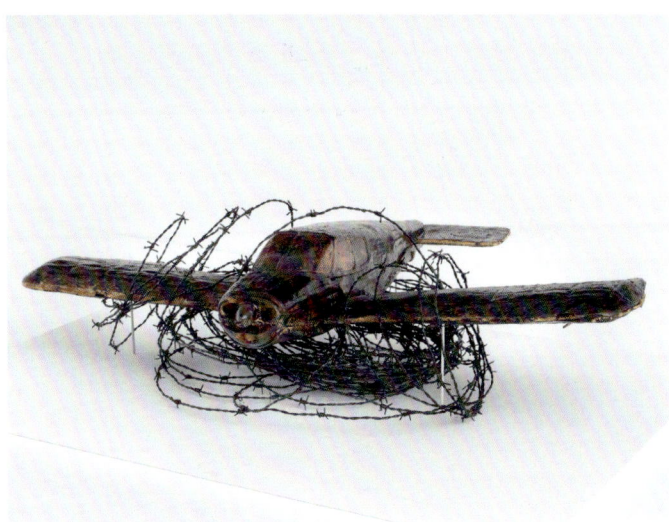

Escape Plan 76 (Brer Plane in the Brier Patch), 1996. Wax, resin, tar, and metal, 12 × 26 × 38 in. Gift of Bruce E. Aldini and C. Richard Becker, New York 2001.18

Meditating on the contradictions of Black social and material uplift, *Escape Plan 76 (Brer Plane in the Brier Patch)* is one of Michael Richards's many engagements with the metaphor of arrested flight. The sculpture depicts a dark, metal-cast, mid-century airplane. Its nose is pitched forward, indicating flying or stasis, rather than angled upward in ascent. Despite the potential for flight, the plane's wings are bent and battered, and the entire object is wrapped in a tangle of barbed wire that coils into a thorny nest beneath the plane's undercarriage. Dappled with tar and resin, the rusty patina of the plane's metal makes it appear both damaged and sticky, referencing, along with the barbed wire, scenes from the Black folktale upon which the work's title and ambivalent "moral" are inspired. In the original tale, the trickster hero Brer Rabbit convinces his foe, Brer Fox, to throw him into the briar patch instead of roasting or drowning him. Though the spiky burrs of the trap prove more navigable to maneuver for the hero, precarity endures through this and subsequent tales.

The strained limitations of mischief and "escape" are referenced in other of Richards's works, but they are echoed most clearly in the theme of halted aviation. In addition to various configurations of feathers and wings, Richards was particularly drawn to the Tuskegee Airmen, an all-Black division of World War II US Air Force pilots whose war hero status netted no peacetime dignity or social reward. For Richards, the Tuskegee Airmen condense the tension between collective Black survival, ambivalent achievement, opportunity pursued, and opportunity denied. Enunciating the frailty of freedom's promise, the bramble-choked fate of Black uplift—or, as it were, "liftoff"—*Escape Plan 76 (Brer Plane in the Brier Patch)* sardonically depicts liberation as an earnest, beautiful, if constantly contested endeavor.

—Jakeya Caruthers

Kara Walker

b. 1969

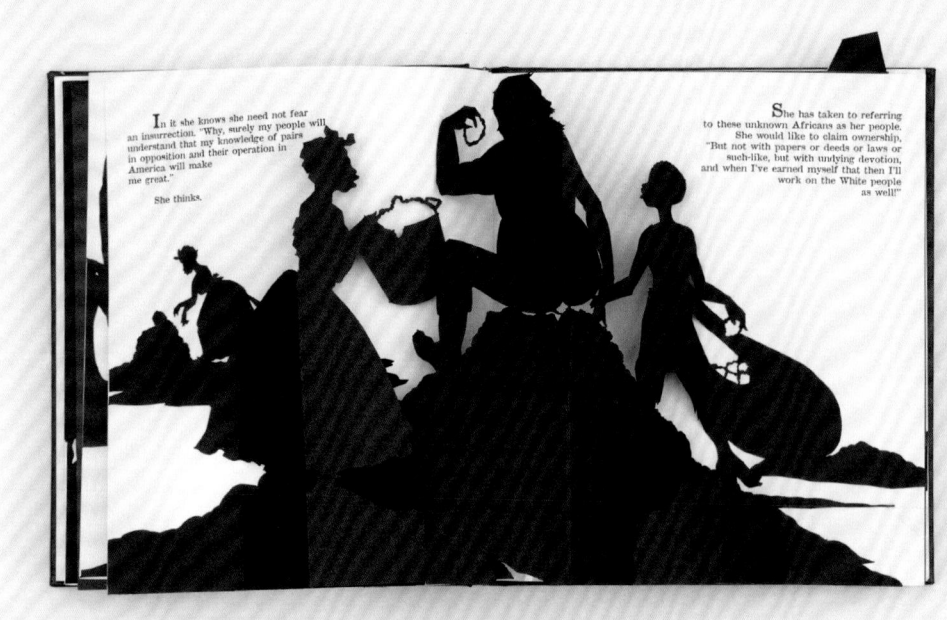

Freedom: A Fable, 1997. Leather bound
silhouette pop-up book; leather on paper,
9 ¼ × 8 ¼ in. Gift of John Nutant Family
1999.3

Kara Walker redefines how blackness is seen and considered within the realm of daily life and art. For Walker, blackness is constructed, not merely a mode for looking at and interpreting history. Her works are daunting to interpret and have haunting effects, illustrating how blackness is quite literally treated, (self-)preserved, and even loved.

Walker uses images along with visual technologies fundamental to the stereotyping and misrepresentation of Black life within the United States. As someone who grew up in Georgia, she was all too familiar with the memorialization of slavery in the South. She is widely known for her black silhouette cutout murals, pop-up books, and films inspired by eighteenth-century Victorian portraiture and Civil War—era cycloramas. Works such as *Freedom: A Fable, Exodus of the Confederates from Atlanta from Harper's Pictorial History of the Civil War (Annotated)*, and *Emancipation Approximation Scene #18* feature Confederate leaders on horseback depicted in ways that contradict and mock their valorization in historical painting and lore. Walker also reappropriates Black minstrel imagery and depicts acts of resistance by the enslaved, whether it be killing their captors, riding their captors' horses, or dancing. Subtle references to the civil rights movement contrast with the violence her cutouts invoke.

In Walker's works, the condition and stakes of freedom are ongoing subjects of inquiry and debate. In her cutouts, women fight for and, if lucky, trek out to freedom. *Freedom: A Fable* contains pop-ups of scenes of an imagined woman character's life before, during, and after enslavement. The use of a text-based narrative materializes the woman's confrontations with oppression after emancipation. A counterpoint to the weighted imagery rises out of the text and is subsumed into the blackness.

Walker eschews a revisionist practice and considers the contradictory rhetoric and imagery associated with freedom. *Emancipation Approximation*, consisting of twenty-seven prints, is a play on President Abraham Lincoln's declaration of freedom for millions of enslaved populations. In this series, Walker melds African American folklore with Greek mythology. *Emancipation Approximation, Scene #18* features a black silhouette carrying a white silhouette of a gentry woman over her head and shoulders—a direct reference to the myth of Atlas, who was forced to carry the heavens as punishment for challenging Zeus's power. Different works in the series illustrate the rape of Leda along with other illicit and nonconsensual relationships between the enslavers and the enslaved that gave way to childbirth and childrearing. Blackness comes in many shades and tones, as illustrated by how the black and white shapes acquire different forms and relationships to each other—further suggestive of the generational imprint of enslavement and miscegenation on freedom.

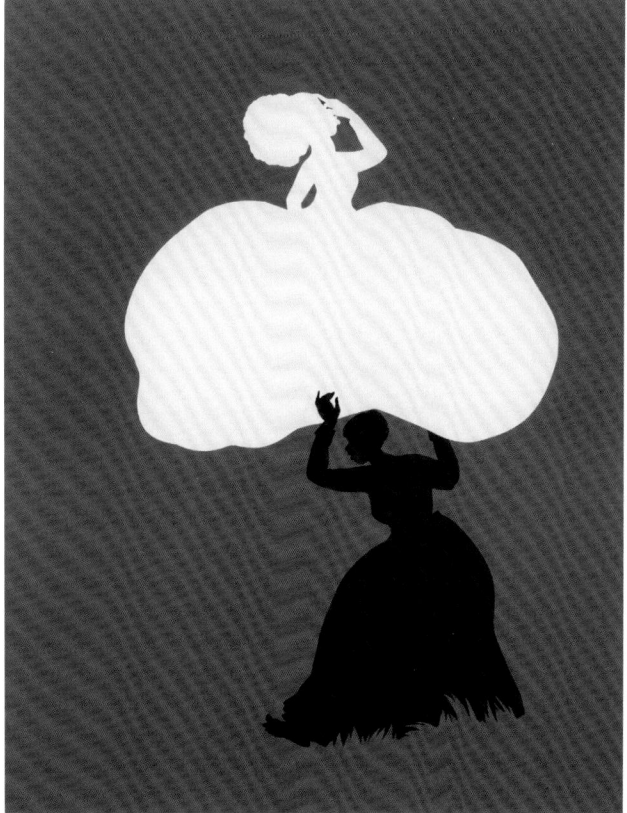

Emancipation Approximation, Scene #18, 2000. Silkscreen on paper, 44 × 34 in. Edition 5 of 25. Museum purchase made possible by a gift from the Peter T. Joseph Foundation, New York 2001.6

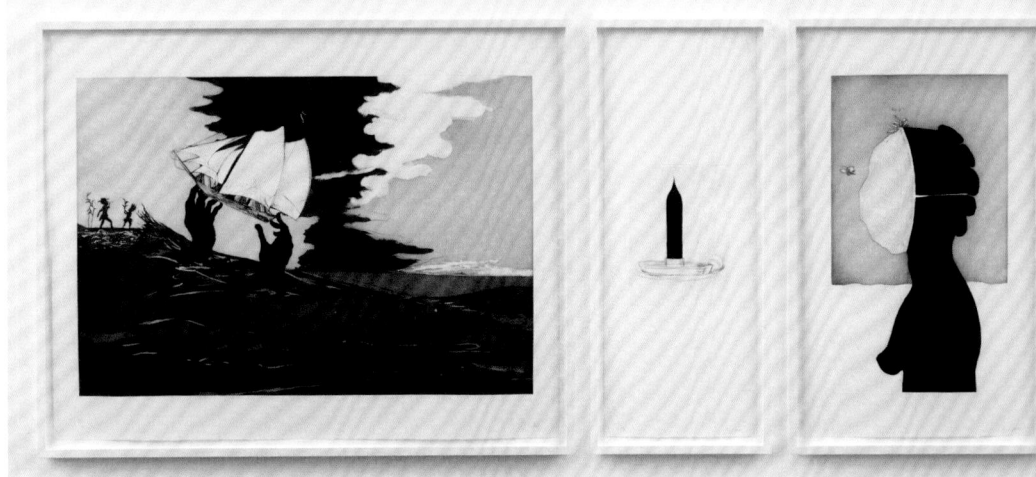

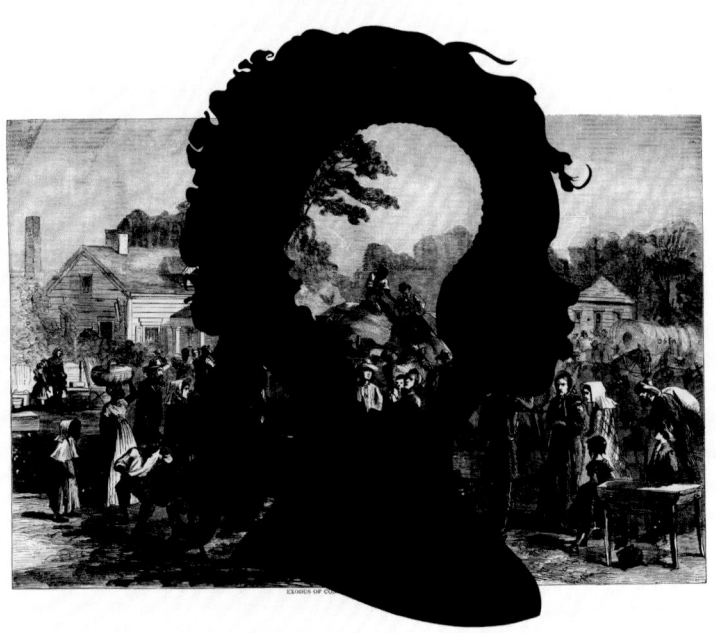

Top: *An Unpeopled Land in Uncharted Waters*, 2010. Etching with aquatint, sugar-lift, spit-bite, and dry-point, printed on Hahnemuhle Copperplate Bright White 300 gsm paper, *no world*: 27 × 39 in., *beacon (after R.G.)*: 27 × 11 in., *savant*: 27 × 17 in., *the secret sharer*: 27 × 27 in., *buoy*: 27 × 35 ½ in., *dread*: 27 × 15 in. Edition 21 of 30. Gift of Fern & Lenard Tessler 2021.26a–f

Bottom: *Exodus of the Confederates from Atlanta from Harper's Pictorial History of the Civil War (Annotated)*, 2005. Offset lithograph and silkscreen, 42 × 55 ¾ × 2 in. Edition 18 of 35. Gift of Ninah and Michael Lynne 2018.44.21

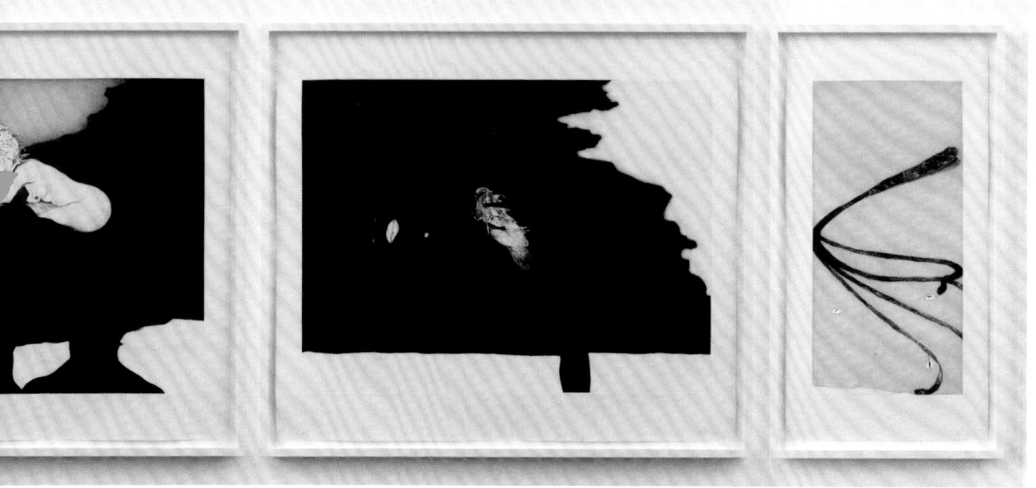

Since the 2010s, Walker has used her earlier works as prototypes and blue-prints to design public art installations, such as *A Subtlety, or the Marvelous Sugar Baby* (2014) at the former Domino Sugar Factory in Brooklyn, New York, and *Fons Americanus* (2019) at Tate Modern in London. Using white substances such as sugar and marble—a contrast to her black silhou-ettes—she enlivens, critiques, and monumentalizes power structures and social relations that continue to incite violence. Freedom is elusive for many of the historical characters whose lives Walker imagines and chroni-cles. There is no better example of this than the series "An Unpeopled Land in Uncharted Waters." One of the prints, *no world*, illustrates an enslaved woman either swimming or drowning in a direction opposite to that of a ship that presumably brought countless unidentified Black people to the Americas.

—Drew Thompson

Vladimir Cybil Charlier

b. 1967   Artist in Residence 1996—97

Picture this: A small aluminum case emerges from a wooden box. When open, the case reveals a religious female deity. She wears a blue veil, necklace, and elaborate halo, all embellished with matching beads and sequins. With a pink heart and two pearl beads, she floats against a pale blue background and is pierced in the chest by a metallic sword. Her accompanying symbolic elements and colors demarcate her as the voodoo goddess of love—Erzulie—in all her forms.[155]

Produced during Vladimir Cybil Charlier's residency at the Studio Museum in Harlem from 1996 to 1997, *Billie Zulie* is a personal and portable shrine dedicated to the celebrated singer Billie Holiday and the Haitian Loa (goddess) Erzulie. Charlier and fellow resident June Clark embarked on a collaborative project that explored New York City's baffling decision to end subway maps at Ninety-Sixth Street, discounting an enormous population living in upper Manhattan and the Bronx. The duo created transportable altars dedicated to their cultural upbringing as an installation. This prompted Charlier to ask herself, "What if the [voodoo] gods landed in Harlem? What would they look like?"[156] Her ensuing works pictured Billie Holiday as Erzulie, Malcolm X as Ogun (the warrior god of iron and war), and Miles Davis as Baron Samedi (the master of the underworld).

Born in Queens to Haitian parents, Charlier grew up equally between Port-au-Prince and New York. On the influence of cultural elements of both locales on her artistic practice, Charlier describes, "It's really in the space in between those two geographic spaces, in the dialogue itself, that the energy and the exchange really reside."[157] Across several media, Charlier employs a visual diasporic language, one that melds symbolic and cultural elements from Black cultures in the United States and Caribbean.

—Habiba Hopson

Billie Zulie, 1997. Aluminum, fabric, acrylic, sequins, beads, and hardware. 8 × 13 × 5 in. Gift of the artist   2022.9

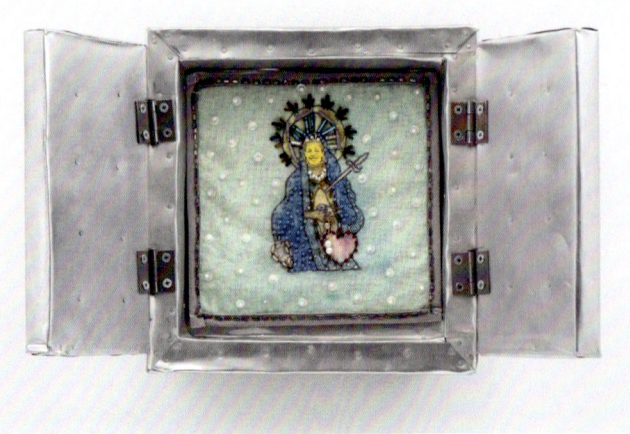

Carrie Mae Weems

b. 1953

1. Window

In *Untitled (Black Love)*, a man and woman encounter each other within the threshold of a doorway. On the left of this triptych, the woman stands alone. The man approaches her in the middle of the composition, and they merge into one figure in the final frame. Across her practice, photographer Carrie Mae Weems asks her viewers to bear witness to moments of intimacy, history, and injustice. The intensely private nature of this work positions the viewer as a voyeur. Mimicking the aperture of the camera, the doorway through which the figures are seen is an opening for reconnection or reconciliation for the couple at the end of a long day. For the viewer, it serves as a reminder of the regularly unseen but grounding quotidian moments, and the critical role that domestic spaces play in relationships.

2. Veil

Continuing her exploration of doorways as transitional spaces, in *Untitled (doorway)*, Weems showcases ancient architecture in Djenné, Mali, one of the oldest cities in sub-Saharan Africa. Weems encountered this site during her first visit to the continent in 1993. She was struck by the organic architectural forms suggestive of women's bodies. In photographing this doorway of a granary from the outside, Weems reinforces the role that women play not only in interior spaces but in life across the city. Its stark presentation of form—without accompanying human

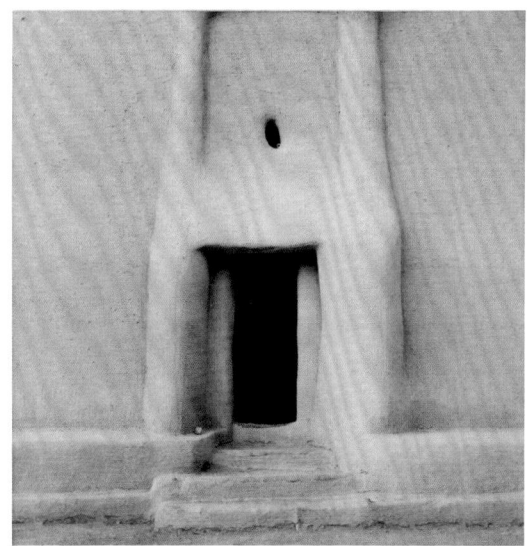

Untitled (doorway), 1997. Digital inkjet print, 8 × 8 in. Gift of Joy of Giving Something, Inc. 2018.47.47

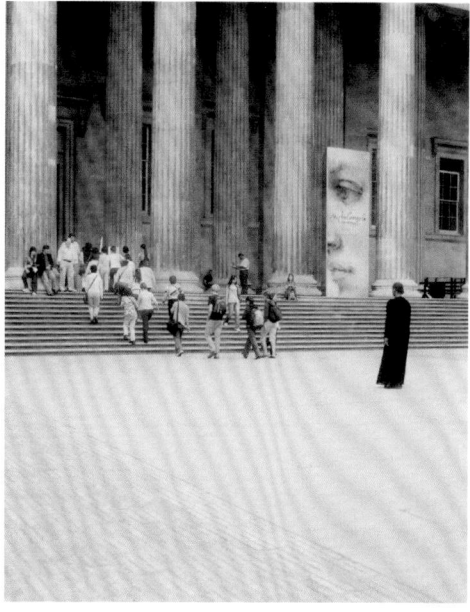

Untitled (from the "Rivington Place" portfolio), 2006. Digital print on Somerset Enhanced Velvet, 30 × 20 in. Edition 1 of 50. Museum purchase with funds provided by the Acquisition Committee 2008.10.7

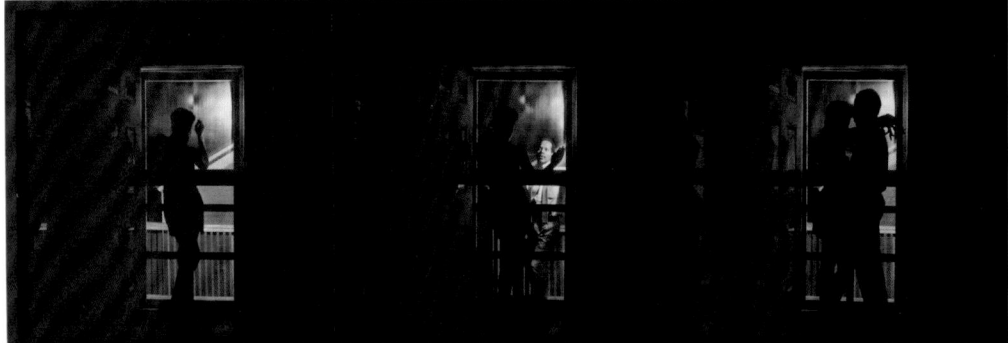

Untitled (Black Love), 1999/2001. Three
gelatin silver prints, each: 15 × 15 in. Edition
1 of 5. Museum purchase with funds
provided by the Acquisition Committee
2002.20.1

figures—frames the unseen labor of the women of Djenné as unequiv-
ocally critical to the structure of the city and society at large. It also
refuses to display their bodies for consumption. Unlike *Untitled (Black
Love)*, the interior space and its inhabitants are left to the imagination.
Much of Djenné was looted beginning in the 1960s, greatly limiting the
information about women and their culture in the once-thriving city. Here,
the doorway simultaneously protects Malian women from the gaze and
invites considerations of a woman-centric history that has been obscured
from the historical record.

3.   Obstacle

For Weems, thresholds are a framing device through which she showcases a moment of encounter between man and woman or past and
present. Expanding on the notion of access, *Untitled*, from "The Rivington
Place Portfolio," points to a doorway as a barrier to entrance. Weems,
dressed entirely in black, stands with her back to the camera and faces
the domineering facade of the British Museum in London. The weighted
appearance of the columns acts as a metaphorical fence, almost entirely
obscuring the door behind them. By juxtaposing her figure with this
Western architecture and with the nearby sign advertising an exhibition
of work by Michelangelo, Weems calls attention to and questions the
historical and contemporary exclusion of artists of African descent within
these institutions and the canon of art history. The doorway is an entry
point visible but inaccessible to the Black artist, a line that defines belonging, recognition, and history.

—Kate Claman

Deborah Willis

b. 1948

Deborah Willis is a photographer, curator, and educator. Her photographs, which are embedded in a rich scholarly understanding of the medium's history, take up themes including body politics, advertising, mass media, and the construction of race and gender.

In *Bodybuilder #4*, professional bodybuilder Nancy Lewis stands with her back turned to the viewer flexing her raised arms and resting one hand on the back of her head, the red nail polish accentuating her black hair. Willis renders her photograph with an extremity of detail, manifesting a stylized, confrontational emphasis on Lewis's physicality. There is a powerful, immediate presence to the sheen of her skin, the shadows carved into her body by muscle, her form protruding from the depthless white background. The beauty with which Willis treats Lewis's muscularity is quietly subversive; it simultaneously flirts with and betrays racist ideologies that frame Black women as less feminine, particularly when their physicality is incongruous with Western ideals of womanhood.

Unlike traditional photographic portraiture, Willis's *Bodybuilder #4* does not lend itself easily to scrutiny of the sitter's identity. Despite the detail and attention lavished on Lewis's sculptural figure, she remains anonymous given her unrevealed face. Additionally, the complexity of gender—in particular the expansive modalities of feminine gender expression—hovers over the image, further complicating our ability to easily define the bodybuilder's identity. While Lewis's hypermuscular body points toward conventional perceptions of masculinity, the shimmer of her metallic bathing suit and red nails signify an alignment with culturally constructed tropes of femininity. Coupled with the obfuscation of her face, the ambiguity of Lewis's body makes for an enigmatic portrait that elides any demand that photographic subjects be readily known.

—Zoë Hopkins

Bodybuilder #4, 1998. Chromogenic print, 19 ½ × 15 ½ in. Gift of the artist 2005.2.1

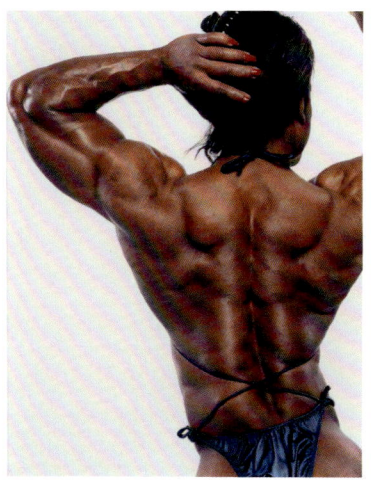

Leonardo Drew

b. 1961   Artist in Residence 1990—91

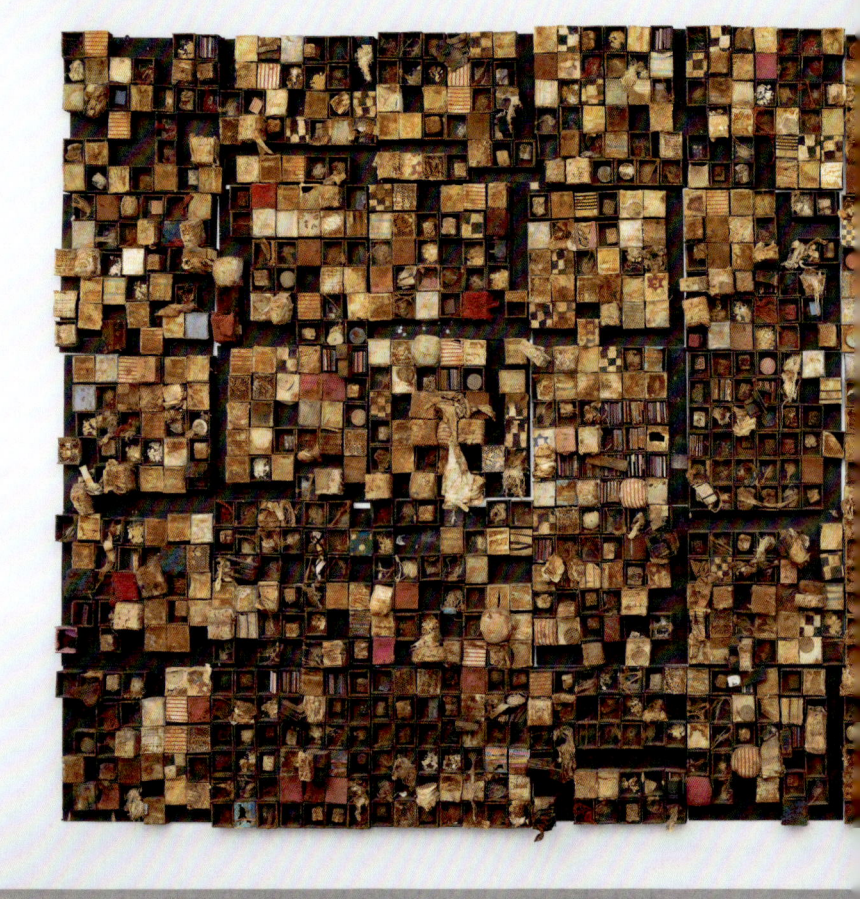

At first sight, Leonardo Drew's *Number 64* appears to be composed of found, ready-made, and discarded materials. Drawing inspiration from the aging process of materials found in abandoned or dilapidated places, Drew meticulously sources and manipulates materials to achieve a "lived-in" quality, infusing his works with history and memory. This act of "becoming the weather," as Drew describes it, symbolizes the passage of time and the transience of life, urging viewers to reflect on the impermanence of all things.[158] He achieves this effect through purposeful decay via oxidation and burning, and meticulous arrangement. While the artist is known for his monumental works often using natural materials, *Number 64* offers a glimpse into his early exploration and eventual break from figuration. It marks a pivotal moment in his artistic trajectory and eventual embrace of abstraction and immersive installation.

This archive-like curiosity cabinet—punctuated by various brightly colored fabrics, wood, and string nestled in its rigid wood structure—provokes introspection, questioning, and contemplation about one's place in the world

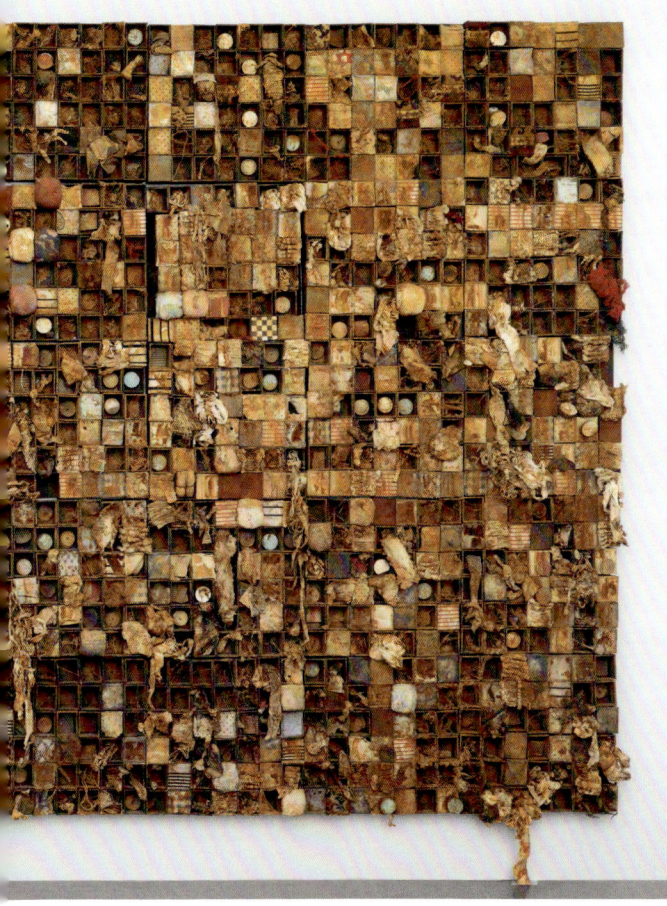

and the connection between the self and the surrounding environment. Central to Drew's oeuvre, the grid-like design connects his works to the intentionality and structure found in city landscapes, while also hinting at the interplay of confinement, chaos and order, abundance and scarcity.

The significance of the grid in Drew's art goes beyond urban symbolism. It represents the structure of life itself—how individual moments and experiences combine to form a larger narrative. Reminiscent of lukasa, the traditional West African beaded wood memory boards of the Luba people used to pass down histories, his work holds knowledge within its intricate layers. Through his meditative and intricate practice, Drew captures the interconnectedness of all things, begins to unravel the complexities of human existence, and offers viewers a mirror to contemplate their place in the world.

—Hanna Girma

Gwendolyn C. Knight

1913—2005

In examining the practice of Gwendolyn C. Knight, one gains invaluable insight into a singular conceptualization of portraiture, landscape, and everyday scenes of urban life that comprise her artistic practice. Amid the dynamic literary and visual developments of the Harlem Renaissance, Knight's work emerged as a site of stillness, interiority, and relationality.

Born in 1913 in Barbados, Knight arrived in the United States when she was seven years old and settled in Harlem six years later. From 1931 to 1933, she studied for a degree in fine arts at Howard University, after which she returned to Harlem and further developed her practice. While there, Knight encountered the works of numerous artists, poets, and writers of the Harlem Renaissance, including Romare Bearden; Claude McKay; Augusta Savage, who would later become her mentor; and Jacob Lawrence, whom she would wed in 1941. Many of the intellectual and aesthetic investments of Knight's contemporaries found articulation in her artwork—namely, the creation of a modernist sensibility that contained what art historian Joshua I. Cohen describes as "clear-eyed attempts to grapple with the sculptural traditions and broader symbolism associated with sub-Saharan Africa" and Afro-diasporic history.[159] Her deliberate considerations of color, form, and subject matter result in works that possess heavy resonance—her pieces speak to internal states of being and external experiences, all while serving as repositories of the personal narratives that encompassed the Harlem Renaissance.

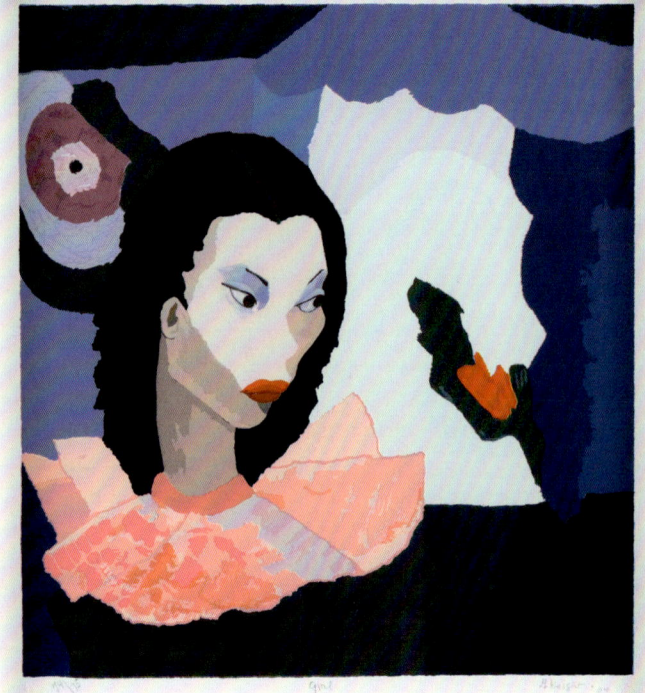

Girl, 2004. Silkscreen on paper, image: 28 × 23 in. Edition 11 of 75. Bequest of Peggy Cooper Cafritz (1947—2018), Washington, DC, collector, educator, and activist 2018.40.157

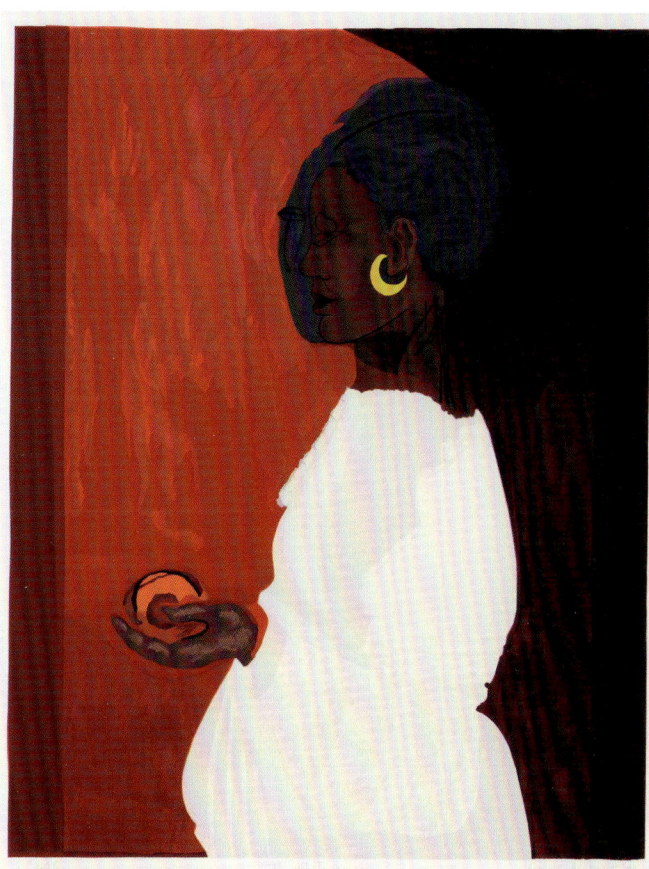

The White Dress, 1999. Screenprint on paper, 28 × 23 in. Edition 49/80. Gift of Francine Seders Gallery, Seattle 2000.4.1

This effect can be seen in several of Knight's works. In *The White Dress*, a woman is shown in profile and her gaze carries an air of serenity and tranquility. She is draped in white fabric and carries what appears to be an apple in her hand. The resulting combination imbues the work with the suggestions of a fairy tale. Knight uses vibrant and crisp colors throughout the work, and the composition of the environment suggests the woman is on a stage—her shadow is cast in a deep indigo, while the background is a rich red. *Girl* also depicts a woman—though in this case we are shown her full visage—with an unreadable expression that creates a degree of distance from the viewer. One is only given a glimpse into the interiority of the subject. Her decorative collar is akin to a jester's ruffle, and the dark drapes and abstract figurations of the background similarly suggest a set-like space. Both works appear to depict a moment of composed stillness before a performance. In these instances, the theme of theater conveys interiority amid a dynamic and complex environment.

These women are likely friends and members of Knight's Harlem community. The methods taken in their representation are informed by Knight's investment in histories of African dance, theater, and sculpture. Her practice is one that engages with the historical, the personal, and the cultural.

—Arese Uwuoruya

Glenn Ligon

b. 1960

Stranger in the Village #15, 1999. Acrylic,
coal dust, oil stick, glue, glitter, and gesso
on canvas, 78 × 132 in. Gift of the Bohen
Foundation, New York 2001.19.1

Coal dust covers the surface of Glenn Ligon's *Stranger in the Village #15*, making it so that blackness obscures the words that appear on this work's surface. The viewer of this work navigates it much like a nightmare—through an experience with glimmers of gesture and meaning in an assaulting, disorienting sequence. The text is excerpted from James Baldwin's 1953 essay "Stranger in the Village," written from his perspective as the only Black man in Leukerbad, Switzerland, in 1951.

Baldwin had left Harlem for Paris in 1948, in part to escape the racism in the United States, finish his first novel, and explore his sexuality in a more liberated environment. In "Stranger in the Village," he compares the experience of being Black in the United States to that of living in Europe. He concludes that the hatred Black people confront in the United States stems from the indifference to his race he found in Europe. Blackness, Baldwin asserts, despite being foundational to the fabric of the United States, is always forcibly separated from the nation's collective history through willful denial and violence. When describing the diasporic Black experience, Baldwin recalls James Joyce's *Ulysses*, in which the narrator, Stephen Daedalus, states, "History . . . is a nightmare from which I am trying to awake."

Ligon has utilized Baldwin's text in many works as a way to extend what it means to be simultaneously visible and invisible, in regard to both the discipline of abstraction and the Black experience. Faint outlines of the letters evoke the contradictions of being read as Black, of being read as strange. By using material abstractions and painstakingly overlaying the lettering with toxic coal dust, Ligon toils with the duality of hyper-visibility and invisibility that defines Black existence throughout history. Coal, from which tar is derived, recalls Baldwin's description of being seen in Switzerland, where his hair was referred to as the color of tar.

Throughout his work, Ligon introduces abstraction and thereby strangeness to this famous text. Like Baldwin's role as a "stranger cloaked in strange-ness" in a small European village where most had never seen a Black person, Ligon is confronted with the roots of US hatred in European indif-ference toward his personhood. The painstaking work of producing and reading *Stranger in the Village #15* collides on one surface. The large scale suggests a horizonless landscape, rife with symbolism, sign, and obstacle.

— Amber Esseiva

Kori Newkirk

b. 1970

In a practice that encompasses installation, painting, photography, sculpture, and video, Kori Newkirk continually expands his sources and materials to explore themes related to Black history, cultural identity, masculinity, and self-fashioning. He brings readily available and popular objects—including artificial hair, plastic pony beads, pomade, and neon lights—into the realm of high art. Often combining childhood memories with social and political commentary, his works blur the division between the personal and the public, suggesting that all individuals face universal challenges.

Alluding to the artist's hometown of Solon, New York, *Solon 6:12* offers a cropped view of a tree line at dusk. This sculpture is part of a body of work that abstractly evokes land- and cityscapes as well as the beaded curtains popular in the 1970s—the decade of Newkirk's childhood— through colored pony beads strung on to artificial hair. *Solon 6:12* more pointedly references the sensationalized press coverage in 1997—three years before the work was made—of Venus Williams's US Open debut. Newkirk began to use pony beads in his work after reading news articles wherein Williams's hair accessories, rather than her play, were the focus of attention. Debates around decorum and permissible hairstyles dominated public conversation about Williams, who was the first unseeded player to reach the US Open Final since Grand Slam tournaments were restructured in 1968. By redirecting attention from her phenomenal ascent within the conservative sport to her hair, the media turned Williams's achievement into one centered on race. Newkirk thus fashions beaded hair into a curtain, a metaphorical doorway, to reconsider this discriminatory characterization.

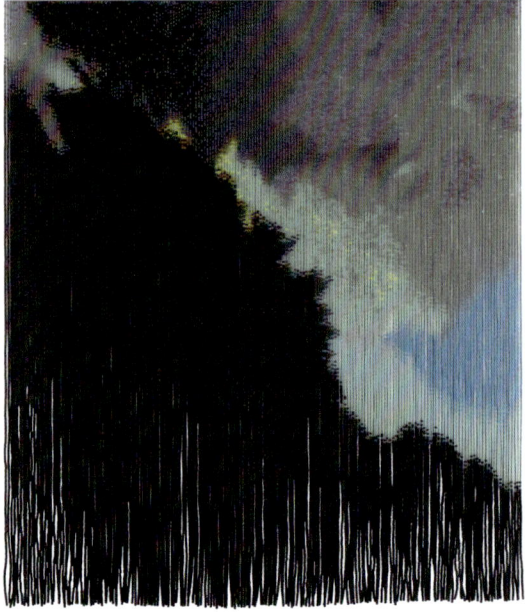

Solon 6:12, 2000. Plastic pony beads, artificial hair, and metal brackets, 81 × 73 ¾ in. Gift of Dean Valentine and Amy Adelson 2009.16

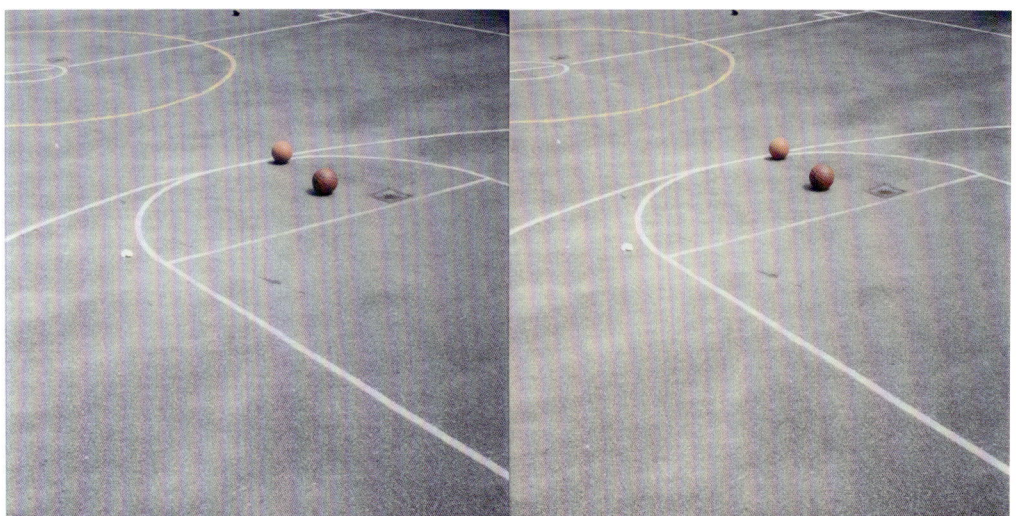

Bumper (diptych), 2001. Inkjet photo
mounted on plexiglass, each: 30 × 30 in.
Edition of 3. Museum purchase with funds
provided by the Acquisition Committee
2001.22a-b

Sports have been a subject the artist consistently returns to, largely due
to an impulse to confront its various tropes around blackness and Black
masculinity. *Bumper (diptych)* is a photographic diptych of an outdoor
basketball court, deserted save for two basketballs and various pieces
of litter. The work resembles a stereograph, a nineteenth-century invention of two nearly identical photographs paired to create an illusion
of a three-dimensional image when viewed through a device called a ste-
reoscope. The slight difference between the two images is discernible but
unsettling to the viewer's eye, thereby compounding the emptiness of the
court. Newkirk here challenges the expectations of athleticism placed
on tall Black men like himself and the assumption that sports are the only
viable option for them. A sense of loneliness prevails in the work, hinting
at the isolation that can be felt even within a team.

While not always physically depicted, the Black subject is present throughout Newkirk's practice, with the implication of the body driving meaning.
In works such as *Solon 6:12* and *Bumper*, the artist investigates the material
signifiers of blackness, grappling with their historical and popular associations and their cultural meanings to address faults and prejudices within
society. Although divorced from their racialized subject, these materials
are still understood as coming from Black culture, emphasizing the fraught
visibility of blackness in the United States.

—Connie H. Choi

Raymond Saunders

b. 1934

Untitled, c. 2000. Mixed media on panel, 63 ½ × 48 × 2 in. Museum purchase with funds provided by the Acquisition Committee, in honor of Nancy L. Lane, and Greater Harlem Nursing Home and Rehabilitation Center, Inc. 2022.15

By way of his polemic essay "Black Is a Color," Raymond Saunders positioned himself not only as an artist but as a thinker invested in blowing open the perennial discourse around the question of the Black artist's role in society.[160] Penned in 1967, the essay proposes that the political function of an art object must cede to the prioritization of the artist's own proclivities, which are informed but not determined exclusively by the question of Black subjectivity.

"I'm an American. I'm Black. I'm a painter," uttered Saunders in 1994, before going on to say, "So all those things enter into what it is that becomes [the work] I present."[161] Here, Saunders articulates a polyphonic understanding of himself that carries into the contrapuntal nature of his oeuvre. As in the case of *Untitled*, the measured intellectualism of pure formalism, as expressed by the layered hard edges of the board as well as Cy Twombly—esque marks, is fused with an elemental and instinctual awareness of the pulse of the world beyond the studio. This is evinced by the inclusion of a concert poster that appears to have been torn from its original surface and affixed to the painting.

Saunders's strategy of assemblage, one that brought formalism and improvisation together, speaks to his investment in evading externally enforced expectations and the narrow interpretive frames such expectations espouse. That he has laid a swath of black paint over the lower portion of the poster acknowledges the overlap of street and studio, wherein the clamor and contradictions inherent to contemporary life may be clarified by way of his creative pursuits.

—Camille Bacon

Dave McKenzie

b. 1977   Artist in Residence 2003—04

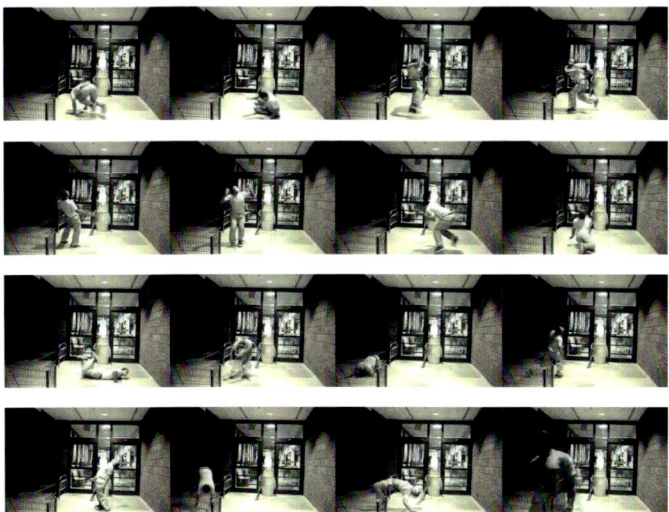

Edward and Me, 2000. Single-channel video projection, looped, TRT: 00:04:25. Edition 2 of 4. Museum purchase with funds provided by the Acquisition Committee 2001.12

Through endurance, exhaustion, and humor, Dave McKenzie illuminates the seriousness of play in art making. With a background in printmaking, McKenzie finds an animating force in repetition as a dynamic, disorienting, and vital technique. His art engages with and questions ideas, images, and language using his principal tool—his own body. His performances, both live and for the camera, are characterized by showing an awareness of a voyeuristic audience, incorporating the built environment, taking risks, and intervening in the public sphere.

Edward and Me, made while McKenzie was participating in the residency at Skowhegan School of Painting and Sculpture, exemplifies his aesthetic inclinations. Filmed outside of a grocery store, McKenzie choreographed his movements based on a gesture from Edward Norton's character in the film *Fight Club* (1999). One of the artist's earliest videos, the work explores performance in real time and what it means to record, rearrange, filter, and layer movement through editing, doubling himself in the process. The work is also influenced by the artist Chris Burden, whose art included sculpture, video, and installation, and who is especially known for his extreme—physically and psychically—and demanding live art. *Edward and Me*, McKenzie's early experiment in performance for the camera, was featured in the Studio Museum's iconic survey *Freestyle* in 2001.

—Adrienne Edwards

Martin Puryear

b. 1941

While teaching at Fisk University—a historically Black college in Nashville—in the early 1970s, Martin Puryear read Jean Toomer's 1923 novel *Cane*, written during and after Toomer's time as a principal at a Black school in rural Georgia. Puryear and Toomer were both born in Washington, DC—albeit nearly fifty years apart—and both experienced the South as educators. Widely considered a modernist masterpiece for its vignette structure that alternates between narrative prose, poetry, and script-like passages, *Cane* impacted and echoed Puryear's experience of the South, despite the decades separating the two. In the late 1990s, Puryear named the Harlem Renaissance novel as a book he would be interested in visually responding to. The resulting 2000 edition of *Cane* features ten woodblock prints by the artist, with seven representing women in the novel and three responding to the graphic arcs Toomer created to separate the sections of the book. A special edition of fifty (from the larger edition of four hundred) also includes an artist-designed wooden slipcase made from four types of wood and a portfolio of seven woodblock prints.

Puryear, an artist known for labor-intensive, handmade sculptures primarily in wood, returned to woodblock printing, which also requires carving, for this project. The prints exemplify Puryear's commitment to abstract organic forms that are often familiar but that evade definition. The works are not mere likenesses but instead evocations of the strength and complexity of these characters, including young Black women lusted after by men and a white woman ostracized for having biracial sons. In collapsing the abstract and the figurative in these portraits, Puryear nods to *Cane*'s experimental fusion of drama, poetry, and prose.

—Connie H. Choi

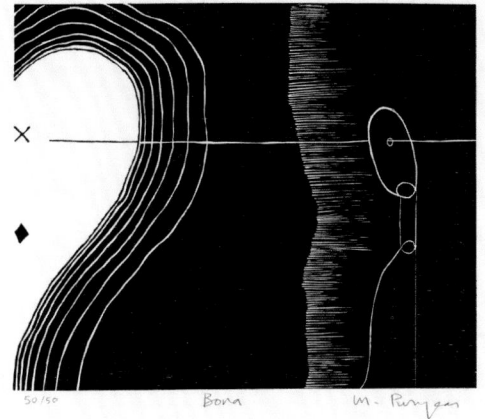

Bona (from *Cane* by Jean Toomer, Arion
Press Editions), 2000. Woodcut on
Kitakata paper, image: 10 ½ × 12 ¾ in.,
sheet: 17 × 20 ½ in. Museum purchase
with funds provided by the Acquisition
Committee 2001.8.1

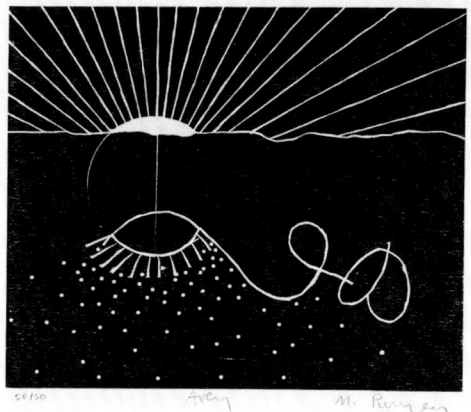

Avey (from *Cane* by Jean Toomer, Arion
Press editions), 2000. Woodcut on
Kitakata paper, image: 10 ½ × 12 ¾ in.,
sheet: 17 × 20 ½ in. Museum purchase
with funds provided by the Acquisition
Committee 2001.8.7

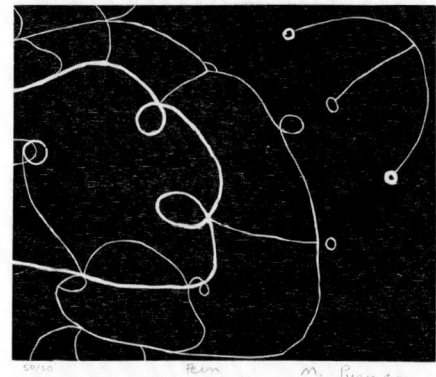

Fern (from *Cane* by Jean Toomer, Arion
Press editions), 2000. Woodcut on
Kitakata paper, image: 10 ½ × 12 ¾ in.,
sheet: 17 × 20 ½ in. Museum purchase
with funds provided by the Acquisition
Committee 2001.8.5

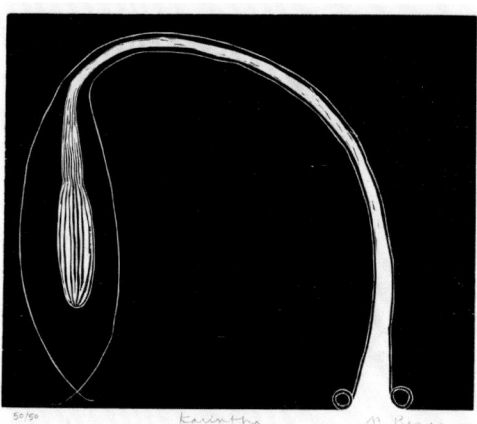

Karintha (from *Cane* by Jean Toomer,
Arion Press editions), 2000. Woodcut on
Kitakata paper, image: 10 ½ × 12 ¾ in.,
sheet: 17 × 20 ½ in. Museum purchase
with funds provided by the Acquisition
Committee 2001.8.4

Yinka Shonibare

b. 1962

Since the late 1990s, Yinka Shonibare CBE RA has created sculptures, photographs, and videos of figures dressed in Victorian-inspired clothing made of brightly colored Dutch wax fabric. Often headless, the figures' poses and costumes offer a nuanced approach to national identity and the legacy of colonialism.

Hopscotch presents a surreal scene of three children playing a centuries-old game of skill and strategy. Their pinafores, petticoats, and bloomers are styled after fashions from the height of Britain's empire and the "Scramble for Africa," the late nineteenth-century period when seven European countries seized control of most of the African continent. The identity of these headless children is ambiguous, as they represent neither the colonizer nor the colonized. The Dutch wax patterns on their clothes are often associated with "Africanness," as this patterning is most popular in West Africa. The origins of Dutch wax, however, trace back to batik patterns found in Indonesia. During the Dutch colonization of Indonesia, the Dutch attempted to market inexpensive replications of the batik process on printed fabric. While this proved to be a commercial flop in Indonesia, Dutch wax fabric found mass appeal in West Africa. For over two decades, Shonibare has incorporated Dutch wax fabric into his artworks as a signifier of colonialism that acknowledges crisscrossing trade routes, the globalized nature of commerce, and the appropriation of colonizers' tools by people of color.

Shonibare's biography and artistic practice are grounded in transnationalism and upend essentialist definitions of what is African or British: born in London; raised in Lagos, Nigeria; educated at prominent British art schools with a master's degree from Goldsmiths; and, since 2019, the founder of a residency program in Nigeria through his Guest Artist Space (GAS) Foundation. Shonibare's complicated relationship to empire extends even to his name. Though he questions the role of monarchy, he proudly carries the honorific title of CBE: "Commander of the British Empire."

—Miranda Lash

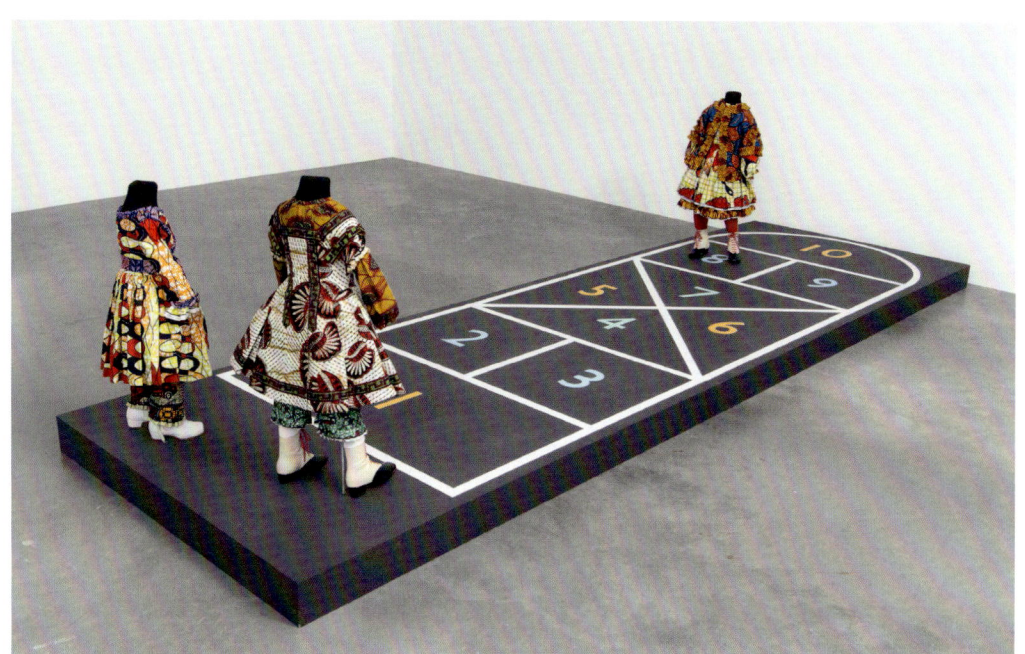

Hopscotch, 2000. Wax-printed cotton textile
and wooden plinth, 41 × 54 ½ × 176 in. Gift
of Ninah and Michael Lynne 2018.44.18

John Bankston
b. 1963

John Bankston's paintings present scenes from life in the "Rainbow Forest," an imagined environment heavily influenced by everyday people in San Francisco, where the artist lives and works. In this magical forest, a variety of characters explore their idyllic world in expressive and often colorful dress. In *Taking Sun to the Clouds*, a young Black man wears an orange uniform with a thick black belt tightened around his oversized pants. He rests one hand on his hip and raises a large bulging sack containing his hopes for a bright future to the golden cloud that hovers above in the distance.

Taking Sun to the Clouds reflects Bankston's interest in revisiting the visual language of coloring books. The painting's deceptively childish form creates a space for play and discovery. Bankston organizes his oil on linen painting with thick black lines that define the composition, the man's expression, his bag, and the sparsely foliated landscape. They also leave room for the artist's loose brushstrokes to create blocks of color that shape the composition. In this way, Bankston's work engages viewers through the common childhood experience of coloring a picture while unfolding a narrative.

As a large-scale painting, *Taking Sun to the Clouds* stands as a singular work of art but also retains its place in an ongoing story of a thriving community of characters who are figuring out their place in the world.

—Bridget R. Cooks

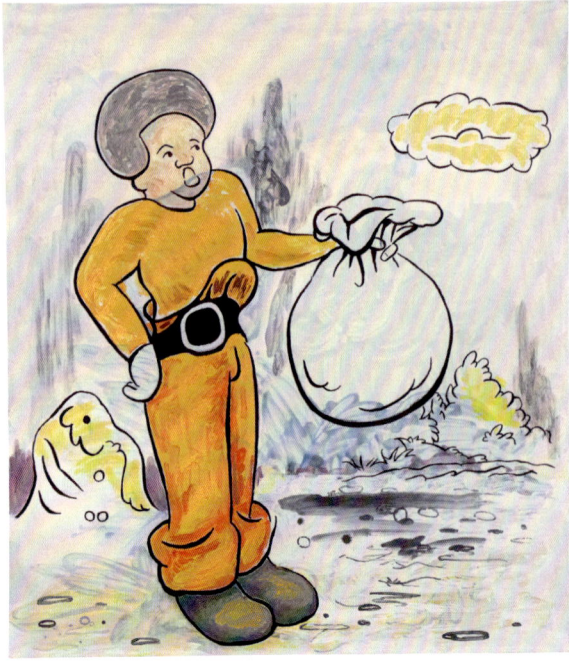

Taking Sun to the Clouds, 2000. Oil on linen, 54 × 48 in. Museum purchase with funds provided by the Acquisition Committee 2001.7

Mark Bradford

b. 1961

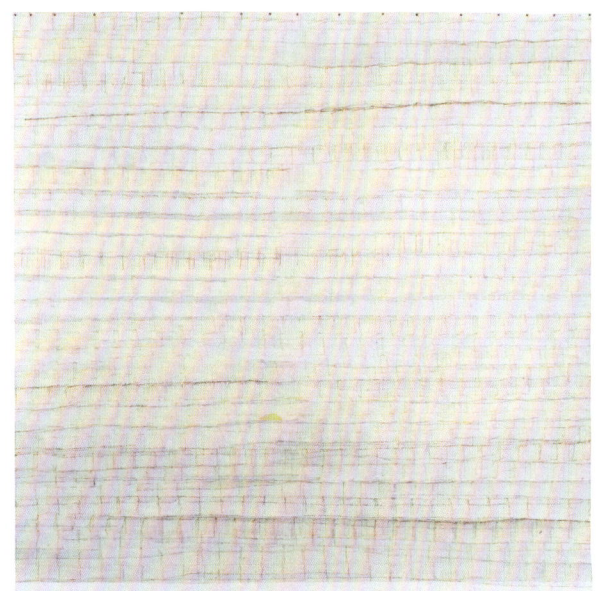

Enter and Exit the New Negro, 2000. Mixed media on canvas, 99 ¼ × 100 in. Museum purchase with funds provided by the Acquisition Committee 2001.9

In a practice frequently described as "social abstraction," Mark Bradford employs material and process to explore histories, spaces, and structures that have impacted or been influenced by marginalized populations. An early work, *Enter and Exit the New Negro* utilizes endpapers, a material Bradford began experimenting with while a student at the California Institute of the Arts in the 1990s. Endpapers—small translucent papers that protect hair ends from heat damage during the perm process—hold a special significance for the artist, who grew up in his mother's beauty salon and became a hairdresser himself. By using a readily available object imbued with both personal and cultural meaning, Bradford pushes and expands traditional definitions of abstraction and painting.

The endpapers inspired the artist's later use of other types of paper also associated with urban neighborhoods, including billboards, advertising broadsides, and movie posters. Known for the accumulation and subsequent excavation of surfaces in these later works, Bradford here suggests a similar kind of process. The layering of the tissue-like papers creates a sense of depth, which is furthered by the undulations of cream and soft yellow. With the thin sheets of endpapers affixed in a staccato rhythm across the canvas, *Enter and Exit the New Negro* recalls familiar and accessible things, such as gridded notebook paper and music sheets. Reflecting the world around the artist, the painting does not attempt to conceal the original context of its primary material. Instead, it becomes a celebration of Black beauty salons and the communities created and nurtured in those spaces.

—Connie H. Choi

Adia Millett

b. 1975   Artist in Residence 2001—02

In Adia Millett's *Inventing Truth* installation, seven gilded frames hang salon-style, each displaying a needlepoint of a single object. Reading clockwise from uppermost left: a quarter pint of Popov; a brown porkpie hat; a pink rose stem; a US twenty-dollar bill, the White House side facing up; white high-rise underwear briefs; a pack of Newports; and a rifle. The use of needlepoint (here on mesh) is apt, as Millett stitches together objects to present a portrait-in-fragments. For the artist, an object is an animate thing and therefore always implicates its use and owner; an object indicates identity and builds a character in place of an absent "subject."

"There are a variety of ways that leftover traces of the past continue to linger in objects and spaces—the fabrics of the blankets we use, old heirlooms, reconstructed buildings . . . . We remember the colors, but forget the shapes or we replace the old idea of who we were with who we are now," she states.[162] Some items in *Inventing Truth* represent purchases unduly associated with Black men—in 1964, when the FDA banned the tobacco industry from targeting youth under twenty-one, the companies turned their efforts toward Black communities, pitching menthol as a tastier and stronger form of nicotine; the vodka for the cheap but accessible booze wrongly associated with rates of alcoholism in Black men. Meanwhile, the rifle stands out among the arrangement. This is the gun of white people, used against Black men, before, during, and in the ongoing aftermath of chattel slavery. The title offers a guide: these objects invent a truth about someone, but whoever this someone was, surely he was acted upon.

Using a medium deemed "women's work" to address masculine terms, Millett's cross-stitching drags these symbolic objects across time, animating them anew as either venerated icons or anthropological exploitations of a forgotten man.

—Meg Whiteford

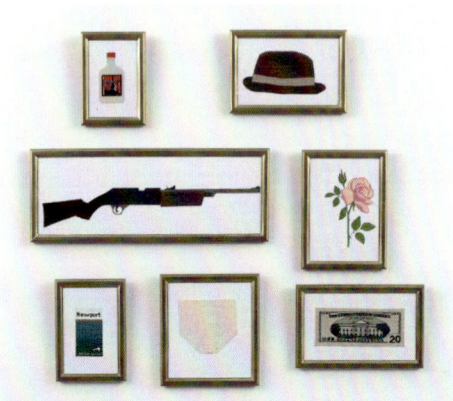

Inventing Truth, 2001—02. Thread on mesh in giltwood frames, installed: 35 ½ × 41 × 1 in. Museum purchase with funds provided by the Acquisition Committee 2002.10.17a-g

Kehinde Wiley

b. 1977   Artist in Residence 2001—02

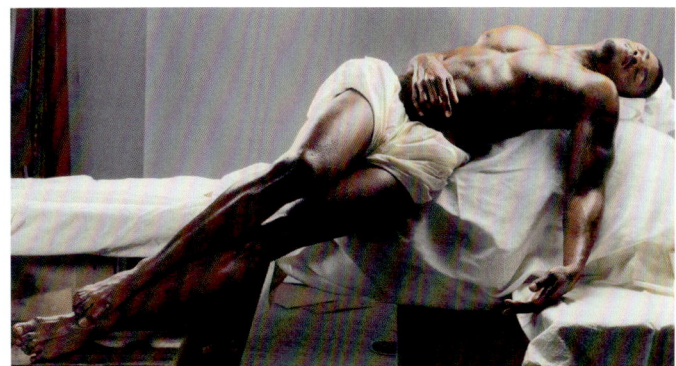

After Jean-Bernard Restout's "Sleep" (from the "Black Light" series), 2009. Archival inkjet print on Hahnemule fine art paper, 30 × 50 in. Bequest of Peggy Cooper Cafritz (1947—2018), Washington, DC, collector, educator, and activist 2018.40.374

Kehinde Wiley's paintings of contemporary Black men in anachronistic poses critique centuries of racist art history and challenge viewers to consider how contemporary representations of Black men often reflect and perpetuate race and power relations. Wiley's visual language makes obvious the specialness of his Black subjects. His veneration of the Black-man-off-the-street is radical because, in the face of visually coded white supremacy, it celebrates the joy and power of self-determination.

Aspects of Wiley's signature formula are present in his early painting *Conspicuous Fraud Series #1 (Eminence)*. In it, a central Black figure claims space within the art historical narrative, which has long excluded Black artists and subjects. Wiley presents a stylized Black man in stark contrast to the media's sensationalized representation of Black masculinity, and the figure's self-expression is conveyed, in part, by contemporary fashion. Wiley underscores his painting's artifice by situating the Black figure in an undefined space and using a decorative element, in this case the figure's expansive and meandering hair, to blur the distinction between subject, background, and foreground.

Shortly after making this painting, Wiley developed his now-standard practice of "street casting" Black models to mimic the power poses of the white gentry memorialized in centuries of European painting. By 2006, Wiley's approach had solidified and matured, and a vigorous demand for his work inspired him to expand the reach of his practice. He established a studio in Beijing, the first of many international production outposts, and he began work on *The World Stage*, what would become an eight-year global exhibition series. At the same moment, Wiley branched into new media and made his work available to a wider market through a partner-ship with Cerealart.

Cerealart "developed, produced, and distributed" three-dimensional multiples for artists who were interested in the "possibilities presented by consumer culture." With Cerealart, Wiley created his first sculptural busts and tapestry. Wiley modeled *The Gypsy Fortune-Teller* after François

Boucher's eighteenth-century tapestry *The Collation*, a romantic pastoral depicting white gentlefolk lavishly enjoying their privilege in an idealized garden setting. Wiley's interrogation of the visual language of white power extends easily to the tapestry format, which—like painting—has been used by European aristocracy to display wealth and power since medieval times. Wiley's eight-foot-wide tapestry retains many of Boucher's signs of luxury and relaxation: languid poses, opulent jewelry, an empty wine bottle, the bent posture of a servant. But unlike its French inspiration, Wiley presents contemporary Black men, two of whom directly stare at the viewer, daring a reaction to the mix of seemingly incongruent visual cues. Why don't we see or celebrate the outdoor leisure activities of Black men?

Today, Wiley collaborates with and nourishes a network of artists to build new global discourses about Africa and the African diaspora. Through Black Rock Senegal, a residency program in Dakar, Wiley brings together artists from around the world to engage in cross-cultural dialogue and multidisciplinary creative processes. As culture writer Touré points out in his essay on the artist, "It's revolutionary work that Kehinde is doing, but the real revolution is not happening with his brushes but within his mind, where he sees us as beautiful and then figures out how to get the world to see that."[163] Wiley's work is much more than his virtuoso brushwork, or even his love/hate relationship with art history. Those are just the means. His mission is much bigger than that.

—Whitney Tassie

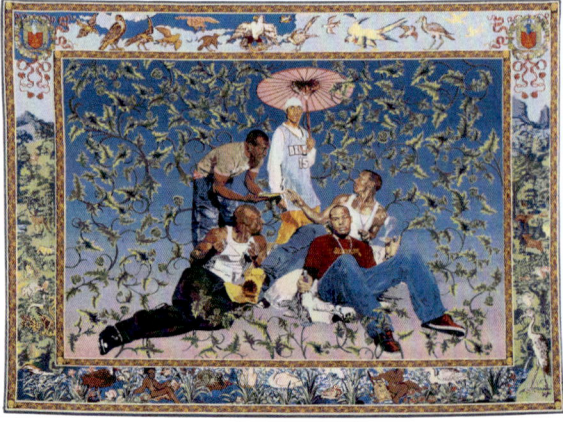

The Gypsy Fortune-Teller, 2007.
Jacquard tapestry, 70 ¾ × 99 ⅛ in.
Bequest of Peggy Cooper Cafritz
(1947—2018), Washington, DC,
collector, educator, and activist
2018.40.376

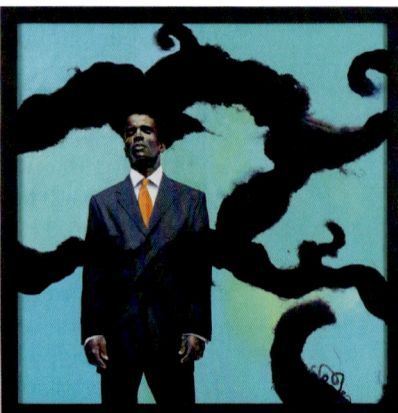

Conspicuous Fraud Series #1 (Eminence),
2001. Oil on canvas, 72 ½ × 72 ½ in.
Museum purchase made possible
by a gift from Anne Ehrenkranz
2002.10.14

Whitfield Lovell

b. 1959

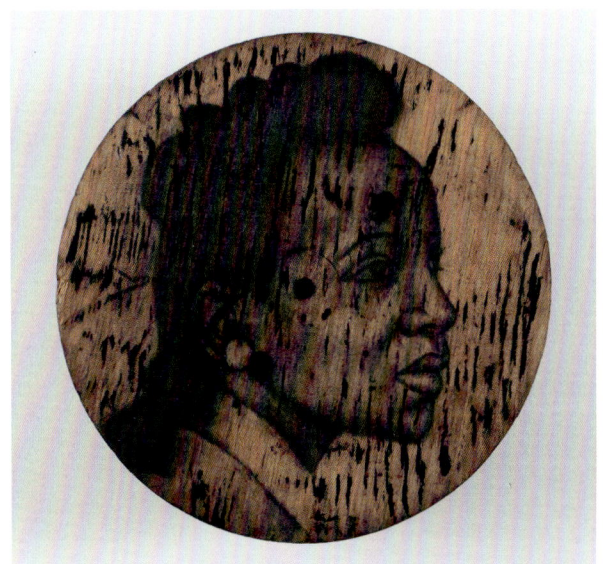

Coin XXIV, 2002. Charcoal on wood,
5 × 9 ½ in. Gift of a private collector
2002.25.3

Whitfield Lovell's exquisite drawings of African Americans have set the standard for realism in contemporary art. Lovell selects his figures from antique photographs he finds at flea markets—he is fascinated by the forgotten histories of Black individuals from twentieth-century North America and is inspired by the facial expressions, fashion, and poses through which they present in photographic portraiture. Lovell renders these people on carefully selected paper and wood, often pairing his drawings with objects, such as playing cards, toys, and other domestic objects, to create conceptual artworks. These choices reanimate the unknown sitters and begin a conversation between the figure and accompanying objects.

Coin XXIV is one in a series of works in which Lovell portrays the faces of African American people on cylinders of wood. The woman pictured looks aspirationally upward. Elegantly coiffed and accessorized with a crisply ironed collar and button earring, she exudes optimism and hope. The color and texture of the wood enhance her lifelikeness. Three diagonally arranged holes offer a clue to the wood's former function as a gear. Thus, the material suggests a relationship between the woman and the history of Black labor.

Lovell's "Coins" honor anonymous sitters by presenting them on currency usually reserved for political or allegorical figures. Larger than monetary coins, their size argues for greater appreciation of the significance of everyday Black people past and present, known and unknown. The form also addresses the value of African Americans and their roles in building the wealth of the United States as enslaved people.

—Bridget R. Cooks

Odili Donald Odita

b. 1966

Refuge and Flight, 2002. Acrylic
on canvas, 75 × 80 in. Gift of
David Alan Grier, Los Angeles 2007.2

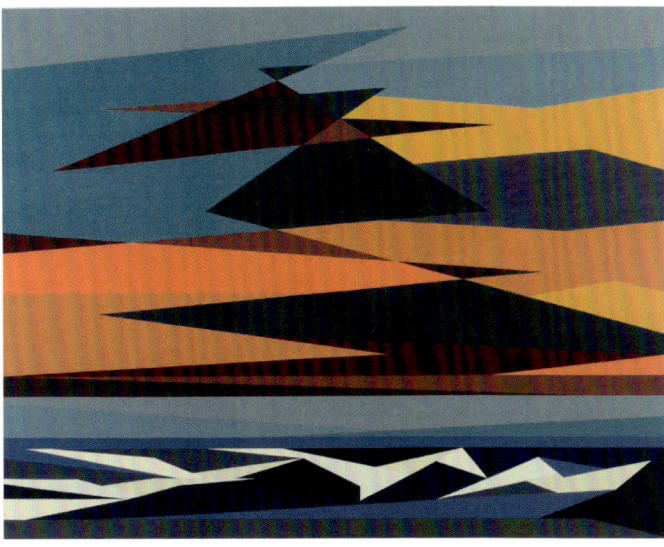

The peaks and valleys that are endured to escape, to persevere, to survive,
are so vast in Odili Donald Odita's *Refuge and Flight* that their shadows
and reflections produce even more shadows and reflections. This landscape visualizes an essence of the expression: How far? How far has one
gone to arrive at this encounter; how far must one go to arrive at the next?

To flee is as sharp as life can be, demonstrated through Odita's pointed,
geometric, triangular shapes. Though it has been done countless times
by countless people around the world, and for as much as the path has
been trodden, the terrain remains sharp enough to pierce skin, to draw
blood, to leave scars. For those who do make it to the other side, a new
journey has only just begun.

The boundlessness of *Refuge and Flight*—an abstracted configuration of
a body of water running parallel to an orange landscape running parallel
to the sky, each one composed of blocks of colors that stretch onward,
upward, over one another, and downward—suggests that forced migration never ends. Just as there are layers and contradictions within Odita's
painting, there are layers and contradictions embedded within calling
a site of displacement a home. Does where one is ever negate where one
is from? Is home only a place to which one has returned? Still, the ability—the blessing—to arrive at a place of refuge is, with all its complexity,
to arrive somewhere safer than where one once was.

—Nectar Knuckles

Nadine Robinson

b. 1968   Artist in Residence 2000—01

For *Black*, Nadine Robinson presents a glimpse of her practice at a more intimate scale. Created after her 2000 to 2001 participation in the *Artist-in-Residence* program at the Studio Museum, the work is one of the artist's "sound paintings" and features a single black speaker centered on black-painted canvas. While the minimalist aspect of this work differs from her other monumental installations, it nonetheless demonstrates key elements of her practice: engagement with sound, modernism, and blackness.

Robinson is an artist best known for large-scale works, particularly those engaging with sound and light, that combine multiple historical and cultural references from the Black urban experience, Afro-Caribbean spiritual practices, hip-hop music, and the legacy of modernist art. Her sound installations typically feature stacks of sound speakers that emulate the "House of Joy" wooden speakers that energized Jamaican dance halls in the mid-1950s. These installations, as well as sound paintings such as *Black*, amplify and reverberate with her own audio arrangements—she creates compilations that borrow from hip-hop sampling techniques with combined snippets of music and voices pulled and recorded from a variety of disparate sources. These presentations offer an expanded sensorial engagement with art and an appreciation for the speaker, not only for its technical capacity to emit quality sound, but as an art object worthy of close listening—and thus, close looking.

Robinson's practice is in dialogue with the tradition of modern artists such as Ad Reinhardt and Robert Ryman, whose monochromatic and abstract paintings are evoked through *Black*'s uniform color. By additionally incorporating the speaker and boom box, objects associated with Black music cultures, Robinson's work attempts to both critique and expand modernism's exclusionary history.

—Kiki Teshome

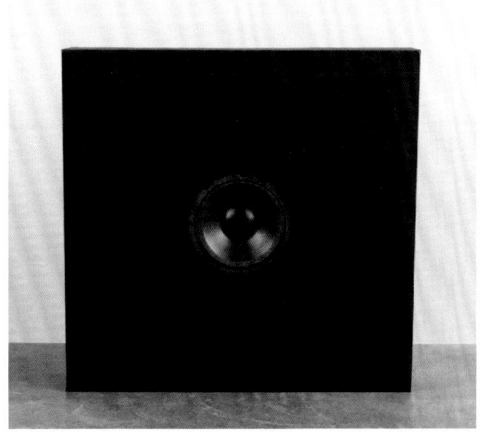

Black, 2002. Acrylic on canvas, speaker, CD player, and amplifier, 42 × 41 × 7 ½ in. Museum purchase with funds provided by the Acquisition Committee 2002.10.15

Mary Lee Bendolph

b. 1935

Mary Lee Bendolph is a quilter, printmaker, activist, and textile artist based in Boykin, Alabama, also known as Gee's Bend. Gee's Bend is home to a lineage of artists with diverse aesthetic and technical approaches to quilt-making that have been passed down through several generations. Bendolph's quilts often feature striking geometrical compositions made of a variety of textile swatches. They range in visual complexity, with some artworks featuring upwards of twenty thousand strips of fabric. In 1972, Sears Roebuck established a long-term contract with quilters in the region to fabricate corduroy pillow shams. The influx of corduroy made the fabric easily accessible, and it was soon introduced into quilts. The varied textures highlight differences in tactility and give the artworks a sense of dimensionality through contrast, such as when velvety ridges of corduroy abut worn patches of denim.

While Bendolph often employs a combination of textures, *Blocks and strips* is constructed entirely of corduroy. The striking combination of navy and aqua stripes provides the visual framework of the quilt. The stripes radiate toward the center in a mazelike configuration. Bendolph resists symmetry, varying the sizes of the strips and punctuating the two colors with occasional fragments of pink and orange. At the center of the work, a winding shock of red fabric acts as both the visual anchor and a counterpoint to the complimentary shades of blue. Bendolph frequently uses repurposed materials, including clothing worn by members of her community. The quilts give the clothing fragments a new purpose while imbuing the artwork with the history and experiences of those who once donned them.

—Mia Matthias

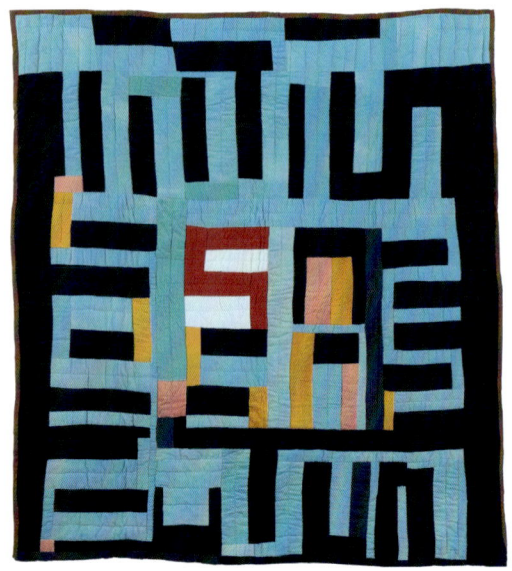

Blocks and strips, 2003. Corduroy, 77 × 71 in. Gift of the Souls Grown Deep Foundation, 2020 2020.12.1

Isaac Julien

b. 1960   Artist in Residence 1990—91

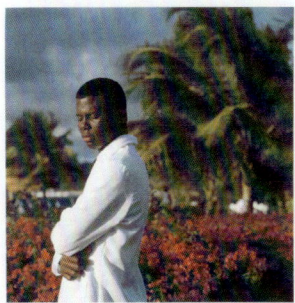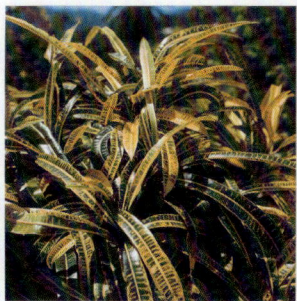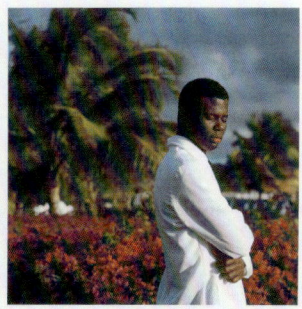

Omeros / Paradise, 2003. Digital color print,
image: 15 × 45 in. Edition 30. Museum
purchase with funds provided by the
Acquisition Committee 2004.6.14

Across the practice of multimedia artist Isaac Julien, queer Black desire, migration, ecology, and diaspora meet as interconnected waters. He emerged in the orbit of the Black British cultural studies shaped by Paul Gilroy, Stuart Hall, and Kobena Mercer, a model of study that challenged the legacies of colonialism and imperialism by asking questions about popular media's depictions of race, ethnicity, and belonging. Formally enriched by the influence of photography, the artist also takes from collaging, painting, choreography, and sound, finding his home in multiscreen video installations.

The trajectory of Julien's filmic practice unfurled from the Black Cinema workshops of the 1980s during Thatcherite Britain, an electrified era in which he cofounded Sankofa Film and Video Collective in 1983. He shifted to an independent solo career with his lyrical meditation on Langston Hughes, *Looking for Langston* (1989), a seminal film on desire among gay Black men. Inventively following the elliptical structure of a dream, the film uses visuals and sound as vehicles for a mythic imagining of the Harlem Renaissance.

Julien's compositional elegance and astute cinematic language—as well as his play with audiovisual expressions of Black memory and what Saidiya Hartman has termed "critical fabulation"—are exquisitely displayed in *Vagabondia*, of which the Studio Museum holds a photograph of the same name.[164] Set in Sir John Soane's Museum in London, this double-projection installation demystifies the imperial and colonial underpinnings of such collections. A Black woman conservator and a vagabond-trickster-dancer operate as disruptive presences—they expose pervasive structures of domination by troubling the authority of that space with, respectively, her very presence as a custodian and his unruly choreography. Accompanied by an untranslated voiceover in Saint Lucian Creole, Julien's piece loosens the architecture of the museum, as its claims to ownership are unsettled. *Vagabondia* combines marionette-like dancing, reanimated statues, mirrored doublings, kaleidoscopic movements, fluid camera movements, and shifting shadows.

Baltimore (2003), a multiscreen installation that includes *Incognito*—the uncanny sculptural likeness of Melvin van Peebles—engages a similar matrix of museums, blackness, and history by resurfacing the slick visuals and Black urban iconography of Blaxploitation, with touchstone appearances of such figures as Martin Luther King Jr. and Malcolm X.

Nestled between *Vagabondia* and *Baltimore*, the video triptych *Omeros / Paradise* illuminates the importance of the aquatic in Julien's practice. The title, after Derek Walcott's book-length poem, infuses this mesmerizing video with a fantastical, epic tone. The narrative centers on a young Caribbean man and toggles between the sunny paradise of Saint Lucia and a chilly, gray, industrial London. This work manifests Julien's attention to hybridity and the tensions of diasporic displacement and so-called "post-colonial" identities, which he continues to address through his interrogations of globalization and its ecological consequences. Across all their themes and forms, the global currents and diasporic tides of Julien's practice are entrancingly experimental, fragmentary, atmospheric, and multisensory.

—Yasmina Price

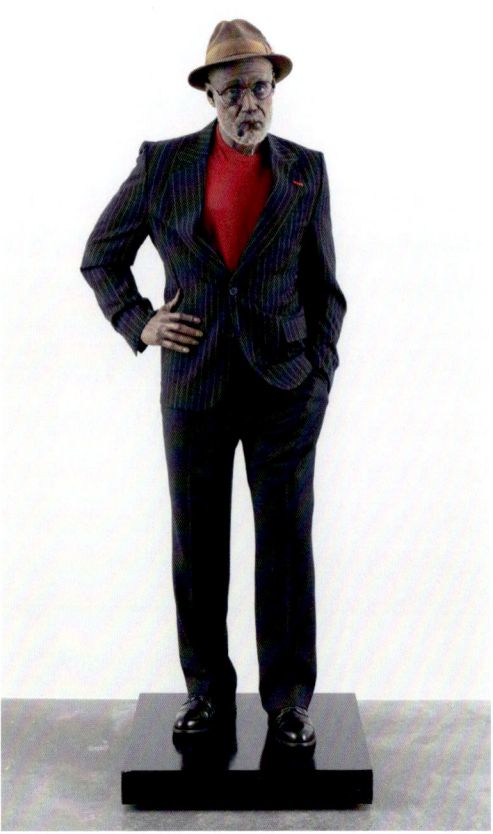

Incognito, 2003. Plaster, urethane foam, urethane plastic, acrylic paint, cloth, and human hair, 73 ¼ × 29 ½ × 19 ¾ in. Edition 1 of 3. Gift of the artist and Mr. Melvin Van Peebles 2004.5.24

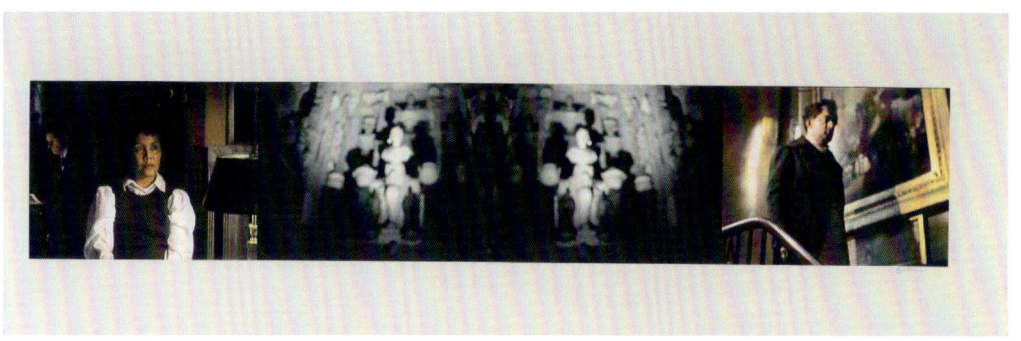

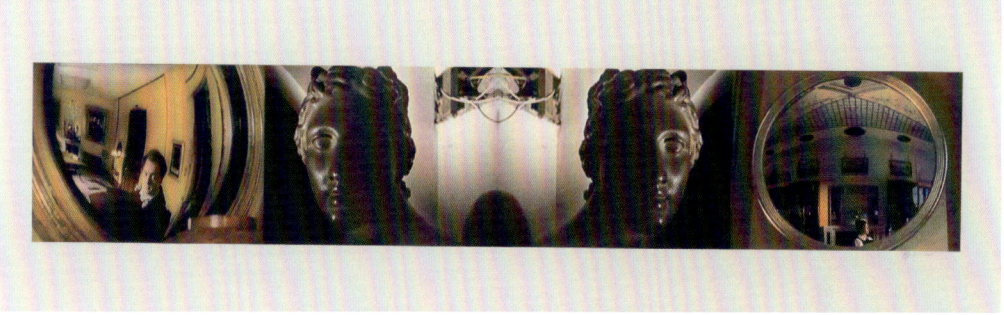

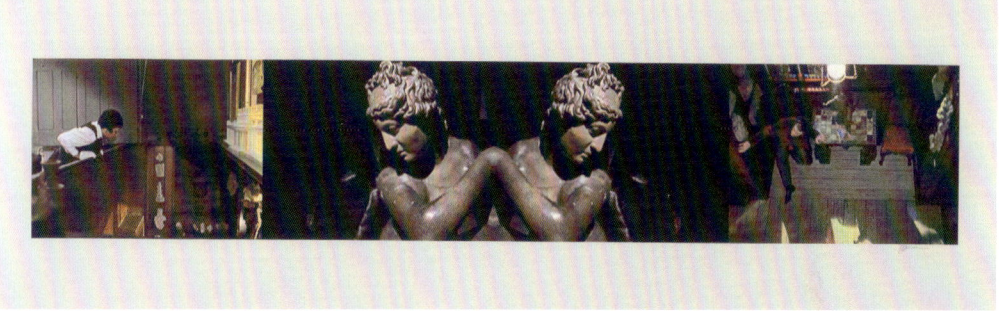

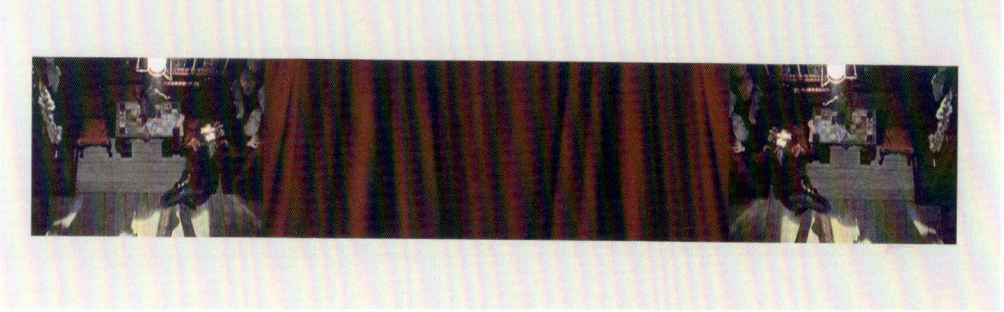

Untitled (film stills from *Vagabondia*),
2000. Four digital prints on Arches paper,
13 × 41 in. Edition AP 1. Gift of the artist
2000.12a–d

Hank Willis Thomas

b. 1976

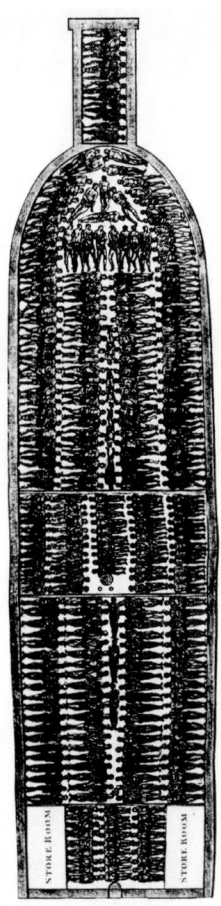

Absolut Power, 2003. Inkjet print on canvas, frame: 40 ¼ × 27 ¾ × 1 ½ in. Bequest of Peggy Cooper Cafritz (1947—2018), Washington, DC, collector, educator, and activist 2018.40.336

COLLECTION

ABSOLUT POWER.

A question of value animates Hank Willis Thomas's conceptual art practice. In his new media works, he appropriates the language and imagery of consumer culture to interrogate themes of identity, history, and popular culture. Works such as *Absolut Power* display a unique preoccupation with the ambiguous social status of Black life. In this work, Thomas repurposes the iconic Absolut Vodka ads, which debuted in 1981, to inquire about the legacies of new-world slavery and its commodification of the Black body. Thomas's print adheres to the conventions of the media campaign as he maintains the brand's spelling and distinctive font. However, unlike the vibrant colors and playful marks of, say, Andy Warhol's 1985 commissioned portrait of the bottle, Thomas explores the racial logics that have given rise to the modern capitalist economy with an overlay of an eighteenth-century abolitionist print that portrays the diagram of the British slave ship *Brookes*. Thomas meanwhile deploys slightly askew lines and uneven pigmentation to mimic the effects of the wood engravings in the letterpress that give eighteenth-century printmaking its distinctive style. By combining the aesthetics of the print and the ads, Thomas casts the economy of slavery as a predecessor to present-day marketing strategies. He fills the bottle up to its neck with Black figures and retains the two empty spaces from the original print marked "STORE ROOM," so that, as in the *Brookes* diagram, the figures are nothing more than units of value that illustrate how profit motives transformed Black people into objects of exchange. Thomas's forging this ship in a bottle uncovers a disturbing resonance between past and present and considers how racism is embedded in the design of the modern capitalist economy.

In *Priceless*, this practice of appropriation aims at implicating the viewer. Following the murder of his cousin Songha Willis in Philadelphia in 2000, Thomas used a photograph from the funeral to create a banner modeled after Mastercard's famous "Priceless" ad campaign. Presented as a billboard outside of his 2007 exhibition at the Birmingham Museum of Art, the image of his grieving family is accompanied with superimposed text that reproduces the ad's iterative structure and tagline. The placement of phrases such as "3-piece suit: $250," "gold chain: $400," and "9mm Pistol: $80" recalls the cadence of the ad until the tagline appears at the bottom of the image: "Picking the perfect casket for your son: [. . .] priceless." Whereas the Mastercard ad seeks to remind the consumer that "there are some things money can't buy," *Priceless* explicitly reflects on the question of value that Black life embodies. In this instance, pricelessness signifies the inherent value of the lost loved one expressed in the family's grief and the disposability, or nonvalue, of Black life within the racial order of capitalist modernity. By displaying the image as a billboard, Thomas confronts the public with their indifference to the quotidian violence that Black people endure.

—Nijah Cunningham

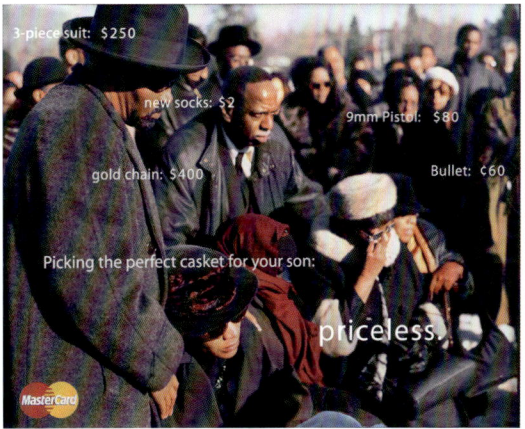

Priceless, 2004. Lambda photograph,
48 × 60 in. Bequest of Peggy Cooper Cafritz
(1947—2018), Washington, DC, collector,
educator, and activist 2018.40.344

Nontsikelelo Veleko

b. 1977

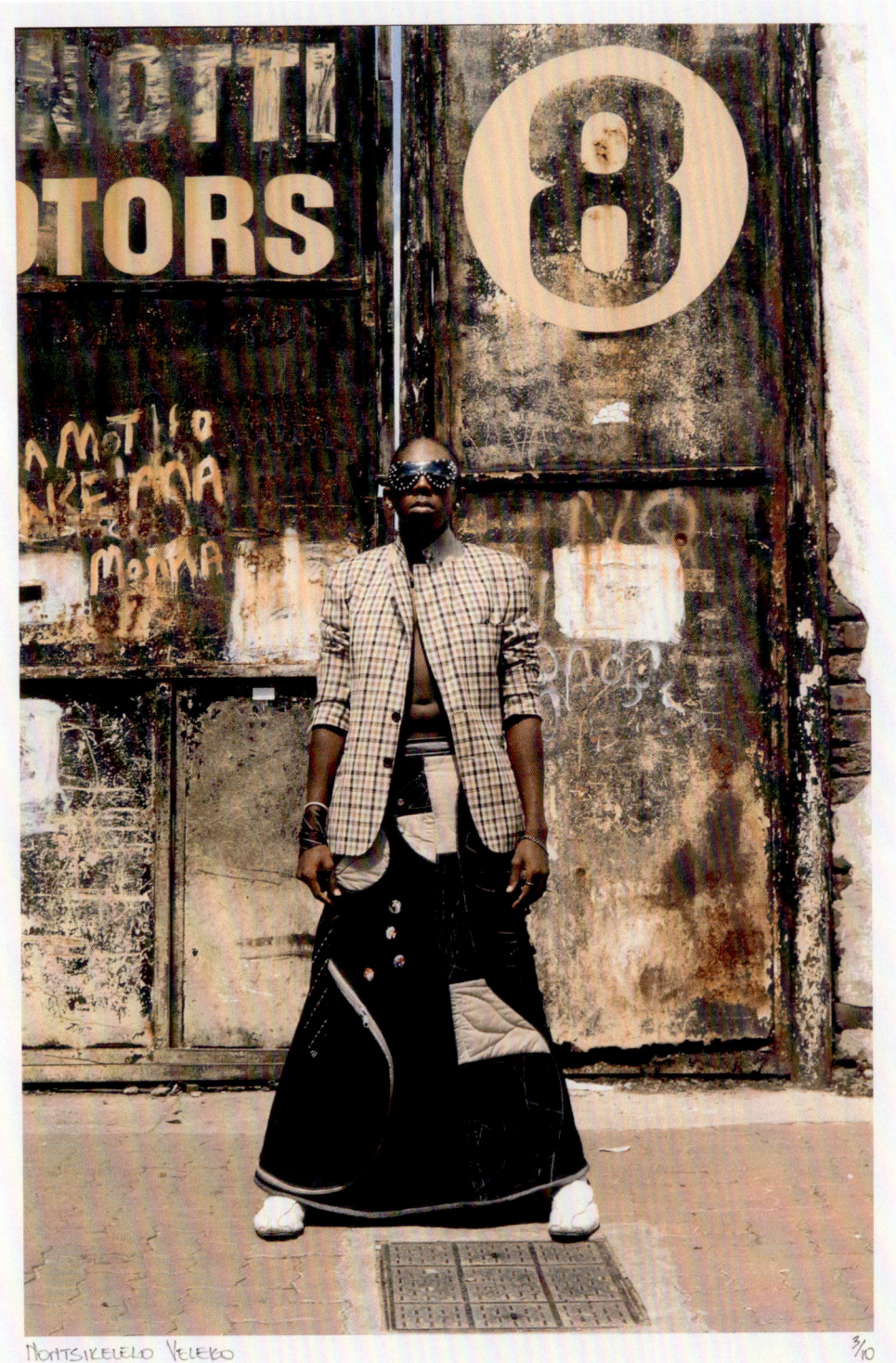

Nontsikelelo Veleko

3/10

Sibu IV, part of Nontsikelelo "Lolo" Veleko's series "Beauty is in the Eye of the Beholder," introduces the burgeoning youth fashion culture of Johannesburg. Veleko uses street photography to provoke the question of what is considered "Black enough," confronting the stereotype of how young, Black, urban individuals should look in a post-apartheid era.[165] Jean-Paul Sartre's concept of bad faith (mauvaise foi), understood as self-deception where individuals deny their freedom and responsibility to avoid the anguish of radical freedom, is extended by Lewis Gordon in his analysis of anti-Black racism to reveal how society perpetuates a collective bad faith by constructing Black people as fixed, inferior Others, thereby denying their existential agency and humanity. This portrait moves beyond the constraints of bad faith through self-expression and one's own lived experience. In this view, the portrait is a site where the subject reveals and discloses itself, while simultaneously entering a state of partial concealment, even when fully visible.

Posing as if they are on the pages of their own high-fashion magazine, the subjects in this series gaze confidently into the camera with a sense of "coolness" and individuality.[166] The subjects' confident and inventive looks defy the expectation that fashion is primarily about showcasing wealth or adhering to Western beauty standards. Veleko's muse in *Sibu IV* is undoubtedly in vogue—wearing sunglasses, a beige plaid jacket, and a black-and-beige patchwork ankle-length skirt. They stand with their legs wide apart in front of a rusted metal gate, reflecting their inventiveness rather than wealth or social status. Thus, through a street-style documentary approach, Veleko captures how the people of South African urban areas employ fashion as a means to express, construct, and challenge prevailing notions of identity. In Veleko's street scenes, fashion is used as a conduit for rethinking post-apartheid society and celebrating the agency and creativity of the "born free" generation.[167] Instead, Veleko's subjects use flamboyant outfits as tools of protest—a rejection of monolithic representations of African aesthetics to instead embrace a diverse and multifaceted visual representation of their own.

— Terrence Phearse

Sibu IV (from the series "Beauty is in the Eye of the Beholder"), 2003—06. Pigment ink print on cotton paper. Image: 11 ½ × 7 ¾ in., sheet: 14 × 9 ¾ in. Edition 3 of 10. Promised gift of Nancy L. Lane PG.2023.010.100

Ellen Gallagher

b. 1965

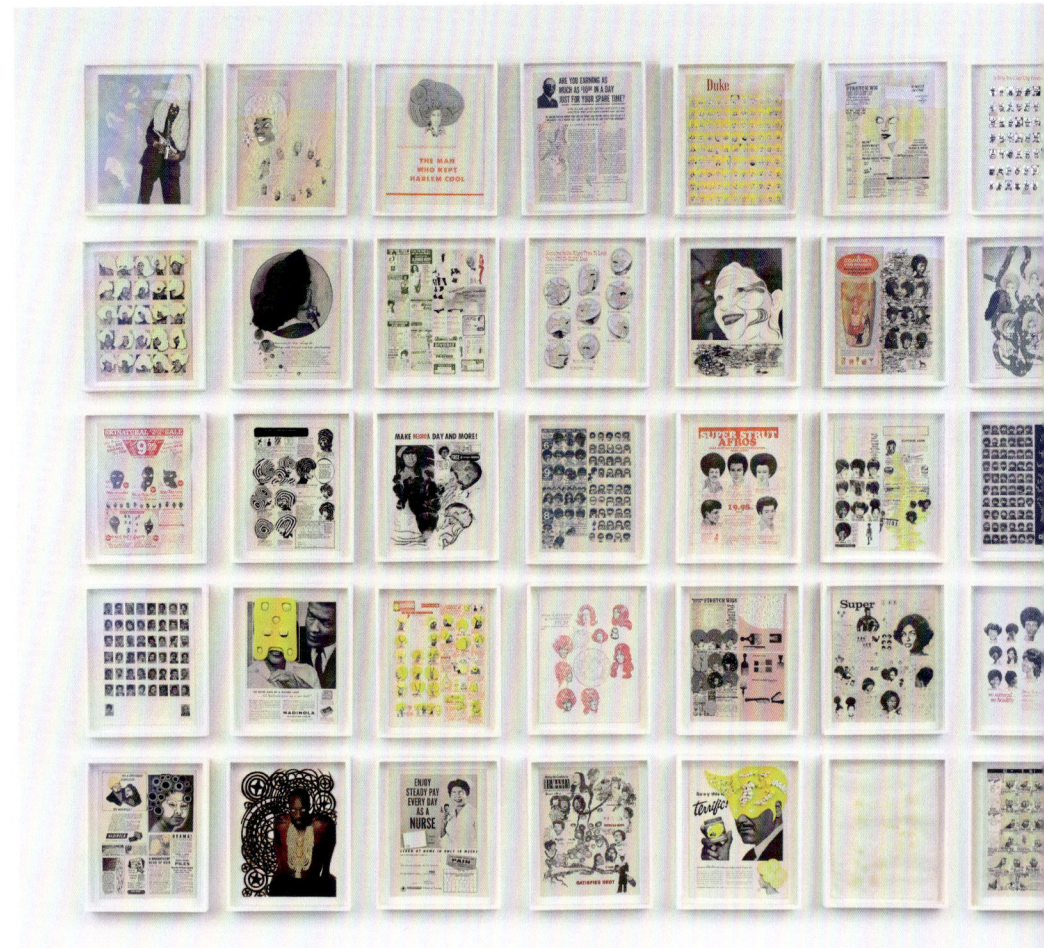

Comprising sixty framed panels reimagining mid-twentieth-century magazine advertisements and articles, Ellen Gallagher's *DeLuxe* serves as a formal and conceptual investigation of identity and transformation. *DeLuxe* emerges from Gallagher's careful research into and collection of magazines aimed primarily at African American audiences. These publications offered dignified portrayals of Black life but often featured ads promoting racialized beauty tips, such as chemical hair straighteners, wigs, and skin-bleaching creams. These ads perpetuated harmful beauty standards rooted in Eurocentric ideals and pressured Black individuals to conform to a white criterion.

Gallagher transforms the ads into photogravures, a printing technique employed in mass production and historical dissemination of cultural narratives. The artist enhances each panel with etching, collage, Plasticine,

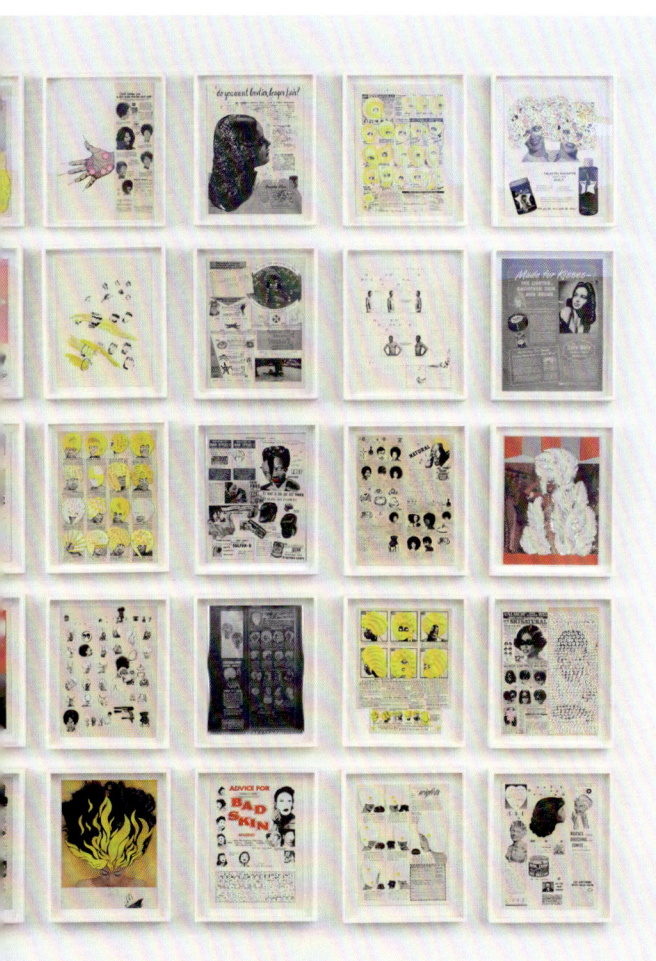

DeLuxe, 2004—05. Grid of sixty photogravure, etching, aquatint and drypoints with lithography, screenprint, embossing, tattoo-machine engraving, laser cutting and chine collé; some with additions of Plasticine, paper collage, enamel, varnish, gouache, pencil, oil, polymer, watercolor, pomade, velvet, glitter, crystals, foil paper, gold leaf, toy eyeballs and imitation ice cubes, each: 13 × 10 ½ in., overall: 86 × 179 in. Edition 7 of 20. Museum purchase made possible by a gift from Thomas H. Lee and Ann Tenenbaum, New York 2005.8a-hhh

beads, and glitter, creating tactile, customized surfaces that resist the impersonal slickness of the original ads. The grid format, while modernist in design, functions as a subversive visual device. Its neat, orderly structure suggests cohesion, yet the diversity of techniques used across the panels disrupts any expectation of uniformity, reflecting the multifaceted nature of identity.

More than a collection of altered advertisements, *DeLuxe* reflects the many dimensions of the Black experience and confronts viewers with the complexities of personal evolution and the challenge of societal expectations. *DeLuxe* is a powerful reminder of art's ability to interrogate, influence culture, and reshape narratives.

—Phillip Edward Spradley

Meschac Gaba
b. 1961

In *African Artist with American Inspiration: Citigroup*, Meschac Gaba proposes a new form of currency by comedically imposing images of his artwork and himself on to enlarged copies of United States paper bills. The work exemplifies his conceptual art practice, which examines and contrasts Western and African visual culture and commerce. He is best known for his playful reuse of found objects and imagery that considers the global economy, museums, and public space as sites of exploration.

The digital prints were presented as part of his 2004 solo exhibition at the Studio Museum, *Meschac Gaba: Tresses*, which featured the artist's altered presentation of hair and paper money. Gaba observed the prevalence and success of West African hair braiding businesses in Harlem and linked the popularity of shared hairstyles between Black women in New York and on the continent. Inspired, the artist worked with hair braiders to recreate iconic buildings in New York and Benin using braided hair extensions.

Gaba further explores the saliency of commerce as a means for autonomy and liberated self-expression through his conceptualization of a new form of currency. By imposing his self-portrait and images of his tresses on to six prints, Gaba raises the issue of the exalted value of the US dollar against the depreciating West African CFA franc. In this work, the Great Seal of the United States, featured on the reverse of the dollar bill, has been conspicuously replaced: the Eye of Providence floating above the pyramid has been swapped for Gaba's architectural creations and the bald eagle with its outspread wings has been discarded to spotlight Gaba's head. By inserting himself into a place normally reserved for symbols of national significance, Gaba points to discrepancies between economic and cultural value across the globe, as well as the way these values have been fortified through visual signifiers now rendered shallow.

— Kiki Teshome

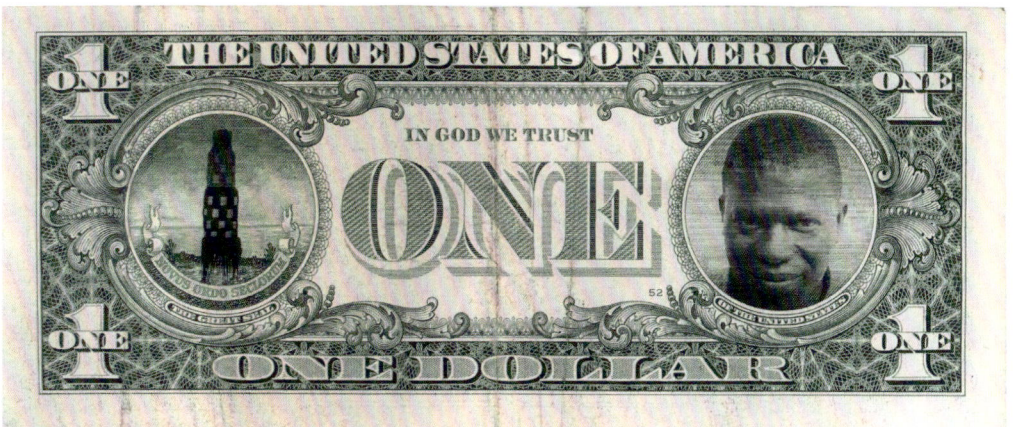

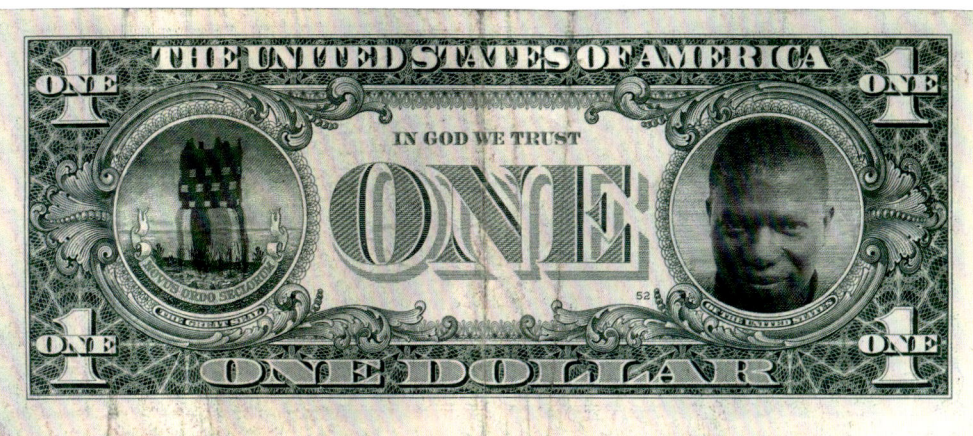

African Artist with American Inspiration:
Citigroup, 2004. Digital prints,
Each: 17 ⅞ × 34 ⅞ in. Gift of the artist
2005.6.2e, b

Leslie Hewitt

b. 1977   Artist in Residence 2007—08

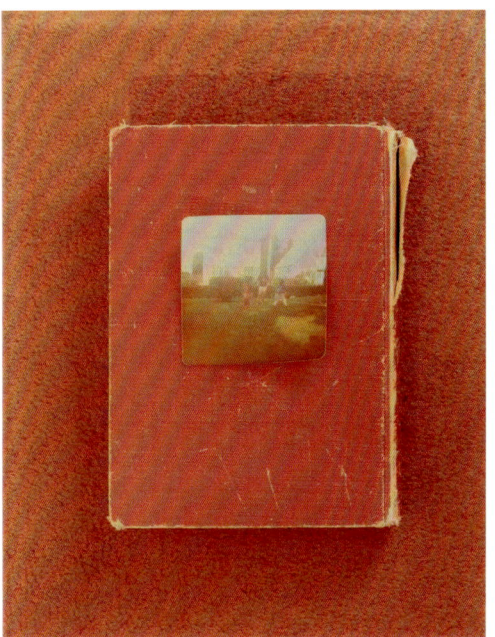

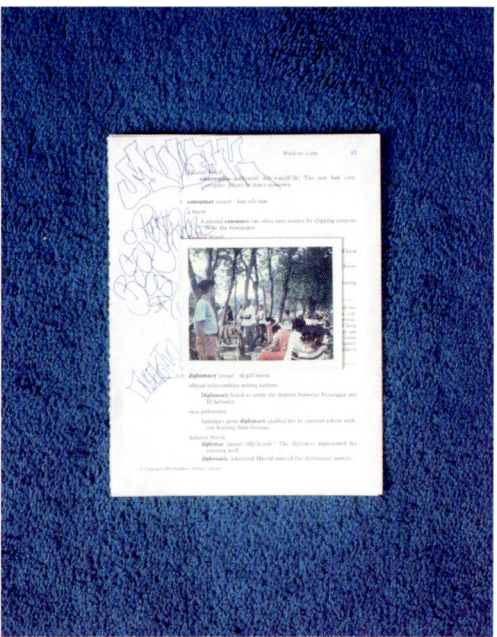

Riffs on Real Time (1 of 10), 2002—05.
Digital chromogenic print, 30 × 24 in.
Gift of Martin and Rebecca Eisenberg
2011.11.2

Riffs on Real Time (4 of 10), 2004.
Chromogenic print, 40 × 20 in.
Promised and partial gift of Martin
and Rebecca Eisenberg, Scarsdale, NY
PG.2005.1.9

Born in the Queens neighborhood of St. Albans in 1977, Leslie Hewitt
came of age in a transformative moment in New York City's history.
Within that decade, the city saw its economic and social realities entirely
reconfigured, as it encountered high rates of unemployment, white flight,
and crime. At the same time, technological advancements allowed for
new grooves, gadgets, and gizmos. The 1970s saw the birth of hip hop,
while electronic devices—such as boom boxes and Polaroid cameras—
became increasingly portable and affordable. With the advancement
of cameras came their quotidian use: personal photography and photo
albums became cornerstones of Black familial heirlooms. For Hewitt,
who was a part of the first generation of Black people in the United
States to experience cultural moments such as the civil rights movement and its aftermath largely through photographs, the camera bore
a revolutionary potential.

Spanning photography, sculpture, site-specific installation, and film,
Hewitt uses myriad, hybridized approaches to image-making that reify
the conceptual weight of an image. Her often-serialized work takes the
form of interventions and reflections on the evolution of the camera,
twentieth-century protest literature, and seventeenth-century Dutch

still-life painting—demonstrating a continued interest in how cultural meaning is derived through images across a broad historical context. She draws on personal and found photographs, ephemera, and artifacts to map time and place, expanding—if not repositioning—one's point of view.

Completed between 2002 and 2009, Hewitt's series "Riffs on Real Time" stacks time. In this series of ten color photographs, Hewitt creates a succinct compositional system for an anachronistic layering of images and artifacts. In each, carpeted or hardwood flooring serves as a background upon which a piece of printed ephemera (such as a newspaper, magazine, book, or manila envelope) is centered. Hewitt then places a photograph, either found or personal, upon this larger print material. This compositional order creates a dialogue between setting (the floor), mass culture (print ephemera), and personal life (photograph). Though its title suggests an improvisational creation, "Riffs on Real Time" intentionally plugs public into private memory; mass media moments into intimate histories; and global into local.

In *Riffs on Real Time (4 of 10)*, Hewitt places a Polaroid photograph of an outdoor gathering atop a page seemingly torn from an educational textbook. The page heading reads "Words to Learn" before glossing over vocabulary words such as "catastrophe," "consumer," and "diplomacy." The personal vintage photograph, detailing a moment of Black communion, bristles against US pedagogies offered on the page. The two elements emerge from opposite spheres: the public space of the US education establishment, which is plagued by systemic racism, and the private space of Black family celebrations. Blue shag carpet backgrounds the photograph and page, placing this visual dialogue in the 1970s, when brightly hued carpeting was ubiquitous. Here, this layering acts as a visual topography. In juxtaposing disparate images and settings, Hewitt challenges the viewer to reconsider how collective histories might be rewritten.

—Yume Murphy

Camille Billops

1939—2019

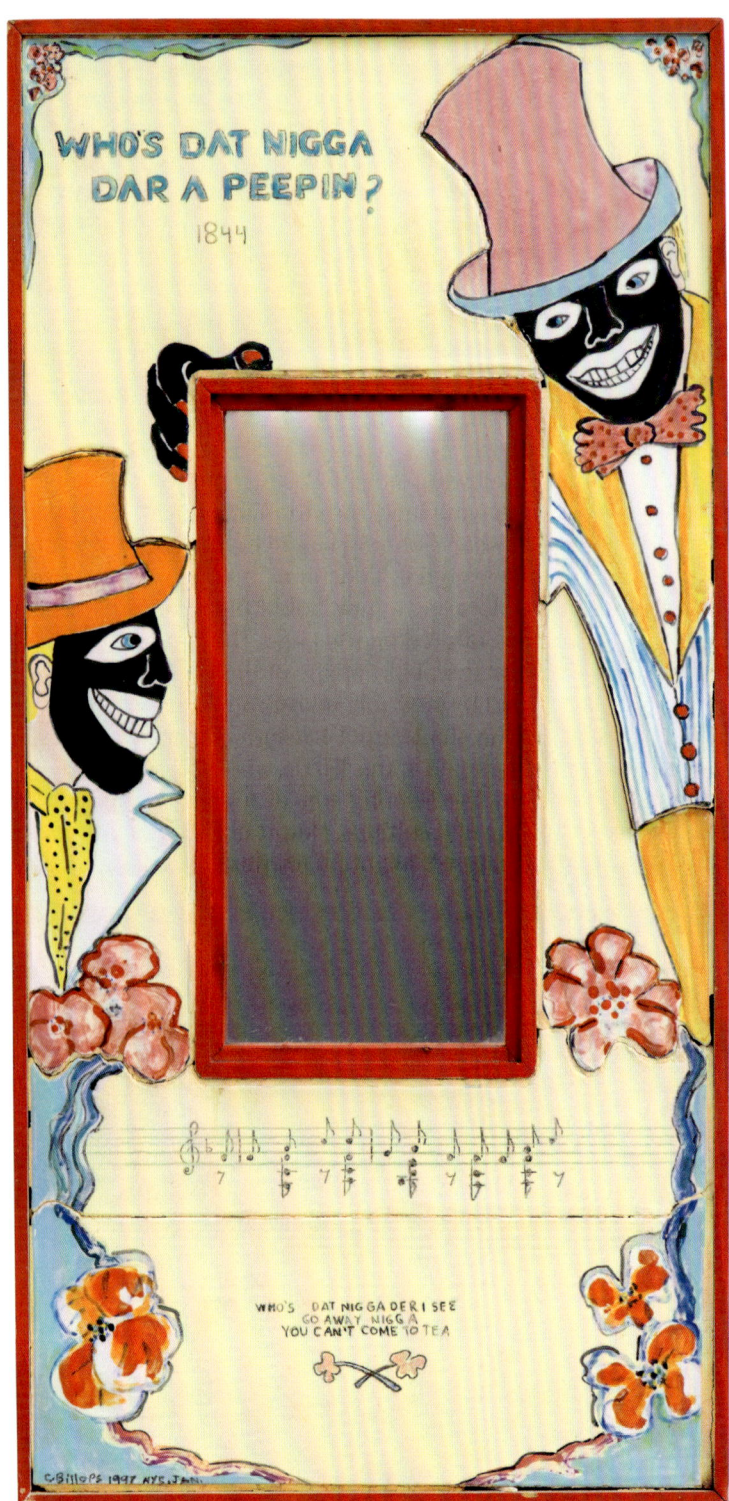

Created in 2004, *Who's Dat Nigga Dar a Peepin'* is one work from Camille Billops's "Minstrel Series," which she began over a decade prior in 1993. The series references blackface minstrelsy—a racialized and racist theatrical performance whereby performers painted their faces with burnt cork, hog fat, and black shoe polish to caricature African Americans. Performing exaggerated, erroneous, and stereotypical behaviors associated with formerly enslaved African Americans, these performances, which began in the nineteenth century in the wake of the Civil War, reinforced and justified anti-blackness and white supremacy in the United States. In *Who's Dat Nigga Dar a Peepin'*, Billops renders a mirror framed by two white minstrel figures donning blackface and attire associated with minstrelsy performance: pink and orange top hats, blue and yellow suits, and bow ties. Below the mirror is a sheet music staff with key signature and notes. This and the title reference a popular minstrelsy song from 1844.

The "Minstrel Series" debuted at the Kenkeleba House Inc. and Wilmer Jennings Gallery in New York City, a gallery that has supported work by African Americans since its founding in 1974. The press release and statement for the show states, "[Camille Billops] invites you to peek behind the mask, and to speculate who was hiding there . . . and why."[168] Given Billops's extensive film work, this series could be viewed as a social critique of American filmmaking, an industry with a legacy rife with minstrelsy tropes and racist propaganda that furthered the agenda of white supremacy after Reconstruction and Jim Crow terrorism in the South.[169] The work also questions modes of authorship regarding who has had the power to narrate their own subjectivity and the subjectivity of others.

— Taylor Renee Aldridge

Who's Dat Nigga Dar a Peepin' (from the series "Minstrel Series"), 2004. Ceramic and mirror, mixed media on board, 21 ½ × 10 ½ in. Bequest of Peggy Cooper Cafritz (1947—2018), Washington, DC, collector, educator, and activist 2018.40.37

Pope.L
1955—2023

Throw out words like Dada, conceptualism, satire, and absurdity, and some or all might catch the artist Pope.L. One might cast him in a production of Samuel Beckett's *Waiting for Godot* playing Vladimir opposite Franz Kafka as Estragon. "Thinking is not the worst," Vladimir says. To which Estragon replies: "Perhaps not. But at least there's that." Beckett's absurdist works emerged as a reaction to the political atrocities of World War II ("After Auschwitz, to write a poem is barbaric," so says cultural critic Theodor Adorno), whereas Pope.L's language drawings, the "Skin Sets," chronicle the travesties of United States circus-politics from the Clinton era onward.

Court poet of the art world since the late 1970s, Pope.L began his "Skin Sets" in 1997.[170] For this series, he writes a color of skin paired with a set of descriptors that together form a declarative sentence on letter-sized graph paper. Like textual pointillism, what might at first blush seem like nonsense comes into definition when stepping back. Such is the paradox of absurdity—its nature works at its converse. Its illogic makes things crystal clear. These are no possibilities or maybes—these are arche-types. He asserts that entire peoples ARE something; something within faulty systems of language and race. The artist has produced over 3,500 of these sets. The amount of work correlates to the amount of material at hand—this is an ongoing project of considering (at the level of syntax) the ongoing-ness of racial stereotyping.

Three particular works, made from 2003 through 2004, declare the following:

· White People Are Angles on Fire (translation: in the geometry of racial systems, white people don't hold their weight; the grammar mistake indicates that this group's veneration might be an error).

· Black People Are the Window and the Breaking of the Window (translation: broken windows theory reference; the policing of "low-income", i.e., Black, communities is, in fact, racial profiling and does not, in fact, solve crime).

· Green People Are Hope Without Reach (translation: our earth is fucked; we're placing faith in the unreached cosmic beyond rather on what can be accomplished on earth).

Every time these "Skin Sets" are exhibited, they are arranged in a new order. This shuffling subverts the expectation of a larger narrative to the works, and the prospect of progress over time. In this way, their tracing across decades, presidential cabinets, skin color, and semantics points to the asinine feedback loop of history and how it is communicated. Where was meaning, for example, when in 2003, as the artist drew *Green People Are Hope Without Reason*, the US government invaded Iraq and two months later George W. Bush declared, "Mission Accomplished," only to have the war crawl on for over twenty years thereafter. Or a year later, when Pope.L scrawled "White People," something called "TheFacebook" launched, something called "Opportunity" landed on Mars, and the largest earthquake in the twenty-first century devastated Sumatra, Indonesia, with something called a "Mercalli Index IX" deemed as "violent." Language, for this artist, is both a tool and an inherently meaningless mark, a way to classify time and a way to conflate it—insomuch as it is humans who use and abuse it. It is the most fallible way of communicating as we bide time for change. Still, or because of that, it is perhaps the thing most worthy of talking about.

—Meg Whiteford

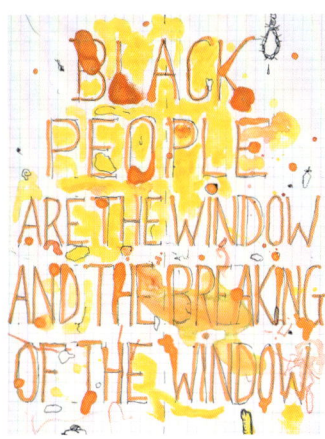 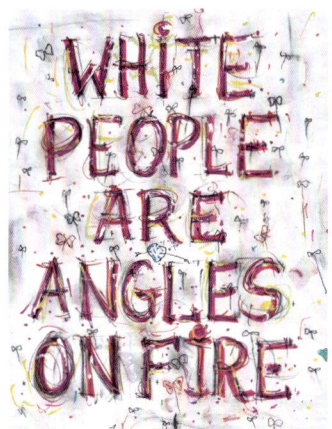 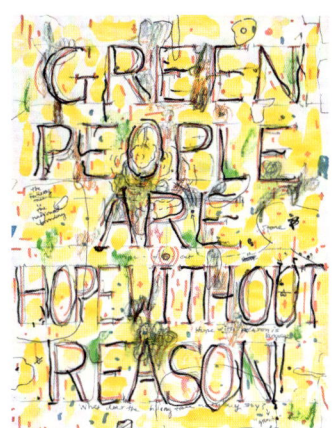

Black People Are the Window and the Breaking of the Window, 2004. Pen and marker on paper, 11 × 8 ½ in. Museum purchase made possible by a gift from Barbara Karp Shuster, New York 2005.4.2

White People Are Angles On Fire, 2003. Pen and marker on paper, 11 × 8 ½ in. Museum purchase made possible by a gift from Barbara Karp Shuster, New York 2005.4.3

Green People Are Hope Without Reason, 2003—04. Pen and marker on paper, 11 × 8 ½ in. Museum purchase made possible by a gift from Barbara Karp Shuster, New York 2005.4.1

Wardell Milan

b. 1977   Artist in Residence 2006—07

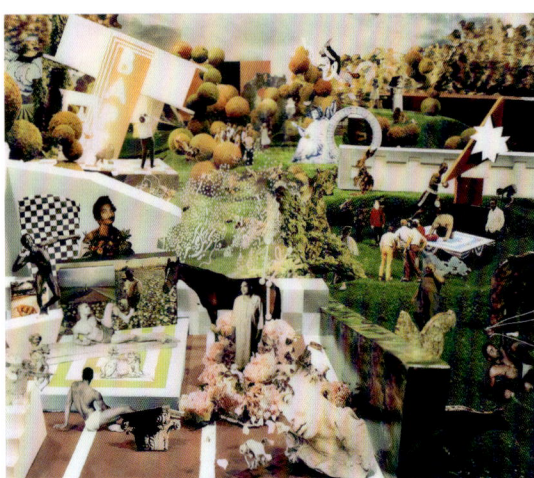

COLLECTION

"Broken hegemonies" refers to the historical unraveling of dominant principles or metaphysical systems that once claimed universal authority, revealing their inherent contingency and fragmentation. Once challenged, these principles lose hold over people's ways of being, paving the way for new possibilities.[171] In this way, Wardell Milan develops "methodologies for alternative histories," as illustrated in *Untitled (Love Part 2)*, by using photo montage to reterritorialize images through appropriation and reassembly, taking fragments from the external world and merging them into a single composition.[172]

Milan furnishes each image in this series as a chapter of a novel, as part of a love story, by combining images from Robert Mapplethorpe's *Black Book*, pictures of slavery in the Southern United States, family photographs, and photos of Black boxers with cutouts of ancient Roman and Greek sculpture and architecture, surreal landscapes, and whimsical objects.[173] In *Untitled (Love Part 2)*, Milan intricately weaves elements of the imagination, tangible realities, and abstract concepts around a specific theme— that is, the love of the subtitle, to reorient visualizations of race, gender, and identity. The image entwines elements of object reality with an inner process that resonates with the depths of psychoanalytic discourse, unveiling the unconscious around the displacement of the past within our imaginations. Through this construction, a utopic space teetering on the brink of reality emerges, although it remains firmly anchored in both ancient and modern themes. Milan's decontextualization of these images demands that their juxtapositions become discontinuities; their perceptions are no longer as they were previously perceived from one era to the next. The artist presents this utopic space with a sense of openness and imaginative freedom that invites viewers to explore the symbolic, metaphorical, and expressive qualities of love, identity, race, and sexuality. The image portrays a phantasmic world of broken hegemonies.

—Terrence Phearse

Kalup Linzy

b. 1977

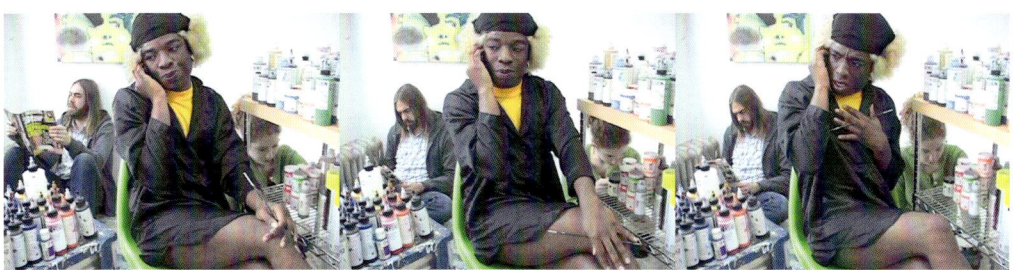

KK Queens Survey, 2005. Digital color video with sound. TRT: 00:07:00. Gift of Alvin Hall in honor of Thomas Lax 2018.49.4

An uncanny undertone runs like a live wire beneath the setting of Kalup Linzy's films. Linzy's voice-dubbing, on the one hand, creates a kind of ventriloquy, wherein characters might be seen as ghosts or puppets orchestrated from both within and outside the scene: "When they're all looped into my voice, it doesn't matter how their body moves." The narrative allows Linzy to circumnavigate the pressures of the market and its violence of representation that crowds out Black, queer, trans, transgressive, and avant-garde art—"If you tell an interesting story, then I guess it will make people forget about certain production values."[174]

In *Conversations wit de Churen III: Da Young and Da Mess*, a Black soap opera unfolds. The opening music might be a version of the song "Tonight, I Celebrate My Love" by Roberta Flack and Peabo Bryson. This film is about forms of aesthetic and social failure, where the ruse of white heteronormativity, ironically staged and parodied by queer characters, implodes and shatters. Linzy's films often parody US exceptionalism and the desire to "make it" in the racial, capitalist, libidinal, and political economy. He does so here through a melodrama of a provincial girl who wants to make it big, except Linzy also serves a read of the nuclear family and individuation. *Conversations wit de Churen III: Da Young and Da Mess* opens with a daughter calling to tell her mother she is getting married. Yet instead of marriage being an achievement, it becomes a crisis. An ex tries to sabotage the proposal. "You want me to come up with a plan to destroy Taywan? Hector Jones, you are becoming more like your mother every day," says his sister, joining in on the plan.

In *KK Queens Survey*, an artist deals with a pestering problem: a phone survey question asked of artists that is also asked by LGBTQIA+ public health officials—"male or female?" The artist responds: "Five years ago I got my dick cut off and replaced with a good pussy; you decide." The character's rejection of the question serves as a metaphor for Linzy's gender nonperformance in many of her pieces. She rejects the protocols of gender conformity. Instead, there is a slippage that one could historicize as gay and Black, wherein figures such as Marsha P. Johnson used all pronouns and was trans, as in between gender(s), and therefore refusing any claim to cis subjectivity. The survey continues: "madam or sir?" The artist replies: "Just list me as homo [long pause] sapien." She is asked about the art scene, where she fits in, the nodes she occupies, how many shows she has had, and if they have been solo or group shows. These metrics are then used to calibrate her social currency in the political economy of the art world.

The parody intensifies. So too does the parrhesia: "Metaphorically speaking, how many asses do you kiss a week?" The art world industrial complex, like any other form of social hierarchy, requires flattery. The artist is always at work. Linzy's ironic and queer reading of the figure of the artist makes plain both the ways the artist's surplus labor is captured and how sociality persists in excess of valuation.

—Che Gossett

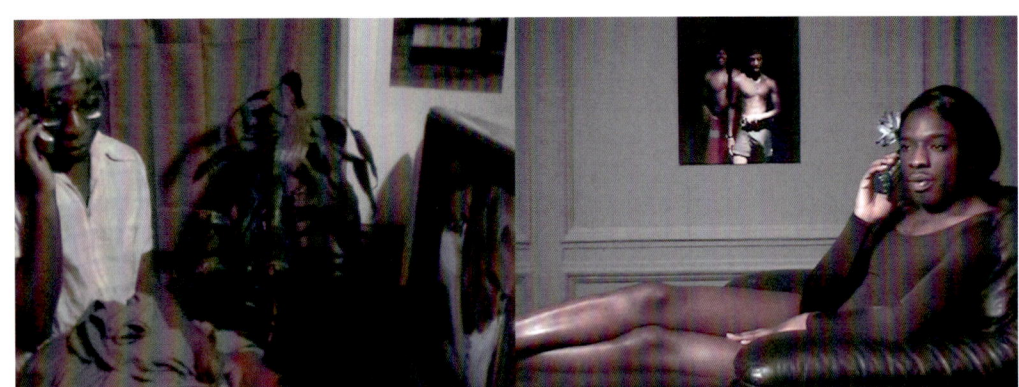

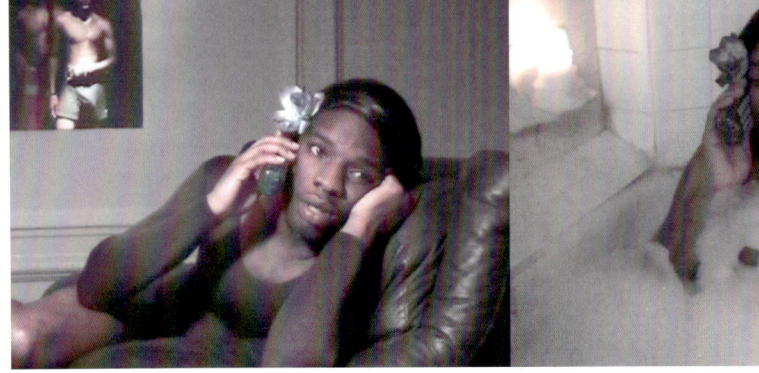

Conversations wit de Churen III: Da Young and Da Mess, 2005. Single-channel video projection, TRT: 00:16:55. Museum purchase with funds provided by the Acquisition Committee 2006.2.4

Clifford Owens

b. 1971   Artist in Residence 2005—06

A white woman (Joan Jonas) drags a Black man (Clifford Owens) over six pieces of paper arranged in a colored grid lying on a studio floor. Charcoal and graphite are affixed to the man's feet and hands. The woman yanks the man by his limbs across the papers to draw unsophisticated circles and lines. The woman has a history of using drawing as a method in her performances and videos. The man has a history of inviting famous performance artists to his studio to create "a unique performance for that audience of one."[175] In the background, Bjork's "Hidden Place" plays, in which she sings: "He's the beautifulest / Fragilest still strong /Dark and divine /And the littleness of his movements / Hides himself / He invents a charm / That makes him invisible."

Part of the artist's "Studio Visits" series performed at the Studio Museum during Performa Biennial05 (the first New York biennial to focus on performance art), *Studio Visits: Studio Museum in Harlem (Joan Jonas)* is a genius gesture against art's obsession with the "Genius"—anti-authorial with clear authorial intent. Since the 1990s, Owens has used his body to create what he calls "abstract figurative drawings"—an oxymoron that suggests erasure of delineation between abstraction and figuration, body and tool. Owens has also made it a practice to both invent a lineage of Black performance art and bring to light that this lineage always already exists: Benjamin Patterson's Fluxus work, 1960s; Maren Hassinger and Senga Nengudi's collaborations, 1970s; Pope.L's crawls, 1970—2023; David Hammons's snowball sale, 1980s; Houston Conwill's *Cakewalk*, 1980s; Clifford Owens, interactions, 2000s—. In this assembly of Black artists, Owens stresses the iterative work of the collective. This anarchic approach is practiced in *Studio Visits: Studio Museum in Harlem (Joan Jonas)*, as the artist allows a figurehead of the medium to literally write him into the canon of performance art.

—Meg Whiteford

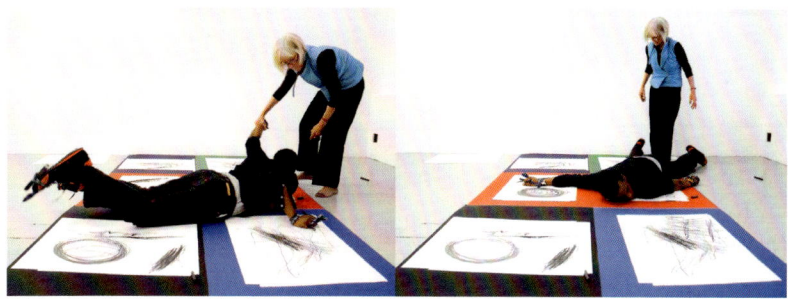

Studio Visits: Studio Museum in Harlem (Joan Jonas), 2005—06. Single channel video with sound, TRT: 00:03:11. Museum purchase with funds provided by the Acquisition Committee 2006.19.9

Robert Pruitt
b. 1975

Through typically oversized figurative drawings, Robert Pruitt blends temporalities and incorporates an eclectic range of references from African and African diasporic visual culture, including ancient civilizations and science fiction. *Pretty for a Black Girl* depicts a slender, bikini-clad figure with a sash and bouquet—attributes of a victorious beauty pageant contestant. Her head and shoulders, however, are obscured by a sizable West African mask. The imposing figure's heels, long limbs, and overall conical form emphasize vertical uplift and fill the sheet. The title cites an expression reflecting a racialized hierarchy of beauty that denigrates, commodifies, and fetishizes Black women and girls. Considered along with the prominent mask, the title also evokes the paradoxical appropriation and disavowal of traditional African art in the development of twentieth-century European and American modernism.

The figure is rendered on brown butcher paper instead of the default white, and ghostly vestiges of a feathery shawl surround her shoulders like Futurist force lines or comic-book depictions of motion, the streaky marks heightening the contrast between her lower and upper halves. In concert with the abundant fingerprints dotted throughout, these pentimenti are Pruitt's signature evidence of his process made visible. A graphic inversion of Frantz Fanon's book *Black Skin, White Masks* (1952), the figure's scrubbed skin contrasts the gleaming ebony of Pruitt's variant of a Nimba or D'mba mask from Guinea. The mask's attenuated breasts, associated with fertility and the harvest, both confine her outlook and assert agency. Poised for approbation, yet shrouded from view, the figure espouses contradiction.

—Akili Tommasino

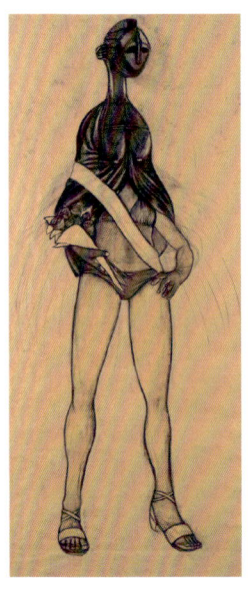

Pretty for a Black Girl, 2005. Conté crayon on butcher paper, 85 × 33 ¾ in. Museum purchase made possible by a gift from Jeanne Greenberg Rohatyn, New York 2005.20

Shinique Smith

b. 1971

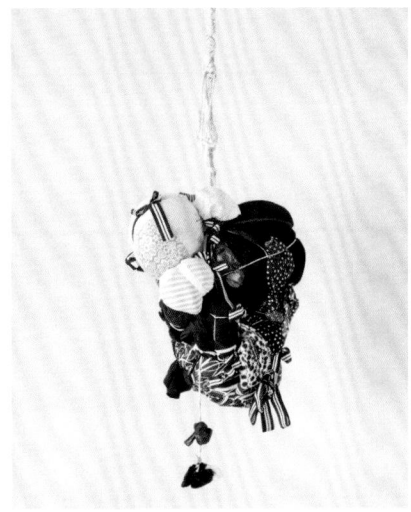

Black and White Floaty, 2006.
Clothing, accessories, fabric, ribbon
and rope, 47 × 23 × 23 in. Gift of
Martin and Rebecca Eisenberg in
honor of Christine Y. Kim 2011.10.17

Shinique Smith is best known for her hanging and monumental fabric
sculptures and abstract paintings and murals incorporating calligraphy
and collage, but her multimedia practice extends to include installation,
video, and performance. Smith embraces the possibilities of abstraction
as "a better way for [her] to communicate life, rather than depict it,"
using form, material, and language as points of entry.[176] Fabric became
the foundational material of her sculptural work in the early 2000s.[177]

Bundles of fabric come together as a single organic mass in one
of Smith's early suspended sculptures, *Black and White Floaty*. The sculpture is composed of numerous black and white fabrics, with smaller
bundles of contrasting colors and black and white ribbons tying them
together or cutting across the bundles. "I have found that mostly the
materials I'm using determine form," notes Smith, "how things can
be physically bound together also affects the finished product."[178] Smith,
not unlike artists who moved beyond Minimalism in the late 1960s,
embraces the organic qualities of her materials to inform the final result.
Floating—as the title suggests—like a buoy in the sea, *Black and White
Floaty*'s amorphous form also offers up less picturesque comparisons,
such as discarded trash masses often found in oceans. Smith's use
of fabric, clothing, and other mass-produced objects for the bundles and
her other works, including her monumental bales, are often understood
as meditations on capitalism's dependency on overconsumption, and the
artist's choice of often-discarded materials presents examples of industries participating in unrestrained production. And yet, the use of these
materials to create art affirms recycling and repurposing as ways to rein-
scribe meaning and value.

—Zuna Maza

Henry Taylor

b. 1958

At the core of Henry Taylor's practice is an ongoing relationship with memory. Including painting, drawing, mixed-media installations, and sculptures, Henry Taylor's works explore ideas of endurance, self-determination, and belonging. Taylor's works blend art history with his own life as a means of reflecting critically on how notions of self, of collectiveness, and of place—both real and imaginary—can introduce new realities. Through varying source materials, his practice enshrines collective narratives, personal stories, and intergenerational knowledge. His works act as annotations capturing the subtleties and truths of Black lives. His compositions depict moments of social, personal, and cultural narratives. Still, his work propels beyond the representational, alluding to a state of unknowing and curiosity that persists as he pushes further the possibilities of painting, object making, and drawing to capture and render life at once.

Drawing from his immediate environment and people he meets, Taylor visualizes stories. Read as social commentary by some and as an acute visual repository of the Black experience by others, the artist's works capture a variety of lived experiences in all their complexities. With *Homage to a Brother*, Taylor remembers Sean Bell, who was killed by five plain-clothes New York Police Department officers on the eve of his wedding in 2006. After revisiting the site of the murder, the artist kept tokens

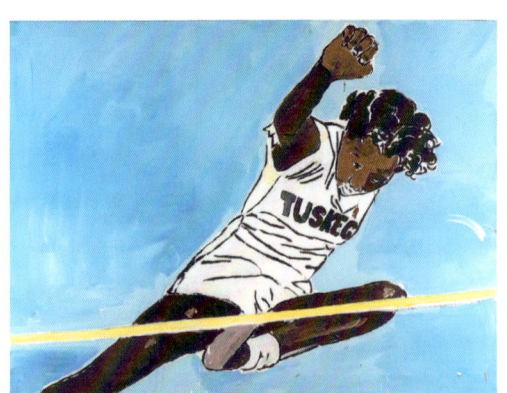

Left: *how i got over*, 2011. Acrylic on canvas, 56 ⅛ × 75 ½ in. Gift of Martin and Rebecca Eisenberg 2013.11

Bottom left: *The Tide is High*, 2008. Acrylic on cardboard, 3 × 5 ½ × 1 ¾ in. Bequest of Peggy Cooper Cafritz (1947–2018), Washington, DC, collector, educator, and activist 2018.40.333

Bottom right: *Brother, Brother, Brother*, 2009. Acrylic on suitcase, 28 × 9 ¼ × 21 in. Gift of Martin and Rebecca Eisenberg 2014.15.29

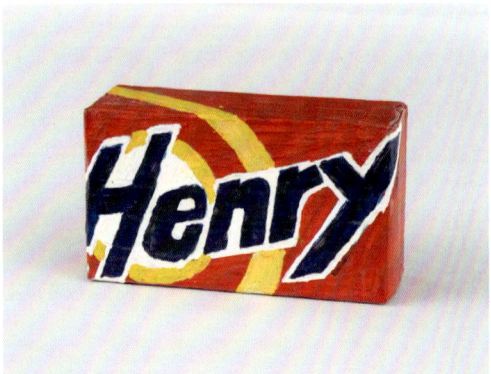

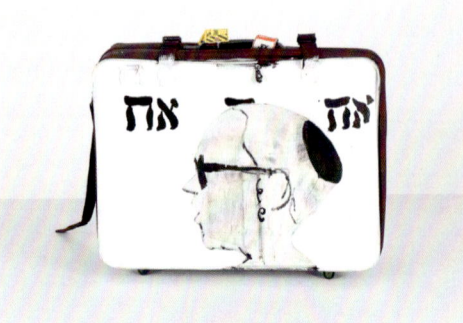

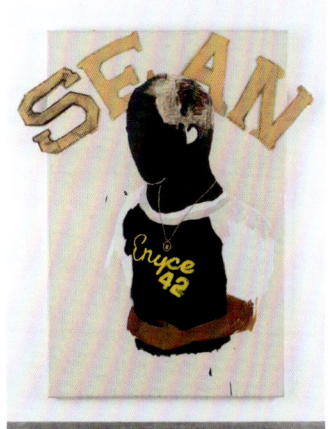

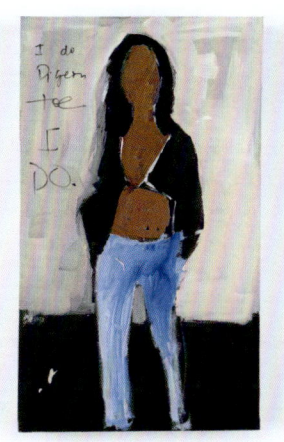

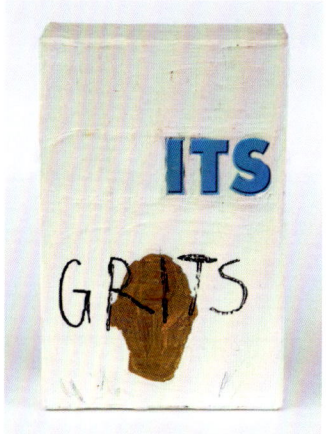

Homage to a Brother, 2007. Acrylic and collage on linen, 95 ½ × 79 ½ × 3 ¾ in. Gift of Martin and Rebecca Eisenberg 2007.13

I Do Pigeon Toe, 2006. Mixed media on canvas, 30 × 17 ¾ × 2 ½ in. Gift of Dana and Stephen Sigoloff 2008.25

It's Grits, 2008. Acrylic on cardboard, 6 ½ × 4 ½ × 2 in. Bequest of Peggy Cooper Cafritz (1947–2018), Washington, DC, collector, educator, and activist 2018.40.332

from the victim and incorporated them into the work. With this memorial portrait, the artist reinforced the importance of historical painting as a mode of advocacy, and that history needs to be told, to be written, and to be seen. One of the interesting tensions in his work is a deep sense of purpose. The brushstrokes are energetic and bold, yet there is a palpable, pronounced precision and an intentionality in his choices. Taylor makes evident that the political can coexist with familiar figures, demonstrating that personal histories are inextricable from shared memories.

With paintings such as *I Do Pigeon Toe* or *how i got over*, his works explore transformation and adaptation as means of manifesting intimacy, dreams, and collective experiences to the fullest. With *It's Grits*, and *The Tide is High*, he paints his own advertisements on cereal and Tide boxes, respectively, allowing him to remain nimble in his formal research beyond the canvas. Taylor has traded these works with peers throughout his practice. Through these abstract yet tangible depictions of everyday realities riffing on household items and found objects—as seen in his painting on a suitcase, *Brother, Brother, Brother*—the artist declares that quotidian elements hold power, and that something unexpected can grow from a pure exploration of form. Through experimentation and imagination, Taylor invites considerations of race as a complicated spectrum through which one can articulate and take up the challenges to revisit, reimagine, and recontextualize the past in relation to a deeply anchored and felt sense of the present.

—Daisy Desrosiers

Charles Gaines

b. 1944

COLLECTION

Charles Gaines has been an influential figure in the conceptual art movement since the 1970s. His work, which includes drawings, works on paper, and photographs, uses formulas and rule-based systems to explore both objective and subjective experiences of aesthetics, identity, politics, and language.

Randomized Text, History of Stars #2 juxtaposes a star-filled night sky with carefully handwritten white text on a black background. Sourced from two important books—Gabriel García Márquez's *Love in the Time of Cholera* (1985) and Edward Said's *Orientalism* (1978)—the text reads legibly yet illogically at the same time, as Gaines selected phrases and sentences from both books at random to create an entirely new narrative. In doing so, Gaines comments on the arbitrary nature of words and language—symbols and sounds assigned with various and changing meanings over time. Although the sentences might appear chosen at random, Gaines employed a randomizing system whereby he selected sentences from each text based on the letter of the first word in the previous sentence. By pairing this newly created text with a depiction of the expansive night sky, Gaines invites the viewer to ponder the human instinct to assign meaning to that which we do not understand.

The work is part of his series "Randomized Text: History of Stars" (2006—08), which continues his interest in language and the written word, previously expressed in the series "History of Missiles" (2006), "Canceled Checks" (1997—2000), "Submerged Text" (1990), and "Incomplete Text" (1979). This work is part of Gaines's ongoing exploration of how the arbitrary assignation of meaning can be manipulated into untruths. According to Gaines, "Usually, when there is symmetry between form and expression, we are convinced that this is proof of the reality and truthfulness of the discourse and/or the image. But by arbitrarily combining them, I want to show the fallacy at the heart of our ideas about reality; rather than being based in truth, the real is a political (cultural) construction."[179]

—Naima J. Keith

Randomized Text, History of Stars #2 (from the series "Randomized Text: History of Stars"), 2006. Digital print and color pencil on paper, 51 ⅞ × 19 ⅞ in. Museum purchase with funds provided by the Acquisition Committee 2007.21.1

ON LES APERCEVAIT TENANT LEURS IDOLES ENTRE LEURS BRAS COMME DE GRANDS ENFANTS PARALYTIQUES. "SOMETHING EVEN RARER," SAID DR. URBINO. AS HE APPEARS IN SEVERAL POEMS, IN NOVELS LIKE *KIM* AND IN TOO MANY CATCHPHRASES TO BE AN IRONIC FICTION, KIPLING'S WHITE MAN, AS AN IDEA, A PERSONA, A STYLE OF BEING, SEEMS TO HAVE SERVED MANY BRITISHERS WHILE THEY WERE ABROAD. IN THE DISTANCE, ON THE OTHER SIDE OF THE COLONIAL CITY, THE BELLS OF THE CATHEDRAL WERE RINGING FOR HIGH MASS. BECAUSE WE HAVE BECOME ACCUSTOMED TO THINK OF A CONTEMPORARY EXPERT ON SOME BRANCH OF THE ORIENT, OR SOME ASPECT OF ITS LIFE, AS A SPECIALIST IN "AREA STUDIES," WE HAVE LOST A VIVID SENSE OF HOW, UNTIL AROUND WORLD WAR II, THE ORIENTALIST WAS CONSIDERED TO BE A GENERALIST (WITH A GREAT DEAL OF SPECIFIC KNOWLEDGE, OF COURSE) WHO HAD HIGHLY DEVELOPED SKILLS FOR MAKING SUMMATIONAL STATEMENTS. IN THE PARLOR WAS A HUGE CAMERA ON WHEELS LIKE THE ONES USED IN PUBLIC PARKS, AND THE BACKDROP OF A MARINE TWILIGHT, PAINTED WITH HOMEMADE PAINTS, AND THE WALLS PAPERED WITH PICTURES OF CHILDREN AT MEMORABLE MOMENTS: THE FIRST COMMUNION, THE BUNNY COSTUME, THE HAPPY BIRTHDAY. SINCE WORLD WAR II, AND MORE NOTICEABLY AFTER EACH OF THE ARAB-ISRAELI WARS, THE ARAB MUSLIM HAS BECOME A FIGURE IN AMERICAN POPULAR CULTURE, EVEN AS IN THE ACADEMIC WORLD, IN THE POLICY PLANNER'S WORLD, AND IN THE WORLD OF BUSINESS, VERY SERIOUS ATTENTION IS BEING PAID THE ARAB. ON THE DESK, NEXT TO A JAR THAT HELD SEVERAL OLD SEA DOG'S PIPES, WAS THE CHESSBOARD WITH AN UNFINISHED GAME. *ORIENTALISM* WAS COMPLETED IN THE LAST PART OF 1977, AND WAS PUBLISHED A YEAR LATER. AT SIX THAT MORNING, AS HE WAS MAKING HIS LAST ROUNDS, THE NIGHT WATCHMAN HAD SEEN THE NOTE NAILED TO THE STREET DOOR: *COME IN WITHOUT KNOCKING AND INFORM THE POLICE.* YET I WOULD NOT WANT TO SUGGEST THAT, CURRENT THOUGH SUCH VIEWS AS LEWIS'S MAY BE, THEY ARE THE ONLY ONES THAT HAVE EITHER EMERGED OR BEEN REINFORCED DURING THE PAST DECADE AND A HALF. IT WAS A HALF-TRUTH, BUT THEY THOUGHT IT COMPLETE BECAUSE HE ORDERED THEM TO LIFT A LOOSE TILE FROM THE FLOOR, WHERE THEY FOUND A WORN ACCOUNT BOOK THAT CONTAINED THE COMBINATION TO THE STRONGBOX. AMERICANS WILL NOT FEEL QUITE THE SAME ABOUT THE ORIENT, WHICH, FOR THEM IS MUCH MORE LIKELY TO BE ASSOCIATED VERY DIFFERENTLY WITH THE FAR EAST (CHINA AND JAPAN, MAINLY). "IT'S THE THIRD TIME I'VE MISSED SUNDAY MASS SINCE I'VE HAD THE USE OF MY REASON," HE SAID. HAVING SAID THAT, ONE MUST GO ON TO STATE A NUMBER OF REASONABLE QUALIFICATIONS. SO HE CHOSE TO SPEND A FEW MINUTES MORE AND ATTEND TO ALL THE DETAILS, ALTHOUGH HE COULD HARDLY BEAR HIS INTENSE LONGING TO SHARE THE SECRETS OF THE LETTER WITH HIS WIFE. *THE DISTINCTION BETWEEN PURE AND POLITICAL KNOWLEDGE.* ONCE THE STORMY YEARS OF HIS EARLY STRUGGLES WERE OVER, DR. JUVENAL URBINO HAD FOLLOWED A SET ROUTINE AND ACHIEVED A RESPECTABILITY AND PRESTIGE THAT HAD NO EQUAL IN THE PROVINCE. RECALLING THE

Adam Pendleton

b. 1984   Artist in Residence 2008—09

To: A son of the South who made it up north

From: A daughter of the South who got up too

Dear   _____,

Too much has happened. Oh, my people, my people, my people. What's become of me, of us? Time has done what time does. Honestly, I'm embarrassed and ashamed of my shifting behavior, my jading perspective. How often am I now walking on by, no sister sparing dimes, crisscrossing 110th Street, keeping my eyes looking straight up at Adam Clayton Powell? Rather than see, speak, check, help that body, that person, this hu(ed)man sprawled, splayed, crumpled, frozen, nodding on the sidewalk, the seat, the doorway before me, beside me, behind me? I wasn't raised like this. Church didn't teach me to behave like this. We witnessed too much, fought too much, learned too much. We *could* be this. Have I become too blasé? But really. What *can* I do now? What *should* I do? *What* is expected of me, of us? What would it be to live as *those people* seem so easily to? Tuning in and showing up when they have the time. Tuning out and standing down when they haven't. Those people rushing, enjoying, and scrolling. Pausing for the requisite photo take. I walk these wide avenues often, alone. Wishing you were here.

"Um, excuse me? Can you...?" they ask. "Not now," I say. *Not now.*

—

to: d
from: s

hold   people
      time   must
                          side by
                              hold   light
                              lord   trust
                                          turn   stand
                                                    struggle
                                                    on! [180]

—Daonne Huff

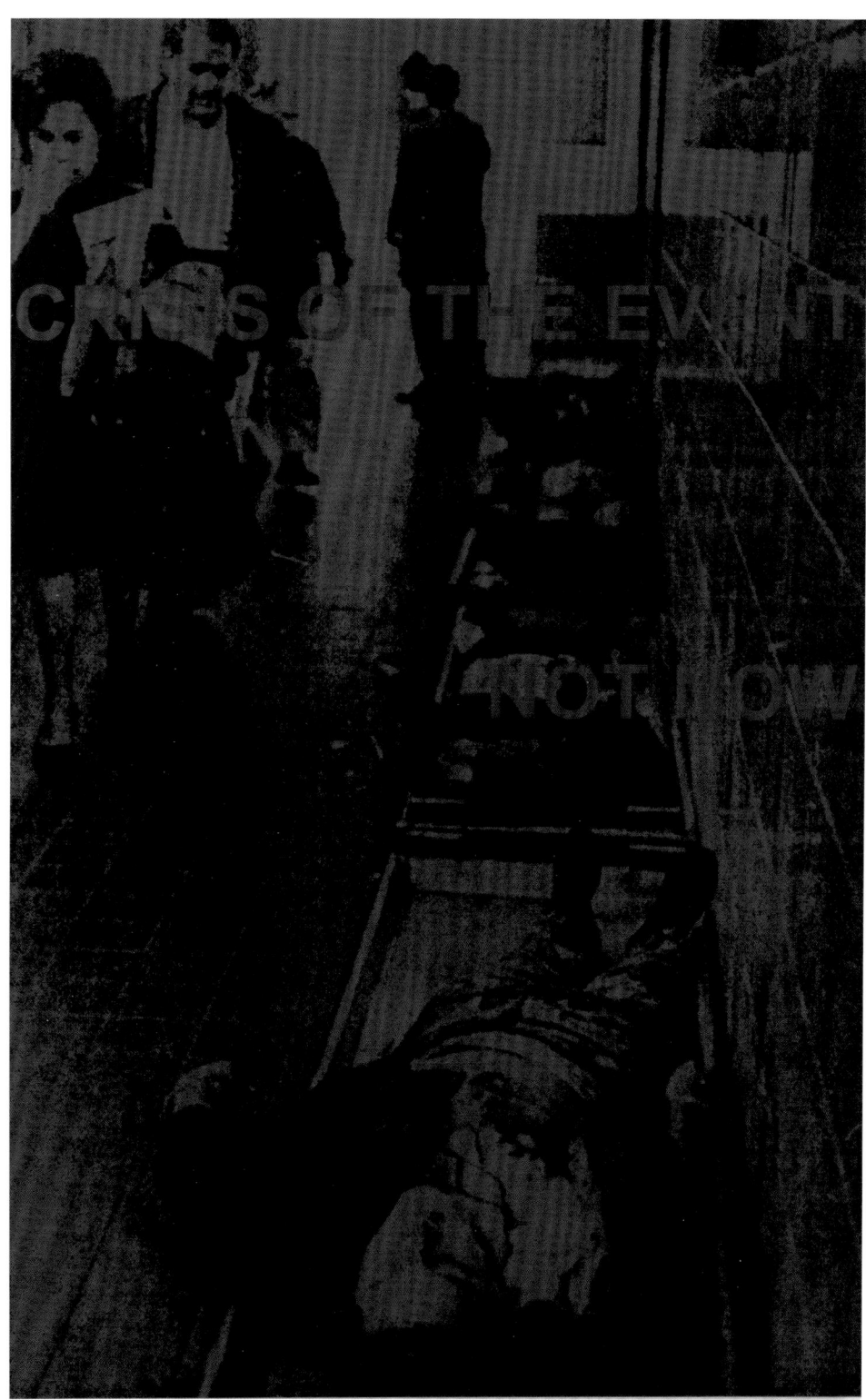

Crisis of the Event Not Now,
2006. Silkscreen on canvas.
75 ¾ × 48 ¼ in. Gift of Ninah and
Michael Lynne 2018.44.16

LaToya Ruby Frazier
b. 1982

Over the course of thirteen years, LaToya Ruby Frazier created "The Notion Of Family" (2001—14), a series of photographs chronicling the artist's family, community, and environment. The series is situated in Frazier's hometown of Braddock, Pennsylvania, where the decline of the steel industry and the environmental impact of industrialization are acutely felt by the majority-Black residents. Frazier draws on the history of social documentary photography to portray her surroundings, referencing artists such as Dorothea Lange and Gordon Parks.

Frazier ascribes a sense of agency and authorship to those photographed; she considers her mother and grandmother, who are frequently depicted, to be her collaborators in the process of creating "The Notion Of Family." Frazier's long-standing commitment to building community and conducting in-depth research is evident across her many bodies of work. There is a palpable sense of mutual respect, understanding, and trust between the artist and those depicted in her photographs. As a result, Frazier captures unmediated moments of tenderness and vulnerability, as in *Grandma Ruby and JC in her Bathroom*. Grandma Ruby, the matriarch of the family, embodies the caretaker while bathing the relaxed JC in the tub, a testament to a sense of comfort between the child, his grandma, and Frazier. In her signature style, Frazier captures a multidimensional composition: Grandma Ruby and JC's heads bend toward each other, and the charged negative space between them anchors the center of the composition. A shower curtain, floral bouquet, and doll surround the figures, forming a layered scene of domestic comfort. Images such as this add a deeply personal and intimate perspective to the effects of environmental racism and deindustrialization, countering the erasure that occurs when systemic issues are discussed in the abstract.

—Mia Matthias

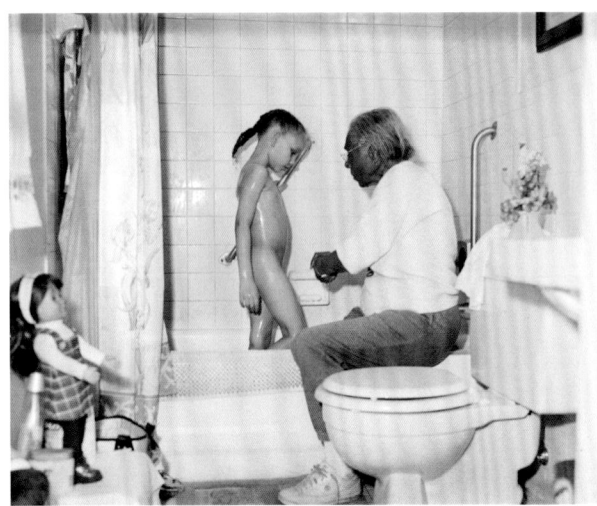

Grandma Ruby and JC in her Bathroom (from the series "The Notion Of Family"), 2006. Gelatin silver print, 16 × 20 in. Bequest of Peggy Cooper Cafritz (1947—2018), Washington, DC, collector, educator, and activist 2018.40.89

Mickalene Thomas

b. 1971   Artist in Residence 2002—03

Mickalene Thomas produces beautiful and complex depictions of Black women in stimulating environments using collages, photographs, paintings, and installations. Her kaleidoscopic living rooms, family rooms, and gardens set the stage for her powerful subjects. The viewer does not merely watch the varied hues of brown and Black women lying in leisure; no, a conversation is had between the viewer and the viewed. These women, dressed in the boldly colored attire of olive greens, sunset oranges, mellow yellows, fire engine reds, and bright plaids and prints, gaze out as much as they are gazed at. They force viewers to see them as individuals to be appreciated, admired, and desired, rather than as bodies to be visually consumed.

In *Kalena* and *Can't We Just Sit Down (And Talk it Over)*, Thomas combines the rich textures of animal prints and shag carpets with a close cropping, thus generating an intimate scene for deep conversations. She pulls source material from personal memories, Black American popular culture and style, 1970s editions of *Jet* and *Ebony* magazines, and her rich knowledge of historical European painters of the female nude, including Jean-Auguste-Dominique Ingres, Henri Matisse, and François Boucher, among others. Thomas also depicts women, semi or fully clothed, lounging on couches and chairs in their personal spaces. In the print *Can't We Just Sit Down (And Talk it Over)*, the partially clothed, singular female crosses her legs and looks calmly toward the viewer. The title augments her unconcerned demeanor, which draws in her unknown onlookers, suggesting they "talk" as she entices them with private teasing.

In the photograph *Afro Goddess with Hand Between Legs*, the artist features herself wearing a dress in a colorfully constructed setting. She also lies on her side on a couch and gazes directly outward attentively, with her legs bent and one hand placed above her genitalia, as if she might pleasure herself. The title also reiterates that she controls the scene.

Can't We Just Sit Down (And Talk it Over), 2006. Screenprint in twenty-eight colors, 27 × 37 ½ in. Edition 6 of 40. Museum purchase with funds from Raymond J. McGuire 2007.14

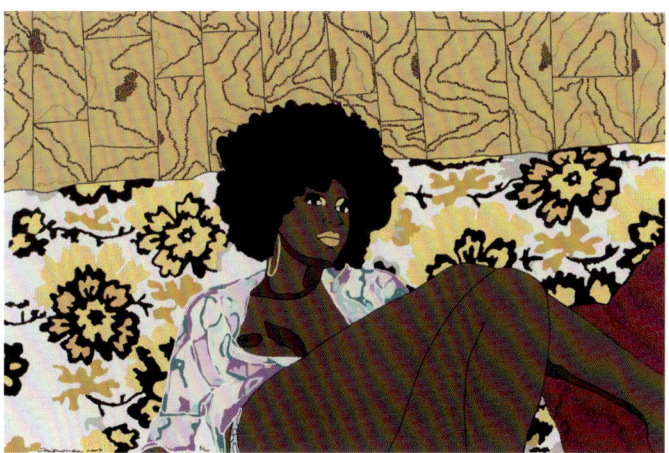

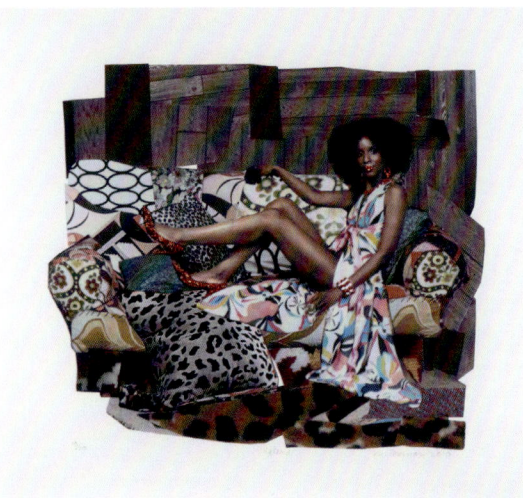

Kalena, 2009. Archival inkjet print with hand-painted applications, sheet: 13 ½ × 15 in. Bequest of Peggy Cooper Cafritz (1947—2018), Washington, DC, collector, educator, and activist 2018.40.349

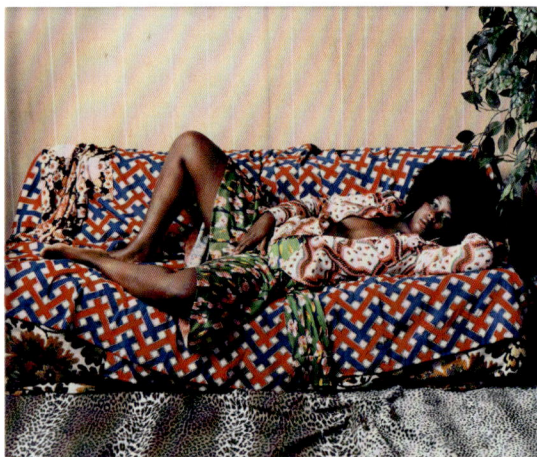

Afro Goddess with Hand Between Legs, 2006. Chromogenic color print, 16 × 20 in. Edition 5 of 6. Museum purchase with funds provided by the Acquisition Committee 2007.6.3

COLLECTION

Interestingly, Thomas's use of collage enhances the shift in tone of these images from passive to active. She crafts various materials, colors, and shapes together with lines of rhinestones in different orientations. At first glance, the construction produces a sensuous spectacle. However, the various techniques and elements call attention to the work as something the artist fabricated, not a fantasy. The lack of cohesion between person and scene allows the eye to roam across the composition, jarring the viewer out of the narrative in their head.

Ultimately, Thomas's works are seductive, as the arrangement forces the viewer to see an image first, and the figures do not offer themselves as bodies on display. Instead, they participate in a conversation with the looker. The women give hints of their self-actualized sexuality with covered curves and body positioning. These women entice, but they make the viewer work to earn their favor. The figures hold the power, and they will use it to get what they please. In this way, Thomas shifts the balance of power so that those looking want to be the woman who has taken control.

—Kimberli Gant

Titus Kaphar

b. 1976   Artist in Residence 2006—07

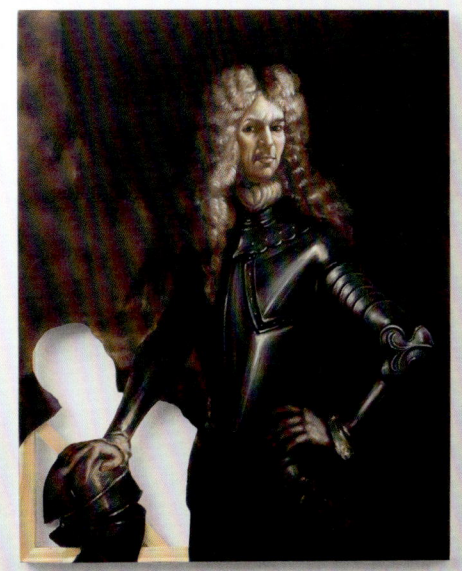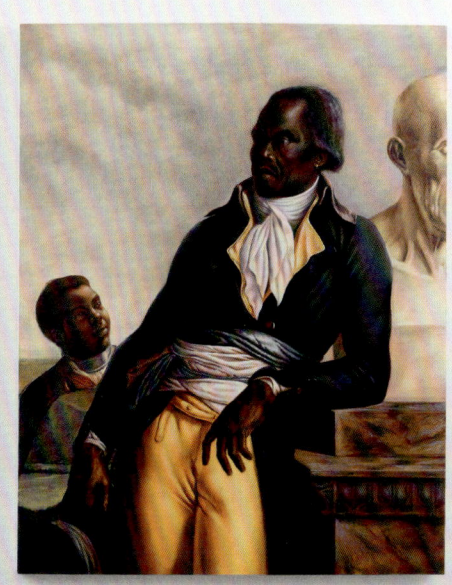

Conversations between paintings #3: Descent,
2007. Oil on cut canvas, 60 × 113 in. Museum
purchase made possible by a gift from
Jeanne Greenberg Rohatyn 2007.22a—b

Titus Kaphar's figurative work implicates the viewer by exposing how Black figures have been depicted within the art historical canon. Kaphar invokes a wide range of tactics to call attention to blind consumption of these representations. Visible holes, cuts, folds, layers, and crumples of canvas are necessary traces of Kaphar's manipulation. He creates a confrontation between past and present to simultaneously rewrite history and document the devastating impact of erasure.

In the diptych *Conversations between paintings #3: Descent*, Kaphar explores the power dynamics among figures on the basis of race and political status. Before Kaphar's intervention, the Black boy's sole purpose is as an indicator of wealth of James Drummond, 2nd Duke of Perth, as represented in Sir John Baptiste de Medina's c. 1700 portrait. Unlike the boy's position in the shadows, Black Saint Dominican (present-day Hispaniola) revolutionary Jean-Baptiste Belley is centered prominently as the subject of this portrait created by Anne-Louis Girodet de Roussy-Trioson c. 1797. Belley's portrait remarks on his fight to secure his freedom from slavery, and later his ascension to French council member status, the first Black man to hold this position in the French government. Kaphar deceptively alters Girodet de Roussy-Trioson's recognizable portrait by reorienting Belley's position so that he directs his gaze to Drummond. Kaphar extracts the boy from the duke's servitude, and places him into an empowering scene with Belley, affirming his dignity and offering an alternate reality for the viewer to consider. While

Kaphar's diptych imagines a rewritten history, the viewer must still face the ghost of the Black boy in the duke's portrait—the hole at the bottom left corner of Medina's portrait is an ominous reminder of the boy's original position and a reference to slavery's lasting imprint on the visual language of European artistic traditions.

With its visible canvas and stretcher supports, is this work a painting or a sculpture? Does this individual represent power or labor? Such questions expand visual culture and ultimately define new, critical ways for viewers to engage with artwork and histories. These themes are also on display in *Glass Blackened, Green Molding Mold.* This is one of Kaphar's more conceptual depictions of the dangers of erasure, likening the unseen labor of producing a glass bust to enslaved people's experiences, as their captors relied on their labor to amass large amounts of wealth and, therefore, political influence. Like his exposed canvases, Kaphar peels back the curtain to reveal the often-ignored manufacturing process and materials that uphold and produce artwork. *Glass Blackened, Green Molding Mold* enshrines the plaster cast of George Washington's bust—the site of an intense process wherein glass is smashed, melted, fired, and refined into its cavity. The byproduct of such a process is often discarded, despite the fact that the successful reproduction of the bust depends upon the labor required for the process to work. Images of Washington appear throughout Kaphar's body of work, as the first US president has been emblazoned into the consciousness of US citizens. Kaphar uses Washington as one vehicle to stage his indictment of the intentional practice of erasure within historical visual frameworks.

—Elana Bridges

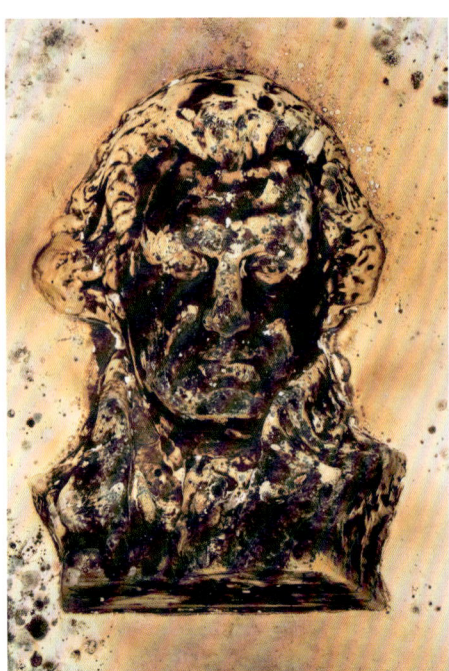

Glass Blackened, Green Molding Mold, 2016. Photograph, 33 ¼ × 23 ¼ in. Bequest of Peggy Cooper Cafritz (1947–2018), Washington, DC, collector, educator, and activist 2018.40.142

Steffani Jemison

b. 1981   Artist in Residence 2012—13

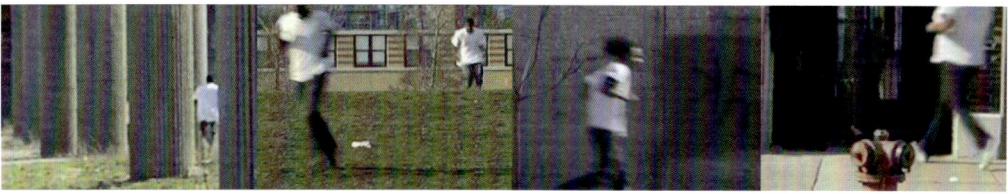

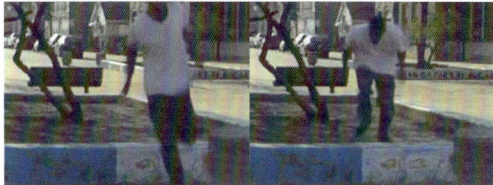

Maniac Chase, 2008—09. Digital video, endless loop, Edition 1 of 3 + 2AP. Museum purchase with funds provided by the Acquisition Committee 2013.13.1

Steffani Jemison's award-winning works in photography, sound installation, drawing, writing, and video demonstrate how situating a praxis within the quotidian while simultaneously remaining grounded in the historical is a delicate and necessary negotiation between the sublime and surreal. Her time-based media work *Maniac Chase* interrogates linear approaches to time and narrative, which, as she explains, allows her to examine "prog-ress and its alternatives."[181] This video is presented as a continuous loop and features four individuals (who appear to be Black men) dressed identi-cally in white T-shirts and denim jeans. Through a series of shots, they run on sidewalks, up and down hills, and through gated doorways and green spaces on a bright day in an unnamed location. In lieu of dialogue, sound comes as ambient street noises like passing cars and slamming gates. The runners' destination is unknown, presumably never-ending, and the repeated actions are hypnotic, daresay, mesmerizing and manic—a meta-phor for those existing within the confines of a neoliberal society, perhaps.

In numerous ways, *Maniac Chase* allows the viewer to be "haunted by logics of recursion and repetition."[182] While watching the scenes on a loop, for example, one experiences a feeling of foreboding. In the wake of Black Lives Matter and the ease with which heinous acts of racial violence are witnessed via social media and other means, the nonstop running con-jures up instances of seeing Black and brown individuals being chased, harassed—or worse—by police. Jemison's work also recognizes the histori-cal cinematic trope of the comedic chase from the silent film era, therefore offering a different proposition. Maybe the individuals are running *toward* possibility and promise? Either way, this film offers the viewer a sense that everything and nothing are happening simultaneously—just like life.

—Rhea Combs

Saya Woolfalk

b. 1979   Artist in Residence 2007—08

Worldbuilding runs throughout Saya Woolfalk's conceptually rich and materially varied artistic practice. As she summarizes her artistic strategy in a 2017 interview: "How do you build a logic that people can enter so that their perceptions of these things can be transformed slowly through repeat engagement through a narrative arc?"[183] Woolfalk works in an iterative and layered way, creating large-scale narrative projects that build on one another. Inspired by anthropology and science fiction, she uses the methods and modes of expression of both to interrogate disciplinary structures and institutions like museums and to invite viewers to imagine future worlds and forms of interspecies connections. Yet, her narrative works do not resolve the tension between utopias and dystopias.[184] Instead, as scholar Nicole Fleetwood has argued, Woolfalk's work "recognizes struggle and tension as necessary processes to forming human collectivities."[185]

Much of Woolfalk's work in these modes reaches back to her project "No Place," which she began while living in Brazil from 2004 to 2006. There, Woolfalk was interested in the movement of flora and fauna between the "Old" and "New" Worlds and began to imagine a future world that was

No Placean Anatomy, 2008. Gouache on paper, sheet: 14 × 10 ½ in. Museum purchase with funds provided by the Acquisition Committee and a gift from Rodney Miller 2008.22.3g

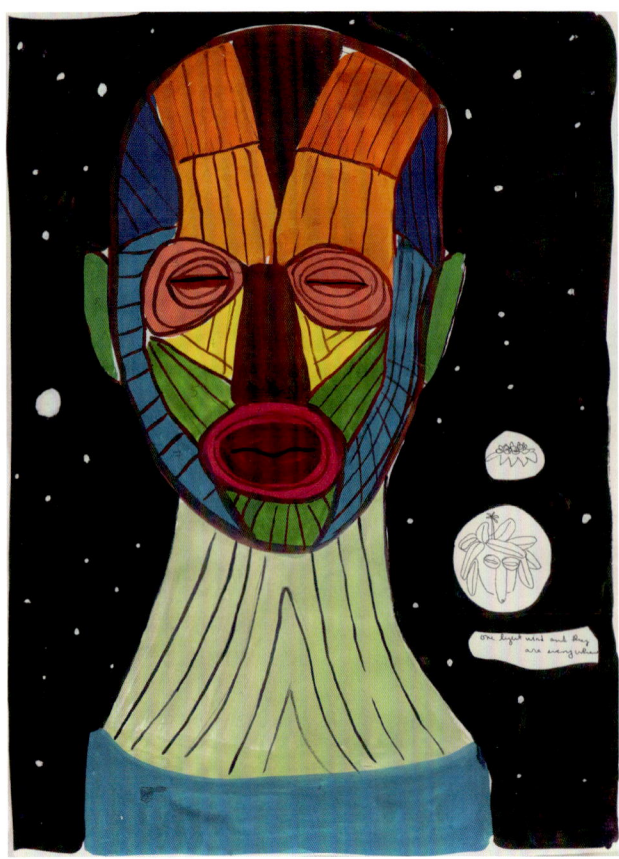

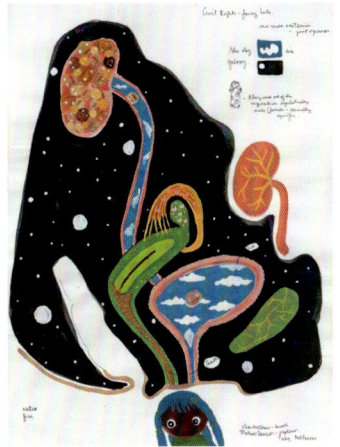
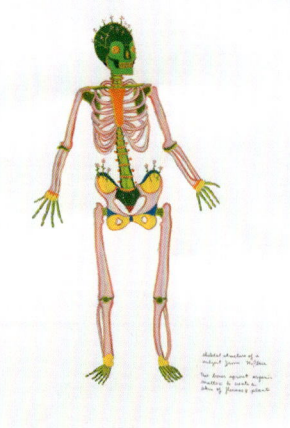
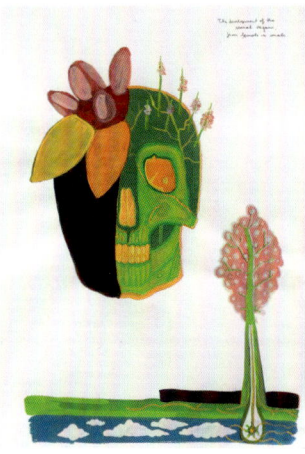

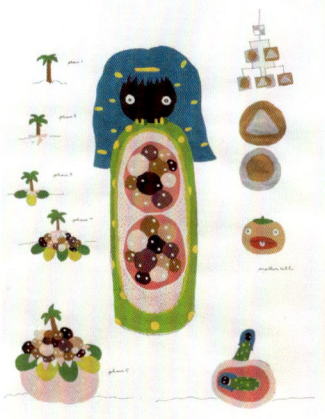
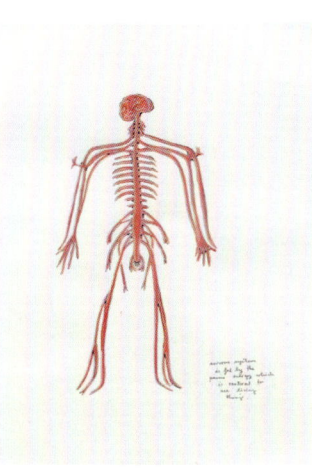

No Placean Anatomy, 2008. Gouache on paper, sheet (each): 14 × 10 ½ in. Museum purchase with funds provided by the Acquisition Committee and a gift from Rodney Miller 2008.22.3a, d, c, h, e

"part plant and part human."[186] She developed "No Place" in collaboration with anthropologist Rachel Lears as a future world populated by "No Placeans." In the narrative Woolfalk developed for "No Place," an anthropologist enters their world through a portal located in Queens and attempts an ethnography of "No Placeans." "No Place" found its first full expression at the exhibition for her 2007—08 residency at the Studio Museum. With brightly colored gouaches on paper, Woolfalk created the anatomy and cartography of "No Place," blending anthropomorphic and botanic forms to envision, for example, generations, the development of the inhabitants' sexual organs, or the functioning of the nervous system.

"No Place" provided the foundation for subsequent multiyear-long projects, such as "The Empathics" and "ChimeTEK." Both are multimedia projects that include installation, video, performance, sculpture, printmaking, and storytelling, and that grew out of Woolfalk's interest in utopian communities, how beings create a sense of togetherness, and how utopias become dystopian.[187]

—Emma Chubb

Noah Davis

1983—2015

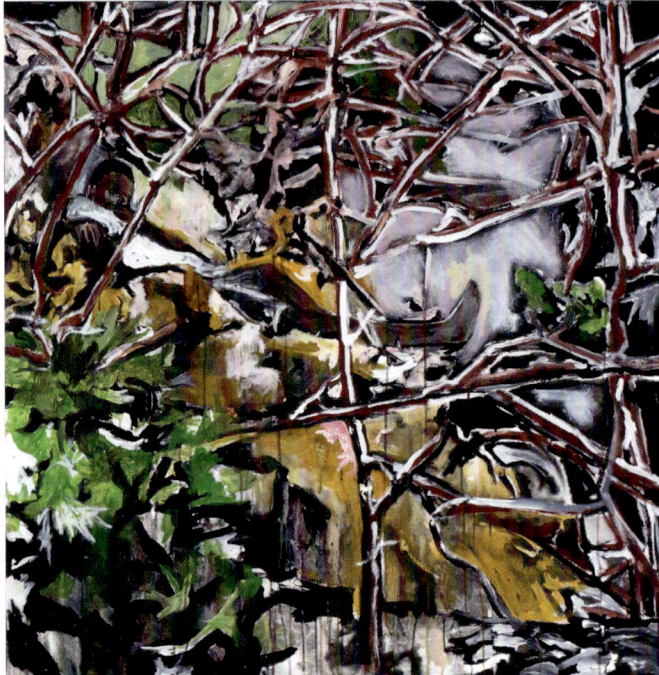

COLLECTION

At once haunting and ethereal, Noah Davis's work challenges notions
of Black subjectivity through an approach to figuration that embraces
the surreal and the abstract. His figures often appear limitless in space,
their bodies rendered in impossible relationships to the environments
around them as if to suggest a divine or spiritual presence. While unteth-
ered by reality, Davis's paintings often draw from photographs taken
by friends and family, events of historical resonance, or everyday moments.
By blurring his figure's edges and rendering their faces with minimal
detail or specificity, Davis engages in a careful act of withholding. His
paintings thus trouble the viewer's engagement with intimate and profound moments of Black life. Through their illegibility, Davis maintains the
enclosure of their interiority.

In *The Gardener*, a solitary man lies within the verdant foliage of a large
tree; his body traces the movement of its trunk. The painting's title
is inspired by Osiris, the Egyptian god of the afterlife and resurrection,
and is part of a larger body of work based on the legend of the ruler whose
coffined body fertilized a miraculously growing tree and of his wife Isis,
who searched for his remains and brought him back to life temporarily.
Through his painterly practice, Davis engages imagination and mythology
to explore Black histories of individual and collective determination, evolution, and remaking. In describing this work, Davis recalls painting's ability
to transport, noting that "elements of fantasy may arise from my need

to 'break the spell,' or the constraints of art theory, and move more into the realm of mysticism."[188]

This approach to image-making blurs temporal distinctions between past, present, and future, and is evident across Davis's work. One such painting references Greenwood, the African American neighborhood in Tulsa, Oklahoma, once renowned as "Black Wall Street." In 1921, a white mob destroyed this affluent and prosperous community by burning it to the ground in an event often referred to as the "Tulsa race riot." Though the devastation of this historical moment is not fully pictured in *Black Wall Street*, several of the figures in Davis's image lie lifeless on the ground. Across his practice, Davis blends truth with elements of the surreal as a means to grapple with complex Black histories as well as moments of interiority and the ecstatic.

At the time of his passing, at the young age of thirty-two, Davis had created over four hundred paintings, sculptures, and collages. A prolific and ambitious maker, Davis left an artistic legacy that continues to influence and inspire—not only through his artistic practice, but through his engagement and commitment to community and space-making. In 2012, Noah Davis cofounded the Underground Museum with his wife Karon Davis in the historically Black and brown neighborhood of Arlington Heights in Los Angeles. This Black-owned museum served as a communal hub, connecting art with diverse audiences and underscoring Davis's commitment to accessibility and inclusivity in the art world.

— Yelena Keller

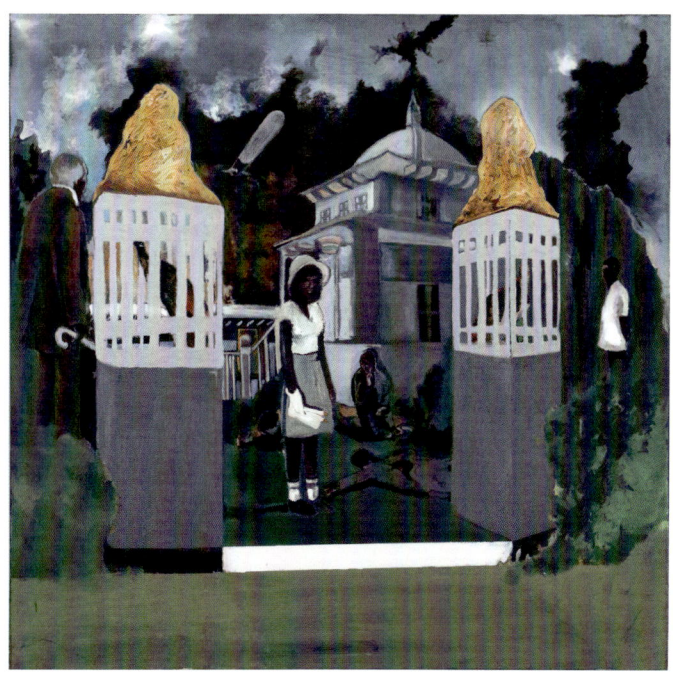

Black Wall Street, 2008. Oil and acrylic on canvas, 60 × 62 in. Gift of David Hoberman 2014.17.2

Narcissister

b. 1971

Untitled (Zagreb # 8), 2009. Chromogenic color print, 24 × 18 in. Edition 1 of 3 + 2 APs. Museum purchase with funds provided by the Acquisition Committee 2013.7.2

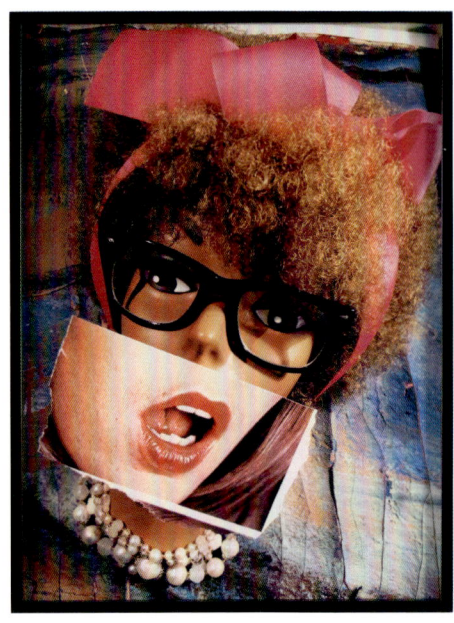

In an image-saturated, digital world where transparency is marketed as the antidote to precarity, Narcissister plays with what it means to intentionally mask one's body. Known for wearing a Barbie mask, wigs, and a merkin, and never revealing her "real" identity, Narcissister has created over two hundred collages depicting the chasms that result when hybridity and ambivalence collide. Cutting, pasting, sewing, and scavenging comprise the core of her creative process. The artist's collages, such as *Untitled (Zagreb # 8)*, some of which are research studies for future sculptures and performances, rhyme with her live works where a multitude of orifices—mouth, vagina, anus—alternately embrace and refuse their physiological function.

In *Every Woman* (2008/9), she performs a reverse striptease to Chaka Khan's "I'm Every Woman," pulling clothing and accessories from between her legs, her mouth, and oversized Afro wig. Her humor, pop song choices, elaborate costumes, and trademark mask upend the idea that physical (and social) transformation is possible, or even desirable. For Narcissister, a focus on the racialized gendered body also necessitates a focus on sex. Sex toys, sex organs, simulations of self-sex, and stereotypical symbols of sexual desire and fetish culture—cherries, lace, latex—all figure prominently in her collages, sculptures, performances, and moving image works. Climax does too, albeit artificially and incompletely; though she performs with flair and skill, she also frequently fakes it or fails to finish. In so doing, she upends conventional representations of womanhood and femininity in fine art, dance, fashion, and pornography.

—Tiffany E. Barber

Stanley Whitney

b. 1946

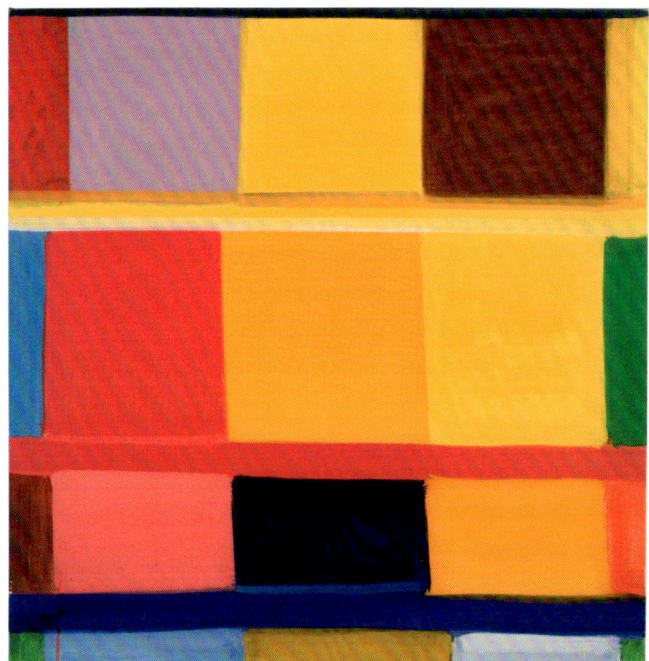

Lightnin, 2009. Oil on linen, 40 × 40 in. Promised gift of Martin and Rebecca Eisenberg PG.2015.19

Throughout his artistic career, Stanley Whitney has evolved a signature style that makes his paintings and works on paper instantly recognizable. Whitney's paintings and artistic practice are deeply influenced by music—particularly improvisation and call-and-response. His colors speak to and lead each other in a system that Whitney has honed over time. Care and rhythm exist within his work, both through the ways he creates each composition and how he allows the viewer in.

Color is a gateway into Whitney's work. In *Lightnin*, yellows and oranges take up multiple boxes and lines. Then come the pinks and reds and the blues. Whitney's paintings and drawings captivate; his commanding use of color is one reason why it is often impossible not to get lost in the worlds he creates in every artwork. Whitney's titles are also gateways into his works. As a curator, I often spend a lot of time thinking about titles: titles of essays, titles of exhibitions, email subject lines (a type of title of its own). Because of this, I also spend a lot of time impressed by artists who can title their works well. Whitney is one of these artists. Early in his career, Whitney would title his works *Untitled*, but in the 1990s he began to title the works with specific words or phrases. His titles provide a window into his interests and his influences. "Lightnin" is also the name of country blues singer, songwriter, and guitarist Lightnin' Hopkins—many of Whitney's titles come from blues and jazz and the variety of musical interests that have had an ongoing effect on his practice.

—Lauren Haynes

Nick Cave
b. 1959

Nick Cave created his first Soundsuit—the artist's signature series of sculptures-cum-costumes—as an instinctive protective reaction in the wake of Black motorist Rodney King's 1991 beating by the Los Angeles Police Department. Cave, feeling powerless and vulnerable under the condition of police violence against Black men, sewed an ersatz suit of armor from twigs he found in a Chicago park. The term "Soundsuit" comes from wearing the object, with the artist stating: "Once I put it on and moved in it, I realized that was [a] protest—the sound it made."[189]

The Soundsuits have since expanded in their visual and material vocabulary to encompass all manner of humble materials, as seen in this particular piece with crochet squares, scraps of fur, and stuffed animals, and elsewhere with beads, plastic trinkets, buttons, flea-market toys, shoelaces, secondhand clothing, and kitschy decor. Cave's use of found materials is an ethical, as well as aesthetic, consideration—with the skill of a couturier, he gives discarded things a second life as dazzling art objects. Crucially, almost all the Soundsuits are meant to be worn for performances that conceal the performer's race and gender identity and transform them into fantastical, powerful creatures. Inspired by a breadth of social gatherings, such as West African masquerade rituals, Caribbean Carnival, Chicago house music, Ballroom culture, and the funk futurism of Sun Ra's Arkestra and Labelle, Cave's public performances and installation projects foreground the Soundsuits' potential for shared exuberance.

Yet, for all their potential as power objects, the Soundsuits frequently mark tragedies in the United States. Several Soundsuits are dedicated to victims of homophobic and anti-Black violence, underscoring an ever-present anxiety lurking beneath their exuberant veneer. As the world perpetually contends with fatal inequities, Cave creates futuristic totems that catalyze joy and celebration as forms of protest.

— Naomi Beckwith

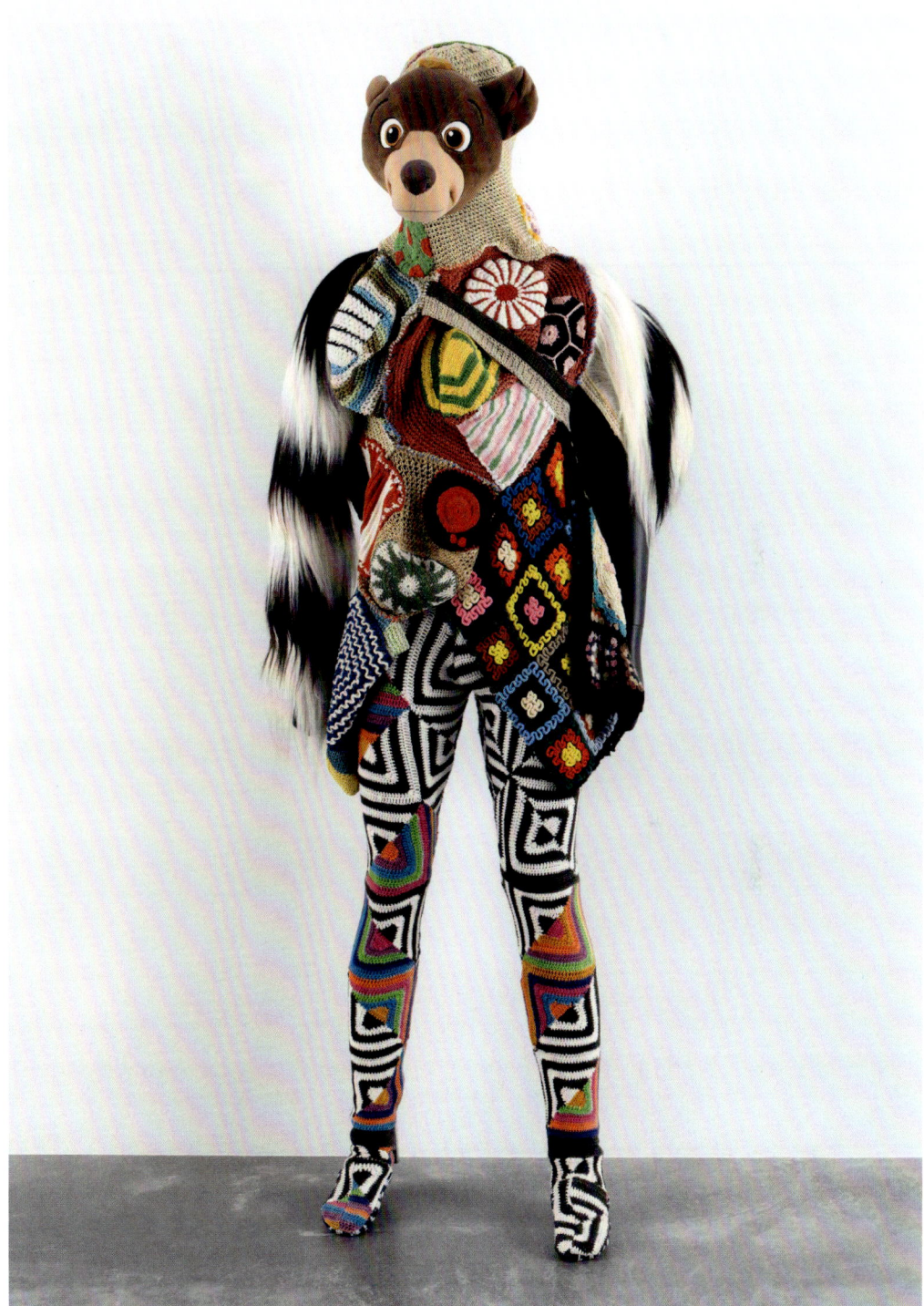

Soundsuit, 2009. Mixed media including
synthetic hair, fabric, metal, and
mannequin, 75 × 25 ¼ × 16 ¾ in. Bequest
of Peggy Cooper Cafritz (1947—2018),
Washington, DC, collector, educator, and
activist 2018.40.53

William Villalongo

b. 1975   Artist in Residence 2003—04

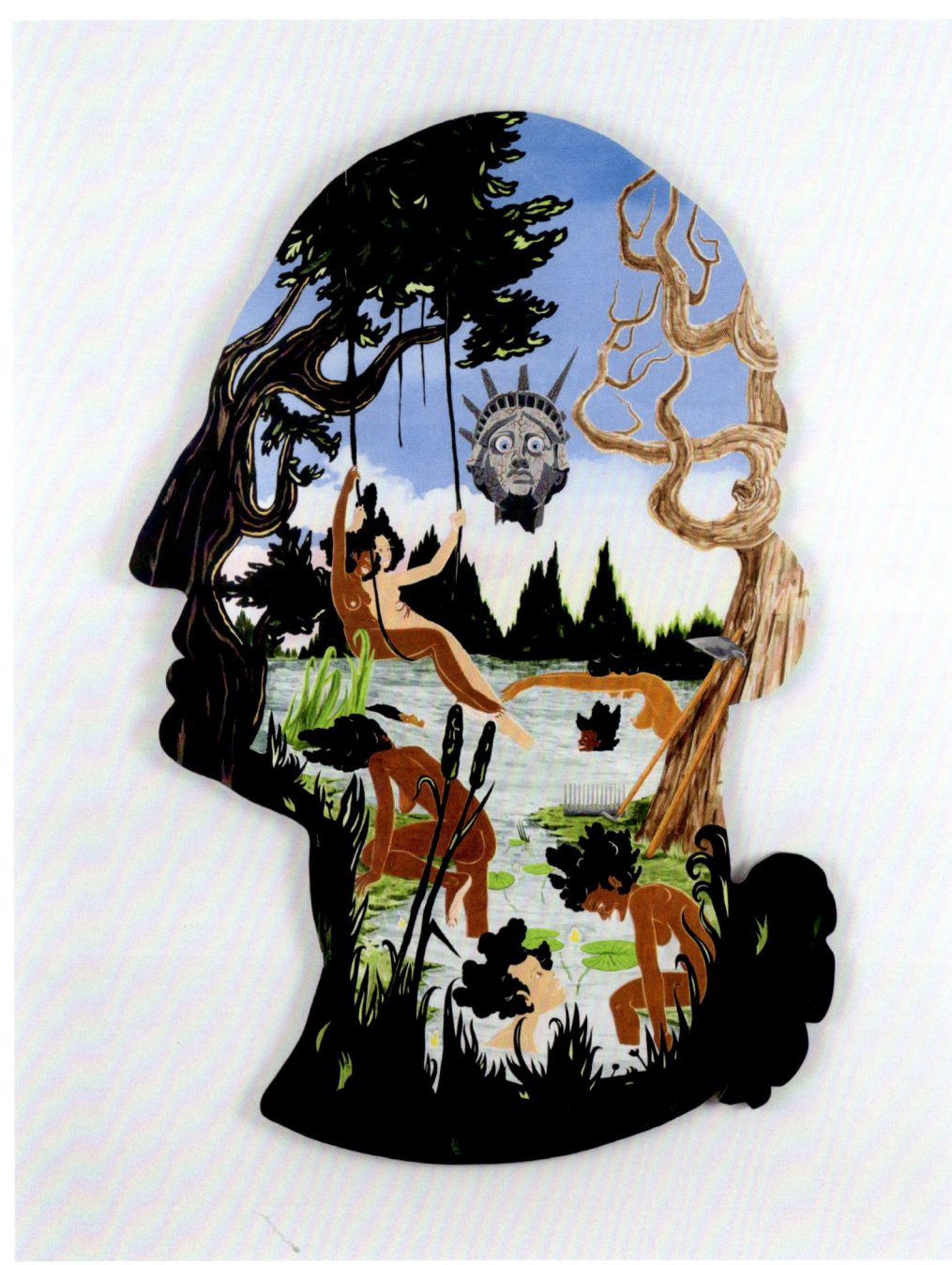

Father I Cannot Tell a Lie, 2009. Acrylic,
velour flocking, and paper on wood
panel, 97 ¼ × 60 ½ × 1 ¼ in. Bequest
of Peggy Cooper Cafritz (1947—2018),
Washington, DC, collector, educator, and
activist 2018.40.362

William Villalongo is known for his attention to the historical erasure of Black subjects from the art historical canon. In *Father I Cannot Tell a Lie*, a group of nymphs populates a landscape layered with United States folklore, Greek mythology, and Rococo motifs, thus interposing a free and sensuous black-ness into Western cultural histories and aesthetics.

Through a signature collage style—combining paper, painting, and velvet—and uniquely shaped canvases, Villalongo's early works, such as this, subvert the neutrality of flatness and the rectilinear picture plane to emphasize material as an integral point of engagement. Cut in the shape of George Washington's side profile, *Father I Cannot Tell a Lie* references the classic US tale of George Washington and the cherry tree. The story, first fabricated by early Washington biographer Mason Locke Weems, tells of young Washington's confession to damaging his father's prized cherry tree with a newly gifted hatchet. This tale of honesty and righteousness extolls the first president as a man of virtue. With a kitschy flare, Villalongo flips the script on this story by satirizing the white patriarchal foundations of so-called American values.

Contrasting these ideals, Villalongo's water nymphs exude desire, femininity, and pleasure. Under the stressed weight of the American Dream—embodied by the scandalized, floating face of Lady Liberty—the women swim, bathe, and play in iridescent waters. To the left, an interracial pair swings above the pond, recalling the central woman in Jean-Honoré Fragonard's *The Swing* (1767). Commenting on the Rococo artist, Villalongo states, "When I look at a Fragonard painting, I am swept away by its romance and lyricism. I can chuckle at its unashamedly decorative zeal; however, I am very conscious of the painting's historical . . . context. It's the height of the African slave trade, a time of mass brutality and extreme accumulation of European wealth."[190] Villalongo frames his diverse mythological subjects within the whimsy of the forest, rearticulating the lush style of the French aristocracy with an incisive pop wit.

—Sheldon Gooch

Kenyatta A. C. Hinkle/Olomidara Yaya

b. 1987

Traversing photography, drawing, and painting, Kenyatta A. C. Hinkle's art is a deeply researched practice of historical excavation that often foregrounds imagery tied to the violences of colonialism and the slave trade in order to seek redress from these systems. Hinkle made *Elixir* after encountering ethnographic photographs and postcards produced by French colonists during the late nineteenth and early twentieth centuries. These images—which often included nudity and were taken without the knowledge of the photographed person—were manufactured to calcify colonial fantasies of Africa and its people. These fictions were then transported back to Europe, where they were widely circulated among people to trade as collector's items.

Here, Hinkle covers a photographic postcard of an unidentified African woman with threadlike patterns of ink that lattice across the woman's body and spill beyond the postcard's edges. Resembling plants and flowers, Hinkle's brushstrokes intervene on the narrative the photograph asserts. Though she leaves areas of the image unobscured—including the woman's strained smile and direct stare—Hinkle's ink denies unfettered access to the pictured woman's body. This gesture disables a spectatorship that treats images of colonized and Black people as possessable and tradeable. In covering the body, she simultaneously adorns and protects it from the violence embedded in the otherizing gaze that the photography originally served. Stated otherwise, Hinkle not only covers the photograph, but also works to re-cover from the brutality that precipitated its making: her ink emerges as a material for healing from the physical and psychic wounds of colonialism. This strategy of repair is accentuated by the title of the work, which resounds with a curative association and activates a gaze centered on caring for the body rather than violating it.

—Zoë Hopkins

Elixir, 2009. India ink on nineteenth-century ethnographic postcard, 13 × 8 in. Gift of Arthur Lewis and Hau Nguyen 2018.48.2

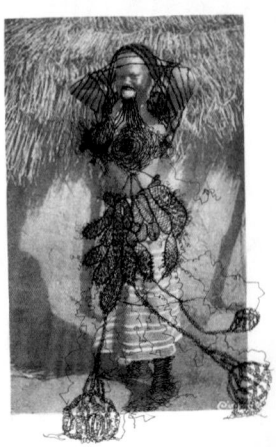

Radcliffe Bailey

1968—2023

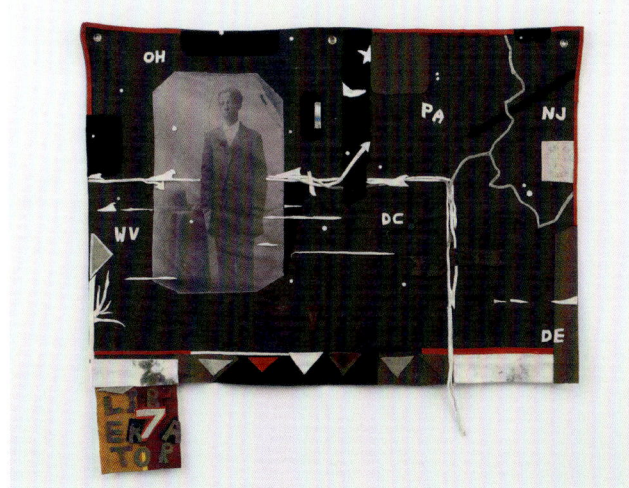

History runs deep in the work of Radcliffe Bailey. Raised and based in Atlanta, Bailey created work with references to the American South, transatlantic slave trade, the Underground Railroad, the Civil War, and the achievements and memories of Black individuals from the last three centuries. Often employing found materials, his careful selection of objects and symbols channeled the profundity appropriate to exploring the effects of slavery and its ongoing legacies.

In *Mason Dixon*, Bailey used felt to create an abstracted map of the Mason-Dixon Line: the boundary created between eighteenth-century British colonies in the United States that in the nineteenth century became famous as the border between the Northern "free" states and the Southern states where slavery remained legal until 1865. Like many of Bailey's cartographically inspired artworks, this work also pays homage to the Underground Railroad. Abbreviations and fabric strips demarcate state lines, while white dots double as potential city markers and stars from the constellations that helped guide slaves escaping at night. The fabric's layers and triangles allude to the importance of quilt-making as a communal tradition and as a tool for communicating encoded information about the Underground Railroad. A reproduced archival photograph of a Black man in an elegant suit dominates the left half of the composition, his image bisected by the jagged boundary between North and South. Situated on both sides of the border, the man stands at a "crossing over" state of migration or schism. Bailey has shared: "Both sides of my family came from Virginia, then, through the Underground Railroad, settled in New Jersey, where I was born."[191] His practice fostered a fluidity between personal and universal stories, acknowledging that these shared histories shape what the United States is today.

—Miranda Lash

Lynette Yiadom-Boakye

b. 1977

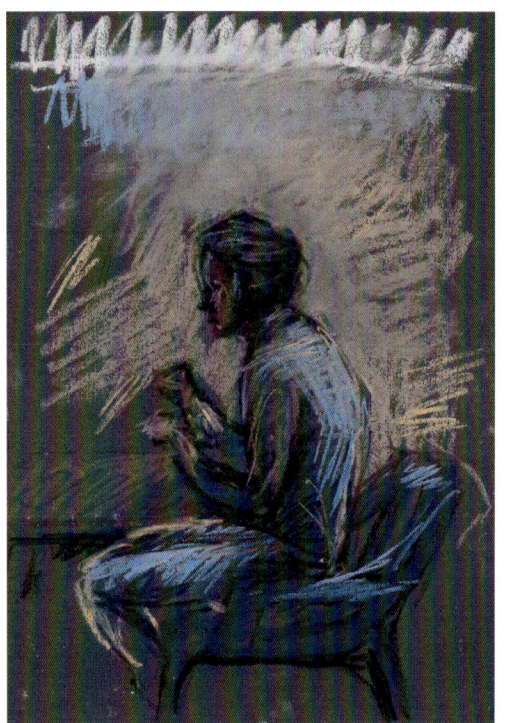 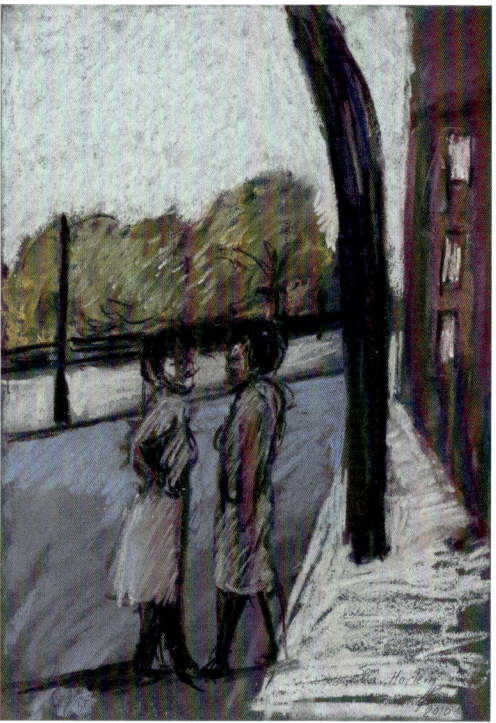

Breakfast East Harlem, 2010. Pastel on paper, 16 ½ × 11 ⅝ in. Gift of the artist and Jack Shainman Gallery, New York 2011.14.10

5 pm Harlem, 2010. Pastel on paper, 16 ½ × 11 ⅝ in. Gift of the artist and Jack Shainman Gallery, New York 2011.14.8

In November 2010, Lynette Yiadom-Boakye arrived in Harlem as the inaugural resident of Studio Lab, a new program at the Studio Museum designed as an incubator for ideas in formation. For two weeks, she traveled across the five boroughs with a stack of paper and pastels in hand. The resulting works, though visually divergent from her typical approach, provide profound insight into the development of the characters that occupy her canvases.

Since the early 2000s, Yiadom-Boakye has created thoughtful paintings of fictional subjects. They are amalgamations—memories, photographs, her imagination—whose clothing and surroundings are suggestive of time periods and locations but refuse easy identification. In *No Head for Violence*, a woman, wearing a maroon dress, ruffled collar, and flower headpiece, looks just off to the side. Instead of emphasizing a reason for her dress or pose, the work opens space for the viewer's projections onto a character. The sparse details of the subject offer only the beginnings of a narrative; they prompt the viewer to fill in the rest.

During her short-term residency with Studio Lab, a strikingly different art-making process unfolded. Unlike her days in her studio—building up canvases with repeated layers—Yiadom-Boakye responded to the scenes she encountered across the city, creating a series of works centered around intuitive mark-making and a painterly style defined by its immediacy. In *Breakfast East Harlem*, two figures sit at a table. The swift strokes (coupled with the work's title) suggest a table with a kitchen wall or window above, but could also be read as a cloud of disorganized thoughts. The suggestion of place—seen more explicitly and vividly here than in *No Head for Violence*—doubles as an expression of thought and emotion.

In *5 pm Harlem*, two women in front of a brownstone on a tree-lined street turn their heads toward a passerby who has seemingly interrupted their conversation. Behind this intimate moment, the particular and distinct setting becomes a character unto itself. With New York as another protagonist alongside its inhabitants, the series is a model not for site-specific, but for site-responsive art making. Yiadom-Boakye's works on paper mirror the ephemeral quality of New York: the speed and nature of her mark-making indicate an environment that, while familiar, rapidly changes from moment to moment.

Yiadom-Boakye's site-responsive working style, as exemplified in these works on paper, is just one of the many ways she develops visual sources. She does not transpose drawings directly on to her canvases; she translates them such that the setting dissolves into the characters and compounds with her many source materials. In this way, her fictional figures are combinations of tens if not hundreds of individuals. The figures stand as open prompts for the viewer's imagination, while also carrying the characteristics of the diverse places, such as New York, from which they came.

—Kate Claman

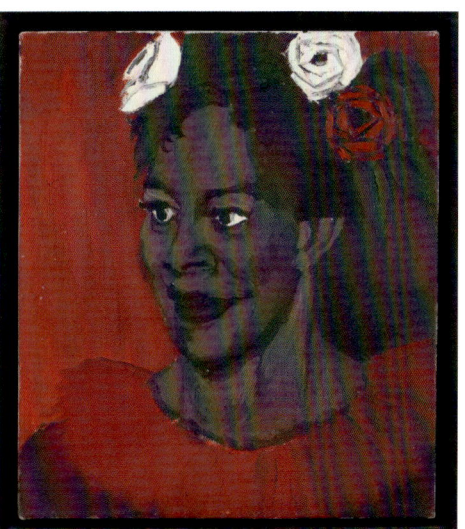

No Head for Violence, 2011. Oil on canvas, 17 ¾ × 15 ¾ in. Bequest of Peggy Cooper Cafritz (1947—2018), Washington, DC, collector, educator, and activist 2018.40.388

Deana Lawson

b. 1979

In *Roxie and Raquel, New Orleans, Louisiana*, Deana Lawson offers a glimpse into a photographic process that she calls "half-staged."[192] Lawson's skills as both director and storyteller are central to this approach. She meticulously composes each image through the careful arrangements of sitters, locations, outfits, and props. In this way, Lawson places her viewers in a state of narrative limbo between fantasy, fact, and fiction—candid moments and orchestrated scenes—finding visions of home throughout the diaspora as she constantly refers back to her first visual reference: the Black family album.[193]

The subjects in Lawson's photographs evoke a haunting familiarity, with piercing eye contact in uncanny settings. Her works often use a mirroring motif—the reflections and symmetry that appear throughout Lawson's works stem from her relationship with her twin sister, Dana. Though the viewer may not know their connection, Roxie and Raquel are inextricably linked by both the infinity loop their postures form and through Lawson's lens. In this way, Lawson unveils the unifying and cyclical elements that connect humanity. Within the context of Black domesticity, her work brings new dimensions to the banal. She offers intimate glimpses into sitters' spaces in various states of composure and disarray. In *Roxie and Raquel, New Orleans, Louisiana*, the room is stripped bare, heightening and focusing on the connection between these sisters, cousins, lovers, or friends. Whether exploring disheveled spaces, peeling paint, or messy beds, her large-scale images monumentalize her figures. Lawson brings radiant beauty and passion to states of abandonment and desolation.

At the heart of Lawson's artistic vision lies the essence of light. Photography, she believes, is intrinsically bound to the interplay of light and shadow.[194] In her delicately composed compositions, the body is the central protagonist.

—Hanna Girma

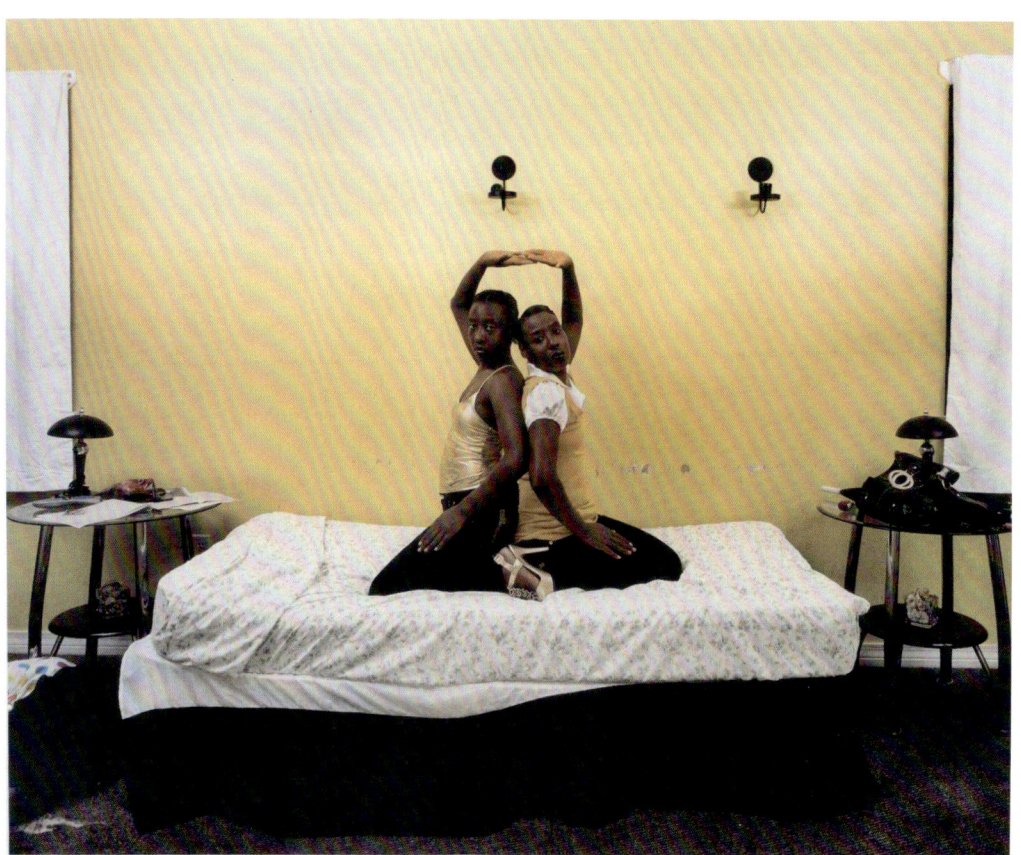

Roxie and Raquel, New Orleans, Louisiana,
2010. Inkjet print, mounted on sintra,
35 × 43 in. Edition 4 of 6 + 2 APs. Bequest
of Peggy Cooper Cafritz (1947—2018),
Washington, DC, collector, educator, and
activist 2018.40.173

Lauren Kelley

b. 1975   Artist in Residence 2009—10

Once upon a time, there was an artist. She lived in a home unlike any other. People would come from far and wide to see what was inside, and it brought her great happiness. "Come in, come in," she would say glee-fully as people gathered around, joining her in play. She was fierce, and her intellect was matched by her insightful ability to know what to call into her space, curating environments that were, yes, beautiful, but more importantly, meaningful, malleable . . . magical. She would never tell anyone what things meant, why she put something there, or something over here, that was for them to decide. The room was vibrant, with electric blue couches calling out for people to join them. Intricate geometric orange wallpaper hugged those who entered to mingle among magnificently eerie sculptures.

Yet although her home was full of freedom to play, to wonder, to explore, to rest, to dream . . . something ominous lurked beneath the surface. All alone, with the lights out, dreams shapeshifted into nightmares, as darkness descended, as sculptures loomed in the background, watching, waiting, listening for those who had departed, for those who had yet to arrive, for those ready to step into the space of undefined nostalgia, self-definition, and self-determination. She hoped they would embrace the dreams once past, turning the darkness into daylight once more. Although time here seemed to stand still—as the last drink had been sipped, the last bite had been taken, and people departed, the space now empty—the home was in reality always quite full with the energy of those whom it had once embraced; energy reminiscent of a time, place, and space tethered to transformation.

—Chloe Hayward

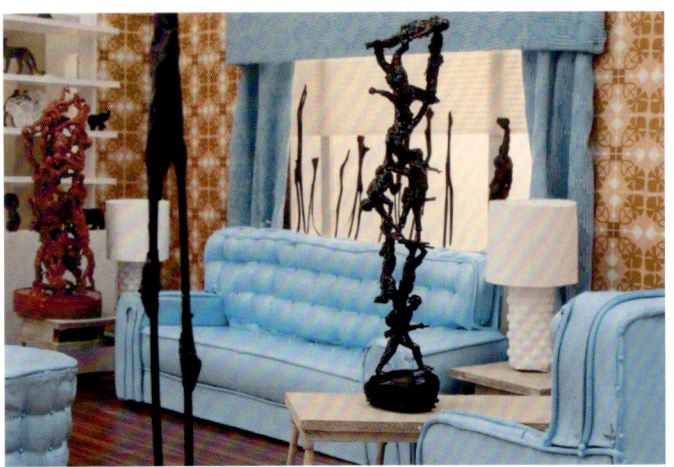

Lindy Lane, 2010. Digital chromogenic color print, 24 × 36 in. Edition of 6. Museum purchase with funds provided by a gift from Jerome and Ellen Stern and Nancy D. Washington 2010.17.2

Abigail DeVille

b. 1981   Artist in Residence 2013—14

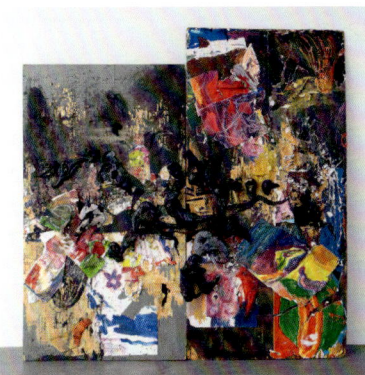

Harlem World, 2011. Found wood panels, latex enamel, tempera, paper pulp, paper, and tape, 72 × 96 in. Museum purchase with funds provided by the Acquisition Committee   2014.12.3a-b

A sculptor and installation artist, Abigail DeVille transforms found objects into dynamic artworks and environments that critique dominant yet incomplete historical narratives. With a focus on enduring cycles of racial oppression and cultural erasure in the United States, DeVille's intricate bricolages celebrate blackness as both a concrete subject and an abstract object. She excavates, studies, and conserves discarded materials from gentrifying cultural meccas to illuminate the divide between US history as it has been documented and the living histories of the African diaspora encoded within these objects.

In *Harlem World*, DeVille intuitively combines trash from the streets of Harlem with children's paintings of superhero universes to assert abstraction as a strategy for reenvisioning an ever-evolving shared reality. These paintings give *Harlem World* its color, street rubbings give it its texture, and a creeping, black, tar-like substance gives it its rhythm. Most legible is a painting of a purple-and-pink flower growing skyward through concrete that delivers a spirit of resiliency to the work. Its two panels of differing heights lean unassumingly against a wall, inviting viewers to more readily see themselves reflected in its narrative.

Like many of DeVille's sculptures, *Harlem World* both marks a specific time and place and proclaims blackness as infinite, expansive, and indestructible. It translates a hyperlocal consciousness into an object of universal significance that—in its transformation from trash to art—can be neither overlooked nor erased. DeVille's sharp powers of observation and cultural commentary steer our attention toward sociopolitical issues, such as racist practices of displacement and disinvestment, often selectively omitted from the dominant historical narrative. By moving stories of Black life from margin to center, DeVille prompts viewers to renegotiate their relationships to historical facts, fictions, and fantasies, and she subverts mechanisms of cultural erasure so often wielded by the Western art canon.

—nico w. okoro

Wangechi Mutu

b. 1972   Artist in Residence 2003—04

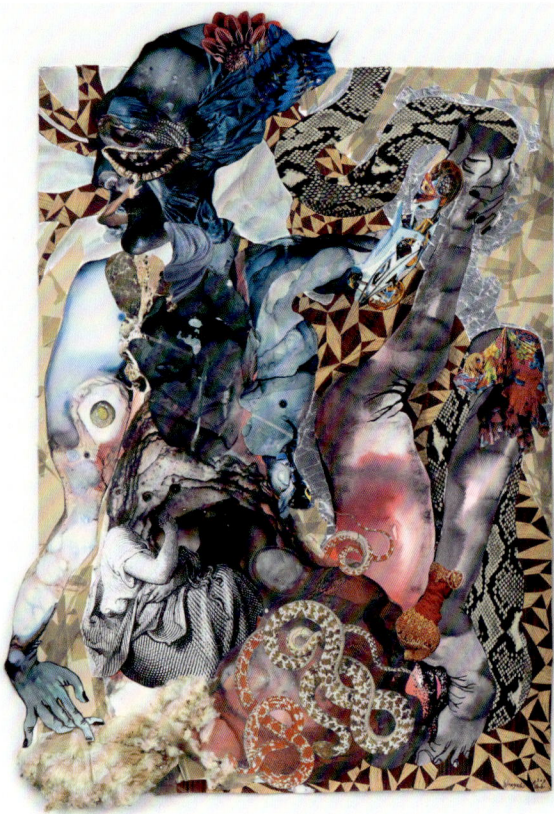

The Mother of all Snake Dreams, 2011. Mixed media on paper, 33 × 23 ½ in. Gift of the artist on the occasion of the Romare Bearden (1911—1988) Centennial and *The Bearden Project* 2012.11

Multidisciplinary artist Wangechi Mutu creates fantastical worlds shaped by her African, ecofeminist perspective. Working with collage, drawing, sculpture, installation, performance, and video, Mutu builds otherworldly environments. Her works are primal and futuristic; tropical and postapocalyptic; beautiful and grotesque; unnerving and empowering. They are always female-dominated and matriarchal. Mutu emphasizes hybridity in her mythical creatures and settings to underscore the interdependence of all things in existence—combining human, animal, plant, land, water, and the supernatural to illustrate this connectivity.

Mutu's belief that everything in the universe is composed of interconnected forces is a central tenet of the spiritual philosophy of the Kikuyu, aligning her work with her cultural heritage. She also partially attributes her long-standing love of nature to her being Kikuyu and her people's deep relationship to the natural environment. At the same time, she is an active citizen of the African diaspora, living between Nairobi and Brooklyn with her feet and heart split between multiple worlds. In her work, she explores this extensively, paying respect to and adapting the visual, cultural, and spiritual practices and traditions from cultures across the African continent and the Black Atlantic.

In works such as *The Mother of all Snake Dreams* and *Chocolate Nguva*, Mutu brings her hybridized, supernatural beings to life through collage and sculpture, respectively. Serpents and sirens from aquatic worlds recur throughout her work, illustrating the artist's ongoing interest in bodies of water as transformative realms and sites of origin, uncertainty, sustenance, peril, and regeneration. On paper, *The Mother of all Snake Dreams* depicts a female figure surrounded by snakes. Despite its uniquely composite, maximalist, collaged aesthetic, the work is visually similar to popular imagery of the transcultural water spirit Mami Wata ("Mother Water" in pidgin English). Celebrated throughout much of sub-Saharan Africa, the Caribbean, and Brazil as a snake charmer or mermaid, Mami Wata is a potent water deity who is seductively beautiful, possesses great healing and protective power, and can also be dangerous.

Chocolate Nguva possesses a more restrained form as a small bronze sculpture, but the work's mermaid-like presence, with its aquatic tail and webbed hands, similarly connects it to African water spirits and deities. The word "nguva," in Kiswahili, means "siren"; the mythical water woman is believed to be derived from the East African dugong, a marine mammal of the Indian Ocean. The dugong is related to the manatee, but instead of a paddle-like tail, the dugong's is fluked, giving it a whale-like appearance that may have inspired early mermaid tales. *Chocolate Nguva* also recalls Yemoja, the Yoruba orisha of water and rivers, goddess of motherhood and protector of children. Her swollen stomach speaks to her role in fertility and all things maternal. In West Africa, she is primarily affiliated with its rivers, but in the syncretic African-derived religions of the Americas, she is celebrated as the goddess of the ocean and the restorative waters that connect the shores of the Americas to the African continent.

Through her hybrid creatures and culturally intertwined, feminine worlds, Mutu encourages considerations of transformation and adaptation as essential means of survival, as well as tools for transcendental navigation of the complexities of the real world.

— Trevor Schoonmaker

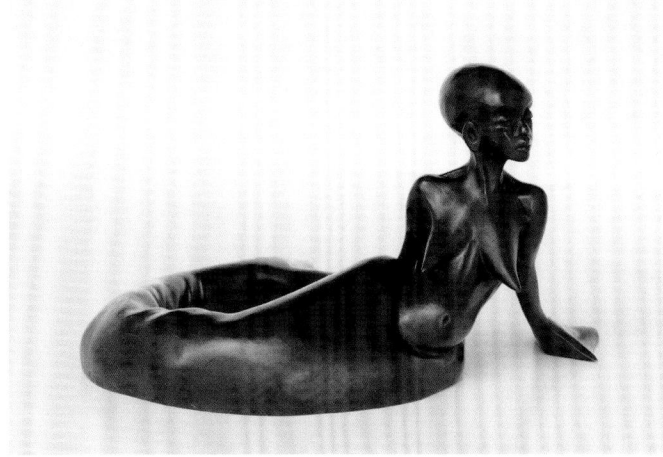

Chocolate Nguva, 2015. Patinated bronze, 16 × 14 × 10 in. Edition of 9 + 3 AP. Museum purchase with funds provided by Holly Peterson 2017.23a-b

Lonnie Bradley Holley

b. 1950

COLLECTION

Lonnie Bradley Holley, an artist based in Birmingham, Alabama, has dedicated his artistic practice to the creation of site-specific sculptures since the age of twenty-nine. Drawing inspiration from his environment and experiences, Holley was initially renowned as a tombstone sculptor and assemblage artist. Holley first created objects for heartfelt tributes to lost loved ones, creating an immersive site-specific sculptural environment in his yard. His artistic trajectory took an unexpected turn when the expansion of the Birmingham Airport triggered a protracted legal battle, resulting in the loss of his property.

In a manner akin to fellow artists Thornton Dial and Ronald Lockett, Holley's assemblage works not only reflect his deep Southern roots but also delve into the intricate tapestry of the region's history. By interweaving rural and industrial elements, the history and symbolism of the modern civil rights movement, and African diasporic ritual traditions, Holley constructs powerful visual narratives.

Reaching My Gold exemplifies these thematic connections. This captivating piece features a vertical marble block adorned with a metal pipe, funnel, and pickaxe, all securely affixed with wire. The pickaxe, traditionally used for breaking earth or rock, contrasts with the industrial pipe, a feature of modern indoor plumbing. Both objects cross through the funnel, with the pipe partially emerging on the other side. This poignant composition metaphorically portrays the metamorphosis of farming communities into bustling iron and steel mill towns during the twentieth century, with particular emphasis on locations such as Birmingham and nearby Bessemer. The presence of a concrete plinth within the artwork evokes both architectural and funerary references, while the horizontal orientation of the pickaxe subtly alludes to the Christian crucifixion and even racial violence, which forms a part of the city's complicated history. The eventual economic downturn led to the decline and eventual demise of these very communities, rendering them shadows of their former selves.

—Shawnya Harris

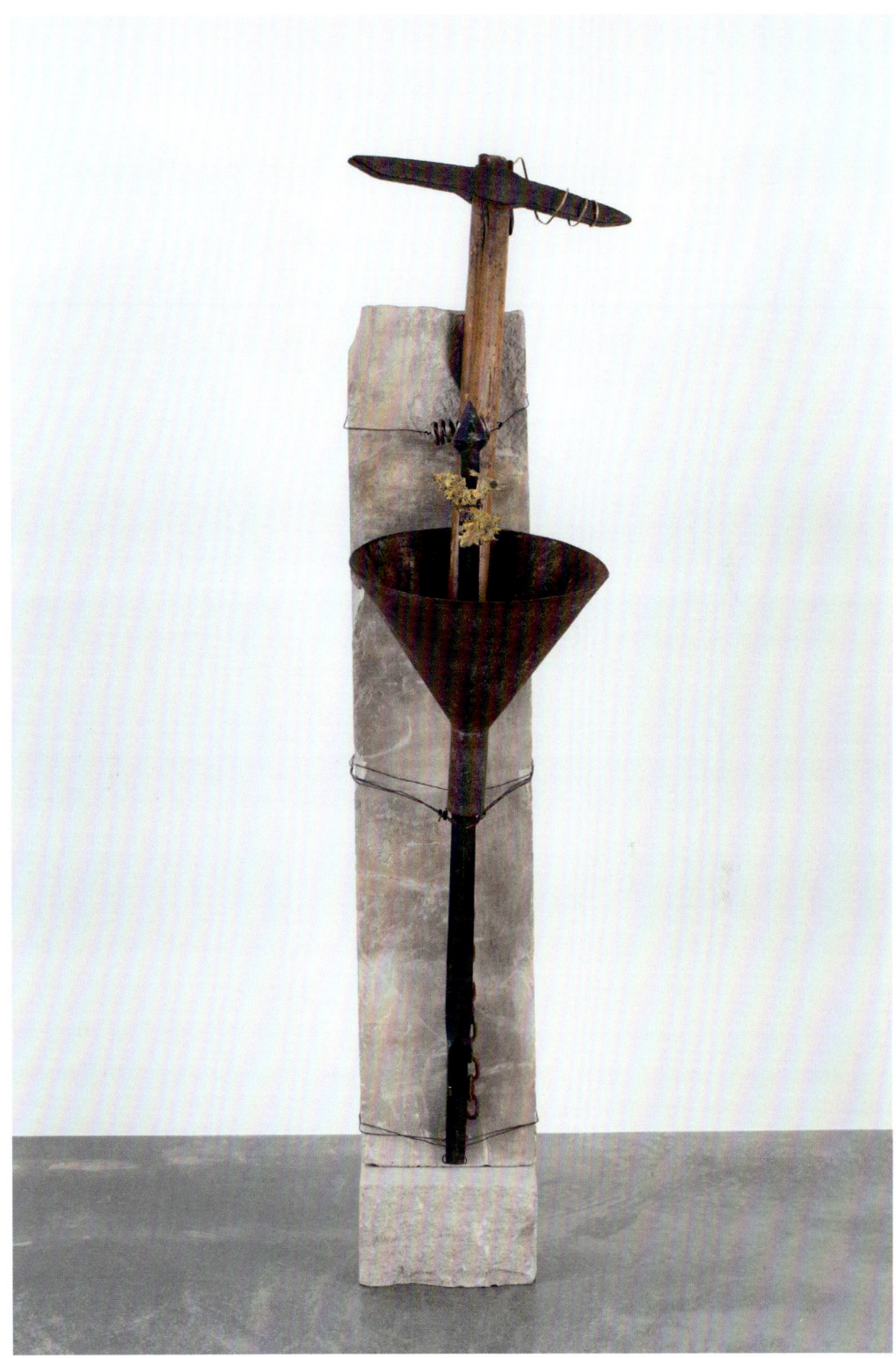

Reaching My Gold, 2011. Mixed media,
50 × 15 × 14 ½ in. Gift of Martin and
Rebecca Eisenberg in honor of Thelma
Golden 2023.39.5

David Hartt

b. 1967

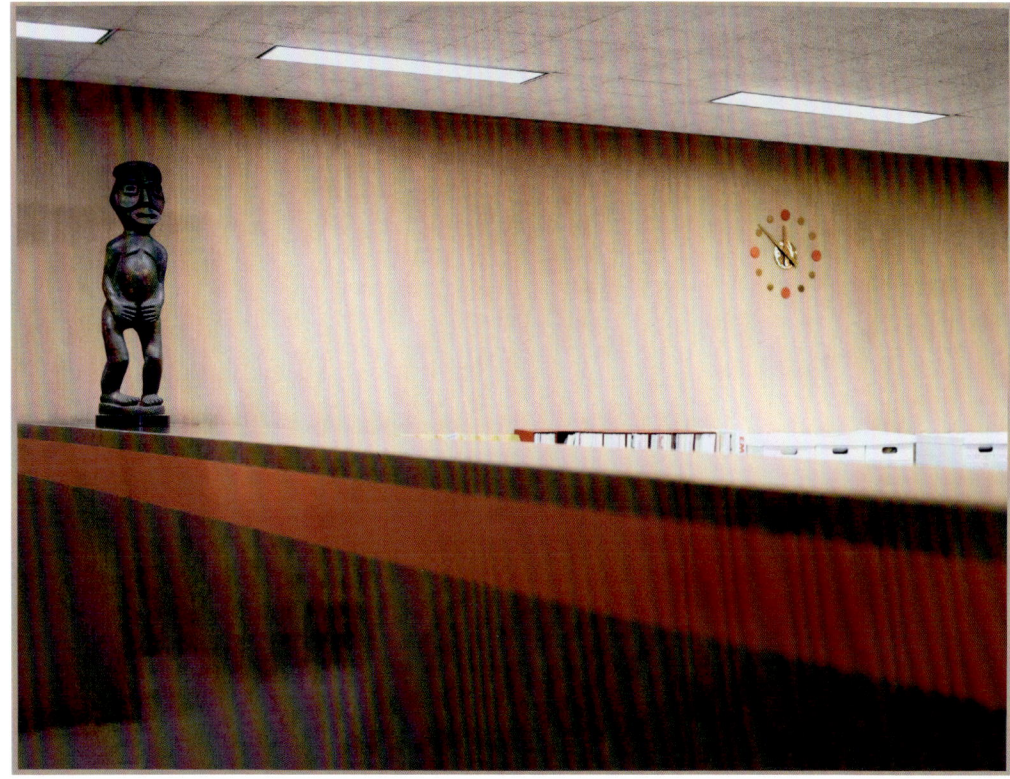

*Archive at the Johnson Publishing Company
Headquarters, Chicago, IL* (from the series
"Stray Light"), 2011. Archival pigment
print mounted to Dibond, 60 × 80 × 2 in.
Edition 5 of 6 + 1 AP. Museum purchase
with funds provided by the Acquisition
Committee 2013.12

David Hartt reaches beyond that which is immediately visible to reveal the mutable nature of history and ideology. Taking a seemingly objective approach with his films and photographs, the artist creates a critical distance between subject and document, opening up a space in which to consider the social, cultural, and economic circumstances that frame our perception.

Hartt's project "Stray Light," named after a technical term for light that interferes with an optical system, captures the iconic Chicago headquarters of the Johnson Publishing Company through photography, film, music, sculpture, and installation. Designed by the African American architect John Moutoussamy in 1971, the eleven-story building boasted a highly stylized interior featuring bold colors and modern design by Arthur Elrod. Home to *Ebony* and *Jet*, leading publications in African American culture, the Johnson building became a "culmination of a set of ideals," or what founder John Johnson and his wife and business partner Eunice envisioned as a successful, modern, Black-owned business.[195]

Hartt was granted access to document the Johnson offices shortly before they were sold in 2011. The artist found the space dutifully preserved, just as it was in 1971. The large-scale print *Archive at the Johnson Publishing Company Headquarters, Chicago, IL* portrays the manifestation of an aesthetic and philosophical vision, and the impact that such a vision has today. Taken at an oblique angle, the subject lies just beyond view: a vast repository of African American culture in files and boxes that remains inaccessible to the viewer. An African sculpture belonging to the Johnsons' personal art collection stands atop a dividing wall. A mid-century modern clock, frozen at just past 11:50, hangs opposite. The photograph serves as a monument to a particular moment in time and to the personal and collective aspirations of African Americans. Yet Hartt also illuminates a different reading: peering from the outside in, the artist calls into question what might be considered a "Black aesthetic," instead revealing an ongoing negotiation.

—Eric Booker

Martine Syms
b. 1988

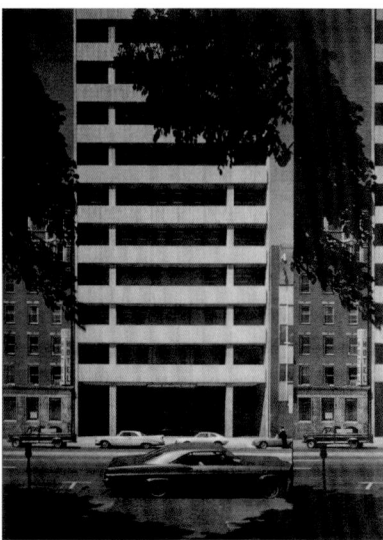

At an initial glance, Martine Syms's *Johnson's Publishing Company Building,
1971* appears simple enough. Scanning the image from the left, the eye
follows the edge of a sidewalk from which tall city buildings—including
a hotel—sprout up prominently. The street below the towering structures
is lined with cars and trees; the latter cast ominous shadows along the
bottom of the composition. As the rest of the image comes into view,
something marvelous happens: before the eye reaches the right edge,
the entire image starts over from its beginning, resulting in a layered
or duplicated effect.

Syms created this altered inkjet print from a black-and-white archival
photograph of the Johnson Publishing Company shot by Hedrich Blessing
Photographers. Founded in Chicago in 1942, the celebrated publisher
of *Ebony* and *Jet* magazines eventually settled into its headquarters along
South Michigan Avenue in what became the first Black-owned building
in Chicago's downtown area.

Syms's use of repetition at this section of the print, which centers the
publishing company's office building, hints gently at a notion of continuum.
The appearance of the Johnson Publishing Company followed immediately
by another iteration of itself provides a powerful and optimistic conceptual framework and suggests a possibility of sustained replication. The
placement of the iconic building can also be read as a foretelling symbol
of the new entities that may follow in the footsteps of the Black-owned
publishing company. Additionally, it looks ahead to the lasting impact and
legacy that the Johnson Publishing Company developed within a larger
Black cultural context.

—Daria Simone Harper

Derrick Adams

b. 1970

Derrick Adams's *Head #4* captures what can be constructed through deconstruction. As a multidisciplinary artist working across painting, sculpture, performance, and installation, Adams considers the way color, symbols, and media fabricate meaning and inform perception, particularly of Black people. His investment in challenging inaccurate conceptions and images of Black life through depicting Black joy takes the form of figurative works that draw from Cubism—and its African art influences—Pop art, and Romare Bearden's collages. Characterized by his signature use of bold, flat, colorful shapes, this work contains the playful quality that makes Adams's work distinctly imaginative and captivating.

Head #4 is one work in the artist's "Deconstruction Worker" series. Begun in 2011, the series comprises collaged portraits made using contact paper, which is traditionally used in architecture and interior design. For this work, the artist assembled cut sections of wallpaper and wood-grain paneling into a head in profile. The variation of colors and patterns that makes up the figure's Afro and face suggests the many tones and textures present in hair and skin. By presenting these materials removed from their intended context, Adams creates a direct parallel between the construction of race and the built environment and suggests how perception is informed by both. The resulting composition attempts to edify a positive self-image. The artist remarks that "as a Black man, I am aware of my vulnerability and susceptibility to trauma and oppression on a daily basis . . . there are images that are less important for us to see than images of joy."[196] By deconstructing and reconfiguring the fundamental elements of built structures, and perhaps cemented ideologies, Adams devises a new, more complex understanding of self-perception that leaves room for multitudes.

— Kiki Teshome

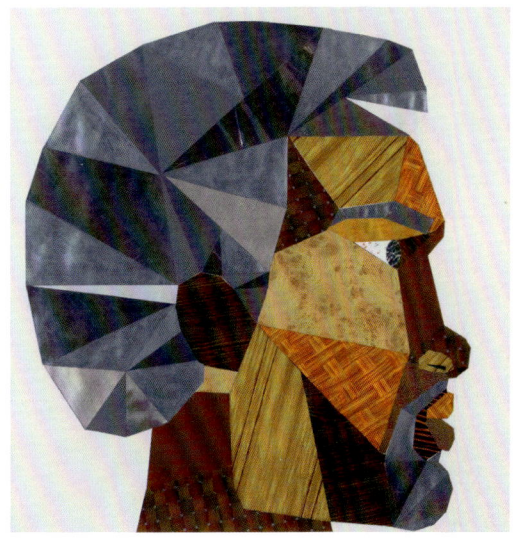

Head #4 (from the series "Deconstruction Worker"), 2011. Mixed media collage on paper, 36 × 35 ¾ in. Museum purchase with funds provided by the Acquisition Committee 2012.17

Ficre Ghebreyesus

1962—2012

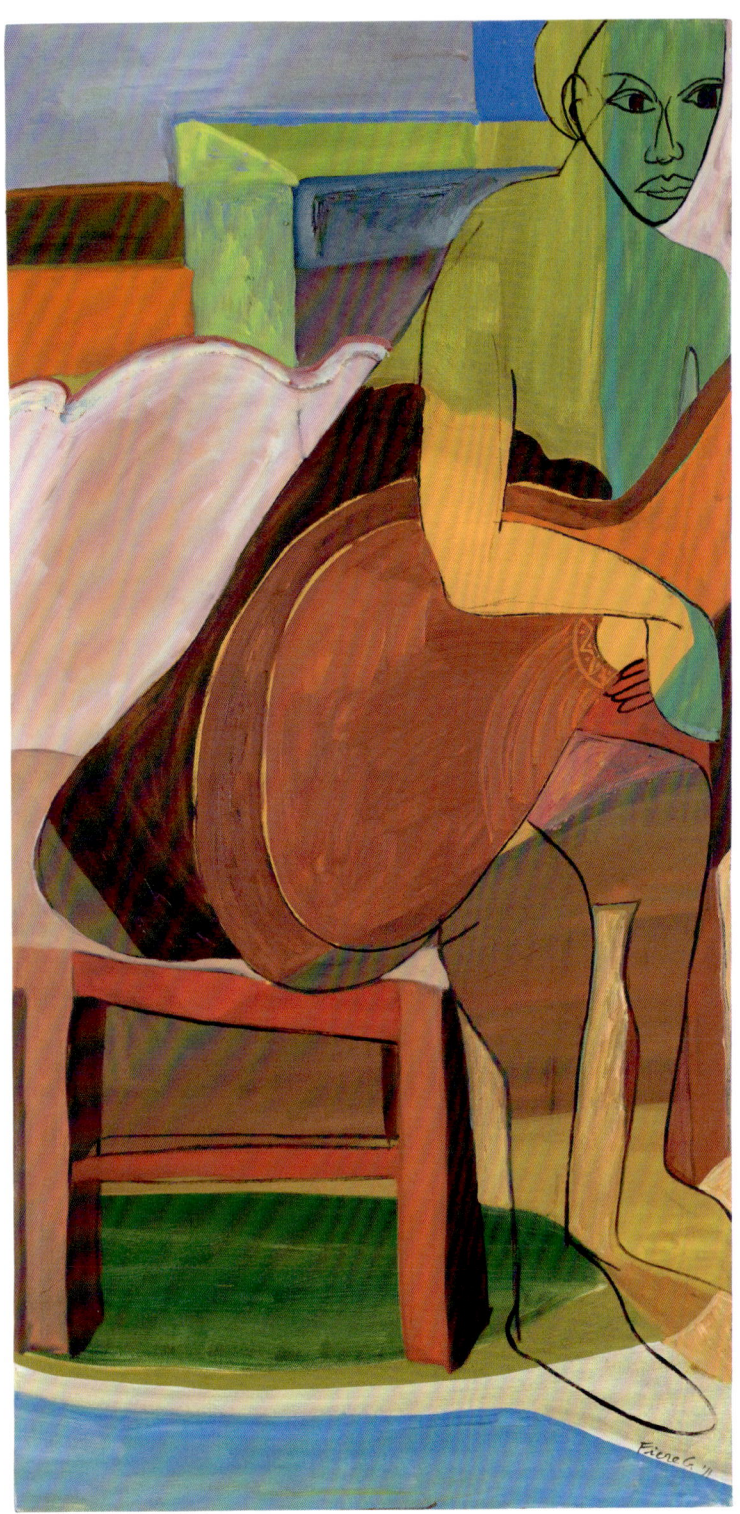

Ficre Ghebreyesus described himself as "a conscious syncretizer."[197] This Eritrean American artist escaped his birth country's thirty-year war for independence as a teenager, passing through Sudan, Italy, and Germany before settling in New Haven, Connecticut, where he opened a beloved restaurant with his brothers. Cooking was but one part of Ghebreyesus's creative practice. Music was another. Versed in instruments from his homeland—including krar (bowl-shaped lyre) and kebero (double-sided drum)—Ghebreyesus also embraced other forms of musical expression, including "Be-Bop, Modern Jazz . . . and polyrhythms of the African diaspora."[198] By 1990, he had also committed to painting.

Seated Musician III depicts a solitary figure against a rectangular form suggestive of an upright piano. Blocks of color appear in a palette redolent of warm spices (cinnamon and turmeric), dried fruits (dates and apricots), as well as jewel-toned blues and greens. The figure cradles a guitar and sits propped on a pink bench with a cloud-shaped back. By framing the figure tightly and outlining it with strong black lines, Ghebreyesus endows the musician with physical grandeur. Yet, the figure's stylized features lend it a timeless quality. Despite precise lines, the musician's body—especially its feet and right hand—dissolves into the background. Further, Ghebreyesus fuses the musician's lower half with the body of the guitar. The figure and instrument become one.

The musician's wide-open, far-seeing eyes gaze outside the frame, placing the true event of the painting elsewhere. This dream like state is underscored by the stringless, thus silent, guitar. Still, a sense of musicality pervades the painting. Here Ghebreyesus manifests his abilities as a "syncretizer," using paint to evoke the effects of sound. The interplay of sinuous and angular forms conveys the rhythmic progression of musical scores, as does Ghebreyesus's application of paint, which oscillates between translucent washes and dense brushstrokes. Together, these elements evince a sonic flow that sweeps across the composition.

This work, painted a year before his sudden, untimely death, exemplifies Ghebreyesus's deftness in portraying inner worlds. It captures the transportive effects of art as a conduit between tangible worlds and transient memories, to which he, as a displaced person, must have been especially attuned.

—Tamara H. Schenkenberg

Seated Musician III, 2011. Acrylic on canvas, 48 × 24 × ¾ in. Gift of Elizabeth Alexander 2019.31

Renée Green
b. 1959   Artist in Residence 1988—89

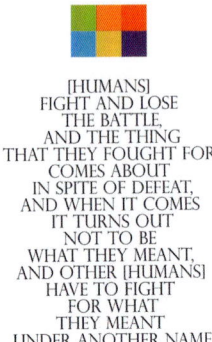

William Morris (from the series "Sigetics Color"), 2011. Letterpress and digital pigment print, 22 × 18 in. Museum purchase with funds provided by the Acquisition Committee 2011.3

[HUMANS]
FIGHT AND LOSE
THE BATTLE,
AND THE THING
THAT THEY FOUGHT FOR
COMES ABOUT
IN SPITE OF DEFEAT,
AND WHEN IT COMES
IT TURNS OUT
NOT TO BE
WHAT THEY MEANT,
AND OTHER [HUMANS]
HAVE TO FIGHT
FOR WHAT
THEY MEANT
UNDER ANOTHER NAME.

"My work has much more to do with association than anything literal or a direct way of going about things," says artist, writer, and filmmaker Renée Green. "My approach is circuitous, which resonates with a life trajectory that is not linear—going in circles and then coming back to things, ideas, and places, seeing them at different times, recombining variables."[199] Working across media to create complex installations, Green explores "circuits of relation" and the exchange of ideas, in part by revisiting and restaging earlier artworks with new ones, thus building a genealogy of references and formal approaches.[200]

William Morris, a print from Green's "Sigetics Color Series," illustrates this process.[201] The artist quotes from English writer, artist, and socialist William Morris's novel *A Dream of John Ball* (1888), which she reproduces in an all-caps serif font centered on a white background.[202] In *A Dream of John Ball*, a man in the nineteenth century dreams he encounters John Ball, a fourteenth-century radical English priest whose sermons bolstered the Peasants' Revolt of 1381. The narrator informs Ball that his dreams of an egalitarian society remain unrealized. Green quotes the narrator in her print, a technically sophisticated combination of letterpress and digital printing processes.[203] *William Morris* continues ideas from the artist's multimedia installation *Endless Dreams and Water Between* (2009), in which, across different media, fictional and historical characters (including Morris) interrogate "how imagination and negotiation of our place in the world collide and corrupt, charging projections, fabulations, and dreams with the complexities of the present."[204] These prints also incorporate symbols and colors from previous projects—in *William Morris,* a six-cell grid of colors is situated like a header. This grid originally functioned as a digital navigational device in Green's early CD-ROM work, *The Digital Import/Export Funk Office* (1996), itself a rethinking of her installation *Import/Export Funk Office* (1992); and the grid continues its migration into *Early Videos* (2010) as a wall painting behind the six DVD players, to now, under another name, *William Morris.*

—Zuna Maza

Xaviera Simmons

b. 1974   Artist in Residence 2011—12

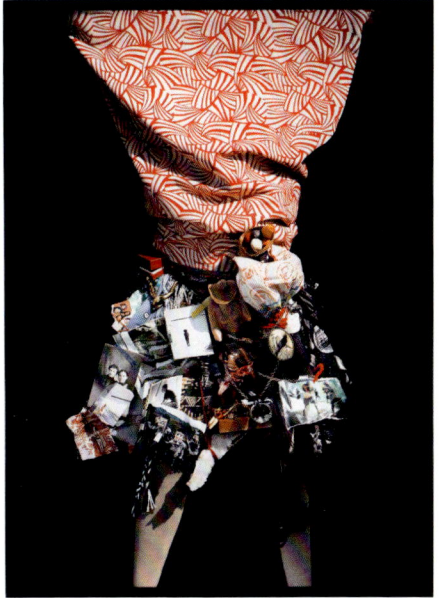

Index Three, Composition Four (from the series "Index / Composition"), 2012. Color photograph, 56 ¾ × 41 ½ × 2 in. Edition 1 of 3. Museum purchase with funds provided by the Acquisition Committee 2012.25

Since her inclusion in the 2005—06 Studio Museum exhibition *Frequency* and her subsequent participation in the Museum's 2011—12 *Artist-in-Residence* program, critics have described Xaviera Simmons's work as potent, unsettling, jarring, and elliptical in its cutting-edge exploration of blackness and its construction. Combining her training in fine art and fashion photography with acting and directing, Simmons shifts the cultural, aesthetic, and political perceptions of portraits, vinyl records, landscapes, and the body as containers of information and selfhood.

In her ongoing series "Index / Composition" (2011—), found images and artifacts—postcards; braided hair; textured materials from the African diaspora such as raffia, typically used for clothing and adornment—hang like totems from the waist of the body pictured. Like a cocoon, the upper half of the figure is wrapped in minimally patterned or solid fabric. But none of the items are easily identifiable, nor is the body. This arrangement creates two contiguous yet distinct object worlds that draw attention to the body's topography, with emphasis on its surface rather than its substance. In some of the works, the body's skin color is visible; in most, however, neither the body's race nor its gender is easily discernible, a motif present in *Index Three, Composition Four.* As the series progresses in number and aesthetic logic, the backgrounds, including wood paneling and black, white, and solid colors, remain fairly mundane, while the fabric patterns and totem configurations grow more sophisticated and more complex. The focus of the series, consequently, is the body and its various states of becoming.

— Tiffany E. Barber

Jennie C. Jones
b. 1968

Jennie C. Jones's interdisciplinary practice embraces the sonic and the visual. Her multimedia work incorporates painting, drawing, sculpture, and sound by repurposing acoustic equipment such as acoustic absorbing panels and noise-canceling cables. Jones's art is informed by her upbringing during the culture wars of the 1980s and 1990s; the legacies of Minimalism and abstraction; and the under-sung avant-garde jazz music by Black musicians in the 1950s and 1960s. The artist has said that she attempts "a merger of art history and black history, with the realm of the abstract languages they constructed—at its core of my practices is a search for neo-modernism."[205] Limited square footage of Jones's studio prompted the artist to examine the notion of space, which became a subject and touchstone in her work. In 2012, the artist began to create acoustic interventions, site-specific works that experiment with and respond to architecture and ubiquitous, paradigmatic white cube galleries and museums.

The act of listening goes hand in hand with her studio practice and is a key element in her work. Jones explains: "Listening is a conceptual practice all its own. It's a strategy that asks, rather than demands, your attention."[206] The title *Shhh and Electric Clef* is a dichotomy and metaphor. The artist says (to paraphrase) there is a constant "back and forth between silence and noise . . . a push pull" in the highly active gestural mark-making of this work and others in the "Shhh" series.[207] The tangling of the cables into a treble clef symbolizes the tensions between order and disorder; between silence and sound; and within the refrain of refusal as dictated by the "shhh."

Early in her career, Jones searched for her place in the narratives of art and Black histories. In many ways, her art making is a continuum of the avant-garde and is an expanded and inclusive narrative. Amid the often-distracting white noise that permeates the politics of the day, Jones's art deploys a resonance that, through its visual minimalism, invites full presence via looking, listening, and reflecting.

—Anne Collins Smith

Shhh and Electric Clef (from the series "Shhh"), 2012. Canceling instrument cable, cable ties, end pin jacks, 58 × 7 in. Promised gift of Nancy L. Lane
PG.2023.010.22

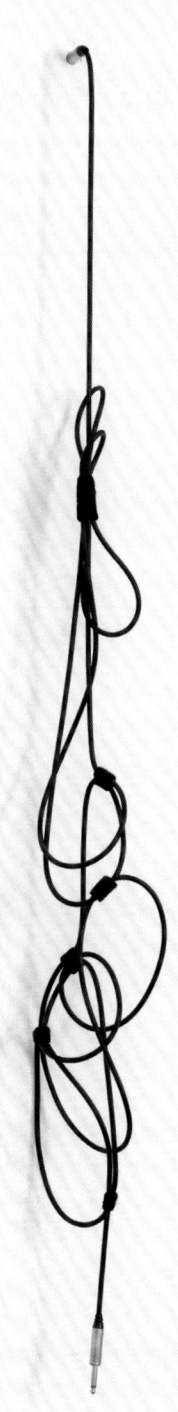

Njideka Akunyili Crosby

b. 1983   Artist in Residence 2011—12

Interior scenes, familiar domestic activities, averted gazes—there is often an intimacy to looking, a sense of intruding on a moment, when viewing a work by Njideka Akunyili Crosby. She seeks the beauty in the everyday, with seemingly quotidian aspects of daily life elevated to moments worthy of being pictured. In *Nwantinti*, Akunyili Crosby offers a glimpse into a bedroom, where two figures—the artist and her husband—gaze lovingly at each other as they lounge on a bed. The haphazardly cast flip-flops on the floor and the open closet doors in the background are additional indicators that this moment is a private one between the couple, an interpretation furthered more so by the title's reference to *Love Nwantinti*, Nelly Uchendu's popular 1976 Igbo album about beginning the journey to love.

Akunyili Crosby, however, complicates a singular reading of her work by incorporating areas of photo-collage throughout. She thereby creates a densely layered composition using the album cover art for *Love Nwantinti*, personal photographs, and images of Nigerian politics and popular culture taken from the internet, various magazines, and advertisements. The combination of image sources is both a nod to the artist's complex cultural identity—having spent sixteen years in Nigeria before coming to the United States—and a visual reminder that people are shaped by a rich fusion of personal and public experiences. Akunyili Crosby places the images alongside flat planes of color, crisp patterning, and loose applications of pastel and charcoal to produce a work with texture and depth, one that revels in the productive tension between love, popular culture, memory, and the formal techniques of painting.

—Connie H. Choi

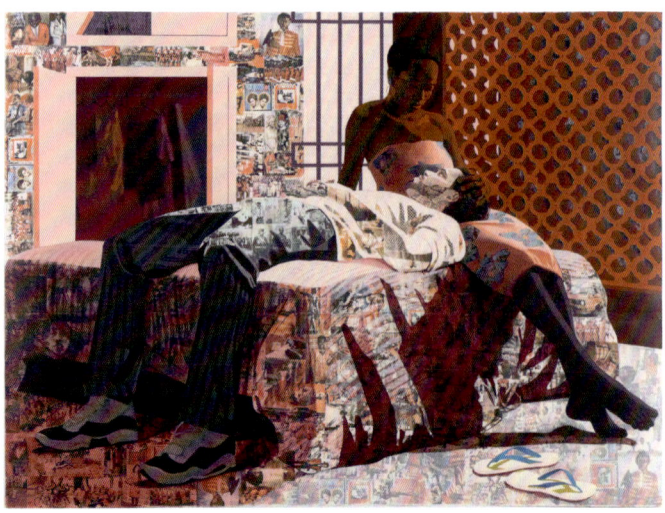

Nwantinti, 2012. Acrylic, pastel, charcoal, colored pencil, and Xerox transfers on paper, 69 ¼ × 96 in. Museum purchase with funds provided by the Acquisition Committee and gift of the artist 2012.35

Nina Chanel Abney

b. 1982

In *Untitled* by Nina Chanel Abney, choreography seeps into the canvas of a systematically convoluted scene. The familiarity of the minimalist shapes couples with Abney's many explorations of duality: abstraction/figuration, planned/improvised, transparent/opaque, black/white, woman/man, and so on.

This composition extends into an optical journey of dissonant communion—the work ricochets from one element to another, like the cadence of free jazz, gospel, or rap (the artist notes sonic influences as a primary component to her method of creation). The result is twofold: a glimpse into a world of the artist's making and the reflection of a recognizable cultural ethos. In the work, Abney disperses saturated shapes of various colors among numbers, sayings (such as "coop" and "YO"), and multiple faces in profile that nearly spill from the parameters of an arched frame. A composition such as this functions as a conduit, something akin to what bell hooks has described as a work that "returns us to experience, to memory."[208] Thus, Abney's work is as timely as it is nostalgic. Her multicolored shapes recall elementary artistic endeavors: lying on classroom floors, playing with blocks, cutting out shapes of all kinds, and coloring vigorously. Abney's bold symbols summon early inscriptions of favorite numbers, sayings, or nicknames sprawled across notebooks with meticulous deliberation or angst.

Abney's works are containers of musicality, wherein her brushstrokes conduct scores of both levity/weight, elation/reflection; her paintings are choreographies on canvas. Her work embodies a "third space" where stylistic methods of expression—whether painted, written, danced, or sung—can reside in dissonant communion and communal dissonance.

—Jenée-Daria Strand

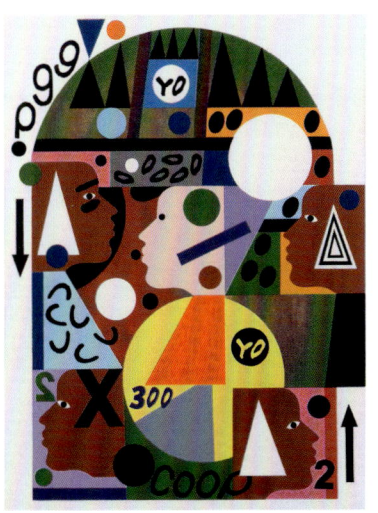

Untitled, 2012. Acrylic on canvas, 48 × 36 in. Bequest of Peggy Cooper Cafritz (1947—2018), Washington, DC, collector, educator, and activist 2018.40.1

Simone Leigh

b. 1967   Artist in Residence 2010—11

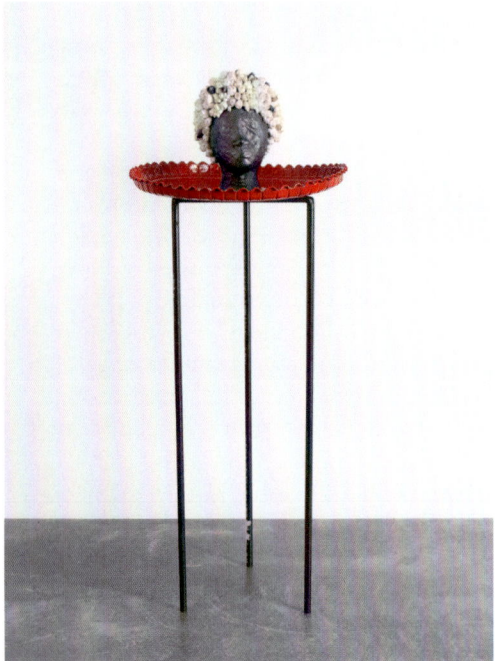

Head on a Platter, 2009. Porcelain, terracotta, copper, silver, automotive paint, steel, graphite, 13 × 9 ½ × 10 in. Bequest of Peggy Cooper Cafritz (1947—2018), Washington, DC, collector, educator, and activist 2018.40.175

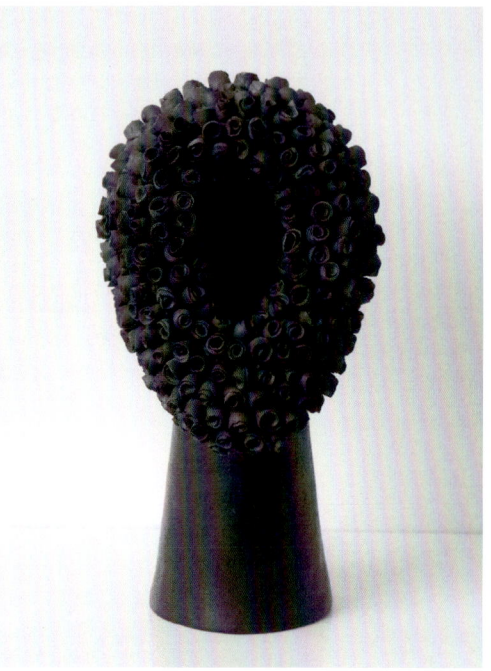

No Face (Black), 2015. Terracotta, colored porcelain, and epoxy, 15 ¾ × 7 ½ × 8 ¼ in. Bequest of Peggy Cooper Cafritz (1947—2018), Washington, DC, collector, educator, and activist 2018.40.176

Simone Leigh uses sculpture, video, performance, and social projects—defined by the artist as "social sculptures"—as vehicles to communicate with her primary audience: Black women. Her deep engagement with the archive of African and African American histories, Black feminist theory, diasporic iconography, and architectural and ceramic practices informs her approach to making. Demonstrating what writer Saidiya Hartman calls "critical fabulation," Leigh's research-based practice allows for a creative intervention in the archive. As a result, Leigh uses her chosen material, primarily clay, to reflect upon, fill in, or call attention to the histories and inner lives of Black women—both real and imagined.

For *Untitled (Cowrie)*, Leigh employed the centuries-old method of salt-firing, a largely obsolete pottery technique once lauded by US potters. These cowrie shell sculptures, molded from watermelons, have become a ubiquitous symbol of Leigh's artistic oeuvre. Often considered purely decorative in their contemporary function, cowrie shells were used as currency for the buying of goods, services, and slaves on Africa's western coast. Leigh's seamless fusion of disparate cultural histories and artistic techniques embodies what writer Jessica Lynne calls "a transatlantic loop of remembrance . . . like a ring shout."[209]

Head on a Platter presents a sculptural, eyeless head adorned with cream and black rosettes for hair. The head sits on a red fluted platter atop an iron stand. Building on this visual language, Leigh's later work *No Face (Black)* displays no face at all. Instead, where the face should be is a garland of roses. In this way, Leigh makes palpable both presence and absence; speech and silence. She forces a confrontation with a void and what can be discovered in the abyss. To engage with Leigh's sculptures is to undergo "the work of witnessing . . . the work of enduring discomfort and facing it head on."[210]

Produced alongside her three-dimensional works, *Breakdown* engages another aspect of Leigh's practice: video and performance. The nine-minute scene, made in collaboration with Liz Magic Laser, features opera singer Alicia Hall Moran in an abandoned theater. To create the score and libretto, the artists gathered snippets from film and television featuring women characters in states of hysteria. A superb mezzo-soprano, Moran oscillates between exclamations of joy and a slew of haunting incantations. Her repetitive, chilling exclamation, "I've always performed! I've been performing my whole life!" emphatically articulates the performative behaviors enacted daily and how this performativity might take a toll on Black women. Witnessing Moran's breakdown, the film reminds viewers of a key aspect of Leigh's practice: considerations of Black women's physical, emotional, and intellectual labor. As Leigh herself notes, "My work is about what they did from those compromised positions—the labor, the care, the love, the ideas."[211]

—Habiba Hopson

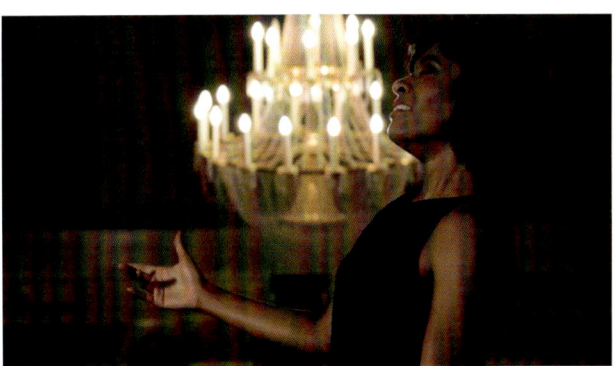

Breakdown, with Liz Magic Laser, in collaboration with Alicia Hall Moran, 2011. Single-channel video (color, sound; 9:00 minutes). Museum purchase with funds provided by the Acquisition Committee 2011.6

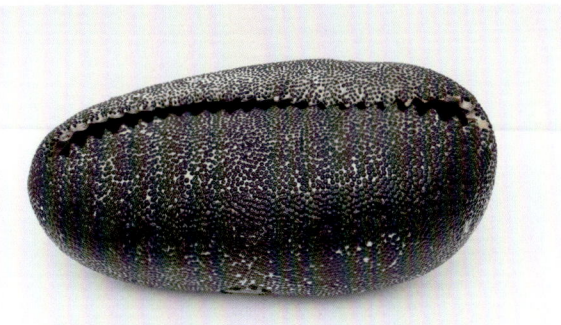

Untitled (Cowrie), 2012. Stoneware, 6 ½ × 15 × 7 in. Bequest of Peggy Cooper Cafritz (1947–2018), Washington, DC, collector, educator, and activist 2018.40.174

Theaster Gates

b. 1973

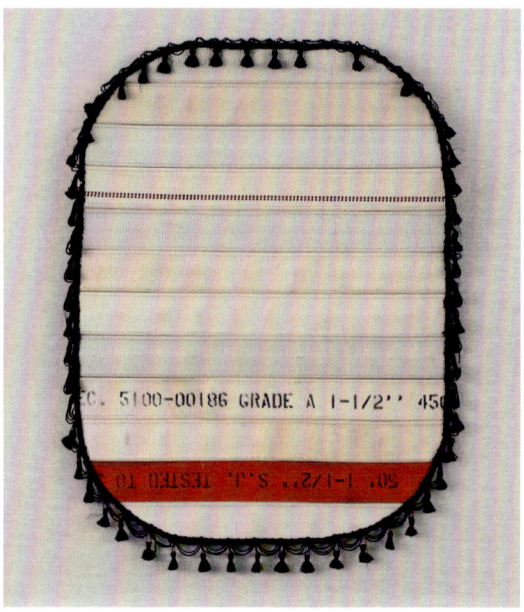

Civil Rights Throw Rug 7200.45, 2012. Decommissioned fire hose and trim, 32 × 28 in. From an edition of 20 unique variants + 3 APs. Bequest of Peggy Cooper Cafritz (1947—2018), Washington, DC, collector, educator, and activist 2018.40.94

Decommissioned fire hoses, flattened and pieced together, comprise the bulk of this editioned work by the artist Theaster Gates. With a title that directly names the struggle for civil rights in the United States, Gates reminds the viewer of the 1963 Birmingham campaign, an organized nonviolent endeavor to call attention to the Alabama city's segregated systems. The campaign brought national attention to the civil rights effort after high-pressure fire hoses were directed at Black children attempting to peacefully march into downtown Birmingham. Gates calls on the multiple associations of his chosen medium—instruments meant to fight destructive fires and save lives that can be turned on innocent youth—to allude to both the nation's fraught history and the ongoing precarity of Black life.

The work makes several art historical references as well. The rows of fire hoses recall the stripes found in Minimalist paintings by artists such as Frank Stella, while Gates's use of discarded objects with symbolic resonances finds precedence in assemblage and collage works by artists including Robert Rauschenberg and Betye Saar. In an additional layering of meaning, Gates suggests the possibility for Civil Rights Throw Rug 7200.45 to be both art and decor—blurring the division between high art and functional object—as its title suggests functional use as a rug. Furthering connections to the domestic, when the work is installed vertically, its black tassels evoke funerary trim often found along the edges of mourning clothing, perhaps another reference to the long history of systemic physical violence against Black people in the United States. In bringing together the political and the art historical, the exterior and interior in his work, Gates expands the possibilities of art as social practice.

—Connie H. Choi

Jennifer Packer

b. 1984   Artist in Residence 2012—13

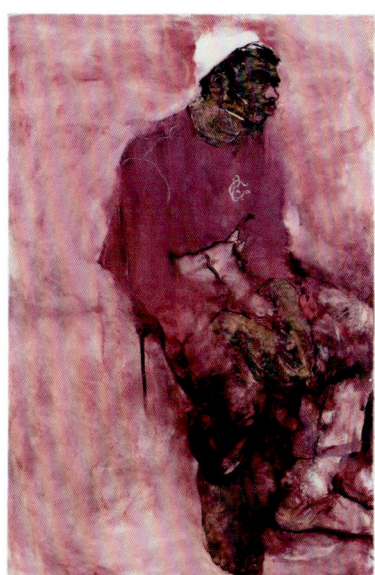

Ivan, 2013. Oil on canvas, 36 × 24 × 1 in.
Museum purchase with funds provided by
the Acquisition Committee 2013.13.3

Jennifer Packer's *Ivan* is entire. Composed to fill up the frame as foreground and background: being is sensory information designed from the
Black climate of a color-filled, visual-sonic ecosystem. Blackness is not
abstracted to be merely elegiac, is not fodder for color blindness; it is more
than and against absence. Packer diffuses the usual seeing and hearing
of Black being hinged on US myths of liberty and racial marking. In *Ivan*,
what shakes is not Black precarity but the whims of portraiture's usual
visual hierarchy. In this seeing, one must forget the eyes. What is Ivan—
the person—thinking, feeling, coming into being, or synchronously fading
into the environment that becomes *Ivan* the painting? An ecology of being
is suggested by his exposed skin, legs, toes, neck, and face with piercing
eyes, a pronounced magenta nose, and large hands. An animacy is in those
large hands, resting without urgency on his lap. Packer retunes the demand
for the Black hand as a tool for defense. Apart from the small white
hat, a toque maybe, Ivan's whole world is a gentle violet monochrome.
It matters little what the thing between Ivan's loosely shaped hands might
be in a world where bone- and rust-colored skin is a beauty and salve,
anti-fear. The world of walls for backing up with a harsh voice ordering
your hands above your head is here displaced. In *Ivan*, Packer's hands are
at work and her intimate seeing open at every stroke into tenderness.
Ivan is not anonymous, could not have been Lewis, Michael, or Philando,
trained as the eye is to receive archetypes amid the sociality of racial
terror. Not any name, those that fill up allegories of racial composition. The
whole painting is gentle, in hue, in perspective, in vernacular, gentle and
taut as skin. Ivan will have his world. This Black man will have his inner life,
unalienated. Approach.

—Canisia Lubrin

Ralph Lemon

b. 1952

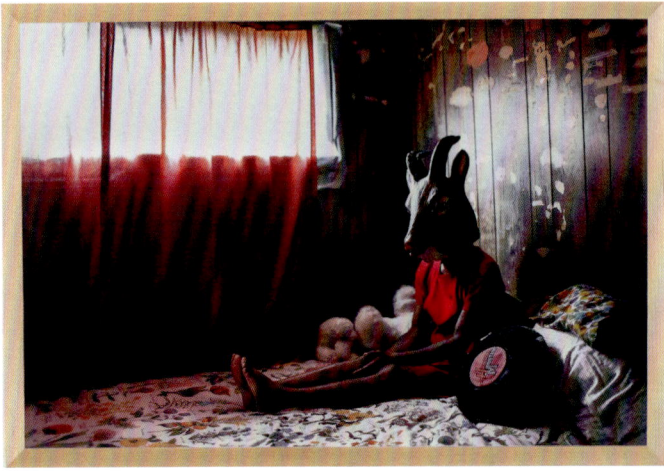

Untitled, 2013—14. Archival pigment print, 14 × 21 in. Museum purchase with funds provided by the Acquisition Committee 2014.7.4

Ralph Lemon's practice defies categorization. Working across dance, visual art, writing, and choreography, Lemon unfurls his understandings of self—as a Black person, an artist, and a practitioner. His works pose more questions than answers, such as "How can I decompose form as I know it and maintain something that is shared as an experience?"[212]

Born in Cincinnati, Ohio, Lemon spent his early years training rigorously in various forms of dance—including ballet and modern—as well as studying literature and theater. In 1985, he founded the Ralph Lemon Dance Company, which he disbanded a decade later. This shift from the company structure marked a significant turning point in his career—liberated from the constraints of a single form, Lemon embraced disassembly.

In the years that followed, Lemon retooled his approach to the stage, creating interdisciplinary, research-based projects often made in concert with others. His landmark *Geography Trilogy*—comprising *Geography* (1997), *Tree* (2000), and *Come home Charley Patton* (2004)—serves as a profound exploration of the intersections between personal and collective history. Including performers from West Africa, South and East Asia, and the Southern United States, this trilogy delves into the painful legacy of slavery and into Lemon's family history, memory, and genealogy.

In 2002, while conducting research for the third part of the trilogy, Lemon met Walter Carter, a hundred-year-old ex-sharecropper living in the outskirts of Yazoo City in Little Yazoo, Mississippi. Carter, who was introduced to Lemon by Jimmy "Duck" Holmes, was described by Holmes as the oldest man in Yazoo City. Born and raised in Mississippi, Carter provided an entry point to a complex history embedded within the landscape. Until Carter's passing at age 103, Lemon recorded Carter, his wife, Edna Carter, and their family in their home on Cessna Road. In a series of untitled photographs taken between 2013 and 2014, Lemon dressed Edna and

Walter, and their extended family members Betty Clifton and Albert and Geneva Johnson, in animal costumes and had them perform for the camera. Lemon provided drawings and performance scores, which the family was to interpret. The resulting images captured their intuitive responses. Within this series of photographs, Lemon engages domestic space as both the site of Carter's family home and a place entrenched in the history of the Mississippi Delta as a means to explore the culture of the South in the wake of US slavery. Throughout this work, Lemon engages lineages of spirituality and mysticism within the Black tradition as well as the concept of land as an index of history. These saturated images of people dressed as familiar figures, such as Br'er Rabbit, and invented characters, including Goat Girl and Space Dog, in domestic space form surreal snapshots. Through their enigmatic stillness and elaborate costuming, Carter and his family appear to be simultaneously in and out of this world.

—Yelena Keller

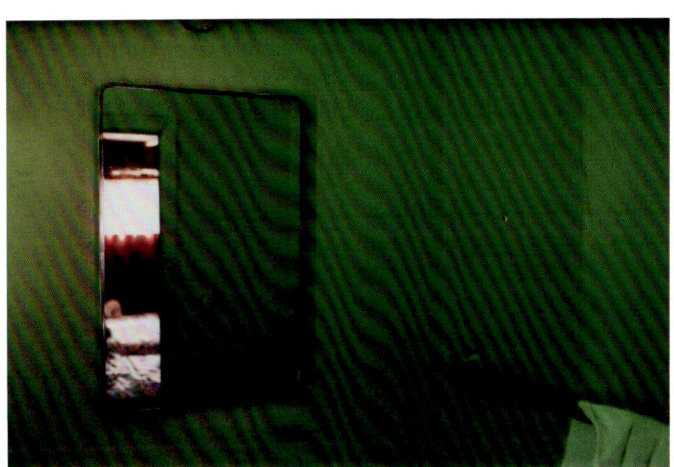

Untitled, 2013—14. Archival pigment print, 14 × 21 in. Museum purchase with funds provided by the Acquisition Committee 2014.7.2

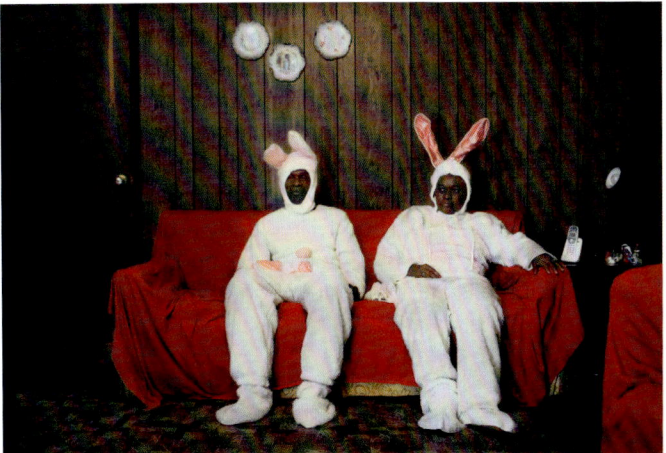

Untitled, 2013—14. Archival pigment print, 20 × 30 in. Museum purchase with funds provided by the Acquisition Committee 2014.7.3

Zachary Fabri

b. 1977

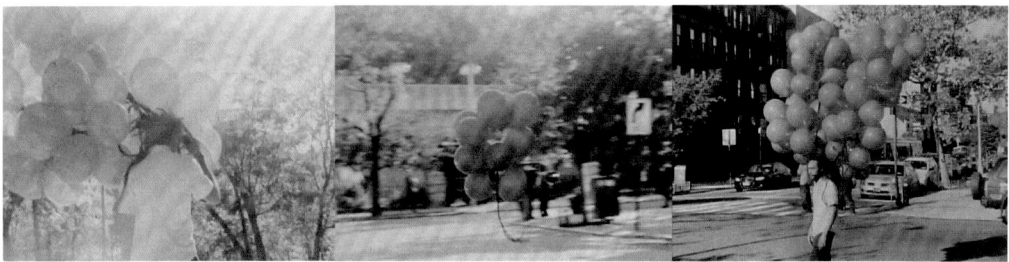

Forget me not, as my tether is clipped, 2013.
16 mm film transferred to video, TRT
00:14:50. Edition 1 of 5. Museum purchase
with funds provided by Isaac Julien and
Mark Nash 2013.16

How do our bodies hold a place and how do places hold us? In *Forget me not, as my tether is clipped*, Zachary Fabri documents himself moving ritualistically throughout historic Harlem streets and seated at Marcus Garvey Park at the corner of 125th Street and Fifth Avenue. Fabri's dreadlocks, grown for fifteen years, are tethered to a large collection of balloons. Over the course of the film, he cuts his locs and the balloons drift up and out, dispersing after their time in the sky. The work—shot on 16-mm film—recalls early black-and-white footage developed for modern cinema and anthropology purposes alike.

The balloons become symbolic of Fabri's articulation of a Black Harlemite identity, which disperses after his procession. Between 2000 and 2013, when Fabri developed the work, the median income in Harlem rose by 35 percent, followed by rezoning laws that were expected to decrease affordable housing by 40 percent in the same neighborhoods.[213] Since 2013, the combination of rezoning and citywide rent hikes exacerbated the gentrification, and by 2023, over eight thousand Black residents had left Harlem, in comparison with an influx of twenty-two thousand white, Asian, and Latinx newcomers amid a moment of political redistricting at the end of 2022.[214] Much like early-to-mid-twentieth-century artists, such as photographer James Van Der Zee, Fabri documents the artistic and interpersonal histories at stake as neighborhoods change. Van Der Zee portrayed the neighborhood through his portraits of others, while Fabri presents his form as the intergenerational vector in *Forget me not, as my tether is clipped*. In documenting moving through and out of Harlem, he offers his body as a stand-in for the shifting presence of the Black community in the neighborhood. He clearly articulates that his tether is "clipped," past tense. Yet, through his work and his presence, Fabri asserts the intangible, lasting connection of Black artists within Harlem.

—Lilia Rocio Taboada

Nona Faustine

1977—2025

Standing in the Financial District of Manhattan, a darker-skinned, volup-
tuous, naked woman stands upon an upturned wooden crate. She faces
forward with her gaze turned downward. Metal shackles bind her hands,
and she wears bright white heels. A seemingly early morning, noted by the
streetlamp, the scene is uncanny—one does not normally see a naked
woman posing this way in the New York City streets.

The subject stands proudly, despite markers of imprisonment and her
location of business suits and briefcases. The figure, Nona Faustine, also
the artist, composes a moment of contemplation. What does she have
to do with the environment around her? Why is she associating slavery
with Wall Street? In fact, Faustine narrativizes the location of global finance
where she has placed herself. The artist's presence serves as a reminder
of the hidden histories of New York—during the eighteenth and nineteenth centuries, it was a major exporter of enslaved Africans and their
descendants to the Caribbean and southern parts of the United States.
She asserts that the economy of the northern part of the country was
built upon, and continues to be inextricably linked to, the South and the
globe. Faustine remarks that the concrete jungle that surrounds her would
not have been possible without the invisible labor, physical and sexual,
of millions of enslaved Black women whose critical legacies in the development of New York are all but forgotten and ignored.

—Kimberli Gant

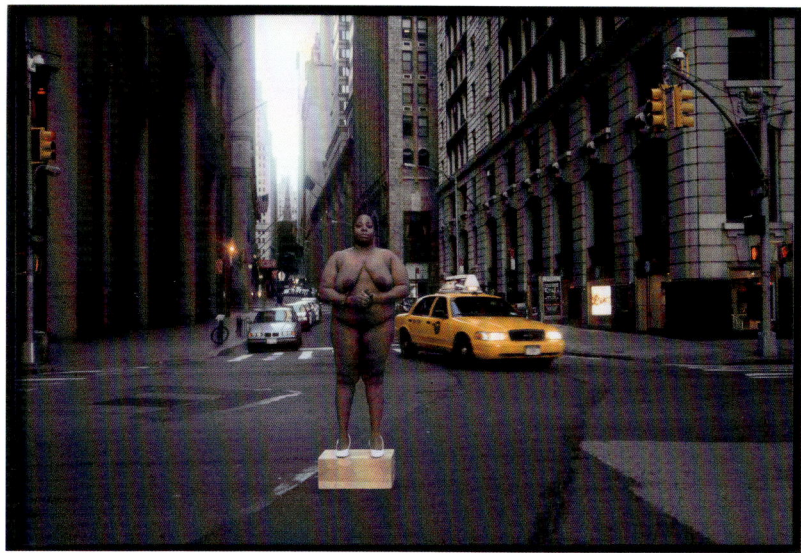

*From Her Body Sprang Their Greatest
Wealth* (from the series "White
Shoes"), 2013. Archival pigment print,
30 × 40 in. Museum purchase with
funds provided by the Acquisition
Committee 2016.7

Kevin Beasley

b. 1985   Artist in Residence 2013—14

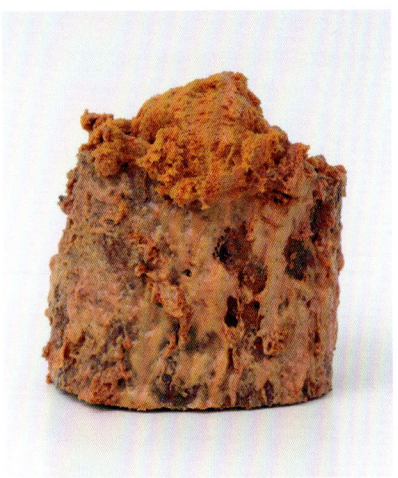

Untitled (Swallow), 2013. Foam, 8 ½ × 8 × 7 in.
Gift of David Lusenhop 2020.25.1

Through sculpture, installation, sound, and performance, Kevin Beasley reframes everyday objects and the cultural references that accompany them. Using sculpture, the artist considers possible transformations of a material and the histories embedded within. *Untitled (Swallow)* is composed of polymer foam, the same material used for car seat cushions. Thus, the work invokes the history of Detroit's car industry, and by working with the language of abstraction, Beasley reimagines the life of things beyond their initial functions.

By transforming material such as foam, Beasley reveals new meanings and layers—personal, historical, and social narratives inherent to how discarded objects and mediums can be reintroduced. *Untitled (Swallow)* demonstrates the artist's skilled exploration of techniques as a way toward a deeper understanding of the intricate web of social issues and histories connecting us to materials. In her essay "How to Be Complicit with Materials," Petra Lange-Berndt states, "To act with the material and to be complicit means to investigate societal power relations."[215] Informed by sculptural traditions, the history of abstraction, and sonic explorations, Beasley's installations manifest this argument. His works draw attention to the power of his main source material and underline the links between modification and interpretation. *Untitled (Swallow)* makes clear that commonplace objects can also function as extensions of a shared history. Beasley's work indexes the erasure of Black bodies from public spaces while developing an alternate language to ensure they are seen and their histories of labor are acknowledged.

The title, *Untitled (Swallow),* plays with different meanings—from its connotations of consumption, engulfing, polymorphing. The title, like the work, suggests a maze of meanings. It elucidates that new modes of abstraction are possible and that nothing is neutral.

— Daisy Desrosiers

vanessa german

b. 1976

Self-described "citizen artist" vanessa german repurposes human-made objects to create what she calls "power figures," often figures of Black women, that honor and reflect "the spiritual, intellectual, and political impulses" of her practice.[216] *Reality Check: To Call Police Use This Phone* is one such sculpture the artist formed from a variety of discarded objects gathered from her former longtime neighborhood of Homewood in Pittsburgh, Pennsylvania.

A single figure, what the artist calls "a figure of protection," painted black stands on a wooden sawhorse and is flanked by two ebony African sculptural figures. From her head protrude other African figures and white ceramic heads that come together like a headpiece. On the figure's face and body, the assortment of materials and objects continues with, among other things, cowrie shells as lips; cowrie shells and button anklets; and a small blue, white, and orange bird perched on one arm. The figure wears a skirt made of a variety of objects and materials, such as worn-out shoes and toy guns. The artist's use of discarded materials within her assemblage practice imbues her work with the possibility of social critique through the embedded connotations of the chosen objects and materials.[217] Placed directly at the center of the figure is a vintage sign with text that reads, "To Call Police Use This Telephone." The power figure holds up a disconnected corded phone and, in the other hand, an off-white handheld mirror facing outward—two gestures that may resonate with or implicate the viewer. Through these carefully selected objects, *Reality Check: To Call Police Use This Phone* summarizes for its audiences the fraught relationship between systematically disenfranchised communities—not unlike Homewood—an entrenched history of abuse, and selective neglect spanning decades and zip codes.

—Zuna Maza

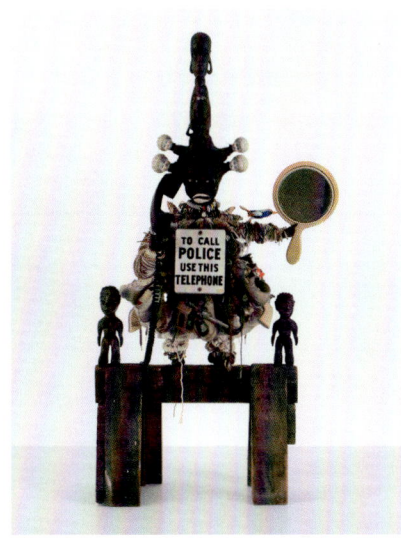

Reality Check: To Call Police Use This Phone, 2013. Mixed-media assemblage, 46 × 24 × 14 in. Bequest of Peggy Cooper Cafritz (1947—2018), Washington, DC, collector, educator, and activist 2018.40.96

Sanford Biggers

b. 1970   Artist in Residence 1999—2000

Piecing together scraps of mostly floral-printed fabrics, Sanford Biggers seems to have made this exuberant collage with an eye toward mixing dissonant readymade patterns and colors into a harmonious ensemble. Red dominates the palette, with accents of vivid yellow and shades of blue. A square fragment from a vintage quilt appears in the upper left, while a narrow border of small black-and-white checks surrounds the entire composition. An amorphous blue shape overlaid with stylized black lines animates the lower half of the composition. The title, *Haute Mess*, is a term used to talk about fashion around the time this piece was made. It describes a slightly disheveled style of self-presentation, one cobbled together from unlikely combinations of clothing. But, as Biggers's collage reminds us, the appearance of not trying too hard is achieved only through practiced skill.

Collage exemplifies Biggers's approach to art making in a variety of other media, including sculpture and painting on quilts. The technique is based on putting disparate things side by side to produce new meanings. The preexisting fragments often embody personal or cultural histories. The tendency toward the mash-up was already evident in Biggers's early days with the Studio Museum. He made a collaborative, short, single-channel video with Jennifer Zackin composed of footage from important family occasions drawn from their respective home movies. The video, *a small world . . .* (1999—2001), was included in *Freestyle*, a 2001 exhibition that opened the decade with the work of "young pacesetters and the next generation of indicators," as characterized by Lowery Stokes Sims in the catalogue. Created later in his career, *Haute Mess* exemplifies Biggers's ability to innovate and improvise while remaining true to his artistic roots.

—Eugenie Tsai

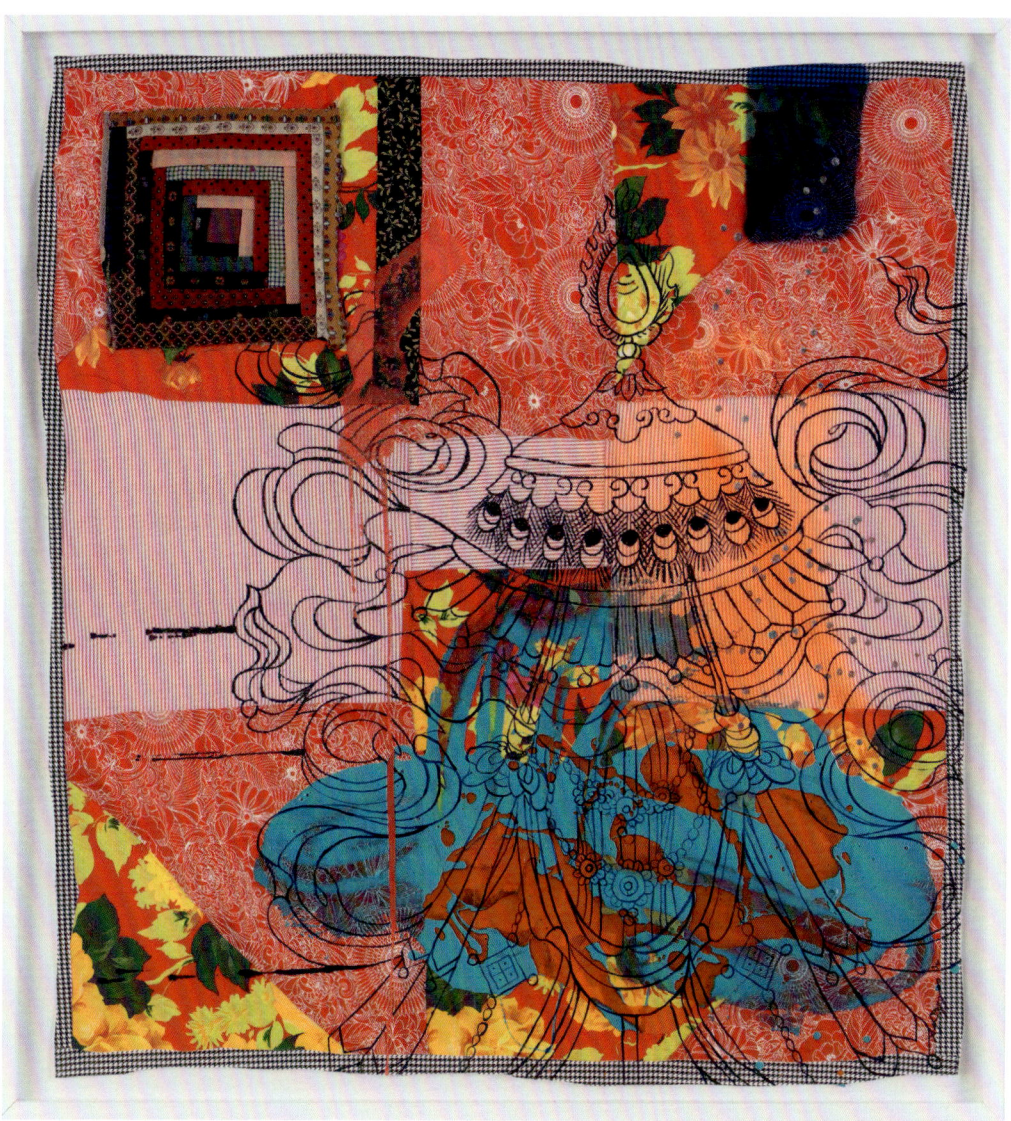

Haute Mess, 2014. Antique quilt fragment, assorted textiles, mixed media on archival paper, 39 ½ × 37 in. Bequest of Peggy Cooper Cafritz (1947—2018), Washington, DC, collector, educator, and activist 2018.40.35

Bethany Collins

b. 1984 Artist in Residence 2013—14

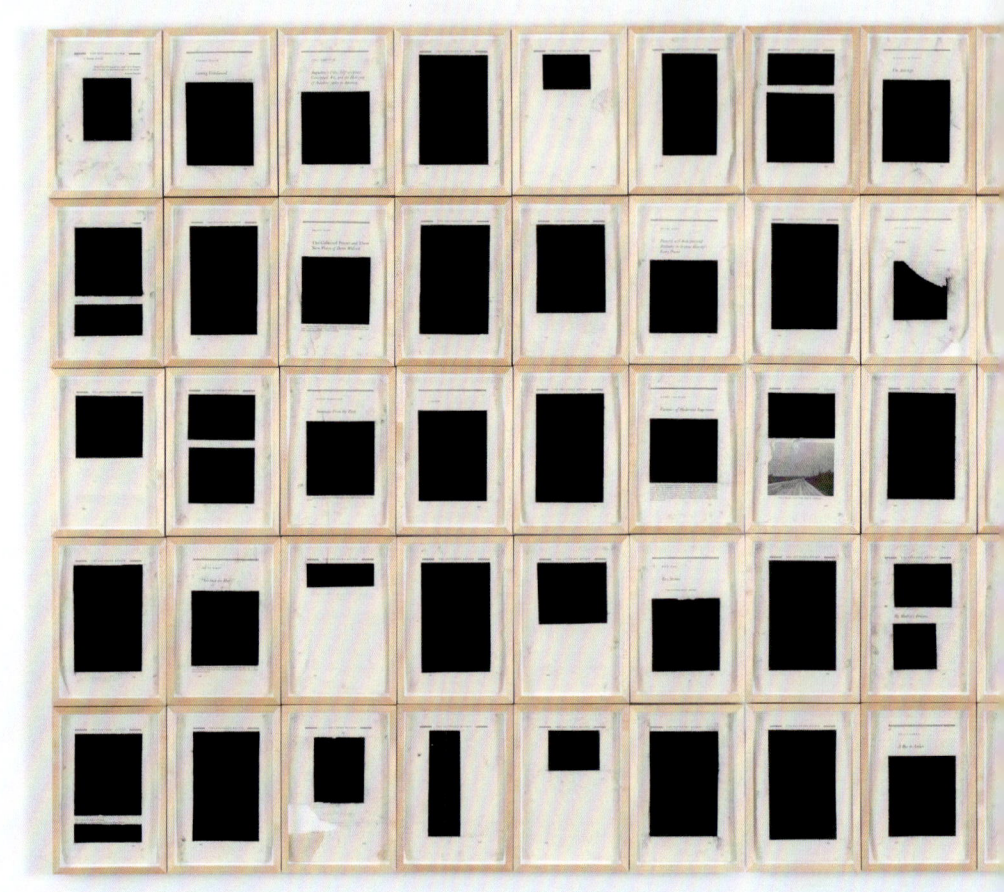

In being asked to write about Bethany Collins's work *Southern Review, 1987*, I am taken back to a very specific moment in time. This work, made up of sixty-four individual framed pages of the *Southern Review*, with specific sections of the text blacked out, was created in 2014 when Collins was an artist in residence at the Studio Museum. During that time I had the distinct pleasure of managing the residency and organizing the exhibition that included *Southern Review, 1987*. The exhibition, *Material Histories*, included Collins's work alongside her fellow artists in residence, Kevin Beasley and Abigail DeVille. Developing a title for a show of three artists with very distinct practices and visual styles is always a challenge, but for their exhibition, it came easily. All three artists were (and continue to be) engaged with materials that have vivid histories and backstories before their transformations at the artists' hands.

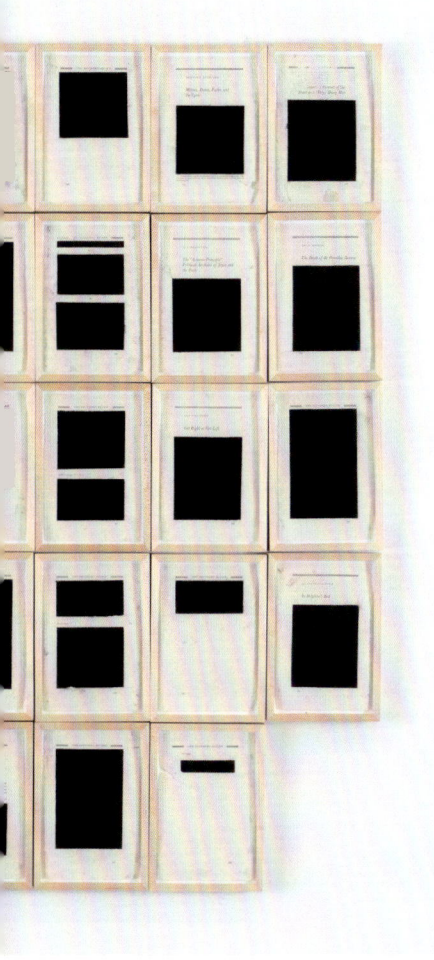

Southern Review, 1987, 2014. Charcoal on paper, 32 ½ × 130 in. Museum purchase with funds provided by the Acquisition Committee 2014.12.2a-lll

Collins's use of pages of the *Southern Review* magazine is no exception. The *Southern Review* is a well-known literary journal in circulation since 1935—and published by Louisiana State University Press since 2011—and includes, among other things, fiction, nonfiction, and poetry written by both emerging and established voices. In *Southern Review, 1987*, Collins has covered much of the text under charcoal, and what remains is a title, an author, caption information, an image, and a page number. Collins's interest in language is a constant in her practice, and this work, as well as the overall series, delves into her explorations of what it means to be an artist from the South. On each page, one can see the artist's hand, sooty fingerprints, and tears. For Collins, her imprint shows she is putting herself into narratives of the South.

—Lauren Haynes

Derek Fordjour

b. 1974

The work of Derek Fordjour, seen here in *Untitled (Red Reverse)*, speaks to a longing for visibility and the integration of all parts of the self—who one is, what one knows, and perhaps even who one longs to become. Through the materiality of this work, Fordjour taps into the deep, often subconscious desire of humanity to know oneself and to be known by others. The process of tearing, carving, and constructing functions as a metaphor for what it means to transform oneself, something achieved by those whom Fordjour often depicts in his work: athletes, performers, and those who connect with ritual and rites of passage. The repetition in the application of the materials is almost a meditative act, and as the surface accumulates, the body becomes visible, tangible, emotive. Although the face of the figure cannot be seen in this work, it is almost as if the viewer has arrived just in time at the moment when the figure will turn, revealing all of who they are. Collage is a process of pulling apart, arranging, and reconfiguring what once was into something entirely new altogether. It is a transformational process, a parallel process to that of the lives of those Fordjour often depicts. To take what one has been given, what one finds, what one knows; to break down, assess, shape, and shift, ultimately bringing together the parts of the self, once fragmented, now whole. Standing in truth. Standing in power. Living with joy.

—Chloe Hayward

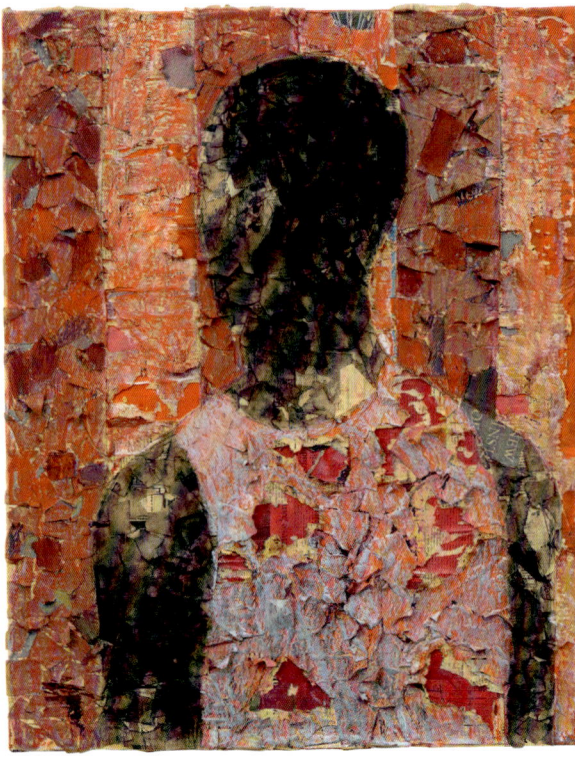

Untitled (Red Reverse), 2014. Oil pastel, charcoal, acrylic, and newspaper mounted on canvas, 30 × 24 in. Bequest of Peggy Cooper Cafritz (1947—2018), Washington, DC, collector, educator, and activist 2018.40.86

Juliana Huxtable

b. 1987

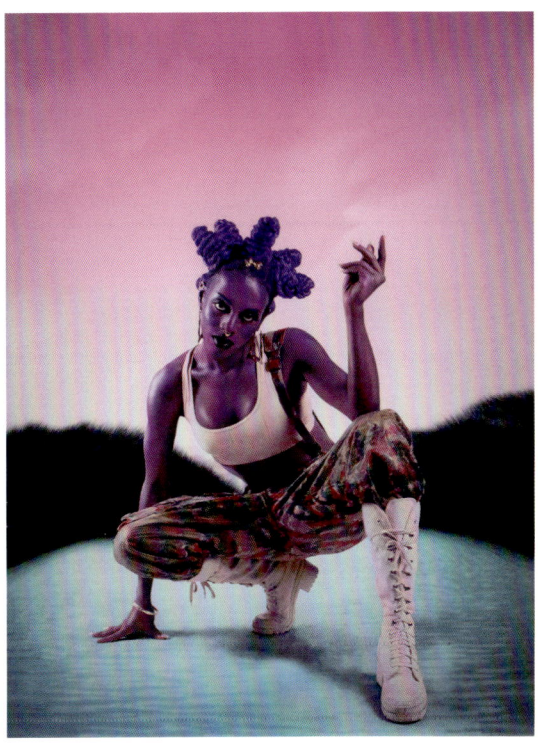

Untitled (Psychosocial Stuntin'), 2015.
Color inkjet print, 40 × 30 in. Edition AP.
Museum purchase with funds provided by
the Acquisition Committee   2015.8.1

To stunt means to shine. A stunt tilts the psychosocial coordinates
of the world (as a symbolic network of social signifiers and protocols)
off axis. If anti-blackness is the ground for the racial genre of human,
as Saidiya Hartman and Frank Wilderson so incisively trace, how might
this ground dissolve?

The natural setting of *Untitled (Psychosocial Stuntin')* is denatured by its
otherworldly saturated color. On what could be the entrance to a beach,
except this beach is not of and would not exist in this world, Juliana
Huxtable poses defiantly, fiercely. There is a glow to Huxtable and to the
psychedelic and also serene setting, blue sand, black grass, pink sky.
Her purple braids hold as much of a presence as her form, but the purple
is subdued, functioning as a kind of bioluminescent richness.

Huxtable's portrait couples the exteriority of the extra-natural scene
with interiority. How are the psychic and the social mutually constituted?
We might anticipate that the artist's invocation of the psychosocial indexes
Frantz Fanon's canonical work on the psychic life of blackness. There
is a resolute affirmation of stunting in Huxtable's self-assured pose, which
reverses the terms of the look. She is not being looked at sans control,
but making a scene such that the audience is forced to reckon with her.

—Che Gossett

Sadie Barnette

b. 1984   Artist in Residence 2014—15

Untitled (from the series "Untitled"),
2014. Graphite on paper, 20 × 16 in.
Museum purchase with funds provided
by the Acquisition Committee 2015.14.2

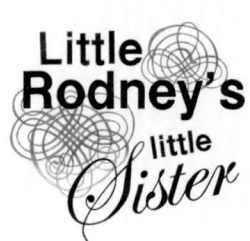

COLLECTION

Sadie Barnette's 2014 "Untitled" series tenderly illustrates the artist's relation to different family members through a set of six drawings. As opposed to rendering family lineage through a conventional family tree or ancestral pedigree chart, Barnette playfully presents a new way to think about relation: through the stylization of text. She draws with graphite, using stencils to replicate the technical precision of graphic design. Her manipulation of the text's appearance through experimenting with different fonts, sizes, opacities, and placements results in compositions that express the personalities of her loved ones. For example, she emphasizes the arc of her matrilineal heritage as "Cassandra's great great granddaughter" through stark, large, white text against a black background.

The names of the family members also respect the honorifics and nicknames of family cultures. To be the daughter of "Uncle Rodney" acknowledges the role parents play in raising other children; to be the little sister of "Little Rodney" recognizes the perpetual youth of younger relatives, no matter how old they get. Typographical styles communicate

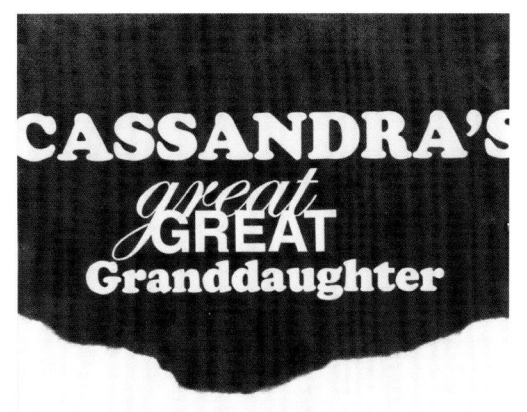

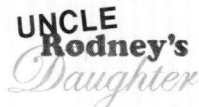

Untitled (from the series "Untitled"),
2015. Graphite on paper, 20 × 16 in.
Museum purchase with funds provided
by Pippa Cohen 2015.14.6

Untitled (from the series "Untitled"),
2015. Graphite on paper, 20 × 16 in.
Museum purchase with funds provided
by the Acquisition Committee 2015.14.4

certain messages and associations, and Barnette's choices suggest how individuals and text can be read in relation to each other.

Many of her works are inspired by her father's legacy—Rodney Barnette founded the Compton, California, chapter of the Black Panther Party in 1968 and opened San Francisco's first Black-owned gay bar in 1990. His activism made him a target of FBI surveillance during the 1970s. Since 2016, the artist has used these surveillance files in her installations, often by reproducing and embellishing the documents. By presenting the files as artworks, Barnette subverts the covert activity of their creation. She alters her father's records to include artwork that memorializes his life and his contributions to his community and family. In this manner, Barnette treats her art not just as an individual creative endeavor but as a method to honor her familial legacy.

—Kiki Teshome

Zanele Muholi

b. 1972

In representations of women's figures throughout the art historical canon, the sitter is looked at, while their gaze is often indirect or directed away from the viewer. Famously, Édouard Manet's *Olympia* (1863) reverses this with the primary subject staring back at the viewer. Treated as secondary, the servant, a model now identified as Laure, acts as a foil to the titular courtesan reclining nude on the bed. Laure is fully clothed and holds a bouquet of flowers that acts like a shield between her, Olympia, and the viewer. Across centuries, *Olympia* has captivated viewers as a portrait of a woman who stares back, creating agency within her gaze. In Zanele Muholi's self-portrait photograph *Bona, Charlottesville*, their gaze is directed introspectively toward themself. In the way Laure gazed at the spectacle of Olympia, Muholi becomes the spectacle themself, a duality of both onlooker and source of attention.

They lie supine and nude on a bed. As they peer into a mirror, the viewer becomes secondary. The artist is fully self-contained. The setting of the room is largely undefined, the bedding and furnishings nondescript as those found in hotel rooms, with the exception of a brocade curtain behind the bed. Thus, the viewer's focus fixates on Muholi. This work is one of a series, taken during the artist's travels, in which they pose with objects found in locations they journeyed through. In *Bona, Charlottesville*, Muholi's bold stare centers on themself within the mirror, and their eyes hold the viewer, deftly occupying both the internal and external. They are a magnetic figure. This inward glance of self-examination plays with the trope of the docile figure found in historical works. Translated from Zulu, "Bona" means "see," and in this case, the artist is absorbed in seeing themself, while the viewer is left unconsidered. The stripped-down setting throws the power in their gaze into stark relief and magnifies their gesture to fashion a representation that is simultaneously soft and alluring, strong and impenetrable.

—Adeze Wilford

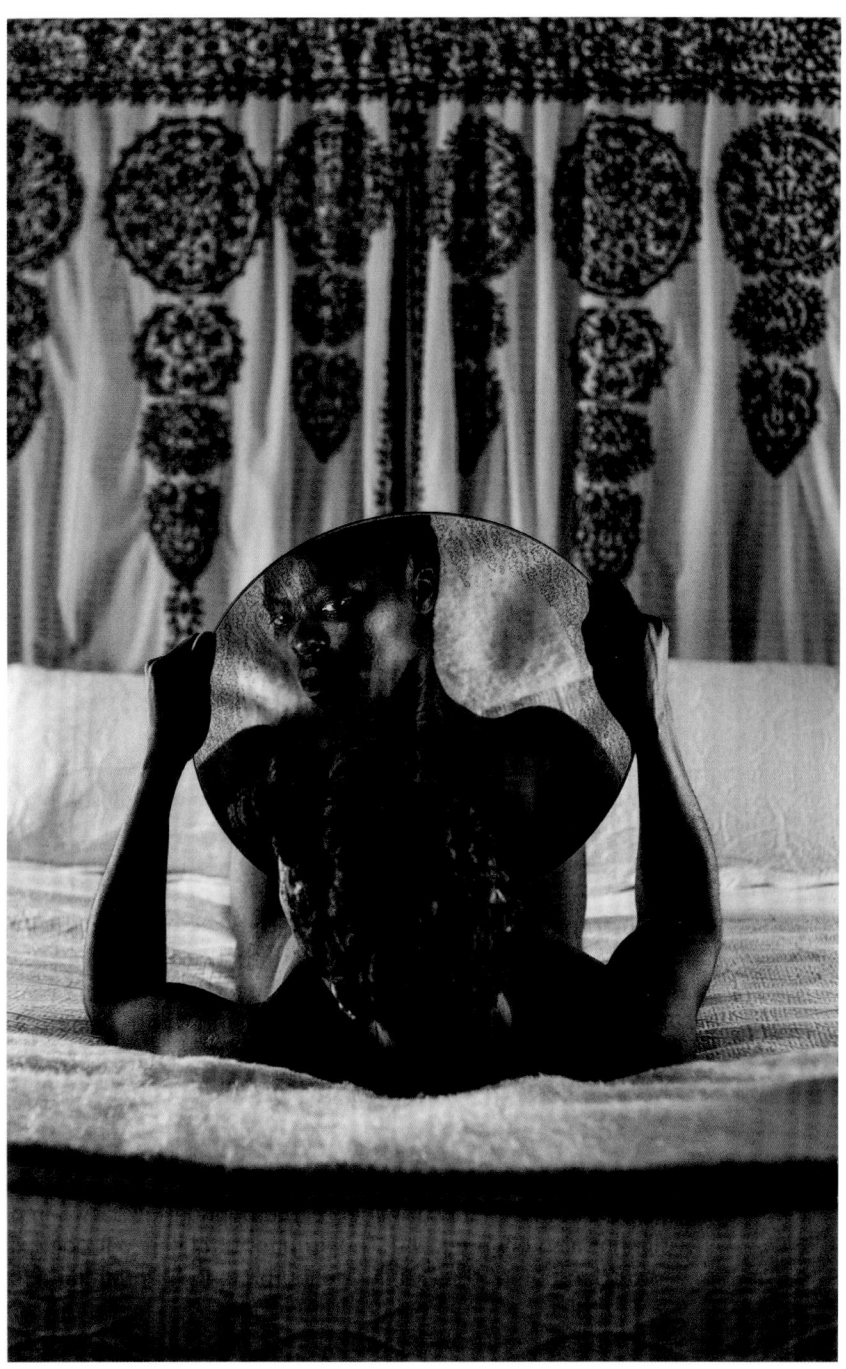

Bona, Charlottesville (from the series
"Somnyama Ngonyama"), 2015. Gelatin
silver print, 35 ¼ × 24 in. Edition 7 of 8.
Museum purchase with funds provided
by the Acquisition Committee 2015.26

Eric N. Mack

b. 1987   Artist in Residence 2014—15

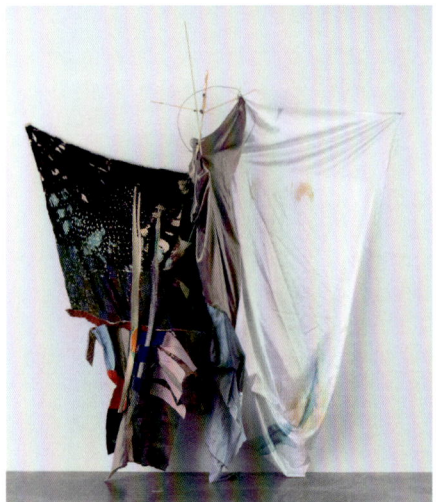

Palm, 2015. Dye on bleached cotton, silk, felt, with metal armature, wood, decorative palm fronds, and paper, 77 × 77 × 38 in. Museum purchase with funds provided by the Acquisition Committee 2015.16

Produced during Eric N. Mack's residency at the Studio Museum, *Palm* converges the worlds of painting and textiles. The work exemplifies the artist's innovative approach to materials and form. Its foundation lies in sourcing various mass-produced fabrics including silk, felt, and cotton. Mack uses acrylic paint and bleach to uncover the hidden layers of dye, giving the store-bought materials a painterly, gestural quality.

By incorporating elements from both fashion and popular culture, Mack invites a sensorial engagement with the work, as familiar fabrics trigger personal associations and experiences. The artist's fascination with ritual and repetition is evident in *Palm*. Through the transformative acts of dyeing, weaving, and draping, Mack infuses the work with ritualistic significance and invokes a form of meditation present in commonplace labor. In integrating everyday substances such as bleach, he introduces notions of cleansing and rebirth into the artistic process.

Mack's work not only transcends the boundaries between painting and textile but also engages with the architectural space it occupies. The artist's consideration of the Studio Museum's long corridor in its former building led to the creation of a piece that emanates a sense of belonging. The title, *Palm*, refers to the artist's continued interest in the material "as a spatial gesture," a material of protection and shelter.[218] The work's makeshift tenting composition of ethereal materials, often utilized in Mack's work, conjures a postapocalyptic yet utopian aesthetic. *Palm* offers a balance of light and dark, rigidity and flexibility, contrasts and tensions, and softness and structure, encouraging a sensual encounter with the fabrics. The piece becomes a conduit between the viewer's world and the symbolic references the fabrics evoke.

—Hanna Girma

Devin Allen

b. 1988

With one viral image, self-taught photographer Devin Allen was thrust into US history. A native of West Baltimore, Allen captured an uprising following the murder of Freddie Gray by Baltimore police in the back of a patrol wagon.

Nearly escaping the frame, a figure runs through the street away from a crowd of police officers. A dark bandana obscures his face to render him anonymous. Opposite the figure, others run and rush to escape the terror of the officers in pursuit. Clad in riot gear and armed, each police officer moves menacingly down the street. The photograph's foreground, middle ground, and background—as well as its form, space, and rhythm—all work together. For some, it may call to mind Henri Cartier-Bresson's notion of the "decisive moment"—Allen captured a fleeting moment, (hopefully) never to happen again.

Over the seventeen-day period known as the "Baltimore Uprising," Allen took ten thousand photographs, but it was *Untitled* from "A Beautiful Ghetto" that went viral online. The photograph was featured on the May 11, 2015, issue of *TIME*. In the magazine's one hundred years, Allen is only the third amateur photographer to snag a cover, and when cropped for publication, his composition, timing, and instinct collectively captured history. His photograph spotlit the city of Baltimore and its age-old corrupted police system. The image is a conversation starter—and breaker—about the ongoing plight of Black people in the United States.

—Jayson Overby Jr.

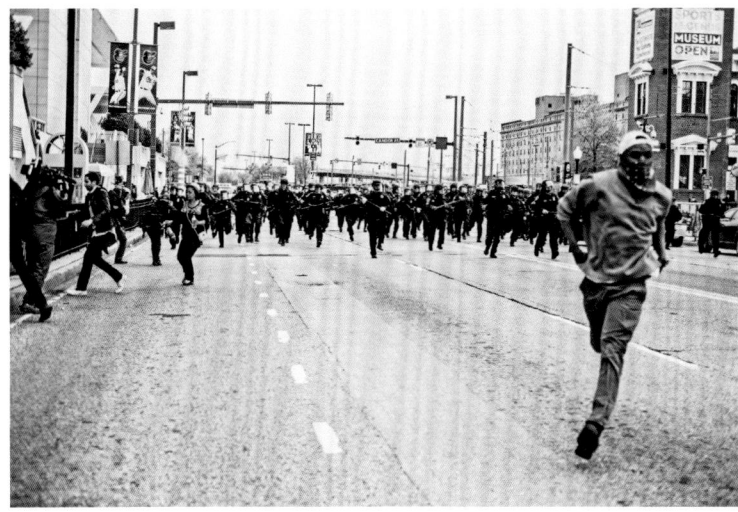

Untitled (from the series "A Beautiful Ghetto"), 2015. Chromogenic color print, 20 × 30 in. Museum purchase with funds provided by the Acquisition Committee 2017.8

Tony Lewis

b. 1986

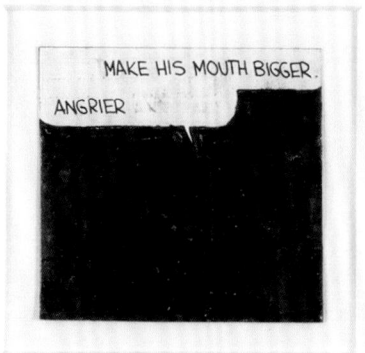

Make His Mouth Bigger, Angrier, 2015.
Graphite powder and correction tape
on paper, image: 2 ⅜ × 2 ⅜ in., frame:
20 ⅞ × 20 ⅜ × 1 ¾ in. Museum
purchase with funds provided by
The Lumpkin-Boccuzzi Family 2016.8

The formal language of drawing can be very different than that of sculpture. The intention to create space and dimension on the flat page excites me. For those who can make compelling reflections on a page, it becomes a world of direct communication, emotional witness, meditation, and tempered promise that reverberates into the future. In Tony Lewis's case, the path toward communication is more literal and absolutely coded—the core of the artist's way of making.

Make His Mouth Bigger, Angrier evinces Lewis's investment in drawing and redaction. Scrubbing out a comic strip panel from *Calvin and Hobbes* (published June 15, 1986) with one of his primary devices—graphite with rubber cement—Lewis builds a landscape of obfuscation. This landscape of graphite introduces Lewis's humor and skill, and offers a Black intervention into the suburban depiction of everyday youth.

Over the many conversations I have had with Lewis, rarely have I felt impropriety or dishonesty; it is equally rare that I have received a straight answer. This illusiveness is at the heart of the personality of the work, an illusiveness that feels wholly cultivated and instinctual to who the maker is. Many make marks that begin with something much more emotional; Lewis constructs worlds through redaction, rigor, and humor. At first encounter with Lewis's drawings, I asked if he considered them paintings or if he considered himself a painter. He said, "These are drawings, and I am a draftsman." I asked, "What are these objects' relationship to illustration?" He replied, "I like to draw." Lewis has long been a fan of comics, in particular of Bill Watterson, author of *Calvin and Hobbes,* the comic strip syndicated in over 2,400 newspapers. It is through this lens that one can more deeply understand Lewis's sensitive approach to narrative, critique, and craft.

—Theaster Gates

Elizabeth Colomba

b. 1976

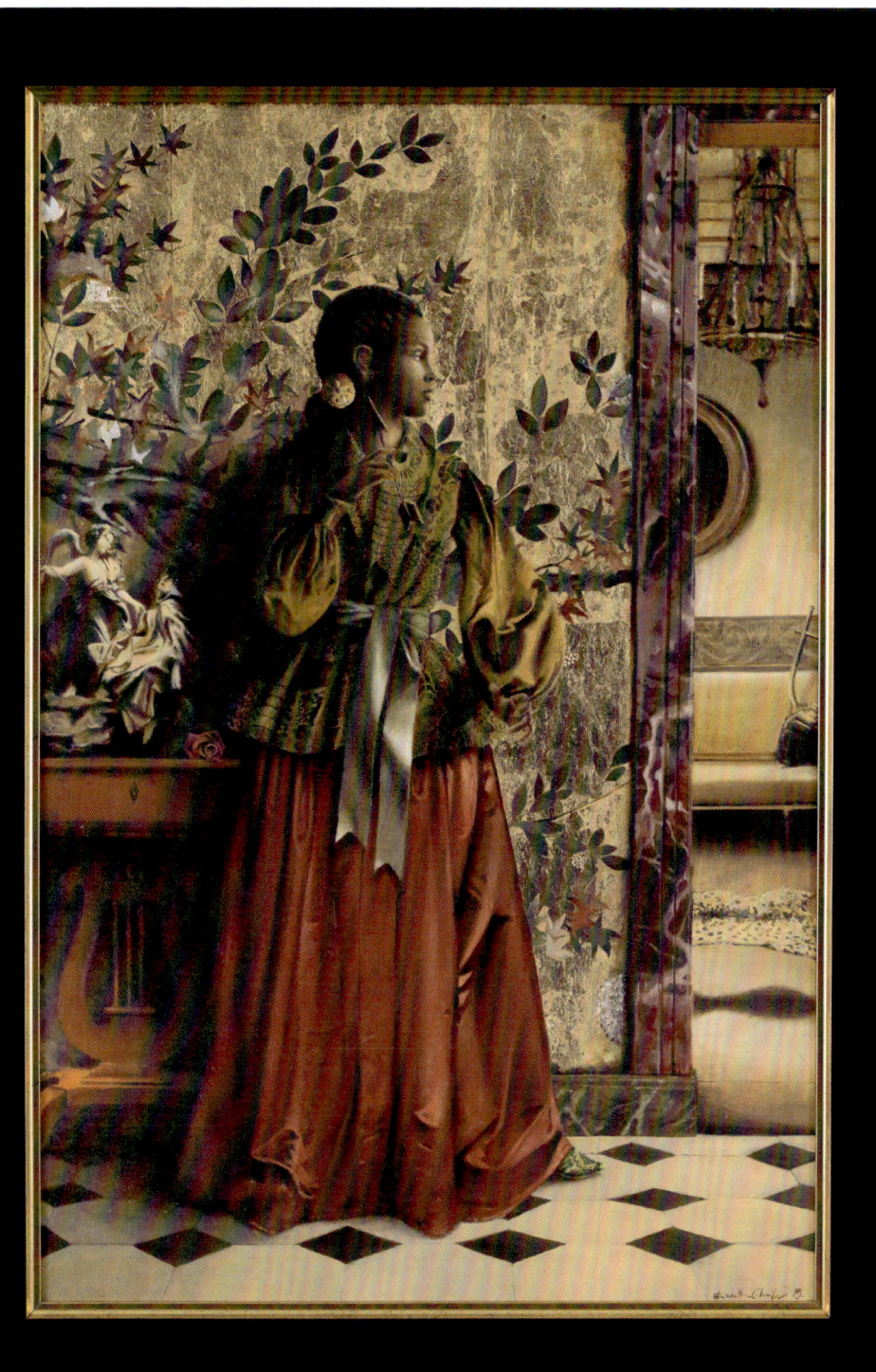

On painter Elizabeth Colomba's canvas, the mythological Greek naiad (a freshwater nymph) Daphne is a fierce and imperturbable Black woman. In Ovid's *Metamorphoses*, Daphne is the victim of Eros's retaliation against the god Apollo, who mocked the archery skills of the god of love and desire. Shooting arrows that filled Daphne with revulsion toward Apollo, and him with infatuation toward her, Eros sealed his cruel revenge. According to the myth, when Daphne tired of running from Apollo, her father, Peneus (a river god), transformed her into a laurel tree, from which the unrelenting Apollo took a crown of leaves and branches.

In *Daphne*, Colomba subverts this progression of Daphne from victim to fugitive to captive by placing her directly in Apollo's home, self-determined and poised for action. She confidently twirls Eros's arrow between her fingers. A miniature of Lorenzo Bernini's *Ecstasy of Saint Teresa* sits atop a table with a lyre base. The statue shows St. Theresa being struck with an arrow, foreshadowing Daphne's next move to reverse the curse and reclaim her life.

Colomba generates meaning by layering complex histories and relations into compelling visual narratives. Following an allegorical tradition, Colomba wields signs, symbols, and pigment, bringing timeless stories rich with iconography to contemporary audiences. Part of the artist's "Mythology" series, where Black women protagonists exist within palatial and Renaissance-inspired surroundings, Colomba's Daphne lurks near a lavish pink marble door frame. Laurel and sweetgum branches, symbols of protection and victory, creep along the golden wall behind her. Transcending substitution or proxy, Colomba reconfigures stories that have profoundly shaped Western art and its histories. Through allegory, she makes visual the heroism and resistance of women across the African diaspora.

—Stephanie Sparling Williams, with research assistance from Grace Billingslea

Daphne (from the series "Mythology"), 2015.
Oil and gold leaf on canvas, 36 × 24 in.
Museum purchased with funds provided by
Neda Young 2017.2

Ja'Tovia Gary

b. 1984

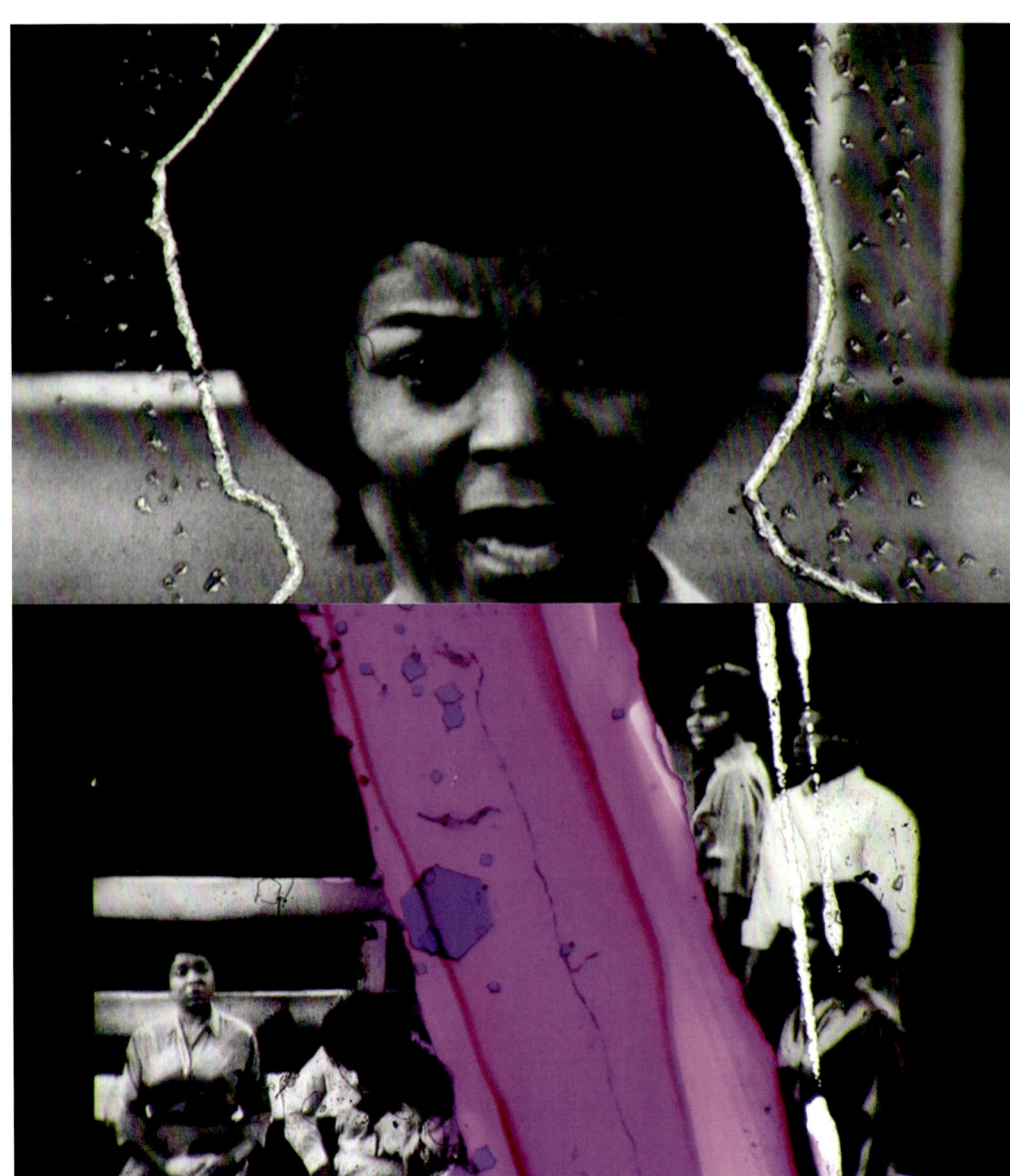

An Ecstatic Experience, 2015. Film, color,
TRT: 00:06:11. Edition 5 of 7 + 1 AP. Gift
of the artist, galerie frank elbaz, and
Paula Cooper Gallery 2019.21

A list of materials:

- Scratchy film
- Archives on archives from the Federal Writers' Project
- Collected slave narratives from the 1930s Works Progress Administration (WPA)
- Ruby Dee as Fannie Moore telling stories about her mother, who was on a plantation/praising the end of slavery in advance of the end of slavery

Master: What you doing? You ain't out here to be hoopin' and hollerin'!

- Ecstatic vision that freedom is nigh
- *History of the Negro People* TV miniseries (1965)
- The Negro Ensemble plus Ruby Dee plus Ozzie Davis
- Resistance footage

Questions:

- What is the relationship between ecstasy and spirituality?
- How can spirituality be used toward liberation?
- How can ecstasy be metaphysical and spiritual?
- Can it move into the realm of the political?

SCENE 1: JA'TOVIA is making salsa in Dallas. AUTUMN is on a laptop in Tangier.

JA'TOVIA
(sneezes)
If you ain't sneezin', it ain't seasoning!

The call to prayer to Allah 5:16 blasts from speakers, blankets the medina in Tangier while JA'TOVIA mixes salsa ingredients.

JA'TOVIA
Baby Suggs (*Beloved*) makes a clearing space in the woods where Black people/slaves could go and have an ecstatic experience outside of the bounds of white eyes and white laws.

JA'TOVIA
This looks good. You finna be maaad at me!

AUTUMN
Send me a photo.
What's your salsa recipe? I make guacamole, not salsa.

JA'TOVIA's Salsa Recipe: Tomato (small cherry), cilantro, green onion, minced fresh garlic, onion powder, garlic powder, fresh cracked black pepper, pink Himalayan sea salt, a dash of apple cider vinegar, and fresh-squeezed lime.

She shows AUTUMN a picture of a newly purchased church pew. (Sculpture to come.)

AUTUMN
Oh, you deep in it.

JA'TOVIA
You can use the pics of salsa and church pew. If you are a spiritualist, you need to be sitting at your altar every day.

—Autumn Knight

Elle Pérez

b. 1989

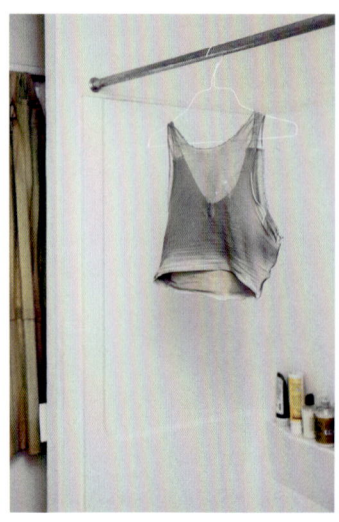

Binder, 2015—18. Archival pigment print, 44 ⅜ × 31 in. Edition 3 of 5 + 2 APs. Museum purchase with funds provided by Neda Young 2019.4

Elle Pérez's binder hangs soiled and stained, enumerating its longevity as a modality of transcendence and becoming. Their photograph *Binder* delves into the intricate themes of private reflection and identity formation. The garment suggests that identity is not definitive—the binder provides a chance for emancipation via restriction.

The photograph singularizes a worn, graying chest compression binder hanging on a white wire hanger in an empty shower stall. Pérez remembers the "sweat and pain" visible in the fabric's details, recalling that the object once constricted their body.[219] The image takes on a symbolic role as a self-portrait without the presence of a body. It instead encapsulates the essence of the person and their desire for gender fluidity and self-determination, and the binder itself exudes a palpable sense of presence. By displaying the binder this way, Pérez inverts an otherwise concealed object.

According to Martin Heidegger, in Greek philosophy, "aletheia" *refers* to "unconcealment," or truth.[220] It discloses the hidden or concealed aspects of Being, thereby allowing beings to show themselves as they are. In this instance, Pérez's binder enacts unconcealment, becoming more than a utilitarian undergarment; in its prominence in the photograph, it brings forth the artist's private struggle at the same time that it allows the same for others in their community. The binder's signs of age, wear, and discoloration provoke contemplation about the passage of time and the temporality of objects. These visual elements prompt questions about the binder's history, the journeys it has accompanied, and the stories it holds within its fabric.

—Terrence Phearse

Turiya Magadlela

b. 1978

In *Untitled 8, 10, and 7*, Turiya Magadlela uses pantyhose to signify the trials and tribulations of femininity and womanhood. These two states of being require endurance in every society and culture, and this composition demonstrates that capacity. The monotony and monochrome palette allude to the reality that, while shared, still subjects us to difference—the pantyhose are various shades of black and gray, with some cotton, others nylon; each stretches vertically, but some remain slim, while others are stretched wide. Here and elsewhere in her "Inequalities" series, Magadlela's manipulation of the everyday material signifies that many women, while enduring patriarchy and gender oppression, stretch to maintain composure—until they cannot.

Magadlela's layering of pantyhose is its own reference to societal hierarchies. Whose progress rests upon whose? Whose priorities overshadow whose? Who remains behind on the path toward the progression of women's rights, the decolonization of gender, and the prevention of gender-based violence? It is easy to get lost in this monochrome mass whose layers resemble a nighttime forest. The confusion in these untitled works mirrors that of the struggle for equity and equality for those who have been historically oppressed, a process that at times feels cyclical, opaque, repetitive, and far-stretched.

——Nectar Knuckles

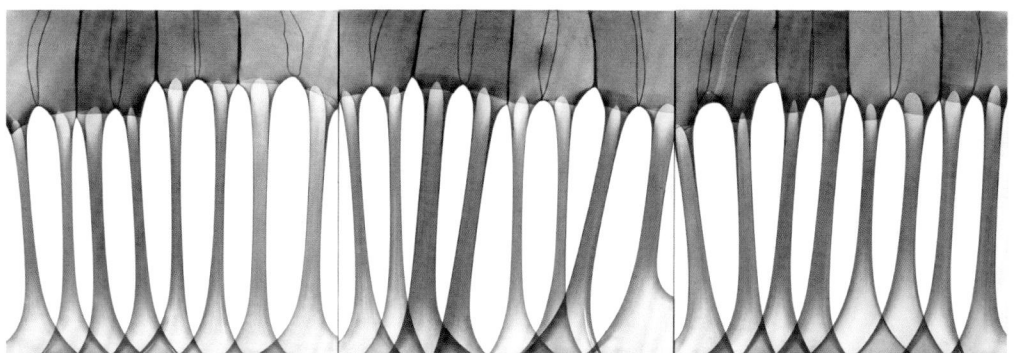

Untitled 8, 10, and 7 (from the series "Inequalities"), 2016. Nylon and cotton pantyhose, thread, and sealant on canvas, each: 46 × 46 × 1 ¾ in., total: 47 × 142 in.
Museum purchase 2016.13

Rodney McMillian

b. 1969

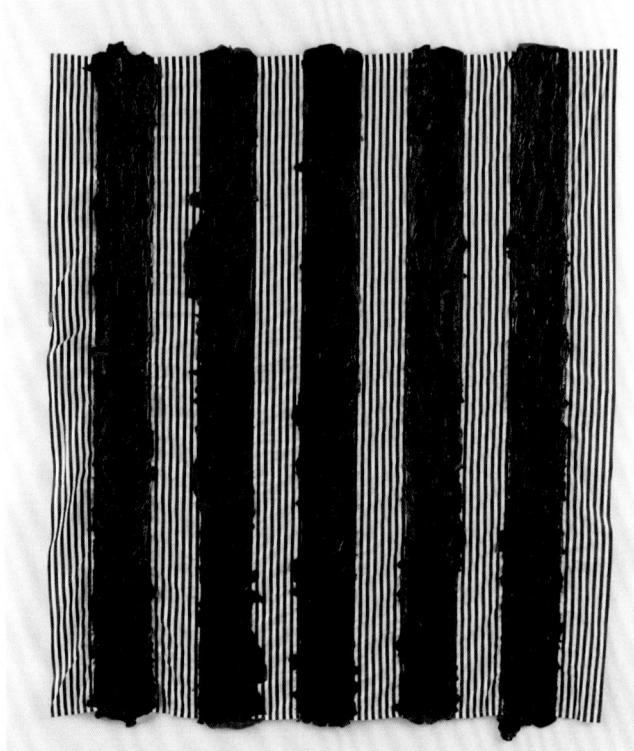

Stripes, 2016. Latex on bedsheet, 92 ½ × 79 in. Museum purchase with funds provided by the Acquisition Committee 2016.23

Rodney McMillian creates sculptures, paintings, installations, videos, and performances that explore how the politics of race, gender, and class shape experience, identity, and a sense of place. He often uses found, everyday objects as his medium—postconsumer materials that relate to personal histories, the home and domesticity, and the socioeconomic associations therein—to construct works that address cultural and political narratives. Through his performative reinterpretations of political texts, historical events, oral records, and popular culture, McMillian confronts the social and economic legacies of race-driven actions and oppression.

Stripes is composed of a used bedsheet and latex. Dark latex paint is applied on top of the black-and-white-striped sheet in five thick, vertical, evenly spaced strips. The inherent differences in the materials—a soft, malleable bedsheet overlaid with hardened, rough latex that disrupts the sheet's smooth surface—evoke feelings of intrusion and discomfort. The artist sourced the sheet from a thrift shop and the leftover paint from construction supply stores; the work brings an object typically reserved for the privacy of a bedroom into public scrutiny. One of McMillian's conceptual interests lies in discarded objects once associated with the human body that are now marked by that body's absence. A used bedsheet possesses myriad intimate histories created by the presence of people and, when presented outside of its original context, becomes a potent metaphor for the intersection of interior and exterior lives. "I've always been interested in domestic spaces because they're great locators for conversations about class and taste and how we use materials," McMillian says.[221]

Many of McMillian's sheet paintings upend the tradition of landscape painting—using the ideas of the personal and domestic to interrogate idealized versions of the world written and created by those in power. As McMillian comments, "The home is informed by the outside world. There are real material, economic, and political aspects of the landscape that shape how homes are built, where homes are built, and how people choose to live in them. The landscape doesn't exist apart from those conditions. The notion of a landscape as a vista, a reprieve from urban life, a place to get back in touch with nature—that seems to be a bit of a fiction."[222] As such, McMillian's sheet paintings reflect the landscape of the interior—one drawn by a person yet defined by their absence. By using a domestic object as his canvas, McMillian explores ideas of class and how economic realities are reflected in interior spaces. While these domestic artifacts hold individual, concealed histories, they are intimately and perpetually connected to the surrounding external political landscape.

—Naima J. Keith

ruby onyinyechi amanze

b. 1982

In *The Divers*, ada—the "alien" with fluorescent yellow skin resembling the artist, ruby onyinyechi amanze—looks outward to the viewer.[223] Onlookers are invited by ada to join her in a fantastical world of a floating leopard head, geometrically patterned bodies captured mid-dive, and trailing potted houseplants that evade grasping hands, which are shooting out instead of feet from ada's legs. At first, these features appear disconnected from each other. However, a layer of networks forms a conjoining, multidimensional space in the drawing. The torso of ada shifts toward the divers, while she drapes an architectural grid, or net, downward and simultaneously pulls the houseplants down to the same vanishing point. This tension of counterbalancing movements creates a visual depth to the composition that ushers in this new world.

The Divers is part of a series of drawings by amanze connected through a recurring cast of characters but not with a continuous narrative. Recognizable forms rooted in reality provide a foundation for *The Divers* that allows for a comfortable engagement with the fantastical elements, highlighter-like colors, and disjointed bodies. Reflecting amanze's transnational upbringing, the white picture plane is borderless and enfolds the viewer into her world for an active viewing experience. Although the individual objects and references in amanze's scenes are recognizable, they are removed from their origins and exposed to subjective reactions for an individualized interpretation of the scene.

—Shanna Kudowitz

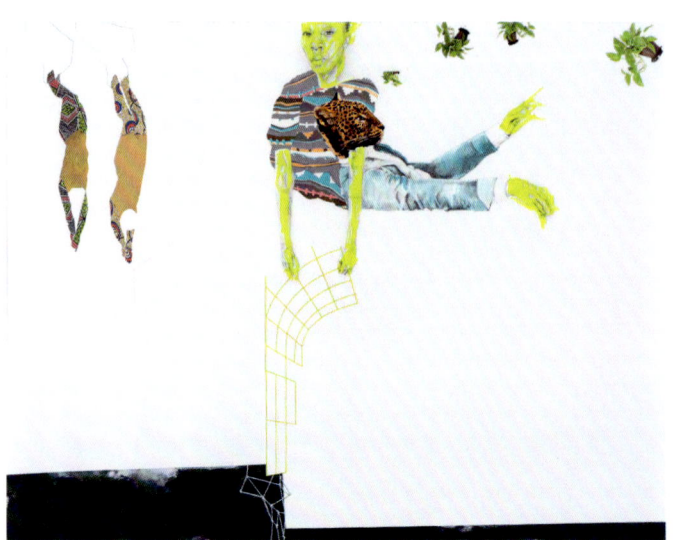

The Divers, 2016. Graphite, ink, photo transfers, fluorescent acrylic, and colored pencils on paper, 38 × 50 in. Museum purchase with funds provided by Nancy L. Lane 2016.29

EJ Hill

b. 1985   Artist in Residence 2015—16

Much of EJ Hill's embodied and performative work is centered in protest. Protest in the form of silence or screaming. Standing proudly upright or, alternatively, at rest. *Surrendered, (A Harrowing Descent)* is part of a suite of collages made at the same time that Hill was conceiving his first durational performance work, *A Monumental Offering of Potential Energy*, for his 2016 Studio Museum *Artist-in-Residence* exhibition, *Tenses: Artists in Residence 2015—16*. An ambitious sculptural installation capturing Hill's lifelong obsession with roller coasters—he has since gone on to realize one to scale at MASS MoCA—this monument was a readymade structure lit with a warm pink glow and made to fit neatly within a museum gallery and accessible to its audience as a recognizable form of entertainment. Atop its undulating wooden track and platform, Hill lay—unmoving, in white—every day that the Studio Museum was open to the public.

While that work was both a form and a performance, Hill's silhouette also clearly referred to what Black bodies carry. The year 2016 was a time of unrest and public protest after the murder of Mike Brown by police in Ferguson, Missouri. Hill's body was a surrender, representing the potential energy and the offering. These works were made at an incredibly charged moment in contemporary US history. Trump had not yet been elected, and protests were omnipresent in the wake of a relentless onslaught of Black death at the hands of police, a continuation of a violent history in the United States.

The people who are pictured on the roller coaster riding against a collaged blue sky display a double reality representing all potential: white bodies at play, emoting glee, intercut with Black bodies willfully filling a charged space. For many, this will immediately call to mind the refrain "Hands up, don't shoot!" This is a call continuing to be heard in the long wake of George Floyd's public murder.

—Amanda Hunt

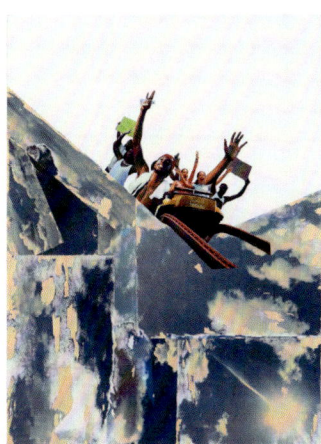

Surrendered, (A Harrowing Descent), 2016. Acrylic, collage, and photo transfer on birch panel, 24 × 18 in. Museum purchase with funds provided by the Acquisition Committee 2016.34

Jordan Casteel

b. 1989   Artist in Residence 2015—16

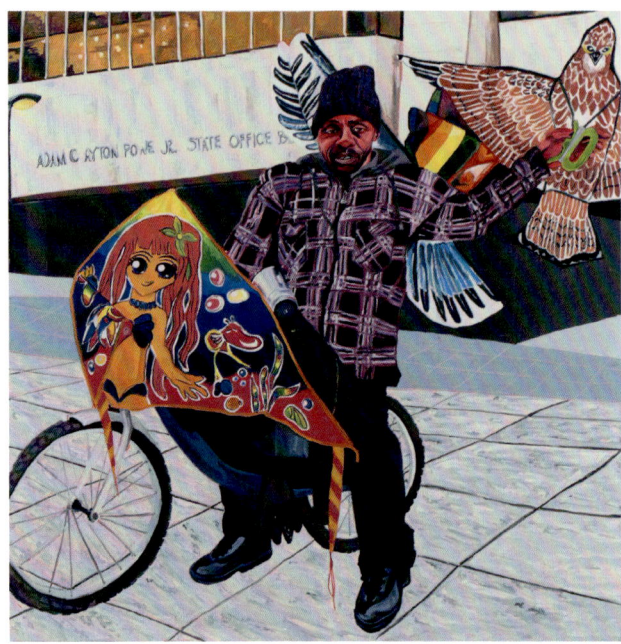

Kevin the Kiteman, 2016. Oil on canvas, 78 × 78 in. Museum purchase with funds provided by the Acquisition Committee 2016.37

Kevin the Kiteman is a Harlem painting. Jordan Casteel's painting is a documentation of Kevin and his kites in front of the Adam Clayton Powell Jr. State Office Building. It is also a record of Harlem at a particular moment because, like many landscapes in New York City, 125th Street between Lenox and Adam Clayton Powell is in a state of flux. A green construction fence in the background acts as a barrier between Kevin and the state office building. Though that key piece of Harlem architecture still exists, Kevin's view across 125th has changed.

The relationships and friendships that Casteel started during the time of this painting still have a major impact on her work and career—both the friendships with her fellow artists in residence and staff members at the Studio Museum, as well as with the Harlem residents who would become her repeat subjects over time. *Kevin the Kiteman* shows Casteel's commitment to getting to know the residents of Harlem and the people she encountered on her way to the Museum and from her studio window. Casteel would often see Kevin and his kites. She eventually went down, introduced herself, told him about the residency, and took some photos that would evolve into this painting. Kevin was there in the courtyard of the state office building to spread the joy of kites to those who passed by. This painting, which depicts Kevin on his bicycle along with his kites in Casteel's signature color palette and style, exemplifies the ways Casteel's time in Harlem and the residency at the Studio Museum have had an immeasurable impact on the artist's practice.

—Lauren Haynes

Autumn Knight

b. 1980   Artist in Residence 2016—17

Autumn Knight works across performance, installation, and video to create participatory experiences that expose and challenge social dynamics. Knight often invites audiences into scenarios that upend expectations, aiming to "put forth inquiries concerning the boundaries of social contracts."[224]

Originally conceived and performed in Galveston, Texas, in 2014, Knight later staged *WALL* at the Contemporary Arts Museum Houston in 2016 and Danspace Project, New York in 2019. Knight drew inspiration for *WALL* from structures around the world that are charged with history and purpose, including the seawall in Galveston that protects Black communities from storm surges; and the Western Wall, otherwise known as the Wailing Wall or Buraq Wall, a holy site in the Old City of Jerusalem. These walls are multifunctional. They simultaneously hold populations in and out; they protect and prohibit; they are sites of memory and loss.

In *WALL*, Knight engages with the notion of walls as both structural and psychological.[225] The cast consists of Black women from the community in which the performance takes place. The ensemble wears blue clothing and sits in a single line to form a wall with their bodies. Knight performs the piece in collaboration with Natasha L. Turner, whose voice joins Knight's in a weaving call and response. Knight, wearing orange, and Turner, wearing red, provide a physical and visual counterpoint to the formation, moving freely through the space and around the ensemble. Knight and Turner's intertwining voices exchange roles and fluidly shift between prompt, response, and duet. Simultaneously, the ensemble cycles through a series of motions and sounds independent of Knight, Turner, and the audience. Over time, the echoing voices and motions build in intensity and morph through fluctuating intonations and signs of exertion. At moments, Knight dissolves the metaphorical fourth wall between herself and the audience or other performers by interacting with each of them directly. Over the course of the performance, the collective builds a space that embodies a wall as something multifaceted—as refuge, obstruction, stability, and protection.

—Mia Matthias

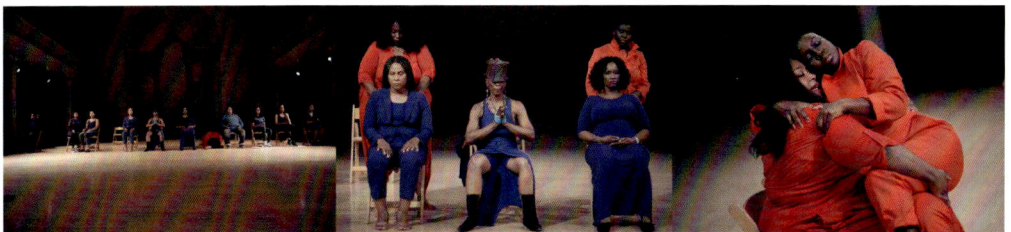

WALL, 2016/2019. Performance.
Museum purchase with funds provided
by the Acquisition Committee
2017.41

Texas Isaiah

Artist in Residence 2020—21

Photographer and "visual narrator" Texas Isaiah (who goes by both names together) creates photographs that center intimacy, care, and collaboration. His images—full of the lives and dreamscapes of Black trans and gender-expansive people—both document his sitters (and himself) and foreground reunion. There is a curiosity and preservation pursued in his work; a generous knowing of his sitters that is captured, brought into composition, cared for. The artist contends with exploitative histories of photography through a restorative study of intimacy—what does it mean, or how does it feel, to be imaged?

My Name Is My Name II is part of an ongoing series that incorporates photography and installation, wherein individual portraits accompanied by altars explore how one might be transformed by communal space. As a ritual practice, the artist considers altar-making (the placement of ephemera that invokes the spirit of oneself and one's ancestors) "a system of celebration." This dimly lit self-portrait depicts a silhouetted figure standing in profile in the center of the frame between three large windows that overlook the Bay Area. Diffuse light passes through the window blinds into a dark room full of shadows; a string of colorful tissue paper hangs above the middle window like papel picado. Even in the image's opacity and stillness, Texas Isaiah's body contains levity and movement. Gently holding the brim of his cap, tilted slightly upward, he looks up toward something. The artist often asks what there is to know about a place, and how this site ties to cultural identity, selfhood, ritual, and queer kinship. Here, he is in communion with himself. Of this work, Texas Isaiah asks: "What does it mean to practice mindfulness with yourself and others?"; "How do we navigate protection when we are creating portals of openness?"[226] Emerging within his images are conversations of celebration and relation—spiritual, ancestral—that are bound by the present but care for the lifelong legacies of his community.

—Angelique Rosales Salgado

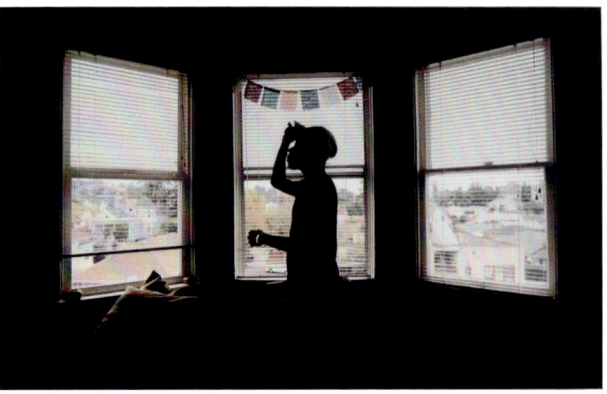

My Name Is My Name II, 2016. Giclée print on archival paper, 20 × 30 in. Museum purchase with funds provided by the Acquisition Committee 2017.48

Ebony G. Patterson
b. 1981

Death is a reality that evokes sublime feelings of joy and pain. Throughout the African diaspora, various Black peoples have found beautiful, poetic, and transcendent ways to conceive of death in the wake of chattel slavery, extractive capitalism, and state-sanctioned violence. To be severed from this world, as it is, is to sacrifice corporeal ills and social evils and instead embrace an inconceivable freedom. These sublime feelings are nearly unbearable when we consider the death of a Black child. Our collective complacency, in keeping this world as it is, reflects on us, rendering our "regrets" our "condolences" and our "gone too soon" mere pretenses as children die around us every day. To confront that reality, the incalculable violence that befalls Black children, physically and psychologically, is what the beauty of Ebony G. Patterson's mixed-media installations aims to do.

Patterson weaponizes beauty. She manipulates the desire to consume beauty, pleasure, and joy through bricolages of brightly colored fabrics, shining rhinestones, and glitter. Varied textures compel the viewer to touch—to feel the fabrics reminiscent of old bedsheets, wallpaper, and auntie's jewelry boxes. Clashing floral patterns, overlaid with faux flowers and fauna, appear to organically erupt from walls. The bedazzled pinks, blues, and golds are too vibrant to be real, too ostentatious to be priceless. The effect is multisensory overstimulation, which can make way for anxiety and mistrust. Strewn throughout the wilds of the installations are trappings of youth—toy race cars, googly-eyed cartoon animals, butterfly barrettes. These subtle reminders of play, joy, and

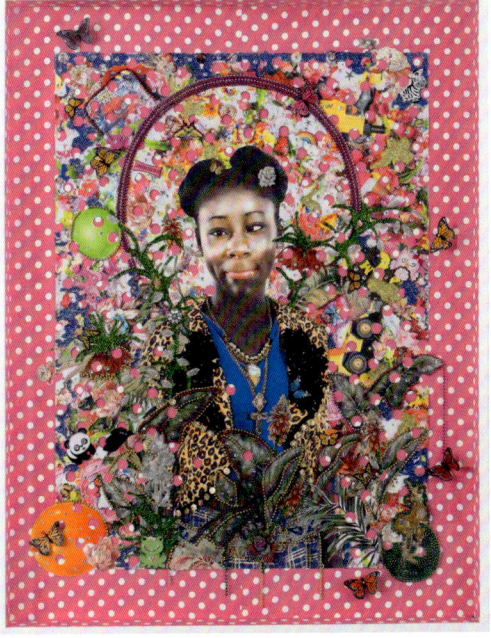

14 (. . . when they grow up . . .), 2016.
Beads, appliques, fabric, glitter, other embellishments, plastic letters, feathered butterflies, and glue on digital print on hand-cut watercolor paper, 61 × 49 in.
Gift of Arthur Lewis and Hau Nguyen
2020.22.8

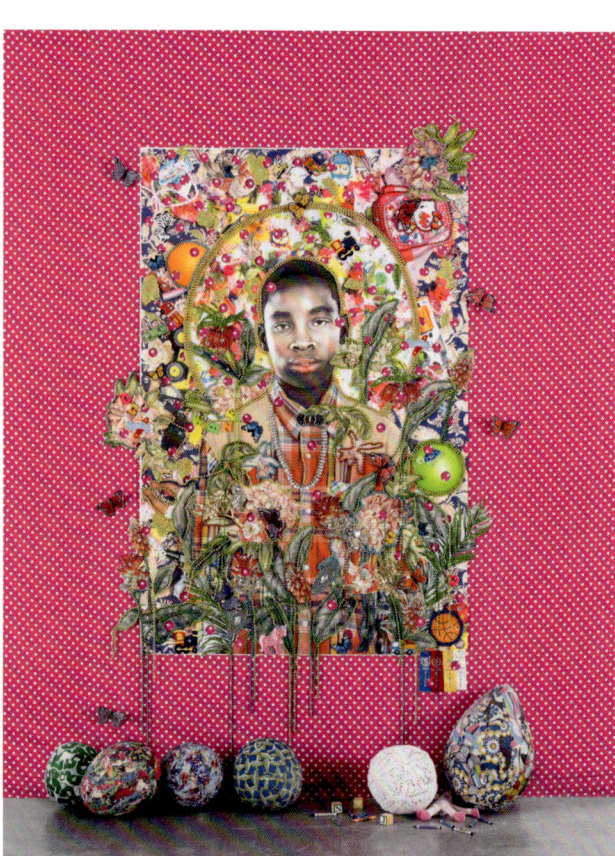

12 (. . . when they grow up . . .), 2016. Beads, appliqués, ribbons, fabric, glitter, buttons, costume jewelry, trimming, rhinestones, toy car, plastic letters, feathered butterflies, and glue on digital print on hand-cut watercolor paper, image: 73 × 51 in., installation dimensions variable. Gift of Arthur Lewis and Hau Nguyen 2016.28

imagination take the mind to a space of nostalgia, a space where one can imagine they once felt free. These are the worlds Patterson creates to frame photographic images of Black children lost to violence. She frames the unthinkable in a beauty so sweet it is sickly.

12 (. . . when they grow up . . .) and *14 (. . . when they grow up . . .)* feature the photographs of a boy and girl, respectively, installed at a child's height. Radiant tactile halos, the iconography of divinity and purity, illuminate their gentle expressions. Adult visitors will look down on these installations and be immersed in the beauty of the children presented as saints. For those raised in or near Black communities, these multimedia installations might evoke the same complex feelings of street shrines erected after someone has died. These shrines intermingle the secular and sacred to create a hallowed ground adorned with teddy bears, balloons, and handwritten signs proclaiming that a community has lost one of their own. The difference is that Patterson's public shrines endure rain and heat. On the street, the balloons sag, and teddy bears mold over, forcing sanitation workers to eventually sweep away the mourning place and allow memory to fade. Patterson's installations, bright, garish, and beautiful, will not allow us to forget these children or our collective failures to protect them.

—TK Smith

Arthur Jafa

b. 1960

Love Is the Message, The Message Is Death is an archive of the archive of what was, an archive of technologies that are now defunct, an archive of the technologies of the body that live on, an archive of feeling.

Love Is the Message, The Message Is Death is a compendium of the crisis and the ecstatic, the hallucinatory and nightmarish, the out-of-body-ness and the embodied, the required virtuosity, the heightened rim of living, the heightened pitch of living required, demanded, and threatened and killed. We are here somewhere between "virtuosity and despair."[227] The dancing bodies are of another world, like the Afflicted Yard,[228] the two innocents—the frightened baby boys and the "beautiful thugs and too fast girls"[229] who must be taught and taught and taught about the dangerous body, about the dangerous world, about the dangerous desire to live. And then there is the sun's ten-thousand-degree Fahrenheit burning.

Love Is the Message, The Message Is Death's method is compilation, compression, juxtaposition, cut, fade, blur, jump, and the slow-down. The method holds together all of the tempos of Black life—making fun, hustling, getting by, just living, and dying. The visceral, biophysical tempos of Black life that lodge and linger in the sternum and the gut, the solar plexus and the spirit. The tempos of Black un/living that remain as heat, as afterimage, and aftersound.

Love Is the Message, The Message Is Death is a compendium, is a Black architecture, is a Black inhabitation.

—Christina Sharpe

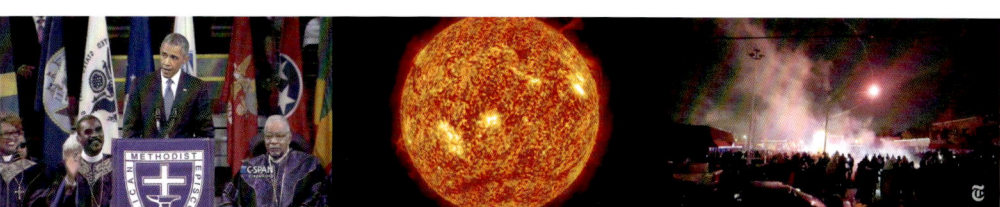

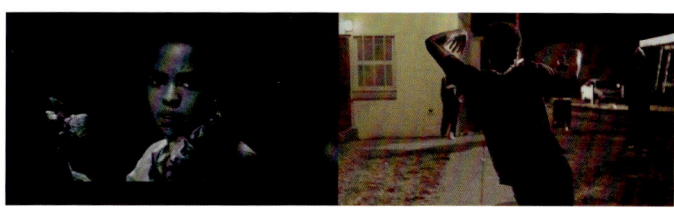

Love Is the Message, The Message Is Death, 2016. Single-channel digital video, color, sound, TRT: 00:07:25. Edition 1 of 13 + 2 APs. Gift of the artist 2018.15

Samuel Levi Jones

b. 1978

Samuel Levi Jones deconstructs academic reference books to critique and scrutinize cultural and political systems of knowledge. The artist dissects these tomes in what he has described as a cathartic process—he carefully separates the jackets and covers from the pages and then transforms the materials into abstract paintings or sculptures. In *Inclusion*, Jones stitches together covers from encyclopedias and law books in an abstract grid composition, recalling both the art of quilting as well as the visual interest in "the grid" that runs across twentieth-century abstract painting into today's contemporary art. The artist considers paper, fabric, and cardboard as his paint, and he uses the torn and raw edges of his materials to create gestural marks. This composition challenges the subjective high value once embedded in painting over other media.

For Jones, the work begins with sourcing. He collects books—old encyclopedias, medical textbooks, law reference books—from various sources across the internet, often for free or at a low cost. That these outdated volumes are aplenty indicates how rapidly systems of knowledge and expertise expire. The ubiquity of these books also reflects the changing valuation of the printed word in a world that increasingly relies on digital modes of holding and generating information. By physically dismantling the books, Jones symbolically breaks down the authority and inherent biases within their contents. The artist's practice at once devalues traditional, often exclusionary voices that enact historical erasure, while generating renewed purpose of his transformed material.

—Doris Zhao

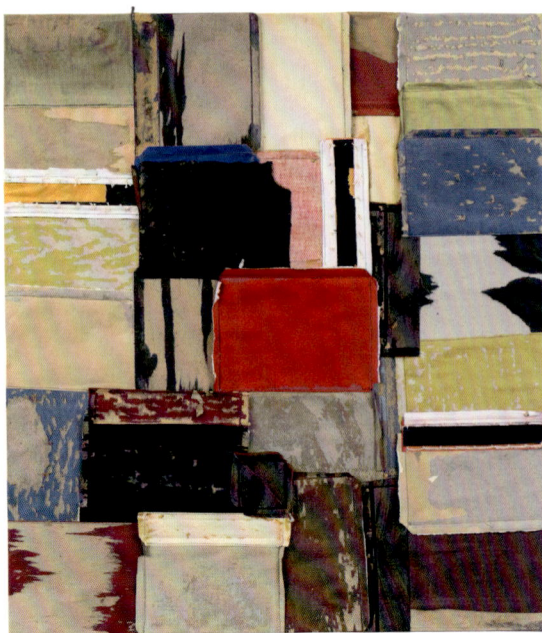

Inclusion, 2016. Encyclopedia and law book covers on canvas, 44 × 39 ½ in. Bequest of Peggy Cooper Cafritz (1947—2018), Washington, DC, collector, educator, and activist 2018.40.128

Julia Phillips

b. 1985   Artist in Residence 2016—17

Donning her famed "banana belt," Josephine Baker beguiled French audiences with her "Danse Sauvage," rising to fame first in Paris in the 1920s. As noted by K. Allison Hammer: "For many critics, the belt symbolizes either her agency or her submission to primitivist caricature and racial/sexual objectification."[230] Julia Phillips's *Exoticizer, Worn Out (Josephine Baker's Belt)* invokes a third reading of Baker's expression of sexuality grounded in the Black feminist principle of holding contradiction, wherein the sculpture establishes a both/and equation that articulates how "agency" and "submission" are entangled points on the parabola of Black femme being.

The tension embedded in Baker's legacy is translated directly on to the formal qualities of the sculpture itself: Phillips's use of brass hardware and ceramic illuminates the belt's ostensible function (to "exoticize") as one that is both weighted (as is brass) and fragile (as is ceramic). Additionally, the sculpture's open clasp and the absence of a body create an indeterminate interpretive frame in which viewers are left to imagine a scenario where Baker has abandoned the belt and one where she is about to wear it. Similarly, as noted by architectural designer and scholar Tomi Laja, there exists a titular contradiction: "worn out" as a signifier of depletion (read as: submission) and "wearing" the belt "out" (read as: agency).[231]

Following a performance in a metropolis that at the time still maintained colonial holdings across the Continent and the Caribbean, Baker exuberantly uttered, "Oh! What an intoxication to dance in the sun with practically nothing on."[232] She thereby communicated a kind of insouciance toward the reductive racial imaginary that informed her audience's delight. Ultimately, Phillips's sculpture provides a physical avenue to consider how Baker's self-generated ecstasy can be understood as a tool to subvert the normative power structures that have long accumulated upon Black femme flesh.

—Camille Bacon

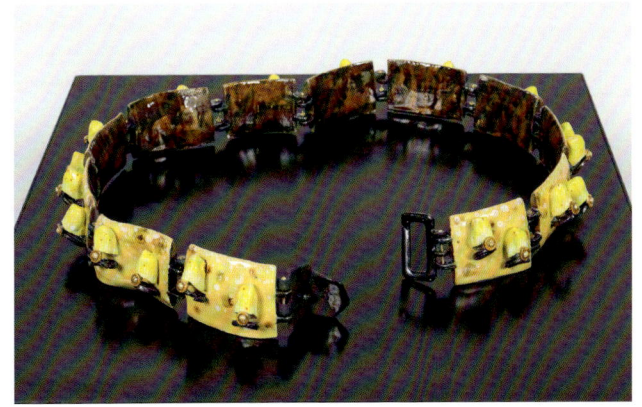

Exoticizer, Worn Out (Josephine Baker's Belt), 2017. Ceramic, brass hardware, and metal pedestal, 39 × 18 × 18 in. Museum purchase with funds provided by the Acquisition Committee 2017.43

Genevieve Gaignard

b. 1981

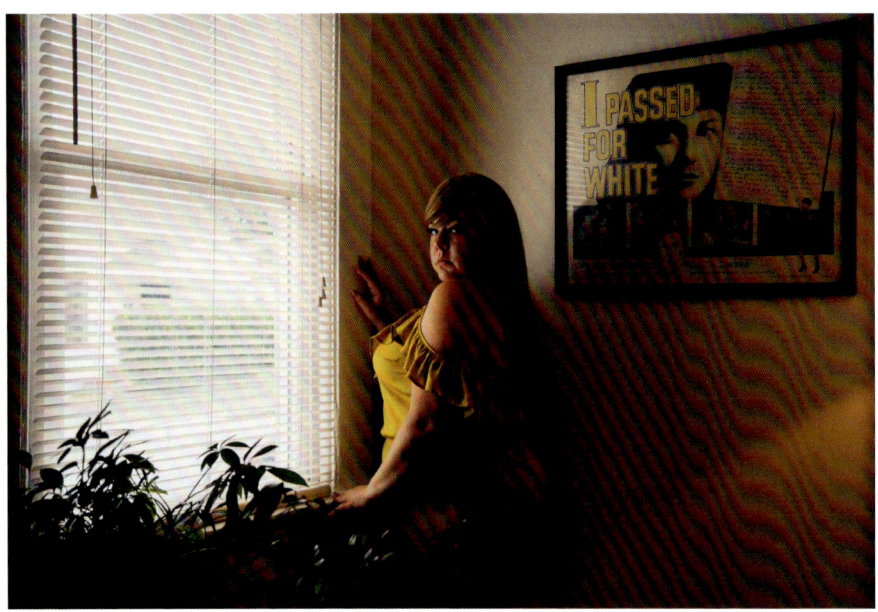

Colorblinds, 2017. Chromogenic
print, frame: 24 × 36 × 2 in. Gift of
Genevieve Gaignard Grassroots 2018.1.1

In this self-portrait, Genevieve Gaignard conjures a metaphor of "blinds" as manipulators of light. These blinds symbolize the choice between visibility and invisibility—privacy and exposure—in a metaphor that speaks to Gaignard's overarching exploration of race, identity, and societal perceptions within the United States.

In the image, Gaignard's yellow dress, blond hair, and skin merge with the wallpaper. The poster for the 1960 film *I Passed for White* hangs on the upper right side of the composition. Adapted from Reba Lee's novel of the same name, this film follows a Black woman navigating the complex terrain of racial frontiers by assuming the guise of a white woman.

Gaignard's title, *Colorblinds*, contemplates the notion of colorblindness as either an ideal or an illusion. The image compels viewers to question whether genuine racial equity can be achieved through the act of disregarding racial differences, even as this act perpetuates a deafening silence surrounding the historic and contemporary forms of violence that shape the United States. Gaignard's direct gaze at the viewer lays bare the power of sight: she exposes the potential for violence inherent in the act of seeing. "Do you see me?" she asks, both hopefully and apprehensively. The artist urges an embarkation to introspection, an urgent plea to delve into who can and should be seen in their entirety.

—June Kitahara

Andy Robert

b. 1984   Artist in Residence 2016—17

Andy Robert describes himself as "working at the edge of representation," with his style "balancing abstraction with recognizable imagery."[233] This tension is clearly demonstrated in *Check II Check*, a composition made during his 2016 to 2017 residency at the Studio Museum. Hovering on the brink of total abstraction, Robert's nocturne relies as much on surface texture as on the application of color to delineate form. The painting's rich palette of blues, reds, pinks, and browns drips, swirls, and blends, making the boundaries of one object virtually indistinguishable from its surroundings. Instead, in a stylistic reference to Beauford Delaney's impasto paintings, Robert layers paint on to the canvas, creating dimensions that communicate shifts in form, while maintaining a tonal palette.

During his residency at the Studio Museum, Robert paid homage to the storefronts of Harlem. Like the work of the Ashcan School of painters a century before, Robert dedicates this lush canvas, with its thick paint, to an everyday entity, a check-cashing store, rather than more conventional, storied landmarks in Harlem. Seen at night through a watery lens, *Check II Check* evokes the feeling of walking around Harlem—of people's day-to-day lives—and captures a snapshot of the neighborhood in an era of rapid gentrification. As Robert notes in the title, many of the figures visiting the check-cashing place are living paycheck to paycheck. He thus sees cashing a check as a kind of nighttime ritual—getting the funds to prepare for the upcoming days and securing the future of the neighborhood for those who have been there for generations.

—Hallie Ringle

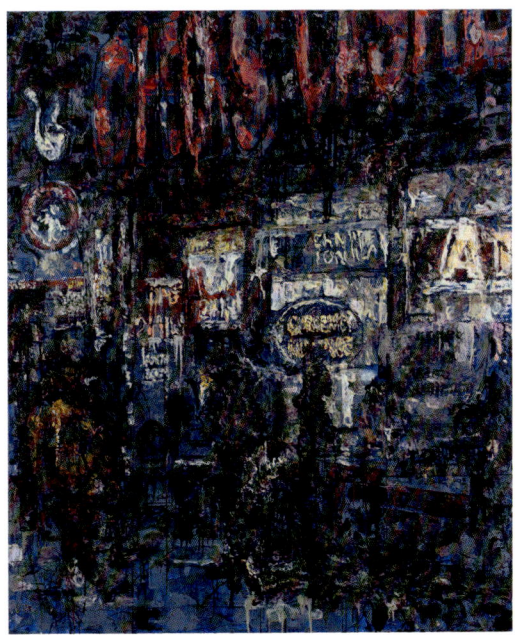

Check II Check, 2017. Oil on canvas, 71 × 59 ½ in. Promised gift of Nancy L. Lane PG.2023.010.34

Aria Dean

b. 1993

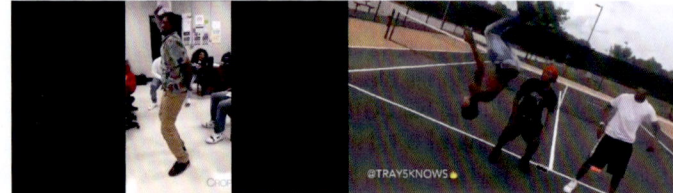

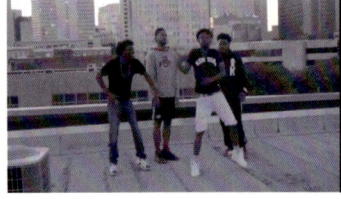
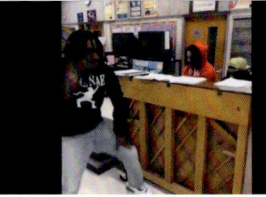
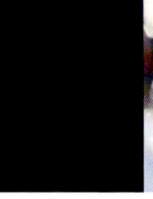
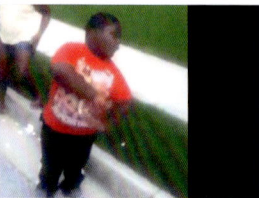

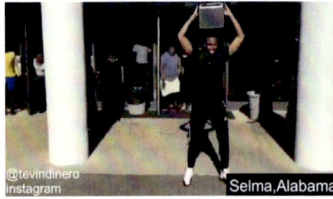
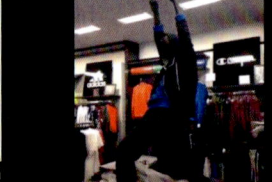
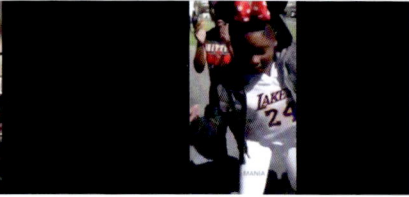

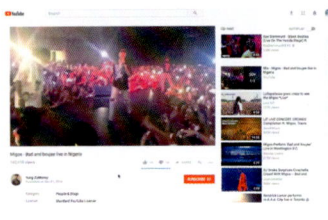
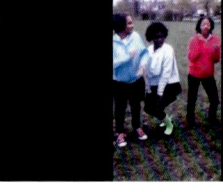
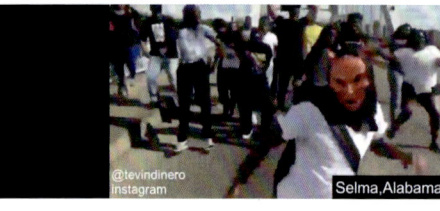

Eulogy for a Black Mass, 2017. Single-channel video, with sound, TRT: 00:05:54. Edition 2 of 5 + 2 APs. Museum purchase with funds provided by the Acquisition Committee 2019.1

Supported by a deep intellectual engagement with various theoretical and philosophical traditions—including Minimalism, post-structuralism, and Afropessimism—Aria Dean's work considers the social and material impacts of art on the ontology of blackness. Her video essay *Eulogy for a Black Mass* explores how memes and digital culture engage with questions of Black labor, authorship, ownership, access, and circulation.

The work adapts Dean's 2016 essay "Poor Meme, Rich Meme" into visual form. We see a compilation of videos—mostly dance and movement reels pulled from online platforms such as Vine, YouTube, and Twitter—interspersed with typing text. The artist's voiceover replaces the cacophony of sounds that usually emerges from a rapid social media scroll. "On a very practical level, there is a blackness to claim," Dean says, "a blackness related to intellectual property and labor . . . . There is an imminent theft to be guarded against." Dean is interested in the ways memes function through blackness—as self-referential images and videos that are not defined by what they are in and of themselves, but by their transmission. Here, memes become an object lesson. To expand the dialogue, Dean also reads from Fred Moten's *Poetics of the Undercommons* (2016) and Hito Steyerl's "In Defense of the Poor Image" (2009) for their resonances with online Black audiovisual vernacular and the movement and acceleration of Black culture, where blackness emerges as a site of contestation.

Memes change and grow, and they are reuploaded and compressed across platforms to form one node in a network of infinite circulation independent of the body. With this in mind, Dean proposes there is no essential referent to blackness: "How do you describe something that is at once just itself and everything?"; "Can we bilaterally think blackness through memes and memes through blackness—both smear, mar, blur, ontological integrity?" The virality of these images and videos illustrates a lack of fixity, which Dean names at the start of the video: "In death, new beginnings." *Eulogy for a Black Mass* questions the imbalances of an attention economy entrenched in interminable circuits of power and capital, as well as the relationship between labor and identity in a digital world that increasingly affects our reality.

—Angelique Rosales Salgado

Lezley Saar
b. 1953

Throughout her career, Lezley Saar has developed bodies of work that speak to the experience of marginalized figures beyond binaries of race, gender, sanity, and religion. Her works draw from varied sources in the space where the historical and the critically fabulated come together, much in line with her family of Black feminist artists including mother Betye Saar and sister Alison Saar.

I dream the body . . . is part of the "Gender Renaissance" series featuring portraits of people who frequented Molly Houses—historically known as meeting places for homosexual men in eighteenth- and nineteenth-century England. The tapestry in material and composition is situated in the past and speaks to Saar's dedication to creating images for marginalized figures in the present. The monumental work opens up the world of a figure, racially ambiguous and gender nonbinary, with eyes closed and dreaming. *I dream the body . . .* is ripe with symbolism that peeks into the figure's most intimate thoughts, beginning with the patterned toile backdrop of a romantic landscape—the dreamworld scene for figure and viewer. The person imaged recalls Helen Ann Windman, known as "The Albino, or White Negro Girl," whose likeness was distributed as spectacle via nineteenth-century cartes de visite. By the logic of the tapestry structure, Saar shows glimpses of the figure's thoughts within each vignette's depiction: the Château de Chambord—a French Renaissance manor; a bowl of red roses; and a hunting scene. The château became King Francis I's hunting lodge, a potential inspiration for the scene on the right side. The manor also has a long history of grandeur and disrepair since it was first constructed in the 1500s.[234] The history of the building is analogous to the dissonance between the roses as symbols of love and passion and the hunting scene—a scene of leisure but also of pursuit and unrest. The figure sees a full life for themself, one of challenge but unbound by the biases of binary systems—dreaming of life on their own terms.

—Lilia Rocio Taboada

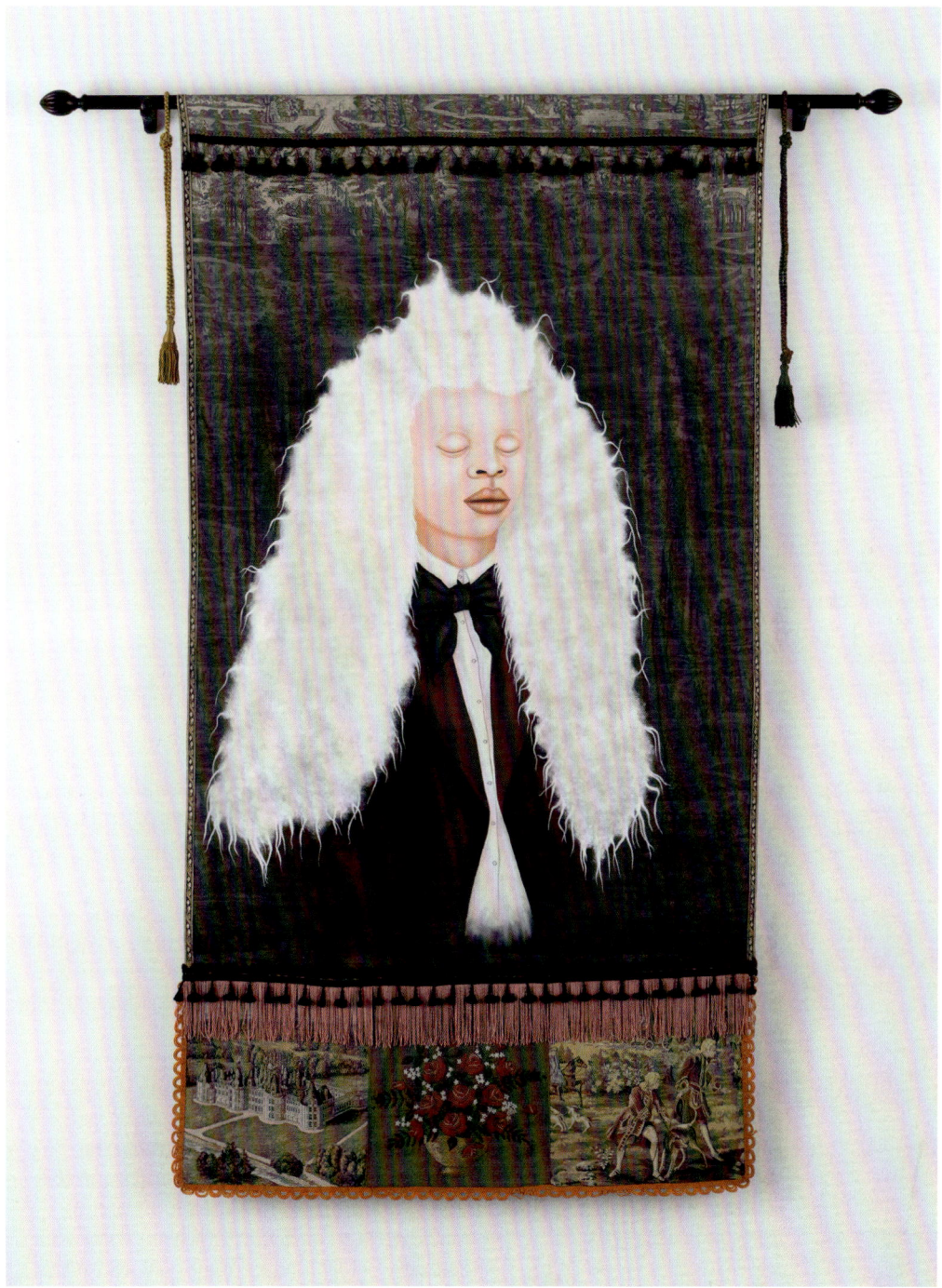

I dream the body . . . (from the series "Gender
Renaissance"), 2017. Acrylic on fabrics with
fringing, braided tassels, and curtain rod,
101 × 55 in. Museum purchase with funds
provided by the Acquisition Committee in
memory of David Beitzel 2019.11

Kameelah Janan Rasheed

b. 1985

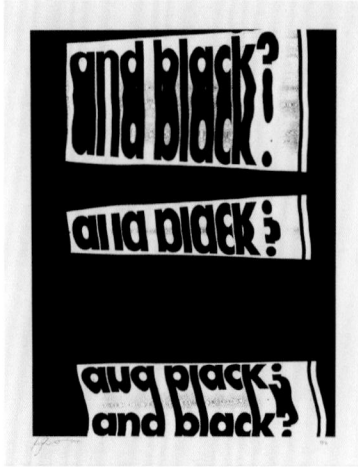

And Black?, 2017. Silkscreen on paper,
23 × 19 in. Edition of 20. Gift of
Art+Culture Projects with support
by Larry Ossei-Mensah 2018.12.4

Kameelah Janan Rasheed identifies as a learner, and it is the circuitous process of learning that informs her artistic practice across printmaking, sculpture, installation, and photography. Pulling from a variety of literature, Rasheed cuts, collages, hand-writes, and photographs fragmented text to create poetic works that encourage inner wanderings and interpretation.

Each of the three white blocks in the silkscreen print *And Black?* contains a different abstracted iteration of the titular phrase. The elongated and mirrored appearance of the text, alongside the presence of smudged black ink, demonstrates the artist's experiments with printmaking and deep interest in the processes of mechanical and digital reproduction. How a text appears influences the way it might be read and understood. By manipulating the words "and black?," the artist considers the ambiguity in a question that is as tricky to answer as it is to ask. What black? Whose black? Black people? Black colors? Black…?

Rasheed's interest in writing, intertextual analysis, and unique typefaces informs much of her work in deconstructing and refiguring knowledge production. Fascinated by racial nomenclature and taxonomies, the artist created this as a print for Art+Culture Projects, drawing from the writings of W. E. B. Du Bois, whose work informs Rasheed's research on how people of African descent came to self-identify from the twentieth century through the present day. Similarly, *And Black?* builds on her artwork *Punctuated Blackness* (2013), which lists the word "black" followed by a series of different punctuations. Like many artists working with text, Rasheed engages with different modes of legibility through her interdisciplinary and intuitional approach to information gathering. She trusts that even if the meaning of a fragmented text is currently unclear, its intent may be revealed later.

—Kiki Teshome

Toyin Ojih Odutola

b. 1985

Toyin Ojih Odutola creates worlds, narratives, that are rooted in the familiar but exist outside of time and place. *The Proposal* is part of a series that explores the lives of two fictional aristocratic Nigerian families—the UmuEze Amara Clan and the House of Obafemi—united through the marriage between two men. The work's title suggests that it captures either a business meeting or the moment of engagement between the noblemen, who sit side by side at a table with the remnants of a meal in front of them. The intimate scene is recognizable, yet the story is improbable, for Black wealth, Black leisure, Black lives have been permanently impacted and shaped by the transatlantic slave trade and colonialism. However, in the insistence on depicting the trappings of affluence and privilege—seen here in the gold tiered dessert stand and the plush seats—the artist posits a different reality, one that offers up possibilities for the future.

Ojih Odutola is known for her labor-intensive process of applying pastel, charcoal, and pencil on paper to create meticulously rendered and variously textured marks. In *The Proposal*, the artist illustrates fabric, metal, glass, and foods using her signature shading and mark-making, a technique she began using while an undergraduate at the University of Alabama, Huntsville, in the early 2000s. Ojih Odutola builds up the paper with layers of color and line that often weave together in intricate patterns, particularly when depicting Black skin. The resulting surface features rich tonal gradations that suggest a natural radiance to the characters who inhabit her world.

—Connie H. Choi

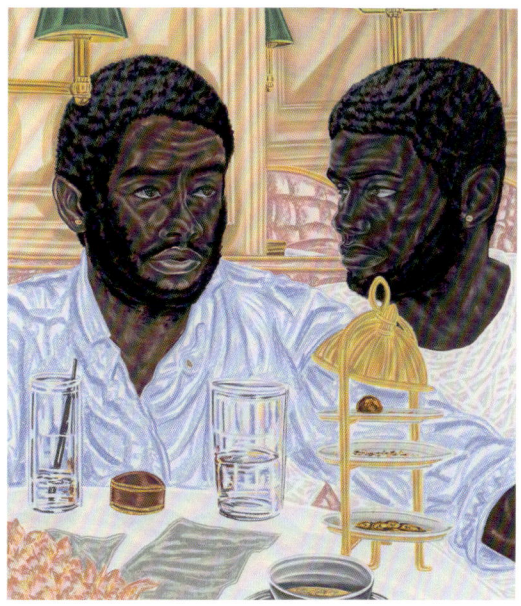

The Proposal, 2017. Pastel, charcoal, and pencil on paper, 53 ½ × 47 ⅞ × 2 ½ in. Bequest of Peggy Cooper Cafritz (1947—2018), Washington, DC, collector, educator, and activist 2018.40.237

Ibrahim Mahama

b. 1987

Navrongo is an example of Ibrahim Mahama's ongoing series of jute sack paintings (Mahama originally trained as a painter) and is named after a northern Ghanaian city on the border between Ghana and Burkina Faso.[235] The patchwork's weathered texture carries traces of the material's original function as bags for transporting commodities. The frayed edges, cuts, tears, ink stamps, and smudged marks evince both the goods these sacks moved and the hands that carried them. Mahama became interested in the material after watching the bulk movement of packed jute sacks across the Ghanaian border in 2011, recalling the economic and colonial histories that have largely framed Ghana's contemporary position in global trade.

Within Ghana, the jute sack—often sourced from South and Southeast Asia or other African nations—is associated primarily with the domestic shipment of natural resources such as cocoa and charcoal, which stain the fabric to such a degree that the sacks eventually become unusable. Mahama intervenes in the material's circular economy, bartering with traders to exchange their worn sacks for his newer ones, and working with a team of studio collaborators and assistants to sew these reused scraps into both small- and large-scale tapestries for his sculptures and installations. "I'm interested in the point where the relationship between the material and society, or the space it finds itself in, breaks down," explains Mahama. "I'm interested in these voids in history. We're like time travelers: we now know how history plays out, how capital becomes more brutal. What decisions could we have made differently?"[236] In recent years, Mahama has also undertaken a series of ambitious building projects, founding an art center in his hometown of Tamale, Ghana, and purchasing a disused food silo—an architecture synonymous with the country's economic aspirations—to convert into a cultural center. These endeavors extend the making of artwork to the remaking of social relations, as they too bear the marks of capital and industry.

—Anni A. Pullagura and Ruth Erickson

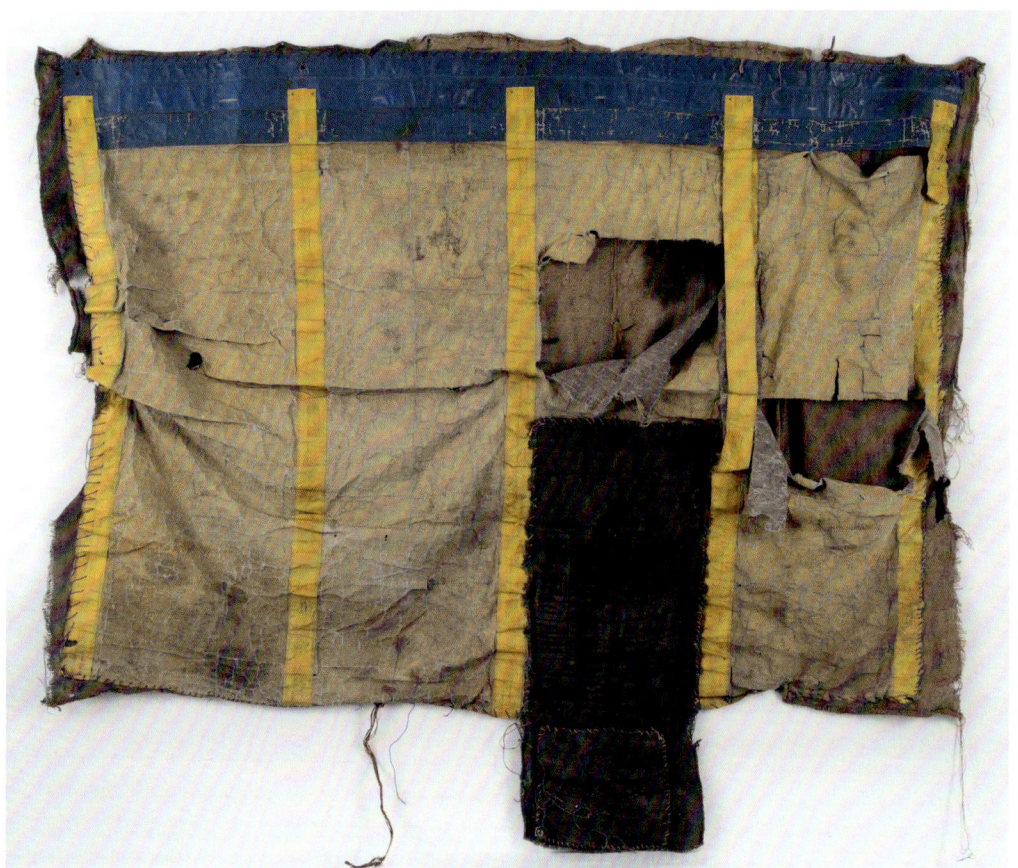

Navrongo, 2017. Mixed media, tarp, burlap,
string, and plastic, 106 × 128 in. Gift of
Lloyd F. Bean and Ursula M. Burns 2022.2

Dread Scott

b. 1965

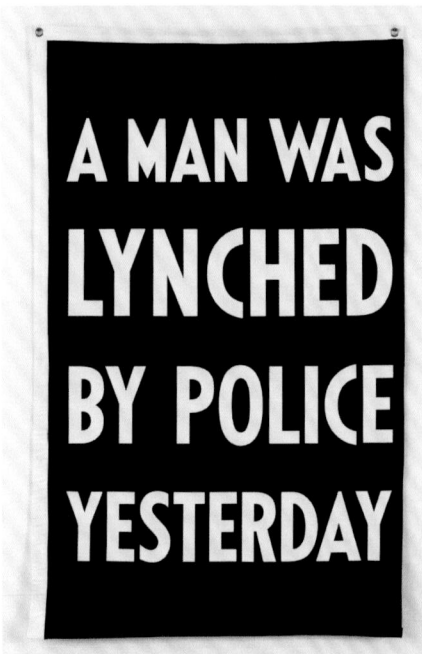

A Man Was Lynched by Police Yesterday, 2017. Screenprint on canvas, 59 × 37 ½ in. Edition 4 of 10. Bequest of Peggy Cooper Cafritz (1947—2018), Washington, DC, collector, educator, and activist 2018.40.284

From 1920 to 1938, the National Association for the Advancement of Colored People (NAACP) flew a flag that stated "A man was lynched yesterday" from its national headquarters in New York City to raise awareness of lynchings—public killings without due process—of Black men and women in the United States. Referencing the NAACP's flag, Dread Scott created this editioned work after the 2015 murder of Walter Scott by the police in North Charleston, South Carolina. By adding "by Police" to the text from the original flag, the artist makes a connection between the violence of the present to that of the past, invoking a long legacy of racial injustices in the United States. The addition of text thus calls attention to the complicity of officials then and now, and to the continued brutalities perpetrated against Black people by those sworn to protect them.

A Man Was Lynched by Police Yesterday, as with Scott's multidisciplinary practice as a whole, criticizes the systemic and structural racism found in US economics, governance, politics, and society. The work is not the first time the artist has employed the flag as a medium for challenging deeply ingrained histories and ways of being. Flags, with their high visibility and various uses as both symbol and signal, hold meaning and carry a significance that Scott utilizes to further the weight of the seemingly simple statement found in this work. For every day that the flag is exhibited, the viewer is reminded of the many yesterdays that have passed, and therefore, the many lives that have been unjustly taken.

—Connie H. Choi

Tourmaline and Sasha Wortzel

b. 1983

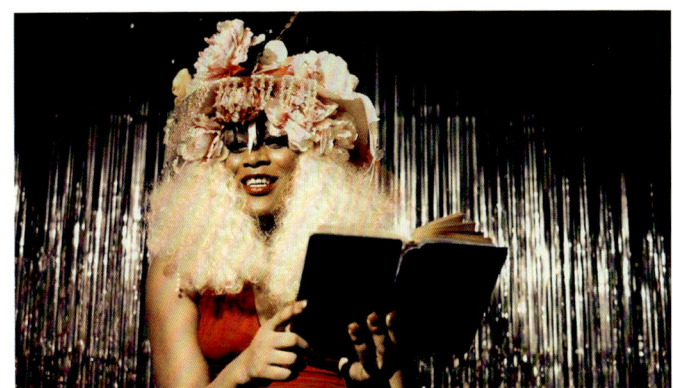

Happy Birthday, Marsha!, 2018. Written, directed, and produced by Tourmaline and Sasha Wortzel, TRT: 00:15:00. Museum purchase with funds provided by the Acquisition Committee 2020.7

Tourmaline and Sasha Wortzel's *Happy Birthday, Marsha!* celebrates the life and legacy of Marsha P. Johnson, a Black transgender woman and central figure in the gay liberation movement of the late 1960s. Johnson played a pivotal role in the 1969 uprisings at New York City's Stonewall Inn[237]—this short film offers a fictional depiction of the hours leading up to that watershed evening. Contrary to historical records, the film places the pivotal event on the eve of Johnson's twenty-fifth birthday. *Happy Birthday, Marsha!* begins with Johnson, played by Mya Taylor, attempting to throw herself a birthday party. When her plans do not come to fruition, she is persuaded to go to the Stonewall Inn instead. In a heartbreaking rendition of the painful realities of being a Black trans woman, Johnson's character, who should be celebrating, faces several violent encounters with the police. The persistent reminder of her life's fragility thus starkly contrasts with the day that honors her becoming. Spliced with archival footage of Johnson in one of her iconic bejeweled ornamental head-pieces, the film weaves dreamlike reenactments with tender recordings of the legendary activist. In one clip, she exclaims "I try!" after being told by a person off-camera that she always seems to "have it together." "It's expected!" she replies with a smile. Despite oppressive marginalization and violence from both within and outside the gay liberation movement, Johnson and the other transgender activists she stood alongside were a consistent force in the fight for trans rights, often positioning them-selves directly on the front lines. In 1970, Johnson cofounded STAR (Street Transvestites Action Revolutionaries) with her friend Sylvia Rivera, who is also featured in the film. The video climaxes with Johnson's character onstage at the Stonewall Inn just before the police raid. She recites: "I'm not saying that it's easy to shine, to love, to twirl. I'm not saying that it don't hurt to be awake in this world . . . . That river keeps on glowing shining light right back at you, so stay awake my darlings, it's all we've got to do."

—Yelena Keller

Cauleen Smith

b. 1967

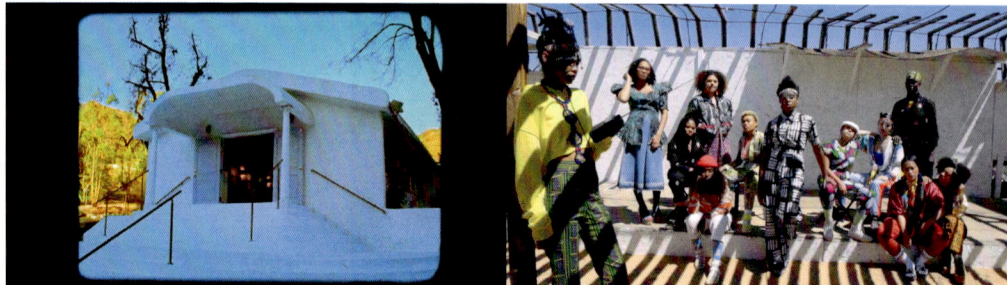

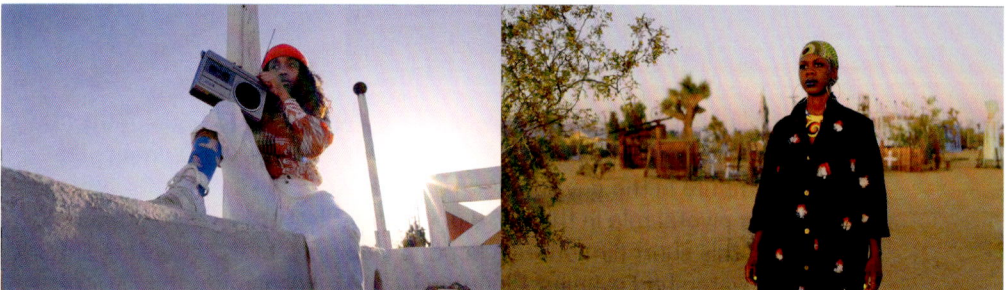

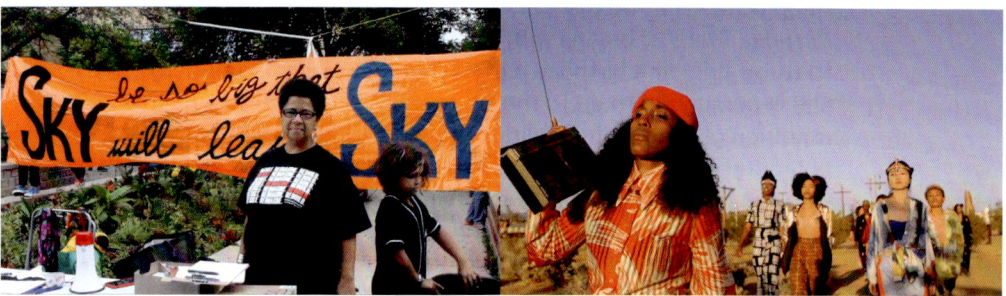

Sojourner, 2018. Digital video, color, sound,
TRT: 00:22:41. AP 3 of 5 with an edition
of 5. Gift of the artist 2021.25.2

Black women are making rituals in so many forms, recognizing how holy it is when we breathe together, listen together.

In 2018, Cauleen Smith released a seed packet, a ritual, a short film titled *Sojourner*. It is a time-travel dose of visual medicine, where every location is both familiar and foreign, memory and projection. It is a green, vibrant bridge connecting art and organizing, a reminder that there are new ways to tell the truth—even if the truth is words we have heard before—from within and without. One by one, I fell for the faces and voices and silhouettes of organizers, artists, and thinkers who have changed and are changing the world. So many have done that work—this is quilt-work, ancestral and alive.

The world has tried to swallow us, to convince us to be satisfied by the conforming weight of domestication, to shrink ourselves into the roles cast by those who need our service. To achieve anything of our own in these conditions requires heroics and help. So we are running to the ocean and listening to what the waves sing into our skin. Salt and water we are. Air reminds us that some parts of us can fly. We sit in the bowl of earth; before we belonged to anyone else, as bodies, minds, desires, or expectations, we belonged to earth.

We sit in circles, creating and finding structures open enough to hold us so we can reach back and reach forward. We send each other earmarked books, playlists, and seeds we can use to cultivate our corner of our col-lective liberation garden. We place the seeds among the living and dead things in the heart of our circle.

Watching *Sojourner* is receiving the seeds, the gift and reminder of what we know and how we know it, what we need and how we can give it to each other, and how underneath the crises there is still so much beauty.

—adrienne maree brown

Tavares Strachan

b. 1979

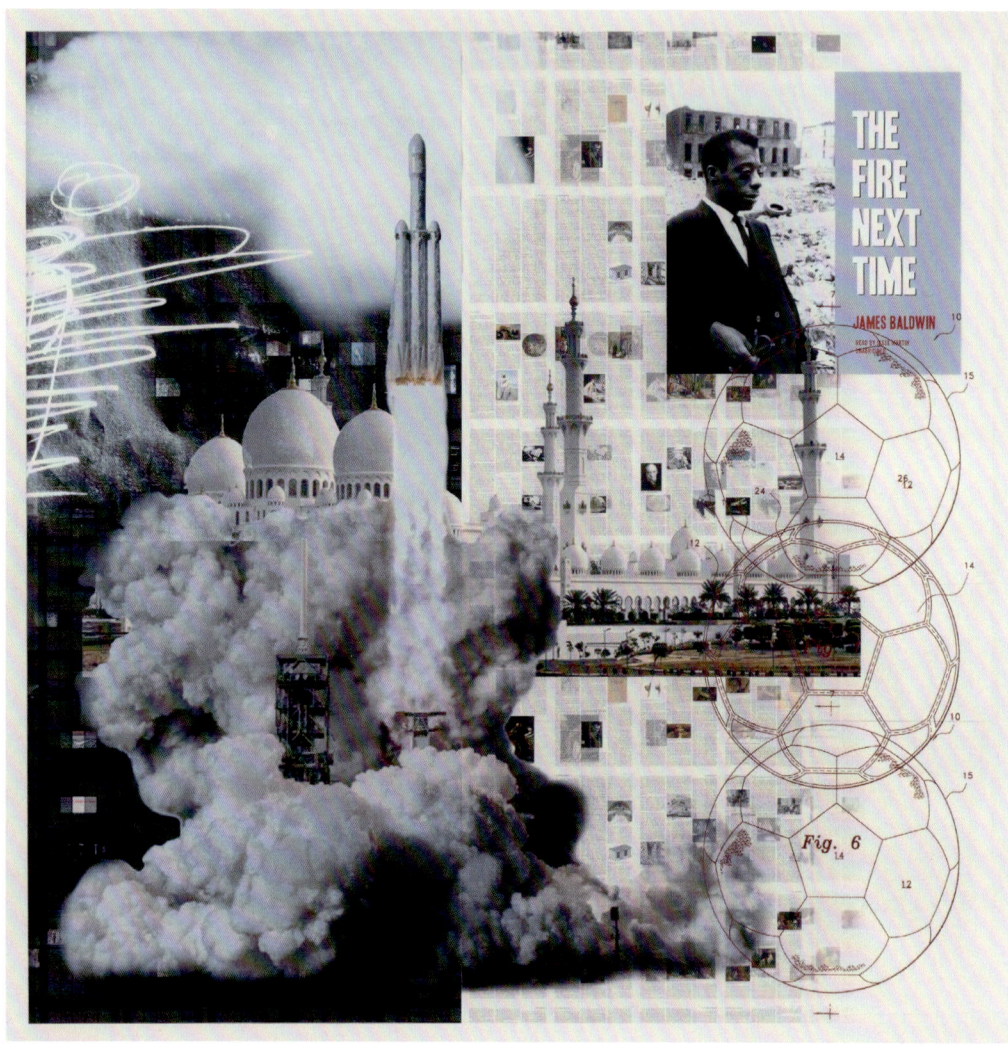

Next Time, 2018. Mylar, matte paper,
pigment, spray paint, acrylic, oil stick,
enamel, vinyl, and graphite, 84 × 84 in.
Gift of Ivor Braka Limited 2019.6

Tavares Strachan makes visible the historically overlooked. In doing so, he exposes systems of oppression that perpetuate the erasure of nondominant groups. Many of Strachan's artworks, including *Next Time*, investigate subjects from his *Encyclopedia of Invisibility* (2018). Produced over eight years, the 2,400-page tome counters the *Encyclopedia Britannica*'s false promise to neutrally represent all knowledge when, in fact, it furthered a Western, colonizing worldview. Strachan's *Encyclopedia of Invisibility* includes fifteen thousand entries on subjects often omitted from historical records, among them writer and social critic James Baldwin and the first African American astronaut, Robert Henry Lawrence Jr.

The base of Strachan's aggregate image *Next Time* comprises pages from the *Encyclopedia of Invisibility*, with the left half printed in negative. Strachan describes his multilayered images as akin to dub music or street festivals for their integration of varied cultural references, in that he sources from historical photographs, vintage advertising, schematic drawings, geometric patterns, and various digital media. Further challenging the biased structure of the "encyclopedia," his cumulative strategy engages nonlinear thinking by juxtaposing seemingly disparate things that share visual and conceptual connections.

Baldwin's book *The Fire Next Time* became a national bestseller upon release in 1963. Its description of his experiences with racial injustice galvanized the emerging civil rights movement. In the upper right of *Next Time*, Strachan includes the marketing image for the 2008 audio release of *The Fire Next Time*, emphasizing that Baldwin's teachings remain just as urgent today. To the left of Baldwin's portrait, a central rocket echoes three towering minarets. Thrusting upward, these white cylindrical forms nod to the early but oft-marginalized contributions of Islamic scholars to astronomy. The rocket, SpaceX's Falcon Heavy, announces Strachan's five-year effort to recognize Lawrence, whose tragic death in a 1967 training exercise prevented him from flying to space. After debuting *Next Time*, Strachan launched *ENOCH*, a 24-karat gold urn bearing Lawrence's likeness, into low Earth orbit using a SpaceX Falcon 9 rocket. This time, Lawrence made it into space. This time, Strachan made sure Lawrence was seen and recognized for overcoming barriers in his pursuit of exploration and knowledge.

—Whitney Tassie

Devin Troy Strother, in collaboration with Alima Lee and Mandy Harris Williams

b. 1992, 1986, 1988

In *The Worst Witch*, a collaborative two-channel video by Devin Troy Strother, directed and edited by Alima Lee, and with dialogue written by Mandy Harris Williams, a witch sits on a couch with a cat named Rashad, played by a human wearing a cat mascot head. The witch recounts to Rashad how a spell recently backfired because it lacked clarity. In turn, she feels like she cast a spell on herself (which she admits happens often). She improvises a wry, quasi-monologue (Rashad's meows interrupt periodically) in which she shares things she's "so over": the weather; her green makeup; her witch wig; the fact that she has to "perform as a witch, in order to justify [her] magicality"; that the Good Witch in *The Wiz* (1978) was light-skinned; and that former president Barack Obama is reduced to the "Magical Negro" trope.

The video switches between a single-screen feed, a split screen, a superimposed screen, and a single-screen feed with large multicolor text echoing what the witch speaks: "COUNTER SPELL," "BLACK," "GREEN," "WITCH," "CLASSICAL MAGICAL NEGRO." Here, Strother, Williams, and Lee consider why Black power(s) and magic are perceived as suspect forces. The witch, a highly politicized body and symbol of power, is a figure of popular and mystical interest. In this vaguely fantastical world, the artists enact superlative associations of identity to scrutinize what informs "goodness" or "badness" as it relates to one's subjectivity. They render the juxtaposition of dark and light and perceived good and bad energies as twisted when, in response to Rashad asking why Harriet Tubman never appeared on the twenty-dollar bill, the witch replies: "Poof! White Magic.... White Magic is like saying a thing is going to happen, but it doesn't happen. That's why they call them white lies." The witch upends definitions of Black Magic—a witchcraft typically understood to invoke "evil" spirits for "evil" purposes—to call out the ways whiteness carelessly makes promises, but rarely meets those intentions. Taking off her wig, the witch concludes, "Black magicality is a ceaseless font, from whence so much creativity can be derived. And so it is."

—Angelique Rosales Salgado

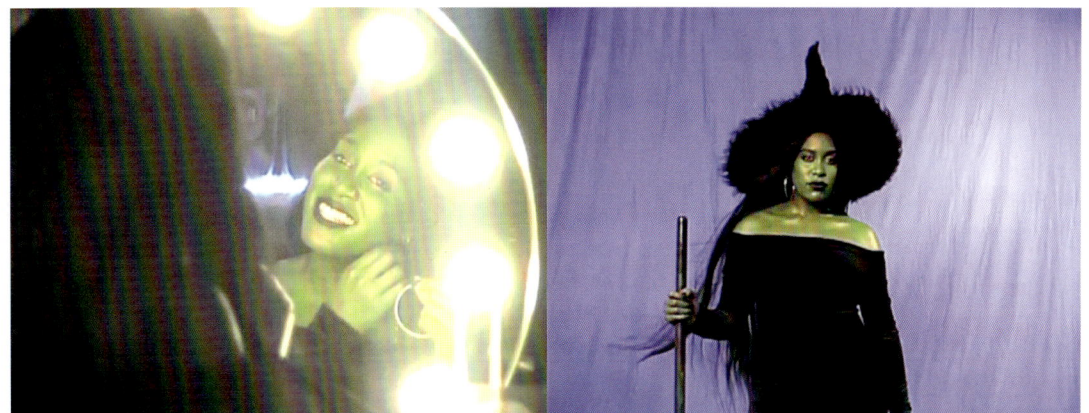

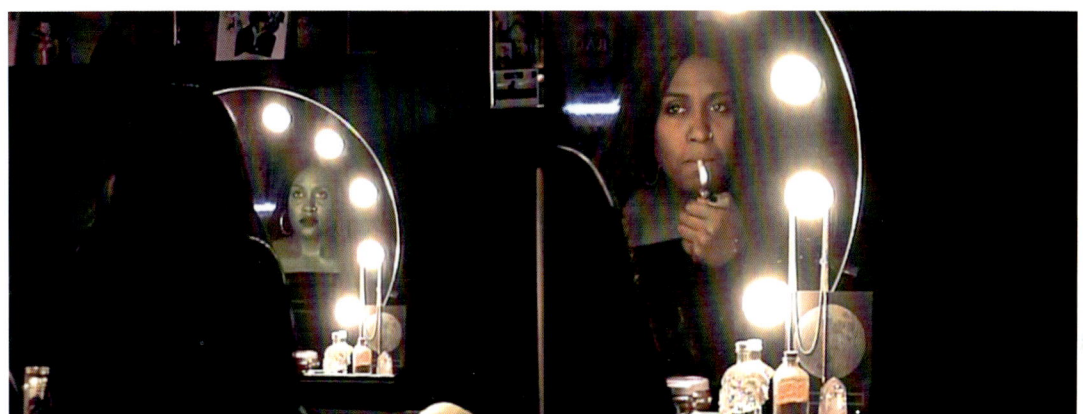

The Worst Witch, 2018. Two-channel video, color, sound, TRT: 00:08:06. Edition 1 of 3 + 1 AP. Museum purchase with funds provided by the Acquisition Committee 2022.25

Firelei Báez

b. 1981

Born out of the artist's engagement with the archives at the Schomburg Center for Research in Black Culture, *Elegant gathering in a secluded garden (or the many bridges we crossed)* was part of a larger installation that combined imagined interactions within spaces of leisure with historical documents and figures. Representations of prominent Black cultural artists, writers, and musicians, such as Zora Neale Hurston and Mary Lou Williams, intersperse with representations of lesser-known women to bring their lives into a larger conversation of history and storytelling, giving them the same gravitas as their more famous counterparts. In this way, Firelei Báez elevates each woman's story much like Hurston, who took vernacular folktales and brought them into the literary canon. The artist's practice frequently mines history and primary documents that she reworks into statements about understandings of colonial heritage. These are then combined with imaginative retellings of the past—told through the lens of a feminist perspective—that are often left out of dominant discourses. In Báez's painting, women are depicted in moments of joy and communion with one another. Comprising smaller groupings, each segment of the painting presents intimate interactions between the women. Within the foreground, figures are shown mid-speech or song, while others gaze upon them reverently, smiling peacefully. This gathering—a reference to an eighteenth-century painting by Yuan Yao[238]—can be read non-linearly with its figures' lives unfolding across time. Throughout each vignette, Báez threads texts from the women's diaries and excerpts of documents found in family papers, including letters, across the canvas. She gives these long-hidden words new life, breathing energy into an archive waiting to be activated by the connections uncovered by Báez.

—Adeze Wilford

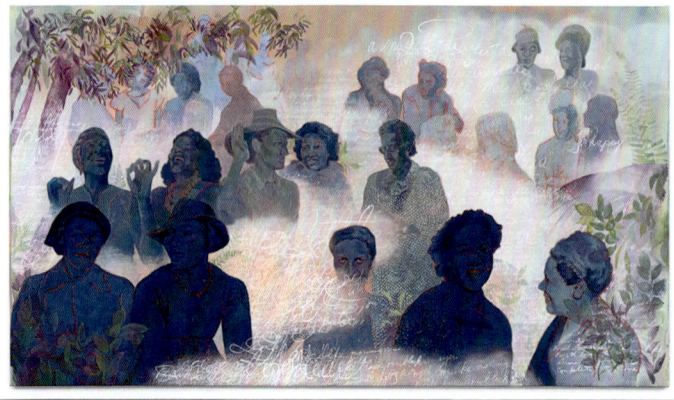

*Elegant gathering in a secluded garden
(or the many bridges we crossed)*, 2018.
Acrylic on canvas, 108 × 192 in.
Museum purchase with funds provided
by the Acquisition Committee
2018.28.1

Cy Gavin
b. 1985

From the painting's edge, you can tell the water is rough today. Cy Gavin's *Untitled (Wave)* challenges you to dive in anyway. Each gestural brushstroke of this composition on denim is a reminder that water can be sharp; it can slap and carve. The painting's large-scale wave obliterates the blurred edge of the horizon. Its churning lines that barrel upward recall standing before the sea. But what comes after the sea is gone? This painted water froths with history, present, and future. It knows the colors of the sea never look quite the same from one breath to the next. It is a red, black, blue, and gray sea sliding in and out, slicing through gravity, horizon, and time. There are millenniums between these layered colors and still just enough time in this composition for one deep breath. Inhale, then the wave meets us with its own open mouth, water everywhere, the abyss. Exhale.

Gavin's practice is connected to a long line of Black artists, gardeners, sailors, farmers, and scientists who have stewarded, preserved, and healed land, sea, and shore. *Untitled (Wave)* is an energetic abstraction and a seascape. The subject of the wave recurs in Gavin's practice. This painting is informed by the time the artist spent in the country of his father's birth, Bermuda. There, he conducted sandy material and archival research, sometimes sleeping in limestone caves along the shore once occupied by the fugitive formerly enslaved. Gavin is as invested in archival documents as oral histories and understands that the indigo-dyed cotton of denim, the cave, the dirt, and the salt water are their own archives.[239] He states: "At times I have felt the land of Bermuda itself to have had anti-colonial designs. Tempestuous weather phenomena and perilous reef systems kept empires at bay until the early seventeenth century."[240] This artwork is in conversation with a lineage of Black transatlantic scholarship and sub-marine poetics that knows sea, sand, and shoal as foundational to creative and resistance practices and that understands landscapes are always political sites.

—Jennifer M. Harley

Untitled (Wave), 2018. Acrylic and gesso on denim, 57 × 92 × 2 in. Gift of Barbara Gladstone 2018.45

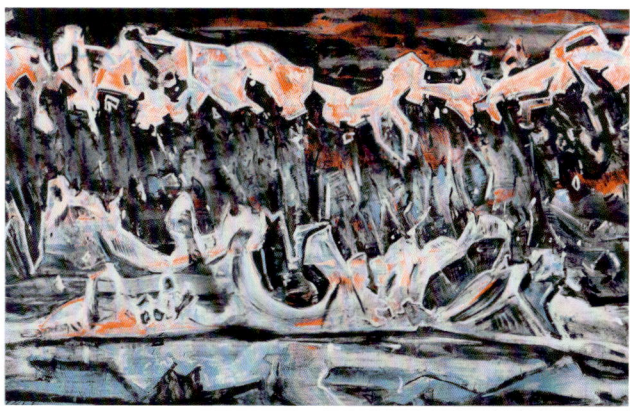

Allison Janae Hamilton

b. 1984   Artist in Residence 2018—19

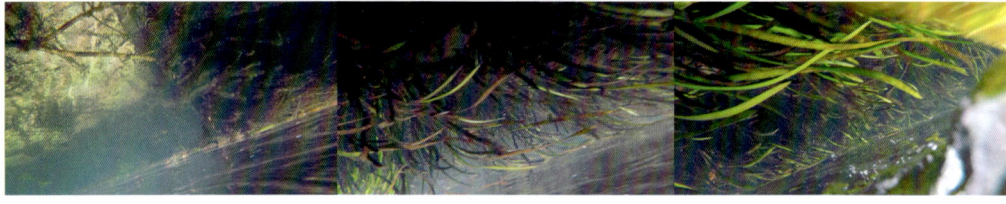

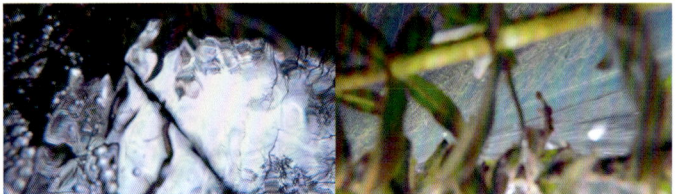

Wacissa, 2019. Single-channel video projection, TRT: 00:22:54. Edition 1 of 5. Museum purchase with funds provided by the Acquisition Committee 2019.22

Allison Janae Hamilton's large-scale video installation *Wacissa* immerses the viewer within a series of human-made rivers in North Florida. These rivers are connected by the region's Slave Canal, named as such for the enslaved people who shaped these pathways to connect Georgia to the Gulf of Mexico via the Florida Panhandle. For this work, Hamilton submerged her camera underwater as she kayaked these rivers capturing the danger and beauty of the currents. The viewer is at the mercy of the water, dragged along upside down past aquatic plants, debris from a recent hurricane, and fallen tree branches. The waterscape—both protagonist and antagonist in this story—captivates, as moments of light shimmer through the currents. It also frightens, as one struggles to resurface. The rising and falling sounds of rushing water further transport the viewer into this at once sublime and terrifying landscape. Although this work is entrenched in a specific local history, Hamilton's exploration of and passage through water links to the Black Atlantic, the transatlantic slave trade, and resulting diaspora across the Americas, Caribbean, and Europe.

Through her multimedia work, Hamilton interrogates how the landscapes of the rural South impact, and are impacted by, the lived experiences of Black people in this region. Born in Kentucky, raised in Florida, with maternal connections to western Tennessee, Hamilton also draws inspiration from the memories, folktales, and traditional Baptist hymns of her upbringing to construct mythic scenes that contextualize the relationships between land and the life it bears. Today's challenges with climate change and environmental justice are just as present in her work as the legacies of displacement, enslavement, and exploitation. At the same time, her appreciation of natural beauty and environmental bounty are ever-present, furthered by her incorporation of found organic materials, such as wood, feathers, bones, and animal hide, into her compositions. Hamilton thereby creates evocative experiences that immerse the viewers in her fantastical and haunting myths.

—Doris Zhao

Tschabalala Self

b. 1990   Artist in Residence 2018—19

A woman's bulbous legs, adorned with slick, black, knee-high stiletto boots, are planted in a wide stance. Her fitted jean shorts accentuate her long stride, which advances toward a secret destination. With one hand on her hip, a sequined purse hooked into her elbow, and the other hand pressing a joint to pursed lips that hover over her shoulder, the subject has secured her most prized possessions for her journey. While the red color field in the figure's background suggests she exists outside of a particular place or time, the Yankees baseball cap and gold hoop earrings act as anchors. It is clear in her stance, her style, and her searing side-eye that she holds a degree of affinity for New York—much like the maker herself. Tschabalala Self was born in Harlem in 1990 and continues to look to the cultural beacon as material for making.[241] At times, as in *Dime*, such material has a greater emotive effect than spatial recognition. Self uses liminality as a device to fore-ground the subject's interiority; as locality markers recede, the subject's physical and sensorial essence take precedence. She is masterful at guiding the viewer's attention along a spectrum of invisible and recognizable spatial markers, but what remains central is the subjects' continual acts of self-realization—and their pleasure in doing so.

Through pose and positioning, Self transfers the once absolute power of the viewer to the subject as a mechanism to upend traditional practices of portraiture. In *Dime*, and across a number of Self's works both painterly and sculptural, she depicts the subject with averted eyes and a turned torso. As bell hooks said of Lorna Simpson's *Waterbearer* (1986), Self also

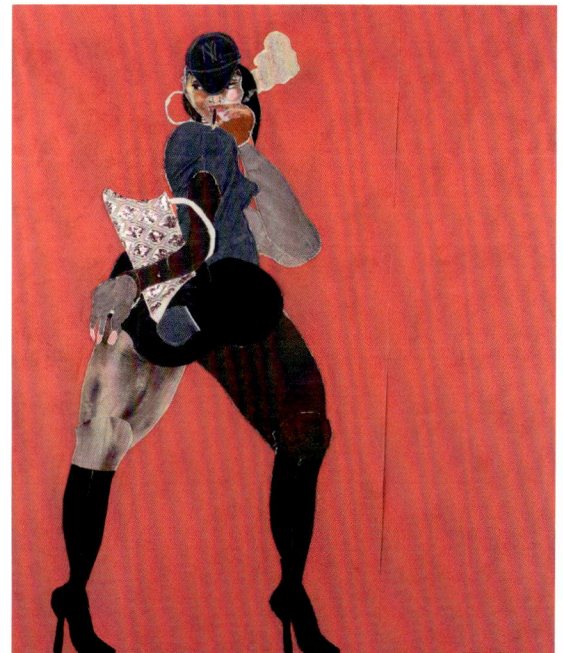

Dime, 2019. Fabric, acrylic, Flashe (vinyl emulsion paint), and painted canvas on canvas, 84 × 72 in. Museum purchase with significant funds provided by Komal Shah and Gaurav Garg and the Acquisition Committee 2019.23

"turns her back . . . on art practices that have been traditionally informed by racist and sexist ways of thinking about both the female image and blackness." By doing so, the artist creates an alternate reality where she is both "self-defining and self-determining."[242] Self has found refuge in the fold where refusal meets reclamation.

This transference of power is also seen in *Entwined*, in which a nude figure (an avatar, as the artist calls them) is accompanied by another figure only partially seen—their limbs rest on the shoulders of the central avatar. The avatar's angular pose suggests an implied movement—she passes through planes and spaces inferred. Just as her limbs fold on themselves, her attention turns inward to enclose her personhood. Though Self's avatars are acutely aware of surveillance, any internalization of visual consumption remains disregarded. Self captures the human body's interstitial movements to further reject posing or fashioning for the delight of the spectator. She asserts it is the viewer who got caught, not the subject.

Akin to the ethos of Harlem, Self's paintings embody kinetic amalgamation in material, form, and concept. She extends her gaze, gumption, and authority to the avatars in her alternate world, where a new imagination of the iconography of Black women materializes. Her imaginings prove vital for a progression toward a collective Black future.

—Jenée-Daria Strand

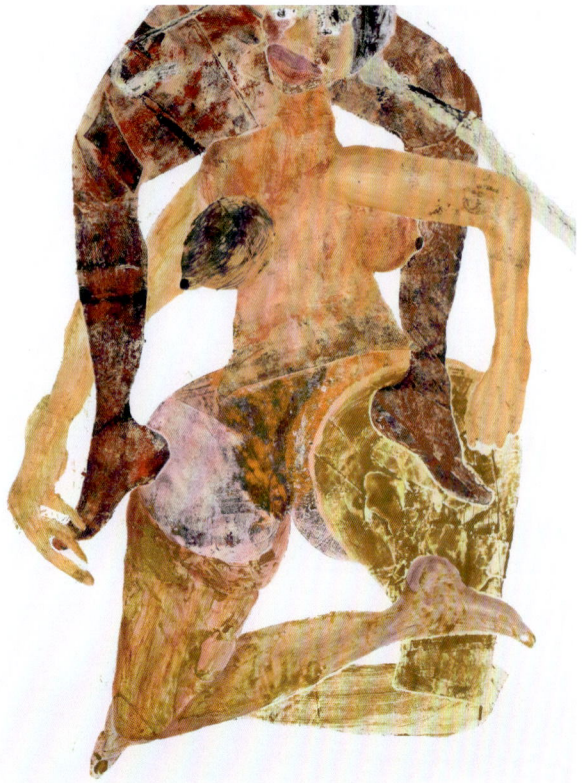

Entwined, 2014. Oil paint and gouache on paper, 49 × 38 in. Bequest of Peggy Cooper Cafritz (1947–2018), Washington, DC, collector, educator, and activist 2018.40.290

Tomashi Jackson

b. 1980

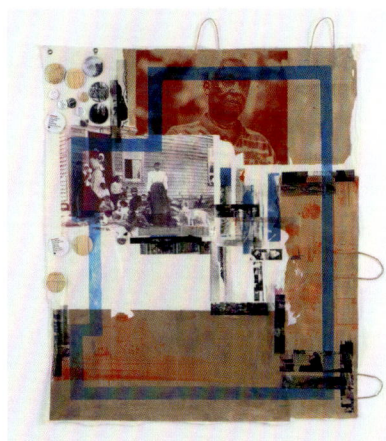

John Brown's Body (Mr. Dorce in Red), 2019.
Mixed media and collage on paper and
muslin, 58 ¼ × 50 ¼ in. Museum purchase
with funds provided by the Acquisition
Committee and John H. Friedman 2020.6

A multimedia artist, Tomashi Jackson strategically uses color theory, material experimentation, and archival research to investigate what she terms in her artist statement as "the selective valuation of human life." Often producing works in series, Jackson critiques institutional racism and its mechanisms by resurfacing and recontextualizing historical ephemera to visualize buried Black stories in their full dynamism and complexity.

In *John Brown's Body (Mr. Dorce in Red)*, Jackson collages layers of buttons, photo transfers, and architectural drawings atop muslin and brown paper bags to tell the story of McConnell Dorce, a Brooklyn homeowner whose properties were seized by the city under the predatory Third Party Transfer program. The work explores the dark nuances of political culture in the United States, such as the government's use of eminent domain to dispossess and displace Black homeowners in New York. Jackson washes Mr. Dorce's portrait in red, a color associated with both love and rage, later painting a thick blue line across his face that could be interpreted as part of a blueprint of Dorce's former home. Here, blue—a color often associated with freedom—subversively frames a broader scene of freedom revoked, including a reproduction of a vintage photograph of a Black family taken in front of their Seneca Village home before being forcibly displaced, alongside other Black property owners, to pave the way for the creation of Central Park in the 1800s.

In both its overt and covert gestures—which includes mention of "John Brown's Body," a folk song and later marching song written in tribute to the famed abolitionist—the work bridges nearly two hundred years of US history, questioning the limits of so-called "freedom" in practice for African Americans. Through its expertly interwoven layers, the work also points to racial identity, collective memory, and dominant histories as social constructs that must be surveyed for gaps, fictions, and outright omissions.

—nico w. okoro

Sable Elyse Smith

b. 1986 Artist in Residence 2018—19

With *Cornering*, multidisciplinary artist Sable Elyse Smith continues her ongoing critical engagement with the insidious violence of the carceral apparatus. Created during Smith's residency at the Studio Museum in Harlem, *Cornering* is a sculpture made of hexagonal tabletop surfaces. Each is hinged and bolted on one side so that together they connect into a new hexagon standing six-feet tall (more precisely, a hexagonal prism, given that the conjoined edges of each table jut outward). The logic of "congenial" punishment is betrayed by the sculpture's angles. Despite a powder coat of soft, if sterile, sky-blue paint, the sculpture's sharp joints and abrupt intervals recall the unyielding angularity of state infrastructures. All attempts at something like a circle—or something like care—are ultimately refused by the lack of smoothness or gentleness of a curve.

Each tabletop hosts a "leg" made of a single steel gray rod that is projected into the interior of the open sculpture and on to which a thinner rod is transversally affixed. On each end of these thinner rods sit small, perfectly round discs that punctuate the sculpture like buttons. In their original context, these discs are meant to be seats; but they too are fastened to each other by metal bars in a paradox of forced attachment and separation. Modeled from the modular units of all-in-one institutional tables found in the inside/outside space of prison visiting rooms, the sculpture ensures that each would-be sitter is disconnected from the next. The bars interrupt any possibility for touch, relation, or intimacy, including with oneself, as the sculpture's labyrinthine interior shows how easily the tables tangle and confuse which legs belong to the human and which belong to the institution. Beyond the choice to title the work with a gerund verb that conjures claustrophobia and the menacing threat of encroachment, the web of seats and their iterative creation of more hexagons reinforces the prison system's vicious echo. In this way, *Cornering* evinces the vexing magnitude of carcerality's deceptively unsentimental, shockingly unexceptional, totally atmospheric system of violence and unfreedom.

—Jakeya Caruthers

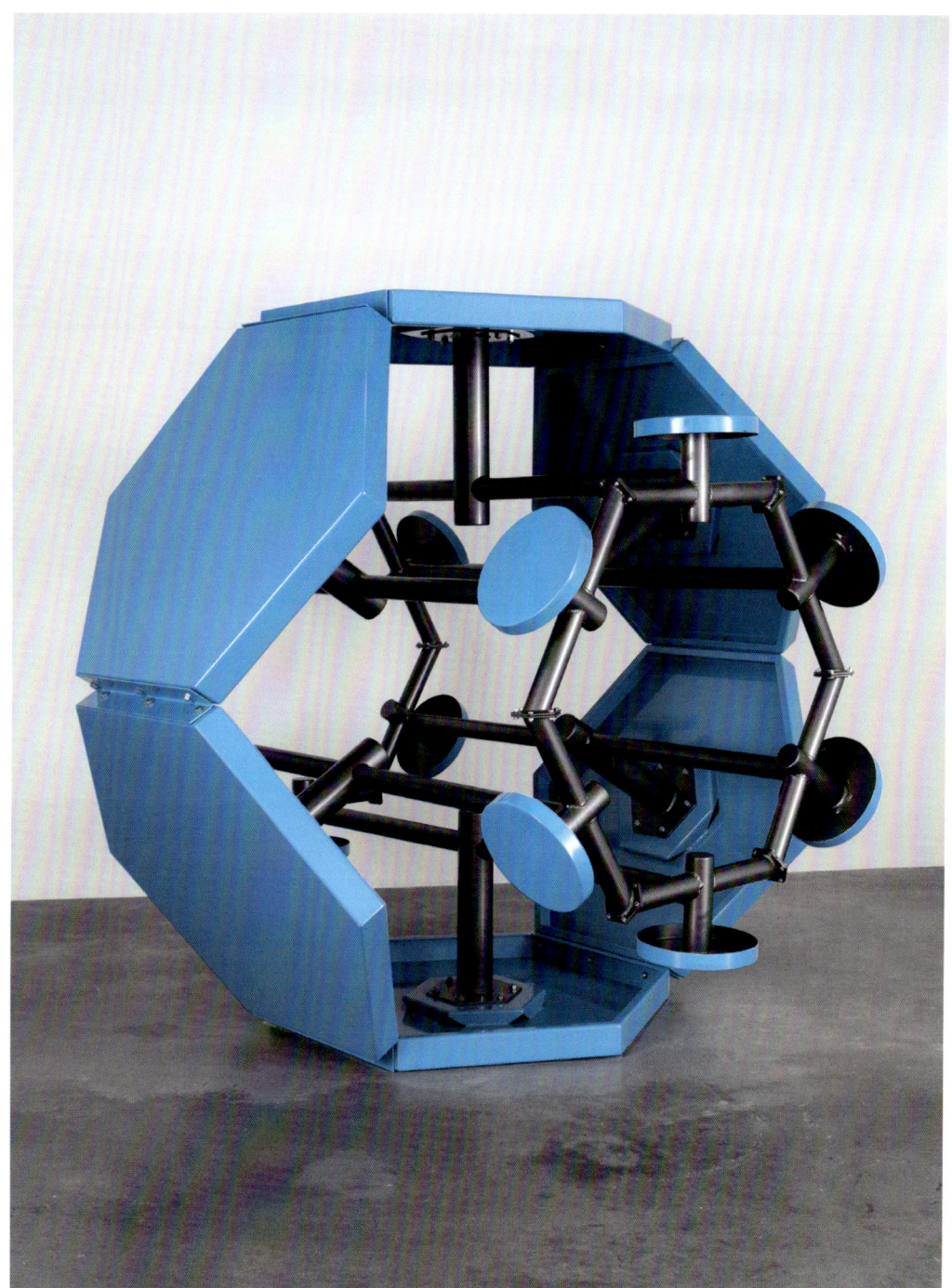

Cornering, 2019. Powder coated aluminum,
75 × 80 × 77 in. Museum purchase
with funds provided by the Acquisition
Committee 2019.24

Deborah Roberts

b. 1962

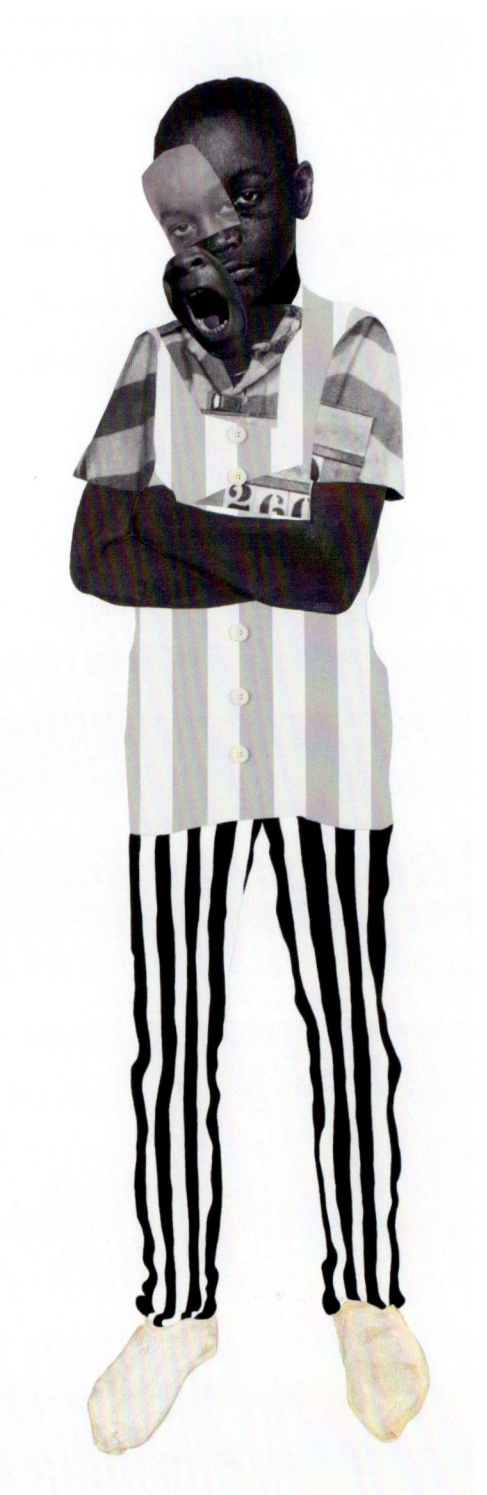

Deborah Roberts constructs singular images of Black girls and boys by integrating found images—mostly black-and-white—with drawings, painted colors, and Pop art patterns set against blank backgrounds. Roberts's *Stinney* is from a series of paintings the artist made in honor of George Stinney Jr., the fourteen-year-old executed by electric chair in 1944 for a murder he did not commit and who remains the youngest person to be executed in the United States. Decades later, the state of South Carolina exonerated Stinney, but his story of injustice and violence emblematizes the deaths of countless Black boys before and since. Roberts recalls being compelled to make this work when she came across Stinney's story: "I didn't want to—I was called to do it," she said.[243]

In this painting, a slim figure crosses his arms and stands to the right edge of the white canvas, a compositional arrangement that intensifies his short height of just over five feet tall. A compelling mix of striped clothing refers to the subject's incarceration (the striped short sleeves and collar come directly from the mugshot) and more broadly indicates the criminalization of Black boys. The most striking elements are the two fragments that overlay Stinney's intense, direct gaze. A smaller set of sienna-tinged eyes covers his right eye as if to place another figure—perhaps a former self—in visual dialogue with Stinney's drawn expression. Such doublings, which recur throughout Roberts's work, speak to her interest in depicting the multiplicity and dimensionality of Black identity. To the left of the figure's face, Roberts has overlaid a fragment of a gaping, or screaming, mouth; its placement powerfully evokes sound projecting into space, a call, shriek, or angry shout. This mouth connects Stinney with contemporary demands for justice and for reforming racist prison and judicial systems in the United States. *Stinney* exemplifies Roberts's figuration of Black childhood as a layered assemblage of images, histories, and ideals. The work negotiates forms of representations as well as what modes of self-representation and self-making are available and accessible for Black youth.

—Anni A. Pullagura and Ruth Erickson

Stinney, 2019. Mixed media collage
on linen, 65 × 45 in. Gift of the artist
2019.26

Jessica Vaughn

b. 1983

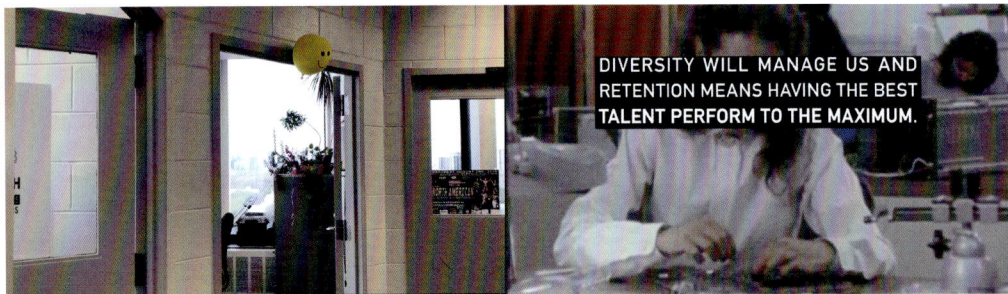

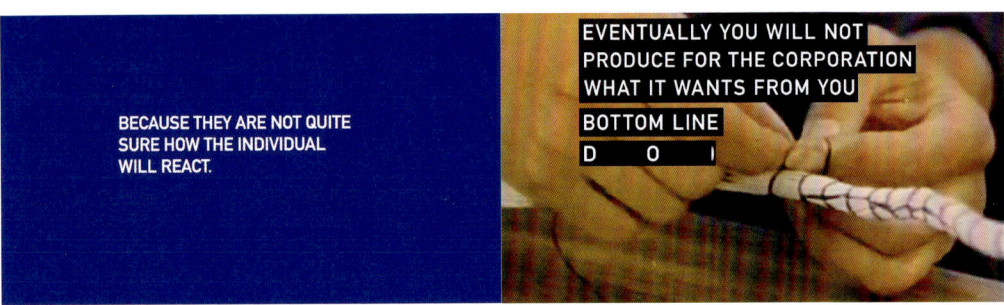

Our Primary Focus Is to Be Successful, 2019.
2-channel, HD video installation, sound,
loop, TRT: 00:07:39. Museum purchase
with funds provided by Martin Eisenberg
and Suzanne McFayden 2020.21

Jessica Vaughn's *Our Primary Focus Is to Be Successful*, a piece charting diversity and equity practices in the workplace, takes on new meanings in the wake of the Supreme Court's decision to strike down affirmative action in 2023. The video installation is a compilation on race, labor, and capitalism in the late twentieth and early twenty-first centuries. Composed of low-fi employee training videos, footage of office spaces taken by the artist, and found text from government occupational reports and diversity training procedures, Vaughn's work serves as a poignant critique on the standardization of people, processes, and architectural spaces.

The diversity and equity practices illustrated in the source material ultimately serve the managerial narrative that hard (and more importantly, *efficient*) work will make a better workforce. The message is maximum diversity, maximum productivity, maximum profit. Yet Vaughn's rearticulation of these materials exposes their promises as falsehoods, undermining the myth that people of color placed in majority-white workplaces can improve the environment without detriment to themselves.

The video also goes after homogenous office culture, incorporating the artist's footage of cubicles, desks, and rooms together with on-screen text outlining Rem Koolhaas's theory of typical architectural plans, a US archetype for standardized office space.[244] Over image and text, the video plays hold music, designed to fill the silence while a caller waits for the next available operator. The tempo of the tinny, milquetoast selections emphasizes procedure, providing a surreal soundtrack for the mundane operations on-screen. Vaughn's work serves as a public service announcement for anyone gulled by the empty promises made by institutions and corporations alike.

——Amber Esseiva

Sanou Oumar

b. 1986

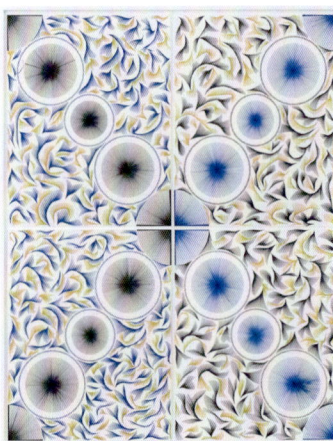

6/5/19, 2019. Pen on paper board in four parts, 87 × 71 ½ in. Museum purchase with funds provided by the Acquisition Committee   2021.13.a–d

For Sanou Oumar, drawing is a daily practice, a devotional act borne out of the artist's experience of displacement as an asylum seeker in the United States. Using simple drafting materials such as pen and paper, Oumar traces the world around him. Popsicle sticks, an ID card, Q-tips, and coins all become formal guides for the artist's intricate abstractions, each made within a single day and titled by its date. Executed without preparation or modification, Oumar's compositions unfold with an automatic virtuosity that renders the spiritual and mundane in equal measure.

As a student at the University of Ouagadougou in Burkina Faso, Oumar admired the university building's tessellated facade—along with other modern structures, including the Central Bank of West African States— noting, "There was nothing missing. I could see all the lines in the building: rectangles, circles, triangles, everything included, each one following its own order."[245] This sense of architecture is present throughout his work: drawings composed of individual, interconnecting marks become a means of interpreting the world through color, line, and form. Recalling a vast range of cultural references such as mandalas, African textiles, and the work of artists Emma Kunz and Bodys Isek Kingelez, Oumar's work defies conventions and instead finds common ground in the meditative and transformative act of making.

The large-scale *6/5/19* comprises four drawings arranged in a grid. Circles descend on a diagonal axis, meeting in cosmic alignment at the four corners in the center. Densely drawn lines radiate from the inky centers of each circle, while blue, gold, and black flourishes dance across the composition. Oumar inscribes his colors, patterns, and forms with personal significance, whether it is an architectural detail he has observed living in New York or the artist's memories of his late mother. Evident in the details is a daily sublime journey.

—Eric Booker

Michael Armitage

b. 1984

In the lead-up to the 2017 general elections in Kenya, Michael Armitage accompanied a local television crew filming an opposition party rally in Uhuru Park, a recreational park in Nairobi, the country's capital and largest city. *The Chicken Thief* is part of a series of works he created inspired by this experience. Here, a gap-toothed man in midstep struggles to hold on to several chickens. Rendered with the barest of brushstrokes, the chickens appear as ghostly apparitions in an otherwise colorful scene. The flaming, monkey-like creature that trails the man becomes the literal "monkey on his back," perhaps hinting at the reason for the man's crime and what he strives to flee from.

Featuring lush colors and soft, often dreamlike passages, Armitage's paintings initially lull viewers into a sense of complacency, only to disrupt any easy reading with compositions that expose the daily lived realities for many in East Africa. This juxtaposition of form and content calls attention to the region's significant disparities in wealth, social mobility, and political power and voice. Armitage's choice of surface, lubugo, a bark cloth traditionally used in ceremonies by the Baganda people of southern Uganda, unsettles the viewer further by bringing a material with deep historical and cultural value into the realm of art. Lubugo, made from the bark of the Mutuba tree or natal fig, features stitched sections and natural imperfections, such as holes. Armitage works with, and often honors, these irregularities, acknowledging the materiality of his painting surface. In using this bark cloth, the artist pushes against the associations with and expectations of canvas for painting, thereby both subverting the traditional hierarchies of the medium and nodding to the geographic specificity of his subjects.

—Connie H. Choi

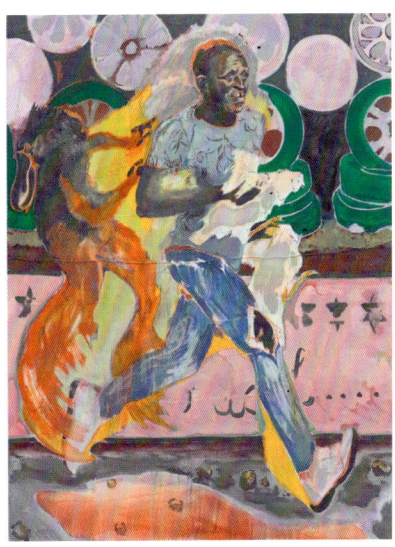

The Chicken Thief, 2019. Oil on lubugo bark cloth, 78 ¾ × 59 ¹⁄₁₆ in. Promised gift of Martin Nesbitt and Anita Blanchard
PG.2021.5

Garrett Bradley

b. 1986

When Garrett Bradley talks about her film *America*, the weight of the title and what she wants the work to—how she wants the work to—enter and shape understanding in visual and sonic registers, she sometimes speaks of the strategies employed by Bert Williams in *Lime Kiln Club Field Day*, "the first feature-length film with an all-Black cast and an integrated production." Williams wore blackface so that the rest of the cast could not. Bradley says that this was an exercise in generosity.[246]

In *America*, a Klan robe taken from its owner becomes a sheet floating above the heads of boys who are playing and running, jumping for and missing it; becomes a bedsheet drying on a line; becomes the object men and women on horseback practice with; becomes the christening gown and the white cloth covering the face of a baptized congregant.

A little girl comes in from school, goes to the table, turns on the radio, puts her head down on her arms. She closes her eyes as a twirling baton signals, and we see a girl in a band uniform twirling two batons. Then baseball players from the Negro League and a little boy at a table adjusting the dials of the radio. They dream.

Bradley's *America* is a twelve-chapter poetic dream of a vision of Black life in deep relation to other filmmakers and photographers, to histories and presents of filmmaking and photography, to movement and sound—Roy DeCarava's *The Sound I Saw* and *The Sweet Flypaper of Life*, Isaac Julien's *Looking For Langston*, Ming Smith's photographs, Julie Dash's *Illusions*, and Charles Burnett's *Killer of Sheep* find their resonance here.

Here in Bradley's particular and perfect grammar is loss, presence, time and rhythm and pacing, practice, solemnity, and joy. Bradley's *America* is also an exercise in generosity. A holding open of a beautifully ordinary "mundane and poetic space."[247] Such joy. What attention.

—Christina Sharpe

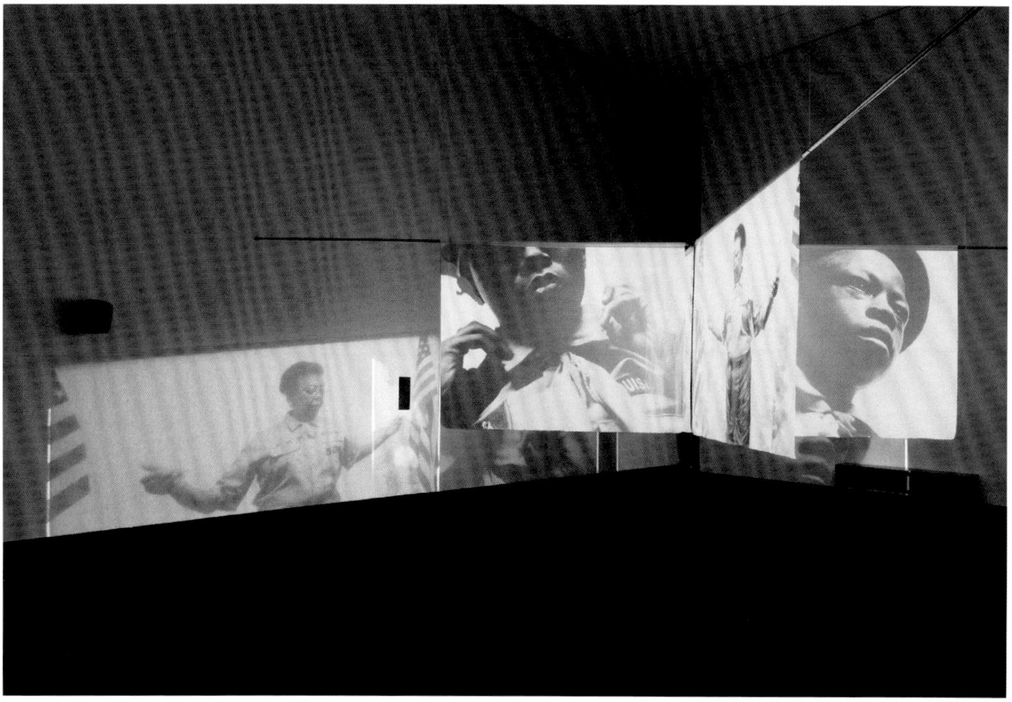

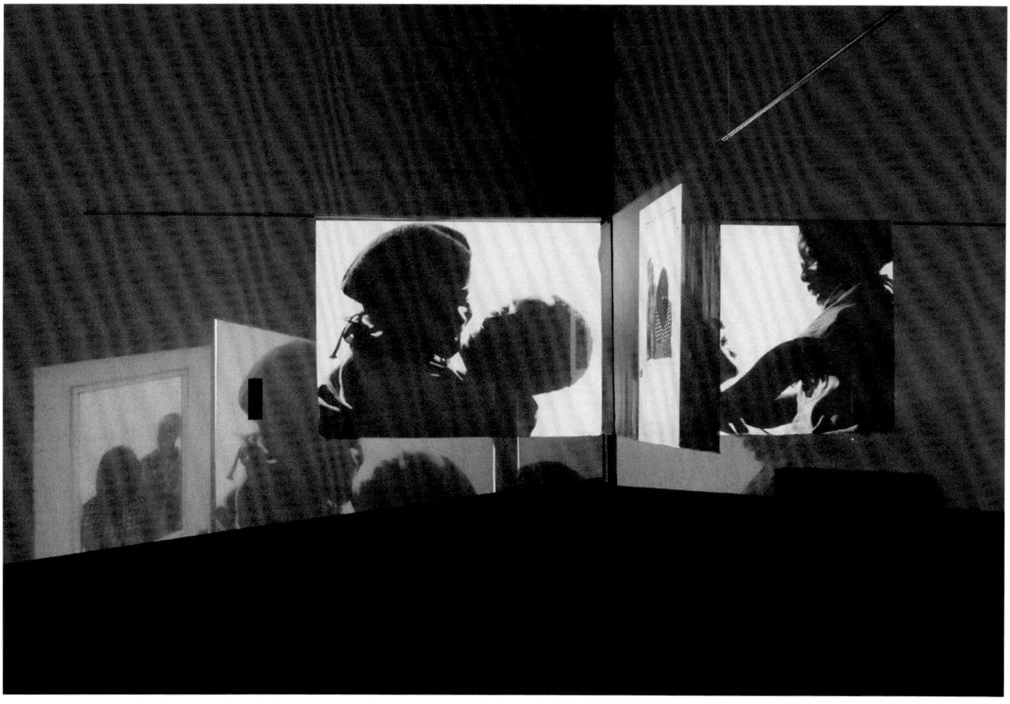

America, 2019. Two-channel video
projection (black and white, sound), TRT:
00:23:55. Studio Museum in Harlem
and the Museum of Modern Art, New
York; purchased jointly by the Museum
of Modern Art, New York and the Studio
Museum in Harlem through the generosity
of an anonymous donor 2023.20.1

KING COBRA

b. 1986

Artist KING COBRA creates visceral sculptures and tattoo design as a form of reclamation to expose and, alternatively, redress the historical violences—and their enduring consequences—enacted on Black women's bodies in the United States. Her practice remains interested in the flesh, often coupling the grotesque with that which shines.

The sculpture *Henrietta: After the Harvest* references the life of Henrietta Lacks. In 1951, Lacks, a young African American mother of five, was undergoing treatment for cervical cancer when her cancer cells were sampled and harvested without her consent at Johns Hopkins Hospital in Baltimore, Maryland. The cells harvested are the source of the "HeLa" cell line, the first immortalized human cell line, which remains widely used in scientific research. *Henrietta: After the Harvest* enshrines Lacks's irradiated cervix in great pink-hued detail to make an alluring spectacle of the site of Lacks's medical exploitation.

Tiny metal pins dot plush layers of coral and salmon foam bounded by prickly barbed wire. Glistening red ribbons of silicone turn gooey black at the sculpture's center. The sculpted organ festers where radiation tubes, like those used in Lacks's treatment, are fixed. Here this marvelous wound is splayed open, compelling viewers to look more closely at an event that much of history has turned to look away from.

—Yume Murphy

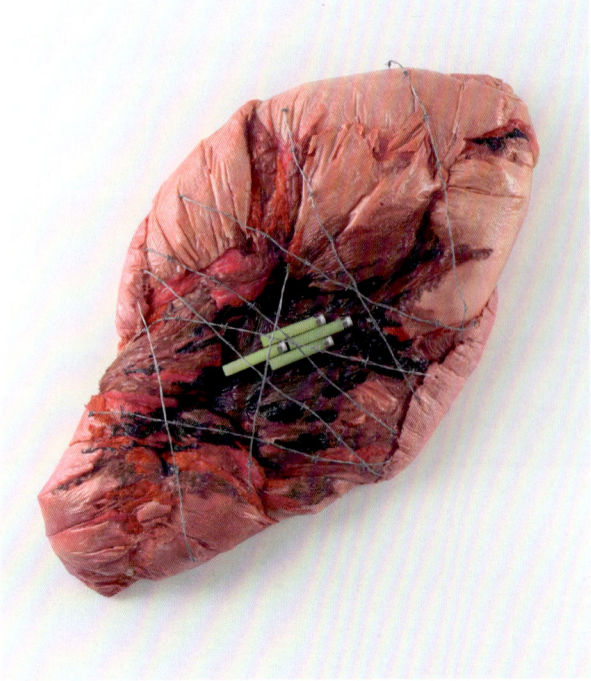

Henrietta: After the Harvest, 2019. Urethane foam, silicone, urethane plastic, steel pins, barbed wire, and glass beads, 71 × 38 × 10 in. Museum purchase with funds provided by the Acquisition Committee, Miyoung Lee, and Charles Boyd 2020.20

Jadé Fadojutimi

b. 1993

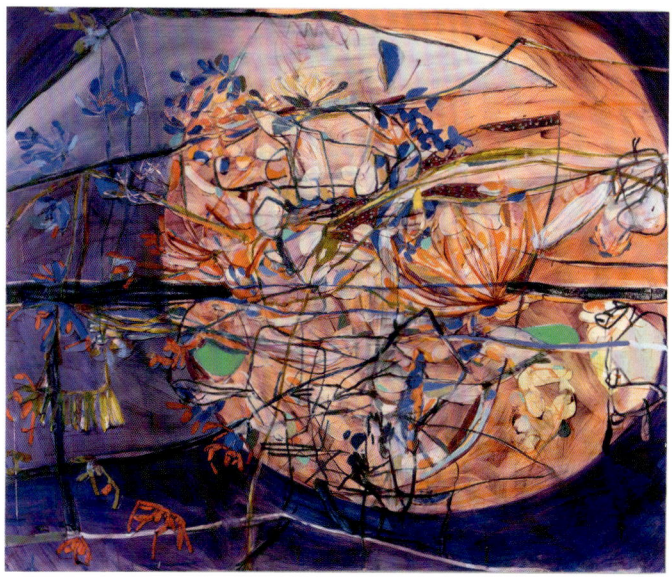

Does a glorious world exist? If that question does not resonate and nothing glorious comes to mind, try to imagine it. It is not the current world, is it? If it were, what would it take to get there, to have it, to breathe it, to feel it— this glory? What would freedom mean in this glorious world? What would it take to get to a place of beauty, abundance, magnificence, and pride? This world, the land imagined—what is its name? Would it need a name? What if its name was the sound of collective joy ringing out at once?

Jadé Fadojutimi's *There exists a glorious world. Its name? The Land of Sustainable Burdens* is an evocative and abstract painting bursting off the canvas with colors as vibrant as fireworks of deep orange, purple, and blue. The colors and hues vibrate in place, like all of the histories, memories, and struggles that vibrate in each person when called upon. The paint layers and marries to reveal this interior world. Fadojutimi is inspired by what is in her studio, flowers she recently bought, and her memories and experiences of this space. Her use of forms and color results from what she sees and feels, which together with her love of poetry and writing, make for an abundance of ideas in this work.

Let us imagine the world she is in when she is painting. What would this world smell like? Would it look like the past or force a contention with an unknown but anticipated future? Imagine touching the oil paint; to stroke its layers might feel like caressing the swaying wheat stalks in a meadow. This land, the land, this hopefully freeing land—what would it take to realize the land of sustainable burdens?

—Ilk Yasha

Diedrick Brackens

b. 1989

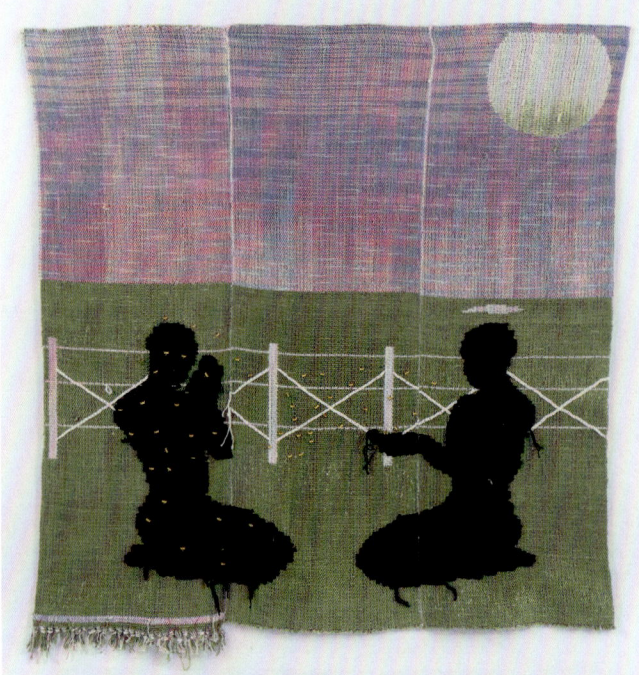

blessed are the mosquitoes, 2020. Woven cotton and acrylic yarn, 82 × 79 in. Museum purchase with funds provided by an anonymous donor, the Acquisition Committee, Amelia Ogunlesi, Patricia Blanchet, Pippa Cohen, Iva Mills, and Lise Wilks 2020.13

In front of a white fence in a green field, two black silhouettes kneel facing one another. Behind them, the moon hangs low and full in the blue and pink sky, bathing the pair in mystic light. Their poses are devotional—one kneels with hands clasped, perhaps in prayer, while the other extends cupped hands, as if ready to receive or give something. Around one, dozens of golden mosquitoes flutter. The scene swells with Southern heat.

Diedrick Brackens's *blessed are the mosquitoes* meditates on history and memory, intimacy and tragedy. The work is woven cotton and acrylic yarn, a choice that speaks to the material history of Black Americans and Brackens himself. His grandmother, from whom he learned to sew, picked cotton as a child in Texas, so works such as *blessed are the mosquitoes* merge the artist's lineage with his practice. Further, the work calls on the extended history of Brackens's identity as a queer Black man. Made in response to staggering reports of the ongoing, disproportionate effects of HIV on Black and Latinx communities, the tapestry literalizes the virus, rendering it as bugs sitting on and buzzing around one of the figures. Brackens avoids passing judgment on this figure, though. One silhouette reaches out toward the other and both perform ritualistic gestures, filling the work with a deep spiritualism echoed by the otherworldly glow that lights the scene. The two bodies coexist, sharing a moment of tender closeness in a moonlit field.

—Simon Ghebreyesus

Chase Hall

b. 1993

Although similar in staging and title to the 1930 Grant Wood painting it references, *African-American Gothic* subverts messages of the original painting, as themes of power and labor—not architecture—are focal points of this portrait of African American life. Hall's signature style comes from his use of coffee as a painting medium throughout his work. He paints with African coffee beans to add a layer of complexity to his representation of Black figures. As he does so, Hall links the exploitation pervasive in the coffee industry to the forced labor that enslaved Black people endured for centuries. The figures in *African-American Gothic* share a lineage with that traumatic history. At the same time, Hall's use of coffee illuminates the figures' resistance in the face of inequality, as the brown hue takes up significant space on the cotton canvas, yet another material reminder of white supremacy.

The pair resists erasure and stereotyping. The two Black figures stand together at the center of an indiscernible rural landscape; both figures return the viewer's gaze. The architectural structures behind them, their clothing, and the accessories they wear tie them to their respective roles. There is a glimpse of a barn in the background behind the man, who wears deep blue overalls and holds a rake. The woman's left hand meets her hip atop her white apron, a symbol of her domestic responsibilities. While the figures' clothing communicates gendered roles, Hall's *African-American Gothic* balances power between the man and woman—they are positioned equally within view and stand on the same ground. This intentional departure from the original composition offers a more nuanced view of the family unit.

—Elana Bridges

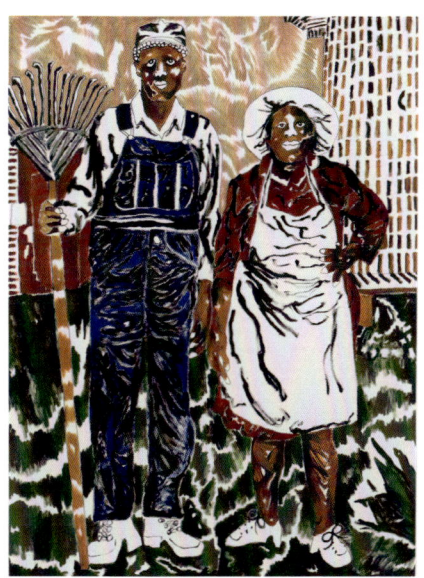

African-American Gothic, 2020. Acrylic and coffee on cotton canvas, 48 × 36 × 1 ½ in. Museum purchase with funds provided by Martin and Rebecca Eisenberg 2020.16

E. Jane

b. 1990   Artist in Residence 2019—20

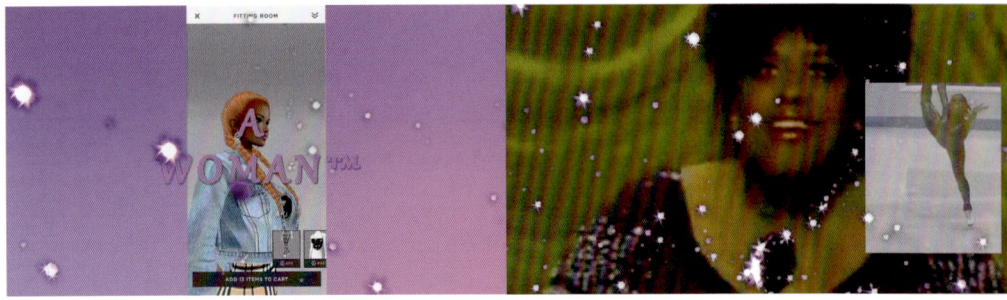

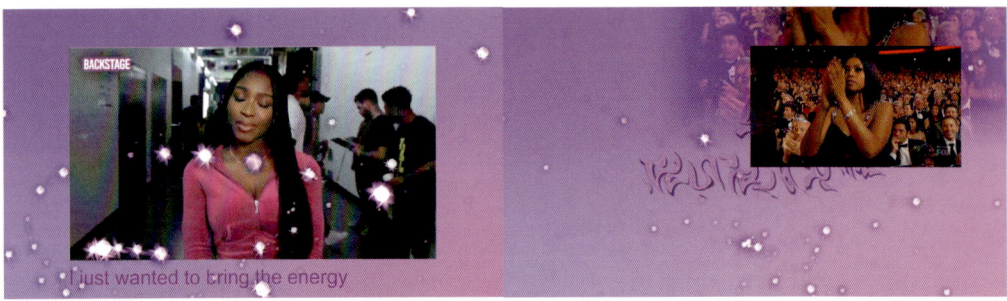

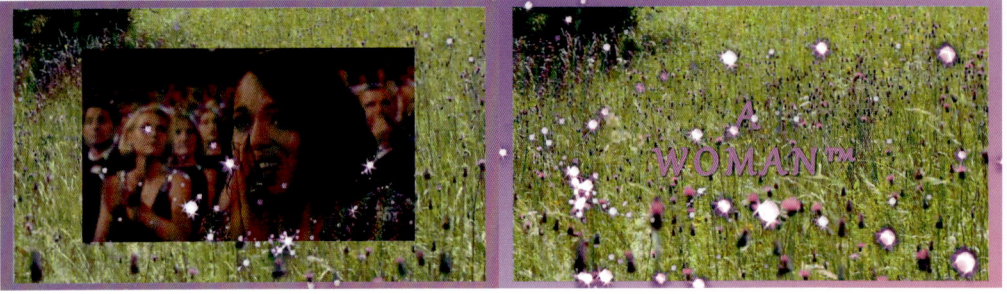

LetMEbeaWomanTM.mp4, 2020. Single-channel digital video, color, sound, fabric, monitor, TRT: 00:06:56. Museum purchase with funds provided by the Acquisition Committee 2021.2

In the video *LetMEbeaWomanTM.mp4*, interdisciplinary artist and musician E. Jane crafts what might be called, after Audre Lorde, a "biomythography"—an exercise in creating a self-fashioned Black femme performance. The Black Diva, specifically the notion of the R & B songstresses of the 1990s, is a central archetype within E. Jane's practice. The artist channels this cultural figure through their persona MHYSA, a diva and underground pop star. The video assembles a playful visual vernacular from found footage of music performances; ice skating routines; interviews; speeches; figures such as Diahann Carroll, Viola Davis, and Jennifer Holliday accepting awards; Summer Walker on Instagram Live; and Laverne Cox interviewed on *Ellen*. E. Jane's honeyed impression of a 1990s R & B ballad scores the piece, which has the formal qualities of the digital baroque: boldly ornamental, theatrical tempos, and a dramatic, layered composition. Overlaid with lavender starbursts, the video creates a queer, Black, divine, virtual terrain on which to situate their devotion to the Black Diva.

E. Jane mobilizes this archetype with the plurality of being and expressions of Black femmes. By actively tracing a genealogy, this video is a historicizing project that exalts a figure whose performance is rarely recognized as a technology of knowing and theorizing. E. Jane has the Black Diva appear in multiple performance arenas in a subtle read of how her figure is almost always in a state of hypervisibility and vulnerable exposure due to the dangers of extreme extraction and consumption. Yet, with care and serious priority, E. Jane sees the Black Diva as an always creatively shifting, consciously and autonomously self-styled being rather than only consumable entertainment.

— Yasmina Price

Naudline Pierre

b. 1989   Artist in Residence 2019—20

Naudline Pierre's dreamlike paintings are imbued with vibrant narratives and rich symbolism. Exalting the Black femme figure, Pierre's work exists within a fictional world that oozes, blends, and transforms, creating portals into the sublime. Through her practice, Pierre gestures toward a vision of that which has not yet been seen and engages imagination as an instrument of survival.

In *A Source of Power,* the central figure has three sets of wings—on its head, back, and ankles—a departure from her previous paintings with a new character within her worldbuilding. Hovering in a bed of silhouetted flames and fortified by the embrace of cherub-like characters, the ethereal central figure exudes both vulnerability and strength. Pierre's work provides sanctuary and invites explorations into the depths of spirituality and humanity. The angelic being, with its fur-covered chest and black wings that arch off its back and turn inward in a protective enclosure, transcends simple binaries and refuses legibility. A conduit to another realm, it is at once tender and fierce in its infinite potential.

Evident in this work is Pierre's adept use of color, which cascades from crimson red into a luminous neon yellow. Created during her time as an artist in residence at the Studio Museum, this painting builds on a body of work that explores the symbolism of fire (and, elsewhere, water) in Black history. Pierre grapples with how fire is used for burning and destruction by reclaiming the flame as both a source of power and mode of rebirth.

Pierre's paintings explore the resistive acts of care and trust. They are encounters with an expansive world, wherein Black femme celestial beings hold on to one another, extending limb, heart, and soul as either ancestor, angel, or avatar. In doing so, this work prompts consideration of what potential for healing emerges when one is pushed to the edge of possibility.

— Yelena Keller

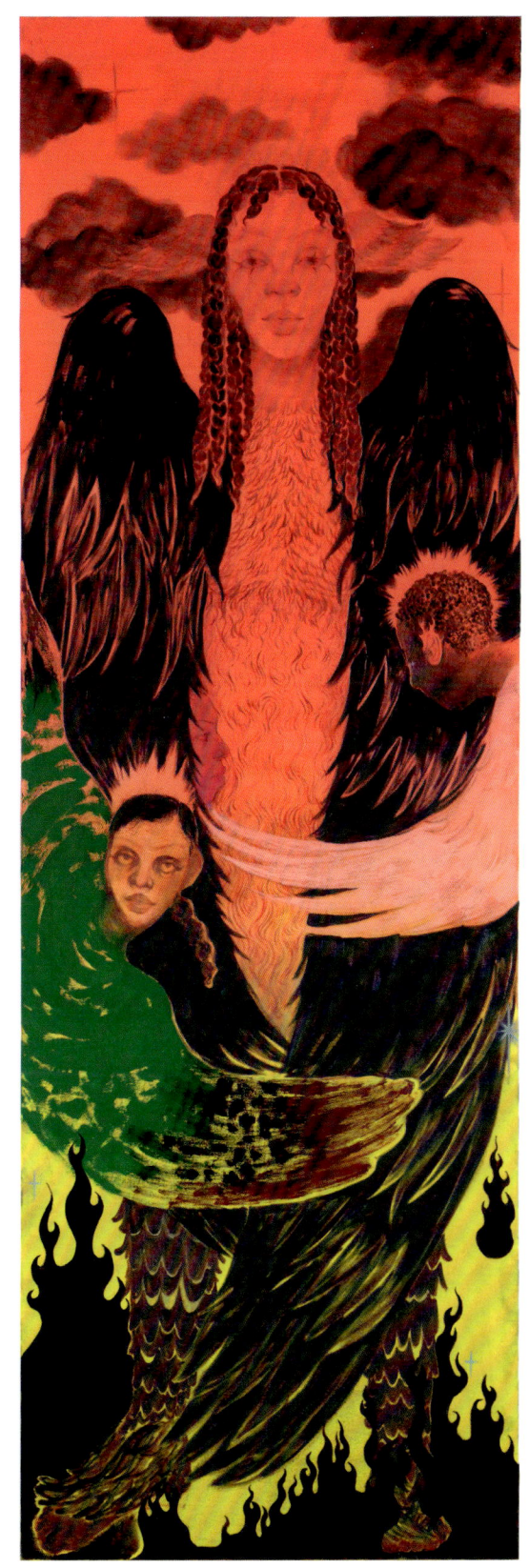

A Source of Power, 2020. Oil and acrylic on canvas, 108 × 36 in. Museum purchase with funds provided by the Acquisition Committee, Komal Shah and Gaurav Garg, Suzanne McFayden, Frank Ahimaz, Lise and Jeffrey Wilks, Godfrey Gill, and Martin M. Hale Jr. and Philippa Lord 2021.5

Elliot Reed

b. 1992   Artist in Residence 2019—20

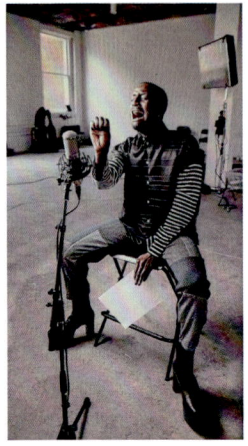 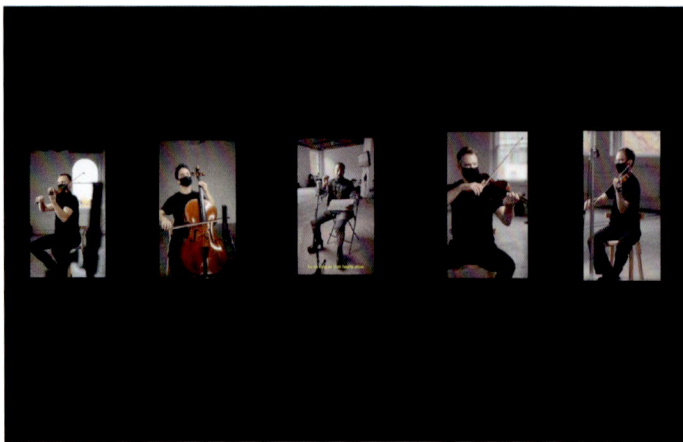

Supernumerary (L: detail, film still; R: installation view), 2020. Five-channel video with sound, performed with JACK Quartet, TRT: 00:24:06. Edition 1 of 1 + 2 APs. Museum purchase with funds provided by the Acquisition Committee 2021.6

Elliot Reed works in performance, video, and sculpture to examine how the body—both as a corporeal being and a collective entity—is a central component within systems of power and subjugation. "Time is my material," the artist states, "and my embodied self is the medium."[248] In 2014, Reed established Elliot Reed Laboratories, a conceptual production office located in their body that holds a copyright with the Library of Congress and a business license with Los Angeles County.

Reed's *Supernumerary* is a five-channel video and sound installation featuring the artist performing alongside the Brooklyn-based JACK string quartet, with each performer contained within individual screens. Sitting in front of a microphone, Reed begins their performance making an array of guttural sounds, groans, slurps, and other noises before stopping to read aloud their written text, "In an Attempt To . . . " The text recounts the stories of Gemmel Moore and Timothy Dean, two Black gay men murdered in West Hollywood by former Democratic party donor and businessman Ed Buck, a white man. Throughout their monologue, Reed periodically conducts the quartet—comprising four white men—as they play sequences of sustained chords both harmonious and cacophonous, as well as brief interjections of Katy Perry's "California Gurls." *Supernumerary* situates Moore and Dean's deaths within a larger history of racialized violence, abuse, and exploitation. As a Black queer person, Reed also reflects on their own position within this matrix of racial and sexual power, using their body as a proxy or vessel through which Moore and Dean's memory survives.

—Adria Gunter

Elliott Jerome Brown Jr.

b. 1993

In this evocative ode to everyday gestures, two seated people embrace at a table. Held within a tight shot focused across a large depth of field, the enclosed, elliptical force of the embrace is echoed by the knuckled hold on the arm of a chair. The closeness of the frame allows the eye to roam across cartographies of information. Affixed to the underside of the table is a gold number-six birthday candle, colored-in outlines, and words on printed pages. The embraced sitter wears glasses. The sitter embracing has an ear gauge the same hue as a colored-in character's hair. The table reveals itself as the border between two worlds. The play space of a child is being intruded on; the table's apron and the orthogonal arm of the embraced sitter form a balanced, if offset, bridge. The more we look, the more we see that this is a work concerned with holding, being held, and the holding (out) of hope.

In an expansive photography practice informed by assemblage, cinema, collage, performance, poetry, sculpture, and social media, Elliott Jerome Brown Jr. continues to refine strategies for negotiating the frame of the pic-ture plane. In the artist's experimental mise-en-scènes of Black and queer intimacy and vulnerability, the viewer sees a rigorous technician at work. Employing a tool kit of Dutch-, high-, and low-angled shots; multiple light sources; theories of color; and a plethora of surfaces and textures, Brown pulls information from the periphery of a photograph into a saturated, active center that demands prolonged engagement.

It is through Georges Braque, Jasper Johns, Deana Lawson, Lorna Simpson, and Carrie Mae Weems that we can trace Brown's hermeneutics of atten-tion to both geometries of dimensional forms and the refusal to let the margin stay settled. In a 2020 interview with *W*, Brown reflects: "Working with the margins at first grew out of a political positioning, recognizing that the margin is an important way to read the center. And what's held at the margin—there's a lot of power there."[249]

—Horace D. Ballard

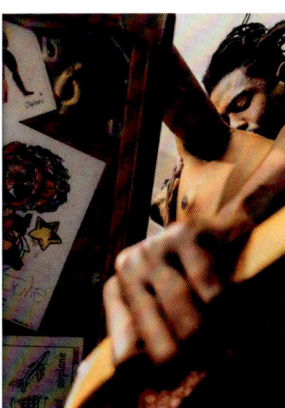

I want to impress leaves on paper with colors they could only know there, where cherries blossom in jacaranda blue., 2020. Archival inkjet print, 40 × 30 in. Museum purchase with funds provided by the Acquisition Committee 2021.12

Rachel Eulena Williams

b. 1991

Rachel Eulena Williams works between painting and sculpture. Her intuitive and improvised compositions are hand-glued, often stitched and sewn, knotted together, and always painted. The artist begins her multimedia process with drawings and then searches for objects that can fill the shapes of her sketched marks and lines. *Orange Blood* is a large-scale work made up of four focal yet opposite circles, unraveling accretions of ropes and knots, and curved edges that seem to rotate like a supple pulley system. The metal wires the artist uses to create her lines expand into armature for the cut canvases that she later sews into the work. The chromatic fields of color (vibrant yellows, oranges, whites, purples, and blues that call upon her time spent growing up in Miami) and scattered symbols within this reconfigured canvas create depth and allow the material to sink both into gravity and into the flatness of the wall.

Williams's interest in repetition emerges continually (although subtly) in the ways she paints the backside of her works—fluorescent pigments reflect the light on to the wall, haloing each element of the work. Her assemblage-like practice echoes artists such as El Anatsui, Al Loving, Howardena Pindell, and Betye Saar, who transgressed aesthetic conventions of abstraction to give new meanings to collage. Consider even Joan Miró's hand-knotted wool tapestries, which are both two- and three-dimensional. Williams's webbed layers hold form by way of the artist's own performance of abstraction: an act of gathering and placement that imbues different actions and embedded histories into her material choices.

—Angelique Rosales Salgado

Orange Blood, 2020. Acrylic paint and dye on canvas, panel, and cotton rope, 60 × 98 × 3 in. Museum purchase with funds provided by the Acquisition Committee 2021.15

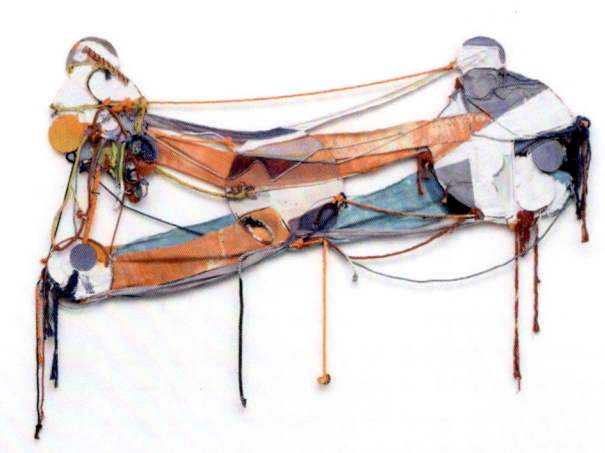

Nate Lewis

b. 1985

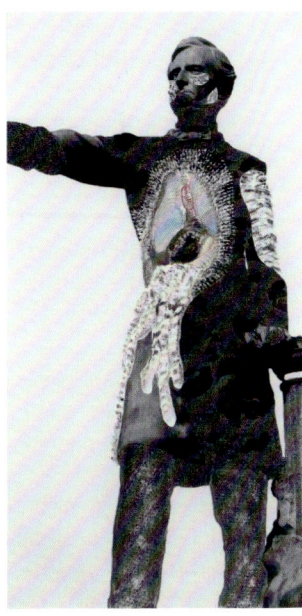

For nearly a decade, Nate Lewis worked as an intensive care unit nurse in Washington, DC. This experience with the human body and medical diagnostic tools, such as X-rays, CAT scans, and electrocardiograms, informs Lewis's practice. Through his mixed-media works that intersect photography, sculpture, drawing, and embroidery, he examines his subjects to investigate the vital functions of their being and surrounding contexts. Lewis has described his process as "clinical"—with surgical precision, he slices the surfaces of inkjet prints and grafts in motifs and patterns to evoke cells, internal organs, or topographic anatomy. With these additions, Lewis symbolically assesses the health and values of his subjects.

The 2019—21 "Probing the Land" series comprises nine distinct works all created during an unprecedented period of a pandemic, hostile politics, and the resurgence of right-wing groups throughout the United States. Lewis photographed statues of Confederate officers that formerly stood along Monument Avenue in Richmond, Virginia. In *Probing the Land VII*, Lewis incises a photo of a monument of Jefferson Davis—the first and only president of the Confederate States—that was removed in 2020 by protestors against systemic racism and police brutality. Lewis acknowledges the living significance of this inanimate monument and its embodied violence. He uses graphite, ink, and paper cutouts in toothlike patterns to expose the statue's lungs, muscles, and internal organs as a method of diagnosis. As if in a search for an infection or poison, his cuts and additions turn this bronze object into vulnerable flesh. The artist's investigative process is rational and precise—his aim is to expose what is broken or ill.

—Doris Zhao

Vaginal Davis
b. 1969

Found paper. Hamamelis Wasser with Mandrake. Henbane and Datura. Hydrogen peroxide. Glycerine. Watercolor pencils. Discontinued over-the-counter medicine, including Anacin and Lydia E. Pinkham Health Tonic. Coconut oil. Nail polish. Enamel. Perfume. Aqua Net Extra Strength hairspray.

The list of non-art stuff that Vaginal Davis used to make her drawing *Nella Larson* seems comprehensive. The dozen-plus items account for materials in both English and German (Hamamelis Wasser is German for witch hazel) and even include a strength of hairspray: Extra. And yet, Davis leaves off some of the information constituting the work. Beneath the figure's bust, for example, is the name of the Geneva hotel that lent its pad of paper as support to the drawing: the Hôtel Adriatica, named for a sea approximately ten hours away by car from the Swiss city. Embedded in Davis's small painterly gestures are the nail-polish brush fibers she used to apply the pigments, as well as a longer strand of black hair.

Let's narrate the list of materials she used to make the drawing as an order of operations: Check into a hotel room. Order yourself some room service. Bring what you need with you, poisonous nightshades included. Get your hair and nails done. Finish with a spritz of scent.

Now, let's turn the list of materials she used to make this drawing into a biography—to describe the process of constructing an image; to describe the person who created the picture. The nail polish—in Davis's hand, in the hotel room—gives the figure her red hair. The drawing is titled *Nella Larson*, after the novelist who wrote *Quicksand* (1928) and *Passing* (1929); her name is creatively respelled in the artwork title. Though Larsen did not have red hair, Irene—the light-skinned Black woman who animates *Passing*, Larsen's story of racial dissimulation—is *Irene Redfield*. The color and its cognates recur in the book: Red arch. Red gown. Red lips. A flame of red and gold. Geranium red. Dusky red. Mahogany-colored. Rose-colored. Reddened. Colored. The red one. Isn't it a dream?

—Thomas (T.) Jean Lax

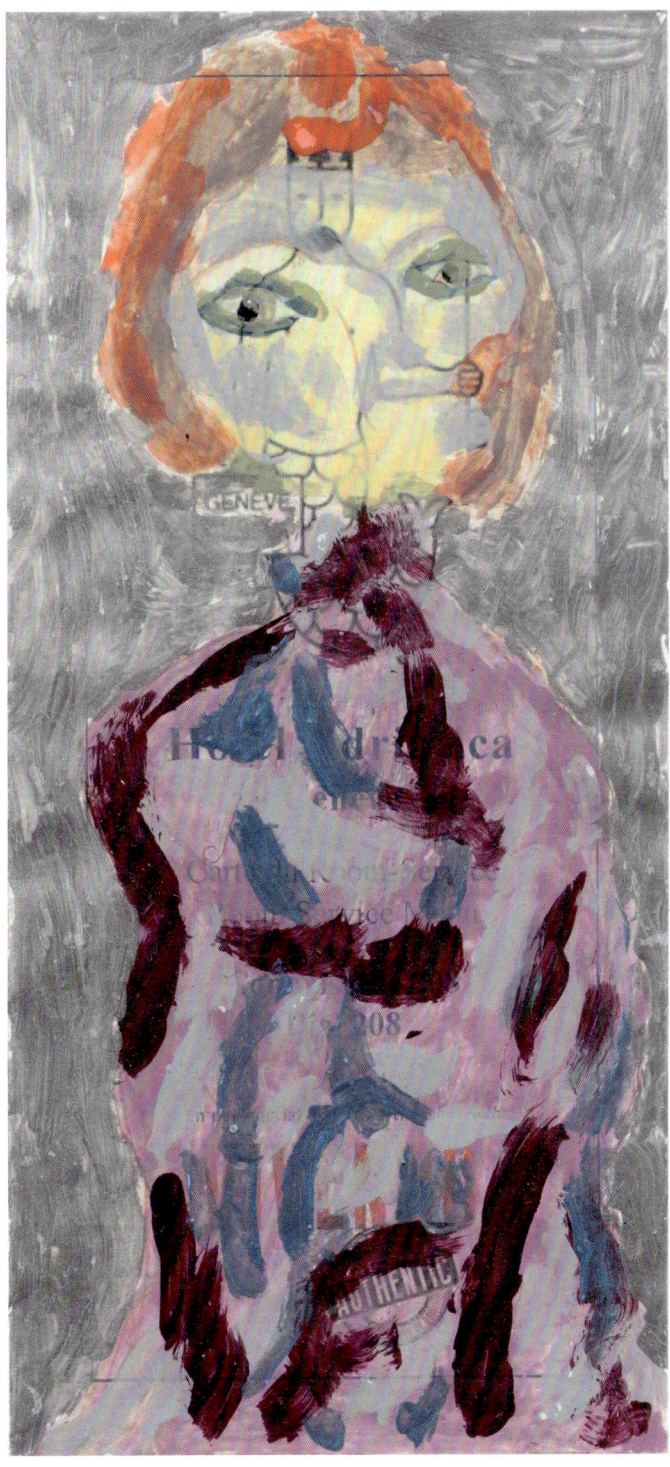

Nella Larson, 2020. Found paper, Hamamelis Wasser with Mandrake, Henbane and Datura, hydrogen peroxide, glycerine, watercolor pencils, discontinued over the counter medicine including Anacin, Excedrin, and Lydia E. Pinkham Health Tonic, coconut oil, nail polish, enamel, perfume, and Aqua Net Extra Strength hairspray, 7 ⅞ × 3 ⁹⁄₁₆ in. Gift of Burton Aaron 2023.22.1

Andile Dyalvane

b. 1978

Andile Dyalvane's contemporary ceramic sculptures are inspired by a deep spiritual tie with his Xhosa ancestors. Born in the Xhosa village of Ngobozana in the Eastern Cape province of South Africa, Dyalvane first trained at the Sivuyile Technical College in Gugulethu, a Black township in the Western Cape province of South Africa. In 2003, he obtained a national diploma in ceramic design from the Nelson Mandela University. "The minute you touch clay," the artist says of the life-affirming material, "you are open to the energies and ready to receive . . . . That's how powerful clay is as a medium of healing, as restoring."[250] Clay grounds him to the earth and ancestral practices. With the medium, he chronicles his personal life and honors his Xhosa heritage. A 2019 residency at Leach Pottery studios in the United Kingdom inspired the artist to further push his creative boundaries by incorporating an expanded repertoire of forms and making his clay vessels more sculptural.

uBuhlanti (Kraal) is a key work from the groundbreaking "iThongo" series, which the artist created during Covid-19 lockdowns in 2020. "iThongo," meaning "ancestral dreamscape" in Xhosa, comprises eighteen handmade low terracotta stools. Each stool is based on a glyph from a pictographic system invented by the artist that represents words that describe aspects of Xhosa life. Dyalvane embeds this symbolic language and cultural memory in the objects. For *uBuhlanti (Kraal)*, he takes his design cue from the rounded form of a traditional South African kraal, or cattle hut. The back rest is suggestive of thorn bush branches of the kraal enclosure. The seat takes the shape of a cow's large femur, and its textured surface is suggestive of dried animal dung. Glaze drips from the lower edges of the seat to the terracotta underbelly. The aesthetic appeal of *uBuhlanti (Kraal)* overshadows its otherwise utilitarian function.

—Smooth Nzewi

uBuhlanti (Kraal) (from the series "iThongo"), 2020. Earthenware, 24 ½ × 41 ¾ × 26 ½ in. Gift of Ann Tenenbaum and Thomas H. Lee 2022.16

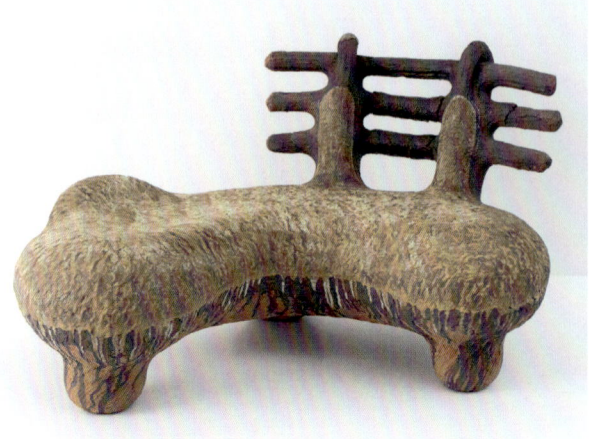

Moshekwa Langa

b. 1975

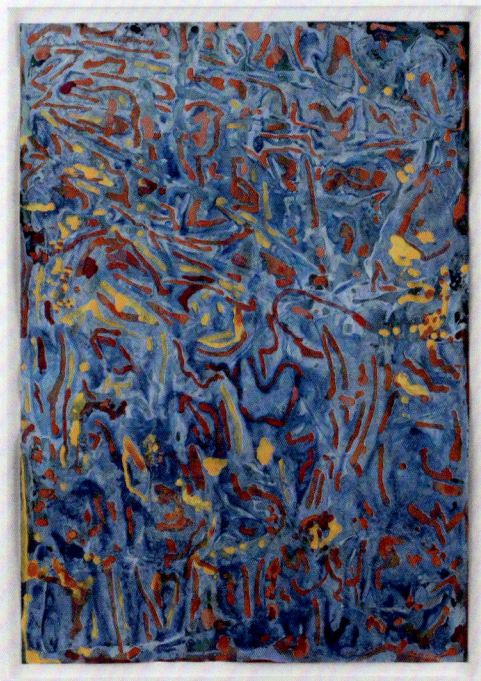

The pond, 2020/2021. Mixed media on paper, 55 ⅛ × 39 ⅜ in. Museum purchase with funds provided by Martin and Rebecca Eisenberg 2022.14

The pond has a linear embodying structure that is present in much of the installation work that Moshekwa Langa has made over the years—from the profound *Temporal Distance (With Criminal Intent). You Will Find Us in the Best Places*, first seen in Okwui Enwezor's Second Johannesburg Biennale in 1997, to the sublime *The Sweets of Sin*, which was on view at the Andrew Kreps Gallery in November 2021. The lattice-like structure that Langa embeds in *The pond* builds the space of color. In this work, color is made up primarily of red and yellow resting on a background of blue; this in turn sets up an emotive and contemplative condition within the picture space. When looking closer, it is intriguing to see how Langa's hand responds to the tactility of the paper surface. One can experience the quickness of thought in his marks and strokes on the painted surface. The colors selected are of a specific and distinct choice in this painting. Langa is not just utilizing the primary color scheme of red, yellow, and blue; rather, he is making concise decisions about where the color and marks are placed. Langa paints blues on to blues to deepen the space with a voluminous quality of light—a low yet intense light accented with a section of golden-yellow among an overall arrangement of muted red and orange brushstrokes that intensifies the richness of the blue. *The pond* can be seen as a reflection into an abyss that remains forever undefined, and a space of wonder to contemplate and experience the spectacle and glory that resides within.

—Odili Donald Odita

Julie Mehretu

b. 1970   Artist in Residence 2000—2001

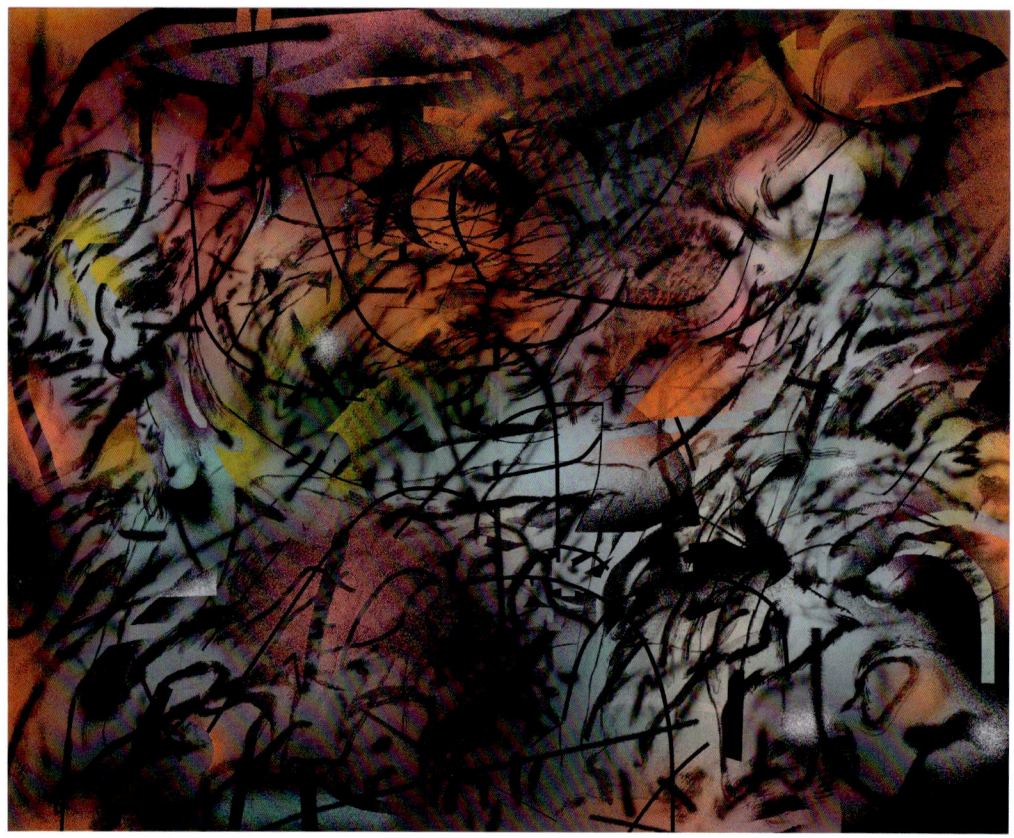

Among the Multitude VI, 2020—22. Ink and
acrylic on canvas, 48 × 60 × 2 in. Promised
gift of Komal Shah and Gaurav Garg
PG.2022.3

Among the Multitude VI is one in a suite of nine abstract paintings by Julie
Mehretu that exudes the collective chaos, grief, confusion, and panic
from the global crises of 2020 to 2022. More intimate in scale than the
larger canvases she is best known for, *Among the Multitude VI* evokes
a window to the exterior world, like the windows from which we peered
out upon deserted streets—interrupted frequently by loud sirens and
flashing lights of ambulances—during the Covid lockdown and the visual
cacophony of television-screens and devices repeating news footage and
images of crowded hospitals, masked protesters, and death toll reports.
As citizens, we remained trapped in a version of the Cretan labyrinth. *Among
the Multitude VI* reflects a destabilized confrontation with an experience
of interiority, with the markings on the surface of the canvas reminiscent
of an MRI image detecting old markings of trauma on the brain.

Mehretu has perpetually turned to the history of painting, literature, and
belief systems to understand and incorporate divergent languages and

to underscore how human conflict, tragedy, borders, and communities comprise civilization. Whether Greek mythology, petroglyphs, Chinese calligraphy, tattoo design, airport maps, or architectural grids, she has channeled myriad modalities, structures, and forms in her abstractions. Since 2016, she has been employing blurred and cropped photographs of global crises and conditions as starting points for her canvases. Recirculated news images, such as the deadly California wildfires and the burning by security forces of the Rakhine State in Myanmar, for example, made their way into *Hineni (E. 3:4)* (2018). An image of police in riot gear during the aftermath of the murder of Michael Brown vibrates under the layers of paint in *Conjured Parts (eye), Ferguson* (2016). Mehretu's gestural abstraction—which includes washes of color, airbrushing, digital spray screenprints, and ink marks—amplifies and disables the incomprehensibility these photographs consider as they exist simultaneously within and outside our bodies and consciousness like a nightmare that lingers into wakefulness or a social media feed that persists in a dream state.

The photographic foundation of *Among the Multitude VI* is of EMT workers during the lockdown in full protective gear, akin to silver astronaut spacesuits, captured wheeling a stretcher across a blockaded street, with lights flashing in the background. Mehretu was interested in the apparitions created by the ghostly figures in this photograph. The painting's colors—orange, fuchsia, white, black, and hospital-scrubs green—vibrate with a catastrophic and transformative energy. The palette, recalling alerts or alarms according to Mehretu, also conjures the twelfth canto of Dante's *Inferno*, the first of three sections of his fourteenth-century epic poem *Divine Comedy*, in which Dante and the poet Virgil journey through hell, purgatory, and heaven. In this canto, the powerful yet demonized Minotaur, a mythical half-bull, half-man creature, guards the layer of hell reserved for perpetrators of violence, patrolling the souls immersed in the river of blood. In *Among the Multitude VI*, the Minotaur—said to represent our "primal fear of the unknown, deeply seated in the human psyche"—coalesces with the fear, anxiety, threat, and confusion of the early days of the pandemic.[251]

—Christine Y. Kim

Reggie Burrows Hodges

b. 1965

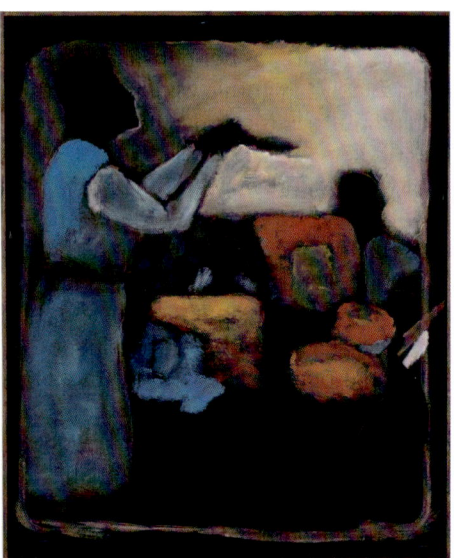

Community Appreciation: Symphony, 2020.
Acrylic and pastel on linen, 61 ⅞ × 51 ⅞ in.
Gift of Martin and Rebecca Eisenberg
in honor of Thelma Golden 2022.19

Set against a black matte background overlaid with a foggy, golden hue, a poised figure stands in profile, mid-movement. The figure is dressed in blue, wand raised in hand. A group of individuals—rendered with no defining features and soft shapes boldly painted in red, orange, and blue—awaits the leader's instruction. A thin gold outline surrounds the full composition, which sharpens the otherwise dreamlike haziness of the picture. With prolonged viewing of the canvas, bodies and shapes make themselves known as a conductor and musicians performing a symphony.

Reggie Burrows Hodges's *Community Appreciation: Symphony* uses space to help a narrative take form. Starting with a raw canvas painted in all black, Hodges's scene materializes as bodies, faces, and shapes emerge from the background. Forms expressively painted with vivid, bleeding colors add an ethereal quality to the otherwise heaviness of the painting. Connected by the voluminosity of the blackness, these figures bring the feelings, memories, and emotions that give a story life. Breaking away from the idea that black space is inherently a void, the space in this work is instead a foundation for connections that unite a composition.

With an educational background in theater and film, Hodges is an expert in the power of using environment and setting as the foundations for developing a story. This scene appears as if it is a fragment of a memory shrouded in a forgetful haze. The space that gives life to the symphony also leaves the viewer to determine if this is the beginning, middle, or end of the concert.

—Shanna Kudowitz

Jonathan Lyndon Chase

b. 1989

The universe-bending, time-come-to-a-halt, don't-know-up-from-down energy that comes with having a crush will have you step out of your body and work up the courage to do just about anything. Maybe even gently ask someone to sleep over after dinner. Jonathan Lyndon Chase's *Sleep Over after Dinner* has all the cinematic qualities of a tender love story I want to watch.

At the tail end of a sweet summer evening, the charcoal in the grill crackles and the music thumps. You've been hanging with your friends all day. An afternoon barbecue turns into a nighttime fete, as we finally (maybe) cool off from the heat. It is in this respite that we remember how generous summer can be. We're so present. Shirts off. Sweat. Skin. Friendship. Love. The last of the dishes are coming out, even though we're all so full, but the ribs were marinating for hours so we must reap our reward for patience. You see them—your crush—tidying up the table to make room and decide to help, which doubles as a reason to keep flirting.

You stack dirty plates.
You make eye contact.
They tell you they love the song that's playing.
You tell them you do too.
You turn up the volume.
They start to dance.
You both dance.
You giggle and laugh.
You embrace.
You work up the courage to ask, "Sleep over after dinner?"

—Salome Asega

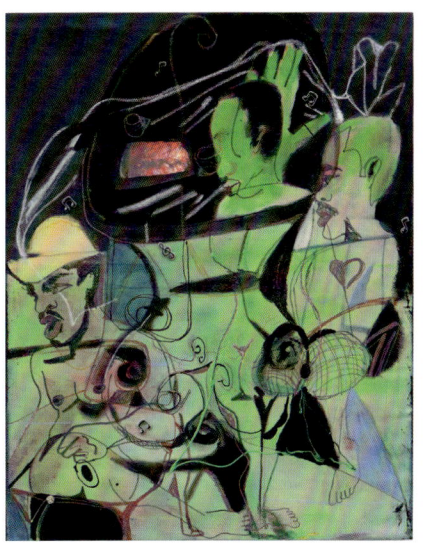

Sleep Over after Dinner, 2020. Acrylic paint, marker, watercolor, photo paper collage, and pastel on cotton polyester, 30 × 24 in. Museum purchase with funds provided by Alan Wang, 2020.27

Cassi Namoda

b. 1988

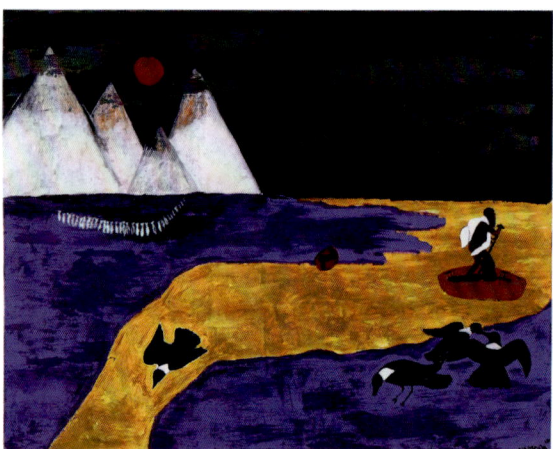

Landscape with child crossing the Styx, 2021.
Acrylic and resin on cotton poly, 48 × 60 in.
Museum purchase with funds provided
by Harry and Lana David 2021.16

At the foot of the mountains in *Landscape with child crossing the Styx* stands a line of carapau, or mackerel fish, an accessible and thus common meal for many during Mozambique's second civil war. In dire circumstances, that which is available to nourish and sustain communities is contingent upon environmental, financial, and political conditions. Facing the—at times harsh—reality of what food can be eaten, which education can be pursued, and what jobs can be had can generate a desire to leave one place in search of another.

During wartime, periods of instability, and the era of climate change, traversing a body of water is as monumental as crossing the afterlife's River Styx. Acknowledging a journey away from home that is as frightening as it is liberating, as desperate as it is optimistic, Cassi Namoda transforms water into lava—both are capable of viscous movement, ready to engulf, to harm.

Still, the pure white cloth that drapes the man and child as they search for safety seems to protect them from danger. Even within this otherworldly landscape that encapsulates their distress—marked by a black sky with gray clouds, at once wispy and ragged, and a blood moon indicating an environment deprived of direct sunlight—life prevails in vibrant purples and yellows, and with the figures. The hovering vultures testify to this. For these birds do not prey on the living; they prefer the dead.

In many ways, Namoda's painting differs from Flemish Renaissance painter Joachim Patinir's similarly titled *Landscape with Charon Crossing the Styx* (c. 1515—24), in which a figure chooses the path toward Hades rather than Elysium. Namoda depicts the man and child crossing away from the land that no longer serves them, suggesting they are on their way to Paradise. The docked boat that remains suggests others can follow suit.

—Nectar Knuckles

Christina Quarles

b. 1985

Painter Christina Quarles creates figures that traverse physical, visual, and temporal planes. Referencing the multiplicity of her identities as mixed-race and queer, Quarles creates images that rely on visible complexity and opacity, rather than figurative legibility. Long sprawling limbs stretch and fragmented bodily forms loom before swatches of pattern and color that float aimlessly against a white void. Quarles's figures hover in impossible contortions and appear simultaneously trapped and liberated by perpetual movement. Her paintings and drawings are arresting in their grotesque exploration of human forms and the gorgeous ways those forms intertwine.

Don't Let It Bring Yew Down (It's Only Castles Burnin') is an acrylic painting that evokes dwindled hope in the face of perpetual despair. Two interwoven figures hold fast to each other in a gentle yet desperate embrace. Their limbs, composed of varied color and density, appear to spiral like climbing vines from lanky torsos, further interlocking arms, legs, and feet. Another pair of figures grasps at each other across an intersecting brown plane. The figure on the left extends their arms in an open gesture toward another, more conservatively posed figure. Against a bright yellow sun, they join their hands and feet in a choreography akin to Henri Matisse's *Dance* (1910). The title of Quarles's painting makes a direct reference to a 1970 Neil Young song, which may infer that the blind maintenance of the status quo relies on each figure's willful momentum.

—TK Smith

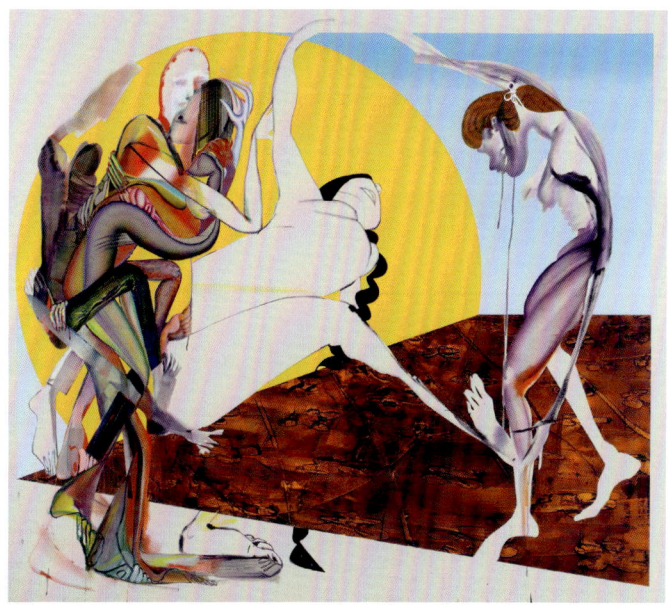

Don't Let It Bring Yew Down (It's Only Castles Burnin'), 2021. Acrylic on canvas, 84 × 96 × 2 in. Museum purchase with funds provided by Gina and Stuart Peterson 2021.24

Kudzanai-Violet Hwami

b. 1993

The main figure in *Travellers 3* is imaged in the nude and sits upon a small pedestal, conjuring the image of Auguste Rodin's *The Thinker* (1904). Both men are depicted lost in thought, but whereas Rodin's thinker carries the weight of his thoughts in his posture, Kudzanai-Violet Hwami's figure embodies ease while occupying an interior scene and gazing fondly at a portrait he holds close to his body. Two figures in the background, visible from the shoulders up, seemingly on video conference, integrate into this intimate moment. While the two cropped figures occupy the same canvas as the main figure, their physical whereabouts are not clear. Perhaps they are there in real time through a video call, or perhaps their images are merely icons of their presence. Still, they are embedded in the space. Thus, *Travellers 3* presents a space that embraces solitude, even as it negates loneliness.

Here, Hwami stages a setting wherein the internal and external, absent and present, alone and accompanied all ebb and flow and, as the work's title suggests, where the subject travels between these dichotomies with movements further altered by the digital realm's interference. *Travellers 3* offers a site of interiority—one particular enough for a potted plant, two full glasses, and a record player to bundle together on the floor; for areas of a painting to appear as a screenprint; and for negative space to be made of layered brushstrokes—where gain, loss, and change occur simultaneously. The element of collage-making in Hwami's painting brings these fragments together, perhaps toward harmonization or a manageable coexistence, but ideally toward a liberation that derives from allowing one's many layers to flourish without absolute alignment.

—Nectar Knuckles

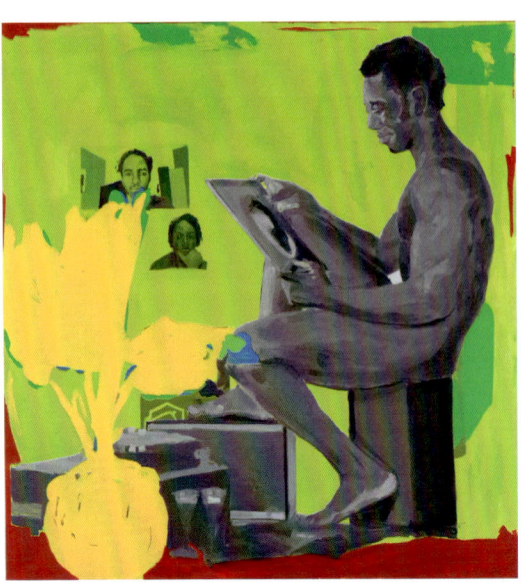

Travellers 3, 2021. Oil on canvas, 62 ⅜ × 59 ⅛ in. Museum purchase with funds provided by Rahul M. Sabhnani 2022.11

Jacolby Satterwhite

b. 1986   Artist in Residence 2020—21

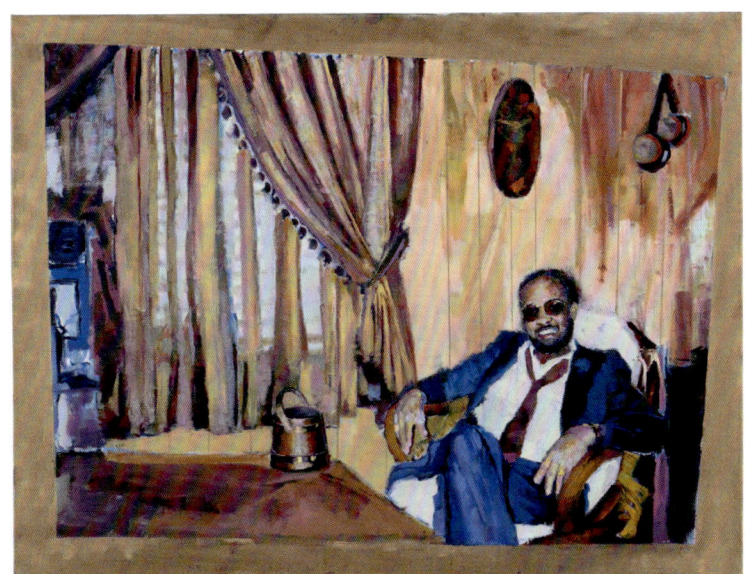

The Father, 2021. Oil on canvas, 38 × 40 in.
Museum purchase with funds provided by the
Acquisition Committee 2022.8

Jacolby Satterwhite's *The Father*—created as a 2020—21 artist in residence at the Studio Museum in Harlem—introduces a lesser-known figure within the artist's practice, and through an unexpected format. For over a decade, Satterwhite actively engaged, in absentia, his late mother, Patricia, as a key collaborative, matrilineal, and creative influence. In addition, the artist has been widely recognized for the expert application of digital- and time-based media within his practice.

In *The Father*, the viewer encounters two new directions. First, Satterwhite's departure from Patricia as his primary partner, who is intertwined and encrypted throughout the lush density of his work; and second, the artist's return to painting, the medium in which he was academically trained and has extensively studied. For the first time, the viewer visits with Satterwhite's patrilineage. The artist first captures a casual domestic encounter with his father via photograph, and then shapes an image by re-presenting the photograph in an acrylic palette of yellow ochres and browns. The artist's father radiates, wearing a blue suit, a loosened tie, and Ray-Ban sunglasses despite sitting indoors. As it is named *The Father*, the work carries forward Satterwhite's ongoing exploration of religious iconography and spiritualism within his broad body of work, suggesting an unnamed trinity in what is left unsaid: a hovering presence of the Son and the Holy Ghost in dialogue with the artist's parent, priestly and propped within the frame, set on to the throne of an ordinary armchair.

—Legacy Russell

Widline Cadet

b. 1992   Artist in Residence 2020—21

Widline Cadet works with photography, video, and multimedia installation to explore the complexities of Black diasporic experience, migration, and displacement. Born in Haiti and partially raised in the United States, Cadet grounds her practice in her embodiment of the tension between belonging and unbelonging. Much of Cadet's work aims to correct and fill gaps within her ancestral memory—as images of her family are sparse, the artist strives to both steward and expand her familial archive through artistic engagement. Reflecting on the foundations of her practice, the artist recalls, "I think my practice started as a way of thinking about these things I didn't have access to and how I'm trying to build something for myself as a means of knowing past generations and as a means of being known to future generations."[252]

Si Ou Ta Dwe Bliye Wout Lakay Ou (Lè Tout Limyè Yo Etenn) (Should You Forget Your Way Home (When All the Lights Go Off)) is a photographic corner diptych depicting the backs of two figures wearing matching blue-and-white gingham dresses, referencing the school uniform Cadet wore while still living in Haiti. The figures emerge from the rightmost edge of the frame as they walk, perhaps trepidatiously, through a dense bush of wildflowers that nearly subsumes them. As seen here, Cadet often doubles figures through posing and/or clothing as a visual device, invoking what Toni Morrison in her 1987 novel *Beloved* terms "rememory," or the re-living and reassembling of a memory. This doubling takes further effect in the titling of her works, which pairs phrases in Haitian Creole with their English translations. "Should you forget your way home (when all the lights go off)" might be imagined as words of encouragement spoken by the two figures, reassuring the viewer that, although their identities are inaccessible, they act as guides through what remains to be seen.

—Adria Gunter

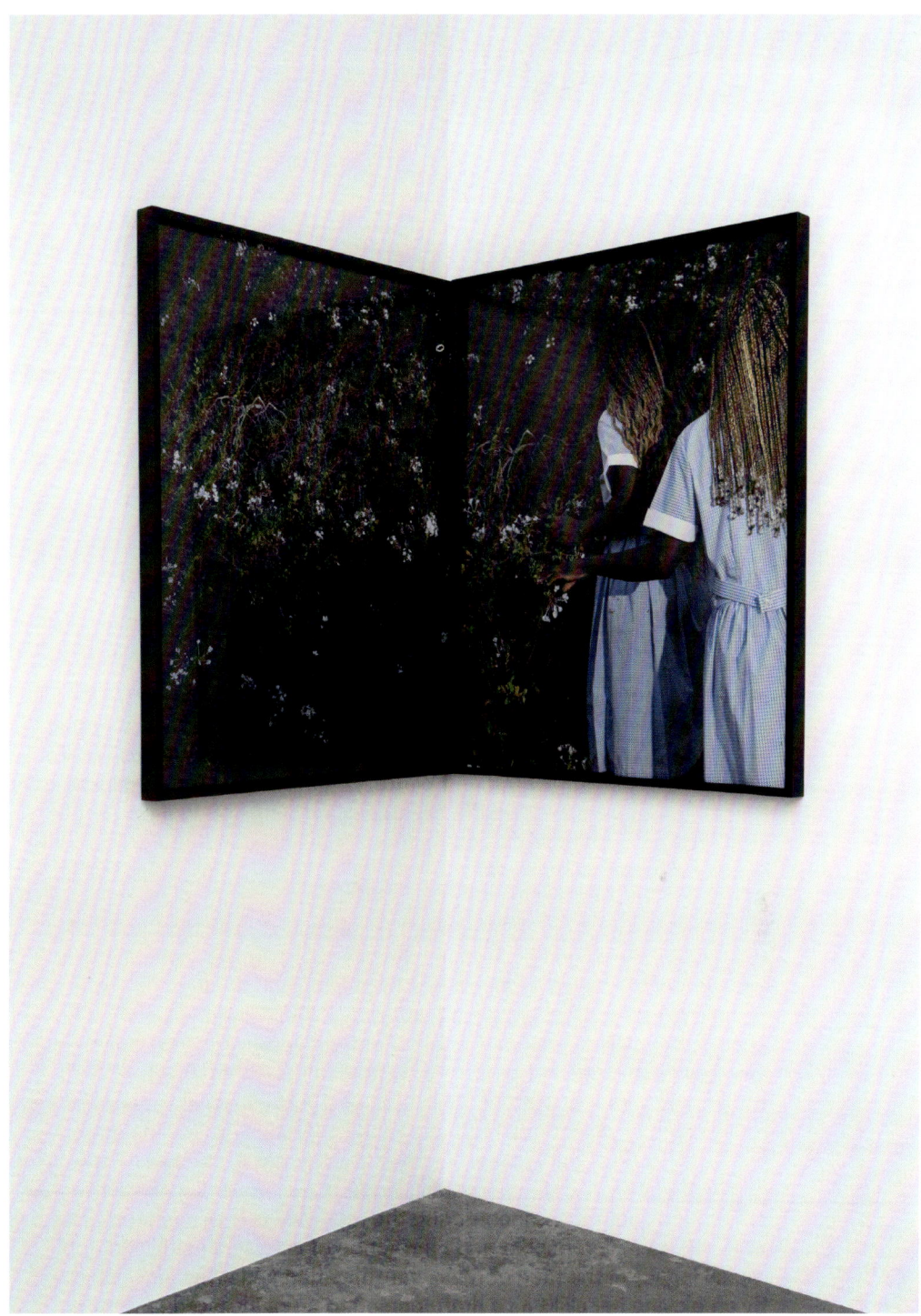

*Si Ou Ta Dwe Bliye Wout Lakay Ou (Lè Tout
Limyè Yo Etenn) (Should You Forget Your Way
Home (When All the Lights Go Off))*, 2021.
Archival inkjet print, artist frame, 40 × 32 in.
each. Museum purchase with funds provided
by the Acquisition Committee 2022.4a-b.

Lauren Halsey

b. 1987   Artist in Residence 2014—15

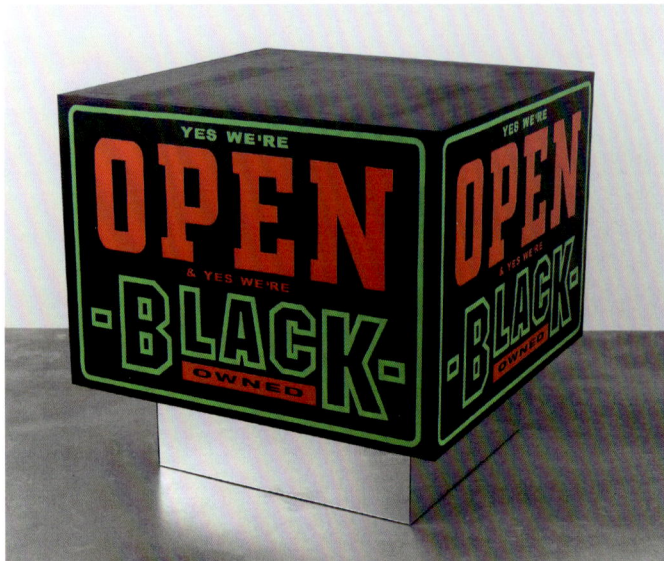

yes we're open and yes we're black owned, 2021. Acrylic, enamel, and mirror on wood, 47 ½ × 49 ½ × 48 in. Gift of Beth Rudin DeWoody 2024.35.1a-b

In 2020, Lauren Halsey founded Summaeverythang Community Center, an evolving hub and warehouse that makes organic produce grown on local California farms accessible weekly to the Los Angeles neighborhoods of South Central and Watts. Organized and run by a local team of neighbors and friends, Summaeverythang connects Halsey's studio to her community through intentional collaboration that plants the seed of a future to be sown.

As an extension of her commitment to community and land, and of her trust in her site-specific practice, Halsey's sculpture *yes we're open and yes we're black owned* exudes Black ownership and commands space with its bold green and red enameled lettering. Channeling the lasting influence of her neighborhood of South Central, Halsey embeds the nostalgic typography of local mid-century advertisements within this work. The titular phrase is repeated on each side of the black acrylic square block, reminiscent of commercial signage found in African American communities at the turn of the twenty-first century. The box is stacked on a smaller mirrored platform, which potentially reflects the viewer's feet as they walk around the sculpture encountering the repeated text at each turn. The work serves as a reminder and affirmation of access, wealth, and communal legacy in the face of mass gentrification and urban development. By employing her skills as a draftsperson to erect idealized structures, Halsey reimagines South Central's past as present.

—Starasea Camara

Tunji Adeniyi-Jones
b. 1992

Moments of intimacy, transcendence, and interplay permeate Tunji Adeniyi-Jones's *A Flashy Encounter*. Loaded with visual and spatial complexity, the work depicts two figures in close proximity amid vibrant flora and fauna. Bodies merge, limbs twist and extend, and colors blur into one another. Adeniyi-Jones's multicontinental artistic formation and Yoruba heritage inform how he conceives the body as a tool to convey layered narratives and communication. His art finds its location in the aesthetic traditions of West African visual culture, while also serving as an expression of his personal investment in dynamic imagery.

In *A Flashy Encounter*, two androgynous figures stand face-to-face. The figure on the left turns only their head toward the other, while their body leans away toward the left, with knee bent and arms extending in a manner that suggests a pause in forward momentum. The character on the right, however, appears to have a somewhat greater interest in the encounter. Though the edge of the canvas cuts off the entirety of their form, one can still view the indicators of their surprise: an elongated neck, arched back, and elevated fingers. Deep greens and indigos, vibrant magentas, and rich blacks and ochres are seen throughout the bodies and the environment. In the upper left, a flame licks across the paper.

The encounter depicted represents an exploration into both the dimensions of watercolor, ink, and acrylic and the narratives that surround an interpersonal meeting. The ambiguity in the precise nature of the figures' relation opens up the work to a personal engagement with the viewer. In the moments preceding recognition, intensity emerges.

—Arese Uwuoruya

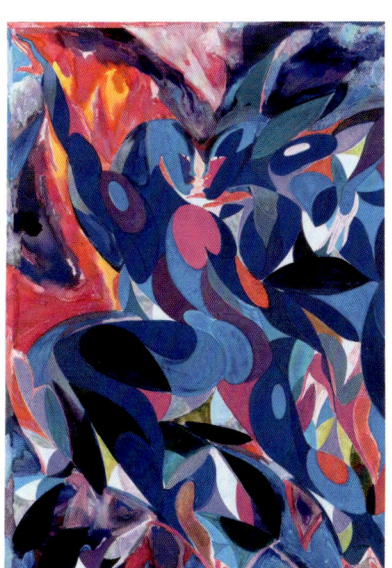

A Flashy Encounter, 2021. Watercolor, ink, and acrylic on paper, 16 ½ × 11 ⅝ in. Museum purchase with funds provided by The Lumpkin-Boccuzzi Family 2022.17

Caroline Kent

b. 1975

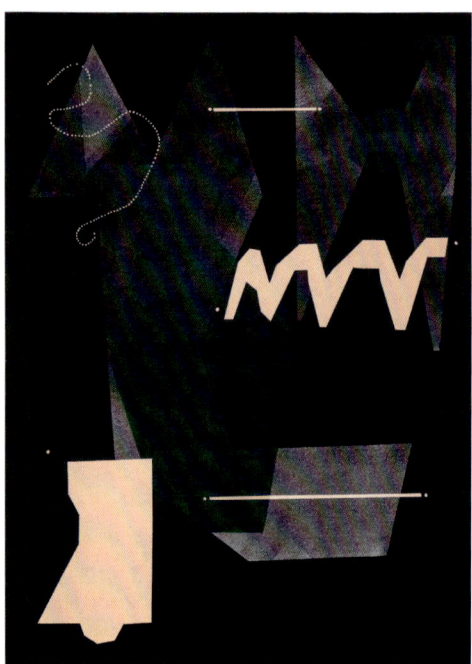

Temptation, 2021. Acrylic on canvas,
47 ½ × 34 ¾ × 1 ¾ in. Promised gift of
Carol Sutton Lewis and William M. Lewis Jr.
PG.2022.2

Caroline Kent's abstract painting vocabulary functions like a language, albeit one that tests the limits of legibility. "When I started making abstract paintings, I was fascinated by the fact that you can create a visual language that is coded. Where it puts everyone on the outside of interpretive meaning," the artist explains.[253] If, in its everyday usage, language categorizes, regulates, and reifies, Kent's intuitive practice exploits language's capacity for openness, multiplicity, and spontaneity. Kent composes her improvisational pictures by cutting shapes from sheets of paper. She then meticulously arranges these hard-edged geometric forms into dynamic configurations that serve as guides for her paintings. The paintings form a growing and extensive library of abstract structures that serve as the basis for subsequent works.

In *Temptation*, overlapping shapes approximate the logic of a diagram. Faded charcoal forms dissolve into the painting's black background, while opaque candy-pink polygons sit on the painting's surface, obscuring the layers beneath them. Throughout, a system of lines and dots acts like punctuation, marking points of emphasis or pause. Like parentheses or quotation marks, these forms function as signifiers or containers waiting to hold language. While the painting invites—tempts, even—meaning-making, the object of desire remains just out of reach. Transparency and opacity become ciphers for a larger exploration of communication systems, illustrating how language reveals and conceals.

—Jadine Collingwood

David L. Johnson

b. 1993

David L. Johnson recontextualizes found objects, continuing the legacy of the Duchampian "readymade" with a political charge addressing how social injustice is embedded in the built environment. *Loiter (Hersel)* is a part of Johnson's ongoing series "Loiter" begun in 2020 in which he extracts spiky metal armatures that have been applied to standpipes, windowsills, and other urban structures that could otherwise be used as makeshift seating. Property owners install these apparatuses to prohibit loitering, in turn policing bodies and contributing to the rampant privatization of public space in New York. In an act of resistance, Johnson appropriates and exhibits hostile architecture, simultaneously restoring possibilities for public seating and elucidating the menacing intent behind these innocuous yet pervasive instruments of discipline and control.

The parenthetical title of each work in the series, in this case, "Hersel," indicates the first name of the owner of the building. Thus, the displaced objects register both the materials and perpetrators of social regulation, functioning as a critique of property. Embodying the precarious divide between public and private space, each lifted structure is installed at the original height it occupied on the standpipe from which it was removed, rendering its corresponding absence visible. These accumulated absences replenish possibilities of loitering and reveal how everyday choreographies of urban life are modulated by design. Johnson walks the streets of New York extensively to locate these restrictive hardwares, turning part of this sculptural practice into an ambulatory exercise. Part flâneur, part bandit, and part bricoleur, Johnson surveys, seizes, and retools the seemingly banal mechanisms of structural violence.

—Jordan Carter

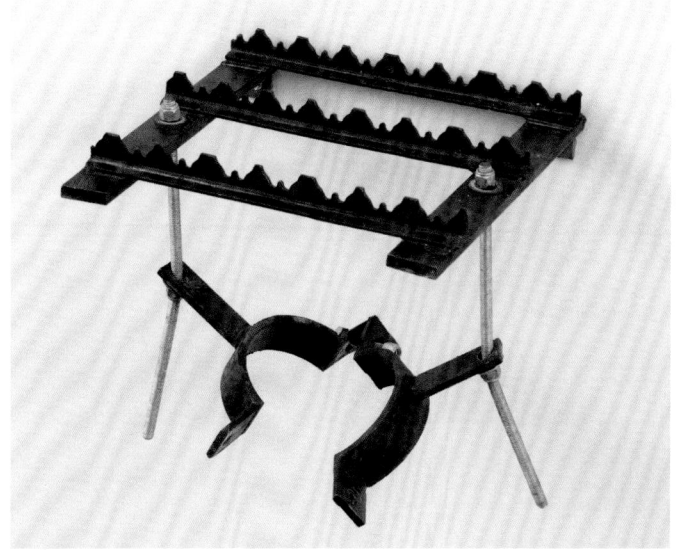

Loiter (Hersel), 2021. Removed standpipe spike, 12 ½ × 14 ¹¹⁄₁₆ × 12 in. Museum purchase with funds provided by an anonymous donor 2022.22

Tony Cokes

b. 1956

Evil.13.5 (4 OE)

the legacy of how this relationship to design has been mostly confined to the **artisanal,**

So we have to really **rethink** all these different concepts

Evil.13.5 (4 OE), 2022. HD video, color, sound, TRT: 00:19:40. Edition 1 of 5 + 2 AP. Gift of an anonymous donor 2023.24.1

has been **confined** to types of production

that one might conceive not as within the **vocabulary** of contemporary design.

Tony Cokes's colorful video installations employ a style and pacing reminiscent of both PowerPoint presentations and slide-tape performances common in audiovisual works from the 1970s to 1990s. Cokes's moving-image works often feature a soundtrack that acts as a counterpoint to the visual material being presented. For him, these videos are all about the United States, and he thinks of them as "Word Portraits" in that they are composed of language by or about public figures, especially politicians and artists.

Evil.13.5 (4 OE) is one in a series of videos concerning the work of mourning as informed by Jacques Derrida's various theories of hauntology. Derrida's hauntology, as conceptualized in *Specters of Marx* (1993), indexes hegemony, which contains the shadows of all that it is not, as well as a past that is always indistinct, indeed inseparable and inextricable from what we might call a present or a future—even under erasure. Here Cokes's research considers the social implications of the work, rhetoric, and activities of curator and writer Okwui Enwezor. In particular, the video examines questions related to design, consumption, economic forms, technology, recycling, and Africa. The text is excerpted from an interview Enwezor held with curator Amelie Klein on the occasion of her 2015 exhibition *Making Africa—A Continent of Contemporary Design.* Enwezor discussed how design on the continent necessitates a rigorous reimagining of concepts and language to capture and reflect its particularities. Cokes was given access to some of Enwezor's library; however, he chose to transcribe this interview, which he found on the internet, because of Enwezor's elegant use of keywords as a structuring device and how his discourse on the subject illuminated aspects of his larger cultural practice from unusual angles. The text animation is set to a compelling polyrhythmic Chicago footwork soundtrack by DJ Hank.

—Adrienne Edwards

Qualeasha Wood

b. 1996   Artist in Residence 2021—22

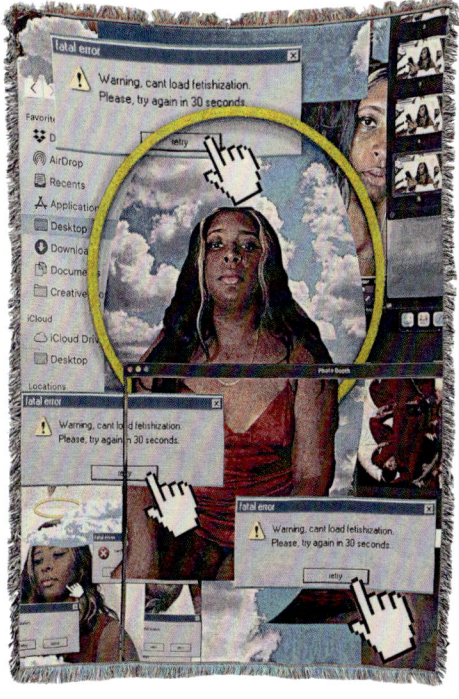

Error404, 2022. Jacquard woven cotton, glass seed beads, 86 ¾ × 59 in. Museum purchase with funds provided by the Acquisition Committee 2023.32.1

A stitch is one in a series of repetitive single loops that together reveal a graphic or pattern through interloping and interlacing thread. A pixel is a single dot that makes up an image on a computer or digital screen. The stitch and the pixel are each reliant on their "neighbors" to illuminate a sum larger than itself. In Qualeasha Wood's *Error404*, stitch meets pixel to reveal an image of Wood angelically framed by a mouse pointer halo and floating in desktop clouds between MacBook applications. The textile also reveals a fatal error: "Warning, can't load fetishization. Please try again in 30 seconds." The pop-up dialog prompts the viewer to click "retry," but the way Wood looks down from her perch suggests this error is a permanent glitch, one that keeps the viewer working to resolve something they think is possible to fix.

In Legacy Russell's *Glitch Feminism*, the glitch is framed as "an active word, one that implies movement and change from the outset; this movement triggers error."[254] Fatal errors are delivered when a computer reads a program attempting to do something unknown or impossible. Wood repossesses her desktop by leveraging this fatal error as a tool of protest, a means to end the very normal and routine fetishization of Black women in image-making and culture. The only other option is to exit out of the dialog box and accept there is no fetishization in Wood's desktop metropolis.

—Salome Asega

Jacob Mason-Macklin

b. 1995   Artist in Residence 2021—22

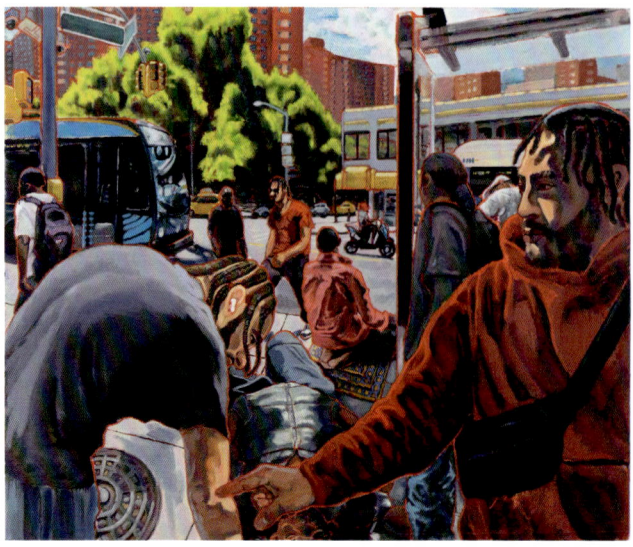

Nirvana's Beneath the Pavement, 2022. Oil on linen, 60 × 72 in. Museum purchase with funds provided by the Acquisition Committee and the Ed Bradley Family Foundation 2023.31.1

There have always been spaces and environments that seem imbued with a certain electricity. Fueled in part by what many believe to be a spiritual residue, these spaces can feel as though there is a current pulsing through the ground itself. This rhythm—this reverberation—is reflected in Jacob Mason-Macklin's *Nirvana's Beneath the Pavement*. Set in the midst of one of Harlem's most prominent intersections, West 125th Street and Amsterdam Avenue, the vibrant and complex scene provokes lines of inquiry surrounding perspective, surveillance, and the act of looking.

Who are the individuals that fill this teeming crosswalk? What have they witnessed in the day leading up to this moment, and what lies ahead as they disappear from view? The two most foregrounded characters appear preoccupied; while one of these men glances toward something beyond the frame, the other hunches over a partially obscured body lying flat on the city sidewalk. The man standing up could be responsible for the fallen figure below him, or he could be leaning down to offer assistance or reaching for something else entirely. The busy figures are unaware that they are being gazed upon from any perspective.

With each daily movement—a brisk skip to reach the bus before it chugs down the block or a barefooted kneel on a prayer rug in daily ritual—Mason-Macklin subtly reveals the transient aspect of spectatorship. Two small surveillance cameras rest inconspicuously near the top of a street sign in the upper left corner of the scene. The inclusion of these devices—and their position in the frame—hints at the artist's investigation of the stakes of living under increasingly normalized surveillance.

—Daria Simone Harper

Danielle Mckinney

b. 1981

In *Guardian*, a woman with a meditative gaze and pulled-back hair rests her head on a wood table. She gazes not at the spectator, but at herself (via a mirror) or toward a horizon (through a window).[255] On the table's surface lies a cupped oyster shell with two lustrous pearls, the white color juxtaposed with the brown desk, the melanated pigment of the figure's face, and the background's taupe hue.

As a skilled photographer, Danielle Mckinney is no stranger to the task of capturing a moment or creating images guided by intuition. A self-taught painter, Mckinney still relies on photography, mainly images from social media, for inspiration to portray intimate and cinematic scenes of Black women. Mckinney's practice by and large reflects a deep investigation and extension of old masters and Impressionist painting techniques. She does not prime her canvases with clear gesso, as is common with preparatory work. Instead, Mckinney begins each composition with a black background to allow her colorful muses to emerge from the shadows. Her striking facility with chiaroscuro, or the effect of contrasting light and darkness, brightens the protagonist and foregrounded objects in *Guardian.* And while she overlays the desk with loose brushstrokes, she adorns the figure's visage with complex washes of orange, red, and brown, exemplifying the complexity of a Black person's skin despite the flat and monolithic implications of the racial classification.

Steeped in allegory, *Guardian*—from its title and subject matter—prompts considerations of what and who are deemed most valuable. In Mckinney's image, the woman shields an oyster, itself a guardian to the semiprecious gem and a symbolic reference to protection and transformation. *Guardian* asks, "What do you guard? What is precious to you?"

—Habiba Hopson

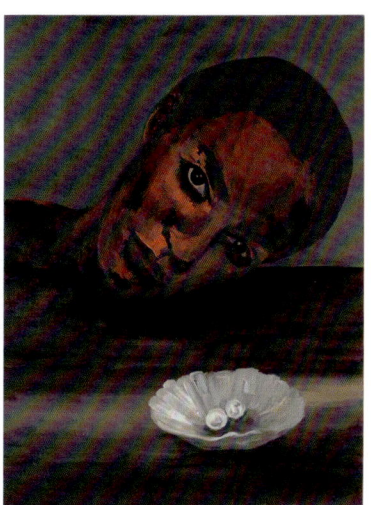

Guardian, 2022. Acrylic on canvas, 24 × 18 in. Museum purchase with funds provided by The Lumpkin-Boccuzzi Family in honor of Nancy L. Lane 2022.13

Nikita Gale

b. 1983

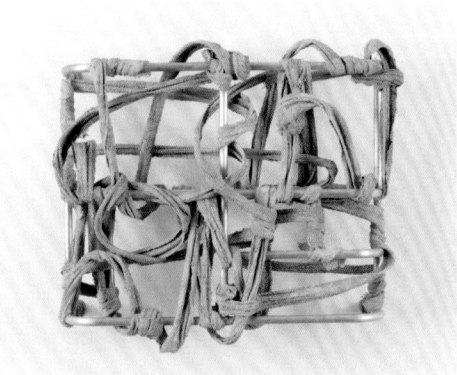

Nikita Gale's long-standing interest in sonic environments finds the artist gesturing to the stages, rigs, and platforms that support and separate performers from crowds. Gale's works are ruins for a sonic culture that is still very much alive. Each sculpture is a relic of its recent past, resonating with scenes belonging to a weekend's past, and each work environment is frozen with remnants of the concluded event. Though soundless and unpopulated, these objects still evoke familiar environments of recording studios, concerts, and performances. Each work awakens scenes where the fluidity between performer and listener enables the active exchange of energy in one cacophonous atmosphere.

The tension between fluidity and stiffness animates many of Gale's works, particularly the artist's "RUINERS" series. Beginning in 2020, Gale's "RUINERS" take on various abstract orientations. *RUINER XIX* utilizes music production materials, including sound-dampening cloth wrapped around repurposed crowd-control barricades. The stiff materials, such as terrycloth and audio cords, travel from each work in the series to create an ongoing language made of staging, rigging, and recording equipment. The austerity of each sculpture directly opposes the original environments from which the materials are sourced—clubs, concert venues, and studios.

The cloths, encased in concrete and draped while wet on aluminum, generate a cold, scaffold-like object. Stiff and twisted, the object resembles both wreckage and prosthetic. The cloths recall a mummified corpse, while the aluminum barricade creates a scaffold for the parts it holds. Each sustains the weight of a multitude.

Here, silence and the memory of noisy spaces are bedmates in one object. Like the debris left behind by a crowd leaving a stadium, these objects resemble what is left in spaces after the stillness of the ending, a void as a memory of bygone hungry audiences. The decay holds bodily data: damp towels, empty cords, and barricades.

—Amber Esseiva

Cameron Granger

b. 1993   Artist in Residence 2021—22

Cameron Granger's installation, built of wood found in Harlem, is a structure that reimagines its material's original purpose. The story and journey of the material are complicated—from trees, to two-by-fours, to building support structures and police barricades, to, finally, art. Granger was born and raised in Columbus, Ohio, and his work considers the journey that neighborhoods, specifically Black ones, go through as they contend with economic and cultural change.

The documentary-like film *Before I Let Go* layers Granger's gentle narration over varying interviews of Columbus residents, open-source government footage, archival material, and first-person footage from across the city. Granger's work contends with the monstrosity that is capitalism and the politics surrounding the architecture of race and urban renewal. Just as "Before I Let Go" is Beyoncé reimagining the Frankie Beverly and Maze classic, Granger's installation reimagines and repurposes materials, subject matter, and characters to show audiences that gentrification is not abstract.

Maybe there is a reason we are told that monsters live underneath our beds and come from inside a home's inner chambers—they are built into our domestic life and are inescapably close. The wooden installation that is the backdrop to Granger's film evokes the warmth of a grandmother's house and, at the same time, the eerie alienation felt when your grandmother struggles with the forces of gentrification—because she is poor or Black or, worse yet under capitalism, both! Could governments collectively care for their populaces, and could they preserve their neighborhoods and generational experiences like some grandmothers sheath their furniture in plastic—to keep and cherish? It turns out, it is a privilege to find what we left behind when we return home.

—Ilk Yasha

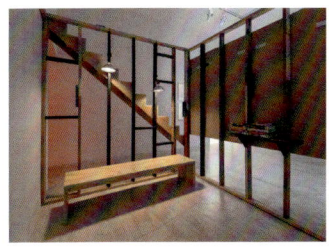
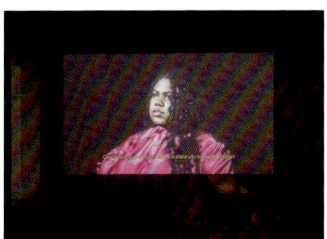
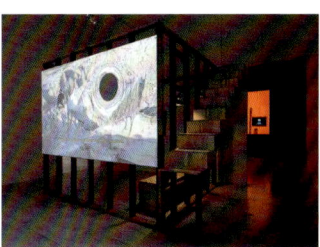

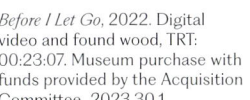

Before I Let Go, 2022. Digital video and found wood, TRT: 00:23:07. Museum purchase with funds provided by the Acquisition Committee 2023.30.1

417

Jeffrey Meris

b. 1991   Artist in Residence 2022—23

Multidisciplinary artist Jeffrey Meris takes to his thoughtful practice with a deep sense of care and compassion. He is fascinated with material culture and the ecology of quotidian objects.

Suspended from a large-scale steel wire hanger attached to a steel support structure, and cast in a cement base, *Black woman* is a molded silicone torso, hands, and arms of a full-figured woman—the artist's mother. This work was first paired alongside *and child* (2023), a sculpture of Meris's molded torso. He cloaks the cement base with the silicone mold as if it is a second skin. In the interest of repurposing everyday objects, the artist uses a wire hanger as a tool to hang the sculpture, but also potentially as an instrument of care that braces *Black woman* for longevity.

Examining the nuances of their relationship, he immortalizes his mother with this sculpture, showcasing the profound bridge between mother and son. The work is also an approach toward mending that parent/child relationship—Meris's mother came to represent a complicated relation to family, the artist's immigrant identity, and displacement. The artist deliberately chose silicone to cast her—as a reward for winning an essay writing competition titled, "Why Is Your Mom the Greatest Mom in the World," Meris received a silicone Tupperware set.

These chalky-white molds are related to works from the artist's series "Now You See Me; Now You Don't" (2020), which includes multiple plaster body casts rendered in the same color. Through this collection of work, Meris concludes that Black bodies are not a monolith, but rather "these collective hieroglyphs."[256] They are a meeting point where intersecting narratives and histories converge and blend. Meris embraces the complexities, differences, and familial histories of both he and his mom—him, Haitian-born and Bahama-raised; and her, Bahamian, born during British colonization.

—Jayson Overby Jr.

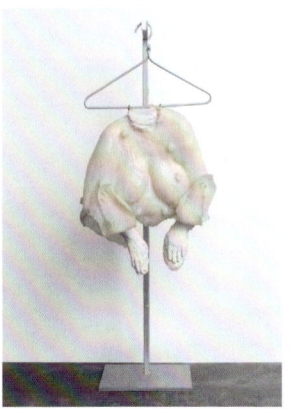

Black woman, 2023. Silicone, Hydrocal gypsum cement, and steel, 67 × 21 × 24 in. Fabrication support: Michael Fadel and Cyle Warner. Museum purchase with funds provided by the Acquisition Committee 2024.27.1

Rashid Johnson

b. 1977

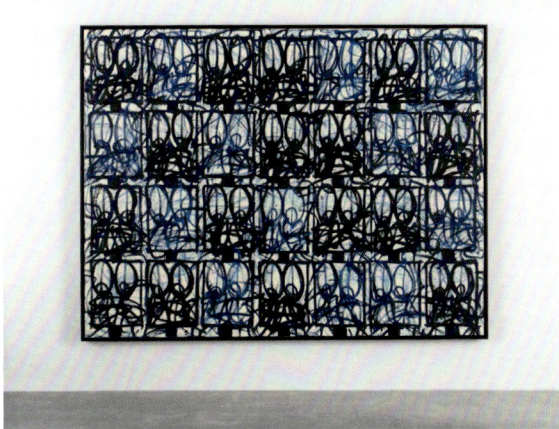

Bruise Painting "Tarmac," 2023. Oil on linen, 72 × 96 × 1 ⅝ in. Museum purchase with funds provided by Greg Mondre and Lise and Jeffrey Wilks TD.2021.38

Rashid Johnson's "Bruise Paintings" demonstrate the artist's reckoning with the aftermath of the simultaneous pandemic and social justice uprisings of 2020. A bruise typically signals the transitory process between injury and repair; it is this liminal space that Johnson considers as the possibility for healing. Developed from a series of similar works made in the pandemic titled "Anxious Red Paintings," the "Bruise Paintings" render the inscrutability of the post-pandemic moment and thus complicate its understanding as a historical event marked by a discrete beginning and end. While the series was initially presented during the artist's 2021 exhibition *Black and Blue* at David Kordansky Gallery, *Tarmac*'s creation in 2023 signifies the continued desire for healing and repair.

The "Bruise Paintings" feature grids covered in frantic lines of light to deep blue—the variation is a result of deep blue oil paint layered across the oil-coated canvas. Each grid cell repeats the artist's signature "Anxious Man" motif. First appearing in his work in 2015, the motif—consisting of two ovals for eyes and a rectangle for a mouth filled or covered with scrawled lines—has come to represent the artist's turn to figuration and the anxiety he faces as a Black man amid police violence and protests in the United States. The motif has taken on a variety of iterations—from its first form as works of African black soap and wax on white ceramic tile to jewelry talismans, to paintings and prints, to its development as mixed-media mosaics featuring "Broken Men," which move away from mark-making to render anxiety through fragmented shards.

Johnson works across multiple media and often references and directly inserts materials that draw from African American culture, art history, and his personal background. It is this expansive knowledge of material and media that allows the artist to deftly capture personal and collective experiences.

—Kiki Teshome

Devin N. Morris

b. 1986   Artist in Residence 2022—23

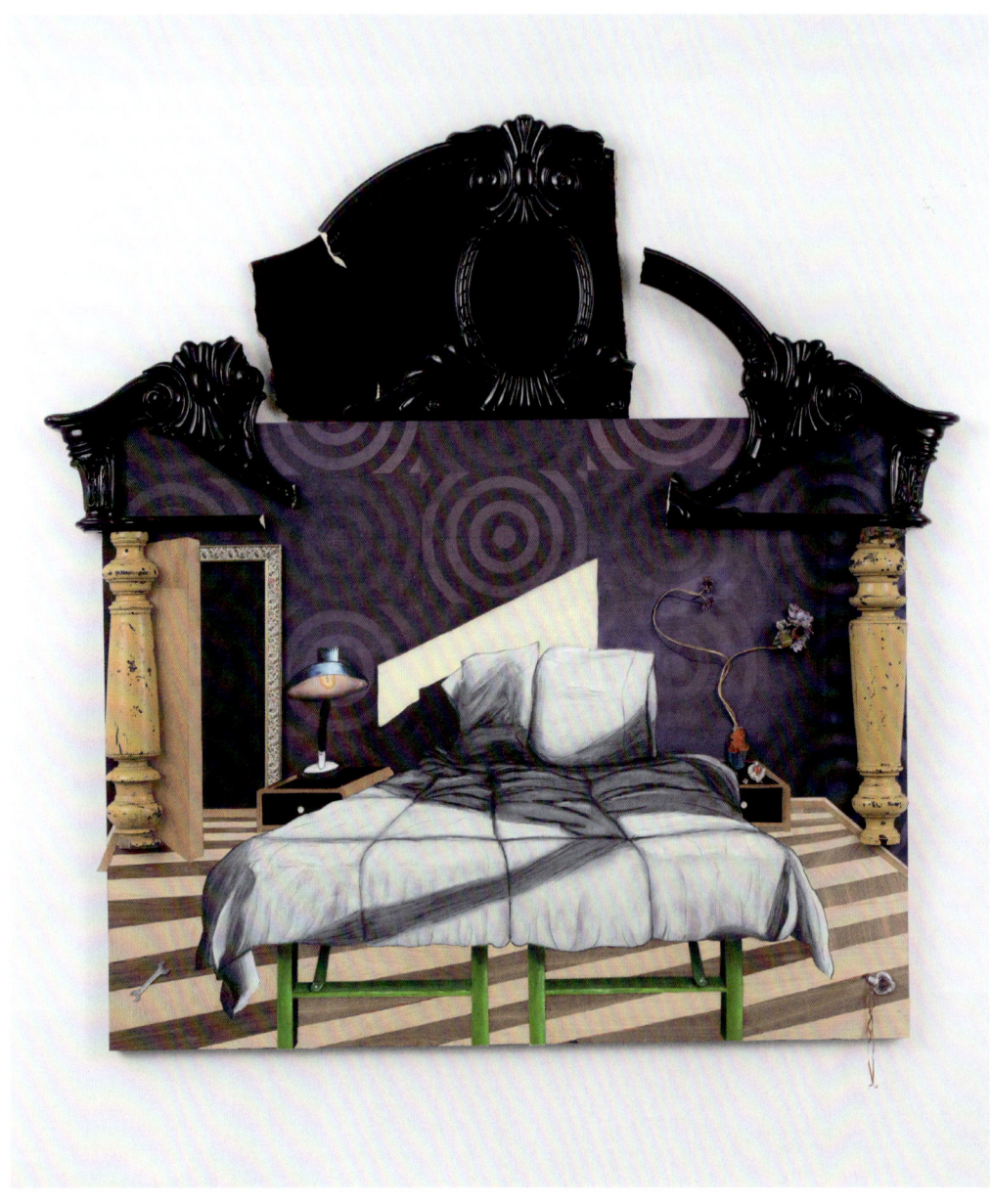

A Little Above the Head, 2023. Felt,
Target bags, oil pastel, oil stick, support,
headboard, wood veneer, a break,
shards, nail polish, nail polish bottles,
her nails, his bed, picture frame, acrylic,
wrench, lamp cord, seashell, a drip, vinyl,
hair barrette, cassette tape film, plug,
plastic, bottle, glass, color pencil, static,
dangerous flowers, newel post, oil, and
knobs on wood panel, 88 ½ × 91 × 5 in.
Museum purchase with funds provided
by the Acquisition Committee
2024.26.1a-b

Working across installation, sculpture, and painting, Devin N. Morris conjures imagined scenes of intimacy, communion, and vulnerability. Fueling a profoundly improvisational practice, Morris gathers materials he collects from daily walks throughout Harlem—relics of his personal life, memories, and conceptual curiosities—to construct painterly and sculptural universes. He describes his practice as "one of looking; looking down, specifically looking around."[257] As such, Morris invites discarded matter of the urban landscape that are imbued with usage history to become newly functional as key artistic accouterments. As seen in *A Little Above the Head*, Morris appropriates detritus such as nail polish bottles, hair barrettes, and cassette tapes as the artwork's material.

A Little Above the Head represents Morris's bedroom in Harlem—which he rented during his residency at the Studio Museum from 2022 to 2023. The painted bedroom situates the bed at center, with two identical drawers on either side. Pasted directly against the canvas, repeated concentric circles from purple-dyed Target bags—collected for years by the artist—evoke the room's wallpaper. Fragments of a disposed headboard surround the work's top edge. Morris's preoccupation with interiority as both an emotional and physical space is laid bare through his application of domestic items: loose acrylic fingernails appear ornamental beside the bed; a picture frame outlines the exit door; and emerald-colored felt comprises the mattress's support structure. Often a deeply nourishing space for the soul, a bedroom is synonymous with privacy, respite, and dreaming—through his depiction of his resting place, the artist lures viewers to access a therapeutic state of mind.

—Habiba Hopson

Charisse Pearlina Weston

b. 1988   Artist in Residence 2022—23

Charisse Pearlina Weston works across sculpture, photography, and writing, and is best known for her use of glass as a medium to consider the conditions of Black life. She is drawn both to the material properties of glass—its fragility and transparency—as well as its use in anti-Black surveillance tactics, as evidenced in the broken windows theory, which suggests that visible signs of disorder like broken windows encourage crime and justify increased policing.

Her work *when in the echoed deep of nightfall, we populate the crater* comes out of the artist's 2022—23 artist residency at the Studio Museum and her research into the 1981 New York Housing Preservation and Development program Occupied Look. During the 1980s, city workers applied photographic decals on to windows of abandoned buildings in the South Bronx to give an external appearance of occupancy and beautification. In response to learning about this program, which neglected to consider the needs of neighborhood residents, Weston created glass sculptures that feature photographs the artist took in domestic spaces while looking out of windows. This sculpture in particular features images taken from the apartment of fellow 2022—23 artist in residence Devin N. Morris, demonstrating the artists' collaborations and close relationships formed during the residency. The warped glass sheets and distorted images serve as a form of concealment—a formal and conceptual approach that considers Black interiority and domestic space as sites of resistance. Given enduring heightened scrutiny on Black communities, Weston obstructs any easily legible reading of her sculptures, symbolizing how concealment, folding, and interiority can function as modes of Black resistance to surveillance.

—Kiki Teshome

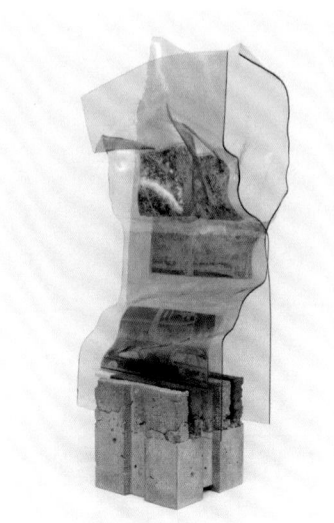

when in the echoed deep of nightfall, we populate the crater, 2023. Photographic decals, slumped glass, etched text, and concrete, 40 ¾ × 10 × 18 ½ in. Museum purchase with funds provided by the Acquisition Committee and Martin and Rebecca Eisenberg 2024.25.1a–c

Karon Davis

b. 1977

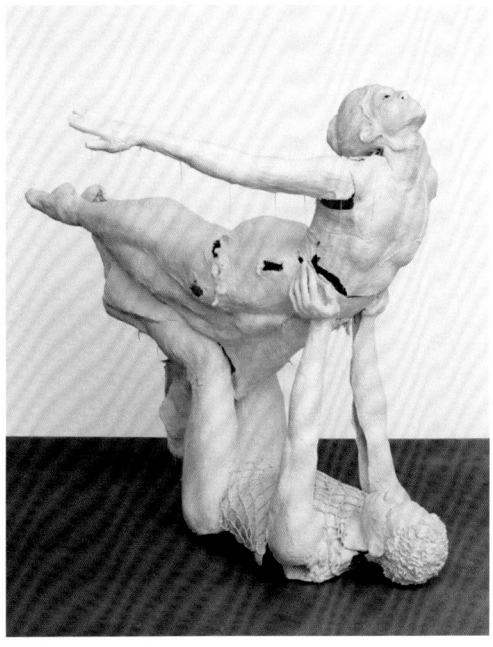

Echo & Narcissus: Love Bomb, 2023. Plaster, steel, tulle, glass eyes, and chicken wire, 66 × 58 × 53 in. Museum purchase with funds provided by Kathryn and Kenneth Chenault 2024.22.1

Karon Davis's sculptural and multimedia practice explores issues surrounding race, history, violence, and memory. Reflecting a long-standing interest in ancient Egyptian mummification, Davis often works with plaster as her primary medium, casting friends, family, and herself in action. The artist gestures to her dance and theater background via the installation of these resultant spectral figures, methodically staging them to convey narrative scenes both real and imagined.

Davis's *Echo & Narcissus: Love Bomb* is part of a larger body of sculptural work in which figures enact pivotal moments from various ballet productions. Her imagined "sculpted ballet" *Echo & Narcissus* chronicles the ancient Greek myth of obsession and unrequited love through dance. Here, the two figures, cast from dancers Fabricio Seraphin and Vicky Lambert, embody a pose seen in Alvin Ailey's *Revelations*, in which Lambert balances on Seraphin's knees with her arms outstretched, as if in flight. By synthesizing a moment in Ailey's magnum opus with an ancient myth, Davis reimagines both narratives as part of her fictive sculptural tableau. Davis's enduring interest in ballet dancers as subject matter is informed by her experience with the labor and preparation that is critical to the sport. She is especially concerned with depicting Black ballet dancers as a corrective to their erasure within dance, noting, "The ballet world is a white, elite, European environment, and Black dancers have to conform and sacrifice to thrive in it."[258] In doing so, the artist challenges the Eurocentricity of ballet culture and insists upon Black dancers taking center stage.

— Adria Gunter

Bequest of Peggy Cooper Cafritz

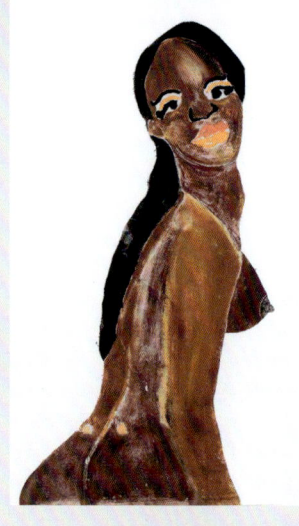

3

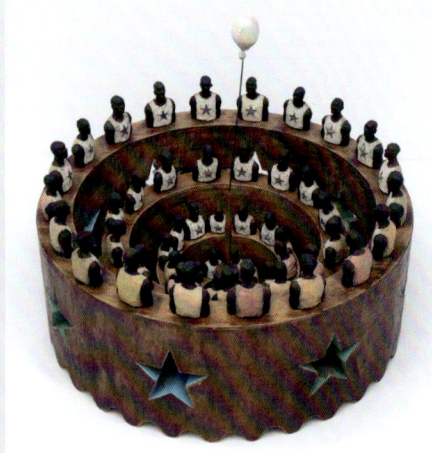

1

2

4

In 2018, the Studio Museum received an extraordinary bequest of over four hundred works from Peggy Cooper Cafritz (1947—2018), a Washington, DC, arts patron, civil rights activist, and educator. In addition to her gift to the Museum, Cooper Cafritz also left more than 250 works to the Duke Ellington School of the Arts, a public high school in DC dedicated to arts education that she cofounded in 1974. The gift—the largest given to each organization and the most ever of contemporary works by artists of African descent—had a transformative effect on the two institutions.

The bequest to the Museum dramatically increased its holdings, bolstering and adding depth to the existing permanent collection. As Cooper Cafritz's dedication to fostering the careers of Black artists aligned with the Museum's mission, her works naturally shared a lot of overlaps with the Museum's collection and exhibition program. Many artists represented in Cooper Cafritz's gift have been featured in exhibitions at the Museum, and over twenty are alumni of the *Artist-in-Residence* program, including Sanford Biggers, Titus Kaphar, Simone Leigh, Mickalene Thomas, and William Villalongo.

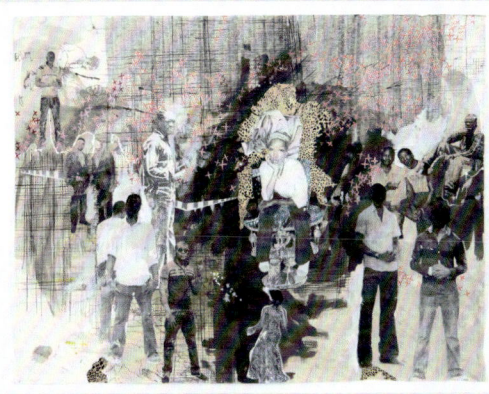

5

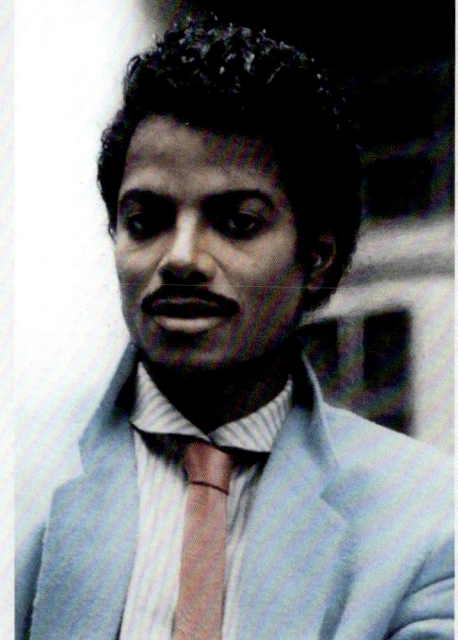

7

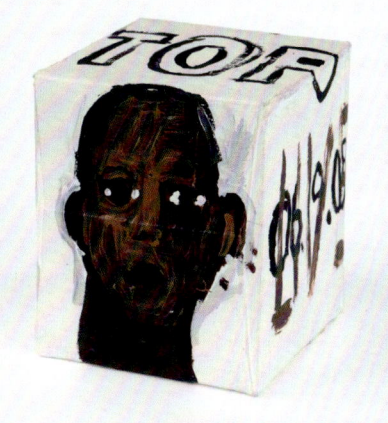

6

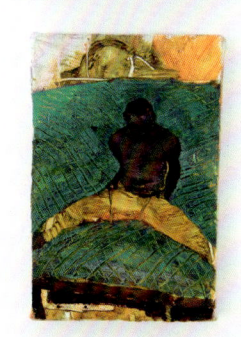

8

1. Emory Douglas, *Untitled (All Power to the People)*, 1969. Poster, 23 ¾ × 30 × 1 ½ in. Bequest of Peggy Cooper Cafritz (1947—2018), Washington, DC, collector, educator, and activist 2018.40.71

2. Derek Fordjour, *Huddle*, 2014. Wood, terracotta, glass, acrylic, and vinyl paint, 20 × 28 × 28 in. Bequest of Peggy Cooper Cafritz (1947—2018), Washington, DC, collector, educator, and activist 2018.40.85

3. Tschabalala Self, *Coco*, 2013. Oil paint on paper, 43 × 27 ¾ in. Bequest of Peggy Cooper Cafritz (1947—2018), Washington, DC, collector, educator, and activist 2018.40.289

4. Allison Janae Hamilton, *The March*, 2014. Chromogenic print mounted on sintra, 24 × 30 in. Bequest of Peggy Cooper Cafritz (1947—2018), Washington, DC, collector, educator, and activist 2018.40.107

5. ruby onyinyechi amanze, *Man-Queen [Na so it be]*, 2012. Photo transfers collage, pencil, ink, metallic pens, colored pencils, fluorescent marker, 50 × 38 in. Bequest of Peggy Cooper Cafritz (1947—2018), Washington, DC, collector, educator, and activist 2018.40.10

6. Henry Taylor, *Four-Headed Fool*, 2008. Acrylic on cardboard, 5 ⅛ × 4 ½ × 4 ½ in. Bequest of Peggy Cooper Cafritz (1947—2018), Washington, DC, collector, educator, and activist 2018.40.331

7. Hank Willis Thomas, *Time Can Be a Villain or a Friend*, 2009. LightJet print, 71 ½ × 50 ¼ × 2 in. Bequest of Peggy Cooper Cafritz (1947—2018), Washington, DC, collector, educator, and activist 2018.40.345

8. Jennifer Packer, *The Acrobat*, 2012. Oil on canvas, 6 ¾ × 5 in. Bequest of Peggy Cooper Cafritz (1947—2018), Washington, DC, collector, educator, and activist 2018.40.251

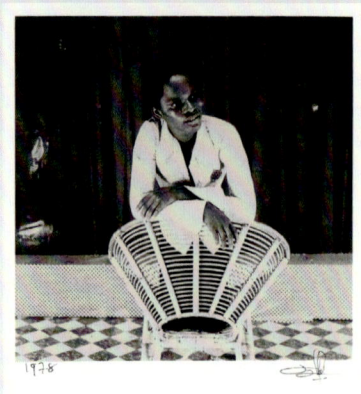

9

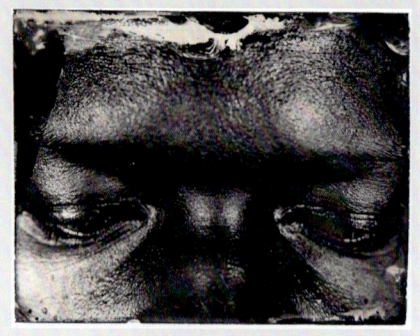

12

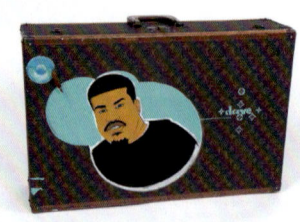

10

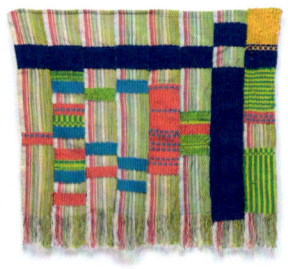

11

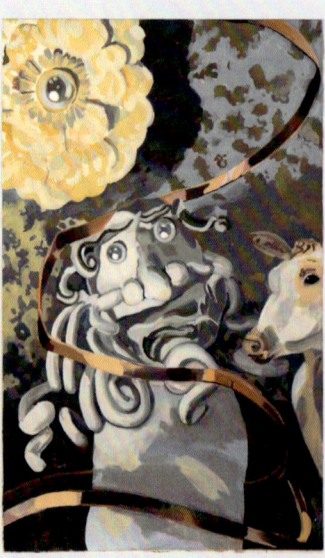

13

The addition of works by alumni of the program enabled the Museum's collection to more fully represent the practices of artists affiliated with the institution from earlier in their careers.

Cooper Cafritz's gift also endowed the Museum with objects by over one hundred artists not previously represented in its collection, and artists who were often considered "emerging" when she first engaged with their work. In the years since the bequest, the Museum has acquired more recent work by several of these artists, including Diedrick Brackens, Derek Fordjour,

and Allison Janae Hamilton, demonstrating a commitment to supporting Black artists at all stages of their careers. Cooper Cafritz shared this commitment, expressed most poignantly in her advocacy of graduates of the Ellington School. Her collection included work by many of the school's alumni, such as Hank Willis Thomas, and these objects are divided between the Studio Museum and the Ellington School.

While her collection focused largely on works by contemporary artists, Cooper Cafritz celebrated the diversity of artists' practices across multiple generations. She

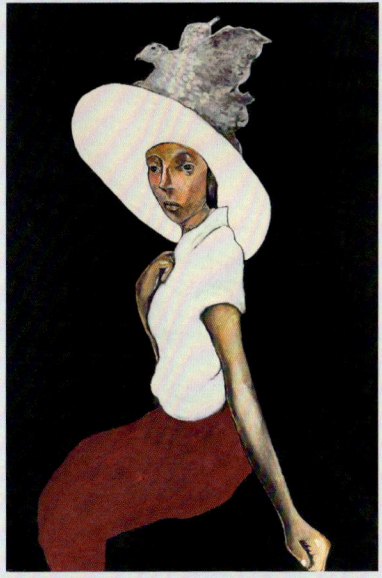

14

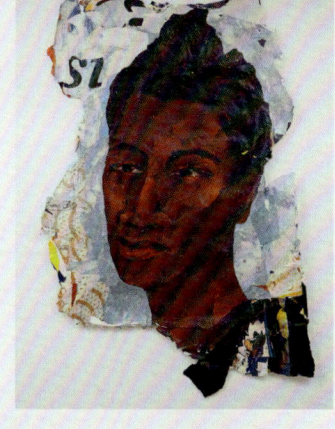

16

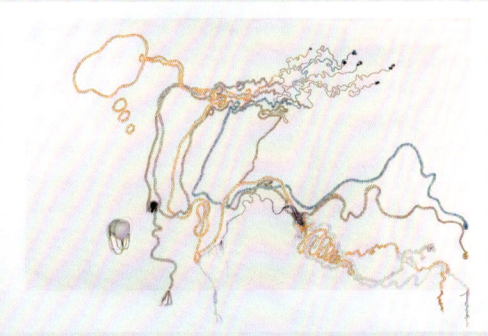

15

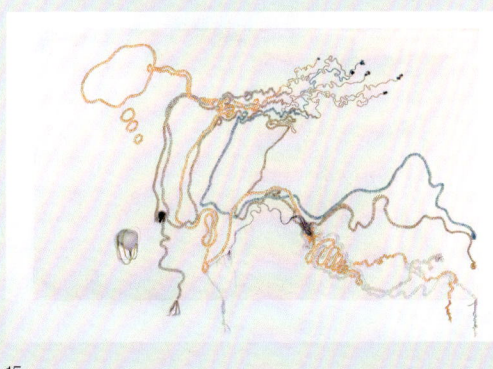

17

9. Samuel Fosso, *Self Portrait*, 1978. Vintage gelatin silver print, 9 ⅜ × 7 in. Bequest of Peggy Cooper Cafritz (1947—2018), Washington, DC, collector, educator, and activist 2018.40.88

10. Rozeal, *Dave, Dove*, 2013. Acrylic on Louis Vuitton suitcase, 21 × 31 ½ × 9 in. Bequest of Peggy Cooper Cafritz (1947—2018), Washington, DC, collector, educator, and activist 2018.40.44

11. Diedrick Brackens, *to know what angels eat*, 2014. Hand-dyed cotton warp, hand-woven cotton, and acrylic yarn, 46 × 51 in. Bequest of Peggy Cooper Cafritz (1947—2018), Washington, DC, collector, educator, and activist 2018.40.40

12. Myra Greene, *Untitled (Ref. #86) from Character Recognition*, 2006—07. Black glass ambrotype, 3 × 3 ¹³⁄₁₆ in. Bequest of Peggy Cooper Cafritz (1947—2018), Washington, DC, collector, educator, and activist 2018.40.101

13. Caitlin Cherry, *Leonardo da Vinci*, 2013. Oil on canvas, 36 × 50 in. Bequest of Peggy Cooper Cafritz (1947—2018), Washington, DC, collector, educator, and activist 2018.40.54

14. Noah Davis, *Black Widow*, 2007. Acrylic and gouache on canvas, 36 × 24 × 3 ¼ in. Bequest of Peggy Cooper Cafritz (1947—2018), Washington, DC, collector, educator, and activist 2018.40.67

15. Nicholas Hlobo, *Thoba utsale umnxeba*, 2008. Ribbon, organza, embroidery anglais, embroidery thread, rubber, buttons, and dust mask on Fabriano paper, 58 ⅞ × 98 ½ in. Bequest of Peggy Cooper Cafritz (1947—2018), Washington, DC, collector, educator, and activist 2018.40.118

16. Kay Hassan, *Untitled*, 2013—14. Paper construction, 93 × 63 in. Bequest of Peggy Cooper Cafritz (1947—2018), Washington, DC, collector, educator, and activist 2018.40.114

17. Samuel Levi Jones, *Nina Simone* (from the series "48 Portraits (Underexposed)", 2012. Inkjet print on pulped encyclopedia paper, 24 ½ × 22 in. Bequest of Peggy Cooper Cafritz (1947—2018), Washington, DC, collector, educator, and activist 2018.40.131

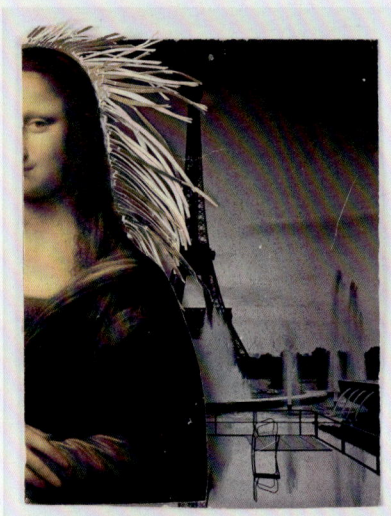

18

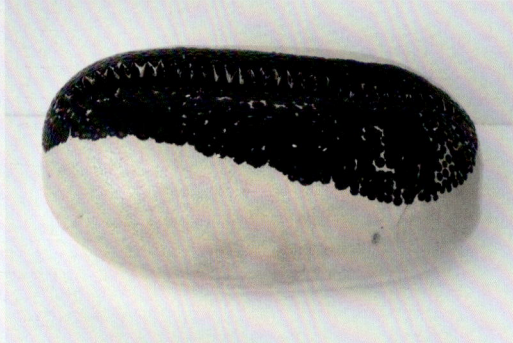

20

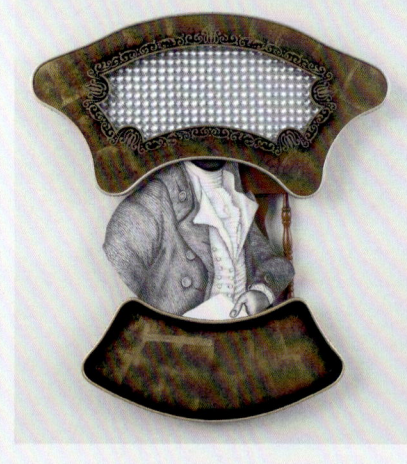

21

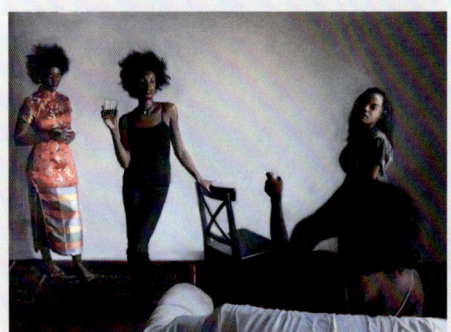

19

collected widely and across media—with abstraction and figuration equally present, and paintings, photographs, sculpture, video, and works on paper all well represented. The earliest work in the bequest is a c. 1920 photograph by James Van Der Zee, while the most recent are from 2017, just a few months before her passing. Despite this range in content, media, and time periods, a core underlying thread across much of the collection is a celebration of color, of spirit, and of artistic exploration.

As a lifelong champion of African and Black American artists, Cooper Cafritz estab-

lished deep and long-lasting relationships with many artists, which is reflected in the depth with which she collected. These works therefore tell an expansive story of how she engaged with artists in her collection—as friend, as mentor, as patron—adding a vibrant history to the ways these objects live in the world.

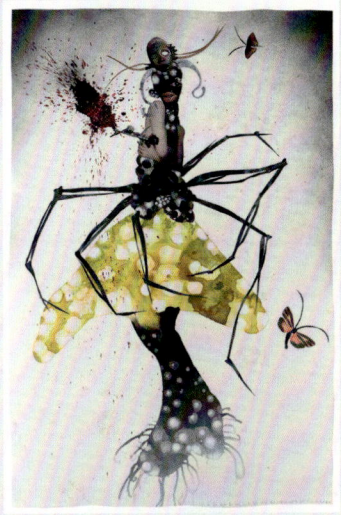

22

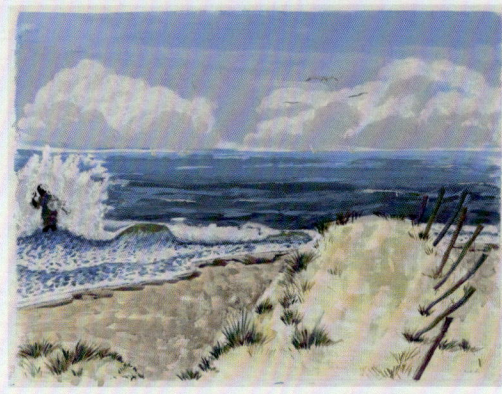

24

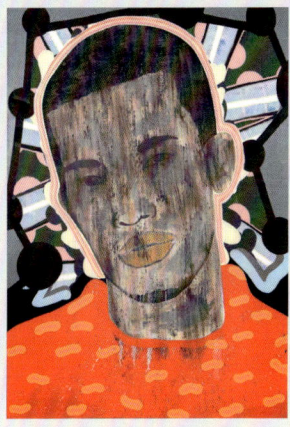

25

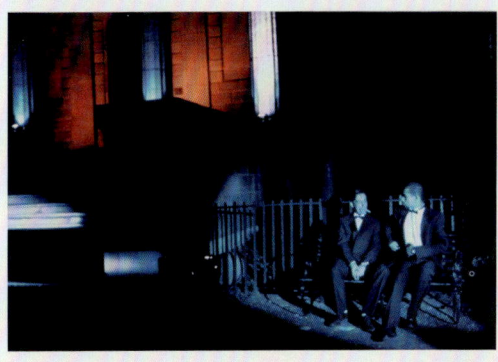

23

18. David Hammons, *Untitled (Mona Lisa)*, 1989. Paper collage, 5 ¼ × 4 ⅛ in. Bequest of Peggy Cooper Cafritz (1947—2018), Washington, DC, collector, educator, and activist 2018.40.110

19. Jas Knight, *A Conversation*, 2017. Oil on linen, 22 ¾ × 32 in. Bequest of Peggy Cooper Cafritz (1947—2018), Washington, DC, collector, educator, and activist 2018.40.159

20. Simone Leigh, *Untitled (Cowrie)*, 2012. Stoneware, 8 × 16 × 7 in. Bequest of Peggy Cooper Cafritz (1947—2018), Washington, DC, collector, educator, and activist 2018.40.177

21. David Shrobe, *Ethereal Plane*, 2016. Oil on wood, wood antique coffee table parts with gold leaf and metal, wood chair parts, mirrored vinyl, glass, and graphite on paper mounted on carved wood, 47 ½ × 42 ½ × 3 ½ in. Bequest of Peggy Cooper Cafritz (1947—2018), Washington, DC, collector, educator, and activist 2018.40.300

22. Wangechi Mutu, *It's the little things that hurt…it's the little things that make us fight!*, 2004. Mixed media collage on Mylar, 35 ¼ × 23 in. Bequest of Peggy Cooper Cafritz (1947—2018), Washington, DC, collector, educator, and activist 2018.40.220

23. Isaac Julien, *Untitled (Newcastle-on-Tyne)*, 1990—99. Chromogenic print, 15 ¾ × 23 ⅛ in. Bequest of Peggy Cooper Cafritz (1947—2018), Washington, DC, collector, educator, and activist 2018.40.136

24. Kerry James Marshall, *Untitled*, 2008. Watercolor on paper, frame: 29 ¼ × 36 ¾ × 1 ½ in. Bequest of Peggy Cooper Cafritz (1947—2018), Washington, DC, collector, educator, and activist 2018.40.197

25. Mustafa Maluka, *We built this city*, 2005. Acrylic and oil on canvas, 72 × 52 in. Bequest of Peggy Cooper Cafritz (1947—2018), Washington, DC, collector, educator, and activist 2018.40.196

James Van Der Zee Archive

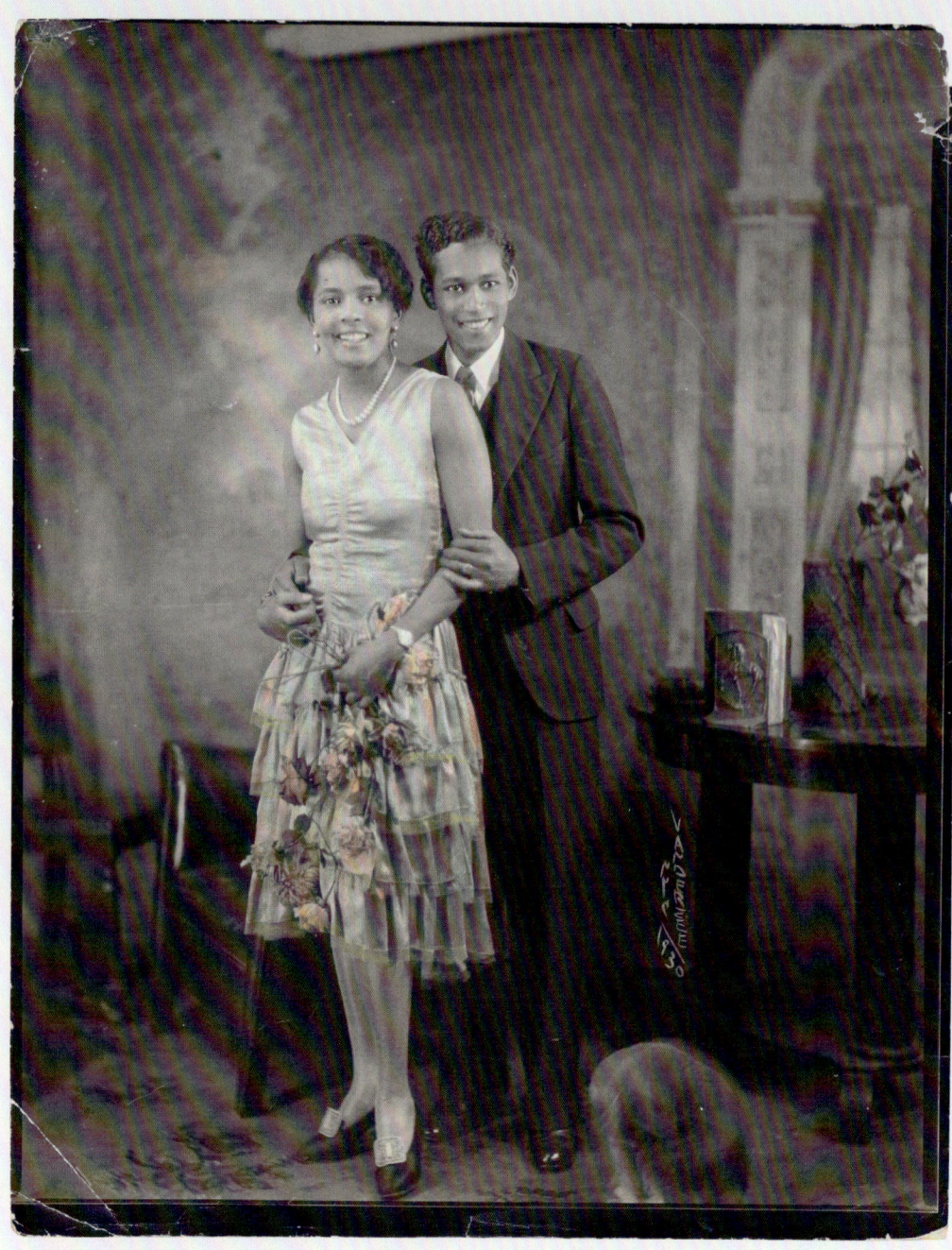

James Van Der Zee (1886—1983), *Amy Brown and John Pyatt*, 1930. Gelatin silver print with applied color, image: 9 ¾ × 7 ¾ in., sheet: 10 × 8 in. James Van Der Zee Archive, The Metropolitan Museum of Art; print from the shared collection of the Studio Museum in Harlem (2021.30.1) and The Metropolitan Museum of Art (2021.444.1)

On December 10, 2021, the Metropolitan Museum of Art and the Studio Museum in Harlem jointly announced the establishment of the James Van Der Zee Archive, a landmark collaborative initiative to research, conserve, and provide full public access to the vast catalogue of photographs by James Van Der Zee.[259] Holding some twenty thousand prints and thirty thousand negatives—as well as the artist's papers, camera equipment, and related ephemera—the archive comprises one of the world's largest single-photographer collections and presents a rich panorama of photographic practice in Harlem from the first decades of the twentieth century to the early 1980s. Collectively, the photographs render an expressive, multifaceted portrait of Black life in the United States as seen through the lens of a virtuoso studio photographer.

The archive includes portraits of young children with their parents; adolescents alone and posed with their peers; baptisms, communions, confirmations, and school graduations; military service members before, during, and after each of the two World Wars; brides, grooms, and their entourages; sports teams, social clubs, and literary salons; musicians, dancers, blues singers, nurses, and beauticians. Van Der Zee also created a celebrated series of funerary tableaux of the dead in their caskets.[260] Reflected in the eyes of Van Der Zee's sitters, we see their ambitions and his own; their modernity and his attuned awareness of the psychological language of portraiture; their social connections and the artist's unwavering belief in the power of photography to preserve the depth, breadth, beauty, and richness of a community.

Born and raised in Lenox, Massachusetts, Van Der Zee excelled in music and the visual arts. In 1900, at age fourteen, he purchased a camera and began his long career. His arrival in New York City in the mid-1910s coincided with the dramatic shift in US cultural life that became the Harlem Renaissance. As Black individuals and families moved to northern cities to improve their circumstances or start anew, Van Der Zee began making their portraits at 109 West 135th Street, the first of his many studios.[261] Although he is now recognized for his photographs of illustrious subjects, from Marcus Garvey to Jean-Michel Basquiat, Van Der Zee is more accurately lauded for his elegant portraits of middle-class people in the US, whose names may likely remain unknown. Nonetheless, it is The Met and the Studio Museum's hope that, with dedicated research, names will in time be reassociated to many of these marvelous faces. The photograph of the young couple featured here—one of some six thousand photographs jointly held by the two museums—is a useful example. After the stylishly posed and delicately hand-colored photograph appeared without identification alongside a suite of others in the *New York Times,* The Met immediately received an email from a New York City teacher who identified her maternal grandparents:

In the 1930 photo, my grandparents are betrothed, but not yet married. He was John Pyatt, Sr., originally from Charleston, South Carolina, who came north in the Great Migration of African Americans from the South years earlier. She was Amy Brown, born in San Jose, Costa Rica, and raised in Kingston, Jamaica, WI. They never lived in Harlem, New York. They resided further uptown, in Mount Vernon, Westchester County, NY, and in the Bronx, NY.[262]

This generous and inspiring note marks the prophetic beginning of the long-term scholarly endeavor to preserve the achievement and legacy of James Van Der Zee. It suggests that with the public's assistance, the institutions can indeed realize their goals.

—Jeff L. Rosenheim

Endnotes

1   "A Museum Is Born in Harlem," *New York Amsterdam News*, September 21, 1968.

2   Mary Schmidt Campbell, "Introduction: The History of Collecting at The Studio Museum in Harlem," in *The Permanent Collection of The Studio Museum in Harlem, Volume I, 1983* (New York: The Studio Museum in Harlem, 1983), 5.

3   Ibid.

4   Quoted in Valerie J. Mercer, "Twenty-Five Years of African-American Art from The Studio Museum in Harlem's Collection," in *The Studio Museum in Harlem: 25 Years of African-American Art* (New York: The Studio Museum in Harlem, 1994), 6.

5   Kinshasha Holman Conwill, "Director's Statement," in *The Studio Museum in Harlem Annual Report 1991–1992* (New York: The Studio Museum in Harlem, 1993), 2, 5.

6   Carolyn J. Weekley, et al. *Joshua Johnson: Freeman and Early American Portrait Painter* (Baltimore, MD: Maryland Historical Society; Williamsburg, VA: Abby Aldrich Rockefeller Folk Art Center, 1987), 75.

7   Hélène Valance, "'The Dynamo and the Virgin': Henry Ossawa Tanner's Religious Nocturnes," in *Henry Ossawa Tanner: Modern Spirit*, ed. Anna O. Marley (Berkeley: University of California Press, 2012), 129.

8   Alain Locke, "The Negro and the American Stage," *Theatre Arts Monthly* 10, no. 2 (February 1926): 118.

9   Deborah Willis, *VanDerZee: Photographer, 1886–1983* (New York: Harry N. Abrams, Inc. in Association with the National Portrait Gallery, Smithsonian Institute, 1993), 16.

10 Ibid.

11 Velma J. Hoover, "Meta Vaux Warrick Fuller: Her Life and Art," *Negro History Bulletin* 40, no. 2 (March–April 1977): 679.

12 Patricia Hill Collins, *Black Feminist Thought: Knowledge, Consciousness, and the Politics of Empowerment* (New York: Routledge, 2009), 98.

13 Carl Richard Benson and Thomas Palmer, *O, Write My Name! American Portraits, Harlem Heroes*, eds. Peter Kayafas and Leslie George Katz (New York: Eakins Press Foundation, 2015), 131–32.

14 Ibid.

15 Ibid., 9.

16 Zora Neale Hurston, quoted in Ellen Skochdopole, "Review of *Inventing Zora Neale Hurston: The Shape-Shifting Woman and Her Portraitist*," National Portrait Gallery, January 6, 2017, npg.si.edu/blog/nventing-zora-neale-hurston-shape-shifting-woman-and-her-portraitist.

17 Fern Gillespie, "The Life and Legacy of Lois Mailou Jones," *Howard Magazine* 8, no. 2 (Winter 1999): 8.

18 Jerry Langley, "Overlooked, but Unbowed: Hayward L. Oubre," *The International Review of African American Art* 17, no. 4 (2001): 13–15.

19 Margaret Rose Vendryes, *Barthé: A Life in Sculpture* (Jackson: University Press of Mississippi, 2008), 94.

20 Jerry Langley, "Hayward L. Oubre: Improvisations with Wire," *Art@UMUC Magazine*, (Spring 2019): 13.

21 Leah Ollman, "Review: How Photographer Roy DeCarava Captured Daily Life with Aching Beauty," *Los Angeles Times*, April 29, 2019, latimes.com/entertainment/arts/la-et-cm-roy-decarava-review-20190429-story.html.

22 Elizabeth Bigham, "Issues of Authorship in the Portrait Photographs of Seydou Keïta," *African Arts* 32, no. 1 (Spring 1999): 61.

23 André Magnin, "Seydou Keita," *African Arts* 28, no. 4 (Autumn 1995): 92.

24 "A Portrait of Mali," *The Journal of Blacks in Higher Education*, no. 17 (1997): 34.

25 Though Keïta did take photographs using artificial light, he preferred natural light as he felt artificial light made his subjects look pale (Magnin, "Seydou Keïta," 95).

26 Bigham, 59.

27 Magnin, 91.

28 Keïta took on this role in 1962.

29 Hale Woodruff to Esther Krasny, letter, New York, November 25, 1955, courtesy Swann Auction Galleries, catalogue. swanngalleries.com/Lots/auction-lot/WOODRUFF-HALE-Illustrated-Autograph-Leter-Signed-with-6-ink?saleno=2470&lotNo=260&refNo=739438.

30 Hale Woodruff, interview by Al Murray, "Oral History Interview with Hale Woodruff," Archives of American Art, Smithsonian Institution, November 18, 1968, aaa.si.edu/collections/interviews/oral-history-interview-hale-woodruff-11463.

31 These spaces were all located in Harlem. Augusta Savage's art studio was for a time at 163 West 143rd Street and then at 239 West 135th Street. The Savage Studio of Arts and Crafts grew out of informal classes in her studio starting around 1931, and by 1934 it was the "largest tuition-free art class in New York City." Sharif Bey, "Augusta Savage: Sacrifice, Social Responsibility, and Early African American Art Education," *Studies in Art Education* 58, no. 2 (2017): 133; Utopia Children's House was located at 170 West 130th Street. Harlem Art Workshop at 103 135th Street, now the Schomburg Center; the workshop later moved to 270 West 136th Street. The 306 group was the location of Charles Alston and Henry Berryman's studio space at 306 West 141st Street. Leah Dickerman, "Fighting

Blues," in *Jacob Lawrence: The Migration Series*, eds. Leah Dickerman and Elsa Smithgall (New York: The Museum of Modern Art; Washington, DC: The Philips Collection, 2017), 14–15.

32 Harlem Community Art Center was located at 290 Malcolm X Boulevard (Lenox Avenue). Dickerman, *Jacob Lawrence: The Migration Series*, 12–16.

33 *The Life of Toussaint L'Ouverture* was completed in 1938, *The Life of Frederick Douglass* in 1939, and *The Life of Harriet Tubman* in 1940.

34 Lowery Stokes Sims, "The Structure of Narrative: Form and Content in Jacob Lawrence's Builders Paintings, 1946–1998," in *Over the Line: The Art and Life of Jacob Lawrence*, eds. Peter T. Nesbett and Michelle DuBois (Seattle and London: University of London Press in association with Jacob Lawrence Catalogue Raisonné Project, Seattle, 2000), 209–10.

35 Bob Thompson, quoted in Jeanne Siegel, "Four American Negro Painters, 1940–1965: Their Choice and Treatment of Themes" (master's thesis, Columbia University, 1966), 79.

36 Austin Porter, "Charles Henry Alston," in *The Unforgettables: Expanding the History of American Art*, ed. Charles C. Eldredge. (Oakland: University of California Press, 2022), 168.

37 Charles Alston, interview by Al Murray, "Oral History Interview with Charles Alston," Archives of American Art, Smithsonian Institution, October 19, 1968, aaa.si.edu/collections/interviews/oral-history-interview-charles-henry-alston-11460.

38 Mali gained independence in 1960.

39 Manthia Diawara, "The Song of the Griot," *Transition*, no. 74 (1997): 16.

40 Ibid., 19.

41 Malick Sidibé, "Interview with Malick Sidibé," interview by Jerome Sother, *LensCulture*, 2008, lensculture.com/articles/malick-sidibe-interview-with-malick-sidibe.

42 Ibid.

43 Norman Lewis, interview by Henri Ghent, "Oral History Interview with Norman Lewis," Archives of American Arts, Smithsonian Institute, July 14, 1968, aaa.si.edu/collections/interviews/oral-history-interview-norman-lewis-11465.

44 Tanisha C. Ford, *Kwame Brathwaite: Black Is Beautiful* (New York: Aperture, 2019), 43.

45 Melvin Edwards, interview by Catherine Craft, "Conversation with Melvin Edwards: Extended Version," Nasher Sculpture Center, n.d., nashersculpturecenter.org/art/artists/melvin-edwards-interview.

46 Melvin Edwards, interview by Michael Benson, "Melvin Edwards by Michael Brenson," The Oral History

Project, *BOMB*, November 24, 2014, bombmagazine.org/articles/melvin-edwards/.

47   Betty Blayton, in *Tonnie Jones' Sculptures and Betty Blayton Taylor's Oil Collages: Etchings and Small Sculptures* (New York: Studio Museum in Harlem, 1974), studiomuseum.netx.net/portals/studio-museum-archives/#document/15642.

48   Meredith Shuba Watson, Valerie Cassel Oliver, and Carol Woods Sawyer, "'Spiritual Abstraction': The Art and Work of Betty Blayton," *Materia: Journal of Technical Art History* no. 2 (2022): 33, issue-2.materiajournal.com/watson/.

49   Betty Blayton, "Interview with Betty Blayton-Taylor," interviewed by Halima Taha, November 9, 1997, *Artist and Influence* 17 (1998): 54.

50   Ibid.

51   SHAFT, directed by Gordon Parks (Los Angeles: Metro-Goldwyn-Mayer, 1971), 31:23.

52   "Alright," MP3 audio, track 7 on Kendrick Lamar, *To Pimp a Butterfly*, Top Dawg Entertainment, Aftermath Entertainment, and Interscope Records, 2015.

53   The year also saw the expansion of the—increasingly deadly for African American troops—war in Vietnam, as well as the election of President Richard M. Nixon.

54   The Civil Rights Act of 1968 was an expansion of the Civil Rights Act of 1964. Later amended, it would also prohibit discrimination based on sex (1974), handicap, and family status (1988).

55   The Museum of Modern Art, *New Documents*, February 28—May 7, 1967. Text from wall label accessed by the author on June 18, 2023. See the exhibition files at moma.org. Despite the well-deserved boost offered by the museum show, there was still no reliable market for fine art photography, and Arbus (and her peers) had to rely on commercial work to make their livings. Beginning in 1960 and until her death in July 1971, Diane Arbus published some 250 photographs in a wide variety of outlets. For a nearly complete bibliography of this work, see *Diane Arbus: Magazine Work* (New York: Aperture, 1984).

56   The portrait would appear in the December 1968 issue alongside a poem by Paul Engle. See "On a Photograph of Mrs. Martin Luther King at the Funeral," (December 1968), 106—07. Curiously, Engle's short poem is a direct response to a different photograph of Coretta Scott King, seen in mourning garb seated in a church pew at her husband's funeral on April 9. It remains difficult to determine if this photograph, of Mrs. King wearing a veil, is a work by Moneta Sleet or Flip Schulke.

57   Greta Berman, "Mavis Pusey," in *Gumbo Ya Ya: Anthology of Contemporary African-American Women Artists*, ed. Leslie King-Hammond (New York: Midmarch Arts Press, 1995), 219.

58   Ibid.

59   David Driskell, interview by Cynthia Mills, "Oral History Interview with David Driskell," Archives of American Art, Smithsonian Institution March—April 2006, aaa.si.edu/collections/interviews/oral-history-interview-david-driskell-15943#transcript.

60   Ibid.

61   "465" recalls Williams's 1980s series titled "111 1/2," in reference to his aunt's address in Harlem, and further demonstrates the thematic significance of home and place in his body of work.

62   Michael Rosenfeld Gallery, "Selected Works: William T. Williams: Recent Paintings," press release, August 13, 2019.

63   Nathaniel G. Nesmith, "Doing It His Way: Ademola Olugebefola's Long and Varied Career in the Arts," *New England Review* 42, no. 3 (2021), nereview.com/vol-42-no-3-2021/doing-it-his-way-ademola-olugebefolas-long-and-varied-career-in-the-arts/.

64   Shantay Robinson, "How a Celebrated Artist Redesigned the Stars and Stripes to Mark His Pride in Black America," *Smithsonian Magazine*, July 14, 2022, smithsonianmag.com/smithsonian-institution/how-a-celebrated-artist-redesigned-the-stars-and-stripes-to-mark-pride-black-america-180980401/.

65   "This Is America," MP3 audio, single track on Childish Gambino, *This Is America*, mcDJ and RCA, 2018.

66   Adoration, confession, thanksgiving, and supplication.

67   Emma Lazarus, "The New Colossus," lines 10—11, 1883, Statue of Liberty, New York, New York.

68   David Hammons, "Interview: David Hammons," interview by Kellie Jones, *Art Papers* 12, no. 4 (1988): 39—42.

69   Henry Miller, *The Amazing and Invariable Beauford Delaney* (New York: New Directions Publishing, 1978).

70   Samella Lewis, *The Art of Elizabeth Catlett* (Claremont: Handcraft Studios, 1984), 93.

71   Elizabeth Catlett, handwritten manuscript for a lecture and slide presentation at the New Orleans Museum of Art, October 15, 1983, Elizabeth Catlett Papers, Amistad Center, New Orleans, LA, quoted in Melanie Anne Herzog, *Elizabeth Catlett: An American Artist in Mexico* (Seattle: University of Washington, 2005), 3.

72   *Separation* (1954) closely resembles one of the prints in the series: "My reward has been bars between me and the rest of the land."

73   Samella Lewis and Ruth Waddy, *Black Artists on Art: Volume 2* (Los Angeles: Contemporary Crafts, 1971), 107.

74   Elizabeth Catlett, "The Role of the Black Artist," *The Black Scholar* 6, no. 9 (1975): 10—14, jstor.org/stable/41066392.

75   Anne Melanie Herzog, *Elizabeth Catlett: An American Artist in Mexico*, 88, 140—41.

76   She writes, "Blackness is important as a *part* of the struggle—it is our part—not only of blacks in the US, Africa and the Caribbean, but of Chicanos and Puerto Ricans in the US, and the peoples of Asia and Latin America exemplified at the moment by the Chileans and Vietnamese. Through art we can bring understanding to Black America, Chicano America, Puerto Rican America, etc. of the character of racism, the need for its elimination, our mutual problems and our differences." Catlett, "The Role of the Black Artist," 14.

77   Hunt was only nineteen years old when he participated in the *58th Annual Exhibition by Artists of Chicago and Vicinity* at the Art Institute of Chicago in 1955, frequently showing in other iterations of this exhibition and the Art Institute's American Exhibition in the following years. Hunt's first solo exhibition came in 1958 at the Charles Alan Gallery in New York. John Yau, "Richard Hunt's Indisputable Achievement," in *Richard Hunt* (New York: Gregory R. Miller & Co., 2022), 10—19.

78   Hallie Ringle, *Richard Hunt: Framed and Extended*, 2016, poster, 17 × 22 in. Studio Museum in Harlem, New York.

79   Richard Hunt, "Statements by Richard Hunt," in *The Sculpture of Richard Hunt*, ed. William S. Lieberman, exh. cat. (New York: Museum of Modern Art, 1971), 15.

80   Robert Rauschenberg, *Robert Rauschenberg: Prints 1948/1970*, exh. cat. (Minneapolis: Minneapolis Institute of Arts, 1970).

81   Jeff Donaldson, "AfriCOBRA Manifesto? 'Ten in Search of a Nation,'" *Nka Journal of Contemporary African Art* 30 (Spring 2012): 80.

82   Dindga McCannon in conversation with the author March 2023.

83   Skunder Boghossian, quoted in Tritobia H. Benjamin, "Skunder Boghossian: A Different Magnificence," *African Arts* 5, no. 4 (Summer 1972): 22—25.

84   Anna Kisselgoff, "Dance: A Spicy 'Carmen,'" *New York Times*, March 4, 1976, nytimes.com/1976/03/04/archives/dance-a-spicy-carmen-harlem-troupe-blends-humor-and-calypso.html.

85   Hassinger and members of Studio Z presented work across Los Angeles arts organizations throughout the 1970s and 1980s, from the Woman's Building (1983) to Barnsdall Art Park (1982) to the Los Angeles County Museum of Art (1981), among other organizations, institutions, and alternative arts spaces.

86   Quote by the artist in Jori Finkel, "Q&A: Maren Hassinger & Senga Nengudi," *Los Angeles Times*, November 27, 2011, latimes.com/entertainment/la-xpm-2011-nov-27-la-ca-pst-kellie-jones-interview-20111127-story.html.

87   Quotation from label entry for *Revolution (Angela Davis)*, Brooklyn Museum, brooklynmuseum.org/opencollection/objects/210696, accessed September 8, 2023.

88   Chase-Riboud's fascination with Cleopatra includes the collection of poems *Portrait of a Nude Woman as Cleopatra* (New York: William Morrow & Company, 1987), three mixed-media wall reliefs each titled *Cleopatra's*

Marriage Contract, and five freestanding bronze sculptures (*Cleopatra's Cape* [1973], *Door* [1984], *Cleopatra's Chair* [1994], *Cleopatra's Bed* [1997], and *Cleopatra's Wedding Dress* [2003]).

89   Barbara Chase-Riboud, "Barbara Chase-Riboud: Poet," chaseriboud.free.fr/Poet2004.htm.

90   José da Silva, "Sam Gilliam: A Life Beyond the Frame," *The Art Newspaper*, June 14, 2018, theartnewspaper.com/2018/06/14/sam-gilliam-a-life-beyond-the-frame.

91   Martin Luther King Jr. "I Have a Dream," August 28, 1963, Lincoln Memorial, Washington DC, Transcript, The Avalon Project, Yale Law School: Lillian Goldman Law Library, avalon.law.yale.edu/20th_century/mlk01.asp.

92   Laure Wilson, *Louise Nevelson: Light and Shadow* (New York: Thames and Hudson, 2016), 64.

93   *With Peter Bradley*, directed by Alex Rappoport (Saugerties, NY: Import Media, 2023), 1 hr. 32 min.

94   "Houston Conwill," *Contemporary Sculpture: Selections from the Permanent Collection* (New York: Studio Museum in Harlem, 1986).

95   Kellie Jones, "Now Dig This! An Introduction," Hammer Museum, accessed August 4, 2023, hammer.ucla.edu/now-dig-this/essays/now-dig-this.

96   Betye Saar, *Recent Works by Houston E. Conwill: Juju* (Los Angeles: the Gallery, 1976).

97   Mel Gooding, "Bowling at Spritmuseum: Landscapes of the Spirit," *Frank Bowling: Traingone*, ed. Vera Celander, exh. cat. (Stockholm: Spritmuseum, 2014), 31.

98   Romi Crawford, "Street Portraits: Romi Crawford on Dawoud Bey," *Aperture*, The PhotoBook Review Issue 019, (Spring 2021): 27.

99   Valerie Maynard in conversation with the author, August 13, 2019.

100 BMA Stories, "Honoring Valerie Maynard's 'Human-Beingness,'" September 23, 2022, stories.artbma.org/honoring-valerie-maynards-human-beingness/.

101 Shira Wolfe, "Lost (and Found) Artist Series: Howardena Pindell," *Artland Magazine*, n.d., magazine.artland.com/lost-and-found-artist-series-howardena-pindell/.

102 Nanette Carter, "On Using Scapes," *Black Renaissance/Renaissance Noire* 9, no. 2–3 (2009): 88+. *Gale Literature Resource Center*, link.gale.com/apps/doc/A271406184/LitRC?.

103 Nanette Carter, interview by Cheryl R. Riley, "Oral History with Nanette Carter," Archives of American Art, Smithsonian Institution, November 22 and December 7, 2021, aaa.si.edu/collections/interviews/oral-history-interview-nanette-carter-22116.

104 Ibid.

105 "Presentation and Studio Visit with Artist Nanette Carter," the Art Students League of New York, YouTube, 32:44, April 14, 2021, youtu.be/0if413EMHdA.

106 Carter, "On Using Scapes."

107 Jack Whitten, interview by Judith Olch Richards, "Oral History Interview with Jack Whitten," Archives of American Art, Smithsonian Institution, December 1–3, 2009, aaa.si.edu/collections/interviews/oral-history-interview-jack-whitten-15748.

108 Beryl Wright and Jack Whitten, *Jack Whitten*, exh. cat. (Newark, NJ: Newark Museum, 1990), 10.

109 Whitten, "Oral History."

110 Whitten drew from his interest in sculpture in introducing three-dimensionality to his paintings. He began woodcarving in 1962 and continued creating sculptures at his summer home in Crete until the end of his life. While he kept that body of work relatively unknown and in Greece, Whitten declared that woodcarving was "the single most important influence on [his] painting's plasticity." Jack Whitten, "An Artist's Life: Jack Whitten," Art21, March 21, 2018, video, 9:19, art21.org/watch/extended-play/jack-whitten-an-artists-life-short.

111 Whitten, "Oral History."

112 A 2023 email Q&A between the author and the artist informs much of the writing of this text, including this specific sentence.

113 Faith Ringgold and Josephine Withers, "Faith Ringgold: Art," *Feminist Studies 6*, no. 1 (Spring, 1980): 207.

114 Leslie King-Hammond, *Hughie Lee-Smith: The David C. Driskell Series of African American Art, Volume VIII* (New York: Pomegranate Press, 2010), 42.

115 Jeff Edwards, "The Long Sweep, A Conversation with Ed Clark about His 60-Plus Years in the Art World," ArtPulse, n.d., artpulsemagazine.com/the-long-sweep-a-conversation-with-ed-clark-about-his-60-plus-years-in-the-art-world.

116 John Yau, "A History Waiting to be Written: Ed Clark's High-Spirited, Abstract Paintings," *Hyperallergic*, January 26, 2014, hyperallergic.com/104776/a-history-waiting-to-be-written-ed-clarks-high-spirited-abstract-paintings/.

117 Edwards, "The Long Sweep."

118 Randy Williams, email with the author, July 12, 2023.

119 Artist quoted in David Revere McFadden, "A Season of Abundance," in *Sana Musasama: Ambivalent Beauty* (Hanover, NH: Dartmouth College, Hopkins Center, Jaffe-Friede & Strauss Galleries, 2007), 19.

120 For more information see Deirdre L. Bibby, "Sana Musasama," in *Gumbo Ya Ya: Anthology of Contemporary African-American Women Artists*, ed. Leslie King-Hammond (New York: Midmarch Arts Press, 1995), 184–85; *Sana Musasama*, "House Series," Sana Musasama, sana-musasama.com/gallery/house-series; and "Sana Musasama: Visiting Artist Lecture Series Spring 2021," Art & Art History, CU Boulder, YouTube, 54:42, March 9, 2021, youtube.com/watch?v=m1MQfFTvkiQ.

121 Bibby, "Sana Musasama," 184.

122 "From the Studio: The Studio Museum in Harlem Artist-in-Residence 1984," Schomburg Center for Research in Black Culture, Art and Artifacts Division, New York Public Library Digital Collections, digitalcollections.nypl.org/items/5e3c8320-f0d4-013a-d118-0242ac110003.

123 Lorraine O'Grady and Aruna D'Souza, *Writing in Space, 1973–2019* (New York: Duke University Press, 2020).

124 "Art Is. . ." Lorraine O'Grady, October 11, 2022. lorraineogrady.com/art/art-is/.

125 Ibid.

126 Lorraine O'Grady, "Olympia's Maid: Reclaiming, Black Female Subjectivity," *Afterimage: Journal of Media Arts and Cultural Criticism* 20, no.1 (June 1992): 14–15.

127 Thelma Golden, *Alison Saar: Slow Boat* (New York: Whitney Museum of American Art at Philip Morris, 1992).

128 Judith Wilson, "Down to the Crossroads: The Art of Alison Saar," *Callaloo* 14, no. 1 (1991): 8. See also Barbara C. Matilsky, "Object, Spirit, Nature: Transformation in the Art of Betye, Lezley, and Alison Saar," in *Family Legacies: The Art of Betye, Lezley, and Alison Saar* (Chapel Hill, NC and Seattle, WA: The University of North Carolina at Chapel Hill and University of Washington Press, 2005), 48–49.

129 Alison Saar, "Fighting Flatness," in *Mirror Mirror: The Prints of Alison Saar from the Collections of Jordan D. Schnitzer and His Family Foundation* (Portland, OR: Jordan Schnitzer Family Foundation, 2019), 95.

130 Wilson, "Down to the Crossroads," 108–09.

131 Saar, "Fighting Flatness," 95.

132 Mary Nooter Roberts and Alison Saar, "Conversing Forms: A Dialogue between Artist Alison Saar and Curator Mary Nooter Roberts," in *Body Politics: The Female Image in Luba Art and the Sculpture of Alison Saar* (Los Angeles, CA: UCLA Museum of Cultural History, 2000), 41. See also Matilksy, "Object, Spirit, Nature," 48.

133 Nooter Roberts and Saar, "Conversing Forms," 55.

134 In her groundbreaking critique of Black women's sexuality and embodiment in art, Lorraine O'Grady famously wrote that, in the national imagination, "white is what woman is; not-white (and the stereotypes not-white gathers in) is what she had better not be." Lorraine O'Grady, "Olympia's Maid: Reclaiming Black Female Subjectivity," *Afterimage* 20, no. 1 (Summer 1992), 14.

135 Shawn G. Kennedy, "For Fledgling Artists, a Place to Grow," *New York Times*, Section C (June 18, 1986): 12, timesmachine.nytimes.com/timesmachine/1986/06/18/issue.html.

136 Linda B. Hirsh, "African Permeates Artist's Work," *Hartford Courant*, January 31, 1996.

137 *Oxford English Dictionary*, oed.com/dictionary/shamma_n.

138 Eliana Smith, "Digital Archives as a Black Interior," *Studio*, December 12, 2022, studiomuseum.org/magazine/digital-archives-as-a-black-interior.

139 Lorna Simpson quoted in Joseph Akel, "A Photographic Memory: In the Studio with Lorna Simpson," *Paris Review*, October 15, 2015, theparisreview.org/

blog/2015/10/15/a-photographic-memory-in-the-studio-with-lorna-simpson/.

140 Ibid.

141 "Lorna Simpson in Conversation with Thelma Golden," *Ursula*, May 14, 2019, hauserwirth.com/ursula/24565-lorna-simpson-conversation-thelma-golden/.

142 Alice Walker, "Beverly Buchanan, Artist, 1940—2015," August 4, 2015, alicewalkersgarden.com/2015/08/beverly-buchanan-artist-1940-2015/.

143 Carol Kino, "Letting His Life's Work Do the Talking," *New York Times*, February 17, 2011, nytimes.com/2011/02/20/arts/design/20dial.html.

144 "Thorton Dial," Souls Grown Deep, soulsgrowndeep.org/artist/thornton-dial.

145 *The New Encyclopedia of Southern Culture* 23 Folk Art, eds. Carol Crown, Cheryl Rivers, Charles Reagan Wilson, James G. Thomas, Ann J. Abadie, sponsored by the University of Mississippi Center for the Study of Southern Culture (University of North Carolina Press, Chapel Hill, 2013), 263.

146 Cheryl Finley, "Frank Stewart's International Lens," *Frank Stewart's Nexus an American Photographer's Journey, 1960s to the Present*, exh. cat. (Washington, DC: The Phillips Collection, 2023), 143—44.

147 Mary Schmidt Campbell, "Introduction," in *Frank Stewart's Nexus an American Photographer's Journey, 1960s to the Present*, 15.

148 See other works from this period, including *Cabin Slide* (2000), *Cabin Vision* (2001), and *Ramshackle Tumble* (2002).

149 Maurice Berger, Jennifer A. González, and Fred Wilson, *Fred Wilson: Objects and Installations 1979—2000*, exh. cat. (Center for Art and Visual Culture University of Maryland Baltimore County, 2001), 33.

150 Chris Ofili, *Chris Ofili: Night and Day*, eds. Massimiliano Gioni, Glenn Ligon, Gary Carrion-Murayari, Margot Norton, exh. cat. (New York, NY: Skira Rizzoli: New Museum, 2014), 249.

151 Ibid., 95.

152 Ibid., 243.

153 Tropical Fantasy soda was launched in Brooklyn in 1990, gaining popularity for its forty-nine-cent bottles. A year later a rumor took hold that the drink contained ingredients intended to cause infertility in Black men, leading the city's Black mayor at the time, David N. Dinkins, to drink a bottle on television in an effort to restore calm.

154 Nari Ward and Lowery Stokes Sims, "Hidden in Plain Sight: Nari Ward in Conversation with Lowery Stokes Sims," in *Nari Ward: We the People*, eds. Gary Carrion-Murayari, Massimiliano Gioni, and Helga Christoffersen, exh. cat. (New York: New Museum and Phaidon Press, 2019), 16.

155 Erzulie is the Haitian Vodou Lwa or Loa (spirit) associated with love and femininity. She embodies many forms, from romantic lover to fierce warrior and protective mother, and is often represented with jewelry, heart-shaped medals, a pierced heart, and three wedding bands (one for each husband).

156 Vladimir Cybil Charlier, interview by Habiba Hopson, "New Additions: Vladimir Cybil Charlier," *Studio*, May 11, 2023, studiomuseum.org/article/new-additions-vladimir-cybil-charlier.

157 Ibid.

158 Nargess Banks, "In a Candid Interview, Leonardo Drew Discusses His Latest Art Installation and Why Art Matters," *Forbes*, March 24, 2023, forbes.com/sites/nargessbanks/2023/03/24/artist-leonardo-drew-on-his-yorkshire-sculpture-park-installation-and-why-art-matters/.

159 Joshua I. Cohen, "Harlem Renaissance and Diaspora," *The "Black Art" Renaissance: African Sculpture and Modernism across Continents* (Berkeley: University of California Press, 2020), 98.

160 Raymond Saunders, "Black Is a Color" (self-pub., 1967), *Arts Magazine*, June 1967.

161 "Raymond Saunders Interview," San Francisco Museum of Modern Art, September 20, 2012, video, 13:52, archive.org/details/cocac_000011.

162 "Adia Millett: Objects of What Remains," *Meer*, May 19, 2014, meer.com/en/9254-adia-millet-objects-of-what-remains.

163 Touré, "The Rescuer," in *Kehinde Wiley: A New Republic*, ed. Eugenie Tsai, exh. cat. (New York: Brooklyn Museum, 2015), 52.

164 Julien mainly works in film, but he also produces large photographs taken from the footage. The photographs are distinct works, but they are often titled the same as or similar to the films.

165 Lauren Haynes, "Nontsikelelo 'Lolo' Veleko," in *Flow*, ed. Christine Y. Kim, exh. cat. (New York: Studio Museum in Harlem, 2008).

166 Ibid.

167 Kathleen Madden, "Figures & Fictions: Contemporary South African Photography," *Artforum*, n.d., artforum.com/events/figures-fictions-contemporary-south-african-photography-190450/.

168 Camille Billops, Corrine Jennings, Gloria Rodriguez, "Press Release: Camille Billops and the Minstrel Series," October 20, 1993, Kenkeleba House Inc.

169 Namely, D. W. Griffith's *Birth of a Nation* is arguably the origin and landmark of American cinema, and also the most racist film in cinematic history. Released in 1915, the film features blackface minstrelsy that renders African Americans as violent, lazy, and ignorant. See Sean Axmaker, "The Birth of a Nation Offspring," PBS, February 2, 2017, pbs.org/independentlens/blog/offspring-of-birth-of-a-nation.

170 The artist is perhaps best known for his late 1970s to present-day performance art crawls across New York City on his hands, knees, and belly, in suits and Superman costumes. These crawls intended to bring attention to a large population of unhoused city residents who lost what the artist calls "verticality," or the condition of having enough means and physical ability not to "lose one's ground."

171 Reiner Schürmann, *Broken Hegemonies*, trans. Reginald Lilly (Bloomington: Indiana University Press), 6.

172 Christine Y. Kim, "Wardell Milan II," in *Frequency*, exh. cat. (New York: Studio Museum in Harlem, 2005), 62—63.

173 Ibid.

174 "'It Creates Layers': Watch Artist Kalup Linzy Explain Why He Plays Multiple Roles in His Madcap Performance," Artnet, September 1, 2022, news.artnet.com/art-world/kalup-linzy-art21-2168437.

175 Clifford Owens, interview by Nick Stillman, "Clifford Owens," *BOMB*, October 1, 2011, bombmagazine.org/articles/clifford-owens/.

176 Kymberly N. Pinder, "Unbaled: An Interview with Shinique Smith," *Art Journal* 67, no. 2 (2008): 9.

177 Jane Simon, "Shinique Smith: Objects and Abstraction," in *Shinique Smith: Menagerie*, exh. cat. (Museum of Contemporary Art, North Miami; Madison, WI: Madison Museum of Contemporary Art, 2010), 32.

178 Pinder, "Unbaled," 14.

179 Vielmetter Los Angeles, "Charles Gaines: Drawings from the Explosion Series," press release, May 2008, vielmetter.com/exhibitions/2008-05-charles-gaines-drawings-from-the-explosion-series.

180 From Eddie Kendricks's "My People … Hold On," from *My People … Hold On*, Tamla Records, 1972.

181 Steffani Jemison, "Drafts: Steffani Jemison on the Stroke, the Glyph, and the Mark," *Artforum*, April 2019, 57, no. 8, artforum.com/print/201904/steffani-jemison-on-the-stroke-the-glyph-and-the-mark-78965.

182 Ben Lerner, "Steffani Jemison," *BOMB*, March 15, 2017, Issue 139, bombmagazine.org/articles/steffani-jemison/.

183 The original quote was edited to correct a presumed typo: "through" for "though." Laura Kina, "Chimera: A Conversation on Mixed Race/Mixed Methods with Sita Kuratomi Bhaumik and Saya Woolfalk," in *Queering Contemporary Asian American Art*, eds. Laura Kina and Jan Christian Bernabe (Seattle, WA: University of Washington Press, 2017), 161.

184 Kina, "Chimera," 158.

185 Nicole Fleetwood, "Performing Empathies: The Art of Saya Woolfalk," *Callaloo* 37, no. 4 (2014): 975.

186 Kina, "Chimera," 157.

187 Fleetwood, "Performing Empathies," 975; Kina, "Chimera," 160.

188 Noah Davis and Lauren Haynes, "3Qs: Noah Davis," *Studio*, May 26, 2022, web.archive.org/web/20220526174435/studiomuseum.org/article/3qs-noah-davis.

189 Naomi Beckwith, "Nick Cave: Beyond

an Eye-Level Existence," in *Nick Cave: Forothermore*, exh. cat. (Chicago and New York: Museum of Contemporary Art Chicago and DelMonico Books, New York, 2022), 54.

190 "Fresh Ammunition: The Artist William Villalongo," *Ammo*, November 2010.

191 Daniel Cassady, "On Eve of Basel Unlimited's Debut, Artist Radcliffe Bailey Has His Sights Set on Bigger Things," *ARTnews*, June 12, 2023, artnews.com/art-news/artists/radcliffe-bailey-art-basel-unlimited-history-1234671112/.

192 "Artist Talk: Deana Lawson," the Art Institute of Chicago, November 5, 2015, YouTube, 54:43, October 15, 2015, youtube.com/watch?v=XzjWtGGDkIQ&t=1204s.

193 "Family Values: Eva Respini on Deana Lawson's Portraiture," Mack Books Blog, mackbooks.co.uk/blogs/news/family-values-eva-respini-on-deana-lawson-s-portraiture.

194 "Artist Talk: Deana Lawson."

195 David Hartt, "Shine a Light: Canadian Biennial 2014: David Hartt," National Gallery of Canada, YouTube, 2:18, January 26, 2015, youtube.com/watch?v=gk5WF5qm9sU.

196 *Derrick Adams: Style Variations*, Salon 94, New York, 2021, cdn.sanity.io/files/cpu8yypf/production/cc11ead-693e8089368dcc39e6b0b-e538052a160c.pdf.

197 Lowery Stokes Sims, "'A Conscious Syncretizer': The Connective Tissue of the Career of Ficre Ghebreyesus," *Ficre Ghebreyesus: City with a River Running Through*, exh. cat. (Petaluma, CA: Cameron + Company and the Museum of the African Diaspora, 2019), 21—27.

198 Ficre Ghebreyesus, "Artist Statement," written in 2000 for admission to the Yale School of Art, ficre-ghebreyesus.com/artist-statement.

199 Renée Green, "Artist Pages and Essays: Renée Green," *Whitney Biennial 2022: Quiet as It's Kept*, exh. cat. (New York: Whitney Museum of American Art and Yale University Press, 2022), 128.

200 "Renée Green," Art, Culture, And Technology Program, MIT, act.mit.edu/about/people/renee-green/.

201 Elizabeth Dee, "Renée Green: Sigetics," *Mutual Art*, mutualart.com/Exhibition/Renee-Green--Sigetics/18EFD412AD53BD2D.

202 *Under Another Name*, Studio Museum in Harlem, accessed June 20, 2023, studiomuseum.org/exhibition/under-another-name.

203 "But while I pondered all these things, and how men fight and lose the battle, and the thing that they fought for comes about in spite of their defeat, and when it comes turns out not to be what they meant, and other men have to fight for what they meant under another name." William Morris, chapter 4: "The voice of John Ball," *A Dream of John Ball* (New York: Oriole Editions, 1971), 19. Retrieved from Internet Archive: archive.org/details/dreamofjohnball0000morr/page/16/mode/2up.

204 Lisa Le Feuvre, "From Island Thought to Water Thought," in *Renée Green: Endless Dreams and Time-Based Streams*, exh. cat. (Yerba Buena Center for the Arts: San Francisco, 2010), 17. *Endless Dreams and Water Between* (2009) was commissioned for the National Maritime Museum, Greenwich, London, and later presented at Yerba Buena Center for the Arts in San Francisco in 2010 for the exhibition *Endless Dreams and Time-Based Streams*; See also *Renée Green: Pacing* (Cambridge, MA: Carpenter Center for the Visual Arts; Free Agent Media, 2020), 227—30.

205 Jennie C. Jones, "Artist Statement," *Callaloo*, vol. 37, no. 4, (2014): 899—902.

206 Taylor Dafoe, "'God Forbid We Should Talk About Joy': Jennie C. Jones on Dodging Pressure to Signify Blackness in Her Art, and Finding Her Own Language," *Artnet*, news.artnet.com/art-world/god-forbid-we-should-talk-about-joy-jennie-c-jones-on-how-her-paintings-alter-sound-208559.

207 The Arts Club of Chicago, "In Conversation: Jennie C. Jones and William J. Simmons," *Vimeo*, May 28, 2023, vimeo.com/421596674.

208 bell hooks, "Subversive Beauty: New Modes of Contestation," in *Art on My Mind* (New York: The New Press, 1995), 50.

209 Jessica Lynne, "The Vernacular Revered," in *Simone Leigh*, exh. cat. (Boston, MA; New York, NY: Institute of Contemporary Art/Boston; DelMonico Books, 2023), 202.

210 Tina Campt, *A Black Gaze: Artists Changing How We See* (Cambridge, Massachusetts: MIT Press, 2021), 205.

211 Siddharta Mitter, "Simone Leigh, in the World," *New York Times*, April 14, 2022, nytimes.com/2022/04/14/arts/design/simone-leigh-venice-biennale-us-pavilion.html.

212 "Ralph Lemon Interview," YouTube, Yerba Buena Center for the Arts, www.youtube.com/watch?v=KS1PVIMpwLo

213 The City University of New York has developed electronic portfolios on urban studies, including a site on gentrification developed by professor David Rosenberg in 2018, eportfolios.macaulay.cuny.edu/genyc/harlem/.

214 Thomas Copeland, "Redistricting Forces a Reckoning in Harlem," *Harlem World Magazine*, October 26, 2022, harlemworldmagazine.com/redistricting-forces-a-reckoning-in-harlem/.

215 Petra Lange-Berndt, "How to Be Complicit with Materials," in *Materiality*, ed. Petra Lange-Berndt (Cambridge, Massachusetts: MIT Press, 2015), 15—16.

216 Artist quoted in Daniel Simmons, "Inherent Magic," in *Vanessa German: Miracles and Glory Abound*, exh. cat. (Flint, Michigan: Flint Institute of Arts, 2019), 31. german embraced minkisi (plural), or nkisi (singular)—central African power figures conceived to house spiritual energy or spirits themselves—as ties to her cultural background in the region, with their strength leading her to refer to her own figures as "power figures." See also: vanessa german and Matthew McLendon, "vanessa german," in *Re:Purposed* (New York: Scala, 2015), 59—60.

217 Matthew McLendon, "Introduction," in *Re:Purposed*, 22—23.

218 Sultan Mahfuz, "Interview: Eric N. Mack, the New York Artist Who Paints with Textiles," *Pin-Up*, Spring/Summer 2019, archive.pinupmagazine.org/articles/interview-artist-eric-n-mack-by-mahfuz-sultan.

219 Elle Pérez, "Elle Pérez Works Between the Frame," *Art21*, video, 4:42, March 20, 2019, art21.org/watch/new-york-close-up/elle-perez-works-between-the-frame/.

220 Martin Heidegger, "The Question Concerning Choreography," in *Basic Writings*, ed. David Farrell Krell (New York: Harper Collins, 1993), 318.

221 Andrew Travers, "Rodney McMillian Puts Landscapes to Bed in Aspen Art Museum Show," *Aspen Times*, May 22, 2015, aspentimes.com/entertainment/activities-events/rodney-mcmillian-puts-landscapes-to-bed-in-aspen-art-museum-show/.

222 "Post-Consumer Report: A Conversation with Rodney McMillian," *Art in America*, April 25, 2016, artnews.com/art-in-america/interviews/post-consumer-report-a-conversation-with-rodney-mcmillian-56451/.

223 "ruby onyinyechi amanze," Goodman Gallery, goodman-gallery.com/artists/ruby-onyinyechi-amanze#about.

224 "Autumn Knight," Foundation for Contemporary Arts, 2023, foundationforcontemporaryarts.org/recipients/autumn-knight/.

225 Eric Booker, "Autumn Knight: Wall," brochure, Danspace Project, October 5, 2019, danspace.wpengine.com/wp-content/uploads/2019/10/AutumnKnight_web.pdf.

226 Texas Isaiah, "My Name Is My Name," Texas Isaiah, 2016-ongoing, texasisaiah.com/my-name-is-my-name.

227 Dionne Brand, *A Map to the Door of No Return: Notes to Belonging* (Toronto: Vintage Canada, 2023), 27.

228 David Katz, "The Afflicted Yard, Peter Dean Rickards RIP," Red Bull Music Academy, January 12, 2015, daily.redbullmusicacademy.com/2015/01/peter-dean-rickards-rip.

229 Saidiya Hartman, *Wayward Lives, Beautiful Experiments* (New York: Norton, 2019), 3.

230 K. Allison Hammer, "'Doing Josephine': The Radical Legacy of Josephine Baker's Banana Dance," *WSQ: Women's Studies Quarterly*, 48, no. 1/2 (2020): 165—81, jstor.org/stable/26979211.

231 Tomi Laja in conversation with the author, August 9, 2023.

232 Chris Chase and Jean-Claude Baker, *Josephine: The Hungry Heart* (New York: Cooper Square Press, 2001).

233 Andy Robert, "2019 Fellows: Fellowship for Visual Artists: Andy Robert," California Community Foundation," January 23, 2019, calfund.

org/nonprofits/featured-funds/
fva/2019-gallery/.

234 Following the French Revolution, the
building experienced further demise
and remained abandoned until an
attempted restoration during the
nineteenth century, which led to its
contemporary existence as a popular
tourist destination.

235 *Ibrahim Mahama: Letters from the Void*,
Viewing Room, White Cube,
whitecube.viewingrooms.com/viewing-
room/53-ibrahim-mahama-letters-
from-the-void/.

236 Ibrahim Mahama and Vanessa Peterson,
"How Ibrahim Mahama's Installations
Exhume Political Ghosts," *Frieze*,
October 6, 2021, frieze.com/article/
how-ibrahim-mahamas-installations-
exhume-political-ghosts.

237 The Stonewall Uprising, which began
on the eve of June 28, 1969, in New
York City's Greenwich Village, marked
a pivotal moment in the history of
LGBTQIA+ rights. The uprising began
when police raided the Stonewall Inn, a
popular gay bar, and subsequently led
to six days of protests, confrontations,
and demonstrations by activists and
community members. This event is
often considered the catalyst for the
modern LGBTQIA+ rights movement
in the United States and around the
world, inspiring increased visibility,
advocacy, and legal advancements for
LGBTQIA+ rights.

238 "Firelei Báez: Joy Out of Fire,"
exhibition guide, Studio Museum
in Harlem, May 23, 2018, issuu.
com/studiomuseum/docs/smoh_
brochure_fireleibaez_proof, 12.

239 This expanded understanding of
archives is indebted to Vanessa Agard-
Jones's expert repositioning of sand in
their writing about queer shore spaces
in Martinique. Vanessa Agard-Jones,
"What the Sands Remember," *GLQ: A
Journal of Lesbian and Gay Studies* 18, no.
2–3 (2012).

240 Cy Gavin, "Painting Bermuda's Past:
Cy Gavin Shares the Stories Behind
his Paintings," *Georgia Review*, 2018,
thegeorgiareview.com/posts/painting-
bermudas-past-cy-gavin-shares-the-
stories-behind-his-paintings/.

241 "Hallie Ringle and Legacy Russell in
Conversation," brochure for *MOOD*
(New York: Studio Museum in Harlem,
2019), 3–6.

242 bell hooks, "Facing Difference: The
Black Female Body," in *Art on My Mind*
(New York: The New Press, 1995), 95.

243 Lita Barrie, "Deborah Roberts Explores
the Fragility of Black Masculinity
in Native Sons," Medium, June 5,
2019, cvonhassett.medium.com/
deborah-roberts-explores-the-fragility-
of-black-masculinity-in-native-sons-
3f6628e1fa69.

244 "A typical plan is an American invention.
It is zero-degree architecture stripped
of all traces of uniqueness and
specificity. It belongs to the new world."
Rem Koolhaas and Bruce Mau, O.M.A.,
"Typical Plan," *S,M,L,XL* (New York:
Monacelli Press, 1995), 335.

245 Sanou Oumar quoted in Svetlana Kitto,
"Sanou Oumar," Gordon Robichaux,
March 2021, gordonrobichaux.com/
exhibitions/sanou-oumar.

246 Focus Series, Garrett Bradley discusses
her film *America* (2019), YouTube,
00:01:57, January 10, 2020, youtu.be/
puH26jx-A24.

247 Ibid.

248 Elliot Reed quoted in Sami Hopkins,
"Elliot Reed On Body and
Performance," *Studio*, June 9, 2020,
studiomuseum.org/magazine/
elliot-reed-on-body-and-performance.

249 Michael Beckert, "Artist Elliott Jerome
Brown Jr. on Making Work in the
Margins," *W*, July 7, 2020, wmagazine.
com/culture/elliott-jerome-brown-jr-
photography-interview.

250 Kathy Donoghue, "Andile Dyalvane
Translates his Dreams into Ceremonial
Objects," *Whitewall*, August 4, 2021,
whitewall.art/design/andile-dyalvane-
translates-his-dreams-into-ceremonial-
objects/.

251 Steven A. Diamond, "Why Myths Still
Matter (Part Four): Facing Your Inner
Minotaur and Following Your Ariadnean
Thread," *Pyschology Today*, December 19,
2009, psychologytoday.com/us/blog/
evil-deeds/200912/why-myths-still-
matter-part-four-facing-your-inner-
minotaur-and-following.

252 "In Focus: Widline Cadet's
Los Angeles," *Frieze*, February
1, 2024, frieze.com/video/
focus-widline-cadets-los-angeles.

253 Caroline Kent, "A Form Walks Toward
You in the Dark," St. Catherine's
University, St. Paul, YouTube, 56:21,
October 15, 2018, youtu.be/
IQNBP7pqZSA.

254 Legacy Russell, *Glitch Feminism: A
Manifesto* (London: Verso, 2020), 29.

255 Rarely do figures in Mckinney's works
return the viewer's gaze, a deliberate
choice made by the artist. Danielle
Mckinney in conversation with the
author, August 11, 2023.

256 Erica N. Caldwell, "Practices of Care:
Jeffrey Meris Interviewed," *BOMB*,
June 20, 2022, bombmagazine.org/
articles/2022/06/20/practices-of-
care-jeffrey-meris-interviewed.

257 "2022–23 Studio Museum
Artist in Residence Devin N.
Morris," Studio Museum in
Harlem, YouTube, 00:02:48,
November 17, 2023, youtube.com/
watch?v=QDIJWeNTNbM.

258 Karon Davis, interview by Olivia Manno,
"Artist Karon Davis' New Exhibition
Grapples With the Physicality and Grit
of Ballet," *Dance Magazine*, November
22, 2023, dancemagazine.com/artist-
karon-davis-new-exhibition-grapples-
with-the-physicality-and-grit-of-ballet.

259 The Met acquired the James Van Der
Zee Archive from the artist's widow,
Donna Mussenden Van Der Zee, and
from the James Van Der Zee Institute,
a now-defunct charitable foundation
established in 1970.

260 This renowned body of work is featured
in the artist's third monograph, *The
Harlem Book of the Dead* (1978), which
includes a foreword by the novelist Toni
Morrison.

261 The photographer's last studio was
located at 272 Lenox Avenue (now
Malcolm X Boulevard), at 124th Street,
just one and a half blocks from the
current location of the Studio Museum
in Harlem.

262 The correspondent, Monica Scott
Nichols, also included two other
Van Der Zee photographs of her
grandparents, one in wedding garb at
the time of their marriage in June 1931.
Email correspondence received by the
author, December 10, 2021; see also
the *Daily Argus*, June 19, 1931, a Mount
Vernon, New York, newspaper accessed
via newspapers.com by the author
on June 17, 2023. The Art Institute of
Chicago owns a portrait [2002.99]
solely of Amy Brown who appears in
the same dress and with similar applied
color as seen here.

Index

Contributors

Alexandra E. Adams is a PhD candidate in art history at Stanford University specializing in late nineteenth- and twentieth-century American art, the African diaspora, and self-taught/vernacular visual culture.

Taylor Renee Aldridge is a writer and curator based in Detroit.

Salome Asega is a new-media artist and Director of NEW INC, the New Museum's cultural incubator for art, design, and technology.

Camille Bacon is a Chicago-based writer and Cofounder and Coeditor in Chief of Jupiter Magazine.

Horace D. Ballard, PhD, is the Theodore E. Stebbins Curator of American Art at the Fogg/Harvard Art Museums.

Tiffany E. Barber, Assistant Professor of African American Art at UCLA, is a scholar, curator, and critic whose work focuses on the visual and performing arts of the Black world.

Caitlin Meehye Beach is Associate Professor of Art History at the Graduate Center, CUNY.

Naomi Beckwith is Deputy Director, and Jennifer and David Stockman Chief Curator at the Solomon R. Guggenheim Museum and Foundation. Beckwith was awarded the 2024 David C. Driskell Prize.

Eric Booker is Associate Curator at Storm King Art Center; he was previously Assistant Curator at the Studio Museum in Harlem.

Elana Bridges, an art enthusiast based in Philadelphia, explores the dynamic intersection of creative thought and artistic expression where art and technology converge.

adrienne maree brown grows healing ideas in public through her multigenre writing, her music, and her podcasts.

Eliza Butler is a New York—based art historian who has held positions at Columbia University, Pratt Institute, and the Brooklyn Museum.

Starasea Camara is a Queens-based curator and scholar, and is currently the Curatorial and Public Engagement Assistant at the Institute for Studies on Latin American Art (ISLAA).

Mary Schmidt Campbell, PhD, is President Emerita of Spelman College, Dean Emerita of NYU Tisch School of the Arts, former New York City Cultural Affairs Commissioner, and former Executive Director of the Studio Museum in Harlem.

Jordan Carter is Curator and Co-Department Head at Dia Art Foundation.

Jakeya Caruthers is Assistant Professor of English and Africana Studies at Drexel University and coeditor of a double-volume anthology entitled *Abolition Feminisms Vol. 1 and 2* (2022).

Vladimir Cybil Charlier, an American-born, New York—based multidisciplinary artist of Haitian descent, has a practice that examines the connections and reinvention of Afrodiasporic cultures within postcolonial societies.

Connie H. Choi is Curator at the Studio Museum in Harlem.

Emma Chubb, PhD, is the inaugural Charlotte Feng Ford '83 Curator of Contemporary Art at the Smith College Museum of Art.

Kate Claman is a cultural worker who holds a BA from Middlebury College and MA from the Courtauld Institute of Art.

Phoebe Collings-James is a sculptor whose works function as "emotional detritus" that speak of knowledges of feelings, the debris of violence, language, and desire, which are inherent to living and surviving within hostile environments.

Jadine Collingwood, PhD, is an Associate Curator at the Museum of Contemporary Art Chicago.

Rhea Combs, PhD, is Director of Curatorial Affairs at the National Portrait Gallery, Smithsonian Institution.

Kinshasha Holman Conwill is Deputy Director Emerita of the National Museum of African American History and Culture and is the former Director of the Studio Museum in Harlem.

Scholar and curator Bridget R. Cooks is Chancellor's Fellow and Professor of African American Studies and Art History at the University of California, Irvine.

Aimee Meredith Cox, PhD, is a cultural anthropologist, somatic artist, and Associate Professor in the Department of Anthropology at New York University.

Leslie Cozzi, PhD, FAAR'18, is Curator and Department Head of Prints, Drawings & Photographs at the Baltimore Museum of Art.

Katelyn D. Crawford lives and works in Birmingham, Alabama, where she is the William Cary Hulsey Curator of American Art at the Birmingham Museum of Art.

Romi Crawford, PhD, is a Professor in the Visual and Critical Studies Department at the School of the Art Institute of Chicago and founder of the Black Arts Movement School Modality and the New Art School Modality.

Nijah Cunningham is an Assistant Professor in African diasporic literatures and culture at Hunter College, City University of New York.

Daisy Desrosiers has been the Director and Chief Curator of Gund Gallery at Kenyon College since 2021 and was previously the inaugural Director of Artist Programs at the Lunder Institute for American Art at the Colby College Museum of Art.

Zimbabwe-born Tandazani Dhlakama is a curator who has worked at Zeitz MOCAA and the National Gallery of Zimbabwe, contributing to major exhibitions, conferences, and biennials on the African continent and beyond.

Amber Edmond is an arts worker based in New York City.

Adrienne Edwards, PhD, is Engell Speyer Family

Senior Curator & Associate Director of Curatorial Programs at the Whitney Museum of American Art.

Ruth Erickson is the Barbara Lee Chief Curator and Director of Curatorial Affairs at the Institute of Contemporary Art/Boston.

Amber Esseiva is a Swiss-Senegalese-American curator. Esseiva is currently the Curator at the Institute for Contemporary Art at Virginia Commonwealth University and Curator-at-Large at the Studio Museum in Harlem.

Katherine Fein is Visiting Assistant Professor of North American Art and Architecture at Amherst College.

Kanitra Fletcher, PhD, is a Curator at the National Gallery of Art in Washington, DC, and Landmarks, the public art program of the University of Texas at Austin.

Kimberli Gant, PhD, is the Curator of Modern and Contemporary Art at the Brooklyn Museum.

Theaster Gates is an artist and social innovator who extends the role of the artist as an agent of change and translates the intricacies of blackness through space theory and land art, sculpture, architecture, music, film and performance, and the reactivation of objects, collections, and archives.

Simon Ghebreyesus is a writer and curator based in New York.

A London-based writer and curator, Hanna Girma is currently Senior Editor and Curator of Editorial Projects at Serpentine.

Thelma Golden is Ford Foundation Director and Chief Curator of the Studio Museum in Harlem.

Sheldon Gooch is Curatorial Assistant at MoMA PS1.

Che Gossett is a Black nonbinary writer and critical theorist specializing in queer/trans studies, aesthetic theory, abolitionist thought, and Black study.

Adria Gunter is Curatorial Assistant at the Studio Museum in Harlem.

Jennifer M. Harley is an artist, educator, and PhD candidate at Columbia University in the Department of Art History & Archaeology.

Daria Simone Harper is a Chicago-based art writer and Cofounder and Coeditor in Chief of Jupiter Magazine.

Shawnya L. Harris, PhD, is the Deputy Director of Curatorial and Academic Affairs and the Larry D. and Brenda A. Thompson Curator of African American and African Diasporic Art at the

Georgia Museum of Art, University of Georgia.

Lauren Haynes is a curator and cultural worker based in New York City whose practice focuses on the work of contemporary artists of African descent.

Chloe Hayward, LCAT, ATR-BC, is Director of Education at the Studio Museum in Harlem.

Zoë Hopkins is a writer and critic based in New York, where she is also a graduate student at Columbia University.

Habiba Hopson is Senior Curatorial Assistant at the Studio Museum in Harlem.

Daonne Huff is an arts worker, artist, poet, daughter of the state where the stars fell, and former Director of Public Programs at the Studio Museum from 2019 to 2023.

Amanda Hunt is the Head of Public Engagement, Learning and Impact at the Walker Art Center in Minneapolis. She was Associate Curator at the Studio Museum in Harlem from 2014 to 2016.

Jamillah James is the Manilow Senior Curator at the Museum of Contemporary Art Chicago.

Jordan Jones is an arts worker based in Seattle currently serving as the Director + Curator

of the Jacob Lawrence Gallery at the University of Washington.

Naima J. Keith is the Vice President of Education and Public Programs at Los Angeles County Museum of Art, prior to which she held leadership and curatorial positions at the California African American Museum, the Studio Museum, and Hammer Museum.

Yelena Keller is Assistant Curator at the Studio Museum in Harlem.

Christine Y. Kim is Britton Family Curator-at-Large at Tate Modern, London; she curated Julie Mehretu's survey as Curator at the Los Angeles County Museum of Art in 2019, and was a Curator at the Studio Museum in Harlem from 2000 to 2008.

June Kitahara is the Henry Luce Foundation Publications Fellow at the Studio Museum in Harlem.

Autumn Knight is a New York—based interdisciplinary artist working with performance, installation, video, sound, and text.

Nectar Knuckles is a PhD candidate in art and archaeology at Princeton University.

Shanna Kudowitz is the Associate Director of Digital Marketing & Communications at the Studio Museum in Harlem.

Miranda Lash is the Ellen Bruss Senior Curator at the Museum of Contemporary Art Denver and the Co-Artistic Director of Prospect.6, an international art triennial based in New Orleans.

Thomas Lax is Curator of Media and Performance at the Museum of Modern Art, New York.

Key Jo Lee is an art historian, curator, and educator currently serving as the Chief of Curatorial Affairs and Public Programs at the Museum of the African Diaspora in San Francisco.

A curator and writer based in New York, Alexis Lowry is currently Curatorial Director at Hauser & Wirth.

Canisia Lubrin is a lover of art, editor, teacher, and writer, most recently of *Code Noir* (Knopf Canada 2024/Soft Skull, 2025).

Mia Matthias is a curator and writer based in Washington, DC.

Zuna Maza is a curator from San Juan, Puerto Rico, currently Assistant Curator at El Museo del Barrio, New York.

Rachell Morillo is a Black feminist artist, writer, educator, and arts worker. She is currently DAJ Director of Public Engagement and Research at the Institute of Contemporary Art.

Yume Murphy is a writer, editor, and strategist based in Brooklyn.

Yvette Mutumba, PhD, is Cofounder and Director of the international art platform Contemporary And (C&).

Ugochukwu-Smooth C. Nzewi is an artist, art historian, and the first Steven and Lisa Tananbaum Curator in the Department of Painting and Sculpture at the Museum of Modern Art, New York.

Odili Donald Odita is a Professor in Painting, Drawing & Sculpture at the Tyler School of Art and Architecture at Temple University and is represented by Jack Shainman Gallery, New York; David Kordansky Gallery, Los Angeles; Stevenson Gallery, Cape Town; and Cristea Roberts Gallery, London.

nico w. okoro is an independent arts consultant, curator, educator, and writer, and is the author of *Museum Metamorphosis: Cultivating Change Through Cultural Citizenship*.

Folasade Ologundudu is a writer, curator, and podcast creator seeking to uncover ideas related to the universal human condition through the intersection of art, education, and culture.

Jayson Overby Jr. is an Assistant Curator

at the Studio Museum in Harlem.

Terrence Phearse is the Chief of Staff at the Studio Museum in Harlem.

Yasmina Price is a New York—based writer and film curator completing a PhD at Yale University. Her work centers Black cinema, anti-colonial visual culture, and the experimental practices of women image makers.

Anni A. Pullagura, PhD, is the Margaret and Terry Stent Associate Curator of American Art at the High Museum of Art, Atlanta.

Hallie Ringle is the Chief Curator at ICA Philadelphia; she was formerly Assistant Curator at the Studio Museum.

Deborah Roberts has found her distinctive voice in collage; this has allowed her to dismantle long-held notions of race and beauty.

Jeff L. Rosenheim is the Joyce Frank Menschel Curator in Charge of Photographs at the Metropolitan Museum of Art.

Legacy Russell is a curator and writer.

Angelique Rosales Salgado is a curator and writer from Mexico City based in New York.

Tamara H. Schenkenberg, a Curator at the Pulitzer

Arts Foundation in St. Louis, organizes exhibitions and publishes essays on a range of understudied artists whose work explores issues around land, displacement, and gender.

Trevor Schoonmaker is the Mary D. B. T. and James H. Semans Director of the Nasher Museum of Art at Duke University.

Christina Sharpe is the author of three books, most recently *Ordinary Notes* (2023)—winner of the Hilary Weston Writer's Trust Prize in Nonfiction, and finalist for the National Book Award in Nonfiction, the National Book Critics Circle Award in Nonfiction, and the James Tait Black Prize in Biography.

Lowery Stokes Sims is a curator, art historian, and social catalyst who has been dedicated to bringing diversity and plurality to the art world for over five decades; and the former Director of the Studio Museum in Harlem.

Franklin Sirmans was a Studio Museum in Harlem intern and he is the current Director of the Pérez Art Museum Miami.

Anne Collins Smith is the Chief Curator of the New Orleans Museum of Art.

TK Smith is a curator, writer, and cultural historian.

Stephanie Sparling Williams is the Andrew W. Mellon Curator of American Art at the Brooklyn Museum.

Phillip Edward Spradley is a cultural producer based in New York City.

Jenée-Daria Strand is a curator, writer, and native Brooklynite whose research centers the intersections of Black feminist scholarship, popular culture, and contemporary art.

Lilia Rocio Taboada is a writer and curator based in Brooklyn.

Whitney Tassie is a mom, curator, and community builder working to connect universities with their local communities.

Kiki Teshome is Curatorial Assistant at the Studio Museum in Harlem.

Drew Thompson is an educator, writer, and curator who serves as Associate Professor of Black Studies and Visual Culture at Bard Graduate Center.

Akili Tommasino is Curator of Modern and Contemporary Art at the Metropolitan Museum of Art.

Eugenie Mae Tsai is a curator and writer based in New York City.

Arese Uwuoruya is a London-based writer and curator currently working as the Assistant Exhibitions Curator at Camden Art Centre.

Terence Washington is a freelance writer and curator based in Philadelphia.

Meg Whiteford is Managing Editor at the Studio Museum in Harlem.

Adeze Wilford is the Blackmon Perry Curator of African American Art and Art of the African Diaspora at the Memphis Brooks Museum of Art.

Ilk Yasha is Director of the Studio Museum Institute at the Studio Museum in Harlem.

Doris Zhao is an art historian, curator, and project manager, and she has held positions at the Metropolitan Museum of Art and the Studio Museum in Harlem.

Image Credits

All works are held in the collection of the Studio Museum in Harlem unless otherwise indicated. The works appearing in this handbook may be protected by copyright in the United States of America or elsewhere and may not be reproduced without the permission of the rights holders. The Studio Museum in Harlem has made every effort to identify copyright holders and obtain permission to reproduce their material in this publication. We are grateful for additions or corrections that should be incorporated in future reprints or editions and will work with Phaidon to make such changes at the earliest opportunity.

All photos: John Berens—Brooklyn, NY, © Studio Museum in Harlem, except otherwise noted. Zalika Azim: 98, 120, 260 (*how i got over*), © Studio Museum in Harlem; Sebastian Bach: 214–15, 366, 426 (*to know what angels eat*); Marc Bernier: 85, 99 (*Too Obvious*), 133, 202, 277, all photos © Studio Museum in Harlem; Dawoud Bey: 20; Casey Kaplan Gallery: 410; Theo Christelis: 379, © White Cube; Tony Cokes: 412, courtesy the artist and Greene Naftali, Felix Gaudlitz, Vienna, Hannah Hoffman, LA, and Electronic Arts Intermix, NY; Paula Court: 341, © Paula Court; Aria Dean: 350, courtesy the artist, Greene Naftali, NY, and Château Shatto, LA; Zachary Fabri: 312; LaToya Ruby Frazier: 266; JaTovia Gary: 332, courtesy Paula Cooper Gallery, NY; Scott Geffert: 35; Robert Gerhardt: 101, © 2024 The Museum of Modern Art, NY, 381, © 2021 The Museum of Modern Art, NY; Kris Graves: 417, courtesy MoMA PS1; Allison Janae Hamilton: 368; Arthur Jafa: 345, courtesy the artist, Gladstone Gallery and Sprüth Magers; E. Jane: 386; Simone Leigh: 307 (*Breakdown*), courtesy Matthew Marks Gallery; Kalup Linzy: 255, 256, courtesy David Castillo Gallery; Tom Little: 75; Ray Llanos: 23; Matthew Marks Gallery: 347; Dave McKenzie: 223; The Metropolitan Museum of Art: 430; Alise O'Brien: 129, courtesy Pulitzer Arts Foundation. © Barbara Chase-Riboud and Alise O'Brien Photography; Clifford Owens: 257; Farzad Owrang: 9; Tom Powel Imaging: 398, Julie Mehretu and Marian Goodman Gallery; Elliot Reed: 390; Adam Reich: 116–17, 124, 136, 193, 195, 259, 260 (*Brother, Brother, Brother*), 261 (*I Do Pigeon Toe*), 296, 304; Cauleen Smith: 360; Sasha Smith-Mendez: 39, 149, 225, 253, © Studio Museum in Harlem; Devin Troy Strother: 365; Denis Y. Suspitsyn: 30; Tourmaline and Sasha Wortzel: 359; Unidentified photographers: 16, 247, 248 (*Riffs on Real Time (4 of 10)*), 313, 425 (*Man-Queen [Na so it be], The Acrobat*), 426 (*Dave, Dove; Untitled (Ref. #86) from Character Recognition; Leonardo da Vinci, 427 (*Black Widow, Thoba utsale umnxeba, Untitled, Nina Simone*), 428 (*A Conversation*), 429 (*It's the little things that hurt...it's the little things that make us fight!, We built this city*); Jessica Vaughn: 376; Whitney Museum of American Art, NY: 77 (*Baby*)

Abney: © Nina Chanel Abney; Adkins: © 2025 The Estate of Terry Adkins/Artists Rights Society (ARS), NY; Akunyili Crosby: © Njideka Akunyili Crosby, courtesy the artist, Victoria Miro, and David Zwirner; Alston: © 2025 Charles Alston/Artists Rights Society (ARS), NY; Alvarez: Courtesy the artist and Monique Meloche Gallery; Amos: © 2025 Emma Amos/Licensed by VAGA at Artists Rights Society (ARS), NY, courtesy RYAN LEE Gallery, NY; Andrews: © Estate of Benny Andrews/VAGA at Artists Rights Society (ARS), NY, courtesy Michael Rosenfeld Gallery, LLC, NY; Arbus: © The Estate of Diane Arbus; Armitage: © Michael Armitage; Báez: © Firelei Báez, courtesy the artist and Hauser & Wirth; Basquiat: © Estate of Jean-Michel Basquiat/Licensed by Artestar, NY; Bearden: © 2025 Romare Bearden Foundation/ Licensed by VAGA at Artists Rights Society (ARS), NY; Bendolph: © 2025 Mary Lee Bendolph/Artists Rights Society (ARS), NY; Biggers: © Sanford Biggers; Billops: © Camille Billops, courtesy the estate of the artist and RYAN LEE Gallery, NY; Binion: © McArthur Binion, courtesy the artist and Lehmann Maupin, NY, Seoul, and London; Blackburn: © The Robert Blackburn Trust; Blayton: © Estate of Betty Blayton; Bowling: © 2025 Frank Bowling. All Rights Reserved/Artists Rights Society (ARS), NY/DACS, London; Bradley: © Peter Bradley; Catlett: © 2025 Mora-Catlett Family/Licensed by VAGA at Artists Rights Society (ARS), NY; Chase-Riboud: © Barbara Chase-Riboud. Courtesy the artist and Hauser & Wirth; Clark: © The Estate of Ed Clark, courtesy the Estate and Hauser & Wirth; Colomba: © 2025 Elizabeth Colomba/ Artists Rights Society (ARS), NY; Cortor: © 2025 Eldzier Cortor/Artists Rights Society (ARS), NY; Davis: © The Estate of Noah Davis, courtesy The Estate of Noah Davis and David Zwirner; DeCarava: © The Estate of Roy DeCarava. All rights reserved; Delaney: © Estate of Beauford Delaney, by permission of Derek L. Spratley, Esquire, Court Appointed Administrator, courtesy Michael Rosenfeld Gallery LLC, NY; Delsarte: © Estate of Louis J. Delsarte III; Dial: © 2025 Thornton Dial Jr./Artists Rights Society (ARS), NY; A. Douglas: © 2025 Heirs of Aaron Douglas/Licensed by VAGA at Artists Rights Society (ARS), NY; E. Douglas: © 2025 Emory Douglas/Licensed by AFNYLAW.com; Drew: © Leonardo Drew, courtesy Galerie Lelong & Co.; Driskell: © Estate of David C. Driskell, courtesy of DC Moore Gallery, NY; Edwards: © 2025 Melvin Edwards/Artists Rights Society (ARS), NY; Fosso: © Samuel Fosso, courtesy JM Patras/Paris; Gallagher: © Ellen Gallagher; Gary: © JaTovia Gary, courtesy Paula Cooper Gallery, NY; Gates: © Theaster Gates Studio and Monastery Foundation; german: © vanessa german; Ghebreyesus: © The Estate of Ficre Ghebreyesus, courtesy Galerie Lelong & Co.; Gilliam: © 2025 Estate of Sam Gilliam/Artists Rights Society (ARS), NY; Hamilton: © Allison Janae Hamilton; Hammons: © 2025 David Hammons/Artists Rights Society (ARS), NY; Hlobo: © Nicholas Hlobo, courtesy the artist and Lehmann Maupin, NY, Seoul, and London; Holley: © 2025 Lonnie Holley/Artists Rights Society (ARS), NY; Hunt: © 2025 The Richard Hunt Trust/Artists Rights Society (ARS), NY; Jackson: © The Gerald Jackson Trust, courtesy Gordon Robichaux, NY, and Parker Gallery, LA; Jafa: © Arthur Jafa, courtesy the artist, Gladstone Gallery and Sprüth Magers; Jones: © Samuel Levi Jones, courtesy Galerie Lelong & Co.; Julien: © Isaac Julien, courtesy the artist; Keïta: © Seydou Keïta/SKPEAC; courtesy The Jean Pigozzi African Art Collection; Kent: © Caroline Kent, courtesy Casey Kaplan Gallery; Knight: © 2025 The Jacob and Gwendolyn Knight Lawrence Foundation, Seattle/Artists Rights Society (ARS), NY; Lawrence: © 2025 The Jacob and Gwendolyn Knight Lawrence Foundation, Seattle/ Artists Rights Society (ARS), NY; Lawson: © Deana Lawson, courtesy the artist and Gagosian; Lee-Smith: © Estate of Hughie Lee-Smith/ Licensed by VAGA at ARS, NY, courtesy the artist and Gagosian; Leigh: © Simone Leigh, courtesy Matthew Marks Gallery; Lewis: © Estate of Norman Lewis, courtesy Michael Rosenfeld Gallery LLC, NY; Ligon: © Glenn Ligon, courtesy the artist, Hauser & Wirth and Thomas Dane Gallery; Lovell: © Whitfield Lovell, courtesy of DC Moore Gallery, NY; Loving: © The Estate of Al Loving; Magadlela: Courtesy the artist and Kates-Ferri Projects; Maynard: © 2025 Estate of Valerie J. Maynard/Artists Rights Society (ARS), NY; Mckinney: © Danielle Mckinney; courtesy the artist and Marianne Boesky Gallery, NY and Aspen; Milan: © Wardell Milan; Mutu: © Wangechi Mutu, courtesy the artist; Nance: © 2025 Marilyn Nance/Artists Rights Society (ARS), NY; Nevelson: © 2025 Estate of Louise Nevelson/Artists Rights Society (ARS), NY; O'Grady: © 2025 Lorraine O'Grady/Artists Rights Society (ARS), NY; Ofili: © Chris Ofili, courtesy the artist and David Zwirner; Oubre: The Hayward Oubre Estate, courtesy of Debra Force Fine Art; Oumar: Courtesy Gordon Robichaux, NY, and Herald Street, London; Packer: © Jennifer Packer; Parks: Courtesy and copyright The Gordon Parks Foundation; Patterson: Courtesy the artist and Monique Meloche Gallery; Pettway: © 2025 Estate of Martha Jane Pettway/Artists Rights Society (ARS), NY; Phillips: © Julia Phillips, courtesy Matthew Marks Gallery; Pindell: © Howardena Pindell; Piper: © Adrian Piper Research Archive Foundation; Pope.L: © The Estate of Pope.L; Puryear: © Martin Puryear, courtesy Matthew Marks Gallery; Pusey: © 2025 Estate of Mavis Pusey/Artists Rights Society (ARS), NY; Quarles: © Christina Quarles, courtesy the artist and Hauser & Wirth and Pilar Corrias London; Rauschenberg: © 2024 Robert Rauschenberg Foundation/ Licensed by VAGA at Artists Rights Society (ARS), NY; Ringgold: © 2025 Anyone Can Fly Foundation/Artists Rights Society (ARS), NY; Robert: © The Artist; Rowe: © 2025 Estate of Nellie Mae Rowe/Artists Rights Society (ARS), NY; A. Saar: © Alison Saar, courtesy L.A. Louver, Venice, California; L. Saar: Courtesy the artist and Walter Maciel Gallery; Saunders: © The Estate of Raymond Saunders. All rights reserved. Shonibare: © Yinka Shonibare CBE. All Rights Reserved, DACS/ARS, NY, 2025; Shrobe: Courtesy the artist and Monique Meloche Gallery; Simpson: © Lorna Simpson, courtesy the artist and Hauser & Wirth; Siskind: © Virginia Museum of Fine Arts Smith: © 2025 Ming Smith/ Artists Rights Society (ARS), NY; Lord Snowdon: Photograph by Snowdon/Trunk Archive; Strachan: Courtesy the artist, photo: Jurate Veceraite; A. Thomas: © 2025 Estate of Alma Thomas, courtesy the Hart Family/Artists Rights Society (ARS), NY; M. Thomas: © 2025 Mickalene Thomas/Artists Rights Society (ARS), NY; Thompson: © Michael Rosenfeld Gallery LLC, NY, courtesy Michael Rosenfeld Gallery LLC, NY; Van Der Zee: © James Van Der Zee Archive, The Metropolitan Museum of Art; Walker: © Kara Walker; Ward: © Nari Ward Studio, courtesy the artist and Lehmann Maupin, NY, Seoul, and London, and GALLERIA CONTINUA; Whitten: © Jack Whitten Estate, courtesy Estate and Hauser & Wirth; Woodruff: © 2025 Estate of Hale Woodruff/Licensed by VAGA at Artists Rights Society (ARS), NY

Staff
As of time of print

Allen Accoo

Cierra Allen

Christopher Andujar

Timotheus Ballard

Edith Bolton

River Bunkley

Ally Caple

Kevin Carter

Kevin Chappelle

Connie H. Choi

Sasha Cordingley

Bonfilio Cortez

Victoria Dadet

Maya Davis

Ivette Dixon

Frederick Ellis

Ernest Esparza

Preston Foxx

Chet Gold

Thelma Golden

Abigail Gordon

Adaiya Granberry

Geoffrey Greene

Adria Gunter

Jodi Hanel

Chloe Hayward

Maya Herdigein

Habiba Hopson

Juliana Hunter-Ellin

Cecil Jones

Divine Jones

Yelena Keller

Sorai Kirksey

June Kitahara

Shanna Kudowitz

Vita Kurland

Shanta Lawson

Zachary Little

Natasha Logan

Ashley Mackey

Betsy McClelland

Stacie Middleton Crawford

Christopher Mittoo

Federico Morrobel

Emily Nazarian

Anna Olujimi

Jayson Overby Jr.

Shay Palmer

Chakshu Patel

Terrence Phearse II

Reynold Ri Boul

Lisa Richardson

Robyn Richardson

Quin Sakira

Brianna Sellers

Kesham Singh

Madison Smith

Timothy Stockton

Rebeca Tapia

Kiki Teshome

Leon Thomas

Isabel Varban

Thomas Webb

Debra White

Kevin White

Meg Whiteford

Lindsay Wilkinson

Tony Wong

Isata Yansaneh

Ilk Yasha

Reg Zehner

Phaidon Press Limited
2 Cooperage Yard
London E15 2QR

Phaidon Press Inc.
111 Broadway
New York, NY 10006

Phaidon SARL
55, rue Traversière
75012 Paris

phaidon.com

Published
in association with
Studio Museum in Harlem
144 West 125th Street
New York, NY 10027

studiomuseum.org

First published 2025
© Studio Museum
in Harlem

Cover image: Lorraine
O'Grady, *Art Is. . .(Girlfriends
Times Two)*, 1983/2009.
Chromogenic digital print,
image: 16 × 20 in. Edition
4 of 8 + 1 AP. Bequest
of Peggy Cooper Cafritz
(1947—2018), Washington,
DC, collector, educator, and
activist 2018.40.240

For Phaidon
Commissioning Editor:
Deborah Aaronson
Project Editor: Maia Murphy
Production Controller:
Andie Trainer

For Studio Museum
in Harlem
Editor: Connie H. Choi
Senior Editor:
Meg Whiteford
Copyeditor: Jedd Hakimi,
Point Line Projects
Henry Luce Foundation
Publications Fellow:
June Kitahara
Design: WeShouldDoItAll

Printed in China
This book is typeset
in Studio Museum Black.

ISBN 978 1 83866 934 8
(trade edition)

ISBN 978 1 83729 085 7
(limited edition)

A CIP catalogue record for
this book is available from
the British Library and the
Library of Congress.

Bank of America is the
Studio Museum in Harlem's
lead opening and inaugural
exhibitions sponsor. Major
support for the inaugural
exhibitions and publications
provided by the Henry Luce
Foundation. Support for this
publication is thanks in part
to the Terra Foundation for
American Art.

Bank of America.

HENRY LUCE FOUNDATION

TERRA
FOUNDATION FOR AMERICAN ART